THE
JUST WAR

BOOKS BY PAUL RAMSEY

ETHICS AT THE EDGES OF LIFE: Medical and Legal Intersections
THE ETHICS OF FETAL RESEARCH
THE PATIENT AS PERSON: Explorations in Medical Ethics
FABRICATED MAN: The Ethics of Genetic Control
THE JUST WAR: Force and Political Responsibility
DEEDS AND RULES IN CHRISTIAN ETHICS
WHO SPEAKS FOR THE CHURCH? A Critique of the 1966 Geneva Conference on Church and Society
NINE MODERN MORALISTS
CHRISTIAN ETHICS AND THE SIT-IN
WAR AND THE CHRISTIAN CONSCIENCE: How Shall Modern War be Conducted Justly?
BASIC CHRISTIAN ETHICS

EDITED BY PAUL RAMSEY

ETHICAL WRITINGS (by Jonathan Edwards), forthcoming
DOING EVIL TO ACHIEVE GOOD: Moral Choice in Conflict Situations
(with Richard A. McCormick, S.J.)
THE STUDY OF RELIGION IN COLLEGES AND UNIVERSITIES
(with John F. Wilson)
NORM AND CONTEXT IN CHRISTIAN ETHICS
(with Gene H. Outka)
RELIGION: Humanistic Scholarship in America
FREEDOM OF THE WILL (by Jonathan Edwards)
FAITH AND ETHICS: The Theology of H. Richard Niebuhr

THE JUST WAR

Force and Political Responsibility

Paul Ramsey

UNIVERSITY
PRESS OF
AMERICA

LANHAM • NEW YORK • LONDON

Copyright © 1983, 1968 by
Paul Ramsey

University Press of America,™ Inc.

4720 Boston Way
Lanham, MD 20706

3 Henrietta Street
London WC2E 8LU England

Printed in the United States of America

Library of Congress Cataloging in Publication Data

Ramsey, Paul.
  The just war.

  Reprint. Originally published: New York: Scribner,
1968.
  Includes index.
  1. Just war doctrine.   I. Title.
[U21.2.R33   1983]   355'.02   83-10182
ISBN 0-8191-3356-6
ISBN 0-8191-3357-4 (pbk.)

In
Memory of my Brother
JOHN EARL RAMSEY, SR.
31 July 1902–31 May 1967

Introduction

This volume is a publication with some revision of the hitherto unpublished papers plus certain articles, chapters, and pamphlets on the subject of the just-war doctrine and on the responsible use of force that I have written since the publication in 1961 of my book, *War and the Christian Conscience: How Shall Modern War Be Conducted Justly?* [1] I am told that together these will make an authentic book and that in any case it will be of service to make these "fugitive" writings more readily available between the same two covers. I do not find it in me to disagree with these two judgments.

War and the Christian Conscience may still be regarded as the more fundamental and historical statement of the ethical justification of Christian participation in the use of military force, and of the conditions, tests, and limits of "just war." Still, in the intervening seven years, events have moved on and there have been new problems arising in the international system and confronting the policies of this nation. It has been necessary to *extend* my general analysis of the *morality of war* into new areas, to see whether, in the face of new challenges, the ancient tests governing "just conduct" in war have any longer any illuminating power, and, in some cases, to deepen and to correct my understanding of these ethical requirements.

Some chapters in the present volume articulate once again the principles effective in Christian conscience in regard to participation in war. The reader need not refer back to that older book, though I would hope one would be led to it for his own assessment of the theological development or the worth of the moral argument. However, a number of the chapters in the present volume—for example, the first two chapters of Part Two on "The Morality of War"—are enough to start with.

[1] Duke University Press, Durham, N.C.

Moreover, the use of the same principles of analysis throughout make this a self-contained introduction to the meaning of the just-war teachings in their bearing upon a variety of contemporary political and military problems to which I have been forced to address myself. In the course of these writings it may be that those criteria were given greater clarification.

Yet the present volume does not simply seize new occasions for going over old ground. A theory of responsible action in the international system is elaborated, for example, in the first chapter on "The Uses of Power," and the second on "The Ethics of Intervention" in the section entitled "Political Ethics," which for this reason is placed first in order.

This section concludes with an examination of "Selective Conscientious Objection" (Chap. 5). Here we examine the warrants and reservations to be found in the just-war doctrine, in the nature of political community, and in law in the United States (as presently interpreted) for instituting a system of alternative national service for men who conscientiously object to service in a particular war which they deem unjust.

It may also be the case that some readers will find particular value in the record of discussions included here on the Vatican Council's statement on nuclear war, and my own final assessment of the statement. As many as six chapters (4, 10, 14–17), explore this signal development in modern church teachings, its background, and the lead it gives.

Special mention should be made of the chapters contained in the final part on "Vietnam and Insurgency Warfare" which open up new meanings in the application of traditional moral principles to this urgent new problem in the affairs of the world. Chapters 18 and 19 are taken from a paper "How Shall Counter-Insurgency War Be Conducted Justly?" which has been widely cited but is here published for the first time. This same urgent and present problem is explored in subsequent articles and debates printed in the final section.

I ought to note the single area in which the author is aware of an important change in judgment since that earlier book. This has to do with the *morality of deterrence*. By continuing to confront the grave problem of the meaning of the political responsibilities resting upon the citizens of a nuclear-power nation, and by the discussions of which this is one side of the record, I was forced back upon my premises again to see whether I had drawn from these a proper and adequate and, indeed, the necessary conclusion on the matter of deterrence. This grave and continuing problem is the concern of Part Three of this volume. The question of deterrence is with us earlier, of course, for example in Chapter 8, "The Hatfields and the Coys," where will be found a statement of *the moral problem* of deterrence which seems to entail that the problem itself contains the Christian answer and the only just answer. There was need to go deeper than that, and this is one of the areas the reader may be drawn into by the present volume, in Chapters 11 and 12, as well as the entire section devoted to it. Concerning this change of mind on the morality of deterrence—or rather concerning this further probing and elaboration of the morality of deterrence—I can only say two things. First, in concluding that no sort of force could be retained for deterrence's sake which it would be immoral ever to use, I had not paid careful enough attention either to some of the findings of fact or to some of the findings of moral law that are necessary to show how a *possible* deterrence posture and governing moral principles mesh together. Secondly, I gladly say that, after all, one always needs colleagues with whom to engage if he is to know what he knows when he thinks he knows anything rightly.

In Chapter 17, "Robert W. Tucker's *Bellum Contra Bellum Justum*," I was forced to defend the applicability and meaning of the just-war teachings against an allegedly more *realistic view of statecraft,* while in all other cases it is from another flank that some of my Christian brethren assault the position I hold to be correct.

This chapter, written in reply to a realistic theory of statecraft and printed in Part Four of this book entitled "The Second Vatican Council and a Just-War Theory of Statecraft," as well as other chapters in rejoinder, can be understood well enough by themselves, apart from the original article I was commenting on. If this is the case, it is because I believe that one does social or political ethics by clarifying *the doctrine.* I can only hope that a number of the chapters in this volume will lead some new readers to the original exchange of views in search of a more detailed comprehension of the matters at issue.

These essays have been only slightly revised, and in a few instances a bracketed footnote has been added. Not much revision was necessary, partly because in my judgment one does not do political ethics in the first place by accumulating facts or factual analyses that are going to change rapidly or radically, and partly because it seemed wise to let the record stand and not try to seem altogether up to the minute or to have been always wise. I did—in common with almost everyone else in the English-speaking world—make one stupid mistake in my reading of the encyclical *Pacem in terris,* which is footnoted; and it is the burden of a subsequent chapter to follow out all of the entailments of the corrected reading (Chapter 10: "When 'Just' War Is Not Justified"). Here, as in the case of the morality of deterrence, the reader has an opportunity to learn with me if he wants to; or else he can locate his own position better in the course of the argument.

I hope I need not apologize for the comparatively small amount of repetition between some of the chapters. This could not be eliminated, because anyone whose point of entrance to this volume is at one or two chapters, and not others, needs a completed analysis or argument to be stated on the point he may be interested in.

Perhaps it was simply a predictable result of my reading again, during the preparation of this volume for publication, the written record of my intellectual efforts over these recent years that I should have become convinced that these chapters form a coherent unity on a broad enough scale to warrant the judgments I mentioned at the beginning of this Introduction. There do seem to be several threads that connect them all—several purposes of this authorship, whatever it may be worth.

I shall mention three of these before concluding these introductory remarks.

1. The first came to mind while working on the present volume when I read (rather belatedly and in English translation) the following paragraphs in Ramond Aron's monumental *Peace and War: A Theory of International Relations*.[2] These seemed to me a very good statement of what has actually been one of the guiding threads, the intentionality, of these writings of mine. Aron is speaking of nuclear proliferation:

> Between the two antinomic theses, each of which has its partisans—peace through the generalization of thermonuclear deterrence and the dangers created by the enlargement of the atomic club—I do not hesitate to choose: the first is illusory, deceptively seductive, it has the characteristic appeal of sophistries. In short, it is war which must be saved, in other words, the possibility of tests of armed strength between states rather than eternal peace, which would have to be established by the constant threat of the thermonuclear holocaust. . . .
>
> It is just as bizarre to imagine the industrial societies will live in peace because they will no longer have the means to fight as it is to imagine that they will live in peace because they will all have the means to destroy each other in a few moments. The seemingly opposite intellectual error is actually the same in both cases. The doctrinaire of peace by fear imagines an equality between states by the capacity of the weakest to deal the strongest a mortal blow. The doctrinaire of peace by disarma-

[2] Doubleday (New York, 1966), pp. 640, 646, 649.

ment imagines the equality to consist of the inability of the strongest to coerce the weakest. Neither equality is obtainable. . . .

Such, in effect, is the first dilemma confronting statesmen in our age: do they wish to save war or save humanity from a certain war (thermonuclear war)?

To "save politics" (and war) for purposefulness (and perhaps to save mankind from purposeless violence) is by no means to concentrate on military "efficiency" alone or "realistic statecraft." To "save politics" will require an effective challenge both to native American pacifism in all its manifestations and to our inclination (*connected* with that) to invoke a narrow doctrine of "military necessity." It will require a just-war theory of statecraft to take the place of the policy of more and more war and the policy of more and more peace which are joined together like Siamese twins in the American ethos.

2. Another central theme of this volume is an entire theory of statecraft, of political authority, political community, and political responsibility. Most of these chapters are concerned with the nature of a proper *political act*—of "government"—specifically, with the proper political action of the nation-state in the international system. This view of statecraft only came to expression in the just-war doctrine on the use of force. I trust that this will be attended to, and that what is said below will not be dismissed—because of our present cliché-ridden debates over foreign policy—by attributing to its author an obsessive fear of communism. Very few statements in the pages to follow—and none of the essential ones—depend upon there being such a thing as communism, much less a monolithic, undiversified communist movement in the world. The concern is rather to elaborate a proper political ethics—from right reason and from the perspectives upon the political life of mankind which Christians should share. The *military* doctrine—the just-war theory—is an outgrowth, entailment, or expression of this conception of the relation between force and political responsibility. Whether one moves "from politics to war" or "from war to politics,"[3] it is statecraft that is crucial.

This theory of statecraft with its concept of the just use of military force was a common possession of all the mainline Christian churches—Lutheran and Calvinistic no less than Roman Catholic. Perhaps this ought to be stressed, since a number of the chapters in this book are devoted to the analysis, exposition, and criticism of modern Roman Catho-

[3] See Theodore R. Weber: "Modern War and the Pursuit of Peace" (New York: Council on Religion and International Affairs, 1968).

lic documents. It is true that the tests of *jus ad bellum* (When is war right?) and *jus in bello* (What is right in war?) were first refined by men who have come to be identified as Roman Catholic moralists for the strange reason that they lived and wrote their treatises before the Protestant Reformation. Still the Augsburg Confession (Art. XVI) says, "Our churches teach that lawful civil ordinances are good works of God and that it is right[4] for Christians to engage in just wars, to serve as soldiers . . ."; the Westminster Confession speaks of wars that are "just and necessary"; and left-wing Calvinism elaborated the just-war doctrine into a theory of justifiable revolution which underlay the struggles for human liberty and rights in the British civil wars and the American Revolution. This view of the tempered and limited use of force in behalf of social change and revolutionary justice was productive also of a spirit of mutual accommodation and compromise. It demythologized the ends to be sought in any historical struggle or cause. It inculcated a sense of political community and habitual observance of social due process (not ever to be breached except in the last resort) which underlies the growth of democratic society upon Puritan Protestant soil.[5] Thus, in important measure, both democracy itself and the just-war doctrine on the use of armed force are manifestations of the same fundamental view of the meaning of proper statecraft.

In any case, the myopic identification of the just-war doctrine with Roman Catholicism has definitely to be rejected. This belongs to all Christians who are not sectarians. That is to say, it belongs to all who are not members of the traditional peace churches or who have not joined the new sectarianism known as the New Left. New or old, these believe —whether because men were created originally so good or because their redemption has been so complete—that politics has undergone or may undergo messianic change, that there need be no constant and prudent connection between force and political responsibility, and that the day has already dawned when it is not right for Christians to engage in just wars under the lawful command of civil authority.

The truth is that, historically, Roman Catholicism never went as

---

[4] Note that the Confession does not say merely that it is "permitted" or that it is an "evil necessity" or the "lesser evil" to engage in just wars. A soldier should have "good conscience" in his calling, no less than men engaged in other secular vocations.

[5] One should not begin a revolt unless he sees "near at hand the possibility of establishing a new and better order"—because "the risk of long continued anarchy, which may result in an even worse tyranny, should be in the minds of Christians" (John C. Bennett, *The Christian as Citizen*. New York: Association Press, 1955, pp. 52–3).

far in endorsing the theory of statecraft which this volume is concerned to expound than either Lutheranism or Calvinism. Roman Catholicism never elevated this body of teachings about justice in war by a reference to it in a "confession" of the church—unless the use made of it by Vatican Council II (see Chapter 16 below) is to be regarded as a somewhat comparable authorization.

We should notice that the just-war doctrine on the use of force takes on a significantly different cast in these several religious traditions. This theory of statecraft is held in common by Augustinian interpretations of Christians and the State. Two of the main branches of a fundamentally Augustinian view of statecraft are the Christian natural law theory of the state and the Lutheran analysis of the state as an "order of necessity" (*Notverordnung*). From this arises a not insignificant difference in interpreting the meaning and basis of "the political act." A proponent of natural law and human rights can so stress the common good which politics serves that the component of power seems lost from view; while a Lutheran can so stress the need for restraint of sin that he loses sight of justice and the other community values that also belong to the essence of political authority and the action of rulers. Pope John XXIII's encyclical *Pacem in terris* with its "natural rights optimism" is an example of the first emphasis, and the *real politic* theories that sometimes emerge on Lutheran ground are corrupt examples of the second of these emphases within the main line of Christian political thought. The just-war doctrine on the use of force holds these divergent emphases together in balanced perspective; it is in fact an excellent prism through which to see the several elements of a Christian theory of statecraft.

However, this difference between Roman Catholic and Reformation versions of just-war statecraft can easily be exaggerated. After all, Luther believed that a prince, even though a Turk and without grace or special revelation, could rule with *justice*. Man's natural sense of justice cannot be expunged from the thought of the Reformers, even though it is fashionable today to attempt this. Luther taught, in fact, that the Golden Rule was a republication in Scripture of "another judge," another norm of judgment to which to take a litigant who refuses to be judged by the law of Christlike love; and he states that moral decisions coming from a free mind are "given by love and by *the law of nature, of which the reason is full*." [6] Calvin wrote that "nothing is more common than for man to be sufficiently instructed in a right course by

---

[6] Martin Luther: *On Secular Authority*, in John Dillenberger, ed., *Martin Luther: Selections from His Writings* (Anchor Books; Garden City, N.Y.: Doubleday & Company, Inc., 1961), p. 401 (italics added).

xiii

natural law." [7] It is also well known that Calvinist political doctrines depart radically from the distinctive Lutheran emphasis upon the state as only an "order of necessity," in their stress upon the creation, and upon the integrity of the human. This made possible the growth of doctrines of natural justice, duties, and rights upon the soil of Puritan Protestantism until the time of (and including) John Locke's *Second Treatise on Civil Government*. Therefore, in general, we must once and for all deny the allegation that the theory of just war and the natural justice of politics is a peculiarly Roman Catholic teaching. Instead, this has been until now the common teaching, in one version or another, of all the major Christian traditions.

3. Finally, this volume is everywhere concerned with the question, *How* ought men to make political decisions in the area of foreign policy and military affairs?—not *what* the decision should be in particular instances. For the short or long meanwhile, we are going to have to make judgments concerning the use of armed force. We need first to *clarify the grounds* upon which men should make judgments as to the justice of resorts to war. It is of first importance that Christians decide how we are going rightly to resolve disputes over the justice of war, before disputing over it or delivering ourselves to verdicts that particular uses of force can or cannot be justified. Until we do this, we have little business trying to inform the conscience of the nations. If our criteria are not first defended as informative for statecraft, the particular pieces of advice we give are very apt to lessen responsible resolve, or strengthen it in the wrong direction, or to be dismissed by those who bear the awesome burdens of political office.

A policy of "anticipatory reconciliation" to which we Christians are prone is simply not sufficient in foreign affairs. The counsel this yields is, on all occasions, Stop, Do Less, Let Peace Prevail. It is fruitful of many an explanation that the enemy is always reconcilable and that his paranoia was due to our containment (Nazi Germany or Red China), of attempted corrections of our supposed excessive confidence in the use of force, of ever renewed searches for lesser evil alternatives that are not there. It seeks always to frustrate unilateral national initiative in the use of force, and in doing so may let worse befall. It provides no grounds for supposing (as now seems likely to have been true) that only U.S. initiative in sending a ship to challenge the Egyptian blockade of the Gulf of Aqaba *might* have loosed Jordan from its bonds with Nasser

---

[7] John Calvin: *Institutes*, II, 2, 22.

enough to have forestalled Israel's six-day war, and prevented the increase of garrison states, guerrilla war, and Russian presence in that region of the world for our lifetime. Because so much of Jewish opinion in this country had joined Christian "liberals" in adhering to the opinion that *multinational* action is almost always better than unilateral action (see Chapter 23 below), we had the spectacle of both Christians and Jews seeking some special *religious* reason for swifter or less ambiguous support of Israel! That is no way to make up for our lack of an adequate understanding of possibly proper political actions.

For many men of this generation the "justified" war against Nazi Germany became an episode having a moral equation that is not likely to happen again. The Korean war was fought under U.N. auspice, because the U.S.S.R. was that month boycotting the Security Council (i.e. because of an opportunity not afforded by the Charter!). It was not necessary, therefore, for men of this generation to think through the justification of a possible U.S. unilateral initiation of the costly war against North Korean aggression. Because of this, and the unusually "greater evil" of Nazism, it has not been necessary for many of us, and especially for churchmen, to conceive of the permanent place force has in the nation-state system. Thus has this liberal generation been saved from the need to clarify the grounds for decisions of state issuing in war or peace in an international system that is largely in a "state of nature" (or "state of war," if this means a perpetual inclination thereto, like Hobbes' "bad weather").

Thus, the typical Western liberal holds a tame version of the limited-war doctrine. This view concedes the use of force as an "exception"; at all other times politics is being rightly conducted. This view has not let the constant function of force or the threat of force in the nation-state system sink deeply into consciousness. This view always cries for less or delayed force and trammels action and initiative in foreign policy. It tries to stay at home and not go abroad. It believes that force or the threat or potentiality of the use of force does not serve liberty, order, and justice so much as setting our own house in order. It tends to believe that reconciliation and not radically new international structures, contrition for past "containment" and not world public authority itself capable of *enforcement*, can fulfill a nation-state's present responsibilities. Its only test justifying resort to force is the "lesser evil" in the supposed consequences; hence it is prone to delay, waiting for the rare "exceptional" case which it falsely identifies with the proviso in the just-war doctrine that a use of armed force should be in the last reasonable resort. Such a view tends always to prize later or lower levels of violence over other possibly more prudent and just courses of action. It tends always to urge negotiation before events and the wills of men have been brought to the point where negotiations can produce a "better peace" (Augustine).

We need to have more than this to say in the years ahead. Churchmen can better serve the present age by engaging in the manifold work of reason in articulating the constituent elements of responsible political action on the part of the nation-states, and by enlarging the terms in public debate, than by partisan support of even the best proposals. It is important that we *know what we are doing*, for example, in sponsoring and signing the nuclear non-proliferation treaty, and that the debate over this treaty be enlarged, its entailments for the future made clear. Such a treaty will (if it is a good thing) require more, not fewer, far-flung tacit commitments of the U.S. to guarantee the security of non-nuclear powers (aligned, like Japan; or non-aligned, like India) against direct nuclear blackmail and against conventional or insurgency assaults that are backed by nuclear threat. Credible guarantees probably cannot be transmitted while making progress in nuclear disarmament (as the non-nuclear powers seem to believe); in fact, an anti-missile protection against future Chinese missiles may be required. Russia and the United States cannot reassure the non-nuclear nations by introducing a resolution in the Security Council pledging the Council to act, and at the same time leave many Americans grounds for hoping that mainland China can soon be admitted into the United Nations under conditions that would seat her as one of the great powers. This treaty will be a significant additional step toward *détente* with Russia; it is therefore unavoidably anti-Chinese and necessarily entails continuing U.S. responsibilities in Southeast Asia. All these considerations need to be lifted into view. In the judgment of the present writer, such a treaty would on balance be desirable; but it clearly entails greater, not less, responsibility on the part of U.S. power in the service of an ordered justice and peace in the world. If we do not now think through the tacit commitments of this nation in securing a nuclear non-proliferation treaty, then—when the going gets rough—we will have another agonizing reappraisal, and will pick up our marbles and come home. If we want this treaty, it simply will not be sufficient for us to say that since war is evil the less of it, the less threat of it, or commitment to it the better; or that since God wills the unity of mankind unilateral national action resorting to armed force or to the threat of force should always be frowned upon. We had better begin re-educating ourselves, and the greater or lesser magistrates who will listen to us, in the elements of Christian political realism, and what this means for *how* to formulate the foreign policy of a nation responsibly.

It remains for me to return thanks. My indebtedness to many persons is evident first of all in the explanation at the beginning of each chapter of the occasion on which the address was given or an article written. I am grateful for these invitations to speak or to write, and in some instances to editors who raised no decisive objection when I put my submissions before them.

A very special word should be said about the Council on Religion and International Affairs; its President, Dr. A. William Loos; its former National Field Director, Mr. William J. Cook; its Director of Publications and Editor of *worldview*, Mr. James Finn; and the many participants at the Seminars and Consultations sponsored by CRIA which I have attended for the politically-awakened part of my life. It is evident to all who know the Council on Religion and International Affairs that this organization and these men achieve their purpose to an extraordinary degree. This purpose is to bring into living encounter the moral and religious issues in foreign policy with the expertness that can be gained only from specialized study and from actual responsibility in the preparation of positions of state. If CRIA had not been in existence, or without the cordial support its officers have always given my own professional work and without the opportunity to receive instruction at CRIA Seminars, the present volume would never have been written— nor, for that matter, the 1961 book either. The acknowledgements for permission to reprint a number of these chapters are a sufficient indication of the extent of my indebtedness. I could never adequately express my appreciation for all that CRIA has meant to me—not least of all for many hours of friendly fellowship and hours of informal discussion with people who knew enough not to begin with the answers.

It pleases me at the end of this Introduction to be able, this time in a second volume, to record the fact that I have had the invaluable assistance of my daughter, Marcia (Mrs. J. Warren Wood, III). Without her help (or without paste) I would not have been able to deliver the manuscript on time to Will Davison, Religious Book Editor at Scribners, and to his associate, Dorothy Gilkey Duffy, whom I also thank not only for past favors but also for the care in editing that I am about to receive.

This volume goes forth into the world in the memory of my elder brother, John, who died while it was nearing completion. He was a business man from top to toe, the successful one of the Ramsey boys. I judge that he felt that in his vocation a man is called to exercise vigorously a rational and a charitable will. His wife and two sons, and his grandchildren, have from him a happy heritage. He was also the leader of our family. He now goes with God.

PAUL RAMSEY

Department of Religion
Princeton University
June, 1968

Table of Contents

PART FOUR: THE SECOND VATICAN COUNCIL AND A
JUST-WAR THEORY OF STATECRAFT

PART FIVE: VIETNAM AND INSURGENCY WARFARE

A Fable[*]

Eve let her eyes fall that day upon the figure of her husband. She knew something of both his resolve and his apprehension over the future toward which they were going. Yesterday her gaze dwelt upon him lovingly with the unwavering support of a woman's eyes in a world long ago where there were no others and no distances between. Today it seemed she had not known him then.

"It is as important to launch this agricultural economy you are determined to have," said she to Adam, "from a sound social base as it is to try to launch it from a sound technological base. You have your wooden plow, but that is not enough. The age we are entering must have as the foundation of its great adventure a social platform of friendly competition, cooperation, and mutual respect. . . ."

A silence descended between them, while her words strove mightily against Adam. Eve's imagination—mother to all the living—grew replete with what was yet unborn.

"The age of Abel the keeper of sheep," she murmured quietly with hope, "of Cain the tiller of the ground and the first to build a city, of Jabal the father of those who dwell in tents and have cattle, of Jubal the father of all those who play the lyre and pipe, of Tubal-cain the forger of instruments of bronze and iron, of Nimrod the mighty huntsman, and of all who make brick with bitumen for mortar—this great age must be launched from the social platform of universal responsibility."

Adam looked with downcast eyes at the shadow upon their pathway cast from behind them by the angel's two flaming swords. He knew better than she the shape of the advancing generations. Yet his mind had no relish for this knowledge, and he too wished that this new age might be launched from some other platform than the No-Returning.

* Reprinted from *The Chaplain*, Vol. 15, No. 5 (October, 1958), 27–28; *motive*, April 1959 cover; and *The Christian Advocate*, January 5, 1961, p. 11.

PART ONE

Political Ethics

CHAPTER I

The Uses of Power*

During the 1964 contest for the Presidency between Lyndon B. Johnson and Barry Goldwater, we did not have any good national debate about United States foreign and military policy. The apparent reason for this is that attention was narrowly focused upon particular issues believed to be clear enough. The basic factor, however, preventing profound debate over how we as a people are to discharge our political responsibilties in the present age is the hardened polarization of "liberal" and "conservative" opinion in this country—endemic indeed to the modern mind. This in turn only shows that we lack an understanding of "government"—of what I shall call "political agency."

The "conservatives" and the "liberals" each have a piece of the truth and they make the error each points out in the other. Beyond this, they also share a common error.

The liberals know that in a nuclear age war cannot be an instrument of justice and there can be no "victory' if the means of violence used are disproportionate to any political goals (as well they may be). Therefore they conclude that there can be no positive use of force of any sort or at any level of violence for political ends, that every dispute can and should be settled, and that the only sacrifice for the nation's good that is to be commended is the sacrificial spirit of diplomats who are resolved to negotiate so that negotiation will never fail.

The conservative, on the other hand, knows that there must be a positive use of armed power in the political affairs of mankind. There-

---

* First appeared in *The Perkins School of Theology Journal*, Vol. xviii, No. 1 (Fall, 1964), 13–24.

fore, he seems determined to "win" all the way up the scale of the available violence.

Both believe that peace, justice, and freedom can be preserved by "bluffing"—the liberal with at most his *show* of force at the lower levels and the conservative with his *show* of force at the upper nuclear level. This is the error they have in common. Therefore, they both avoid thinking through the actual *use* of power for positive purposes, and the political morality governing such use.

Of course, a liberal President proved we would "shoot back" in the gulf of Tonkin. This, however, is not enough doctrine for the responsible use of the power of a great nation. It only goes beyond the western gunfighter's morality, which allows the other fellow to *draw* first, by now allowing him to *shoot* first. This is, in fact, the doctrine that permits the Vietcong successes with their "insurgency warfare," which may be defined as hitting the "haves" where they have it not.

The brilliant North Vietnamese General Giap, who never went to war college, was once asked to explain his theory of war. He replied, "The first essential is to have a working politico-military doctrine."

The empires and nations of Christendom used to have such a working politico-military doctrine. Lately, however, political purposes have been split off from military doctrine. The conservatives do this by their asserted willingness to use or threaten force that cannot have any political purpose, by their determination to defend the free world and even roll back communism by simply being resolute enough, and by their belief that if only this nation *sounds* as if it is willing to use its entire nuclear arsenal it won't have to do so. The liberals split politics and military doctrine apart by their belief that only peaceful means serve any positive purpose, and that force has at most the purpose that a show of it stimulates negotiation.

The politico-military doctrine that used to be intact among the peoples of the West is the "just-war" doctrine, which is better called the theory of the *justified* war. This teaching has many aspects, some of which I have explored elsewhere. Here it is important to say that the rules or principles governing the responsible use of armed force, or rather the principles which *anatomized* the nature of a responsible use of armed force, were at the same time a way of understanding human political reality and a way of delineating the nature of *any* use of power (armed or not). The just-war theory was a working politico-military doctrine, and a first essential in the government of mankind. This is the heart of the matter, which I want to discuss in this chapter.

II

The use of power, and possibly the use of force, is of the *esse* of politics. By this I mean it belongs to politics' very *act of being* politics. You never have politics without the use of power, possibly armed force. At the same time the use of power, and possibly the use of force, is inseparable from the *bene esse* of politics. By this I mean that it is inseparable from politics' *proper* act of being politics, inseparable from the well-being of politics, inseparable from the human pursuit of the national or the international common good by political means. You never have *good* politics without the use of power, possibly armed force.

The proposition that the use of power, and possibly the use of force, belongs to the *esse* of politics (its *act of being*) and is inseparable from the *bene esse* of politics (its *proper act of being*, or its act of being *proper* politics) is denied by two views of the state, or of political community. Both of these mistaken views have gained wide currency today— the first only among some Christians, but the second among Christian and non-Christian so-called "liberals." (Myself, I would prefer, if I could, to save that great word from such abuse.)

The first is Karl Barth's Christological view of the *normal* functions of political authority. His radically Christocentric understanding of politics is symbolized and exhibited in his teaching that it is the *polis* that is destined for perfection in the Kingdom of God, while the Church shall wither away. Meantime, this side resurrection, the state derives its meaning from the fact that Jesus Christ has already assumed the human reality which magistrates govern. This means, Barth writes, that "war should not on any account be recognized as a normal, fixed, and in some sense necessary part of what on the Christian view constitutes the just state, or the political order demanded by God." [1]

On a surface reading of it, of course, that statement should never be denied. We should always affirm, with Barth, that "what Christian ethics has to emphasize is that neither inwardly nor outwardly does the normal task of the state, which is at issue even in time of war, consist in a process of annihilating rather than maintaining and fostering life. . . . It is no part of the normal task of the state to wage war; its normal task is to fashion peace in such a way that life is served and war kept at bay. . . . It is when the state does not rightly pursue its normal task that sooner or later it is compelled to take up the abnormal one of war, and therefore to inflict this abnormal task on other states." [2]

---

[1] *Church Dogmatics* (Edinburgh: T. & T. Clark, 1961), Vol. III, Part 4, p. 456.

[2] Barth, p. 458. To circumscribe correctly the war-making power, the last sentence above should be revised to read: "It is when any state or all states do not rightly

Barth, however, means something more profound than this in his apprehension of the task of political authority in the light of Christ and the supernatural *polis*. "It is no primary concern of Christian ethics to say that [the state should exercise power], or to maintain that the exercise of power constitutes the essence of the state, i.e. its *opus proprium*, or even a part of it. What Christian ethics must insist is that it is an *opus alienum* for the state to have to exercise power." [3]

The other, more prevalent and, in my opinion, more naive way of denying that the use of power, and possibly the use of force, is of the *esse* of politics is the supposition that not the advent of Christ but the advent of the nuclear age means that politics can and may and must be conducted without ever invoking power to impose solutions. This view ultimately depends (not upon the "logic" of nuclear weapons, but) upon the myth of the primeval goodness and preternatural wisdom of man. This seems to me to underlie Adlai Stevenson's Dag Hammarskjold Memorial Lecture delivered at Princeton, March 1964, and not inappropriately entitled "The Audacious Dream of Dynamic Order." [4] As we have moved from a policy of Containment to a policy of Cease-Fire, so the world is on the verge, said Mr. Stevenson, of a breakthrough to a policy of Peaceful Change replacing Cease-Fire. Containment meant limited war; Cease-Fire means limited peace. Peaceful Change, no longer static like those former policies, would be true (and I suppose unlimited) peace, because this will be based on "a *dynamic* system of order" which will apply a "curative resolution" to the roots of hostility. ". . . *Perhaps* Korea was the end of the road for classical armed aggression against one's next-door neighbor; *perhaps* Suez was the end of the road for colonial-type military solutions; *perhaps* Cuba was the end of the road for nuclear confrontation."

Missing is any mention of "wars of national liberation" conducted by subversion and insurgency from abroad. Mr. Stevenson simply believes that "we may have *slipped almost imperceptibly* into an era of peaceful settlement of disputes" (italics added). So imperceptible was this passage except to the eyes of faith, that, despite the Ambassador's discussion of improvements yet to be made in the United Nation's peace-keeping machinery, it seems evident that Stevenson's audacious dream of a dynamically changing order changing in an orderly fashion must be based on

---

pursue their normal task [of maintaining and fostering life] that sooner or later a state has inflicted upon it the abnormal task of war." This makes evident how statistically normal this normatively abnormal task may be in a world of finite rulers with limited wisdom (not to mention the consequence of the Fall upon political existence, which Barth's Christological viewpoint rejects as decisively important for Christian political theory).

   [3] Barth, p. 456.
   [4] Princeton Alumni Weekly, Vol. LXIV, N. 20 (June 9, 1964), 26–30.

some myth of the primeval goodness and preternatural wisdom of man. (U.N. peace-keeping machinery provides enforcement for only one policy —the still static one of cease-fire—while the dynamic resolution of disputes, it is hoped, will proceed non-violently.) Concerning "this consensus on recourse to non-violent solutions" only, Stevenson declared, "most of the world is in agreement right now!" He added in all earnestness, and with no sense at all of the tragic irony of his remark, simply this one qualification: "There are a few who would make a small exception of his own dispute with his neighbor."

But neither the western liberal's primeval man nor Barth's post-evil Christ-formed man is the subject of political agency or of political rule *post lapsum* and this side resurrection. Therefore, I say, the use of power, and possibly the use of armed force, is of the *esse* of politics and inseparably connected with those higher human goods which are the *bene esse* of politics in all the historical ages of mankind. This interpretation of political authority is held in common by the Augustinian tradition and its two main branches: the natural law theory of politics and the Lutheran analysis of the state as an "order of necessity" (*Notverordnung*).[5]

Another way to say this is as follows: politics is defined by both its *genus* (community) and its *specific difference* (the use of power). What political community has in common with other communities (friendship, economic associations, professional and cultural groups transcending national boundaries) within the *genus* to which they all belong may comprise the higher human qualities. Every community pursues a common good, or a good in common. But the legitimate use of decisive physical power distinguishes political community from these other communities in the formation of the life of mankind. *Generic* social values are the matter of politics; but so also is the *specific* use of power. You can say that the former comprise the higher values to which the latter is a conditional value; but not that the latter is a merely extrinsic instrument that can be dropped. In fact, in the *definitional* sense of "primary" and "secondary," *generic* community values are the secondary (i.e. the distinctly human) purpose of politics while the use of power comprises the differentiating *species* or the primary (i.e. the distinctive) modality of politics. I mean only to repeat this in the proposition: the use of power, and possibly the use of force, is of the *esse* of politics, and it is inseparable from the

---

[5] It is, of course, possible for natural law teachings so to stress the *bene esse*, the common good, that the component of power is lost from view; and for the Lutheran view to stress restraint and lose sight of justice and the other community values that also belong to the essence of political authority and the action of rulers. Pope John XXIII's encyclical *Pacem in terris* with its "natural law optimism" is an example of the first, and *real-political* theories that sometimes emerge on Lutheran ground are examples of the second, of these divergencies from main-line Christian political theory, of which the just-war doctrine is the chief prismatic case.

bene esse of politics. This entails no derogation of the uniquely human ends, the generic values, the *bene esse,* of political community. Quite the contrary. This puts power in its place in our understanding of politics by definitely placing it within the pursuit of the political good.

The ingredients of this classical understanding of the nature of political society need to be comprehended by citizens and statesmen alike if political action is to be restored to health in the present day. Ours is an era in which "liberals" face down every fact with the myth that there is a non-violent solution to every conflict and in which even hard-headed political "realists" who define politics in terms of power still speak as if political action is therefore intrinsically immoral. The fact is that there is no domestic political action that does not erode or strengthen the power and authority of government and at the same time erode or strengthen the more human purposes of government (the common good). The one is no more "selfish" or otherwise immoral than the other.

Likewise, there is no political action in the realm of foreign policy that does not erode or strengthen the power position of a nation and at the same time erode or strengthen the purposes of that nation in the world community—the international common good as this is viewed and acted upon by that government's power and policies. To enhance the one is no more "selfish" than to do the other; neither can be accomplished without effect upon and causal influence from the other. A political action is always an exercise of power and an exercise of purpose. Power without purpose and purpose without power are both equally nonpolitical.

In the field of foreign affairs, the United States always needs an environment or field of forces favorable to its power in the world, and we need always an environment favorable to our purposes in the world. Broadly speaking, the overriding goal of our foreign policy is to create and sustain a system of free and independent nations. We are in the business of nation-building. This understanding of the international common good is the *bene esse* of our political actions toward foreign powers, while in our physical, economic and other forms of power lies the *esse* of such actions and the way a nation takes responsibility for its purposes. Either requires the other, and each requires an environment favorable to it. To perform the political action that rightly protects our security and power in the power-environment is no more immoral than an act that rightly protects our nationhood by fostering an environment of independent nations. We cannot contribute to the upbuilding of nations and the system of free and independent states without making our power felt; nor can the free nations grow strong without affecting, one way or another, the power and prestige of the United States in the security environment. Thus, the *esse* and the *bene esse* of international political agency, our exercise of power and the actualization of our agreement concerning what is morally and politically right, belong inseparably together and they fluctuate together.

III

This understanding of political action is enough to show that the standards of personal morality are not to be applied without more ado to political conduct. Political responsibility does not mean simply doing all the humanitarian good one can in the world, without prior attention to that which specifically differentiates the political good from the good in general, and without prior analysis of the structural difference between personal moral agency and political agency. This mistake has led many of the best people in the world today (those rather inappropriately called "liberals") to suppose that cultural exchanges, economic aid, and the Peace Corps are the only *proper* modes of politics toward which the nations are or should be moving. That would be to try to launch out toward the *bene esse* of politics without taking responsibility for its *esse*.

This does not mean, however, that personal and political actions are subject to entirely different moral standards, or that there is a double standard for individual conduct and for the actions of states. It only (but definitely) means that they are subject in different modes to the moral requirements governing conduct.

This is further in evidence when, leaving aside the use of power as politics' *act of being* politics, we take up some of the basic ethical criteria which determine politics' *proper act of being* politics.

The state, which is the "subject" of political action, has its responsibility defined by the national common good and by the international common good. These goods are not always the same.[6] There is, to say the least, a dialectic, a tension, a polarity, if there is not an actual or irremediable conflict, between the national and the international common good. The responsibility of the statesman is defined by the area of incidence, or overlap, between them. Allowing for the fact that he should strive always to envision and if possible to establish a larger area of incidence between his nation's good and the international common good, it is still this area of incidence between these goods that defines his responsibility. He is not called to office to aim at all the humanitarian good that can be aimed at in the world. Instead, he must determine what he *ought to do* from out of the total humanitarian good that *ought to be*. He is not even responsible for all of the *ought to be* that *ought to be*

---

[6] Besides Pope John XXIII's omission of sufficient consideration of the problem of power, another way to characterize the defect of his encyclical *Pacem in terris* is to say that he supposed that the national and the international common good are always coincident, or can be made to be coincident in any moment of governmental decision.

politically done, since there are other nations and other political actors in the world. He must locate his political obligation, and that of his nation, within an area of incidence between the national and the international common good.

The theory of political anarchism is false which teaches that those goods are somehow completely congruent, so that these are but two misleading words for the same thing. Only upon a Kantian postulate that somehow the moral universe insures it can it be supposed that the *true* good of the nation (if only one could discern this) is the same as the good of all mankind (if only one could know what that is). In any moment of historical time, it is in any case true that there are more ways to miss the mark than to hit it (as Aristotle said), and missing the mark cannot *simply* be defined as doing less than the international common good alone requires.

Of course, a statesman is in danger of serving a too narrow view of the international common good and *thereby* failing to serve the best possible good of his own nation. And of course he may serve a too narrow national interest and *thereby* fail to serve an international common good that was possible. But there is also the danger that he may try to do too much of the humanitarian good that ought to be politically done, with the result that he does less than he ought to have done for the national common good and renders his own nation less apt to serve either common good in the future.

Nothing can remove from among the awesome responsibilities of magistrates the determination of where to draw these lines. If a "conservative" has any political sense, he will not simply decry all internationalism as naive "do-good-ism"; nor will the "liberal" if he has political sense meet every proposal that the present far-flung commitments of the United States be revised, and some of them liquidated, with the cry of "isolationism." Every responsible political decision involves some precarious determination of how the circles of the national and the international common good are to be drawn. This is the mode in which the ideal humanitarian good (all of which, by definition, ought to be) specifies itself for political choice.

IV

There is another set of terms which are determinative (or the realities to which they point are determinative) of the morality of political conduct. These are "order" and "justice," with a tension or dialectic between them similar to the one we have considered between various "common goods" in our analysis so far of the *bene esse* (the *proper* being) of politics.

Order is not a higher value in politics than justice, but neither is humanitarian justice a higher value than order. Both are in some respects conditional to the other. Order is for the sake of justice since the only real political justice is an ordered justice; yet justice is no less for the sake of order, since the only real political order in which men may dwell together in community and peace is one that is *just* enough to command the love and allegiances of men, or at least their acquiescence and their compliance. Power, which is of the *esse* of political agency, may be a conditional value only; but order and justice, which are ever in tension yet in inter-relation, both are values that comprise the well-being, the *bene esse*, of political affairs and the common good which is the goal of political action.

A decision-maker contemplating, for example, some positive interventionary military action should try to relate the use of power or force rationally as means to the ends of policy; but he should reckon order and justice both—and not justice only—as ends or the effects of responsible action. In deliberations about the order to be conserved or the justice to be done, his reckoning will be in accord with those summaries of political wisdom known as the "principle of proportion" and the rule of "double effect." This may not tell him what to think, but it is how he will think. He will know that "order" and "justice" both are the effects of his action. He will count the cost of one effect upon the other. He will ask how much disorder is worth a calculable preservation or extension of justice (which in turn will make for a new or better political order), or he will ask how much of the injustice in the world (none of which *ought to be*) it is his responsibility to expunge at the cost of disordering the political order in which alone political justice obtains embodiment. Whether justice warrants a disordering action or order warrants the permission of some injustice, nobody can say in advance of statesmanship which rules by what it decrees. The failure of the United States to come to the aid of the Hungarian freedom-fighters may have been an instance of the requirements of order warranting the tragic permission of injustice. If so, this was not only because not all of the *ought to be* (the world political good) ought to be by us done, but only that part of it that is congruent with our national good. It was also because the preservation of political order against graver disorder is a part of the good of politics no less than the defense of justice against injustice.

V

Upon analysis the concept of order breaks down into two types of order that are politically relevant—the legal order and the order of power (for which hereinafter the word "order," or *ordo,* shall be used). This leads to a final characterization of the good of politics, this time involving three terms: *lex, ordo,* and *justitia*—or law, the order of power, and justice.

A Christian understanding of politics will be one that makes use of the concept of *ordo* (the order of power) in its relation to *justitia* on the one hand and to *lex* on the other. *Lex* refers to *the legal order*—the current state of international law and the treaties and agreements between governments and the United Nations with the nation-state system it is built upon. *Justitia* refers to the regulative ideal of all political action summed up, I suppose, in the word "humanitarianism," and to political judgments that are made in terms of the national and the world common good. Between these two stands the *order of power* (for which I use the word *ordo*). There is an area of coincidence or overlap, but not entire congruency, between these three circles: the legal order, justice, and the power realities. Statesmen must take all three into account, but never one or two of them alone or at the expense of the other.

Just as not all *justitia* is legal justice, so not all order is legal order. The *lex* of international agreements and institutions may be understood as an effort to impose coherence upon the order of power, but this coherence also flows from the *justitia* that may be preserved, beyond the legalities, in the relative power positions of nations (the order of power); and there is also a (fluctuating but still definite) coherence inherent in the powers themselves in their encounters and in the mutual limitation of one nation's power of being by that of another.[7]

In the nuclear age the nations of the world seem to have an overriding interest in identifying every actionable justice with *legal* justice, and the principle of all order with the legal order. Nevertheless, a Christian theory of politics (and this was enshrined in the just-war theory as a working politico-military doctrine) will not yield to this tempting prospect. *Lex* and *ordo* and *justitia* stand in a dialectical relationship in all responsible political agency. Doubtless the ideal is to effect the largest possible area of incidence between these norms of politics, and to see to it that every exercise of power is both legal and just.

Still, proper political doctrine will hold open the other possibilities. This is a world in which injustice may have the power and/or it may be legal. The use of power should not always stick by the legal boundaries, else the erosion of the order of power and of realized justice may make worse befall than a violation of the legalities. A responsible political action is never simply a legal act or simply an exertion of power or simply just. It is possible for a statesman to serve the legal order so

[7] Cf. Paul Tillich's analysis of encounters of power in *Love, Power and Justice* (New York: Oxford University Press, 1954).

well that he erodes the power environment and thereby contributes to the weakness even of the legal order in the future far more than he would have weakened it by not literally limiting himself to *lex* in his present action. Likewise, it is possible for him to be so concerned about national security that he fails to see the degree to which this depends on the growth and perfection of international institutions. It is not impossible for him (or at least for the citizens of a modern democracy) to be so concerned about the single norm of justice that they misdirect and trammel political action until the order of power fails to produce from its convergencies and tensions that justice which is attainable in the earthly city.

We may regard it as a triumph of law and of justice that the International Court to which the Republic of Panama appealed used the Universal Declaration of Human Rights for the first time in international adjudication in reaching its decision concerning the strife that broke out in the Zone in January 1964 when a group of students raised the Panamanian flag. But it is not immediately evident that this *lex*, or the treaty which gave us the canal and brought Panama into existence, or the Panamanian contention that its sovereignty reaches back before its birth, or that considerations of abstract justice should (under some conditions of our power responsibilities in the world) require the United States to abandon its power over the canal. If the power realities are now such that it would be a politically responsible act for us *basically* to renegotiate the canal treaty, the same is precisely *not* the case for Okinawa where for the United States to grant self-determination to the inhabitants of that island would be to play false to half the globe. No more was it evident that the last British presence in the Middle East and its legal claims should have yielded to United Nations' intervention in the Suez crisis and to the supposed "injustice" of all but non-violent means. (So said President Eisenhower!) In this last instance, it is significant to note that the new legal order that has emerged has not yet guaranteed access to the Suez Canal to all nations (viz Israel) as effectively as did the old legal order that rested in some measure upon imperial power. It is also not without significance that in 1964 it seemed that Cyprus might be the next domino to fall outside the western defense perimeter, perhaps this time into that of Russia.

It is the awesome responsibility of magistrates to decide, beyond all doctrine but through an adequate political doctrine, how decision is to be made between *lex* and *ordo* and *justitia*, and how responsible political action is to be made out of regard for all three of these criteria. This is the political truth, even if my illustrations do not suggest the best decision to have been made in those instances.

VI

At this point someone may exclaim, "That's all true; but now we have another 'subject' of political action—the United Nations—to take the place of the nation-state. All the foregoing *is* the nature of politics, but in the nuclear age only the United Nations is fit to be the agent of it."

In answer to this one might spend a lot of time talking about the improvement of U.N. "peace-keeping" machinery, and how far this is from accomplishment. Then one might spend more time talking about the perfection of U.N. "decision-making" machinery; and how much more important this is than "peace-keeping" machinery, even if this were a perfect arm; and how defective the United Nations is as a body capable of making the radical and positive decisions that are necessary if this is to be a world in which changes are effected without force.

More important it is to remember the whole fabric of community and the loyalties necessary for there to be government (world or national), and thus the need for far deeper world community if there is to be world political agency or any sustained collective use of force supplanting that of the nation-state.

I will mention only one aspect of the familiar fact that a sense of community and common identity is necessary for there to be politics. This will be to provide an ultimately *religious* answer to the question, Why are we so irresolute? or, Who killed politics? This will also be to go deeper than the "logic" of the nuclear age to explain the alienation of vast numbers of people in our time from the nation and its political responsibilities, and their alienation from giving any thought to the uses of power, its limits, and the perennial need for it to be used.

The "subject" of political agency must be felt to provide a proximate solution to what Paul Tillich calls "the ambiguity of historical sacrifice." [8] The subject acting in political and military intervention must be felt to provide a proximate solution to the problem of the death of an individual. The whole of southeast Asia and Australia to boot are not worth the immortal soul of one American soldier or peasant in his rice paddy cut down in the prime of the life God ordained for him! The reply to this, of course, is that the supernatural end or good and the temporal good of the human person are quite incommensurate dimensions of human life. To say that the whole world is not worth one human soul (Jesus himself said something like that!) is simply to compare the incom-

[8] *Systematic Theology* (Chicago: The University of Chicago Press, 1963), Vol. III, p. 348.

parable. This is true. The "sacred in the temporal" and the temporal common good are quite different things.

But who can deny that there is a strong feeling for the sacred in the temporal person at work delaying and weakening political resolve until a more inclusive entity is vitally challenged—the nation which is felt to be immortal and transcendent over the individual in value and in the perdurance of its life? Thus the nation affords a provisional solution of the ambiguity of finite sacrifice, and only if this is the case does the nation or any other political entity become the "subject" of political agency capable of legitimating finite sacrifice. There can be no supranational political authority capable of supplanting the nation-states in their responsibility for the political ordering of the world by means that must necessarily include the use of force until, among the bonds of community converging in and comprising this authority, it is widely felt that the sacrifice of the finite individual to the on-going, assuredly continuous life of some future "United Nations" is worth it. (No gaseous generality like "humanity" can be the subject of *political* loyalty and sacrifice).

The tragic character of all this I recognize. The people of "emerging countries," e.g. the Congo, remain political only in their tribes which precisely solved for them the ambiguity of finite sacrifice, and indeed of finite individuality. At least, the tribe did so until a short time ago. These people are pre-political within the sometimes nonviable framework of the states they have inherited. There, politics is only the extension of management in another form, and moreover the management of champagne-drinking and other *ersatz* symbols of leadership on the part of the leaders and a way of getting wages on the part of soldiers. A harshly expressed test for this is that they cannot fight a good war, i.e. a war in which force begins and ends in subordination to national purpose and policy, even the purpose of the arbitrament of a civil war waged to determine what the national purpose shall be. The reason the entire outside world has reason to doubt whether the Congo or Cyprus can endure as political entities roots in the fact that great groups of the population do not feel in their hearts and along their pulses that the Congo or Cyprus shall live though they may die. The ambiguity, nay the absurdity, of finite sacrifice has for them no provisional assuagement.

Vast numbers of people in the sophisticated countries of the world have become post-political in their alienation from the nation-state. This may be a period of transition over to the formation of new and higher political loyalties, and to the emergence of another "subject" of political agency that can be vigorous because it will have provided another provisional solution to the problem of finite sacrifice.

I doubt this. In any case, we have to examine where we are, and say this one thing more. The loss, in our secular age, of any vital sense of the sacred in the temporal or of the supernatural end of the human person has profound effect in the confusion of politics, nay, even the death of politics, in our time. Hans Morgenthau has explored one aspect of this in a profound essay entitled "Death in a Nuclear Age." [9]

Morgenthau asks why we are so numb and can't bear to think through to the end the problem of nuclear war. Why are we content with sluggish foreign policy, and so supinely confident of making a *show* of national power combined with diplomacy in the United Nations mode? Why is it *necessary* for us to hope on in this form of secular faith, and not admit to ourselves that, when measured by the radical solutions that are needed, ours is largely "the pastime of children on the rim of the abyss, a wasted effort on the eve of universal disaster"?

It is because ours is a secular age which has replaced the idea of an immortal destiny for the individual with the idea of the "immortality" of the human race in temporal, historical sequence on this planet. A secular age cannot bear the thought that there may not always be others like us to follow us. "To die with honor is absurd if nobody is left to honor the dead. The very conceptions of honor and shame [and, we may add, of resolute and principled political action] require a society that knows what honor and shame mean." The ingression of the nuclear age upon a secular age blasts its mooring in the always-receding future, and "destroys the meaning of life by throwing life back upon itself." Precisely because there may not be any like us to follow us, we cannot bear to think about nuclear war, and the real requirements of politics today.

An age which began by first becoming radically secularized then became "an age whose objective conditions of existence have been radically transformed by the possibility of nuclear death." Thus it must evade "the need for a radical transformation of its thought and action by thinking and acting as though nothing of radical import had happened." We pretend that the possibility of nuclear death portends only quantitative changes in politics, and "not a qualitative transformation of the meaning of our existence." The challenge of nuclear death to our secular values is for us graver and more difficult to face than the threat to political survival. The latter cannot be allowed to awaken us from our former slumbers.

No longer believing in the supernatural life, we are no longer convinced of principles, except as these derive their strength from those like us expected to follow us. No longer believing in the supernatural life, we cannot bring ourselves to think long and soberly about (leave aside the principles of political action) the *facts* of the situation we face. We cannot admit the nuclear revolution of politics, for that goes to where

[9] *The Restoration of American Politics*, Vol. II of *Politics in the Twentieth Century* (Chicago: The University of Chicago Press, 1962), pp. 19–25. First published in *Commentary*, September 1961.

the meaning of our very existence came to rest. Sluggish foreign policies may be the result, by remote but definite connections, of a sluggish secularism at bay!

Thus Morgenthau is moved, if not as a political scientist, then as a contemporary philosopher, "by the concrete issue of nuclear war to reflect on the meaning of death in the atomic age, and that philosophic reflection, carried on for its own sake, can serve to illuminate the actor's mind and, through it, to fashion political action." Can it be that he believes that the revivification of religious conviction in the minds of men today, at the operational level where they live, could have something to do with their capacity for "nobler and weightier acts of political performance"?

An extension of Morgenthau's analysis, and this alone, can fully explain the vain attempt of contemporary Western man to live postpolitically. Secular man has not entirely lost his sense that the person is the sacred in the temporal; he has only lost the conviction that there is an ultimate non-temporal resolution of the problem of historical action and sacrifice. When secular man reduced the sacredness of the person to the "dignity of man," he forgot that men live in two dimensions whose goods are quite incommensurate. Letting go the heavenly city, he held on to the earthly city with infinite passion. He began to make infinite demands of political action. Such action must be worth the sacrifice of a man's life. So modern secular man is unable any longer to look into the heart of the tragic ambiguity of all earthly sacrifice, the meagerness of every political achievement, and the transiency of the common good men serve by means of political power. Art, Music, Philosophy, Religion, and their International Congresses and exchange programs; economics and the Peace Corps; and all other non-violent sources of political change and reconciliation—these comprise all *positive* political actions, even though a little *sinning* by use of *negative* means may still be necessary.

This is the ultimate source of the modern persuasion that all war is murder, and military intervention in defense of the political good wrong unless it is "multilateral" in origin or freely invited and legal. "It's murder, that's what it is," said the mother interviewed in David Brinkley's Averagetown program whose son had been killed in South Vietnam, "What good comes of it?" She meant, of course, that no sufficient good could ever come of it; and in the truest sense, she was quite right.

This is also the ultimate source of our conviction that politics can be conducted without power, of the views of even the social scientists who say that an exercise of national power is necessarily immoral, and of the widespread belief that the only sacrifice that can be worth it is the sacrificial spirit of statesmen who are resolved to negotiate so that negotiation never fails.

Since audacious dreams do not change the nature of politics, this attempt to economize or to spiritualize political action cannot succeed. We cannot bring the heavenly city to earth by our faith in United Nations' forces that act by interposition alone, or by the doctrine that positive solutions are never imposed solutions. I include the "bluff" within the attempted spiritualization of politics which cannot succeed. Even a proponent of an assertedly strong foreign policy such as Senator Goldwater seems compelled in the contemporary period to talk this way. "I pledge from the depths of my heart and conscience," he declared during the California primary, "that as President of this nation I would consider it my foremost duty to keep the peace and to keep freedom at the same time." [10] The final explanation of such a statement is that, in a secular age which has lost all sense that the human person possesses his sacredness in the temporal order by reference to nothing in that temporal order, no one can come right out and say that the fragile freedom of people who grub for life on a small and remote part of the earth's territory could possibly be worth the sacrifice of human life to try to preserve it by the precarious and ambiguous political means that are in our hands.

[10] *The New York Times,* May 20, 1964.

CHAPTER 2

The Ethics
of Intervention*

In politics the church is only a *theoretician*. The religious communities *as such* should be concerned with political doctrine, and with clarifying and keeping wide open the legitimate options for choice. Their task is not the determination of policy. Their special orientation upon politics is, in a sense, an exceedingly limited one. They need to stand in awe before people nowadays called political "decision-makers," or rather before the majesty of topmost political agency. Political decision and action is an image of the majesty of God, who also rules by particular decrees. God says, "Let there be . . ."; and His word becomes deed and actuality. So also earthly magistrates have the high and lonely responsibility of declaring what shall actually be done. Allowing for the limitations that surround even the highest magistrate of a great nation, it is still the case that he creatively shapes events by decisions that must be particular decisions going beyond doctrine. He must actualize what is to be from among a number of legitimate choices. The majesty of political rulership is that it is always a triumph over doctrine through right doctrine, a victory over generalities through the proper generalities. It injects life-giving, or at least actuality-giving, deeds into words over words and beyond words.

* An address before the Religious Leaders' Conference on Peace, held at the Church Center for the United Nations in New York, January 12–14, 1965, first printed in *The Review of Politics*, Vol. 27, No. 3 (July, 1965), 287–310.

The religious communities have a less awesome responsibility; their task is a lesser, or a non-magisterial one. It is to see to it that the word over which and through which statesmanship or government wins its victory is not an inadequate word, that narrow political doctrine does not unduly restrict the range of political choices or false doctrine preclude some decision that might better shape and govern events. When the churches turn their primary attention to trying to influence particular policy decisions (to which they are tempted because every churchman is also a citizen, and therefore a lesser magistrate), they do what they ought not to have done. I think it cannot be denied that in the present day the churches are becoming very legalistic about what they regard as a "consensus" of moral and religious opinion built up by precedents through a series of *specific* position papers that have exceedingly questionable foundation in either theological ethics or political doctrine. In doing this, they are in danger of leaving undone what they ought to have done, namely, to clarify the ground on which government must rest and open wide the articulation of structural elements in that human reality which statesmanship must govern and the range of alternatives it is legitimate for statesmen to have in mind as they rule by specific decree. This does not mean that statesmen and citizens are always wise, but only that they are always the magistrates, which the church is not.

It is within these proper limitations that I address myself to the ethics of intervention. This means that I shall not undertake to recommend interventionary political and military action, or to recommend it not; but only to clarify the grounds, if any, for such possible decisions of state. Political doctrine cannot say what should or must be done, but only what may be done. It can only make sure that false doctrine does not unnecessarily trammel policy choices or preclude some decision that might better shape and govern events.

II

I shall be concerned chiefly with military intervention. The reason for this is certainly not that the use of armed force in political intervention is always its most choiceworthy form; nor is it that a theory of politics can foreknow that military intervention or any other form of interference or aid should be chosen in any particular situation. The reason is rather that the justification of military intervention as among the rights and duties of states unless and until this is supplanted by superior government (which world political authority, if ever it emerges in human history, will have the right and the duty of intervention) will already have traversed the ground for the justification of interventions that today are regarded as less serious, for example, economic assistance, beguiling or imperative diplomacy, propaganda to win men's minds, threats, getting in touch with the "next government," *et cetera.* I will state my personal opinion that it is not obvious that direct political and military aid to South Vietnam or the Congo is somehow more questionable than economic aid to Nasser's Egypt when the latter takes the lead in the political turmoil and military subversion of the Congo. Moreover, it does not appear obvious to me that it is more difficult to discover warrant for military intervention than for that type of interference which takes place when a program of economic assistance (under the auspices, let us say, of the American Friends Service Committee in cooperation with a small Western-educated local elite) conspires with the compulsions flowing from the hunger and desperation of the masses to teach them to raise and plow under leguminous crops contrary to the teachings of the religion that for centuries has informed their culture. This seems obvious only in an age that, in the name of "spiritualizing" politics, has economized both political morality and the higher cultural affairs of mankind. It seems obvious only in an age that has relativized and become skeptical about its judgments concerning political justice while never questioning its notions of economic betterment. In any case we shall be concerned with political intervention, and specifically military intervention; and not with that most Faustian and nineteenth-century program of draining swamps as the way of interfering in the affairs of another state, or with the eighteenth-century program that gave primacy to the increase of knowledge (cultural exchanges) in improving the political life of mankind.

First, several things should be said about the kind of world political situation which today is the context in which we raise the question of possible justifiedness of political and military intervention.

This is politically a bi-polar world, or at most, if you take into account mainland China, a tri-polar world. Recent talk about multi-polarity is, at the least, very misleading as Henry Kissinger showed in his *Foreign Affairs* article. You will have multi-polarity only when in between the great imperial powers there emerge regional powers who are able and willing to assume a leading role in securing the stability and enforcing with justice the government of an entire area, and not simply capable of pursuing their own economic development in independence of the great powers by playing off their strength or weakness. If, for example, India or Australia were nations with the political and military strength and the will to shelter the smaller countries of Southeast Asia, toward which these might lean instead of toward either Red China or the West, and if Malaysia could look to India instead of to Great Britain for political and military aid against Indonesia, then and only then will another power emerge to interpose itself between East and West in the government of mankind. If there were sufficient agreement among the African states, if the Organization of African Unity developed radical decision-making and powerful peace-keeping machinery, then Africa would be a power instead of a dangerous vacuum between the present three great powers. Or—to choose an illustration from within the so-called Western world—if the North Atlantic Treaty Organization had been able and willing to throw a sanitary cordon around Cyprus early in that unhappy conflict which began in 1963 and has not yet been settled, or if Britain (which had the treaty rights to do so) had been willing to do this either in order to enforce the constitution that brought Cyprus into existence or to impose controls on the situation so that the negotiation of a new solution could proceed with some hope of equity and success, that, too, would have been an ingredient of a multi-polar world. (Lacking this, negotiation under United Nations auspices was to a large degree an appeal to the arbitrament of arms on the island.) If Europe became Europe economically, politically, and militarily strong and *not* in alliance with the United States, while the former satellites of eastern Europe gain not only the free play to limit and harass Russia but genuine independence from her, then and only then will there be a real multi-polar world. In short, the luxuriant nationalism of the emerging countries of Africa and Asia and the revival of nationalism on the European continent under the shelter of the stalemate there, called a *détente*, do not as such add up to replacing the era of di- or tri-polar power and responsibility with an era of multi-polar power and responsibility.

A second thing to be said of the age which is the context in which we raise the question concerning the morality of interventionary political and military action is that the United States has inherited responsibilities to which its power is not commensurate. It is not that following the Second World War we were thrust into a position of power we had not sought, though that is true. It is not—as churchmen like to emphasize—that we have great power, and the question is whether we know or can learn to use it responsibly, though that is also true. It is not—as political commentators remind us, now that it is evident that we must reexamine our far-flung commitments—that we must realize that even the power of the United States is limited. The latter is very limited, indeed, if one means usable power that can surely accomplish choiceworthy political goals on a world scale. Even a great actor on the world stage has to acknowledge that not all of what ought to be can be *politically* done; and that not all that politically ought to be done can be done *by us*, since there are other political actors who play a role on that same stage. Still, the conduct of not a few of these political actors only accentuates the fact that there is a great deal that ought to be done politically that is not being done by them; and this only accentuates a statesman's responsibility, and his guilt, if he abdicates or withdraws the power of a great nation before seeing whether effective power can be mounted. The primary reality of the present age and for the foreseeable future is that the United States has had responsibility thrust upon it for more of the order and realized justice in the world than it has the power to effectuate. Since it is quite impossible for the United States to obtain power commensurate with the responsibilities we have inherited, there is nothing we should want more than to be deprived of these responsibilities by the effective organization of countervailing centers of power in, for example, Africa or Southeast Asia, which alone can assume them. Meantime, for us to choose political or military intervention is to use power tragically incommensurate with what should politically be done, while not to intervene means tragically to fail to undertake the performance of responsibilities that are there, and that are not likely to be accomplished by other political actors even when we must judge that there is much political responsibility that simply cannot be assumed by us. Anyone who is impressed only by the immorality and probable ineffectiveness of interventionary action should sensitize his conscience to the immorality and probable ineffectiveness of non-intervention. This is the world which magistrates must somehow govern by particular decrees.

The third thing to be said is that this is a world of protracted conflict and of new conflicts constantly arising. It is a world at war—defining war as the perpetual inclination thereto, and all other time as peace. It is so far a world safe for insurgency warfare, or for so-called "just" wars of liberation. The Russian and the Chinese Communists differ only in the degree and timing of the prosecution of it. When Russia vetoed a moderate "slap on the wrist" resolution in the Security Council condemning Indonesian action against Malaysia, Ambassador Adlai E. Stevenson expressed "regret" and "surprise" that the Soviet Union had prevented the Council from doing its duty; and he sought to convict the Russians of moral and political inconsistency by quoting Premier Khrushchev's oft-repeated words about the importance of avoiding the use of force in any form, direct or indirect, "for whatever political, economic, strategic or any other consideration." Stevenson said the vetoed resolution "did no more and could not have done less" than ask the parties to conform to these principles. Platon D. Morozov of the Soviet Union replied by thanking Stevenson for quoting from "very important documents of the Soviet Union" which expressed "policies the Soviet Union unfailingly supports"; and he quite rightly instructed our Ambassador that these policies as *the Soviets interpret them* "do not exclude but on the contrary provide, just as the Charter does, for the right of all peoples, large and small, to fight against colonialism and for their national liberation, for freedom and independence—and not in the American under-standing of these words." [1]

As the case at bar made plain, "wars of national liberation" are not domestic problems only but are assaults supplied and directed from abroad subverting conventional boundaries. Lest this be not very clearly provided for by the present Charter, one of the points already placed on the record as a Soviet demand in any future revision of the Charter is that such wars of liberation be expressly sanctioned.

Alex Quaison-Sackey, President of the General Assembly, in his address upon assuming office, asked rhetorically whether the United Nations depends upon peace between the great powers or peace between the great powers depends on the United Nations. If only he had included peace between the small powers, the answer to his question would be evident, and evidently the reverse of the one Quaison-Sackey intended. The United Nations depends on peace between the powers great and small—upon the several and collective policies of the nation-states upon which United Nations diplomacy is carefully erected. More-over, it is a fact that peace between the great powers increasingly depends upon peace between the newer nations, and upon their not becoming the advertent or inadvertent agents or subjects of insurgency warfare.

Such peace we have not. Not yet has a sufficient protective retribu-tion been devised and inflicted upon insurgency, much less in such measure as to deter it in the future. The world is still safe for it. In fact, the balance of nuclear terror has dampened war down to the un-conventional level, and forced a spread of conflict at that level.

This is the world in which we must raise the question of the morality of intervention. It is a world in which it cannot but be wrung from a Dean Acheson to "almost say" it would be an "immoral" choice "to deny ourselves the use of force in all circumstances, when our adver-saries employ it, under handy excuses, whenever it seems useful to tip the scales of power against every value we think of as moral and as making life worth living." [2] If intervention can sometimes be immoral as well as tragically ineffective. so also can non-intervention. This is the world magistrates must somehow find a way of governing by their particular decrees. If the churches presume to address any word to them, it must be the whole truth, and not merely a corrective piece of it. In any case, in view of the present state of public opinion in this country, any President of the United States is at least as apt to fail to find a way of using avail-able power in a measure commensurate with what should be politically done as he is apt to use power in excess of the responsibilities that have devolved upon us.

[1] *The New York Times*, Sept. 18, 1964.
[2] "Ethics and International Relations Today," an address delivered at Amherst College, Dec. 8, 1964, and reported in *The New York Times*, Dec. 10, 1964.

The fourth thing to be said is that the right and duty of intervention to deal with breaches of peace and threats to a just peace can be withdrawn from the nation-state only by an actual reordering of the structures of world politics by which this power and responsibility is transferred to higher political authority. Only a world public authority or regional public authorities that themselves rule by means of the exercise of real power can supplant intervention from among the possibly legitimate decisions of the individual nation-states. These two things are opposite ends of the same seesaw: one end (the right and duty to use force to impel another power to do or to forbear) cannot go down faster than the public authority and enforcement of a world or regional political community (the other end) goes up. Until higher authorities in the government of mankind are organized, resolute, and powerful, the responsibilities of national statesmen in our structurally defective international order must still include possible resort to intervention.

Suppose a group of nation-states ostensibly organized around the single principle of non-intervention. That would not be a system that works automatically. It would rest upon non-interventionary *policy.* Thus, even the principle of non-intervention contains an implied right to intervene to bring protective retribution upon any violation of this policy, to compel compliance with the policy prohibiting intervention, and to restore the system of non-interventionary states by deterring future non-compliance.

Does this mean that promises are of no effect, or that pledges, treaties, alliances, and charters announcing the principle of non-intervention are only scraps of paper? Does it mean that the wrong-doing of one party in breach of such a multilateral treaty makes it right—because he did it *first*—for another party to do the same wrong of intervening in the internal affairs of another state? Not at all. It means simply that we have not properly analyzed the meaning of a commitment to non-intervention as a *political promise.* This explicit promise or pledge contains an implied right of intervention to impel compliance with it, unless and until the non-interventionary policy is enforceable by higher authority. The reason no nation-state is committed inflexibly to an abstract principle of non-intervention is that, contrary to the uninformed convictions of apolitical minds, it is impossible to be consistently bound by a political contradiction. In foreign affairs there are no self-enforcing or self-fulfilling policies.

All talk about the nation being a "perfect society" invested with the attributes of "exclusiveness" and "impermeability" as a "judicial person" in the international community is talk that itself aims to secure maximum compliance with the duty of non-intervention so that these rights may be actualized. Such language expresses a non-interventionary *policy.* A non-interventionary system, of course, works largely by virtue of *compliance*, or by the active acknowledgment of the duty of non-intervention on the part of any state that wants to claim for itself the right to be impermeable. But such a system works also, and in the last resort, by active permeation and intervention to compel compliance, whether the source of the enforcing action is a member state or an agency of the collectivity of states. There must be not only compliance, but compulsion to comply, and there must be deterrence of non-compliance. A "perfect society" of mankind will make manifest that every one of its component member states is "imperfect," that is, permeable to intervention by higher public authority and only because of this impermeable to intervention by other member states.

The people of the world were the losers when, because of Russia's use of the veto, it proved impossible for the permanent members of the Security Council to act unanimously in not only putting a stop to breaches of the peace but also foreseeing and correcting threats and dangers to the peace. With the "Uniting for Peace" Resolution, the first of these provisions of the Charter was assumed and in some measure fulfilled by the Assembly; but its "peace-keeping" operations hardly begin to be threat-removing, and the Assembly seems not to be an organ capable of the radical sort of decision-making this would require.

At the present time the people of the world and the profoundest longings of the whole human family seem to be losing again, in the encounter between Russia and the Charter over the issue of payment for peace-keeping operations. This is even being spoken of in our own press as a showdown between the United States and Russia, and not as a showdown between Russia and the Charter or between all the defaulting powers and the hope that the United Nations might become a public authority superior to the nation-state system in taking the action needed to keep the peace and to anticipate and remedy threats to it.

As only one of the member states and as a great power, our national interest alone probably gives us as many reasons as have the Russians not to want to pay for future United Nations actions that we do not approve and which may go contrary to our own estimate of our interests. An argument can be made that we should have sided with Russia and France on this matter, and that our policy was wrong from the beginning. The decision was to side with the Charter and to try to strengthen the United Nations. Unless the smaller nations rally—which now seems unlikely—they will get what seems to be wanted, namely, the United Nations as a forum (however important) and still an ancillary of a luxuriant nationalism.

When one thinks about it, it is not opposition to the United Nations on the part of some Americans that requires explanation but the widespread acceptance and support of the United Nations in this country. Then when one reflects upon this question, the answer must be that the

United Nations has afforded a haven both for properly internationally-minded people and for erstwhile isolationists as well. The latter have found the United Nations to be an apparent way to be involved in the affairs of the other nations without ordinarily being *tragically* involved in them; and this is what was sought to be avoided in avoiding entangling alliances with the rest of the world and its troubles. The question of the warrant for interventionary political and military action seriously arises when one accepts the fact that to be responsibly involved with other nations means to be *tragically* involved with them in world-historical events and action. Whether one decides to intervene or not to intervene one sets out on a course of action that has both good and evil consequences and many unforeseeable results.

In any case, this is a world in which the writ of United Nations intervention would have to extend further than it has in the past if ever a policy of non-intervention in the affairs of other states is to become the single duty of the leaders of the member states, especially the leaders of a nation that has inherited power and responsibility in imperial (if still gravely limited) proportions. The right and duty of intervention can be morally and politically withdrawn from nation-states no more rapidly than this same right and duty is perfected in its exercise by world or regional public authorities. These are two ends of the same seesaw. There is an inverse logical and actual connection between having intervention thrust upon us—sometimes as a responsibility, always as a possibility—and being deprived of any such legitimate option by superior political authority. One good reason for correcting the structural defects of the nation-state system is precisely to avoid having intervention thrust upon us. In the world as it is, however, a doctrine of intervention commensurate with the power and responsibility a nation possesses would not be so much needed if the nations and the international system were anywhere near ready for a world political authority that can make and enforce sound policies.

III

There are ultimate and there are penultimate grounds for the possible justifiedness of intervention; and it is important to keep distinct the ultimate and the penultimate reasons for such possible decisions of states. These do not tell the statesman what to think, but they *anatomize* how he will think in considering the alternatives of intervention or non-intervention in particular situations.

The ultimate justification of intervention, if it is politically wise and right, and the doctrine in terms of which this has to be decided, is what may be called "just-war intervention," I use this expression not for want of a better term, but because there can be no better term for anyone who will take the trouble to investigate without prejudice the just-war theory as a mere summary or prismatic case of the ethico-political and the working politico-military doctrine that was governing in Western thought until just lately.

This means, first, that the statesman must make a decision about the politically embodied justice he is apt to sustain or increase by his choice to intervene or not to intervene. Until there is world community there will be no actual world agreement as to justice. After all, that is a prime ingredient in the definition of community. Until then, to adopt H. Richard Niebuhr's terminology, we have no "universal views" to go by; we have only but definitely "views of the universal." This does not mean subjective relativism. It does not mean that there is nothing worth dying for outside of the contours of our own skin except an unreal universal justice; or that there is nothing at stake in the real justice and the actual communities we have attained with their converging and conflicting "views of the universal." This simply means that general justice is actualized and specified for political choice and action only in these views of the world common good.

A nation that does not stand for the agreement as to justice which constitutes it a people, and the environment of world justice that this entails, is not apt to come into that land where universal justice may become the content of political choices. Universal justice is the regulative ideal of politics; a view upon this universal justice is its substance. The environment of world justice which we define in United States foreign policy in terms of a world system of independently developing peoples and states is as necessary to the justice that constitutes us a people as a favorable security environment is necessary to our power in the world. And it is certainly no more difficult to define that just order of free and independent states entailed in our view of justice and of the universal common good than it is to define the defense perimeter which must be held lest we weaken our own security and at the same time prove false to more than half the globe.

A decision to intervene or not to intervene has, secondly, to be made in terms of an assessment of order as one of the ends power must serve. Order is not a higher value in politics than justice, but neither is justice a higher value than order. Both are in some respects conditional to the other. Order is a means to justice, but also justice is a means of securing order. Order is for the sake of justice, since the only real political justice is an ordered justice; yet justice is no less for the sake of order, since the only real political order in which men may dwell in community and peace is one that is just enough to command the love and allegiance of men, or at least their acquiescence and their compliance. Order and

28

THE ETHICS OF INTERVENTION

justice are ever in tension yet in interrelation; and both are terminal goals in politics' act of being *proper* politics (its *bene esse*).

A decision-maker contemplating, for example, some interventionary or non-interventionary action should reckon order and justice both as ends or the effects of responsible action, and not justice only. In deliberations about the order to be conserved or established and the justice to be politically done, his reckoning will be in accord with those summaries of political wisdom known as the "principle of proportion" and the "rule of double effect" according to which one effect justifies another. This may not tell him what to think, but it is how he will think. He will know that order and justice both are consequences of his decision to do or to forbear. He will count the cost of one effect upon the other. He will ask how much disorder is worth a calculable preservation or extension of justice (which in turn will make for a new or better political order), or he will ask how much of the injustice in the world (none of which *ought to be*) it is his responsibility to expunge politically, at the cost of disordering the political system in which alone political justice obtains embodiment. Whether justice warrants a disordering action or order warrants the tragic permission of some injustice (for example, Tibet, Hungary), nobody can say in advance of statesmanship which rules by what it decrees.

Thirdly, the justifiedness of intervention is to be measured in terms of the national common good and the international common good. These goods are not always the same.[3] There is, to say the least, a dialectic, a tension, a polarity, if there is not an actual and even if there is never an irremediable conflict, between the national and the international common good. The responsibility of the statesman is defined by the area of incidence, or overlap, between them. Allowing for the fact that he should strive always to envision and if possible to establish a larger area of incidence between his nation's good and the international common good, it is still this area of incidence between these goods that defines his responsibility. He is not called to office to aim at all the humanitarian good that can be aimed at in the world. Instead, he must

---

[3] Pope John XXIII's encyclical *Pacem in terris* seems on first reading to teach that the national and the international common good are always coincident, or that these can be made to be coincident in any moment of governmental decision. At least, this is the interpretation of some enthusiastic commentators, who seem to believe there is never any reason for negotiation to fail. To the contrary, the Pontiff rightly emphasizes that "it can at times happen" that "meetings" are actually useful. This implies that it can at times happen that they are not, and that issues fail to be resolved. ". . . To decide whether this moment has arrived . . . these are the problems which can only be solved with the virtue of prudence." Whether the moment for fruitful negotiation (which should always be held open as a possible occurrence) has actually happened is a decision which "rests primarily with those who live and work in the specific sectors of human society in which these problems arise." (¶ 160)

determine what he *ought to do* from out of the total humanitarian good that *ought to be*. He is not even responsible for all of the *ought to be* that *ought to be politically done,* since there are other nations and other political actors in the world. He must locate his political obligation, and that of his nation, within an area of incidence between the national and the international common good.

The theory of political anarchism is false which teaches that those goods are somehow completely congruent, so that these are but two misleading words for the same thing. Only upon a Kantian postulate that somehow the moral universe insures it can it be supposed that the *true* good of the nation (if only one could discern this) is the same as the good of all mankind (if only one could know what that is). In any moment of historical time, it is in any case true that there are more ways to miss the mark than to hit it (as Aristotle said), and missing the mark cannot *simply* be defined as doing less than the international common good alone requires.

Of course, a statesman is in danger of serving a too narrow view of the international common good and thereby failing to serve the best possible good of his own nation. And of course he may serve a too narrow national interest and thereby fail to serve an international common good that was possible. But there is also the danger that he may try to do too much of the humanitarian good that ought to be politically done, with the result that he does less than he ought to have done for the national common good and at the same time renders his own nation less apt to serve either common good in the future.

Nothing can remove from among the awesome responsibilities of magistrates the determination of where to draw these lines. Every responsible political decision involves some precarious determination of how the circles of the national and the world common good are to be drawn. This is the mode in which the ideal humanitarian good (all of which, by definition, ought to be) specifies itself for political choice.

Finally, a responsible statesman, especially one who is the leader of a great power, must include the legal system and international law and institutions among those concentric circles: justice and order and the national and the international common good, concerning which some determination must be made. These are never entirely congruent circles at the time of any historical action. Not all justice is legal justice. Not all order is legal order. The legalities comprise, of course, mankind's attempt to impose some coherence upon the order of power. But such coherence flows also from the justice that may be preserved, beyond or beneath the legalities, in the relative power positions of the nations.

In the nuclear age the nations of the world seem to have an over-riding interest in identifying every actionable justice with legal justice, and the principle of all order with the legal order. Nevertheless, a realistic

Christian theory of politics will not yield to this tempting prospect. Doubtless the ideal is to effect the largest possible area of incidence between these norms of politics, and to see to it that every exercise of power is both legal and just and orderly. Still, proper political doctrine will hold open the other possibilities.

Today religious opinion has been placed rather solidly behind the opinion that in the internal political life of this nation there is a justice above and beyond the law and that this should be established by "direct action," sometimes against the law and more rapidly than available social due process for changing the law would afford. It is an oddity that this same religious opinion often can see no warrant for ever going beyond the law in international affairs where the legalities are far more imperfect and where the social due process for significantly changing the legal system is even more wanting. It must be that within the domestic life of the nation we count on the strength of the law and the procedures established for orderly, legal change to be able to withstand these allegedly justified attacks upon them, or that we believe lawful procedures will be improved and not inundated by such assaults in the name of a higher justice; while in regard to international law and institutions we are content that our statements remain a legalistic ideology having little relation to the dynamic forces that alone sustain these things, or may destroy by overburdening them.

This is a world in which injustice may have the power and/or it may be legal. The use of political power by a nation-state should not always stick by the legal boundaries, else the erosion of the order of power and of realized justice may make worse befall than a violation of the legalities. A responsible political action is never simply a legal act or simply an exertion of power or simply just. It is possible for a statesman to serve the existent legal order so directly, and exclusively, that he erodes the power environment and thereby contributes to the weakness even of the legal order in the future far more than he would have weakened it by not literally limiting himself to the legalities in his present action. Likewise, of course, it is possible for him to be so concerned about national security that he fails to see the degree to which this depends on the growth and perfection of international institutions. It is not impossible for him to be so concerned about the single norm of justice that he misdirects and trammels his political resolution so much that the order of power fails to produce from its convergences and intrinsic coherence that justice that is attainable in the earthly city.

President Kennedy's handling of the Cuba missile crisis was to be admired not only for the combination of firmness and restraint in the action he put forth in the encounters of power. It was also to be admired because of his combination of *initiative* in the order of power with the concurrent (yet *only* concurrent) action he set in motion within the established legal institutions, the Organization of American States and the United Nations. By his initiative in the power encounter, he gave the lead to the political opinion and action that was brought into being within those regional and world authorities. If President Kennedy had failed to place his political action *beside*, and in this sense *outside*, the legalities, it is certain that world public opinion would have gone every which way. No acceptable solution would likely have been reached. World institutions might then have been weakened. The *détente* atmosphere that followed in the wake of his initiative in the order of power would not have been forthcoming. It may also be added that without Kennedy's *initiative* in the power encounter domestic public opinion— especially that of the churches exceeding their mandate by calling for various specific kinds of settlement—would have gone off in all directions.

President Johnson's initiative in the Dominican crisis in April 1965 was not so neat, nor was the crisis *felt* to be so grave or the facts so indisputable. Still, in this instance as well, the location of action, outside or alongside the largely nonexistent or ineffectual legalities of the Organization of American States (in the hope that this would *lead* to concurrences of a collective order) cannot be declared to have been a wrong determination of political responsibility in the concrete, particular case facing the President and in the midst of which he had to govern events or be governed by them.[4] No moral theory or sound political doctrine

[4] [When this statement was written I had quite enough information yet not enough to rely on; I had not exhaustively studied the matter before rushing to judgment. I had only an understanding of political agency according to which President Johnson need not *necessarily* be wrong in the Dominican intervention (because of some *absolute* moral dictum against this), together with a memory of the fact that *The New York Times* reported during those tumultuous days of the civil war that someone in the "democratic" forces arrayed against the military junta apparently thought it more important to destroy the printing presses of allied groups in the "civil war" itself than to fight for their common cause, and a knowledge of Che Guevara's doctrine that if in an uprising you have more than seventy-five or so staunch communist revolutionaries, that is more than enough and you should divide your forces and send some to another republic! The latter understanding prevented me from believing that our government acted from not only ignoble motives but *laughably* ignoble motives when it could only send out the report that there were about this number of identifiably Castro communists involved in directing the "civil war."

All this was possible for anyone to know at the time. Now anyone who says our Dominican intervention was wrong must say this in the face of the remarkable account written by our former Ambassador to the Dominican Republic, John Bartlow Martin, in his book, *Overtaken by Events: The Dominican Crisis from the Fall of Trujillo to the Civil War* (Garden City, New York: Doubleday & Co., 1966). From this I draw only the following observations. The first is to remark upon the fact that Martin (a Stevenson-Kennedy democratic liberal if there ever was one!) could be compelled to believe that *only* U.S. power could guarantee the Dominican people after decades of horrible dictatorship the slim good of not falling under another one—a second chance at democratic nationhood. Secondly, Martin's detailed account of how Bosch's political lieutenants in the democratic movement had all taken refuge in

can, from any general principle, rule his intervention to have been an illegitimate decision; in fact, sound theory must open and hold open possibilities such as this as well as the contrary acts of non-intervention. Then statesmanship must bear the burden of having been prudent and wise.

In sum, it is the awesome responsibility of magistrates to determine, beyond all doctrine but through an adequate political doctrine, how decision is to be made between justice and order, the national and the world common good, and among *lex, ordo,* and *justitia* as all alike the terminal objectives or goals of politics, yet almost never entirely congruent ones.

This is what is meant by saying that decisions to intervene politically or militarily, or not to do so, are made in terms of the understanding of politics that was summarized in the just-war theory.

IV

In turning next to penultimate justifications of intervention, let me first remark upon the relation of these to the ultimate grounds for the possible justifiedness of intervention. The penultimate justifications finally depend upon the validity of particular decisions made in terms of just-war intervention. This does not mean, however, that the penultimate reasons, in their various degrees, should at once be reduced to the ultimate. Because justice and order and the relevant common goods are always needed in the justification, and may be sufficient, this does not mean that these grounds are ordinarily sufficient without having recourse

---

foreign embassies; and, thirdly, the fact that this decisive turn of events took place within the forty-eight hours between our *announced* intervention merely to save lives or to guard the exodus of non-Dominicans and the decision to use our forces, sent in for the former purpose, as inter-positional forces in the civil war.

   ·   Reading this account of the actual events, and of the hard, rapid, ambiguous decisions that had to be made, one way or another, one can only conclude that the Dominican intervention was possibly right. This is *not* to say that it was right. It is only to say that anyone who judges it to have been wrong must do so in the face of *the costs* to the Dominican people, and in the face of the domestic repercussions upon any administration allowing that result. The effectuation of a principle of non-intervention may be worth that, but it must be worth *that*. And this is to say that any U.S. citizen who accuses his government of bad faith or of adding to the "credibility gap" or of Yankee imperialism or of acting as the gendarme of the universe in this intervention does not himself know the meaning of purposive politics or else he does not know the facts of the situation.

   It may be added that anyone who in any degree invokes against U.S. "intervention" in South Vietnam a "sphere of influence" theory and at the same time denounces U.S. intervention in the Dominican Republic has not yet learned to think consistently.]

to the secondary justifications. Even if (as I would argue) we should never let our reasons for intervention become locked in at one of the penultimate stages or exclude the possibility of making appeal to just-war intervention *alone*, it is still the case that there are various penultimate justifications that have a certain additional validity in their own right. These add weight to the ultimate grounds for intervention.

The relation of the secondary justifiedness to the primary justifiedness of interventionary action may be expressed by saying that these secondary reasons set "firebreaks" or establish "qualitative boundaries" which are important to recognize in the logic of intervention. Here there is an analogy with the need for firebreaks and qualitative boundaries that are easy to recognize and can be readily agreed to in establishing acceptable controls over military escalation.

One or another of the secondary justifications may be a quality or a value or a norm in a sense which men in the present age have lost the ability to believe pertinent to politics. Someone may argue (as I would) that such a secondary justification draws a "qualitative boundary" in a sense quite different from the meaning with which this expression is used today in connection with the problem of military escalation (where it means simply a *perceivable gap* in the range of *quantitative* distinctions—there being no normative boundaries that need be taken into account in the conduct of war). Even so, it would still be the case that such a qualitative boundary between a penultimate and the ultimate justification, or between one secondary reason and another, would also serve the purpose in the logic of intervention of providing an easily recognizable boundary which it is important but not always necessary to preserve. Moreover, even if the relation between secondary and the primary justifiedness of intervention is that of inferior to superior norms (and even if the inferior criterion is never merely a technical means to its superior end), it would still have to be insisted that those infravalent considerations, even though they are qualitative in the correct meaning of that word, can never assume the authority of a final court of appeal than which there is none higher.

The first of the secondary justifications may be termed "counter-intervention." The meaning of this in South Vietnam is related to the integrity of the legitimate borders of a country against penetration by hostile subconventional forces. United States involvement in South Vietnam may invoke the implied right to assist a people in its right of self-defense against insurgency forces within that country commanded and supplied in significant measure from abroad. I need not recite here the evidence that is sufficient to establish these facts to be beyond question.

The only question to be raised about the rationale of counter-intervention is whether its apparent but mistaken ultimacy as a criterion does not lead to some very odd self-imposed doctrinal limits. Just as the just-war doctrine cannot be reduced to its relic, the aggressor-defender doctrine, so just-war intervention cannot be reduced to counter-intervention. Counter-intervention only, but definitely, lays down a "firebreak" with its emphasis upon merely countering the initiative assumed by subversion. It provisionally uses the legal borders of the subverted country to circumscribe the range of the countervailing action that may be justified. If it is assumed to be more than this, the doctrine of counter-intervention will sooner or later prove to be counter-productive of fully responsible political and military actions. The ponderous term we use—"*counter-insurgency*"—for the military training at Fort Bragg and for the "advisors" assigned to South Vietnam is more a product of the American ethos than it is of the political realities or a proper doctrine of intervention. Politically responsible action is not to be limited to reaction. Nor should a 12 to 1 disadvantage be imposed as a matter of principle upon military forces by a political policy that assigns false ultimacy to *counter-intervention*. If during these many years of frustrating warfare in South Vietnam, there were targets north of the border by which twelve units of the force that should have been repressed could have been repressed by one unit of insurgency, I see no doctrinal reason why this should not have been done; or any reason, except the value of preserving a quantitative boundary in the logic of the escalation of intervention, why the South Vietnamese and the Americans should be required to wait until twelve units of force were required to repress one unit of the force to be repelled.

It may reasonably be argued that for too many years it was false doctrine that permitted the Vietcong success in their "insurgency warfare" which hits the "haves" where they have it not. The nineteenth-century doctrine of non-intervention across legal borders became a weapon with which the Communists, joined by neutralist nations and a great many Americans, hit the Western powers where they have it not (where we acquiesce in an inadequate politico-military doctrine) while insurgency warfare struck where our power was weakest. By this doctrine, the United States denied itself and its ally legitimate targets north of the border while this novel type of warfare denied us targets by its furtiveness on the south side of the border.

I ask only whether, by assigning false ultimacy to "counter-intervention," we did not yield to and cultivate a prejudice against some of the possible actions that may be included even within this concept itself. Granting that vigorous, positive action falls within a doctrine of counter-intervention provided the "posture" and "intention" of the intervention is defensive, were we not still too much trammelled in coming to any such actual decision?

No authority on earth can withdraw from "social charity" and "social justice" their intrinsic and justifiable tendencies to rescue from dereliction and oppression all whom it is possible to rescue. This is why the traditional just war theory did not hesitate to justify "aggressive war," that is, initiative in the charitable extension of an ordered justice. This justification can never be withdrawn; it can only be limited, supplanted, or put in abeyance. This happens whenever political prudence is tragically compelled to judge that more harm than good will be done in the attempt. This is the reason modern papal teachings have proscribed aggressive war as, under modern conditions, disproportionate to the ends of justice. A legal institutionalization of this moral verdict, however, would require a political authority superior to the nation-state effectively to take over the task of insuring collective justice and security.

Likewise, no authority on earth can subtract from "social charity" and "social justice" the acknowledgment or primary intuition of moral responsibility for military intervention in behalf of what ought politically to be done. No *principle* proscribes this. It is only (but often definitely) estopped by the prudent consideration that tragically more harm than good will actually be done in the attempt. This opens and leaves open the possibility that if interventionary initiatives may often be unjustifiable, they may under some circumstances be justifiable. The statesman has the burden of having to have been right and wise, no matter whether he decides to intervene or to intervene not. Or else the impulse to do the perilous political good sometimes even across legal boundaries has to be transferred to some superior public authority, which then will have the right and the duty of intervention. Doubtless this political responsibility can be alienated from one political "subject" or "agent" to another, but it will not perish from the earth.

It is simply an illusion to believe that there exists or can exist a system of impenetrable nation-states, founded upon an absolute principle of non-intervention, which has removed from among the decisions of magistrates the question whether the political good will be sustained more by intervention or by non-intervention. Thus, *La Prensa* (Peru) called for radical political reconstruction when it pleaded that the special inter-American Conference that opened in Rio de Janeiro on May 20, 1965, should establish an organism within the Organization of American States that will provide "automatic defense" against international crises that threaten to subvert American republics. However, its editorial contention that meanwhile the United States should have proposed "collective measures by the inter-American system" instead of moving on its own (or in advance of motion within that system)[5] may be correct or incorrect as a particular judgment in this particular case; but this is certainly not a conclusion to be drawn from an unbreakable rule of non-intervention.

[5] *The New York Times*, May 3, 1965.

A second and final secondary justification of intervention may be called "intervention by invitation." On this score, United States intervention in South Vietnam is clearly justified. One may put these two formulations together and say that our political and military action in South Vietnam is "counter-intervention by invitation." [6] There is, indeed, an ethico-political quality to be assigned to intervention by invitation, because of the importance of the legal order (*lex*). One criterion of the justifiedness of the action of nation-states—especially today when the ordered justice and the peace of the world depend so much upon the upbuilding of international law and institutions that can guard against the escalation of war—is whether such action has legality.

Still this is not the sole or the paramount or only consideration. In fact it can be said that another reason for supporting intervention by invitation alone is that where such invitation is forthcoming a policy of nation-building linked with the preservation of the order of power does not have to start from scratch. This can be linked with the upbuilding of the international legal order. To base our action in South Vietnam upon the legality of the invitation is both correct and qualitatively important; this action has penultimate justification both because it is "counter-intervention" and because it is "intervention by invitation."

But it would be wrong to assign ultimacy to these criteria alone, separately or together. And if anyone says that the considerations of justice and power or of the relevant common goods, which, as we have seen, comprise the criteria of just-war intervention, only add additional weight to counter-intervention by invitation, but could not be used by themselves in the case of South Vietnam, this seems to me to reverse the infravalent and supravalent reasons. One has to say instead that counter-intervention by invitation adds weight and clarity to just-war intervention, and insures that the intervention in South Vietnam may also directly (and not only indirectly) serve the upbuilding of a legal order. But counter-intervention by invitation is not necessarily the only way in which even the legal order may ultimately be best served, not to mention the other values which political action should secure.

If the ultimate justifiedness is in terms of just-war intervention within a policy that seeks to build a system of freely developing and independent states, then it is better not to begin from scratch but by invita-

---

[6] There is, of course, the prior question of the legitimacy or legality of the South Vietnamese government. On this I will only observe that the legitimacy of the Saigon regime is at least as good as one-fourth of the members of the General Assembly of the United Nations. It is only by a system of double bookkeeping that one could require more secure credentials to legitimate a government in the use of violent means in the international system than would legitimate it in participating non-violently in that system (i.e., in Assembly debates and resolutions). The same can be said of the requirement that governments be democratically representative.

tion, and one main objective will be to strengthen the acceptance by the people of a government that continues to express their general will. On the supposition that the South Vietnamese people did not want their government to exercise this legal right to invite legal intervention, this would doubtless alter *that* right and it might alter one's hope of a successful policy of nation-building; but the possible justice of intervention might still stand (even if it should then be judged unwise to be done). I do not see how ultimacy can be granted to the criterion of "intervention by invitation" without saying either that *lex* is the only criterion or that Chinese-Hanoi-Vietcong "might" makes "right." Where political aid is needed, and many years' time for growth of political maturity on the part of a people, it is quite foolish to demand democratic expression of a people's will before there can be legitimacy in the government to be aided. If, in such a situation, intervention may often be immoral and unfeasible, non-intervention may also immorally abandon a people, and tragically may be no more effective in accomplishing what politically ought to be done. This describes the situation in which the leaders of a great power must determine how best to use power commensurate with the responsibilities that have devolved upon us in the present age.

It is not simply that peace is a "process," a process that sometimes involves resort to arms. That seems too stark a paradox. Peace is not the only political good. It is rather that peace with justice and an ordered liberty is a "process," a process that sometimes involves resort to nonpeaceful means. It is not at all paradoxical that *this* should be the nature of international politics. In mankind's endless struggle for an ordered justice and peace, it is only realistic to expect (even if no one should hope for this) that "the fact that there are different ideas of what constitutes pacem in terris" may be "the final source of human division." [7] So it is to date.

V

One does not need to be a "hawk" to know that the "doves" are not always right politically, just as surely as one need not be a "dove" to discern that "hawks" are not always realistic. It may be the fault of United States policy in Southeast Asia that we did not long ago launch bold "reconciling" schemes. It may equally well be the case that a principal failure was the delay and our too great hesitation in shaping the

[7] John Cogley, "The Encyclical as a Guide to World Order," one of the papers prepared for the planning session of the *Pacem in terris* Conference which was held in New York City, Feb. 18–20, 1965. The paper was inserted by the Hon. Claiborne Pell in the *Congressional Record*, Thursday, May 21, 1964.

force employed to the actual contours of the military struggle going on in that part of the world.

If in any measure the latter was the case, then the root cause is to be found in our incapacity for believing that positive good can ever come from the use of force, or from an increment in the force used. As to that dovelike belief, one need not be a hawk to know that our nation has a long history of letting worse befall before decisive action is taken. Then the objection to current policy in South Vietnam would be not the action now being taken but that this was not begun earlier. Instead, we had further complicity in the laceration of the fragile political institutions of that country and the suffering of the people we intended to help.

As evidence of the *possible* doctrinal trammelling of our earlier policy, consider the following record of official statements. (*Some* explanation must be sought to account for the apparent difficulty these declarations of policy had in coming to congruence with the objective realities of the situation.)

The "message" we sent to the Communist Chinese on May 18, 1964, was that the United States would take "all measures short of war" to preserve the independence of Southeast Asia. This was hastily changed, on May 19, 1964, to read "all necessary measures" (*The New York Times,* May 19 and 20, 1964). Then there was a period in which some significant victories over the Vietcong in South Vietnam, our reconnaissance flights over Laos, and the bombing of Communist positions in Laos by neutralist government forces seemed to make our policy and the "message" clearer. Then on June 28, 1964, President Johnson altered the text of his speech in Minneapolis and said that "when necessary" we would not hesitate to "*risk* war" (italics added) where the text read that we would "use the force necessary" to help maintain South Vietnamese freedom. Max Frankel's analysis of these halting statements and the United States dilemma was entitled "A Crisis of Confidence" and subtitled: "U.S. Shaken by Feeling that *Show* of Power Won't Stop Reds in Asia." (*Ibid.,* May 21, 1964, italics added.) A spokesman (later identified as Secretary of State Dean Rusk) said one day that North Vietnam and Communist China should leave their neighbors alone or face war with the United States; and a few days later he eased the tone of recent warnings by asserting that peace "ought to be possible in Southeast Asia without any extension of the fighting." (*Ibid.,* July 2.) The next day, Max Frankel's comment was: "For the second time in a month, the Administration has called off its warnings of war in Southeast Asia, revised its public utterances to emphasize a passion for peace and blamed the newspapers for the confusion." (*Ibid.,* July 3.) This is almost as agonizing an inability to make an appraisal as the question posed to the President in an advertisement inserted in *The New York Times* (March 28, 1965) by a group of scholars and churchmen in the New York area, who pleaded: "How can we possibly win and yet prevent a widening of this conflict?" (The "In the Names of God, STOP IT" statement, April 4, signed by twenty-five hundred ministers, priests, and rabbis was beneath *political* consideration, and I should say bore few of the marks of responsible citizenship.)

Since I know that it is sometimes necessary to communicate ambiguity to an enemy, I can only ask (without knowing the answer) whether 1964 was such a time and Southeast Asia the place; and I can only ask (with strong suspicion that I know the answer) whether our own policy decisions and announcements do not unnecessarily pull the laboring oar against an ethos that absolutizes "counter-intervention" and against an ill-conceived political ethics? A definite threat, of course, cannot be made lightly since it would have to be honored should North Vietnam and possibly China respond in kind. A heightened "deter-the-insurgency" policy would have to be backed by a corresponding escalation of our "fight-the-insurgency" policy. Still it is we who may have been deterred from responsible military action by unwarranted fears cloaking themselves in a doctrine that denies justice to any initiative in the use of force across boundaries.

Secretary McNamara said in his speech at the Forrestal Memorial Award Dinner on March 26, 1964, after the Hawaii Conference: "Whatever ultimate course of action may be forced upon us by the other side, it is clear that actions under this option would be only a supplement to, not a substitute for, progress within South Vietnam's own border." There is no proper doctrine of intervention that prevented the Secretary, assuming certain findings of fact and the availability of means to the targets, from saying the contrary: "Progress within South Vietnam's own borders is only a supplement to, not a substitute for, acts of intervention in North Vietnam and into those parts of Laos now held by the Communists." Instead of "concentrating on helping the South Vietnamese win the battle in their own country" because "this, all agree, is essential no matter what else is done," the shape of the whole insurgency operation in Southeast Asia *might* be better reflected in the statement that, all agree, it is essential to concentrate on the *source* of its direction and supply no matter what else is done elsewhere.

Early in 1965, we tried to improve our doctrine of intervention. While continuing to try to give "political aid" to the South Vietnamese, United States forces also began to assist in air strikes over Laos. Then President Johnson extended air strikes to North Vietnam. This brought into range *some* of the sources of supply, though not yet the command and direction of the insurgency so far as this comes from North Vietnam. Moreover, we may have sent out so many contradictory signals concerning our policy, that it is mainly we who are deterred. Witness the present low state of the debate over our policy in Southeast Asia. In any case, the foregoing does seem to reflect an excessively *trammelled* course of action.

Without presuming to say whether the war should have been extended or not, it is clearly the case that consideration of this possibility has been hampered by inadequate politico-military doctrine. And it cannot be doubted that a chief weakness in the execution of the present policy is that Hanoi and Moscow and Peking have ample reason to believe that American public opinion will not for long persevere in the support of it.

You cannot win at the conference table anything that *it seems evident* you could not win on the battlefield, or are not resolved to win. General Giap knows this well enough.

CHAPTER 3

What Americans Ordinarily Think about Justice in War*

One of the latest books with the title, *The Just War,* was not on that subject. Instead, subtitled *A Study in Contemporary American Doctrine,*[1] this was a comprehensive analysis of the aggressor-defender concept of war. Taking as our guide this work, by Professor Robert W. Tucker of Johns Hopkins University, I propose in this chapter that we explore the anatomy of the aggressor-defender justification for a nation's resort to armed force, and the shaping influence exerted by this concept of warfare upon this nation's policy, as well as upon discussions of policy among weapons analysts.

My thesis will be that our present nuclear policy has not been determined so much by the new weapons technology, or by technical reason ungoverned by any moral doctrine proposing various schemes for the control of this technology. Instead, the pure reason of our experts and the political wisdom of our policy makers have first been determined by the American ethos with its peculiar doctrine of the aggressor-defender war

---

* First appeared in *Christian Ethics and Nuclear Warfare,* ed. by Ulrich S. Allers and William V. O'Brien (Washington, D.C.: Institute of World Polity, 1961), pp. 108–134.

[1] Robert W. Tucker, *The Just War* (Baltimore, Md.: The Johns Hopkins Press, 1960).

before proposals are ever made for governing the use of nuclear weapons.

The dilemmas we face in nuclear policy are apt, therefore, to be dilemmas already inherent in the aggressor-defender doctrine. These may prove to be surmountable, if at all, only by the abandonment or radical revision of that justification of the use of force. For the idea of the "defensive war" has been the "prior science" or the morality predeterminative of all our policy decisions, and even of apparently pure products of weapons-gamesmanship. If any reader has in mind any other meaning he assigns to "morality," "the moral law," or "the just war," he ought momentarily to put this aside, as we proceed to clarify the aggressor-defender concept of war. This will be found to contain certain elements, which must be exhibited in some detail. Under each heading into which this doctrine may be analyzed, I shall attempt to show that present day nuclear policy and proposals are made in the image of antecedent American doctrine, and that, if indeed this policy is the only option we have because it is determined by the nature of the new weapons, such would tend to demonstrate that, by an amazing coincidence, the moral order of the universe is that expressed in "the moral law" contained in the American doctrine of the aggressor-defender war. If the latter is doubtful, then there must be other options for policy; and we should proceed by manifold action and thought to the hazardous business of revising our doctrine of war and the policies this has shaped.

1. The first point is that war may be justified, and can only be justified, by an overt act of aggression against which the just war is a defense. Thus, "the circumstances immediately attending the initiation of force" must contain the whole warrant for a resort to arms. Ours has been a "singular preoccupation with the overt act of resorting to force" [2]—if aggressive, this is always unjust; if defensive, it is just. This may be called the doctrine of *the just occasion* as the criterion for justifying resort to force. (This first, and seemingly obvious, test of justice in the aggressor-defender war, cannot, as we shall see, be understood without other and not so obvious tenets comprising this doctrine.)

The aggressor-defender doctrine directs attention to the immediate circumstances in which force is resorted to. It finds in that occasion the justice or injustice of war. Other events of longer standing in the past and graver consequence in the future are ruled out as not of decisive importance in determining the morality of war. On the one side, the causes behind an act of aggression are not of paramount importance. On the other side, once war has begun, the objectives for which and manner in which a just war is fought are identified with its occasion in aggression, and forthwith the goals and actions of war are justified, along with the war itself, because of the manner of its inception.

[2] P. 11.

We Americans may have been more concerned than Professor Tucker supposes with the causes that have led to war.[3] We have believed in removing the causes of aggression and have often acted from a belief in the possibility of "anticipatory reconciliation" among nations. Unjust aggression and therefore even the just or defensive war might have been prevented, we do not doubt, by attention to prior causes. Still, whatever the causes that have led to war, whatever grievances remain uncorrected, and despite our realistic predictions that, given severely unjust conditions, war *must* come, all this does not lead us *morally* to justify the act by which it comes.[4] For we do not allow that resort to force is ever the only or the best or a *necessary* and *unavoidable* means of redress. Therefore the state that acts aggressively must have acted wrongly, and avoidably so.

Of greater significance is the fact that, according to its criterion of the just occasion, the aggressor-defender doctrine finds excuse for any of the unspecifiable and therefore limitless purposes for which the just war, once it has begun, may be fought, and for conducting such a war in any manner that may be regarded as militarily necessary or even desirable. Thus, the morality of war's conduct and of its actual objectives are compressed into its justifying occasion, or the immediate circumstances in which it began. Both the means and the ends of war are given their warrant from war's *start*.

Before the outbreak of hostilities, we reject war as an instrument of national policy in the belief that there are always other, political, means for obtaining political objectives. Once force is defensively undertaken against aggression, however, we are quite willing to attain through force political ends which, prior to resort to force by the other state, we insisted must be obtained only by peaceful methods.[5] Before aggression provides the justifying occasion, war is proscribed as a means to gain political objectives; afterward, war becomes precisely such a means. While historical experience may teach us that the actual aggressor may have defensive purposes and the defender aggressive purposes in the actual conduct of war, and while experience teaches that the reluctance a state may display in taking aggressive action is no measure of its aggressive intent thereafter,[6] still the aggressor-defender *doctrine* teaches us that the purposes of the defender are *by definition* defensive and therefore just.

While in traditional views a defensive war was one fought in such fashion as to leave the vital interests of individual states and the interna-

[3] Pp. 11–12.

[4] Cf. p. 31 n. 27: ". . . It is one thing to assert that the proscription on resorting to force will most likely remain ineffective if other means are not found to remedy injustice. It is quite another matter to assert that in such circumstances the proscription on force ought to fail."

[5] P. 63.

[6] Pp. 64, 178.

tional order and balance of power substantially unchanged, the American doctrine has such a *status-quo* orientation only before the occasion. In time of peace the moral law forbids basic change, if this must be brought about by resort to force as an instrument of policy. "But once force is employed in defense against aggression, the same moral law apparently sanctions force as an instrument for effecting the most drastic change." [7] Before an outbreak of hostilities, American doctrine purports "to place narrow limits upon the circumstances in which states may legitimately resort to force." But this same doctrine "places almost no substantial limits upon the specific objectives which may legitimately be sought once force is employed in defense against aggression." This does not mean that we always confess that defensive wars are to be fought for limitless ends. Nor do we expressly condone any conduct in war or any force that may be exerted. But the purposes we do avow—defense and peace—"set no meaningful limitations to the specific objectives that may be pursued in war." So it comes about that, while holding that war ought not ever be chosen as an instrument of policy, "once war has been thrust upon peace-loving nations they may employ force for achieving almost any results. Accordingly, force may be justified as the instrument for achieving almost any policy." [8] For when, we may ask, "has the danger that justified the resort to force been removed?" [9] Thus, American wars in this century have been wars to extirpate the roots of aggression, to make the world safe for democracy and for self-determination, and wars to the end of unconditional surrender. The notable exception to this—the Korean conflict—may be assessed, in terms of American doctrine and even in terms of better doctrine than that, as a too limited war.

The new weapons technology, Professor Tucker declares, "has not had the effect of changing the central tenet of the American just war doctrine, that the just war is first and foremost the war fought in self or collective defense against armed aggression." [10] Nor have nuclear weapons substantially modified the complacent conviction that the purposes sought in war and the manner of employing force may be derived from and sanc-

[7] P. 65.
[8] P. 74. ". . . Once we have entered upon war, there have been few nations more disposed to believe that history can be radically transformed for the better through the instrument of unrestrained violence" (*ibid.*, p. 22).
[9] P. 129.
[10] Internal subversion and ambiguous challenges to our security are simply assimilated to the concept of armed aggression, and any difficulty in locating or defining the justifying occasion of aggression does not alter this doctrine or weaken our adherence to it. "The equation of ambiguous threats with armed aggression is the response of a doctrine which asserts that force need not be employed and therefore ought not to be employed save as a measure of defense against the aggressive use of armed force." (*Ibid.*, pp. 101–102. Cf. pp. 121 and 123 for the "expansion" of the concept of "self-defense" to include "preventive" war.)

tioned by the circumstances in which war is initiated.[11] In fact, we can say more. Systems of deterrence by means of weapons of mass destruction may be viewed as positive enactments of the doctrine of the *justifying occasion,* in the mechanism of the weapons and in the almost impersonal institutions governing their use.

On the one hand, when peace prevails, deterrence is assimilated to the concept of defense in that these systems are designed to renounce the use of force as an instrument of national policy save on the one restricted, justifying occasion. Safeguards are built-in to guarantee certainty that an aggressive act against us has occurred before these weapons are ever used. Meanwhile, the political objectives of the nation are supposed to be pursued by legitimate political means only, under the umbrella of a self-fulfilling renunciation of the use of force.

On the other hand, once aggression has occurred, deterrence systems instantly change their character and the war that follows is objectively offensive in character. The deduction of the justice of any of the military and political consequences from the justice of the occasion has, as it were, been read into a computer. Deterrence, writes Tucker, "—and particularly the more extreme version of deterrence—has been a defensive policy with an offensive *arrière pensée.*" [12] We can say more: deterrence is defense with an offensive *arrière pensée,* without the *pensée.* That a punishing response is certain, more certain, if possible, even than the resolution of men, is indeed what qualifies this scheme as a system of *defense,* and therefore brings it within our notion of the moral law. Of course, the limitless objectives said by definition to be defensive, and therefore just, are not ideal ends, such as peace and the extirpation of aggression. Nevertheless, they are objectively limitless goals, and unconstrained methods of war, whose justice is fully deduced from what occasioned them.

Considered from the point of view of its expected "success," a strategy of massive deterrence looks defensive; but from the point of view of its possible "failure," "if the measures threatened must ever be carried out, the character of the measures taken promises to be more than defen-

[11] *Op. cit.,* pp. 97–98.

[12] P. 158 n. 39. This note continues by quoting from Herbert Butterfield, *Christianity, Diplomacy and War* (Nashville: Abingdon Press), p. 19: ". . . Though your enemy may have attacked you first, and you have a right to defend yourself, his sin does not itself justify you in becoming an aggressor at his expense—does not justify you in carrying on the war for the purpose of destroying the enemy or breaking him up." Tucker comments: ". . . These words may be lost on a doctrine that views the response to aggression as necessarily defensive, and consequently sanctioned by the moral law, whatever the precise character this response may take. Thus, however aggressive in other respects, massive retaliation has always been regarded from a moral point of view as purely defensive."

sive." [13] Indeed, *the more* purely defensive deterrence is as a threat, *the less* likelihood that it can serve any legitimate defensive purpose if ever used.[14] Yet it is of paramount importance to notice that should deterrence fail, it will fail *disastrously;* but according to current American doctrine, it will not have failed *morally.* This is because the morality of war itself is assimilated to its justifying occasion in the aggressor-defender doctrine.[15]

> Thus the policy of "massive retaliation" has been generally interpreted as serving the obviously defensive purpose of preventing armed aggression, and should deterrence fail, the equally obvious purpose of waging a defensive war. That purpose has therefore been held to confer upon peace-loving nations the right not only to threaten potential aggressors with a degree of retaliation far in excess of the force required to repel an aggression but to carry out that threat if expedient.[16]

Upon our premises it was to be expected that we would come at last to the idea of "capital punishment" for the state that by unjust aggression sacrifices its right to life. While some notable scientific discoveries were necessary to develop the mode of execution, and while we may deplore the necessity of carrying out the sentence, there can be nothing *morally* objectionable—upon these premises—in the act of pulling the switch. Nor will the fear of mutual destruction consequent upon the possession of this system by more than one power suffice to fault it morally. Nor will it prove sufficient with Herman Kahn to introduce, in a crevice in the superstructure erected upon the aggressor-defender doctrine, the judgment that only the notion of "bonus damage" built into deterrence is a "basically immoral idea" or sufficient to say merely that if these machines for capital punishment "happened to involve explicitly the annihilation of all humanity it would be totally immoral." [17] Instead, the whole moral foundation of our policy needs re-examination, and in particular the view that compresses the just war into war's start.

It should give us pause that this aggressor-defender doctrine remains intact not only because of our policy-makers and weapons-planners but also because churchmen have spoken more from within the American ethos than they have from any identifiable Christian ethos. Conferences were not held, symposia were not issued, consciences were not awakened so long as this design for war was possessed by the West alone, and it could

[13] P. 177.
[14] Pp. 162 n. 4; 140; 179.
[15] Cf., p. 151.
[16] P. 157.
[17] Herman Kahn, *On Thermonuclear War* (Princeton, N.J.: Princeton University Press, 1960), Lect. II, Chap. IV, p. 171, and Lect. I, Chap. III, p. 96.

be believed that the consequences of exempting war, before and after it starts, from the control of sound policy would be spared these shores.[18]

2. A second point in the aggressor-defender doctrine of war is its pronounced voluntarism. "It is this marked voluntarism in our interpretation of conflict, and not simply a moral aversion to violence, that has given the distinctive character to the American doctrine of just war." [19] Moral aversion to violence as an evil thing has been common to most, perhaps all peoples. "At any rate, a simple moral aversion to violence cannot alone adequately account for the fervor with which we have condemned the recourse to war as an instrument of national policy and the intense moral indignation with which we have looked upon aggressor states. That fervor and indignation stem not only from the belief that war as such is evil but also from the belief that its initiation is an unnecessary evil." [20] The aggressor is not bound to go to war. No "reason of state" compels him to do so, at least none that peaceful means would not better serve. If he goes to war he has not only done something evil, but an evil that he could have avoided had he the will to do so.

Once the entirely unnecessary and avoidable act of aggression has occurred, however, there is a different sort of necessity that impels the defender. This is a "necessity of principle" which requires that the perpetrators of avoidable evil have especially to be restrained.[21] In so doing, a distinction between the "evil few" and the "many good" can be made so long as it is possible to get at the former, for this "is essential to a doctrine that persists in viewing armed conflict as an entirely avoidable feature of history." [22] Thus force functions in the international order to exorcise aggression as it does in the domestic order to repress crimes of violence.[23] Both need never have been. When it occurs, an act of aggression is always the product of a bad will and an ignorant mind; it is "the result of deliberate evil wedded to accident, the accident of miscalcula-

[18] "As long as this nation retained, or was thought to retain, an overwhelming superiority in nuclear weapons and their means of delivery, these implications troubled very few consciences; a threat which envisaged the possible annihilation of an aggressor was readily accepted as having a strictly defensive character and therefore as fully consonant with the moral law. Morality required only that this nation or its allies receive the first blow. The strategy of deterrence has assumed throughout that the decisive blow would be the act of retaliation. In this manner, the moral law would be observed and at the same time military success would be guaranteed; a defensive war according to the moral law would still reap the military advantages otherwise attending a decisive preventive strike" (Tucker, pp. 157–58. Also cf. p. 73 n. 66 and p. 173).

[19] Tucker, p. 21.
[20] P. 23.
[21] Pp. 20–21, 25.
[22] P. 26.
[23] P. 29.

tion." [24] From this stems the special emotional weight behind our justification of a defensive war to correct or punish clearly avoidable evil. From this also stems Dulles' policy of ringing Russia with alliances to make clear to the mind of the enemy what we define aggression to be while at the same time mounting the strength to dissuade his will from doing the evil he need not do,[25] as well as, in large part, Kennedy's meeting with Khrushchev at Vienna in order to make certain that he does not become an aggressor by miscalculating our policy or doubting our resolution. No wonder the President was "somber" upon his return from meeting face to face with a man who believes there are, in the encounters of states, necessities and forces at work, there to be acknowledged, other than the necessities of these principles!

The full meaning of voluntarism in our doctrine of war can be elaborated only in connection with a third element. Before passing on to this, however, we may indicate the sense in which our present policy of nuclear deterrence is built upon this same voluntarism. This pertains both to the aggressor and to ourselves. As to the aggressor, the explanation of our persistent faith that deterrence can be made to work, Tucker points out, "must be found in the conviction that aggressors may readily be deterred precisely because they have no real need to resort to force" [26] Since armed conflict is an entirely avoidable feature of history, and the act of aggression an unnecessary evil, potential aggressors will surely be deterred, provided, of course, that our own minds are clear as to the justification of defense by deterrence and our resolution firm. As to us, therefore, "the strategy of nuclear deterrence has assumed that this requirement of an ever triumphant will could be satisfied, if only because strength of will must somehow be proportionate to nobility of purpose. If our heart is pure, our hand will be steady, or at least steadier than the aggressor's." Thus, our doctrine of voluntarism teaches us that it ought not to be possible actually to degrade any system of deterrence we may have erected that either has "over-kill" built into it or concerning which no one can doubt its capacity to deliver a "barely intolerable" damage. Only faith in ourselves and in our purposes and in the justice on which we stand by virtue of the justifying occasion through which war came should be "needed to achieve the goal of banishing aggressive force from history. . . . To convince the adversary that we would act in the manner threatened, it is indispensable to convince ourselves that we would so respond. As long as we believe, others will believe. As long as others believe,

---

[24] P. 183.
[25] A "political warning system" combined with "selective retaliatory power" (Tucker, p. 40 n. 32).
[26] P. 184.
[27] P. 185.

they will not act. The key to a successful strategy of nuclear deterrence lies wholly within ourselves." [27]

And so the substance of deterrence reduces to increasingly declaratory pronouncements, to the determination to play out this game of wills to the end, and to the will to will to will in accord with the doctrine that a radical voluntarism must prove triumphant in political and military affairs. Our time has even produced an entire science of such voluntaristic games of strategy. For this analysis the question is *not*, What would I do if I were the enemy seeking to enforce some finite national policy by possible resort to arms? The question, in an encounter of wills apart from concrete policy, is rather: What would I do if I were he wondering what he should do if he were wondering what I would do if I were he. . . . ? In the determination of radically voluntaristic military policy the focal point is each side's expectation of what the other expects it to expect to be expected to do. One can be guided only by "what he expects the other to do, knowing that the other is similarly guided, so that each is aware that each must try to guess what the second guesses the first will guess the second to guess and so on, in the familiar spiral of reciprocal expectations." [28] The pity is that perhaps all this has very little to do with real political encounters. It is disconcerting to observe that the enemy, since his will is linked more closely to some national policy in an older plan of war, shows very little inclination to collaborate with us even in obeying the rules that should govern a game of hostile wills in seeking to triumph.

3. The third ingredient in the current aggressor-defender doctrine states that war may be engaged in as an instrument of national policy on the single supposition that this policy aims to banish force as an instrument of any *other* national policies. The perfectionistic goal of banishing force from human history as the only justifying ground for resort to armed force goes along with and is mutually explained by the restriction of the justice of war to the circumstances immediately attending a resort to force and the interpretation of an act of aggression as under all circumstances a deliberate evil action that could and should have been avoided. Were we once to concede, for example, that the grievances and causes behind the act of aggression that gives occasion to a just war of defense might ever justify the initiation of force, then the banishing of force from human history would in principle be placed in jeopardy.[29] Were we once to concede that armed conflict is an unavoidable feature of the life of nations, or that there are any circumstances that warrant the first use of violence, then the banishment of force would in the first instance be impossible and in the second undesirable. And the seemingly simple distinc-

---

[28] Thomas C. Schelling, *The Strategy of Conflict* (Cambridge, Mass.: Harvard University Press, 1960), pp. 54, 57, 87.

[29] Tucker, p. 14.

tion between just defense and unjust aggression is not fully understood apart from these other attendant convictions.

It is a hard saying, but an illuminating one, which asserts that the capacity for destructiveness in modern war is not only the result of science and weapons technology, but also that our obtaining and maintaining this destructive capacity is a consequence of our continuing attempt to banish force from human history and from affairs of states. This is why "deterrence" can be reduced to "defense" only if "defense" is understood to contain this additional objective, in comparison to which "the much more modest purposes in traditional notions of defense must appear trifling." [30] When, however, "defense" is understood in the terms now current in the aggressor-defender doctrine, then deterrence contains all these purposes writ large in the proposals of our experts and institutionalized, if not quite mechanized, in our weapons systems.

Therefore, Professor Tucker rightly points out that the hope of banishing resort to force "has found its expression in a philosophy of deterrence which optimistically assumes that history can be radically transformed for the better simply by confronting would-be aggressors with the certainty of severe punishment in the form of nuclear retaliation should they seek to carry out their evil designs." [31] All-out violence is for the sake of all-out peace.

> *On the level of policy,* there is a world of difference between the endeavor to do away with the violence in the relations of states by promoting treaties that "outlaw" war as an instrument of national policy and the attempt to prevent armed aggression by threatening potential aggressors with annihilation or severe punishment should they seek to carry out their designs. *On the level of doctrine,* however, both policies spring from the conviction that violence is not an inevitable evil in a society of sovereign states, that the resort to force is instead an entirely avoidable means for effecting change or for resolving conflicting interests. This being so, it is the prevention of war rather than its mere limitation that must form the great objective of policy. The Kellogg-Briand Pact and nuclear deterrence may represent radically disparate means for pursuing this objective, but both spring from the same basic aspiration. If war cannot be exorcised by the conclusion of multilateral treaties solemnly invoking that purpose, the prevention of war must be sought by insuring that the reaction to aggression is made sufficiently punishing to leave no potential aggressor in doubt that he would lose more than he could possibly hope to gain by resorting to aggression.[32]

Just a few citations are sufficient to demonstrate that Tucker is cor-

[30] P. 68.
[31] P. 22.
[32] P. 68.

rect. "A theory of deterrence," writes T. C. Schelling, "would be, in effect, a theory of the skillful *non-use* of military forces." [33] And in defense of the Polaris system of (temporarily?) invulnerable missile bases roaming the ocean, Oskar Morgenstern exclaims: "War has to become technologically impossible in order to be stopped." [34] Thus, science and technology have done what religion, morality, and international treaties never could, in fulfilling the American dream and—in my view, what the Christian religion never proposed—of effectively banishing the use of armed force from human history. Even Herman Kahn can and should be so read. Kahn simply knows of no deter-the-war policy or weapons system which he cannot think of ways of degrading unless this is backed by a fight-the-war policy. He wants the latter planned *in order to make deterrence effective.* His analysis falls to the ground only if his various fight-the-war plans are not, as he believes, a truly feasible use of the weapons now in being—feasible enough to make it credible that we can actually deter-the-war and not have to use them. Moreover, at the crucial point he, too, is forced to rely on a mechanistic commital strategy if he is to continue to hope to have skillfully brought about the non-use of these arms. Kahn writes: "If an enemy is lucky enough to destroy 80 percent or more of our striking force, we should devote the remaining force to malevolent (i.e., countervalue) objectives—to punish the enemy in that way which was most hurtful to him." Kahn's apology for this "central war" is as follows:

> The reason I think this contingency plan is reasonable is partly that *every effort should be made to insure that the enemy could not possibly destroy 80 percent or more of our force on his first strike.* If we are successful in this attempt, then, the 80 percent destruction case cannot occur and we do not care if the corresponding plan is reasonable or not. . . . [Yet] in this uncertain world of rapid technological change . . . it is just possible that the enemy, in spite of our best thought and preparation, may (either because he is clever, or because he or we have made a miscalculation) develop a technique which *he believes* will destroy more than 80 percent of our strategic force at the first blow. We wish to assure him that *even if he thinks he can be this successful, he is still in serious trouble.* To the extent that he could rely on our using our small remaining force "sensibly," this might not be true.[35]

To rely on ourselves to do this act (so that the enemy can certainly rely on it, in the spiral of his second guessing these wills of ours that must triumph) it would be well to build this response into computers. Such surely is a politically purposeless act of war, unless we understand that the purpose behind all such proposals is the final banishment of

[33] *The Strategy of Conflict,* p. 9.
[34] *The Question of National Defense* (New York: Random House, 1959), p. 295.
[35] *On Thermonuclear War,* Lect. II, Chap. IV, pp. 184–185.

force from human history. Kahn's book is therefore not the product of technical reason but of such reason rooted in the American ethos. Nor is it (as some believe) the product of a calloused heart, but of a too loftily aspiring one. Should the expected consequence not come to pass and if deterrence fails, it will have failed tragically, of course; but nothing in the moral underpinning of these proposals tells us that it will have failed morally, since from the beginning all justice was concentrated into war's beginning, and aggression was defined as *the* evil to be exorcised. We are not concerned about the morality *of* war because we have concentrated all moral reflection and energy upon questioning the permissibility of any, or certainly the first, use of force. This nation needs to find out and find out quickly whether it agrees with *Time* magazine, that there is "no moral problem in the H-bomb that was not present in the A-bomb, none in the A-bomb that was not present in the mass bombing of cities [so far, so good] and none of these that is not present in war itself, and no grave problems in war that are not present in the basic question of the permissibility of force in any circumstances." [36] Then only can we retrace our steps toward becoming a more mature nation.

"The paradox of deterrence," writes Tucker, "is that it is defensive —or perhaps even less than defensive—as long as the need to employ force does not arise and almost inevitably more than defensive once the necessity for employing force does arise." [37] Searching for an explanation of this paradox, we may say that before the event, deterrence is less than defensive (since it cannot specifically prevent an aggressor from attaining some immediate aim of policy) because already deterrence was for more than defense and was suffused by the far greater purpose of altogether exorcising force; and that after the event it displays its true character of not being defensive in any apt sense of that word, but ultimately on the offensive, because no clearly defined boundaries can be assigned to the pursuit of the evil of aggression.

So far the new technology has provoked no serious re-examination of our doctrine of war. To be sure, we are anxious about the destructive power we possess. But according to Professor Tucker, "the principal effect of that anxiety has been to confirm beyond doubt the conviction that force must be banished as an instrument of national policy and that no circumstances can possibly serve to justify an 'aggressive' resort to force." [38] The new technology serves, therefore, only to deepen and strengthen what throughout this century has been our American doctrine. The moral convictions of this doctrine have begotten two seemingly op-

[36] April 12, 1954, p. 33. Quoted by Tucker, p. 75, n. 68.
[37] Tucker, p. 70. Cf. pp. 176, 180, 182; and pp. 191–198 for a sober treatment of the question whether we should really elect a world from which force had been banished.
[38] P. 98.

posite heirs: the growth of nuclear pacifism and the technical perfection of weapons and arms control plans. Only by harboring the same optimistic expectations as those contained in the aggressor-defender doctrine can either of its sons find seemingly plausible justification for being.

We Americans are nothing if not prone to improve on what comes naturally in love and in war. So, for the life of men in nations in history, even churchmen cry "Peace! Peace!" where between states there is no peace, instead of addressing themselves to the morality of a truly just war. Like Engels, who borrowed it from modern western idealism, we are driven by the belief that "everything that is reasonable within the heads of men is destined to become real, however much it may contradict the existing seeming reality." Yet one of these existing seeming realities seems to be Khrushchev, an "old Russian," who rather likes horsemeat and soldiers and diplomacy with a purpose, who cries "general and complete disarmanent" only because he knows how to fight with almost anything in order to achieve concrete political purposes, who is more skilled in the use than in the non-use of force, and who "stupidly" or "arrogantly" (we suppose) refuses to "collaborate with the enemy" in getting a clean bomb, banishing force, or "stabilizing" deterrence. Khrushchev seems not likely to collaborate with us, at least not (there is evidence) if this means consistently hardening bases, making them invulnerable, letting us help him get a complete Polaris system because the system works better at not working if both sides have one, tacitly agreeing never to withdraw his population from their plight as hostages under our guns, or detailing a battalion of intellectuals to tell him how to insure that force will never be used by correctly anticipating our anticipation of his anticipation, and so on.

4. While the aggressor-defender concept of war is sufficiently summarized in the foregoing consideration of a) its doctrine of the just occasion, b) its voluntarism, and c) its pervasive moral resolve to banish force from history, there remain two additional points in Professor Tucker's analysis of current American doctrine that deserves exposition and comment, in order for our minds to be brought to focus upon the need to revise radically this doctrine, and to undertake the urgent, if hazardous, theoretical and practical task of restoring a truer doctrine of just war. The first has to do with the meaning of "just conduct" in warfare. Our view seems to be that in war military necessity should prevail and that the end justifies the means. That, it might be said, is of ancient lineage and was by no means "made in America." Yet, insofar as we say this about the conduct of war, we do so in a special sense that can be understood only by connecting this with all the foregoing features of current American doctrine.

It is not simply that "the ethics of peace are held to condemn the principle that the end justifies the means" while "the ethics of war are held to endorse that principle." [39] We do not really believe in a double standard, or in two entirely separate realms or periods, peace and war, each with its own criteria for conduct. Nor do we feel the basic contradiction between these, and then remain content in this contradiction out of fear that the only way that could be found to resolve it would be to adopt an ethics of war justifying the means by the end to govern also our action in peacetime. [40] Rather it is essential to our view that these be connected, and compressed into that restricted event in which war finds justifying occasion in an act of aggression. Therefore, the ethics of peace and the ethics of war exhibit the same categorical imperative: that resort to force be banished. Not just any end justifies any sort of means to attain it: this we know well enough in peace or in war. But this single *supreme* end, the exorcism of aggression, justifies any means *necessary* to attain it. Thus do we deduce military necessity from principle. Therefore, as Tucker remarks, "the ethics of war may justify the use of almost any weapons and the employment of almost any methods *which realize the ends and purposes of the just war.*" This does not spring from calloused hearts, but from too loftily aspiring ones, "from the belief that the justification for these procedures has been resolved." We give the conduct of war over to technical reason, not out of immorality or amorality or by adopting a different ethical standard, but out of the belief that, once war has been thrust upon us, "only technical questions remain to be solved." This is the case because the same objective whose commanding presence should control military and political policy in peacetime—the rejection of force as a matter of policy—has already certified any indispensable military means in the conduct of war, provided only that it is just in these terms. "Moral indifference" in the conduct of war "is thus the result of moral certainty." [41] The same moral certainty that prevailed in peacetime to separate force from policy continues to do so in time of war.

Yet it cannot be denied that, from such a view of the justice of war, we have now come around to a reversal of the very meaning of terms such as "just," "good," and "virtuous" when these are applied to weapons systems and war's conduct. Thus Thomas C. Schelling is able to say that "a 'good' weapon—to push this philosophy (of stabilizing defense against surprise attack and eliminating any actual use of force) all the way—is a weapon that can only hurt *people* and cannot possibly damage the other

[39] Tucker, p. 75.

[40] "If we become sufficiently oppressed by the logical inconsistency of our emphasis on the distinction between war and peace, we might repudiate the paradox by accepting the premise of the totalitarians that *at all times* the end justifies the means"—James B. Conant, "Force and Freedom," *Atlantic Monthly*, Jan. 1949, pp. 19–21. Quoted by Tucker, p. 75n., 67. Italics added.

[41] Tucker, p. 75.

side's striking force; such a weapon is profoundly defensive in that it provides its possessor no incentive at all to strike first and initiate a major war." [42] Therefore, in order to bring about a state of affairs in which no aggressor *can* strike because he cannot *want* to, and to eliminate all possibility of resort to force by these means, weapons formerly called immoral are now called "good" and "just" and "virtuous" altogether.[43]

This view may be said to stress the importance of "the virtue of vice," "the humanity of inhumanity." and "the goodness of evil" when these are built in as an "improvement" of the deterrence system, and contribute to its technical perfection (compare the cruciality, for these systems, of committal to policies that have "the rationality of irrationality"). Professor Tucker is quite correct in his comment that these weapons are good, even in Schelling's sense, only so long as they are not used; they are "profoundly defensive" only so long as they are not employed. "Once employed, they undergo the most radical change in purpose. What is wholly defensive as a threat becomes wholly retributive as an actuality. On the other hand, weapons whose capabilities make them useful for preventive war (in Schelling's scheme, weapons 'that can exploit the advantage of striking first and consequently provide a temptation to do so') are less profoundly defensive as a deterrent but may still serve a defensive purpose if once employed in retaliation." [44] This is to say: they become in some measure a counterforce defensive shield between the forces of the enemy and our people should they fail to deter him. It is clear that we have accepted the predicate "good" to apply to such a military system only because the supreme goal of banishing force has already come to be regarded as a good of quite a unique kind in comparison to all other goods or goals of policy. Deterrence provides what pacifism always sought: a substitute for the use of force. The only questions, then, remaining to be raised about such a weapons system are the technical questions: Will it work? How can it be made to work?

It is more difficult to explain the connection between this deduc-

---

[42] "Surprise Attack and Disarmament," in Klaus Knorr, ed., *NATO and American Security* (Princeton, N.J.: Princeton University Press, 1959), p. 179.

[43] ". . . Weapons may be more stabilizing and less aggressive if they are more capable of civilian reprisal than of military engagement. A standoff between two retaliatory forces is in some ways equivalent to an exchange of hostages; and '*inhumane*' weapons, capable of inflicting damage but not able to go after the enemy's strategic forces, *acquire virtue* because of their clearly deterrent function and the lack of temptation they give either side to strike first." In fact, Schelling seems to believe that these weapons may be *more* "virtuous" *the more inhumane* they are since, "if submarine-based missiles have possibly a lesser degree of accuracy as compared with ground-based missiles," this "makes them less of a threat to the enemy's retaliatory forces and more of a genuine deterrent" (T. C. Schelling, "Reciprocal Measures for Arms Stabilization," *Daedalus*, Fall, 1950, pp. 892, 905, italics added).

[44] Tucker, p. 140 n. 26.

tion of military necessity from principle and the theme of voluntarism; yet surely the two are related. ". . . Indifference" to war's conduct, Tucker remarks, "may also stem from the conviction that once force is employed man has moved from the realm of freedom to a world of necessity." [45] Yet, like peace and war themselves, these are not two different, disjoined realms. They are rather internally related to one another, even if confidence in the triumphant freedom of man radically to transform history and his submission to military necessity once war occurs seem to vary inversely with one another in the American ethos, and to alternate in fact. Illustration of this may be found in that remarkable series of editorials written by Charles C. Morrison in *The Christian Century*, declaring after we became involved in World War II that "war is hell," i.e., the inexorable *judgment* of God, from which even the freedom and purification of purgatory has been expelled, while the peace that God's patience allowed us had been our time of trial and of obedience or disobedience.[46] We might also call attention to the fact that in the present day churchmen and other leaders of public opinion alike break into utterance during periods of "thaw" in international relations, advising statesmen that if there is a will there is a way to ransom these times and effect reconciliation among nations, strengthen the United Nations and bring peace, while during periods in which the cold war grows colder they seem *of necessity* to grow strangely silent.

Whatever the explanation, it is in no case an accident that "a markedly voluntaristic interpretation of war itself has been juxtaposed with a markedly deterministic interpretation of war's conduct"; and that

> . . . As a general rule the greater the voluntarism shown toward war, the greater the determination shown toward war's conduct. For there is a direct and obvious link between the optimism which assumes that force can be banished from history and the pessimism which concludes that if the achievement of this end shall prove impossible, it will prove equally impossible to set any meaningful limitations on war's conduct. Thus in recent years those who have professed the greatest faith in a policy of nuclear deterrence as a means for exorcising force from history have unfailingly insisted almost in the same breath that should nuclear deterrence somehow fail it will prove impossible to set any meaningful limitations on war's conduct.[47]

And does not that other son of the aggressor-defender doctrine—the Christian or other nuclear pacifist—in the same breath affirm the same

[45] P. 76.
[46] Charles C. Morrison, *"The Christian and the War"* (Chicago, Ill.: Willett, Clark & Co., 1942).
[47] Tucker, pp. 77–78.

voluntarism and the same determinism? Indeed, against this background, he who would address a radically different doctrine to the people and the leaders of the western powers—one that requires a usable link to be forged between force and policy both in peace and in war—must be prepared to be simultaneously accused of utopianism with regard to imposing limits upon the conduct "necessary" in war and of trying to save war as an instrument of national policy when it was just about to be abolished altogether.

Professor Tucker writes ironically about the singular ambiguity in current American doctrine concerning limits upon the conduct of war.

He rightly points out that "it is a mistake to assume that the acceptance of limited *objectives* must insure the limitation of force as well—that there is a necessary relation between the limitation of the purposes sought in war and the limitation of the *manner* of warfare." [48] He realizes that in the nuclear age, an independent ethics of *means* is crucial: "Whether or not the means will prove discriminating must depend upon the limits directly imposed on the means themselves. . . . There is a distinction—and in the nuclear age perhaps a vital distinction —between the *discriminating use* of weapons and their employment for *discriminate objectives*." [49]

Since, however, current American doctrine voids any limitation upon the conduct of war under the lure of the limitless objective of abolishing war and punishing aggression, we have known only an ethic of means of war derived from the ends alone. This excludes only *wanton* acts of cruelty or destructiveness. ". . . The principle of military necessity surely does not allow the employment of force unnecessary or superfluous to the achievement of the purposes of war. . . . It is the unnecessary infliction of human suffering and the wanton destruction of property that is opposed, not only by the principle of humanity but by military necessity as well." On this view, what will be proscribed as "unnecessary" must largely depend upon the purposes of war;[50] and, given the objective of "unconditional surrender," it was not unreasonable to suppose, by honest conviction at the time of action, that the bombing of Hiroshima and Nagasaki was justified. The fault in this action was in its goal or purpose, not only in the use made of indiscriminate means.[51]

As for elaborating the criteria for limiting the conduct of war, there are two views that vie with one another. The one holds that "the principal purpose for restraining the manner in which hostilities are conducted is not to protect human rights or to mitigate suffering [as such] but to insure that the minimum foundations of order will be preserved

[48] P. 153 (italics added).
[49] P. 153 n. 4 (italics added).
[50] P. 90 n. 82.
[51] P. 91 n. 83.

even in war. . . . These restraints must seek to prevent a war waged in such a manner as to threaten the very existence of the participants [states], thereby striking at the foundations upon which any international order must rest." [52] The other "more modern" and the American view begins with the premise that war always "signifies the breakdown of all order." [53] Hence the purpose of limiting the manner of conducting hostilities will not be to protect the rights of aggressor and defender alike in the existing political order but "to protect the inherent rights of individuals *qua* individuals." This is the "humanitarian" view.[54] This proscribes wanton destructiveness only, and has little or nothing to do with defining *legitimate* military necessity.

While setting these forth at first as discrete positions, Tucker himself points out that the former view (which he prefers) is not unconcerned with or inimical to humanitarian considerations. In fact, he argues that the position faces up more forthrightly to the difficult task "of somehow reconciling the fact of violence with the demands of humanity." [55] The partial collapse of the original distinction between considerations of order and considerations of humanity would not be worth pointing out were it not for the fact that current American doctrine concerning the conduct of war always identifies the distinction attempted to be made between combatants and non-combatants as an implication only of the humanitarian view that seeks to treat individuals *qua* individauls,[56] and then speedily concludes that this distinction is futile.

It is significant that the *memory* of this distinction is still alive in American doctrine, even if this is "not altogether impressive" when accompanied by a doctrine deducing military necessity from the objective of the war, and by our belief that "the central moral problem is war itself and not the weapons and methods of war" and that the manner of responding to aggression is only a technical question.[57] But what we do with the memory of this distinction amounts to a complete annulment of it:

> With a sufficiently elastic definition of a legitimate military objective and a sufficiently broad interpretation of what constitutes "incidental" injury to the civilian population, there is no need ever to deny the continued validity of the principle distinguishing between combatants and non-combatants. In this manner, the World War II bombings of Hiroshima and Nagasaki were justified in that they contained military

[52] P. 81.
[53] P. 82.
[54] Pp. 82–83.
[55] P. 83.
[56] Pp. 84–86.
[57] P. 86.

objectives the destruction of which were alleged to warrant the "incidental" damage done to the civilian population.[58]

That may be compared to the man who, when asked the difference between adultery and fornication, replied that he had tried them both and
so far as he could see there wasn't any difference! With a sufficiently
elastic definition of morality and immorality and of the terms in which
these may be expressed, one can, of course, justify anything; but in both
instances any improvement in moral behavior must stem from clarifying
the categories. To point to "the significant absence of any war crimes
trials in which the accused were charged with terror bombing of civilian
population" does not demonstrate that this was not still a crime (in the
moral and political sense if not a crime before international law).[59] It
only goes to show that the vanquished were guilty of the crime of this
century in American and western doctrine—avoidably starting an aggressive war—and other evils besides; while victors and vanquished alike
were guilty of the other crime.

If it is a "pathetic effort to apply to aerial warfare some remnant
of the traditional principle distinguishing between combatants and non-
combatants," then we are left with only the (now non-existent) limit that
war should be fought only in such a manner as not to strike at the very
foundations of the international order. Professor Tucker has already
indicated that from imposing a limit upon the purpose or objectives in
war alone no limit that is worth the name can be imposed upon the
means or upon the war's conduct. There must be "limits directly imposed
on the means," and a vital distinction must be made "between the *discriminating use* of weapons and their employment for discriminate objectives," [60] or else there are no limits to the manner in which war is to be
waged.

It is, therefore, of crucial importance for us to understand that
the distinction between combatants and non-combatants is no mere humanitarian principle treating individuals *qua* individuals on the assumption that the outbreak of war signifies the breakdown of all order. This
principle, instead, treats individuals as members of states at war. It is
the moral underpinning of that minimum foundation of order to be
preserved even in war. It is, as it were, the "natural law" of warfare that
is conducted justly; and the only ethics of means independent of war's
objectives which specifies the manner in which it ought to be waged. This
distinction is older yet, and the parent of the principle of order which
emerged as the western nations emerged out of "Christendom" and which

[58] P. 93.
[59] P. 155 n. 36.
[60] P. 153 n. 4 (italics added).

60

counseled that the vital interest of states ought not to be at stake in the course or on the outcome of war.[61]

5. Finally, Professor Tucker singles out, among the features of the American doctrine of just war, its vehement rejection of preventive war as wholly unjustifiable under any circumstance. With some boldness and at length, he undertakes, as a contemporary historian and analyst, to describe and expose the ambiguities in our announced attitude toward every case of initiative in the resort to armed force. With yet more boldness (having twice remarked that a thorough examination and correction of America's doctrine of the just war is a hazardous enterprise), I will state the constructive thesis that it will also prove necessary to call in question this assumption; and that a truer doctrine of the just war cannot avoid asserting in its doctrine the possibility of a just initiation of armed force.

In fact, apart from a purely pacifist position, something like the American doctrine of the aggressor-defender war is the only theory of war which finds itself obliged to reject what we nowadays call "preventive" war.[62] Unless the principal tenets of this doctrine are valid, its thorough-

---

[61] Moreover, it is a mistake to assume that the balance of power worked automatically to limit war's conduct and apart from the suasive influence of the moral and political ethos. "Before the balance of power could impose its restraints upon the power aspirations of nations through the mechanical interplay of opposing forces, the competing nations had first to restrain themselves by accepting the system of the balance of power as the common framework of their endeavors" (Hans Morgenthau, *Politics Among Nations*, 2nd ed. (New York: Alfred A. Knopf, Inc., 1954), p. 199). That ethos and balance came to an end when in World War I the German high command ignored the counsel (of the strategists who drew up their original war plans) that, if the thrust toward Paris did not succeed quickly, the Germans should promptly sue for peace; and proceeded to fight a protracted war that became even more purposeless in the trenches. In the case of either the principle of order or the principle distinguishing between combatants and non-combatants, the question is: *Where* (not *what*) is the ethos or the doctrinal agreement among nations that can make *any* attempt to limit war anything more than a "pathetic effort"?

[62] In the following discussion I am bound to the use of this expression only by Professor Tucker's use of it. In my view, the term "preventive war" has already been shaped by the American doctrine that the only imaginable just use of force would be against an act of war itself. We first reject any use of force as an instrument of policy, rejecting any intervention by force of arms even to forestall political developments that may be the cause of an act of aggressive war in the future. We wait for that to justify any resort to military force; or so our doctrine states. A people so determined by doctrine will naturally think first of defensive war, then of war to prevent *war*, and finally only of *pre-emptive* war. The latter, as we will see, comes closest to qualifying as defensive against actual aggression; and we toy with this idea most of all, next to waiting to be drawn into conflict. Most alien to the American mind-set is not even war to prevent *war*, but the possibility of the use or threat to use force, along with diplomacy, etc., as instruments of international policy. To this I refer in speaking of the possibility of initiative in the use of force instead of "preventive war" (already a concept misshapen by the aggressor-defender doctrine).

going rejection of a first use of force will not follow. Thus, Tucker writes that ". . . preventive war as a possible instrument of policy cannot be excluded on moral grounds alone save by a doctrine which insists upon identifying the justice or injustice of war with the acts immediately attending the initiation of force." [63] Nor can this be excluded on moral grounds alone save by a doctrine which insists that better political means of redress are always available, in comparison with which resort to force is always not only evil, but an avoidable, unnecessary evil. The initiative in the use of force cannot be denied on moral grounds alone save by a doctrine of radical voluntarism according to which history can be transformed and force banished from the affairs of states. Unless one or all of these premises are correct, then a first use of force may possibly be just.

Yet there are specific objections to the justice of ever taking the initiative in resorting to force which have to be dealt with, if only in order to show that these objections gain all their force from the foregoing convictions, and are formed by or reduce to the peculiar features of the aggressor-defender doctrine.

It may be said that "a policy of resorting to preventive war is absolutely condemned, among other reasons, because it allegedy assumes the inevitability of conflict . . ." This may be true, in the sense that the advocate of the possible justice in a first use of force will hold that such initiative should and will be a permanent feature of political life, that force cannot be banished from history before banishing the nation-state from this planet, and that the right to have resort to force can only be deposited in some political agency other than states where it will continue to subsist. Here opposing premises are exposed, not an additional argument. But this objection may mean to condemn the permissibility of a first use of force because it allegedly assumes the inevitability of a particular conflict, and "thereby must presumably depend upon an omniscience to know the future that is denied to man." If so, the answer is, in Tucker's words: "In fact, the argument for preventive war does not depend upon any claim to omniscience in reading the future," or upon a war's general inevitability. "That argument proceeds, as all statecraft must proceed, upon an estimate of the future to which a varying degree of probability may be attached." Within that calculation of probability, a policy of resorting to force first does aim to "determine" the future. But these are not sufficient grounds for condemning the policy as "repugnant" and "an ignominious surrender to irresponsibility." Under some circumstances it is possible that the refusal of statecraft to estimate a future danger within some degree of probability and its refusal to attempt then to determine the future may themselves be to surrender to irresponsibility.

[63] Tucker, p. 15 (italics added).

Certainly, the aggressor-defender doctrine has no standing to bring up these objections, since, after war occurs, that doctrine allows the possibility of calculating the future and fighting the war offensively to determine the future. ". . . If preventive war is to be morally condemned" for these reasons, "then it is difficult to see why the same judgment may not be made with respect to a policy that employs force—even though initially in defense—for predominantly preventive purposes.[64] The aggressor-defender doctrine can only reiterate that a preventive war lacks any justifying occasion, that it refuses to concede that resort to force is always avoidable, etc. Any other argument it advances is apt to turn against the aggressor-defender doctrine, or against war itself, even in defense.

A stronger argument (although Tucker does not seem to think that it has greater weight) is the contention that a first use of force "involves the acceptance of a *certain* evil in order to avoid what can only be a less-than-certain danger." Now, in estimating the effects of proposed actions, and balancing them against one another, a less-than-certain evil should always be chosen instead of a more certain or quite certain one, *provided* the *gravity* of the evils is the same. More than the proximity and remoteness, or the certainty or probability, of the good or evil in the effects has to be assessed. The quality of the good or the enormity of the evil has also to be thrown in the balance. The opening sentence of Tucker's reply is therefore not yet sufficient, in that it simply admits that "without doubt, preventive war does involve precisely that," i.e., the choice of a certain evil over a less-than-certain one. If that were all, resort to force ought *never* to be chosen. But Tucker goes on to bring in the enormity of the evils that are in comparison, in order to argue that a less but certain evil *may* be chosen over a greater but less-than-certain one. ". . . If for this reason," he writes, "preventive war is taken to represent a surrender of responsibility, then any action involving the acceptance of a certain evil in order to avoid a still greater potential evil is to be equated with irresponsibility." [65] This is the marrow of the matter. The proscription of a first use of force may very well be a conclusion of statecraft; it ought never to be its universal premise. If I may borrow some terminology from Roman Catholic moral theology (and possibly misuse it), the proscription of a first use of force may very well be a proper "hypothesis" of states; it ought never to be their "thesis."

Finally, Professor Tucker points out that a sweeping proscription of the first use of force gains credence within the aggressor-defender doctrine by virtue of its own identification of war (once it is occasioned), and

---

[64] Pp. 71 n. 65; 105; 107.

[65] P. 108. Ought we *always* to agree with Hanson Baldwin, writing of the concept of preventive war as "alien and repugnant," that "if war has to come it is far better that it come twenty years from now than today" ("The Price of War," *Harper's Magazine*, July 1948, p. 26)?

therefore also any resort to war, with unlimited war. "It is . . . not obvious and has never been obvious why preventive war must be 'by definition' an all-out war with no restrictions placed on the manner of employing force." It is only by means of a "self-fulfilling definition" of war as unlimited that the conclusion is reached proscribing first resort to force under all possible circumstances for this reason.[66] The vehement objection to the first use of force is, therefore, a significant revelation of the anatomy of the aggressor-defender doctrine. Unable to find any link between policy and force after war occurs, this doctrine can find none before it occurs. It passionately rejects, before an outbreak of hostilities, the very thing it bears without any grounds for restraint in its own bosom, and which clearly comes to expression after war has begun, namely, the acceptance of radical evil to achieve a desirable end. "Precisely the reasons used to condemn preventive war become the reasons used to defend the manner and purposes of a defensive war." After war occurs "unconditional surrender" becomes the goal of a clearly "preventive-defensive" war to extirpate the evil of aggression. If one purpose of a *previous* war was to anticipate the future and determine history, "if this purpose necessitated the acceptance of certain evils in terms of the manner of conducting war, which it certainly did, this was never interpreted as a surrender to irresponsibility." [67]

As an analysis, this is correct; as an argument, of course, it would be *ad hominem*, and, if used in support of the possible legitimacy of the first use of force, it would tend to prove too much, or to prove that resort to force is justified without a limiting connection with concrete policy. Still, it is instructive for us to see how the weight of the opposition to the first use of force is drawn from wrong doctrine. Moreover, Tucker is correct in pointing out that many of the advocates of the means-end argument against the first use of force "are not really entitled to its use." For it is clear that they do not have in mind an ethics of means (having some independence of ends) to deny them on moral grounds the use of certain supposed *necessary* means; they simply judge the means to be unnecessary—before war's start.[68]

It should be clear that "a preventive war may be defensive in every sense save for the initially 'aggressive' act of resorting to armed force, and the state made the object of the preventive use of force may wage a war that is anything but defensive except for the fact that it did not literally initiate the armed conflict." [69] There is no possibility of forging a connection between force and policy after war has begun without also re-establishing this connection during the period before war's start. This

[66] Tucker, pp. 105, 106, 106 n. 5.
[67] Pp. 109, 110, 111.
[68] Pp. 112–113.
[69] P. 115.

64

will entail not only a recovery of an understanding of the justice and limitation of wars once begun but also a recovery of the possible justice of their initiation. If ever we emerge from the present period of purposeless war plans, we shall also have to go back to the truth contained in Francis Bacon's words, "Wars preventive upon just fears are true defensives, as well as upon actual invasions," [70] or beyond that, to the more ancient just war theory which found it impossible to exclude this provision.

For it is quite possible that in the world of today, for all its capacity for violence, there is a vacuum not only of usable power but also, at least on the part of the West, of the use of power. The Charter of the United Nations provided that the Security Council was to take action not only upon a "breach of the peace or act of aggression" but also upon its determination that there was a "threat to the peace." That entailed a possible first use of force, i.e. its preventive use. Therefore Tucker comments that it is "not without significance that the one attempt in this century to realize a centralized system of international order and thereby overcome the ambiguities and hazards inherent in contemporary doctrines of self-defense nevertheless sanctioned the preventive use of force subject to no substantive restraint other than that imposed by the necessity of obtaining the unanimity of the major powers." [71] Whether the great powers were expected to act in unanimity only when the cause was just, or justice was expected to be whatever they willed unanimously, this ideal scheme did not neglect to take account of the problem of preserving security and order and justice by resort to first use of force.

Since that failed, states individually, in the collective regional arrangements that have emerged, and in the Assembly of the United Nations, have had to rely on other procedures. The principal legality to which appeal has been made is the provision of Article 51 of the Charter: "Nothing in the present Charter shall impair the inherent right of individual or collective self-defense if an armed attack occurs against any Member of the United Nations . . ." But that was clearly dependent upon the initiative that is now absent, as the concluding words of this article make plain: ". . . until the Security Council has taken the measures necessary to maintain international peace and security." In the absence of Security Council action to put down any "breach of the peace or act of aggression," the exercise of this right and duty rests with states, individually and collectively, and with the Assembly of the United Nations. Then it would seem that, in the absence of Security Council action to forestall any "threat to the peace," the exercise of this right and duty rests also with states, individually and collectively, and with the Assembly, by the initiative this entails, and possibly by a first resort to arms.

[70] Quoted *ibid.*, p. 116.
[71] P. 133.

But, meanwhile, the American aggressor-defender doctrine of the just war has spread, like the rest of the veneer of American civilization, over almost the whole western and neutralist world; and the single cause capable of always securing a mandate in the Assembly is "peace," nonintervention, opposition to aggression *after* it has occurred, and the interposition of a modicum of force between rival forces—which leaves threats to the peace to be dealt with by peaceful resolutions.

So, Dean Acheson, United States Secretary of State, asserted on April 30, 1951, that the United Nations action in Korea "never contemplated the use of force to accomplish its political objective in Korea, which is the establishment of a unified, independent, and democratic country." On June 26, 1951, while admitting that but for Chinese intervention this purpose might have been accomplished, as it were, unintentionally, as an "incidental effect," he gave the following ingenious explanation of the true purpose of the fighting: ". . . there would probably have been a unification of Korea as a result of the combat; but the combat was not for the purpose of doing that. It was for the purpose of eliminating this aggression by rounding up people who refused to surrender and who refused to lay down their arms and refused to do anything except keep on fighting." [72] And President Eisenhower, while stating that the British and their allies had great grievances on their side and had suffered the violation of legal rights which led to the abortive thrust against Suez, remarked: "I do not believe that another instrument of injustice—war—is the remedy for these wrongs." The decisive question to be raised is not whether there was on that specific occasion greater justice on the side of Egypt or on the side of her attackers, but whether, according to our public doctrine, there could be *any* occasion of the first use of force of which it would *not* be said that such an "instrument of injustice" cannot be the remedy for wrong.

Have not these words of Acheson and Eisenhower in effect been repeated time and time again, until we have turned the whole world into a Congo—or rather the Congo into this present world—in which there is force aplenty, and United Nations forces interposed between forces, but no positive policy can be enforced? If Khrushchev in his fury wrecks the United Nations, the remote if not the proximate cause of that may be the fact that the western powers placed upon it a burden it was not able to carry because it is not an originating source of armed power. But more especially, the cause will be that our own policies, reflected in United Nations action, have had no more substance than "rounding up people who refuse to surrender and who refuse to do anything except keep on fighting." The reason we are persuaded that interposition is a policy is

[72] Quoted by Tucker, p. 62.

surely due to our public doctrine which finds the justice of war only in its occasion in aggression.

It is clear that there is today a vacuum in the taking of initiative, possibly by first resort to force and always with the possibility of this, in comparison to that envisaged to be necessary by the Charter of the United Nations. The western alliance has so far found no way, or has not been very much inclined, to forge a link between positive policies and the use of force. This will have to be done, if not collectively then by the individual states, and especially by that nation which has the leadership of the western world in its hands.

A crux of this failure is a flaw in our doctrine. We have, of course, not simply aimed to preserve the peace, but (in the phrase President Eisenhower was fond of repeating) "peace with justice." The flaw, however, is in how in the silent assumptions of our doctrine we understand peace and justice to be related, and guaranteed to be linked by an unseen hand. By a sweeping proscription of aggression and by the renunciation of force as an instrument of national policy, Professor Tucker points out, we never "thereby admit to a concept of international order in which peace . . . may be founded upon injustice." [73] Instead we mean to say that force *should not* be employed aggressively as an instrument of policy "because it *need not* be so employed." [74] The renunciation of force and the according of justice, in the American dream, will proceed hand in hand. There is for us a necessary coincidence between peace and all means necessary to secure justice, as well as between the security interests of this or any nation and waiting for the justifying occasion. [75]

Such convictions can only lead to the immobilization of politics. This may be illustrated by a recent editorial comment in *The New York Times.* [76] Written against some proposal for action by the minority Republican leaders of the Senate and the House, Dirksen and Halleck, this editorial did not say that this or that was wrong with their specific proposal. It said instead—in words that sum up ironically the plight of politics and the plight of justice in the present day—: "The alternative to negotiation is action. The risks that *action* can bring in this thermonuclear world are so great that they are justified only as a last resort." This is not an illogical consequence of a doctrine which first renounced resort to arms as a matter of policy, and then found no difficulty in conscience in accepting weapons plans which promise, before war comes, to prevent the policies of a nation from ever taking up arms, and, after war occurs, to prevent arms from ever taking on any purposeful policy.

[73] P. 30.
[74] P. 34 (italics added).
[75] Pp. 32–39.
[76] June 9, 1961.

While rejecting out of hand the idea of "preventive" war in a sense of a first resort to force for possibly some justifiable reason, the aggressor-defender doctrine is able to accommodate itself to the idea of "pre-emptive" war even if this is for no purpose save punishing aggression. This is the final gruesome contrast between the traditional just-war doctrine and the American doctrine of the just war. A pre-emptive strike can be brought within the aggressor-defender doctrine simply by an extensive interpretation of the act of aggression that justifies resort to force. A pre-emptive attack assumes that the enemy *has already taken the initiative* even if this has not quite yet come to blows. Thus, pre-emption can be reconciled with the absolute condemnation of a first resort to force. Indeed, pre-emption may be said to be morally required by such absolute condemnation of the first use of force and by the determination of war's justice exclusively by its justifying occasion, for "a pre-emptive attack involves an action in which the attempt is made *to seize the initiative from an adversary* who has either already resorted to force or is *certain* to initiate hostilities in the immediate future." [77] Bernard Brodie writes that "this idea has been somewhat unkindly referred to as the philosophy of I won't strike first unless you do." [78] Professor Tucker rightly comments that such "unkind critics" are "not essentially incorrect." [79]

Indeed, it may be said that the capacity to respond "justly" and pre-emptively to surprise attack has been built into the surprise attack weapons themselves. In that familiar spiral in which acts of war arise not out of concrete policy but out of contending wills, each side may be expected to do what it expects to be expected to do because of what it expects the other side to expect to be expected to do. Thus each side begins to suspect that the other is bound to launch a surprise attack, which pre-emption in turn would have to be pre-empted, and so on. Mutual "anticipatory retaliation" (Einstein) against aggression is always about to take control of the system which was supposed always to deter both sides. This is *not* because either side *mis*calculates but because both sides are in danger of *calculating correctly*. "The 'necessity' that is held to justify a pre-emptive attack can no longer be regarded as stemming from a situation both exceptional in occurrence and readily identifiable as a distinct series of acts; in the final analysis this necessity stems less from overt behavior of a potential adversary armed with nuclear-missile weapons than from the mere fact that the adversary possesses the means to destroy with almost no advance warning." [80] The act of aggression and an unlimited "defensive" war have both been built into the weapons

[77] P. 142–143 (italics added).
[78] *Strategy in the Missile Age* (Princeton, N.J.: Princeton University Press, 1959), p. 242.
[79] Tucker, p. 143 n. 29.
[80] P. 145.

system. For, given the capacity of the missiles to destroy, their threat is so enormous as to provide a sufficiently justifying occasion for knocking out these weapons if their bases are vulnerable. The question has now become: "when is a pre-emptive attack *not* justified?"

It was at this point that technical reason was brought to bear upon the problem of devising schemes for permanently integrating these weapons, by mounting them on hopefully invulnerable bases, into prevent-the-war policies and arms control proposals that *will finally succeed* in implementing that other premise of the aggressor-defender doctrine, namely, that force be banished from human history by making its use forever impossible.

Thus have we institutionalized all that we ever believed: that force can be banished, that the justice of war lies wholly in its occasion, and that should force ever be used a state of war supervenes to which no norms or limits apply. This used to be an oscillation in successive periods of time between all-out peace and all-out (aggressor-defender) war. Contemporary proposals for arms control *based on the total deterrent* represent the final product of the American ethos. Their distinctiveness is only that they may claim to have banished force and provided automatically in advance for the irrational use of violence in one timeless scheme.

CHAPTER 4

Pacem in terris*

Of the myriad comments upon the encyclical *Pacem in terris,* the one from Mrs. Dagmar Wilson, the pretty, pert, and freethinking founder of the Women's Strike for Peace, must be prized for its thought-provoking irrelevance. "We've always maintained," said she, "that politics and religion played no part in the struggle for peace, and the Pontiff seems to be supporting the same idea." [1] While the encyclical is addressed "to all men of good will" everywhere, it is obvious on any reading of it that it is pervaded by politics and religion. Moreover, by the principles of the Christian religion—as these are received by Roman Catholics and by many others besides—and by some sound and exceedingly important political truths that were in search of a voice humanly great enough to utter them.

I

Still, there is a defect in the religio-ethical analysis beneath the encyclical, and a consequent defect in its explicit political diagnosis, which need to be pointed out. Its opening paragraphs move swiftly from the praise of God for the place accorded man in the order of creation to the serenity and certitudes arising from the fact that "the Creator of the world has imprinted in man's heart an order which his conscience

* First appeared in *Religion in Life,* Vol. XXXIII Winter 1963–64, 116–135. Copyright © 1963 by Abingdon Press.
[1] *The New York Times,* April 11, 1963.

reveals to him and enjoins him to obey." The encyclical as a whole, then, simply elucidates the contemporary application of the moral laws governing men and states, as these differ from the laws that govern "the forces and irrational elements of the universe." The moral laws governing men and states therefore "are to be sought elsewhere, namely, where the Father of all things wrote them, that is, in the nature of man."

Only two sentences refer in passing to the disordering of God's design by sinfulness; and this factor missing from this statement of the religious perspectives upon human affairs that Christians are given to possess—at least when one encompasses the whole of the Christian witness—accounts for the encyclical's exceedingly slight emphasis (in the same two sentences) upon the exercise of force as the mark distinguishing political community from all other communities that also seek a common good. "How strangely does the turmoil of individual men and peoples contrast with the perfect order of the universe!" the pontiff exclaims. "It is as if the relationships which bind them together could be controlled only by force." This is the last we hear of that!

Lacking is a proper sense that the human, moral world is also a world of "indeterminate, irrational equations," that there is a "surd" and an "indispensable negative" or "minus sign" also located in human nature, which accounts for the fact that we have newspapers (at least *our* newspapers).[2] (In reference to what some Protestant theologians call "demonic" powers, is it to be expected that the Vatican Council may decide that henceforth it is proper to refer to Satan as "our separated brother"?) Lacking, therefore, is that important element in Christian political diagnosis which makes it clear to us that the relationships properly called political which bind men together require always and everywhere that they be controlled *also* by force.

Commenting upon the pope's evident expectation that the communist nations will eventually adopt his views of world order, John F. Cronin, S.S., describes this as "a position that in anyone but Pope John would seem to be one of blind optimism and impractical idealism."[3] If *Pacem in terris* is excessively optimistic and idealist, it is so at a deeper theoretical level in its analysis of the political relationships among nations, and not just in the matter of the "opening to the left" which has been so much debated. And if there is here any failure to comprehend in every way the basic nature of politics, this is an inadequacy in anyone, including Pope John. Montesquieu once predicted that Protestantism would disappear, and that when this happened, Catholicism would become the same as Protestantism. The highest tribute to be paid the

[2] These are the words of the "midnight visitor" to Ivan Karamazov.

[3] "The Encyclical's View of Marxism," *The New World* (official newspaper of the Archdiocese of Chicago), April 19, 1963. Mr. Cronin is assistant director of the Social Action department of the National Catholic Welfare Conference.

encyclical is that—both in tone and in substance—the pontiff sounds so much like a liberal Protestant parson. This is also a way to express succinctly the chief criticism to be made: the encyclical sounds too much like liberal Protestant statements which, while rightly stressing what positively needs to be done for the attainment of the universal common good, fails to grapple with the problem of power except in *those* terms. We cannot fail to take notice of the degree to which the pontiff's powerful expression of the aspirations of the whole of mankind, when these aspirations and their foundation in the moral law stand so nearly alone, becomes a nonpolitical statement in the arena of the actual practice of politics.

For the sake of religious concord and civil peace, Protestants will especially applaud two notes in this encyclical of John XXIII. The first is the pontiff's endorsement of the freedom of assembly for the *public* worship of God in a heretical manner, and presumably the allied freedom to conduct public propaganda on behalf of a faith regarded by Roman Catholics as heretical or schismatic. This theme is introduced almost incidentally, or as an aside, while repeating the ordinary rights of personal conscience ("no one can be coerced to perform interior acts") and the freedom of *private* worship from any restriction or coercion: "Every human being has the right to honor God according to the dictates of an upright conscience, and therefore the right to worship God privately *and publicly*" (italics added).

The second is the pontiff's clear break away from the continuing debate about whether those abstractions, "truth" or "error," have equal rights; and his forthright declaration that it is the person who is the bearer of rights, not what he thinks or believes. "One must never confuse error and the person who errs"—not even when his error has to do with faith and morals. "The person who errs is always and above all a human being and retains in every case his dignity as a human person. And he must always be regarded and treated in accordance with that lofty dignity."

These positions have, of course, long been taken by liberal Roman Catholics; but never before, so far as I know, have these two fundamental points been asserted, without any qualifications that weaken or withdraw them, by the highest teaching authority of the Roman Catholic Church. It may not be advisable to test the practice of these principles right away in every nominally Roman Catholic country.[4] I know, too,

---

[4] In Spain Roman Catholicism is the dominant religion, "which is that of the Spanish state." The basic law of the land provides, however, that "nobody will be molested because of his religious beliefs or the *private* exercise of his creed," while external manifestations by non-Catholic religions are banned. In the wake of the Council, negotiations between the regime and the Catholic Church (with no consultations, it is true, with Protestant leaders) seem likely to lead to a measure that would,

that the debate will continue—now, over what exactly, and as applied to particular cases, the Holy Father meant. Still, the plain words stand in the encyclical; and Protestants can now embrace those who do not like to be called "liberal" Roman Catholics without as much fear as heretofore that this may actually endanger their cause, by confirming the suspicion of conservatives and those in positions of ecclesiastical authority that their liberal brethren have fallen to talking just like wide-minded Protestants.

It is, of course, under the injunction never to confuse error and the person who errs that the pope inserts—without naming the Communists—his famous "opening to the left." I do not propose to intervene in the dispute that has arisen over this among Roman Catholics, nor am I competent to comment upon whether, in exegeting the text, we must take account of the fact that certain passages were poorly translated from the Latin into the vernacular languages or from Italian into Latin. Still, the text of the encyclical at this point tempts one to suppose that, from the basic distinction between error and the person who errs, the sin and the sinner, or between communism and the person who is a Communist (which is a truth in the personal and the religious sphere), one can extrapolate to a historical, political *prediction* that social movements based on dangerous errors will progressively become ameliorated until, at the end of a unilinear development, mankind will arrive at "an order founded on truth, built according to justice, vivified and integrated by charity, and put into practice in freedom."

One cannot reach this conclusion from a major general premise distinguishing erroneous doctrine from the person who errs, not even by means of the minor premise which the pontiff uses, and which, in my opinion, is also true. This is his judgment that "in every human being there is a need that is congenital to his nature and never becomes extinguished that compels him to break through the web of error and open his mind to the knowledge of truth." Doubtless, one cannot interpret aright the turmoil and the struggles for justice in any historical time without taking account of the pressures of the human essence, and of what Maritain calls man's knowledge of the natural law by "congeniality," upon the external arrangements and structures of society. But one has to take account also of another law in our members that wars against the law in our minds, if he is to understand the persistence of evil and of error and the emergence of ever new forms of injustice even in the face of the strong, silent, innermost tendencies of human nature toward the true and the good.

---

among other things, guarantee undisturbed operation of churches and schools (*The New York Times*, May 14, 1963). There have been, of course, significant changes in church-state relations in Spain since the second Vatican Council.

Because of this, it takes more than what the pontiff calls the "pronounced dynamism" of "our times" to explain why "the problem of bringing social reality into line with the objective requirements of justice is a problem which will never admit of a definitive solution." Even that "dynamism," taken alone, is almost enough to require a significant modification of the pope's extreme confidence in the competence of negotiation and in the actual achievement of the impartiality requisite for litigants always to reach settlements. It is correct to proclaim that in this generation John XXIII arose to greatness in that succession of men, which happily no generation has lacked, who have been "interpreters of the very profound longing of the entire human family." He was for all followers of Christ the world over, and of every denomination, their Christian brother, and a great priest in the church where all minister, from faith to faith, to one another; a chief servant of the servants of God, free for all and subject to none. He was indeed a saint, if that class has any members. But anyone is an indifferent political scientist who passes over the problem of power so lightly, and who sees not that the need to bind men together also by forcible arrangements arises from human nature; and that this, too, is inscribed in the human heart in letters that may never be effaced to the end of time.

If one concentrates on the brief passage itself, and not on its framework, one obtains a different interpretation of the pope's "opening to the left." The passage itself is quite relativistic. It is a realistic observation deduced from nothing. In actuality, and on a careful reading of the encyclical, a *rapprochement* with the Communist nations is only, but definitely, a possibility; it is one among the contingencies of history; it may happen because of the dynamism of social movements in the course of time; it is not to be excluded by a dogmatic anticommunism:

> . . . Neither can false philosophical teachings regarding the nature, origin and destiny of the universe and of man be identified with historical movements that have economic, social, cultural or political ends, not even when these movements have originated from these teachings and have drawn and still draw inspiration therefrom.

> This is because the teachings, once they are drawn up and defined, remain always the same, while the movements, working in historical situations in constant evolution, cannot but be influenced by these latter and cannot avoid, therefore, being subject to changes, even of a profound nature.

Therefore "it can happen," and the pontiff simply observed that it can: "It can happen, then, that a drawing nearer together or a meeting for the attainment of some practical end, which was formerly deemed inopportune or unproductive, might now or in the future be considered opportune and useful."

It is important that we see clearly what constitutes the pope's famous "opening to the left." It is a practical possibility not to be ruled out by the opposition between truth and error in theory. "To decide whether this moment has arrived and also to lay down the ways and degrees . . . are problems which can only be solved with the virtue of *prudence*" (italics added). Moreover, these decisions "rest primarily with those who live and work in the specific sectors of human society in which those problems arise." Here, it is true, the pontiff inserts again that such persons are to be guided by the natural law and the teachings of ecclesiastical authority. The specific guidance provided is simply that men should not because of their doctrinaire opinions refuse to be open to historical possibilities for cooperation.

The importance of this for eroding the position of many Roman Catholic "conservatives," and that of other men who out of inflexibility or ill will have sanctified their minds with absolutes of either a natural or the supernatural variety, can scarcely be overestimated. An analysis, however, of the very passage in which the pontiff refers, except by name, to these possibilities within the evolution of communism as a social and historical movement, leaves standing, it seems to me, many degrees of *prudential* anti-communism or of *prudential* collaboration, according as those who live and work in the specific political sector of human society may decide.

The framework of natural-law optimism, however, has led both the Catholic and the secular press to attribute to the pontiff a supine belief that the Communist nations must eventually become convinced of his view of world order. It is striking fact that among Roman Catholics, an unalloyed doctrine of natural law leading mankind on to world justice and, among Protestant liberals, confidence in the power of Christian love pure and undefiled to reconcile every opponent, lead religiously motivated political diagnosis away from the problem of power. In both instances the question to be raised is whether "the very profound longing of the entire human family" *in the modern period,* which knows no other peace than the peace of the earthly city, has not first shaped religious statements.

In any case, Max Ascoli's editorial in *The Reporter,* May 23, 1963, raises significant question about the seizing of the present moment by Catholics that has followed in the wake of the encyclical. John XXIII, Ascoli wrote, "knows the name of the most powerful among the men who err. This man may well agree with the Pope, only the other way round, and think that, after all, some good may even come from the Catholic, un-Marxist error. Immensely different as they are, these two men have one thing in common: they are both sophisticated peasants. Each has done his sowing. But for the harvest, one relies on prayer, the other on history, and never stops giving history a hand." He observes that the Bishop of Rome who "has his heart in Warsaw" has taken a gigantic risk for his church, and not only for his church; and then questions whether "the nearly unanimous effort on the part of Catholics and non-Catholics alike to avoid seeing the risk has, if anything, multiplied it."

Stronger alarm has been expressed by conservative German Catholics. Rudolf Krämer-Badoni protested: "That [Italian] workers and intellectuals, and also an increasing part of the middle classes, saw the door to Communism standing more invitingly open than ever demonstrates the political incompetence of the Pope"; and he concluded by directly addressing the pontiff: "You misuse your office politically. You are throwing our already weakened will to freedom into complete confusion. You wish to rescue the church, and you throw in our freedom as the price. You have no authorization to make politics. Turn back from this path." [5]

Krämer-Badoni, of course, may be quarreling with history, and refusing to see it as a realm of indefinite possibilities; and this the pope rightly struck down as no proper position for lay Catholics to assume in the sphere of political decision. Still, almost the same words might be used by someone who wished only to say that his political prudence differs from the pope's prudence and that his reading of the signs of the time is otherwise. If so, that would be an allowable way to be guided by this encyclical—if we are not to attribute to John XXIII an excessive optimism about the unilinear development of all social movements toward a just world order, or if that stands corrected by a deeper wisdom about political affairs.

For it cannot be denied that in making prudential political estimates as to whether "this moment has arrived," or concerning the "ways and degrees in which work in common might be possible," only the future can determine who was wise. Along one line, we may see Concordats with eastern European governments, the communization of western Europe following the destruction of political Catholicism there, and bitter statements from leaders of the Center who feel their church forsook them, comparable to those of the former head of the Center Party in Germany during the Nazi era. This encyclical having signified the church's willingness, without blessing totalitarian atheism, to live with it in the expectation of outliving it, it may become necessary for some future pontiff to write an encyclical letter like *Mit brennender Sorge* (1937), which broke with Nazism. Then, these future developments will have disclosed that the cost of relaxing the traditional Catholic stand

[5] "The Pope and Politics" in *Die Welt* (Hamburg). See *The New York Times*, May 13, 1963.

was too great to pay; the momentary advantage may only have been to relieve some Protestants of their apprehension that the papacy already has an airplane running, ready to move to Chicago after the next Italian election! [6]

Along another line, it may well be that the pope's "opening to the left" has seized the right historical moment; it may be that a genuine easing of tensions with eastern European nations and with Russia is possible. Then the future will disclose that John XXIII's prudence was right (or the prudence of the statesmen he encouraged), and this encyclical may go down in history for having helped to save Christendom from destruction and the whole world from nuclear holocaust. I know of no deductions from the tendencies in human nature or from the natural law, from faith and from sound morals, that can relieve political decision of its enormous risk-taking. Nor has Christ our Light given any man or priest or saint to see the future. Every historical moment is a time of waiting and of action without idols. This is another reason why *Pacem in terris* should not have failed to address itself to the problem of power as well as to the need for a just world order; and why the prudence of statesmen needs also to be informed by the moral principles governing the use of force when this is required. [7]

II

In his Christmas message of 1944, Pope Pius XII declared, "The theory of war as an apt and proportionate means of solving international

[6] The Vatican keeps busy correcting its correction of previous tendencies. Thus, on August 1, 1963, the Vatican radio went out of its way to remind Roman Catholics and all free men that there can be no compromise with communism. This broadcast was described as "extremely timely," lest the West lower its guard in the wake of the discussion of the test ban treaty in Moscow. "To promote, help and encourage initiatives and understanding that favor peace is a duty," the radio said. "But equally indispensable is the duty of vigilant, constant and indomitable opposition to the Marxist ideology and the duty to block every line of its penetration. There is no international situation, no easing of tension, no historical pretext [sic] that can justify any indulgence or conciliatory attitude toward Marxism and communism."

[7] Without minimizing the significance of the test ban agreement signed in Moscow, August 5, 1963, or the "steps" that may follow this one, one moment's thought will disclose in the present moment that the problem of power, and of how force has to be deployed and when or how used, is a perennial one in human political history. The gap between East and West in Europe has been closed in the degree another has opened between Russia and Red China. Beneath the "reconciliation" between Russia and the West there is the continuing struggle over whether, twenty years from now, West Germany will be allied with East or West; and the new opportunities for negotiation are also new challenges in this struggle over the largest power in central Europe.

conflicts is now out of date." At Christmas, 1948, he condemned "aggressive" war as "a sin, an offense, and an outrage," and modern total war, unless it were in self-defense, as "a crime worthy of the most severe national and international sanctions."

Interpreting Pius's words, John Courtney Murray affirmed that, for all Roman Catholic Christians, "the use of force is not now a moral means for the redress of violated legal rights. The justness of the cause is irrelevant; there simply is no longer a right of self-redress; no individual state may presume to take even the cause of justice into its own hands." But in answer to the question, How can this sin in the moral order, defined by the pontiff, be now transposed into a crime in the international legal order? Murray could only reply: "Pius XII did not enter the formidable technical problem, how this legal transcription of a moral principle is to be effected." And to this he appended the following somber notation: "This problem has hitherto been insoluble." [8]

It is obvious that the spirit and teachings of John XXIII are, if anything, even more set against the right to wage war as an inherent attribute of national sovereignty. When the objectives of nations are in conflict, he writes, "the resulting disagreements must be settled not by force . . . but rather in the only manner which is worthy of the dignity of man, i.e., by a mature and objective investigation of the situation." "Men are becoming more and more convinced that disputes which arise between States should not be resolved by recourse to arms, but rather by negotiation," the encyclical affirms at another point; and "it is hardly possible to imagine that in the atomic era war could be used as an instrument of justice." [9] Because of the ever deepening problem of war in the nuclear age, there is not in *Pacem in terris* any reference to a right of recourse to arms in self-defense, such as there was in Pius XII's Christ-

---

[8] "Morality and Modern War," pamphlet published by the Council on Religion and International Affairs, 1959, p. 10.

[9] [I later learned that a far better translation of this sentence would read: "Thus, in this age which boasts of its atomic power, it no longer makes sense (it is a violation of reason) to maintain that war is a fit instrument with which to repair the violation of justice." My error at this point in relying on the authorized English translation was inexcusable, and it added mistaken strength to my contention that the encyclical was unrealistic in dealing with war and with force as a decisive ingredient in politics. This mistake, however, was shared by a great part of the vocal opinion of the whole Catholic world, and especially by generally liberal and pacifist opinion— which was resolved to believe that in this crucial statement John XXIII had advanced significantly beyond the recent line of pontifical teachings on war. The mistaken translation was not corrected for many months by any available English translation. On the mistaken translation the pope did make an advance, thereby making a political and military judgment that is gravely in error, while on the correct translation he said nothing beyond previous popes and stepped into no grave error. The reader may want at once to read Chap. 10, pp. 192 f. below, where I elaborate the political ethics entailed in one and then the other of these translations.]

mas messages, which removed only the right of redress. War seems now in no case a just resort of policy; and a mature and objective assessment of the situation in order to negotiate seems all that could morally be done by states.

Because of his natural-law optimism, because of the overriding importance today of "the principles of human solidarity," and because of the perfection of justice in the pope's mind by Christian charity, John XXIII believed litigants, even though they are nation-states, to be capable of such dignified "mutual assessment." He went further than Pius XII did toward spelling out how the sin, in the moral order, of using armed force might be transcribed effectively into a crime in the international legal order. Still, a chief question about *Pacem in terris,* now and in the years to come, will be whether to it must not be appended the same somber verdict: "This problem has hitherto been insoluble."

An even more fundamental question is whether John XXIII actually understood how formidable a task it will be ever to create a world order out of the present system of nation-states. There is a good deal of evidence that the late beloved pontiff had little comprehension of the difficulty of transposing into international legal and institutional arrangements the principles of just world order which he enunciated.[10]

Concerning the way to transform our society into any ideal state, William Temple once told the story of an Englishman traveling in Ireland who asked the way to Roscommon. "Is it Roscommon you want to go to?" said the Irishman. "Yes," said the Englishman; "that's why I asked the way." "Well," said the Irishman, "if I wanted to go to Roscommon, I wouldn't be starting from here." Similarly, one wouldn't be starting from the nation-state if one wanted to reorganize the world on a supranational political basis.

So, for one thing, John XXIII didn't start from here, but from some other world. This first becomes apparent in the summary of the four parts of the encyclical which is given in the last paragraph of its in-

[10] The best comments yet to appear on *Pacem in terris* are to be found in the special edition of *worldview,* June, 1963. See especially Will Herberg, Alan Geyer, and William V. O'Brien. Amid the paeans of deserved yet uniformly quite uncritical praise with which Protestants greeted the encyclical, only Reinhold Niebuhr modified his tribute with remarks that went incisively to the heart of the matter. "The difficulty with this impressive document," Niebuhr wrote in *Christianity and Crisis* (May 13, 1963, p. 83), "is that the Church absorbs some of the voluntarism of the social contract theory, which underlies modern liberalism, and speaks as if it were a simple matter to construct and reconstruct communities, not by organic processes of history but by an application of 'the sense of justice and mutual love.' . . . Augustine's criticism of Cicero's universalism, by calling attention to the confusion of tongues in the community of mankind, is not heeded. The encyclical is thoroughly modern in many ways, but particularly in breathing a Pelagian, rather than an Augustinian, spirit."

troduction. The fourth point of this outline reads: "Finally, how, on the one hand individual men and States, and on the other hand the community of all peoples should act toward each other, the establishment of such a world community of peoples being urgently demanded today by the requirements of universal common good." This is a puzzling statement, into which is packed the whole quandary of contemporary international politics. The first part of the statement assumes that it is possible to speak of "the community of all peoples" as an *actor* in politics. There is no such actor on one side, with individual men and existing states on the other, each capable of acting upon the other.[11] If there were, the establishment of such a world community of peoples, to give voice and effectiveness to the universal common good, would not be so urgently demanded.

In another respect the pontiff fails to start from here. "Human society," he writes, "ought to be regarded as above all a spiritual reality"; and it is apparent as we proceed that this "above all" means "exclusively," or substantially so. Therefore John XXIII can make the surprising and quite erroneous statement that "the *whole* reason for the existence of civil authorities is the realization of the common good" (italics added). And concerning the banning of nuclear weapons, he declares: "If this is to come about the fundamental principle on which our present peace depends must be *replaced* by another, which declares that the true and solid peace of nations consists not in equality of arms but in mutual trust *alone*" (italics added). Obviously, if men clearly and impartially apprehend justice in the midst of their disputes, if human society is to such great degree a spiritual activity, if the "whole" reason for authority and power is to realize a common good, and if

---

[11] I am assured by Father Donald R. Campion, S.J., associate editor of *America*. that the various available English editions are all quite reliable and that there is no real obscurity as to the encyclical's teaching on any significant point; but that we also have in the Italian version a reliable guide to an understanding of the Latin. Still, the point made in the text above is stronger when based on the English translation; and it is considerably weaker in the Latin, which reads: ". . . quibus postremo modis inter se contineantur hinc singuli homines et civitates, illinc universarum gentium societas . . ." The words "inter se contineantur" say that individual men and states and the community of all peoples are *interdependent* on or *continuous* with one another; not that they *act toward* one another, or even interact. The Italian version takes the meaning of the Latin better than the English. It reads: ". . . e quelli [i rapporti] fra le singole persone e le Comunità politiche da una parte, e dall'atra, la Comunità mondiale . . . ," where the antecedent "i rapporti" clearly means "relations between." I refrain from withdrawing the point made in the text above, however, because the English translation, which may be misleading at this place, nevertheless succinctly exhibits the objection to be validly made in general against this or any other document on world peace which assumes that it will be comparatively easy for world agencies to fetch themselves forth by the acts and policies of nation-states.

disarmament can be based simply on trust, it may be believed a ready achievement for the common good of nations to be extended to their mutual pursuit of the universal common good. Later in this chapter I shall try to show, in demonstrating the urgent need for world organization, that there is a "structural defect" afflicting the proper use of force in the present day that can and may and must supplement the "structural defect" which the pope points out that prevents the nations from serving the universal common good.

On the other hand, John XXIII started, of necessity, too much from here, from within our multinational world, to which his principle of "subsidiarity" gives protective sanction. He extrapolates from the sound moral principle that "it is not true that some human beings are by nature superior and others inferior," that "all men are equal in their natural dignity"; and from this draws the conclusion that "consequently there are no political communities which are superior by nature and none which are inferior by nature. All political communities are of equal dignity, since they are bodies whose membership is made up of these same human beings." This, of course, is not to be denied in the moral order; and every people's right to share in world justice ought never to be forgotten. But these propositions function in the encyclical as political propositions which *alone* govern the organization of mankind in a coming world community. Herewith, the power realities are forgotten. From this beginning one can end only with the present United Nations organization, with its carefully protected national sovereignties. In this way one gets what we have: an international forum in which the claims of no nation, great or small, are allowed to be forgotten; and at the same time an organization to which no great power can entirely submit its policies.

This is also the defect in the words (at least, the words in English) which the encyclical addresses to the urgent problem of progressive nuclear disarmament, even though in this connection the power realities are recognized in the stipulation that this goal can be achieved only with "an effective method of control." It needed saying that "an equal balance of armaments" for the sole purpose of dissuading others from aggression offers no permanent solution; that "some incontrollable and unexpected chance" could bring the war no nation intended; and that even "the mere continuance of nuclear tests, undertaken with war in mind, will have fatal consequences for life on earth." But the proposal that "the stockpiles which exist in various countries should be reduced *equally* and simultaneously" (italics added) could, if put into effect, only prove disstabilizing—and increasingly dangerous the closer the nuclear powers approached "complete and thorough" disposal of their weapons. Therefore, in one meaning (and the least likely intended meaning) of the word "equally," this is by no means a solution. If, however, "equally" means some complex proportionality,[12] this is the premise of the present negotiations, which are not evidently successful; namely, that staged disarmament must increase, or at least not decrease, the security and the power position of the nations that can agree to it.

The principles of "subsidiarity," the pontiff writes, should regulate "the relationships between the public authority of each [existing] political community and the public authority of the world community." This means that the public authority of the world community is intended to provide existing public authorities new ways of doing things, not a way of curbing them. "The public authority of the world community is not intended to limit the sphere of action of the public authority of the individual political community much less to take its place." This must be set down as a piece of philosophical anarchism—to which natural law optimism comes at last—in no way able to serve as the principle of world organization. Not thus will the universal common good secure a voice and an actor in politics to enter into relationships with men and existing states. The principle of subsidiarity within national societies does operate to conserve "individuals, families and intermediate associations"; but not without *limiting* them and placing them under a higher, *coercive* authority. John XXIII's vision of an emerging world community is altogether too similar to John Locke's "state of nature": as with Locke's individual men, so with the nations: *When their own preservation comes not in competition, ought they, as much as they can, to preserve the rest of mankind.* There is not even a note of Lockean realism in recognition of the fact that to rest international community on carefully protected national sovereignties leaves standing the grave "inconvenience" that each nation must judge in its own case. Not enough is said about the problem of power to produce a truly forceful movement toward the organization of the community of mankind, which will require that the nations find a way of alienating themselves of the right to execute the law of nature. This right to redress injustice by resort to force has been *morally* withdrawn by the teachings of Pius XII and John XXIII. How can there be a legal transcription of these moral principles unless the public authority of the world community *powerfully* limits existing public authorities?

[12] The Latin text reads: ". . . ut bellica instrumenta, quae variis civitatibus praesto sunt, hinc inde, per idemque tempus minuantur." The words "hinc inde" are a more or less colloquial expression, sometimes written "hinc et inde," meaning "from here and from there": "that instruments of war . . . from here and from there (i.e., *everywhere*) and at the same time be reduced." "Reciprocally" takes the meaning better than "equally." So reads the Italian: ". . . si riducano simultaneamente e reciprocamente gli armamenti già esistenti."

III

Undoubtedly the most important section of *Pacem in terris* is the one that bears the subtitle "Insufficiency of Modern States to Ensure the Universal Common Good." Here the pope argues, cogently and clearly, that "the public authorities of the individual political communities . . . no matter how much they multiply their meetings and sharpen their wits in efforts to draw up new juridical instruments, . . . are no longer capable of facing the task of finding an adequate solution to present world problems." This is not for any contingent reason, but "because of a structural defect which hinders them." One analysis of this "structural defect" is a part of the foregoing quotation: "placed as they are on a footing of equality one with the other." It is difficult if not impossible to say how this statement of the difficulty coheres with much else in the encyclical—e.g., its emphasis on the equality of all peoples, bypassing their inequalities of responsibility and power, and its suggestion that existing public authorities need not be limited by the public authority of the world community.

A second, and the controlling analysis, of this "structural defect" that frustrates all efforts on the part of the leaders of the nation-states is simply that "the present system of [political] organization and the way it operates on a world basis no longer correspond to the objective requirements of the universal common good." In any age, "there exists an intrinsic connection between the common good on the one hand and the structure and function of public authority on the other." These must correspond: authority must extend as widely as the problems it has to solve in order to direct society to the achievement of the common good. "Today the universal common good poses problems of world-wide dimensions which cannot be adequately tackled or solved except by the efforts of public authorities endowed with a breadth of powers, structure and means of the same proportions." Perhaps in an earlier age "the common good of the entire human family" might have been sufficiently secured as an indirect result of the action of the public authorities wisely pursuing the common good of their separate people. This is no longer the case. Today there is urgent need for "public authorities which are in a position to operate in an effective manner on a world-wide basis." The use of the plural, instead of reference to a single "public authority," reflects the real usefulness of many of the organs and functions of the United Nations, each of which is, in one degree or another, able to operate effectively on a world-wide basis. But on the paramount issue of security, only a single public authority can match the world-wide dimensions of the threat to the universal common good, especially since the pope had already pointed out that the "structural defect" persists even in face of the multiplication of meetings and the sharpness of wits heretofore in drawing up "new juridical arrangements."

By concentrating attention upon the magnitude of the problems besetting the universal common good which demand new public authorities, world politics is mistaken for a cultural or "spiritual" activity, and political community comes to be viewed rather like other communities that pursue a common good. Yet political community differs from all other human communities by the fact that its authority exercises a monopoly of power. A simple definition of politics by its *genus* (community) and *specific difference* (the use of power) requires that another analysis be given of the "structural inadequacy" which statesmen face in a multinational world; and this needs to be set alongside that of the encyclical before we have delivered the decisive verdict that this world, with its present political arrangements, suffers from a defect not of wit or of will but in its institutions and organization.

The present writer has reason to disagree with the use Roman Catholics make of definition by genus and difference in another department of moral theology—or with the conclusions that seem to them consequent almost as a matter of definition. First, man is defined as a "rational animal"; here the noun refers to the more inclusive and less important genus, and the adjective—rational, spiritual, etc.—refers to that in human nature which distinguishes it from the larger class. But then, when the moral theologian undertakes to define a community of two of these rational animals—namely, marriage—the logic of defining this by genus and specific difference leads to the following odd consequence. What a man and woman have in common in their distinct human quality—their common good, mutual love, etc.—belongs also to the wider genus of human communities—friendship, etc.—while the specific difference that sets marriage apart from these consists of generation (which in the individual belongs to the race and not to him in his essentially human quality). The *specific difference* in the case of marriage requires that the primary, unique, and distinguishing purpose of marriage as such has to be generation, almost as a matter of definition; while the goods that run between the principal parties to this community have to be defined as secondary. This is all that is meant by the primary and secondary ends, and this intends no derogation upon the secondary, and more uniquely human, ends.[13]

---

[13] [This *definitional* primacy—which is all that was ever meant—of the procreative good over the communicative good of marriage was entirely abandoned by the Pastoral Constitution on the Church in the Modern World issued by Vatican Council II. The Pastoral Constitution *Gaudiam et spes*, however, still kept the two

Neither do I intend any derogation upon the uniquely human ends of political community, stressed so eloquently in the encyclical, when I say that the *specific difference*—the exercise of a monopoly of power—ought not to have been dropped from view in a letter dealing with the peace of the world. This is "primary" in politics. It would seem that the pontiff was speaking of *generic* social values, and therefore of the "secondary" essential goods of political life (and was he not speaking rather like a Protestant trying to avoid the traditional definition of marriage in terms of its specific difference?), when he wrote:

> Human society . . . ought to be regarded as above all a spiritual reality in which men communicate knowledge to each other in the light of truth, in which they can enjoy their rights and fulfill their duties, and are inspired to strive for moral good. Society should enable men to share in and enjoy every legitimate expression of beauty, and encourage them constantly to pass on to others all that is best in themselves, while they strive to make their own the spiritual achievements of others. These are the spiritual values which continually give life and basic orientation to cultural expressions, economic and social institutions, political movements and forms, laws, and all other structures by which society is outwardly established and constantly developed.

None of this ought to be denied, but rather affirmed of human society generally. Politics, however, has a more restrictive definition. Yet, these *generic* social values are almost the whole content of the analysis the encyclical gives of the structural defect in the present organization of *political* authority; namely, that this is not proportionate to the attainment of the universal common good. This is *not* the specific difference that defines the nature of *political* community or its primary if not its highest good.

IV

If one wants to make the strongest *political* case for radically changing the nation-state system, he must start and remain with the church's traditional teachings about the just conduct of war. For these criteria are also the principles intrinsic to purposive political action; they specify the moral economy governing the use of force, which must always be employed in politics—domestically within the nations; internationally in the postfeudal, pre-atomic era; and under the public authority of any possible world community that may be established during the nuclear age.

purposes of marriage ultimately inseparable as, I argue, the *esse* and the *bene esse* of politics cannot be separated in principle.]

Among the rules of civilized warfare, and of civil politics or enforcement, the one most pertinent to demonstrate the demand for a new world-wide organization of the use of power is the requirement that there be a reasonable proportion between the injury caused by any use of force and the good effected or the graver evil prevented. On this basis it may be contended that, in the nuclear age, it is impossible for statesmen to establish any rational relation between the ends of policy and the means of violence that are available to them. John XXIII said as much when he wrote: "It is hardly possible to imagine that in the atomic era, war could be used as an instrument of justice." [14] And, in not expressly holding open self-defense as a possible justification of resort to arms (as did Pius XII), the pontiff seems to be saying that in the atomic era there can be no circumstances in which war can be regarded as right, because there is in it no reasonable expectation that one effect will justify another and the good accomplished warrant the evil let loose.

Such a sweeping assertion can be questioned. One interpretation of the papal teachings is that the right of war has been withdrawn more completely than a single world public authority has been adumbrated—and certainly more rapidly than international institutions make it possible for responsible statesmen always to follow the pope's lead. John XXIII's statement that "it is hardly possible to imagine that in the atomic era, war could be used as an instrument of justice" is open to another interpretation. He has provided the *framework* of cost-benefit in which the use of force has always to be calculated, and *not the conclusion* of all argument concerning the possible justification of war. I do not believe that in the whole range of possible resorts to arms by major powers there is none that could be an instrument of justice in the atomic era. But whoever believes this ought not then to conclude that international politics can now be based merely on impartial assessment of justice and upon negotiation. He ought rather to conclude that the nation-state is moribund, and must be rapidly replaced by a more inclusive public authority capable of exercising force in a just and effective manner. Only the public authority of a world community can provide the legal transcription of the tendency of papal teachings to withdraw, morally, the right of war. These two things are opposite ends of the same seesaw: the moral right to use force cannot go down faster than the public authority and enforcement of a world community is organized.

It may be asked what advantages there are from reaching the same conclusion as that of the encyclical, but from the premises of the morality

---

[14] [To say, correctly, that this is hardly possible allows that it may be possible. This is the interpretation which I suggest below, Chap. 10, pp. 192 f. See note 9 above.]

of the use of power? I shall discuss two fundamental strengths that come from taking this approach.

1. In the first place, the basic forces that are tending to make possible better relations with eastern European Communist nations and with Russia—and perhaps, in the future, a new world order—are made clearer. It is not simply that there is a tendency in human nature of all peoples toward the truth, or that political "movements, insofar as they . . . are interpreters of the lawful aspirations of the human person, contain elements that are positive and deserving of approval," or that trust does sometimes work wonders. From the undoubted truth of these propositions, it is impossible to extrapolate any precise guidance for political prudence concerning the nature of any particular historical moment.

The character of our particular moment in history is, instead, determined by the crisis in the uses of power brought on by the nuclear age. This is the interest in common that may make *rapprochement* possible, and perhaps, if men are wise, the establishment of public authorities commensurate with the magnitude of the problem of controlling the force we have in our possession, and new ways of conducting politics in this age. Interesting confirmation of this is to be found in the fact that the Communist "just war" doctrine is undergoing essentially the same revision, or emphasis in its application, as that to be observed in the West in papal teachings, and in contemporary Protestant thought as well.

The Marxist-Leninist doctrine was, and is, that any class struggle leading to war makes that war just; and specifically that "a just war is a non-predatory, liberatory war" which today includes "defensive wars" as well as "wars of national liberation." [15] But the definition of social revolution, and of wars of national liberation today, as "just" wars has proved insufficient to tell Communists when or whether to fight one. What is just, in the sense of licit, is not forthwith to be done. So there has developed a test of expediency which has eroded war's fatal inevitability in Communist doctrine, without, however, discarding the orthodox Marxist-Leninist doctrine of just war. This is the key to Russian revisionism and "coexistence," in contrast to Chinese intransigence.

Thus, Edvard Kardelj, writing in 1960, asserts that the Marxist-Leninist distinction of just from unjust wars was not intended to give "any absolute scientific or political evaluation"; and that this doctrine "cannot possibly mean that the working-class should be for a war or should even fight in a war which may be just." [16]

[15] Y. A. Korovin, *et al.*, Academy of Sciences of the U.S.S.R., *International Law* (Moscow: Foreign Languages Publishing House), p. 402.

[16] Edvard Kardelj, *Socialism and War* (Belgrade: Yugoslavia Publishing House, 1960), p. 89.

> The classics of Marxism and Leninism have always emphasized that it is
> not the mere justifiedness of a war that should determine the attitude of
> the revolutionary proletariat to it, but the part that war plays in the
> whole complex of international developments. Even very just wars can
> have a reactionary effect. For this reason, Lenin considered that it would
> be wrong to support a war, however just in itself, if that war were to
> excite reactionary consequences on a world scale. . . .
>
> The formula about just and unjust war as interpreted by the Chinese
> turns into a peculiar mystification, the sense of which is that you may
> not fight for peace if any war which interrupts peace is a just war.[17]

Obviously there are considerations other than "justice" that have to be
reckoned before determining the final "justification" for engaging in
war.

The foregoing shows the emergence of a stand against war (*jus
contra bellum*), and this development comes from within the Communist
doctrine of just war itself, and from its own moral economy in assessing
the use of force. Perhaps there are other ways of "fighting for peace."
This strikingly resembles the development in papal teachings. Here,
too, it is not the mere "justifiedness" of a war that determines one's
whole attitude toward it. This development was, indeed, contained in
the Western just-war doctrine, almost from its beginning, in its principle of expediency or proportionality.

Thus, it may not be the "justice" of the Communists that is
approaching a meeting with western conceptions of justice. It may merely
be that they are discovering that the use of force has multiple consequences which must be weighed against one another—leading to the
conclusion that it is wrong to engage in a war, however just in itself,
if this leads to greater evil. This is the doctrine of coexistence; and it
can happen that, in the nuclear age, this stand against war will provide
the basis for new institutions with world-wide powers. If so, this will not
be because mankind's "justices" became one but because the common
principle of expediency or proportionality in the use of power requires
it, in order for violent means to be subdued and connected again with
minimal political goals.

2. A second advantage in taking our approach to the need for
world law and order from the problem of power, and from the traditional
moral analysis of the use of force, is that the choice before the people of
the United States can hereby be made sun-clear. This choice is between
world order based on placing the use of physical force within proper
legal limits, under international public authority, and a military posture

---

[17] Kardelj, pp. 89, 91 (for the above, I am indebted to Lynn H. Miller, "The
Contemporary Significance of the Doctrine of Just War," *World Politics*, October,
1963).

based on usable force that can be connected with national policy. We must ask and answer the question: Is "just war" possible today? How can we learn to subordinate violent means to political ends, while still maintaining the nation-state system? If this cannot be done, then a world public authority is the only alternative. If, on the other hand, world public authority cannot now be achieved, and until it is established and the nation-state abolished, the responsibility of statesmen must still include possible resort to arms. For peace and justice are not linked by an unseen hand, as pacifists and the deterrence people both suppose, nor can the political life of mankind endure without the use of force.

At this very moment the American people seem to suppose that there is no need for a national community fall-out shelter program. This would seem to be a necessary component of just or counter-forces warfare (with or without ourselves renouncing nuclear weapons), of the continuation of nation-states in a nuclear age, and of the performance of the political responsibilities of this nation in a multinational world. Yet, so far as I know, the people of Portland, Oregon,[18] and the Congress in its lethargy, have not faced up to the fact that they cannot declare civil defense to be useless without at the same time declaring nationhood no longer to be viable. In a nuclear age civil defense, protecting the population which an enemy may *not* make the *direct* object of attack, is the minimum responsibility of a nation and its leaders charged with "preparing for the common defense"—*even if that nation itself possesses no nuclear weapons.* Else we must prepare for the common defense by taking long strides toward the abolition of the United States of America.

Yet I have not seen many resolutions passed in Oregon or by the Congress or by the peace-loving people of this land indicating their clearly thought-out verdict that this nation must get ready to make massive abdications of its sovereignty in order to establish an international power over us and our weapons. These people, and all of us, need to acknowledge that we are caught between the clinchers of the argument from the crisis—at root, the question how policy is to gain enforcement —which nuclear technology has brought upon politics in our time. The very profound longings of the entire human family are not going to change the nature of political life, even if these longings are in danger of blinding many eyes so that they do not see the need to use force— one way (justly limited war) or another (world order). The peace and order of the world cannot be maintained without usable power, and the use of it in some manner.

In the meantime—in which we may have to plan and strive for both justly limited war *and* world order—this is an age of waiting and of

---

[18] [This city had recently made news by withdrawing from such "civil defense" as this nation attempts to maintain.]

action without idols, not even the idol of peace on earth. The action may be in waiting with an alert consciousness. This simply means that from the principle of proportionate grave reason we seem to be required to judge that it is immoral to resort to force; and from the justice of many a cause, that it is immoral not to use force when all other available means have been exhausted. If this correctly expresses the moral dilemma of the nuclear age, then we must move to give ourselves other means. The most immoral position of all would be to assume—numbed as we are by the intimidation we share in the face of nuclear weapons—that justice and peace no longer require that powerful means be used.[19]

[10] [At this point the reader may wish to go at once to Chap. 16 below, for an analysis of the statement on nuclear war issued by the second Vatican Council.]

CHAPTER 5

Selective Conscientious Objection*

"Is military service in this country's armed forces an option exercisable solely at the discretion of the individual?" This seems to be the proposal many people today are making.

A quick answer to that question would be to say: "That depends on his discretion."

This is to say that whether an individual is apt rightfully to exercise the choice extended him by a system of optional service would depend on how his conscience—his discretion—has been formed and informed. Moreover, whether any government in securing the political common good could ever grant selective armed service at the conscientious discretion of individuals depends on whether the citizens of a nation are more like Socrates, who while suffering imprisonment and death for conscience's sake still effectually acknowledged "the conscience of the laws," than they are like Sophists putting in individualistic claims that their own subjective opinion is the measure of truth. Not everyone who is eighteen or sixty years old has as yet arrived at the age of political discretion.

This, of course, is only to state the problem of conscience in relation to military service. Yet it is a statement of the problem that needs a great deal of repetition and clarification today.

* A shorter version of this chapter appears in *Conflict of Loyalties: The Case of Selective Conscientious Objection*, ed. with Intro. by James Finn (New York: Pegasus, A Subsidiary of Western Publishing Co., Inc., 1968).

This calls our attention to a fundamental fact concerning man in his political existence. The individual is included within the common good of the nation-state (which is to date the most inclusive, actual political community that we have), but he is *not* included in the national common good *to the whole extent of his personhood*. The person transcends the political community, but again *not to the whole extent of his being*. The person does not exist simply to serve the state, but neither does the state (meaning political society, not merely the "government") exist simply to serve an aggregation of individuals. Some human rights touch the person and at the same time the common good so directly that they are absolutely inalienable. Others in the hierarchy of rights are inalienable only substantially: these pertain to the person given certain conditions of fact, but under other circumstances they can properly be restricted. They can be limited so that other rights and social values may better be served. There is, indeed, a distinction between the *possession* of certain human rights, and the claim that one of these rights may now justly be *exercised* in a given way.[1]

This means, for example, that while under some conceivable circumstances the state may secure the common good by directing a mathematician to teach mathematics, the state cannot tell him the mathematical truth he should teach. Similarly, a citizen may be required to serve in the armed forces and to be willing to lay down his life for his country. But this does not mean that his conscience is entirely included within the determinations of public policy. The question is how we are to understand the legitimate claims of personal conscience in conflict or in symbiosis with the legitimate claims of the national common good to which every individual also "belongs" in the very marrow of his humanity.

It is now well established in United States' draft laws that allowance should be made for special status for men who "by reason of religious training and belief" are "conscientiously opposed to participation in war in any form." We shall later take up the recent judicial decisions that may have interpreted "religious" to mean "conscientious." The point here is that, to date, the tangible and readily understood test for either or both is that a man shall be opposed to participation in war in any form, and the further point that this provision of alternate service for the pacifist objector is not a *constitutional* right but a "right" granted by the "grace" of Congress in the positive legislation it enacts.

An individual's spiritual counselors may advise him that by the grace of Jesus Christ he should follow his own upright conscience or even his erring conscience on pain of making himself "good for nothing"

---

[1] Jacques Maritain: *Man and the State* (Chicago: University of Chicago Press, 1951), pp. 101, 117, 135.

(mortal sin). Still the pacifist objector is relieved of the obligation to bear arms in obedience to no constitutional principle, but because it has accorded with the policy of Congress thus to relieve him. Doubtless ours is a better society, the common good is better achieved, because of this. Doubtless Congress also, and not individuals or churches only, should recognize that in the forum of conscience there is duty to a moral power higher than the state. But the Congress is not *legally or constitutionally* bound to do this. In this there is a relic of the fact that while the person is transcendent he does not transcend the national common good to the whole extent of his being.

This means that persons whose responsibility it is to direct the community toward the political good, and the public processes by which the political society acts together, steadily in one way rather than another, have their consciences too. The "right" of pacifist conscientious objection can be granted for the fostering of the consciences of free men only because in national emergencies there are a sufficient number of individuals whose political discretion has been instructed in the need to repel, and the justice of repelling, injury to the common good. No political society can be founded on a principle according *absolute* rights to possibly errant individual consciences. It is the aggregate-individualism of such a view, and not true conscientiousness, that makes such an account of political obligation a radically non-political and an ultimately inhumane viewpoint.

Politically realistic absolute pacifists have commonly recognized this. Some have as members of Congress felt themselves bound to *vote* for military appropriations, or at least not inhibit existing political purposes, even while by their lives and witness they tried to persuade "the conscience of the laws" that another direction might be taken by a political community resolved together to go the way they themselves must tread. While remaining faithful to the dictates of their own consciences, they have not been impelled to a confusion of categories, or made legalistic-pacifist use of the just-war criteria as if that doctrine governing the political use of armed force was designed to make peace by disqualifying one by one all wars. They have not been too ready to sign public manifestoes that contribute to the "credibility gap" while hastily condemning that gap in the present Administration—by, for example, charging that Robert McClosky's recent, rather blundering statement of sound doctrine rests on a "curious argument" or "semantic confusion" or on a "distinction without a difference" between "bombing *Hanoi*" and "bombing military targets" *in* or near Hanoi.

One such pacifist who indeed would have the whole church become pacifist (and who for that matter does not renounce the prospect that the whole citizenry might in principle become members of a pacifist church) is Culbert G. Rutenber. His recent article "Pacifism Revisited" [2] contains some of the most telling demonstrations and vigorous denunciations I have read of quasi-pacifist dissents and actions in the public forum that do not play fair with "the conscience of the laws" or with the conscience directing current public policy.

II

SELECTIVE CONSCIENTIOUS OBJECTION

This brings us to "particular-war" objection or "selective" conscientious objection, which might be the meaning of the proposal that service in the armed forces should be an option exercisable solely at the "discretion" of the individual. The present writer argued as long ago as 1961 that there should be a category of "just-war objection" in the mind of the church and instituted by Congress in the draft laws it enacts. This was long before the current agitation over this matter of selective or particular-war conscientious objection. I may perhaps point this out without undue personal *hubris,* since I only followed the moral argument where it led. It was not necessary for anyone to wait for the American Civil Liberties Union to think of it or for the current widespread disaffection over Vietnam to lend (I shall have to say) somewhat questionable support to the proposition. I wrote then: the church must "make the decision to support its members who refuse to fight because they believe a particular war to be unjust with the same vigor with which it has in recent years supported the pacifist witness within its ranks and within the nation. This would mean that the church will consciously attempt to obtain in military draft laws some status for those who refuse to fight unjustly as well as for those who have conscientious objection to all war. . . . If the decision is reached that the church's doctrine of just or limited war [is addressed only to magistrates or to topmost political leaders and military commanders, and] is *not* addressed to private citizens and soldiers, then, if also penance is good for anything, consideration should be given to reviving the requirement of forty days' penance following participation in any war [!]" [3]

[2] *Andover Newton Quarterly*, March 1966, pp. 38–52.

[3] *War and the Christian Conscience* (Durham, N.C.: Duke University Press, 1961), pp. 128–129, 132–133. It is the purpose of the present chapter now to test this proposal by bringing to bear upon it the full force of a hopefully adequate political philosophy, to analyze the conditions of a possible enactment of particular-war objection, and to think through certain questions concerning the reservations necessary if, upon just-war warrants, selective conscientious objection is choiceworthy and feasible.

Yet the reservations and conditions that must surround just objection to particular wars, and which indeed could make this a possible enactment of Congress, are the same as in the case of pacifist objection. This, too, depends on the "discretion" abroad in the land—on the forming and informing influences upon political consciences in our society. Ralph Potter has written the best study I have seen on the subject of "Conscientious Objection to Particular Wars." [4] He is of the opinion that the granting of status to selective conscientious objectors would "demand a considerable upgrading of the level of political discourse in America." Such an enactment, he believes, would contribute to that goal. A selective objector would have to look to his reasons, and so would the members of his draft or review board. Appeals to *jus contra bellum* and *jus in bello* would require formulation, and empirical knowledge in applying these tests, and not slogans that do not admit the real possibility of *jus ad bellum*. A premium would be placed on the *discriminating* religious conscience and on a higher order of ethico-political reasoning than is fostered by a system that focuses attention, and with less refinement of men's judgment, upon the comparatively simple decision made by an intuitive conscience between participation in war and participation in no war.

I rather think it works the other way round. A considerable upgrading of the level of political discourse in America is among the conditions of the possibility of granting selective conscientious objection. At least, these two things can and may and must go together. The signs of the times are not propitious for either, nor are religious leaders contributing all they could either to the upgrading of public discourse concerning the morality of participation in war or to advancing the cause of conscientious discretion concerning particular wars. In the context of extremist assertions that "this is Lyndon Johnson's war" or "McNamara's war" or that our leaders are committing "murder" and "genocide" or that this is a "race" war of white versus colored peoples, or that this nation's leaders are obsessed with a compulsion to play "world policeman" or are conducting a "holy war" against the legitimate aspirations of an underdeveloped people or are activated by a blind anti-communism—in such a context the proposition that "military service in this country's armed forces is an option exercisable solely at the discretion of the individual" has one sort of meaning.[5] That meaning should be refused by

[4] In Donald Giannella, ed.: *Religion and the Public Order* (New York: Cornell University Press, 1968), pp. 44–99.
[5] This was the package of particulars condemned as misguided and war-prolonging forms of dissent by the Freedom House political advertisement in *The New York Times*, Nov. 30, 1966, and signed by persons as disparate as former President Eisenhower, Senator Jacob Javits, Dean Acheson, and James B. Conant—and the present writer.

anyone who has any conception of the meaning of an individual's political obligation.

Yet in another context precisely this proposition could be defended as a proper enabling ordinance for the discriminating consciences of free men in politics. The question is whether we are nurturing such an ethos. No nation can grant draft exemption to conscientious objectors to particular wars if it is widely believed among the people that tests of the justice of war are mainly ways of securing peace by discrediting one by one all wars. They are rather directives addressed to every generation of young men, no less than to their political leaders, concerning how within morally tolerable limits they can and should protect and secure the relatively juster cause by resort, if need be, to a political use of armed force.

In order to sustain the individual consciences of generations of young men in the determination of the justice or the injustice of their participation in particular wars, there is need for spokesmen of the churches always to remember all the sons of the church wherever they may be—those in the armed services (as did the Vatican Council [6] and as did not the 1966 Geneva Conference of the World Council of Churches Conference on Church and Society) no less than those sons of the church who in conscience protest particular wars. There is need for church leaders when acting severally or collectively as citizens commending some particular policy and exerting strictly political pressure to use their "Reverends" as the regulations of Princeton University require me to use my "Professor," for purposes of identification only. Moreover, there is no profit in the unexplicated verdict of a congress of Christians declaring, as did the 1966 Geneva Conference, that recent United States' actions in Vietnam "cannot be justified," [7] when the need is for the clarification of decision-oriented and action-oriented standards for telling whether any particular war or act of war is justified or not, and for the creation of an ethos in which men are apt to be able to exercise the requisite moral and political wisdom.

To pant after some specific conclusion which is as undiscriminating as the intuitive verdict of a pacifist conscience against participation in war in any form, or to feel compelled to reach an "agreement" regardless

[6] "Those who are pledged to the service of their country as members of its armed services should regard themselves as agents of security and freedom on behalf of their people. As long as they fulfil this role properly, they are making a genuine contribution to the establishment of peace." *Pastoral Constitution on the Church and the Modern World* (*Graudium et spes*), par. 79, quoted from *The Documents of Vatican II*, ed. by Walter M. Abbott, S.J. (New York: Guild-America-Association Presses, 1966).

[7] For a fuller treatment of this too-particular condemnation, see my *Who Speaks for the Church? A Critique of the 1966 Geneva Conference on Church and Society* (Nashville: The Abingdon Press, 1967).

of disagreement in the moral and political premises which are most in disrepair—this would betray the needs of generations of men for strength and instruction in how they should go about forming or informing their own political discretion in matters concerning which conscientious men evidently disagree. Nor is it self-evidently a good thing for the American Philosophical Association (Eastern division, December, 1966) to pass a resolution voicing in the public forum their moral opposition to elements of our present policy in Vietnam, submerging altogether the fact that there is vast disagreement among philosophers concerning the nature of the political good, especially when many members of this profession who voted for the resolution have contributed little lately to the upbuilding of sound notions in our society concerning the meaning of "moral" and "immoral" and when there are many who believe this cannot reasonably be done. Sometimes one wonders who has contributed most year after year to the "credibility gap."

In "workshops" on conscientious objection, sometimes sponsored by ministers and local church councils, has there been as much open and realistic debate over how responsibly to tell political justice in war and peace as there has been simple instruction to young men concerning their rights and privileges under the draft laws? As much concern over how to form *one's own* mature conscience as about how to act on an assumed particular opinion? If not, people's responses to this or any other war are left close to the visceral and emotional level, and our responsibility for constantly upgrading political discourse in this country has simply been abandoned.

No political community can be based solely on accrediting the claim that (in the sense that Nietzsche meant it) "at least everyone claimeth to be an authority on 'good' and 'evil'." [8] The rejection of such individualism was the import of the provision in the just-war theory that to be just, an extension of politics into a resort to armed force must be legitimately or officially declared. That test was never meant to be used in legalistic-pacifist fashion to condemn a war merely because it is not *technically* "declared." It refers rather to the authority of the established political processes by which the political community directs its policy and exerts its united force one way rather than another. Nor was the provision meant *simply* to exclude "private wars" (or *private* peace-making expeditions to Hanoi on the part of U.S. citizens).

Instead, this provision expresses the basic requirement that for there to be a political community, capable of being an actor in the international community, there must be some way of identifying a nation's decisions or commitment, and some measure of internal authority accorded to this "voice" even by those of its citizens who dissent from it.

[8] *Thus Spake Zarathustra*, II, xxvii.

"If the political community is not to be torn to pieces as each man follows his own viewpoint, authority is needed. This authority must dispose the energies of the whole citizenry toward the common good. . . ." [9]

Does this mean that there is no room for effectual conscientious objection to particular wars? Or that only the "upright" conscience should be allowed such rights, or only the consciences judged by legitimate social processes to be activated by a proper political "discretion"? It does not! Still there is a burden upon the consciences of selective objectors that can be identified.

There is, of course, no "third man" to insure that an individual has discerned the true justice and the really responsible political policy in opposition to the public conscience. There is no way to appeal to "objective obligation" beyond the good faith efforts of conscientious men seeking to discern in their sense of "subjective obligation" their real objective duties. Unless, therefore, selective or particular-war objection is granted to possibly errant consciences, it will not be accorded at all; and in no way will a discriminating transcendence of the person over the state be capable of coming into evidence while the state makes war.

If ever talk about "just-war conscientious objection," and about the limits drawn by moral law and the gospel, is to be reduced to action, there must be a manifold work of political intelligence directed toward making this an acknowledged part of citizen responsibility. There can be no question about the *moral* right. In the foregoing, I have spoken mainly about the conditions of the possibility of *exercising* this right, and the prerequisites to granting it *legal* status.

Still there would need to be acknowledged an important ingredient within the subjective consciences exercising objection to particular wars. This is a minimum acknowledgment of the authority of the laws. If political community is not to be torn to pieces between upright and errant consciences, or for that matter between various assertions of upright conscience disagreeing as to the justice of the cause, there must be in each some significant measure of acknowledgment that political authority must dispose the energies of the whole toward the common good as this has been determined by the legitimate decision-making processes of the community. This is simply the bracing requirement that a man should concede the judgments of justice that have been made on behalf of the nation *unless and until,* by looking to his reasons, he is searchingly sure in his own mind that the nation's course of action is unjust. This requires not *certainty* (since there is no "third man" or "impartial observer" to adjudicate between his personal conscience and the conscience of the laws); but it does require a degree of certitude at-

[9] *Pastoral Constitution on the Church in the Modern World, (Gaudium et spes),* ¶ 74.

tained in an inward wrestle for valid moral insight, and accepting a burden of proof favoring the authority of the commitment of the nation to which an individual belongs unless and until he has succeeded in winning his way with integrity to a subjectively sound decision by means of all the sources of enlightenment available to him in forming his own conscience.

This is a slight thing, and the agent's own; but it is no mean requirement. Especially not in a day in which it has become fashionable, as a first move, to disbelieve the moral credibility of one's own government; and when with no sense of political incongruity one young man in an anti-Vietnam protest could declare over television for all his fellow countrymen to hear that, of course, he'd fight in Vietnam if he *knew* the war there was just, but since he didn't know he had to protest its immorality!

III

THE BURKE MARSHALL REPORT ON SELECTIVE SERVICE

A minority on the national Advisory Commission on Selective Service[10] wanted to recommend to the President that exemption be granted to conscientious objectors to particular wars. Their arguments were that: (1) The present statute incorporating the moral position of absolute pacifism accords a "place of privilege as the legal doctrine which alone controls the issue of conscientious objection" to a position which, while "time-honored in American society," is nevertheless "a sectarian position and does not represent the moral consensus of the American people with regard to the uses of military force." (2) "The classical doctrine on war widely held within the Christian community has been based on the moral premise [a "marginal morality"] that not all uses of military force are inherently immoral. . . . In a word, a war may be just; it may also be unjust." (3) While "the decision to make war is the prerogative of duly constituted government . . . and constitutes a presumption for the citizen in favor of the legitimacy of the war" a person should not "abdicate his own conscience into the hands of government. . . . In particular cases, therefore, it can happen that the conscientious moral judgment of the citizen is in conflict with the judgments

[10] *In Pursuit of Equity: Who Serves When Not All Serve?* Report of the National Advisory Commission on Selective Service, Burke Marshall, Chairman (Washington, D.C.: Superintendent of Documents, U.S. Government Printing Office, February, 1967). See pp. 9 and 48–51 for both the minority and the majority positions.

made by government, either with regard to the justice of the nation's cause or with regard to the measure and mode in which military force is to be employed in the defense of the nation's vital interests." The statute should "be so amended as to reckon with, and incorporate, this doctrine on the uses of force." (4) ". . . The objector should be obliged to state his case before a competent panel. The purpose would be . . . to convince his judges that his objection was 'truly held,' in the words of the *Seeger* decision. The hope was expressed that in this fashion the level of moral discourse on the uses of force would be lifted. Young men would be required to reflect on the issues of war and peace, under the guidance of their mentors, and thus enabled properly to form their consciences at an early age." (5) The present requirement of alternative non-combatant or civilian service should continue to be stringently enforced.

From this summary—especially points (3) and (4)—it immediately leaps to the eye that the acceptability of selective conscientious objection depends on the answers to two questions. Its acceptability depends first of all upon whether there exists in the ethos of this country a moral consensus or doctrine on the uses of military force that could be used in determining the statutory grounds for conscientious objection, in contrast to the time-honored doctrine that all uses of military force are inherently immoral. Unless this is the case, it would seem that the proposal for particular-war objection is at bottom a plea for individualistic consciences, all sincerely moral no doubt, each to be able not simply to make his own determination of justice within some minimal agreement about everyone's political responsibilities, but rather free to *determine how he is going to determine* what is just or unjust for him to do, with *whatever degree* of recognition he may *choose* to give to the claims of his nation upon him. The latter view of the person and community and of freedom of conscience never composed the moral substance of political community. This draws our attention to the large issues that may lurk behind proposals of selective objection, and which must be brought to light and resolved before this could become national policy.

The possibility and acceptability of selective conscientious objection depends on not only the nature of the views of political responsibility widely held in a society. It equally depends upon whether we can articulate and reduce to actionable principles the "competence" of panels, mentors, and young men to determine whether judgments are "truly held" in the case of objection to a particular war no less than in the case of absolute pacifism. We must face the fact that no nation (except for extrinsic reasons) can accept an objector's statement that his political beliefs are "truly held" conscientious convictions. We must face the fact that the requirement of opposition to "participation in war in any form" provides some check, some clarification, of the conscientiousness of the objection which is at trial. We must face the fact that a viable substitute for this test that can be "taken hold of" must be found if we are to make provision for objection to particular wars. We must face the fact, in other words, that no political society can allow exemption for purely political objection to its uses of military force, and we must find a way to distinguish between this and refusals to participate on moral grounds if we are ever to legislate exemption for selective conscientious objection. Without the manifold intellectual work that is needed to wrestle successfully with this distinction, the proposal of selective objection will remain an ideological protest—or else one that is based on the optimistic faith of philosophical anarchism that out of the self-determining freedom of individual consciences political community can be composed and its energies effectively disposed one way rather than another in the course of its history.

The National Advisory Commission's recommendations, the position of the majority, seem to have been convinced by the issues that, at least, remain to be solved in regard to allowing particular-war conscientious objection. We, who are proponents of this, need to take seriously the views of this distinguished and presumably morally sensitive group of our fellow citizens, and find the way to answer them, if there is such a way. The Commission said: (1) "It is one thing to deal in law with a person who believes he is responding to a moral imperative outside of himself when he opposes all killing. It is another to accord a special status to a person who believes there is a moral imperative which tells him to kill under some circumstances and not kill under others." Moreover, it observed, the "classical Christian doctrine" on the subject of just and unjust wars, which would be interpreted in different ways by different denominations, is "therefore not a matter upon which the Commission could pass judgment."

Here a partial reply might be that this is a doctrine concerning justice on which more than Christians could and do agree, and also that neither the Commission nor competent panels in the future are required to judge this on its merits (any more than they are required to credit the pacifist's claim) in order to be able to recognize that consciences formed in these terms may be granted exemption. The crux of the obscurity that would need to be cleared up was in the Commission's second point. (2) ". . . So-called selective pacifism is essentially a political question of support or nonsupport of a war and cannot be judged in terms of special moral imperatives." Coupled with this was the judgment that conscientious objection which only goes so far as "political opposition to a particular war should be expressed through recognized democratic processes and should claim no special right of exemption from democratic decisions." To this the Commission added that (3) "the distinction is dim" between selective pacifism and selective disobedience to all laws, or conscientious opposition to the payment of a particular tax [e.g. the presently proposed ten-percent surtax, a chief reason if not the sole reason for which is the cost of the war in Vietnam]. Finally, (4) selective conscientious objection would pose a special problem for men already in the Armed Forces. "Forcing upon the individual the necessity of making that distinction [between the justness and unjustness of any war—or, in the minority's words, "the measure and mode in which military force is to be employed"]—which would be the practical effect of taking away the Government's obligation to make it for him—could put a burden hitherto unknown on the man in uniform and even on the brink of combat, with results that could be disastrous to him, to his unit, and to the entire military tradition. No such problem arises for the conscientious objector, even in uniform, who bases his moral stand on killing in all forms, simply because he is never trained for nor assigned to combat duty." [11]

A reply, and I think a sufficient reply, should be inserted here to the Commission's final point. The Commission is mistaken, at least from the point of view of the just-war doctrine on the uses of military force, in supposing that laws and practices based on notions of *jus in bello* (justice in war) would "take away" the government's obligation to make these decisions for the man in uniform, or would mean that the government would relinquish this primary obligation, or that the soldier on the "brink of combat" would have put upon him the "burden hitherto unknown" of making the *primary* decision concerning the justice of the "measure or mode" of the war's conduct. The presumption would rather be that lawful commands are just unless and until the soldier conscientiously believes he knows they are *un*just. This mistake about the presumption of legitimacy is one that is commonly made today not only in regard to *jus in bello* but also by persons who are too eager to transform *jus ad bellum* (the "just cause" for war) into a doctrine of *jus contra bellum*.

On this understanding of the presumption, the Commission might have been more open to it, particularly since some, at least, of the deci-

_____

[11] I omit the Commission's report of the view of a smaller minority, and its answer to them. These members would have cut through the obstacles in the way of granting exemption to selective objectors by not requiring "that they show that their objection to combatant service is on properly moral ground," and would have coupled a probably generous use of this excusal with the elimination of the present alternative of some form of civilian service. Instead, objectors to particular wars would be "required to serve in a noncombatant *military* capacity, under conditions of hardship and even hazard, and perhaps for a longer period (for example 3 years)." This meat-axe approach to the problem, a "more narrow option" especially occasioned by opposition to the Vietnam war, is indeed an alternative, perhaps the only alternative to the present requirement of opposition to participation in war in any form, unless and until we can show how purely political objection is to be distinguished from moral or ethico-political objection in a system of selective service that allows conscientious objection to particular wars.

sions in an actual war situation have a clarity that can take them out of the shadowy realm of mixed political and moral decisions. It has recently been argued in regard to "opposition to particular weapons" that:

> Here perhaps the question of proof of sincerity and the probable effect on conduct of granting or denying exemption is not so very different from the case of the person opposed to war in any form. The morality of particular weapons is a question that can be rescued from the flux of uncertain facts and relative values, continuity of belief and expression may be demonstrable, and the determination of the objector not to have a hand in the employment of these weapons may be as firm as the determination of the absolute pacifist.[12]

This paragraph speaks, of course, about decisions to go or not to go to war; and it must be said that "opposition to particular *weapons*" would hardly be the discriminations between just and unjust conduct in war countenanced by the just war doctrine on the uses of military force. But Mansfield's point is well taken: this would be a basis of particular conscientious objection which if granted would, because the continuity of belief and expression may be demonstrable, not be subject to the chief reason the Commission found for supporting exemption for objection to participation in war in any form but could not endorse selective pacifism, namely, the lack of ways to distinguish in the latter case between conscientious moral objection and purely political opposition to a particular war. The case of a man already in the Armed Forces who developed this form of particular objection, and had not a continuity of belief and expression to show, would be no different from cases in which now a soldier may apply for release or exemption because he has come to be conscientiously opposed to war in any form.

The main thing to be said, however, is that we should press for the development in our military codes of the possibility of *defenses* that can be entered against a charge of disobedience to a "lawful command" proving that the command was not lawful because it called for an *unjust* action to be done. Even on the brink of combat or in the middle of combat it should be possible for a man who grants the presumption of legitimacy resident in every particular command to have, if he judges that he knows enough to know that the action would be clearly *un*just, the possibility of a defense against a charge of disobedience in the fact that he was commanded needlessly or wantonly to kill prisoners of war, or to perform acts of cruelty, to do something inherently immoral, or to make war in ways that are contrary to international conventions governing

---

[12] John H. Mansfield (Harvard Law School): "Conscientious Objection—1964 Term," in *Religion and the Public Order*, ed. by Donald Giannella (Chicago, Illinois: University of Chicago Press, 1966), pp. 3–81, at pp. 80–81.

warfare to which his nation was a party. So understood, this should not be a burden disastrous to the soldier, to his unit or to the entire military tradition, but a quite necessary element in the marginal morality of warfare.

Having said this, the general proposal that selective conscientious objection be adopted still has to face the main reasons the Commission refused to recommend it. I propose to go more deeply into these questions in the next section by asking:

IV

WHAT HAPPENED ON THE WAY TO SELECTIVE CONSCIENTIOUS OBJECTION?

Two things happened before we got started. These two preconditions are apt to void the current pleas coming from many quarters calling upon the nation to recognize, indeed encourage, more discriminating conscientious judgment concerning the justice of particular wars by instituting particular-war objection. Unless these trends or happenings are reversed, it is exceedingly doubtful whether Congress will grant or should grant exemption, with alternate service, to more selective consciences than the pacifist. Yet both *seem* irreversible.

The first is the steady erosion, for at least the last three or four decades, of shared basic convictions concerning normative structures in social ethics having for religious people final theological warrant. There has been a flight from the use of rational principles of analysis, and a lack of political philosophy or norms governing our deliberation upon moral questions. This means that there can be no fundamental moral consensus among or within the religious communities of our nation. At least a retreat from the articulation of the lineaments of a political philosophy is what happened in Protestantism. Symptomatic of this decline is the fact that the 1937 Oxford Conference on Church and Society, whose participants still shared some articulate principles of justice and knew how to discriminate according to normative delineations, produced a far more impressive body of social teachings than any of our subsequent conferences.

The shared social and ethical convictions in and among the religious communities have suffered the relativization of the times. What has happened in the absence of norms and intervening principles governing action is rather like the hectic game of hurley in Ireland which was once interrupted when the ball went into a tree. All efforts to dislodge it by shaking the tree and throwing stones at the branches having failed, one captain is said to have exclaimed to the other: "Ah, the hell with it, let's get on with the game!" The name of the game is casuistry without principles, decision-making that is believed to be more responsible because situations are so unique that there are no relevant, *specific* norms. Have not such views taken increasing hold among us, leading not to increasing discrimination and refinement in moral judgment but in the very opposite direction on every moral matter, including the morality of war?

Since this thing that happened on the way to selective conscientious objection is only a contingent fact (however forceful), it is not impossible for the claims of conscience to prove more powerful still. But the way we would have to go, if, starting from here, we are going toward selective conscientious objection should be quite clear. This was expressed very well by the Roman Catholic, Protestant, and Jewish theological students who participated in the Seminarians' Conference on the Draft held in Cambridge, Mass., in mid-May, 1967, under the sponsorship of the student Social Action Committee of the Harvard Divinity School.[13] In order to set aside legal "discrimination in favor of those who form their conscience by the categorical method of the traditional pacifist," the Seminarians knew that it was necessary to rest the claims of a more selective conscience upon an articulated doctrinal foundation. The Seminarians' claim was not only that "our ethical decisions are founded on religious traditions" or that generally "God has given us the capacity to reason" in dealing with empirical situations. The claim was also, and more specifically, that "we have principles (which are not arbitrary) on which to base a reasoned discernment of what is right and wrong" and that "ethical decision-making includes *theological and moral principles* through which we view the empirical data . . ." (italics added).

This was almost too good to be true; too *just* to be credited as the prevailing mode of reasoning concerning moral and political questions among religionists. Yet perhaps there was here forecasted some reversal of modern trends that have come close to rendering selective conscientious objection itself indistinguishable from a "categorical" judgment in particular cases, or indistinguishable from purely political opposition or the "merely personal code" which Congress refused to accord exemption under the heading of conscientious objection. In any case, the statement issued a clarion call, and gave one practical reason for it, when it said: "We urge church leaders of different denominations to reach a consensus on the 'just war doctrine'. . . . We cannot expect the Government to recognize selective objection to 'unjust' wars when the religious community cannot agree on the 'just war doctrine'. . . ."

[13] "On Morality and the Draft," excerpts published in *The New York Times*, May 14, 1967.

That doctrine is in fact systematically ridiculed, or radically misunderstood in order to dismiss it as antiquated, in a great many church pronouncements issued in recent years. The Seminarians themselves radically misunderstood this doctrine at one point that would be crucial to expecting the government to recognize selective objection, when they wrote: "The spirit of these principles demands that every war be opposed *until or unless* it can be morally justified in relation to these principles" (italics added). John Courtney Murray, S.J., a member of the minority favoring selective objection on the President's National Advisory Commission on Selective Service, in an address on this subject,[14] said inelegantly that "the dear seminarians have got it backward"! This is true because of the moral authority to be accorded by every individual conscience to the political community in initiating a use of armed force through its established political processes. A particular war should rather be regarded as just, and should be supported, "until and unless" in relation to these principles it must be judged *un*just by a conscience that has formed itself in these terms. This is the meaning of the legitimacy to be accorded by every individual to the decision and initiative of public authority, expressed in ages past in the provision that a just war must be officially, not privately, "declared"—nor "privately" opposed, we may add, because of one's merely personal moral code. Unless this is acknowledged, the Seminarians would be espousing something they plainly mean to disavow, namely, that they were "demanding that the church defend an 'absolute individual freedom' to the detriment of society." Their philosophy would be an individualism—at least "until and unless" a particular war could be accredited to individual consciences in relation to these principles; and so at bottom it would be an individualism still. The mere fact that of course moral men have "a concern for men in their communities" does not, as such, mean an intrinsic respect for orderly authority in the determination of what *that* means. Taken alone, individual moral man's social concerns would accord insufficient authority or priority to government, it would fail to acknowledge the degree of moral authority required by the just-war doctrine to be attributed to "the conscience of the laws" and to established public authority in the conduct of diplomacy and in making war.

[14] "War and Conscience," unpublished Commencement address at Western Maryland College, June, 1967.

V

THE *SEEGER* DECISION

The second thing that happened before we got started on the way to selective conscientious objection was in the legal order. This too is extraordinarily apt to frustrate that conclusion, and in the practical order it may force the religious communities to *choose* between two "revisions" of our draft laws. We may have to decide which of two "liberalizations" we wish to support, selective conscientious objection to particular wars *or* the interpretation lately placed upon the *meaning* of conscientious religious objection by the United States Supreme Court.

In the case *Torcaso v. Watkins,* the Court had before it for decision the matter of a man who, elected Notary Public, refused to take the oath required by the state of Maryland that he believed in a Supreme Being. Instead of resolving this matter equitably on the narrow grounds of appeal to the Ethical Culture Society to which Mr. Torcaso belonged, a group long ago cognized by the courts as a "religion" because of its cult and practices, the Court chose rather to launch out upon an ocean of theological speculation, and it might have assigned Mr. Torcaso a godless religion *without* the trappings heretofore recognized (at law) as also necessary to there being a religion. The Court went so far in a *dictum* as to speak of "Secular Humanism" as also among the religious sects that do not believe in a Supreme Being.[15] *Dicta* of the Supreme Court that are in accord with the trends of the age have a way of becoming law.

The *Torcaso* case with its *dictum* about the meaning of religion almost immediately entered into the decisions of our courts in conscientious objector cases. By a cluster of decisions which we must now review, the Court "constructively" imposed an assertedly constitutional meaning upon legislation enacted by Congress in regard to religious objection to military service. In this way alone could the Court, on the *Torcaso* con-

[15] 367 U.S. 488 (1961), and 495, n. 11. Cited in evidence were watered-down versions of some of the more questionable aspects of the theologies of Paul Tillich and Bishop J. A. T. Robinson. For the box this places the Court in, in ever distinguishing the "secular" purpose and primary effect of *any* legislation from its possibly secondary "religious" consequences, and its difficulty now in stopping short of saying that any instruction in any values in the public schools amounts to an "establishment" of "religion," see Paul G. Kauper, "Schempp and Sherbert," in *Religion and the Public Order,* ed. Donald Giannella (Chicago: University of Chicago Press, 1964), pp. 3–40 at pp. 22–23; and Paul Ramsey, "How Shall We Sing the Lord's Song in a Pluralistic Land?" in *Journal of Public Law,* Vol. 13, No. 2 (1965), pp. 353–400, esp. pp. 385–6.

struction of the meaning of "religion," avoid declaring the more limited and the more probable common sense meaning of legislation enacted by Congress to be unconstitutional.

The 1940 Selective Training and Service Act had granted exemption to those who by reason of their religious training and belief are opposed to participation in war in any form. Then there arose divergence in the decisions of the circuit courts of appeal. Some districts limited exemption to cases showing religious training and belief in an ordinary language sense of these expressions. One circuit, however, went beyond a cult and practices definition of "religion" to require a showing of belief in a Supreme Being to warrant the religious exemption. Because of this lack of uniformity, the Congress in 1948 added to Section 6 (j) of the 1940 Act a statutory definition of religious training and belief, requiring "belief in a relation to a Supreme Being involving duties superior to those arising from any human relation," and specifically excluded "essentially political, sociological, or philosophical views, or a merely personal code."

After that enactment, decisions on appeal in conscientious objector cases proved no more uniform than before. This finally brought the matter before the Supreme Court for resolution during its 1964–65 term. The thing to be noted concerning the Court's resolution of these dilemmas is the fact that, with *Torcaso's dictum* as its premise, the Court drove even deeper into the territory of theological interpretation, and even unfolded a speculative theory of conscience. It did not find a way, if indeed such a way was possible, to bend the uniform interpretation of the 1948 statute back to the more tangible meaning of "religious training and belief," to the meaning "religion" usually has at law in other connections, or to require that some evidence of religious training, practices, or influences be shown upon beliefs held in good faith, and *nothing more.*

The hinge case was *United States v. Seeger.* The applicant had been reared in a devout Roman Catholic home and was a close student of Quaker beliefs, from which he claimed to derive much of his own thought. He frequently attended Quaker meetings. That would seem enough evidence of religious training and belief in the law's ordinary view of these matters. The applicant did not rest his claim to exemption upon these facts, as perhaps he might have done before the 1940 Act was amended in 1948. Still this did not prevent the Court from basing a decision in his favor on these facts had it chosen to do so. The Court might simply have struck down the 1948 requirement of "belief in a Supreme Being involving duties superior to those arising from any human relation" as *unconstitutional.* This would have returned the law of the land in the matter of exemption for conscientious objection to the 1940 Selective Training and Service Act, plus placing the lower courts on notice that the Supreme Court meant for no additional (Supreme Being) test to be required under it.

Instead the Court strained to find the 1948 statute *constitutional*, and it was therefore driven to search in the inner recesses of "conscience" for the equivalent of (lower case) "supreme being" in most or many men. It searched for that paramountcy in natural conscience which the Congress, being composed of reasonable men, must not have meant to exclude by its reference to "a relation to a Supreme Being." Just as in *Torcaso*, the Court's *dictum* created for the applicant "Secular Humanism" as a religion which it might have assigned him, had he not already been a member of the Ethical Culture Society that long has been recognized as a "religion" because of its external cult and practices, so in *Seeger* the Court created for the applicant the equivalent of a relation to a Supreme Being which he disavowed, instead of resorting to the religious training and belief which (certainly in the law's manner of speaking) Seeger claimed, without himself basing the justification of his conscientious beliefs upon these things. The Court did not venture upon what might be called a strenuous effort to construe the findings of fact concerning the origin and descriptively religious nature of Daniel A. Seeger's beliefs in order to bring him under the statute. Instead it made what has been called a "strenuous statutory interpretation" of the 1948 legislation and of "conscience" in order to bring the statute over him. It said in effect that no matter what were Seeger's apprehensions of his own case, he did actually believe in (to use the "lower case" for the idea) the "supreme being" that Congress had in mind. As Professor John H. Mansfield of the Harvard Law School has written, "It is certainly permissible to wonder whether the authority of Congress is really any more respected by the sort of strenuous statutory interpretation that the Court indulged in to avoid a constitutional question than it would be by an outright holding of unconstitutionality." [16] This leaves us with an interpretation of the meaning of "religion" required to be read into Section 6 (j) of the 1940 Military Training and Service Act that would hardly be the meaning of religion where this has been noticed or legislation enacted in most other aspects of our law. And it leaves us with an interpretation of "a relation to a Supreme Being" in the 1948 statute as a certain supremacy or a transcendent element within the structure of a man's conscientious beliefs upon which the last word has certainly not been spoken. Fast upon the heels of this legal history and into *this* understanding of the meaning of conscientious objection, the proponents of selective objection are endeavoring and must endeavor to insert exemption from particular wars as an *additional* qualification.

It should be acknowledged that the Court was dealing with a

---

[16] In *Religion and the Public Order*, p. 6.

mare's nest of religious assertions when it joined two other cases with *Seeger* for decision. In *Jakobson*, the claimant affirmed his faith in a "Supreme Being," "Ultimate Cause," or "Supreme Reality" which is "ultimately responsible for the existence of man." Arno S. Jakobson's appeal had been upheld by the second circuit court of appeals, even though he had stated that his relation to "Godness" was a "horizontal" one "through Mankind and the World," and not a "vertical" and "direct" one.[17] In *Peter*, the applicant for exemption rested his objection philosophically upon his "consciousness of some power manifest in nature" which is "the supreme expression of human nature" or "man thinking his highest, feeling his deepest, and living his best." These beliefs were affirmed to have been derived from reading and meditation upon "American culture, with its values derived from the western religious and philosophical tradition."[18] The ninth circuit court of appeals judged that Forest B. Peter's "respecting and loving . . . livingness in other objects and human beings" did not meet the statutory requirements; this was only a "personal moral code." His exemption was denied.

In the *Seeger* case the issue was presented squarely, since Seeger did not claim that his objection was based on a belief in a Supreme Being in *any* sense. His claim that he simply adhered to "a *religious* faith in a purely *ethical* creed," and that "pacifism . . . is for me a *transcendent* concern and it is in this respect that I consider myself *religious*,"[19] also gave the Court its lead in vastly expanding the meaning of the statute.

[17] *United States v. Jakobson*, 325 F.2d 409 (2d Cir. 1963).
[18] *Peter v. United States*, 324 F.2d 173 (9th Cir. 1963).
[19] *Record*, p. 99, *United States v. Seeger*, 380 U.S. 163 (1965), italics added. In fuller context, these statements read: In contrast to "action taken through fear of God or desire for eternal reward. . . . I feel more respect for this nobler spirit of pagan antiquity [Plotinus], i.e., belief in goodness and virtue for their own sakes, and a religious faith in a purely ethical creed." "Personally, I do not believe that life derives any meaning from cosmic design but I do believe that a person can give his life meaning by doing something worthwhile with it, i.e., by relating his existence in a constructive and compassionate way to the problems of his social environment. In this sense, pacifism, among other things, is for me a transcendent concern and it is in this sense that I consider myself religious." While Daniel Seeger declared that the existence of God cannot be proven or disproven nor his essence be determined, while he stated that "I prefer . . . to leave the question [of belief in a Supreme Being] open rather than answer 'yes' or 'no,'" and affirmed that "in human history the principle of righteousness has emerged very gradually from man's own painful efforts, uncertain and unblessed," he also rather startlingly affirmed that "such personages as Plato, Aristotle and Spinoza evolved comprehensive ethical systems without belief in God, except in the remotest sense" (pp. 73, 99). Coupled with his definition of the view he rejected in becoming a "religious agnostic," i.e. "fear of God and desire for eternal reward," this gave the Court an opening (slender as it may have been in Seeger's total testimony) to have ruled, as the courts have done in other cases, that he was only denying a naive "fundamentalistic" belief in a Supreme Being, which Congress had not

The courts below had all pointed out the difficulty of draft boards distinguishing between "Godness," "goodness," "livingness" at the heart of things, or "a high state of order and even disorder within the physical universe governed by laws which are presently above my ability or that of any man to completely control or completely understand"—which one claimant alleged he believed in.[20] The courts had strongly suggested that if by "Supreme Being" Congress meant to limit the exemption, the statute was unconstitutional. They had drawn upon the ever broadening meanings in contemporary religious thought, and called attention to the fact that many modern men feel the internal demands of conscience as compellingly as the externally derived commandments of God have traditionally been felt. And in granting Seeger's exemption, the circuit court of appeals relied heavily upon a definition given by Judge Augustus Hand in a decision interpreting "religious training and belief" *before Congress added the "Supreme Being" specification* excluding a merely political, philosophical, sociological, or personal moral code: "a belief finding expression in a conscience which categorically requires the believer to disregard elementary self-interest and to accept martyrdom in preference to transgressing its tenets." [21]

It is important to notice that the Supreme Court endorsed in one respect and did not endorse in another respect the decision of Judge Irving R. Kaufman of the second circuit court of appeals in reversing Seeger's conviction and granting him exemption. It did *not* hold that "a line such as drawn by the 'Supreme Being' requirement between different forms of religious expression cannot be permitted to stand consistently with the due process clause of the Fifth Amendment." It did *not* hold that "a requirement of belief in a Supreme Being, no matter how broadly defined, cannot embrace all those faiths which can validly claim to be called religions" [here Kaufman cited *Torcaso*]. Instead, this was exactly what the Court proposed: a broadly defined (lower case) supreme being or transcendent principle in consciences to be called religious in properly grounding the exemption.

The Court, however, did endorse Kaufman's decision in another, crucial respect. The *Kauten* test, wrote Judge Kaufman, recognizes that in today's "skeptical generation . . . the stern and moral voice of conscience occupies that hallowed place in the hearts and minds of men which was traditionally reserved for the commandments of God." "When Daniel Andrew Seeger insists that he is obeying the dictates of his conscience or the imperatives of an absolute morality, it would seem impos-

---

meant to require in the 1948 statute. Instead, the Court took up the notion of Seeger's internal "transcendent concern" or his "religious faith in a purely ethical creed" (which certainly neither Plato, Aristotle, Plotinus or Spinoza possessed).

[20] *MacMurray v. United States*, 330 F.2d 928 (9th Cir. 1964).

[21] *United States v. Kauten*, 133 F.2d 703 (2d Cir. 1943), at 707.

sible to say with assurance that he is not bowing to 'external commands' in virtually the same sense as is the objector who defers to the will of a supernatural power." [22] With this the Supreme Court agreed; but it construed this to be the meaning of the "Supreme Being" test.

Daniel Seeger's *"religious* faith in a purely ethical creed," his *"transcendent* concern" in pacifism,[23] seemed clearly to be a way out of a morass of subtleties, a way to grant Seeger exemption by an extraordinary interpretation of the 1948 statute. So the Court did *not* find that statute to be unconstitutional or rest Seeger's exemption upon his Catholic upbringing or upon the demonstrable influence of Quaker teachings upon him, or the fact that he frequently attended Quaker meetings, or upon the fact that he had a rather limited notion of a Supreme Being (as did, indeed, the government's brief against him) when he said neither "yes" nor "no" to that question. It did *not* revert to the 1940 requirement of "religious training or belief," or require Congress to revert to it. The upshot was rather to make such a reversion to an earlier test impossible, by virtue of the Court's anatomizing the meaning of the conscientious objection which Congress must have meant to require when it passed the 1948 statute. It is hard to see how there *could* be any reversal of this interpretation even if there *should* be.

Mr. Justice Clark, writing for the Court,[24] held that by amending the law in 1948 Congress intended only to clarify the meaning of "religious training and belief," and moreover that this was an expanding clarification and not a limiting one. Where the Congress required "belief in a relation to a Supreme Being," it meant to embrace all "religions," including godless religion. What then is the trial to be made of "religious belief"? The test to determine whether a belief is religious is to ask "whether a given belief that is sincere and meaningful occupies a place in the life of the possessor parallel to that filled by the orthodox belief in God of one who clearly qualifies for the exemption." [25] Thus there must be in the anatomy of a man's conscience some belief that forms its crux, comprises the organizing principle of his practical life, and has the

[22] *United States v. Seeger,* 326 F.2d 846 (2d Cir. 1964). Excerpts printed in *The New York Times,* Jan. 21, 1964

[23] It is high time our Judges and Justices cease citing, as they have done since *Torcaso,* Paul Tillich in support of their interpretation of the meaning of "religion." Obviously, such a thing as "pacifism" must be, for Tillich, of *less than* "ultimate concern"; and the fact that Seeger said "pacifism, *among other things* . . ." would mean that his was not the "transcendent concern" Tillich has written about. Judges and Justices, however, can scarcely learn better when a good many theologians have, after a moment's hesitation, declared these decisions to be in line with some of the best trends in modern theological analysis.

[24] *United States v. Seeger,* 380 U.S. 163 (1965). See also: 326 F.2d 846 (2d Cir. 1964), cert. granted, 377 U.S. 922 (1964).

[25] *Idem* at p. 166.

paramountcy that "a relation to a Supreme Being" used to have or has for others. That, in fact, was what Congress meant to require.

It is not quite clear, we should note, that the Court has reduced *religious* exemption to the test of *conscientiousness.* Yet the Court's functional notion of religious belief comes close to that. "After this decision," Professor John H. Mansfield writes, "one is left to wonder whether there are any conscientious objectors who will not be found, whether they like it or not, to be religious objectors in the meaning of the statute . . ."; concerning the "non-religious conscientious objector," the question still unanswered is "whether under the Court's decision he still exists." [26]

Still there might be forms of conscientious beliefs that the Court in the future may hold to be ones that do not meet the requirement of a kind of religious ultimacy in the structure of conscience as readily as did the "transcendent concern" Seeger placed in pacifism. There may be convictions lacking the sort of paramountcy that can be compared in functional importance to a relation to a Supreme Being in traditionally religious conscience, but which yet are undeniably conscientious. In short, there *may* be some merely political, sociological, philosophical, or personal objections that could not qualify for the exemption.

Still the Court has reduced the religious belief conditioning the exemption to a speculative form of conscientiousness. On this basis it seems very clear that there are *some* conscientious beliefs concerning duties arising from merely human relations that in the anatomy of conscience involve duties superior to those arising from all *other* human relations which Congress did not mean to exclude in seeming to say so,

[26] In *Religion and the Public Order,* pp. 7, 81, Mansfield's opinion is that "even under the Court's liberal construction of the term 'religious belief,' there would still seem to remain forms of opposition to war which although entitled to be considered conscientious are not founded on religious belief" (p. 68). This seems likely enough in the case of a man's affirmation that "his highest obligation is to save his own skin or to pursue his own interests . . ." But on the Court's test of functionally transcendent concern, it becomes less clear how the exemption would be denied in the case of other illustrations Mansfield gives in which a man holds a more general philosophy, even a philosophy of self-preservation or "a philosophy of hedonism or crude materialism" (p. 29). "If a person steadfastly maintains his disbelief in anything beyond the material order and this life, and asserts only that civilization can flourish and the human race improve its condition for a time, before all is snuffed out in an inevitable and mindless catastrophe, it may be difficult for the Court to bring these rather limited hopes within the notion of religious belief" (p. 33). How different is this from Seeger's "principle of righteousness" emerging by painful human effort "uncertain and unblessed"? All these propositions may be "truly held" about the nature of reality and the significance of human existence; and it would seem that in these cases the thing that distinguishes a non-religious conscientious objector from an objector who is *not even conscientious* would also be the thing that enables us to identify the "religious" objector.

and which could henceforth rightfully warrant granting the exemption. Moreover, it can scarcely be denied that there may be *some* political, philosophical, sociological, and personal moral outlooks that function in the lives of those who possess them as once did belief in a relation to a Supreme Being, and which also Congress did not mean to exclude when it went about saying so. It is the supremacy or commanding presence of an ingredient in conscience that has now to be assayed.

The ordinary citizen in his daily rounds—if he thinks about it— may puzzle over why the meaning of "religious belief" is to be settled by "the place that the belief occupies in the life of the objector" and not by "the character of the truths believed." While religion cannot be satisfactorily defined *without* reference to the role belief plays in the life of a believer, he will suppose that religion cannot be defined by that *alone*, with no reference to what is believed.[27] In any case, generally speaking, the character and content of a belief, and not only how it is held, will have some effect upon whether the community will consider it wrong to require a person to act contrary to it.

Public acceptance of the *Seeger* decision, indeed the general commendation of it, has depended not on these intricacies or on the Court's actual ruling but on a consensus that when it comes to exemption for conscientious objection to "participation in war *in any form*" there are "really no convincing reasons why the religious objector should be exempt and not the non-religious objector." [28] The strange manner in which the Court reached this result is of no account; in fact, it is a widely held but false opinion that it reached it simply by saying so.

Nothing in the foregoing account has been meant to raise objection to these developments in juridical law-making. To the contrary, this extension of the meaning of conscientious objection may be an entirely laudable and necessary growth in our understanding and practices in a religiously pluralistic and in a secular age. Our purpose has rather been simply to present this first significant juridical "revision" in the meaning of conscientious objection that had already been accomplished before the peak, at least, of the movement toward adding a second significant revision, namely, conscientious objection to particular wars. It has been necessary for our account to be a rather full one in order to direct attention to the enormous practical problem and indeed the profound doctrinal issue whether any political community can extend the meaning of exemption from military service in both directions at the same time. Only *now* do we have before us the meaning of that conscientious objection which it is *now* proposed be no longer limited to objection to war "in any form."

[27] John H. Mansfield in *Religion and the Public Order*, pp. 9, 33–34.
[28] Mansfield, p. 76.

The acceptability of the result of *Seeger* depended on our moral consensus that *in the matter of exemption from participation in war in any form* no important distinction should be drawn between religious, philosophical, or other personal grounds on which an individual might be driven to *that* conclusion. The fact that he had to enter objection to all wars already exerted its *heuristic* effect; that was clarifying as to whether this was an ultimate for him. He no more opposed one particular war than any other, and no more opposed his own nation's policy than any other. Given this anchorage, given this limit upon the exemption, no distinction should be made or needs to be made between religious and non-religious conscientious objection. With this we all concurred.

If anyone supposes, however, that the courts (or Congress) having just reached clarity on the meaning of religious objection to all wars are going, holding that firm, to plunge immediately into the subtleties of distinguishing between "religious" and "political" objection, he is very naive indeed. The test *itself*—opposition to war in any form—did more than any panel could (except for assaying a man's sincerity) to insure that his was *not* a merely political or strategic or personal opposition to one war rather than another, or against his own country's wars rather than those of some other. This test itself had a clarifying effect upon conscience, and upon what review boards and courts were to make trial of. The fact that this was the meaning of the exemption on one side enabled the courts to extend its meaning on the other. Because the *character* of the belief looked for was opposition to participation in war in any form enabled the courts vastly to enlarge the meaning of the "religiousness" with which this belief has to be held in order to qualify for *that* exemption.

We have several choices before us: (1) This recent "revision" in the meaning of conscientious objection is more important than getting Congress to grant selective objection to particular wars; (2) Objection to particular wars which are believed to be unjust is more important than the extension of the exemption to non-religious objectors; and we should pull the laboring oar back upstream to a far more limited and precise meaning of "religious" to which selective objection could then be attached; or (3) Because *both* of these meanings of conscientious objection are right and just, we must now undertake the manifold intellectual labor of distinguishing between conscientious moral or ethico-political objection to a particular war and merely political opposition to it. It is only the man who gets exhilaration out of being a prophet without really trying who will imagine that there is a fourth alternative, i.e. who imagines that there is any point in simply protesting and petitioning or demanding that Congress grant status to particular-war objectors simply because, taken out of context, there are principled claims that can be made for this.

It is noteworthy that the National Advisory Commission on Selective Service in holding on to exemption only for objection to war in any form also held on to *Seeger*. This at least suggests that if anyone wants to work for particular-war objection with any hope of success he may have to work against *Seeger*. The Commission considered only the question whether there was need for the selective service statute to be amended in order "to assure as a matter of orderly form that the Supreme Court's interpretation of the law as set forth in the *Seeger* decision would be followed." It concluded that such an amendment would be unnecessary because "it is the obvious duty of the Selective Service System . . . to follow the construction of the law which has been placed on it by the highest Court in the land." [29] But the Commission was *not* set up to make recommendations to the Selective Service System! It was making recommendation to the President, who then would recommend to Congress. It might, therefore, have recommended legislation having the effect of narrowing the results of the *Seeger* decision; and I suggest it might have had to do so if at the same time it had endorsed particular-war objection.

In any case, if we are going to show the validity of selective objection without absenting *Seeger*, this can only be by demonstrating with some precision the difference between moral or ethico-political objection to particular wars for cause of conscience and purely political opposition to particular wars. The latter cannot be *inchoately* granted by any nation, certainly not when "religious" or conscientious objection means practically anyone in the population who takes his opposition to a particular war seriously.

The gravity of the problems surrounding the proposal of particular-war objection in the context of this recent extension of the meaning of "religious conscience" can be seen by simply recalling how utterly "categorical" and undifferentiated were many of the philosophical and personal ultimates claimed in the cases the Supreme Court has had before it. These categorical ultimates would now be applied to particular wars without the limiting, more tangible test of "religious training and belief" in any ordinary sense of these words and without the limiting and *heuristic* test that the objection must be to all wars.

Perhaps those objections were "categorical" because the statute now invites only grounds for opposition to war "in any form." It is said in behalf of selective conscientious objection that this would invite conscientious objections that are more thoughtful and discriminating, and might even help to raise the level of public debate over particular

[29] *In Pursuit of Equity: Who Serves When Not All Serve?*, p. 48. See also p. 9.

wars. Certainly no one should say that conscientious objection is any the less "religious" or "conscientious" because *reason* has entered into it. We should reject altogether the notion that an objection is the more conscientious or religious in nature because it is merely intuitive or has, as it were, entrapped the claimant who without giving reasons simply cannot do otherwise. Still the proponents of particular-war objection must see that the very argument advanced in favor of it is an argument against it. The fact that, presumably, particular-war objection would be more reasoned and discriminating is the characteristic of it that makes it, apparently, indistinguishable from any sensible political opposition to the nation's policy. How is a conscientious judgment that a particular war is stupid and therefore wrong to be distinguished from any other opposition to that war?

We noted that the Seminarians' statement acknowledged that we cannot expect the Government to recognize selective objection to "unjust" wars when the religious community itself cannot agree on the just-war doctrine. Do we not need in addition to frame another precondition to the possibility of selective objection, in the light of the Court's venture into the interpretation of "religion" and its speculative anatomization of conscience? Do we not need to articulate with some definiteness the criteria by which claimants themselves and then competent review boards could tell the difference between reasons of a philosophical, sociological, political, or personal nature for opposition to particular wars that qualify as exemptible *religious conscientiousness* and those that do not? Consider the following problematic cases:

A. The year is 1917. I am a German-American and I live in Wisconsin. On Sundays we all go to Lutheran services conducted in the German language, but I do not believe in what is said there about God. This does, however, define essentially who I am. It is my link with the past, and with dozens of cousins in the fatherland. I love this new land, however, and I would defend her. I am not opposed to wars if they must come. But one war I cannot fight in: this would be a war of my new country against the old country where my father and forefathers lived and lie buried. If I were called upon to do this, it would tear my very heart out. Loyalty to my ancestry is the highest loyalty I know. On this point there is for me a *prohibitiva* superior to all duties arising from the human relations in which I now stand. Socrates said there was a voice within him that never told him what to do, but only what not to do. This is my condition. Maybe patriotism or religion and conscience should mean more to me. But more is unproven. Nothing is as transcendent. I admire rather that noble spirit of pagan antiquity who claimed only to know what he could not do. I cannot and I will not fight against Germany.

Such, indeed, were the grounds for one of the earliest proposals that conscientious objection to particular wars be protected. Senator Robert LaFollette offered an amendment to the 1917 Selective Draft Law that would have exempted, in effect, "on ground of conscientious objection to the undertaking of combatant service in the present war," persons of Austrian and German ancestry who had conscientious scruples against fighting those nations.[30] This can be compared to the English case in which Indians were allowed exemption who, while prepared to fight for Great Britain, were not willing to fight for Great Britain so long as India was not free. Would such deeply-felt personal and political objections be identified as of the essence of the meaning of religious or conscientious objection to particular wars, or as a peripheral accommodation alongside "truly held" particular-war objection? Then what is the meaning of the latter, as distinct from political and personal opposition to a war, which may or may not be accommodated?

B. The year is 1940. I live in New Jersey. I am a member of the German-American Bund, as also is my father. Here is my membership card, and there is more evidence I can provide showing that for some years now this has been my devout cause. I have, with no regret, sacrificed a good deal for it—in comparison, say, to my high school classmate Jerry who as this war approached waked up suddenly to political realities and began to conceive that he could not conscientiously participate in war in any form. I would never say that, but I do say that our country should never range itself behind those who continue to perpetuate the injustice of the Versailles Treaty. This is more than a political judgment for me. As I see it, there are salvic moral and spiritual resources for today's world coming only from the German *Volk*. Some may believe that there is a cosmic design or providence behind all this. As to that I say neither "yes" nor "no." But I do feel that here I have a relation to a power commanding my life superior to any other. I cannot and I will not fight in this war. But, of course, I would fight if the U.S. chose to use its military force in behalf of the wave of the future—*for* and not against that future in which mankind can reach true superiority over its present cravenness.

C. The time is the present—an eternal present. I cannot conscientiously fight in this war. Not because, as you may think, I just want to save my own particular skin. I grant that my philosophy may sound very like that, but it is a principle for me. In fact, I am a Christian. Jesus Christ, I believe, came to save those in need. I can plead only *need;* that's all any man can plead. And so, on the highest authority I know, I must simply admit and follow my need. This does not mean that I think I should always save myself from any war. There might be wars in which, tested by this need of mine which for Christ's sake I can not deny, my

[30] 55 Cong. Rec. 1474 (1917), cited by John H. Mansfield in *Religion and the Public Order*, p. 15, n. 14.

need and my country's would be the same. In fact, I think this is usually the case. But this particular war seems to me to go contrary to anything that has any relation to the significance of my life, to anything that could make my life significant. Christ came to save me in my need. This war doesn't.

D. "As Americans of draft age, we face an urgent dilemma because many of us cannot in good conscience support American policy in Vietnam. We are deeply committed to the procedures of majority rule and to action within law. Yet we believe that a great strength of the American constitutional system is its genius for accommodating the dictates of the individual conscience within the framework of the law. In the present situation, we believe that this can best be done by offering alternative service to those who are opposed to fighting in Vietnam. We are convinced that offering such an option would be in the national interest, as well as consistent with the finest traditions of American democracy." [31]

Can "opposition" to the government's policy be simply made the grounds for alternative service? Should this be one ingredient in determining "who serves when not all serve" in the military forces? Would that be *fair?*

E. I live in Los Angeles, and I tell you right now that I believe the whole Federal income tax system is an invasion of human liberty and a violation of man's natural rights. I have formed my conscience and found this lodestar of my political calling by long years of reading on this subject, particularly the classics of Anglo-American liberties. The income tax is an evil and vicious thing.[32]

Or: I cannot and I will not pay this 10% surcharge added to my Federal income tax solely because the government persists in fighting a grossly immoral war in Vietnam.

These cases need to be thought about even if it is the case that to date no individual federal taxpayer or group of taxpayers can gain "standing to sue." This is a technical device by which the Supreme Court keeps out of its domain the determinations of Congress together with other established political processes disposing the energies and policies of the nation one way and not another. Still, philosophically, the issues seem much the same, as the National Advisory Commission reminded us, between conscientious objection to paying taxes in support of particular

[31] Case D is a statement signed by 10,000 students of draft age, including about half of the student bodies of Yale and Davidson colleges and 70% of the Amherst graduating class, and forwarded to President Johnson, June 29, 1967.
[32] Cf. Senator Thomas Kuchel's comment: "I cannot say that they make a religion of these convictions, although some may." 110 Cong. Rec. 21357 (1964), quoted by John H. Mansfield in *Religion and the Public Order*, p. 56.

wars and conscientious objection to serving in a particular war that a man opposes. It can be said, of course, that no "substitute burden" can be devised for an exempted taxpayer which can be compared to the alternative service required of a man exempted from military service. Perhaps the taxpayer could still be allowed to pay up the last farthing, but permitted to designate that his tax go to support other government projects of recognized social value and of which he approves. But would it be *fair*, would it be equitable, to allow some to specify the uses of their taxes, while others must support policies to which they are only mildly opposed? In any case, such a system has within it a tendency to break the nation into many parts, each paying for policies it supported and not for others. Even so, it would seem, selective conscientious objection could lead to only those serving who did or do not oppose a particular use of the war power—so long as "conscientious" objection can be based on undifferentiated religious, philosophical, political, strategic, or purely personal grounds.

> F. I am a Marxist-Leninist, as you know. You know, I presume, because of my name, and that of my father who is one of the leading Marxist theoreticians of the English speaking world. This means, you see, that I was to the manner born; that from earliest youth my conscience was formed to tell the difference between just, anti-imperialist wars and unjust wars. This is what I must do now; I cannot go to this war of yours against the people and against progress. This does not mean that I'm against the use of violence; far from it. Nor that I could not fight in one of this (our) country's wars if ever it were on the right side, which I really don't expect to happen. Still I'm no pacifist, nor am I against our government. I'm just *for* the just cause as I see it; and see it not only subjectively but objectively as a force, as something in the grain of things, working itself out through history. It's greater than we are. I am bound to serve communist justice—like I suppose, people used to obey the will of God. Only my transcendent concern arises from no transcendent source, but an immanent one. The justice I believe in is the livingness in all the objects in the world; this is the true science, it is no religion; and for this reason I cannot participate in this war.

> G. It's the revolutionary impulse upsurging in our era that I see as the bearer of justice, not the *status quo* politics of the U.S. or even the static formulae of Marxist-Leninism. I have a religious faith in this political creed, since—while no fear of God or desire of eternal reward motivates me—it is Man at last who is battering down every establishment. Every now and then, I see our government tentatively siding in some measure with the cause of revolutionary justice that is abroad in the world; so I cannot say I would never fight in my country's wars. And certainly I don't refuse to participate in war in any form. In fact, I believe in revolutionary violence when necessary according to revolutionary standards. But *this* war

H. This war is against X-enemy nation. I believe the cause of X to be just for reasons a, b, c, etc. Justice for me is a transcendent concern; therefore, as I said, for reasons a, b, c, etc., I cannot and I will not participate in this particular war against X, which is unjust. Since this is ultimate for me, it is religious; and I claim exemption on grounds of conscientious objection to particular wars, under Section 6 (j) of the Selective Service and Training Act as interpreted by *Seeger* and amended by Congress in 19—.

How would a competent panel be able to deal with these cases? Let us suppose that, without the searching and clarifying burden upon claimants and panels which was the effect in some measure of the test of opposition to war in any form, it is still possible for them to distinguish the truly conscientious from the un-conscientious holders of these various beliefs. *Then* the question is how to distinguish between merely political opposition (which any political community must require to yield or to find expression only through established political processes) and the conscientious particular-war objection to which it is proposed that exemption be granted. If religious, philosophical, and personal creeds may all, in effect, qualify for religious exemption, how can the paramount claims *thence* arising be distinguished from purely *political* objection which will not be allowed, certainly not in time of war? It is not likely to prove any easier to distinguish one objection from another in the case of particular wars than to distinguish one conscience that is religious from another. But the point here is a *normative* one: if no line should be drawn between the variety of modern man's religiousness, why should any line be drawn between his various grounds for opposition to a particular war? Unless grounds for doing so can be found, selective conscientious objection would in the end mean exemption upon request, with only a determination of the claimant's good faith, sincerity, and deep-feeling in which what *he says* about his opposition has the casting voice. This would seem to be an unconstitutional favoring of those who feel deeply about their politics in determining who serves when not all serve. These are the issues *beneath* the unpersuasiveness of this proposal to the ordinary citizen or statesman. The ordinary citizen will reflect as follows (and so far we have not deprived him of this argument): it is the applicant who in World War II was a devout member of the German-American Bund, or today has formed his conscience quite sincerely according to the tenets of communism, or has found his spiritual home among the Viet Cong of this age or (lest the foregoing be dismissed as another expression of an inflexible anti-communism or of an anti-revolutionary "mystique") who believes with all his heart in the justice of the cause of future national enemy-X, who could most clearly qualify for exemption from one of these particular wars because in his conscience there is an ingredient functionally equivalent to a relation to a Supreme Being involving duties superior to those arising from all (other) human relations.[33] To determine the meaning of a valid conscientious objection to particular wars is certainly not going to be easier than distinguishing between "a relation to a Supreme Being" and "godness" or "livingness" or the "inscrutable order and disorder" that rules in a young man's mind. Nor, certainly, is it any part of the just-war doctrine (which, after all, is a theory of statecraft and of political authority and community) to warrant conscientious objection to unjust wars on a petitioner's claim that he is supremely devoted to "man thinking his highest, feeling his deepest, and living his best." It is no conclusion from the just-war doctrine on the uses of military force to warrant exemption on a number of the cases A–H stated above. How is particular-war exemption to be determined? To this question we have devoted too little attention.

That was an excellent statement of the case for selective conscientious objection made by Professor Roger Shinn representing the Council for Christian Social Action of the United Church of Christ and filed with the Senate Armed Services Committee, April 14, 1967. But one thing in it simply will not do. If we propose to be *going* on the way to selective conscientious objection, and not just "proposing," we cannot fail to face the hard problems, both in practice and in theory, created by endeavoring to relieve *both* of the two restrictions in Section 6 (j)— both the restriction in the legislation that attempted to limit exemption to persons having "religious training and belief" (or who acknowledge "a relation to a Supreme Being involving duties superior . . .") and the restriction of the exemption to objectors to "participation in war in any form." It will not be enough simply to accept *Seeger,* and then ask for more. It will not be enough to pass over lightly the difference made by *Seeger* (as I judge Professor Shinn did) with a commendation of the decision for being "in agreement with contemporary theological scholarship" and with but the expression of some qualms now put behind us: "Our misgivings on this clause are mitigated, if not entirely overcome." Nor is it enough simply to iterate the obvious, that the selective objector would have to make a more discriminating judgment and case for himself. He is less likely to get by with draft dodging in this way than if he in-

[33] The fact that such a man would not make a good soldier is *not* to the point of whether exemption for cause of conscience should be granted. Neither is it to the point to argue that, because of modern military technology, a nation might be able to fight its wars without requiring those conscientiously opposed to particular wars to serve. The question precisely is whether *under these conditions,* when fewer men are needed, opposition to a particular war *should* be an element in determining who will be required to serve. Is selective objection a *fair* national policy, and could it be made consistent with the integrity and disposition of a nation's policy? That is the question.

sincerely declares himself a categorical pacifist. It is true, of course, that men "would have an easier time pretending to oppose all wars than explaining to skilled interrogators why on grounds of conscience they accept some wars but oppose others." But malingerers are not the problem. That is not the crux.

The crux is that it does not yet appear, on the Court's anatomy of conscience, how one would distinguish between political objection and political loyalties, on the one hand, and the exemptible conscientious objection on the other, especially when the former are passionately held in disagreement with the nation's policy. The question is whether selective conscientious objection can be made compatible with the very nature of political community, and a nation's ability to dispose itself one way rather than another while counting that all citizens acknowledge the authority of this disposition until and unless they clearly must say it is unjust. The question is *how*, upon the institution of particular war objection, we could avoid the result that we would become a nation divided into those fighting, and their sons, who supported the war before it started, and those who oppose the war, who are exempted from fighting. It is not enough to say that conscientious objection because of political opposition or alien counter-loyalties may as well be admitted since such a person would count for nothing, or for worse, in the nation's cause. Nor should we avoid the point by observing that the nation's cause must not be worth much if it cannot command the agreement of a majority of young men, or by relying on the fact that military technology may enable a nation to fight wars without a large number of soldiers. The problem of discriminating between merely political and conscientious objection to particular wars cannot be dismissed or avoided. Then the question is whether we *should* thus distinguish between opponents to a given national policy or war, any more than we should favor one religion over another. The point is that the Supreme Court's doctrine of conscience in its recent decisions, coupled with particular ethico-political objection, would (as Rousseau scathingly said of his fellow *philosophes* in the eighteenth century) make us all "men" and not one a "citizen." That was harmless enough when what was at stake was objection to participation in war in any form. Indeed, there may be great value in encouraging these reminders of general humanity with its claims against all wars where one nation or one war is no more faulted than any other by such ultimate appeals. But coupled with the proposal that a nation recognize as well objection to particular wars, it does not yet appear that, as consciences are formed in the modern period, this revision would not have ominous consequences upon our remaining sense of political community and the claims this places upon everyone.

VI

THE WAY AHEAD UPON JUST-WAR WARRANTS

I do not believe that the conclusion from this must be to abandon the case for selective objection. To the contrary, the case for this is an intrinsic moral one while the obstacles are in the empirical order, however deeply embedded these are in our culture and law. They may be so deep within the hearts of non-religious, non-political modern men as to be insurmountable in our time. Still a serious search for a viable implementation of selective conscientious objection is required by our conviction that men live in more than this one earthly city, that life in the kingdom of politics does not encompass men to the whole extent of their beings, and that the character and institutions of these kingdoms should be open to transformation and elevation by that other City to which we, with all men implicitly, belong. The *transcendence of the person* requires us to ask whether this must be manifested only by the insights and vision we strive to put into public debates over national policy. To say this *is* the only bearing of morality upon politics and war is *not* an amoral view of politics. Quite the contrary. Still we should press the question whether in regard to the state's activity involving the killing of man by man, a way cannot be found by which the transcendence of the personal in its claims upon persons can come to expression in yet another way, in exemption granted to conscientious objection to particular wars.

There are only a limited number of options—each difficult to *think through* and difficult to execute—if we really mean to be going to particular-war objection. In listing these alternatives, I assume that John Courtney Murray, S.J., is quite correct in the recommendation he made in the interest of "good public argument": "the issue of selective conscientious objection must be distinguished from the issue of the justice of the South Vietnam war." [34] We cannot think straight about this matter unless these two issues are separated. Unless they can be separated for purposes of this discussion there might even be some question to be raised about the ethics of *the advocacy* of selective objection, since the fact is that not only is the latter issue "muddled and confused" but also it is "misused and abused" in the present atmosphere of extremism in action, reaction and counter-reaction. It "would not be good morality and it would be worse politics," as Fr. Murray said, if the issue of selective conscientious objection is used "as a tactical weapon for political opposition to the war in Vietnam or to the general course of American foreign policy." This can

[34] "War and Conscience," unpublished Commencement address, Western Maryland College, June, 1967. Subsequent quotations are from this address.

be said, and insisted upon, while nevertheless acknowledging that "we all owe some debt of gratitude to those who, by raising the issue of selective conscientious objection, have undertaken to transform the tragic conflict in South Vietnam into an issue, not simply of political decision and military strategy, but of moral judgment as well." But the fact that this political issue is, like most political issues, also a moral matter does not settle—it only opens—the question whether our moral judgments should enter into political decision through the procedures of public debate in a democratic society, obliging us then to support the direction given our nation's action while continuing to dissent from it, or whether the transcendence of the person and fundamental moral claims exceptionally in the matter of war requires that particular-war objection be granted. The premise that a political act is a moral act certainly does not perform for us the manifold intellectual labor required to distinguish in which matters the one or the other of these conclusions is proper. To approach the question of particular-war objection from the point of view of generalized rights of civil disobedience is already to have abandoned political reason. Finally, the morality of the political act does not automatically enable us to know the lineaments of a system of selective conscientious exemption that would be ethico-politically *right,* much less one that would be practicable.

The limited number of difficult options follow, I believe, from the evidence gathered and analyzed in this chapter. They follow also from the warrants and reservations in the just-war doctrine on the uses of military force, which doctrine arose from serious thought about the nature and responsibilities of statecraft in light of the transcendent claims of the person upon the structures of political action. (So did also, of course, the processes of a democratic politics.)

1. It might be the case that, in order to institute a system of selective service that requires no man to fight a war or a mode of war he conscientiously believes to be unjust, we would have to choose at this juncture between proceeding on the way to selective conscientious objection and first attempting to restore to the comprehensions of men the meaning of religious claims, of genuinely transcendent claims, upon conscience.

However, this may not be a necessary or an acceptable disjunction. Fr. Murray does not believe that it is. He has stated that on the National Advisory Commission he advocated "that the grounds for the status of conscientious objector be not only *religiously* or *non-religiously* motivated opposition to participation in war in all forms, but also *similarly* motivated opposition to participation in particular wars."

2. In that case, our task is only the enormous one of re-educating an age in the meaning of political justice and of justice in war. Our nation would have to "make its way to some discriminating doctrine . . .

on the uses of force." "Our national tradition of confused moral thought on the uses of force" would have to be brought to an end, and reversed. We would have to become a people who no longer deny that a nation has *jus ad bellum*, or strive to render this inoperative or unfit as a basis of policy; and who, when the *jus ad bellum* we refuse to acknowledge comes into play, tend then to deny that there is *jus in bello* governing our conduct in war. Granting that those strange, latter-day understandings of religion which we have reviewed have at least the virtue of according to the conscience of every man as man its proper importance, and assuming the recovery of a national capacity for political reason, it would still be incumbent upon us to *show how* selective conscientious objection could be made to work without being destructive of political community (and this means of the nation and its power to act with one will and way in the nation-state system).

The truth is that every time we endorse or propose selective conscientious objection to our fellow countrymen, we are mainly making a proposal to ourselves, and delivering a judgment upon ourselves. This self-incriminating judgment can be summed up in the obvious fact that we who are the vocal voices in church and in academic community have done very little to articulate and transmit an adequate political philosophy in the present day. It may be exhilarating to get behind this reform. But it is another thing again to create the conditions of its possible enactment—or, for that matter, even to imagine how we are going to do this. To raise the level of public debate in any nation of the modern world so that there could be a *proper* adoption of selective objection seems insurmountably difficult. We ought not to think we have made any advance if we succeed simply because modern weapons eliminate the need for many men in order for force to be used, and eliminate in some measure also the need for integral, purposive political community, because opposition to national policy can be shrewdly accommodated by exemption from particular wars. Nor should we rejoice if this proposal commends itself to our contemporaries simply because it is one more step in the erosion of imperative political obligation by an omnivorous individualism and by apolitical optimism about the trustworthiness of men's moral sensibilities.

But can it be expected that in making our way as a nation to some more discriminating doctrine on the uses of force we can really reach the minimum requirement of clarity in recognizing the difference between moral objection to a particular war and political objection to a particular war? *This is the sticking point,* and one which in my judgment Fr. Murray too quickly assumes would be solved by a greater degree of common, articulated, moral and political discourse. There seem to be two obstacles in the way of assuming that political self-re-education would have as one of its fruits that we would learn to draw an acceptable line between conscientious moral and conscientious political objection to particular wars. One difficulty is simply the fact that we are morally a pluralistic political community no less than we are religiously a pluralistic people, and are apt to remain so. Can we come to agreement on what is to count as conscientious moral objection any more than on what counts as a religious belief? The other, and a deeper, obstacle may lie in the fact that moral reasons and political reasons (which are admittedly inseparable) may intrinsically not be distinguishable enough for this to be a foundation of the proposed system.

This brings us to two remaining ways in which particular-war objection might be made possible and determined to be desirable.

3. With certain findings of fact, selective objection might be accorded without attempting to distinguish between moral and political objection, whether because the line cannot be drawn practically or because the distinction is believed to be impossible in principle. Exempt status could be granted as a politically wise and humane accommodation, not as a response to a *moral claim* (transcendent or otherwise), let alone a human or constitutional *right* which Congress must grant. All that would be assayed would be a young man's "sincerity," his "conscientiousness," how deeply he feels his objection to be, whether moral or political, and whatever the nature of his moral or political beliefs, their substance or worth. This seems to be the main thrust of what Vatican Council II had to say on this subject, if its statement is transposed from universal to particular objection. Among agreements which are designed to make military activity and its consequences less inhumane, the Council stated, it also "seems right that laws make humane provisions for the case of those who for reasons of conscience refuse to bear arms, provided however they accept some other form of service to the human community." [35] On condition that this does not frustrate the political purposes of a nation in its legitimate determination to use military force, governments should seek, among other things, to relieve the burdens and frightfulness of war by holding in check the enforcement of military service upon persons conscientiously opposed to service in a particular war. It will be a better political community if this can be done. This would be a political judgment, itself a moral judgment, on the part of a society, to the effect that to extend exemption to conscientious objectors on moral/political grounds to service in a particular war would conserve an individual and a common good that is more important than the degree of unfairness to those who are not so deeply opposed or who support the present direction of American foreign policy. On some suppositions of fact, however, this conclusion could be rebutted, since it is not based on

[35] *Pastoral Constitution on the Church in the Modern World*, paragraph 79. See also Chap. 16 below, pp. 383–85.

an inherent moral claim, as against a distinguishable, "merely" political objection. The judgment would be reversed if to grant the exemption would frustrate the disposition of the energies and will of the nation one way rather than another. Moreover, if the *fairness*-features of the situation seemed uppermost, then the war could be judged less totally burdensome if strong objectors to a particular war were entered into a lottery system along with the college-bound and with high school "drop-outs" alike in determining who must serve when not all need serve.

4. The final possibility seems to the present writer, given the present understanding of religious conscience in our law and given the present understanding of political justice and of the tests of the justice of a nation's war policy, to be the only way in which we might begin to introduce selective conscientious objection as a matter of principle, or as the recognition of a *moral claim*. I put this suggestion forward only as one long *question*. It is a move which I judge calls for thorough investigation and manifold thought.

The proposal is that in thinking about the justice to be invoked or the conscientious objection to participation in a particular war to be explained before a competent panel by claimants to exemption from military service, we would need to move in two different directions at the same time in setting such a claimant's and panel's terms of reference. (a) We should cease to look into the anatomy of conscience itself to find grounds for the conscientious objection which are functionally equivalent to those duties "superior" to any duty arising from human relationships that a traditional religious believer felt were grounded in relationship to a Supreme Being. In that direction we are not going to discover a workable distinction between conscientious moral objection and conscientious political opposition to particular wars, even if this were either a theoretically possible or a morally and politically defensible distinction. Therefore, one of the conditions of the possibility of selective objection based in any measure on the transcendence of the person or on moral principle or the inherent claims of conscience would be that we cease to look for this in political positions that are "truly held."

We should look rather to where the claims of humanity have, in the matter of war, been largely registered and given some shape or form not wholly subject to the passions and strongly-held opinions of the moment, namely, in *jus gentium*, in international law, in agreements and treaties and conventions expressing men's agreements as to justice and governing the conduct of men and nations in war. This would be to build upon Jacques Maritain's suggestion that "knowledge of the primordial aspects of natural law" are known directly by no reason, no conscience, other than God's, and that these elements of a transcendent justice are "first expressed in social patterns rather than in personal judgments"—not simply in any sort of social patterns, but in the *jus gentium*, or the common law of human civilization.[36] Perhaps a system of particular-war objection could be erected upon the double foundation of conscientious inclinations moving a person to claim the exemption and clarifying objective features in the agreements of men concerning justice in war. The proposal is, therefore, that the class of exemptible conscientious objection to participation in particular wars shall be based on opposition to the war because of the claimant's conscientious belief that the war is in violation of international conventions and the "laws of war" and in violation of agreements to which his nation was and is a party. Other sorts of objection to particular wars, which are also, of course, moral appeals and claim moral warrant (as do the opposing and the prevailing opinion), shall nevertheless be regarded as falling wholly within the legitimate due processes of democratic society, from the burdens and outcome of which no participant can claim exemption.

Secondly, (b) those who hold, vaguely or in more precise terms, to the just-war doctrine on the uses of military force should distinguish between what we may call the teleological, or consequentialist, tests in this doctrine and the deontological tests. We should distinguish between what is stupid and therefore morally wrong and what is inherently wrong (even if not stupid). It is one thing to determine whether and when a war is rightful, another thing to determine in *prohibitiva* what is rightful or wrongful in war. It is one thing to determine that the overall "cause" of war is just, another to determine whether the war is conducted unjustly. And between the two tests of just conduct of war, it is one thing to determine whether the mode of warfare is excessive in terms of what is at stake (or is likely to lead to proportionately greater evil than the evil prevented), and it is another thing to determine or conscientiously to believe that acts of war are being "aimed indiscriminately" and are in direct violation of the moral immunity of non-combatants from direct, intended attack. In all these cases, my proposal is that the *second* in these pairs be recognized as a possible basis of a creditable claim to conscientious objection to participation in a particular war, because in these respects the claimant would state his belief that something is unjust no matter what are the good policy-consequences alleged by others or by the government. These policy-consequences, in his own case or that of any other citizen, would not be allowed as bases of a claim to exemption because, while equally a moral claim, such judgments would not be distinguishable from merely political opposition to a particular war or from disagreement with the general course of the nation's foreign policy.

[36] *Man and the State* (Chicago, Illinois: The University of Chicago Press, 1951), p. 92.

Taken together, these two stipulations would constitute a minimal and a somewhat clear, non-sectarian agreement concerning how citizens would go about distinguishing between claims to conscientious objection that may be accorded exemption, on the one hand, and, on the other, their opposition to particular wars or support of them (also properly expressed in terms of verdicts of "just" and "unjust" war) which simply indicate that there are points of view in significant political debate. The one of the latter overruled in the course of determining the nation's policy would have rights of continuing dissent but no intrinsic claim to conscientious objector *status*.

It cannot be too often repeated that, if we have no more objective terms of reference for the meaning of the proposed conscientious objection than the Supreme Court's anatomization of conscience, then all talk of applying this to particular wars is beating the breeze. The proposal then amounts to a claim favoring one religion over another, or one political opposition over another, or stronger dissent over weaker dissent, which will not likely be granted and perhaps should not be granted; or else this would be a claim to normless, individualistic dissent that could not begin to be considered compatible with a citizen's responsibility. Such a proposal will not be adopted by a political community whose people still have a will to be a *people* and have any remaining sense of *res publica*—except as an accommodation hedging for some men the burden of directly serving the cause they oppose, which may prove unfair to men less certain that the current policy is wrong. Hence the proposal that acceptable claims to exemption on grounds of conscience be linked with specifiable features in international law and in agreements governing warfare in the international system to which one's own nation was and is a party. These grounds in *jus gentium* are often the same, in any case they fall within the same range of ethico-political considerations, as the tests of *inherent wrongfulness* (the deontological tests) in the just war doctrine on the uses of military force.

The teleological tests—which would be excluded as bases of claims to status as a conscientious objector—are the test of justice in the overall "cause," the test whether the war was undertaken in the "last" reasonable "resort," and the test of proportionately greater good or lesser evil in the effects. To say that objection on these grounds would not be an admissible claim is *not* to say that opposition to the war for these reasons would be any the less moral. The proposal only recognizes that the course of the nation's policy was set by precisely these same considerations, on which men may disagree who are exercising the same conscience, and that in these respects conscientious moral objection cannot be distinguished from serious political opposition to that particular policy. The place for the interplay of conscience on *these* points is and must remain in the public forum, in continuing dissent until "the conscience of the laws" is persuaded or in conscientious objection that bears the burden of *refusing* to serve.

Here may be introduced an interpretation of "just cause" which, I would say, was its essential meaning in ages past and which, in any case, must be its accepted meaning in today's world if there is any hope of discriminating between conscientious political viewpoints that are the very substance of political discussion (and also the basis that may be equally claimed for any prevailing political policy) and conscientious moral claims that might be allowed special status as grounds for exemption from particular wars. To understand the just-war doctrine we must link together the several teleological tests that a war must be for "just cause," that it must be officially "declared" by proper authority, that war must be in the last reasonable resort, and that not even every just cause is worth the fires of war. These tests are properly linked together because legitimate declaration of war was always thought to entail competent judgment concerning the justice of the cause, the cost/benefits, and judgment as to whether to refrain longer from resort to arms could be only out of a desperate and unreasonable hope for a peaceful solution.

What must this be taken to mean? To answer this question, a choice has to be made between two "models" concerning a judgment declaring a particular war to be just in these respects, warranting its initiation. One model is expressed by "the *tribunal* of war," the other is expressed by "an *arbitrament* of arms."

The idea that just war is a tribunal entails a belief that killing in the war is an "execution" of a court's "sentence." This view seems to require that the justice or injustice of the cause be sun-clear to all observers; that the capital punishment of the "guilty" can rightfully be exacted; that the initiation of the use of force by one side is clearly in accord with an objective distinction between the "guilty" and the "innocent"; that a warrior is only a hangman acting within a quasi-juridical order.

The idea that just war could ever appeal to such a commonly accepted understanding of guilt or innocence may have had some semblance of credibility within "Christendom" with its common understanding of rights and dues. On the other hand, it may well be that the "model" of a "tribunal" of war executing an agreed upon justice and punishing offenders is a romantic notion having no correspondence to any actual state of human affairs in the past or in the present.

In any case, this is not the human condition politically in the modern world. If now one holds in mind the model of war as a "tribunal," and "declaration" as executing sentence upon the "unjust," he goes so far astray as not to be able, on this basis, to be a proponent of selective conscientious objection to wars that are unjust. This model will force one rather to become a pacifist in regard to all wars, and to give up the case for conscientious objection to particular wars;[37] or else it will force one in the direction of justifying all the decisions of proper political authority as the highest decisions concerning political justice that we can certainly know.

I can only assert, therefore, that the requirement that the cause of war be just in all these respects, coupled with the requirement that the war be declared by the authorities or by the established processes of decision-making presumed to be competent to make these determinations, always actually meant resort to an "arbitrament" of arms, not resort to anything properly to be called a "tribunal" rendering its verdicts by the light of an objective certainty as to the universal justice of the cause. In any case, the model of an "arbitrament" of arms is the one that more correctly exhibits mankind's struggles for justice in the nation-state system with its politically embodied justices on which men do not always agree. There would be world political community with an enforcing authority if we did so agree, and no more need to be loyal to the justice we know. It is sometimes tragically necessary to determine the justice of the cause of war by the light of the apprehensions of justice that we have; these apprehensions are always less than the "universal view" presupposed by the tribunal-model.

This does not mean that these tests laid down by the just-war doctrine on the uses of force are of no more avail. Nor does it mean that they are addressed only to the topmost magistrates or political leaders of the nations. In modern democratic society they are addressed to every man who must say whether the war is justified or unjustified in these terms. This does mean, however, that decision as to whether the cause is just, whether the end will be a more just and peaceful order, whether what is at stake is worth the costs paid and exacted, and whether there were better ways out that were *possible,* all these are decisions falling within established political due-processes by which a nation has the political *authority* (which is more than the *power*) to dispose the energies of the whole citizenry toward the realization of its agreement as to the national and the international common good. If we do not stand as a nation for the justice we know, we are not as a people likely to come into that land where a wider, perhaps a universal, view of justice can become known. As individual citizens we are not apt to come into that land

---

[37] This is the legalistic-pacifist use of the just-war doctrine, one example of which is to be found in Gordon Zahn's article "The Test of the Just War," *worldview,* Vol. 8, No. 12 (December, 1965), pp. 10–13. Protestant pacifists also allow the just-war doctrine strength enough to condemn any particular war brought under review, just before its own demise. The question such use of the just-war doctrine as something other than an ethico-political theory of statecraft poses most urgently is: can a pacifist tell a just war? See Chap. 12 below.

either, unless we allow the nation the *moral authority* to do this, even while, it may be, persevering in conscientious dissent on all these points from some particular policy.

I suggest that this entails that as a matter of moral and political *principle*[38] men who feel their conscientious moral and political objection to the prevailing judgment as to the justice of the overall "cause," etc. to run so deep that they cannot and will not participate in a particular war should not claim to be exempted from the consequences of such refusal. Theirs is only another reading of the particular political encounter their nation went to meet, and by an application of the same moral/political tests governing whether war is justified or not.

We are permitted another conclusion when it is not a question of estimating the rightfulness of a war, involving such vast and at the same time uncertain and mixed moral and political calculations of the political good to come. In the matter of estimating rightfulness and wrongfulness in war there may be grounds for distinguishing more clearly between conscientious objection to a particular war based on conscientious claims as moral claims, on the one hand, and, on the other, "truly held" political opposition.

The analogy is with the situation in military justice when a man in the Armed Forces charged with disobedience to a lawful order is allowed to enter as a defense the fact that he was ordered to do something inherently immoral or contravening the "laws of war" to which, in treaties and conventions, his nation was a party. If his commanding officer said "We're going down this valley to take all the territory this side of yon river," and ordered him to go, he is not allowed as a defense to try to prove that this was quite unwise as a tactic, or did not conform to the contours of the strategic encounters going on or to the contours of what was politically at stake in the world. He is not allowed as a defense to try to prove that he conscientiously *believed* the command, in this sense, to be wrong morally and politically. He is not allowed as a defense to state that he believed that he was commanded to use *excessive* force, and therefore that the order was not a lawful one. But he is allowed as a defense against a charge of disobedience to a "lawful order" to show that he was ordered to kill prisoners of war, etc., and that therefore the command was *not* a *lawful one*. For men on the brink of combat or in the midst of combat there is a clear enough difference between the rightfulness of a particular engagement and what would be wrongful *in* that particular engagement. Further to clarify or enlarge the class of such legitimate defenses linked to international conventions and agreements to which his nation was a party would be an improvement in military jus-

[38] I.e., excluding for the moment the possibility that selective conscientious objection could be granted as an *accommodation* to limit the burdens of war. This was option 3 above.

tice. (For example, a defense against a command to use many of the forms of gas or micro-biological warfare.) There are principled reasons for these defenses; they would not simply be an easement of the burdens of obedience for men strongly opposed to some command or tactic. Moreover, such an ingredient in the procedures and decisions of Courts Martial would allow, in some measure, at least, for the growth through case-law of what we do actually regard as rightful or wrongful in war in response to the claim that the order was for the defendant an *inherently* immoral one.

This is only an analogy; crucial differences between defenses against a charge of disobedience in war and recognizing or assessing claims to particular-war objection will have to be brought out. But the foregoing may be a helpful analogy. The differences are that in claims to exemption from the liability of combatant service on grounds of selective conscientious objection the claimant would not be attempting to demonstrate that the war is *in fact* in violation of international law or inherently wrongful in its conduct, nor would he bear the burden of proving that the "laws of war" to which he makes appeal do have in international law the construction he places upon them. Nor would a competent review panel have a duty to make a determination concerning such alleged findings of fact and of law or right. Instead, the claimant would have to show that, beyond the conscientious moral/political nature of his objection, these are his terms of reference, that his conscience has been formed in these terms, and that he cannot participate in a particular war because it is his conscientious belief that the war violates canons of conduct clearly governing nations at war. The panel would have the duty of determining that these are his reasons and that the claimant's conscience has in fact been formed to this sort of objection and not as an excuse for claiming exemption that is actually based on general opposition to the course of the nation's foreign policy or to the judgment that resort to military force was required by this policy in this instance. The claimant would not simply be asserting, nor would a review panel probe his conscience to find out *only* how deeply he feels his conviction, that the nation should not "go down a particular valley" in the political encounters taking place in the world.

His case would not be *wholly* unlike that of the universal pacifist who dissents, as it were, "from the history of nations; his position does not single out his own country for adverse judgment," [39] or this war and not others. True, the selective objector singles out a particular war and not all wars, and he singles out his own country in this war for special rebuke and perhaps not others equally. Still he dissents not from the

[39] Donald A. Giannella: Religious Liberty, Nonestablishment and Doctrinal Development, Part I, "The Religious Liberty Guarantee," *Harvard Law Review*, Vol. 80, No. 7 (May, 1967), 1415.

particular resort to war as such, but from this particular sort of war as a part of the history of warfare and of the history of nations. While he bears the burden of rebuking this particular war and not others or more than others, and of rebuking his nation's war in this particular case more than others, he could gain no standing to enter conscientious objection with any claim to exemption on grounds that single out the entire justice of his own nation's cause in a particular war or the recent course of his nation's foreign policy which later seemed to require a resort to military force. It is the latter and not the former claim that would seem to be indistinguishable from strongly-held political opposition—which belongs to the history of political debate, to the forum of political debate, to the history of democratic determination of national policy by established procedures, and to the history of continuing dissent (from which no man should dissent).

Under the proposed system of selective objection I see no reason why conscientious objection to certain modes of warfare (such as nuclear) might not be allowable grounds (although I myself do not believe a particular weapon-system is the mode of warfare censured on just-war principles). This would certainly become a ground if there were international agreement proscribing the use of nuclear weapons to which one's nation was a party. There would be another arguable ground, under conditions of a supposable particular war, if there is "customary international law" proscribing *first* use of nuclear weapons. But these and other cases I have given are only illustrations. The point is to link exemptible cases with the formation of conscience by reference to ethico-political agreements in the international system to which the nations are parties. In the case of claimants and review panels under the proposed scheme (much more readily than in the analogy I used to defenses in military courts) it is possible to anticipate that, upon claimant's reference to the "laws of humanity" and to something he believes *inherently* wrongful in war on which there is no clear international convention, there would be developed a body of case-law and precedents exhibiting our agreement as a people concerning inhumanity and injustice in war sufficient, at least, for us to be willing to grant exemption from military service to any man who conscientiously believes that a particular war violates man in these particular respects. Again, there would be no burden of showing or of reviewing whether findings of fact or of international law or of a true and actionable universal justice are sufficient to sustain the claimant's judgment, but only a showing that his conscientious objection had in fact these terms of reference.

One thing more should, in conclusion, be observed. It has sometimes been proposed that one "chamber" of the United Nations should be directly elected by the people of the nations, who as entities and actors in the international system of nations would continue to be "represented" in the other "chamber." This would be a step toward achieving an international legislative authority, radically altering the present structure of the United Nations which is carefully erected upon the nation-state system. The same thing can generally be said of the World Court, which serves to interpret the meaning and force of treaties among the nation-states. Even when a nation agrees to compulsory adjudication before the Court, this can be rescinded, even as a decision to act through the United Nations is a national decision. The proposal that one "chamber" of the United Nations represent people and not the nations is an attempt to envision how the nation-state system is going to be able to fetch forth from itself something more than the nation-state system, namely a genuinely public world authority approaching a legislature for mankind.

There is a comparable structural problem in the world *juridical* order. How is the nation-state system going to fetch forth from itself, by the action of nations, a juridical order and international law that is founded in more than agreements between nations and their willingness case by case to abide by these conventions? The proposed scheme of selective objection might be a small step toward making the agreements between states concerning what is rightful and wrongful in war *the law of the land* in the sense of the people's reference to them and not simply the government's. There would be no international tribunal rendering judgment upon the claims of consciences who in the cause of humanity make reference to international agreements and law; such courts would still hand down judgment upon states and treaties, etc. There would, in fact, be forthcoming from review boards acting within the body politic *no* findings of fact or law or justice upon the claims of humanity at work in the conscience of claimants. In fact, the contrary would be the case. In particular-war objection as with objection to participation in war in any form, it would still hold true that "if the government refrains from compelling a person to participate in war over his conscientious objection, it does not thereby accept the individual's judgment on the moral question." [40] The reason it does not do this is that *government,* even in its decisions to resort to military force, is a moral act (strange as this may seem to a typically modern mind).

By enacting the proposed system of selective conscientious objection, however, we would at least have taken the step of saying that a man who forms his conscience in terms of *jus gentium,* and not only in terms of his conscience's own inner demands or in terms of political disagreement with his nation's policy, may have a case in the body politic for exemption from participation in a particular war which, he judges in these terms, is being disposed wrongfully by the country's political leaders in the exercise of their proper authority to decide to go down one "valley"

[40] John H. Mansfield, in *Religion and the Public Order,* p. 39.

rather than another in today's world. This would mean to introduce into the body politic some recognition of the transcendent claims of the person and of humanity as these have taken and are taking specifiable form in the international juridical order. This would be the state's acknowledgment of some transcendence over its particular decisions on the part of this juridical order, resident within its own body politic, even when it does not agree with or think it possible to act in accord with these claims. This would exert some influence on the state's action in shoring up and keeping in repair, up-dating and improving, those conventions and agreements in which it expresses its sense, as an actor in the nation-state system, of the agreements as to justice which are to the world's common good. I should think that a *conscientious* "conscientious objector" would not want his objection to count for less than this, or for exemption to be allowed him as a political easement or because only he knows, or says that he knows, that he represents a higher justice.

PART TWO

The Morality of War

CHAPTER 6

Justice in War*

Question: How do porcupines make love?
Answer: Carefully!
This is a parable of the nations in a multi-national world. They can't get along with and they can't get along without one another. They make love and reach settlements, or they make war when they cannot reach or postpone settlements—all, carefully!

There is nothing more like a pacifist than a believer in massive deterence: *both* think it possible to banish the use of force from human history before banishing the porcupine nation-states from off this planet. To them may be added what Walter Lippman called the "war *whoop*" party in this country, which thinks we won't ever need to use nuclear weapons if only we say loudly enough that we are going to. So do we as a people—whether by confidence in moral suasion and the omnicompetence of negotiation or by confidence in our deterrent technology or by confidence in our superior bluffing ability—avoid facing up to the moral economy governing an actual *use* of the weapons we possess. With peace and the nation-state system as our premises, we have designed a war to end all war: God may let us have it.

Since, however, the porcupine-nations are unlikely soon to be banished, since they are armed with massive nuclear weapons, and since somewhere, sometime, a nation is likely to find itself so vitally challenged

* First appeared in *New Wine*, Vol. II, No. 3 (Spring, 1964), pp. 21–25, published by the Westminster Fellowship, University of North Carolina, Chapel Hill, N.C., and in *A Study of Morals and the Nuclear Program*, Headquarters Field Command, Defense Atomic Support Agency, Sandria Base, Albuquerque, New Mexico, 1964, pp. 23–39.

that it will believe that even in the atomic era war can be an instrument of its justice, we are today forced to reexamine an ancient set of teachings which many people thought was out-of-date. This is the doctrine of the "just war," or the morality governing a resort to arms which is only an elaboration of the morality governing the use of power generally.

One of the "tests" in this body of teachings about the morality of warfare is the principle of "proportionate grave reason," or the justification of one good or evil effect only by weighing the greater good or lesser evil of the other effects let loose in the world. This is a test in terms of consequences, and this criterion has been the focus of significant developments in recent years both in Christian analysis, Protestant and Roman Catholic, and in the Communist theory of "just war." [1]

In this chapter, however, I want to deal with the *origin* and the *meaning* of another criterion for the morality of war's conduct. It is a more intrinsic one, having to do with the justice or injustice of an *act* of war, considered apart from its consequences. In the course of tracing its origin, the systematic meaning of "just conduct" in war will be exhibited. This is the distinction between *legitimate* and *illegitimate* military actions. This distinction cuts across all distinctions among weapons systems and applies to them all, even though it is nuclear weapons that have decisively raised the question whether there are just and unjust acts of war by raising the question whether these particular weapons can possibly be used in a just manner. To learn the meaning of "justice in war" (and its origin out of love-informed-reason) will be to learn what it means to say, in connection with military policy, that the end does not justify the means and that it can never be right to do wrong for the sake of some real or supposed good.

The western theory of the just war originated, not primarily from considerations of abstract or "natural" justice, but from the interior of the ethics of Christian love, or what John XXIII termed "social charity." It was a work of charity for the Good Samaritan to give help to the man who fell among thieves. But one step more, it may have been a work of charity for the inn-keeper to hold himself ready to receive beaten and wounded men, and for him to have conducted his business so that he was solvent enough to extend credit to the Good Samaritan. By another step it would have been a work of charity, and not of justice alone, to maintain and serve in a police patrol on the Jericho road to prevent such things from happening. By yet another step, it might well be a work of charity to resist, by force of arms, any external aggression against the social order that maintains the police patrol along the road to Jericho. This means that, where the enforcement of an ordered community is not effectively present, it may be a work of justice and a work of social

---

[1] See Chap. 4, pp. 87–8 above and Chap. 10, pp. 189–191 below.

charity to resort to other available and effective means of resisting injustice: what do you think Jesus would have made the Samaritan do if he had come upon the scene while the robbers were still at their fell work?

Now, I am aware that this is no proper way to interpret a parable of Jesus. Yet, these several ways of retelling the parable of the Good Samaritan quickly exhibit something that is generally true about the teachings of Jesus—namely, that by deed and word he showed the individual the meaning of being perfectly ready to have the will of God reign and God's mercy shed abroad by his life and actions. These versions quickly exhibit how a social ethic emerged from Christian conscience formed by this revelation, and what the early Christians carried with them when they went out into the world to borrow, and subsequently to elevate and refine, Stoic concepts of natural justice.

While Jesus taught that a disciple in his own case should turn the other cheek, he did not enjoin that his disciples should lift up the face of another oppressed man for *him* to be struck again on *his* other cheek. It is no part of the work of charity to allow this to continue to happen. Instead, it is the work of love and mercy to deliver as many as possible of God's children from tyranny, and to protect from oppression, if one can, as many of those for whom Christ died as it may be possible to save. When choice *must* be made between the perpetrator of injustice and the many victims of it, the latter may and should be preferred—even if effectively to do so would require the use of armed force against some evil power. This is what I mean by saying that the justice of sometimes resorting to armed conflict originated in the interior of the ethics of Christian love.

Thus Christian conscience shaped itself for effective action. It allowed even the enemy to be killed only because military personnel and targets stood objectively there at the point where intersect the needs and claims of many more of our fellow men. For their sakes the bearer of hostile force may and should be repressed. Thus, participation in war (and before that, the use of any form of force or resistance) was justified as, in this world to date, an unavoidable necessity if we are not to omit to serve the needs of men in the only concrete way possible, and maintain a just endurable order in which they may live.

There was another side to this coin. The justification of participation in conflict at the same time severely limited war's conduct. What justified also limited! Since it was for the sake of the innocent and helpless of earth that the Christian first thought himself obliged to make war against an enemy whose objective deeds had to be stopped, since only for their sakes does a Christian justify himself in resisting by any means even an enemy-neighbor, he could never proceed to kill equally innocent people as a means of getting at the enemy's forces. Thus was twin-born the justification of war and the limitation which surrounded non-combatants with moral immunity from direct attack. Thus was twin-born the distinction between combatant and non-combatant in all Christion reflection about the morality of warfare. This is the distinction between *legitimate* and *illegitimate* military objectives. The same considerations which justify killing the bearer of hostile force by the same stroke prohibit non-combatants from ever being directly attacked with deliberate intent.

This understanding of the moral economy in the just use of political violence contains, then, two elements: (1) a specific justification for sometimes killing another human being; and (2) severe and specific restrictions upon anyone who is under the hard necessity of doing so. Both are exhibited in the use of force proper to the domestic police power. It is never just for a policeman to forget the distinction between the bearer of hostile force who must be stopped and the "innocent" bystanders (no matter how mixed-up they are). He may hit some innocent party accidentally; but it would never be right for him to "enlarge the target" and deliberately and directly kill any number in the crowd on Times Square *as a means* of preventing some criminal from injurious action. Nor do we allow the police the right to get a criminal's children into their power as hostages and threaten to kill them in order to "deter" him. Yet the source of the justification of such limited use of force is evidently to be found in "social charity." This is clear from the fact that a man, who in one situation could legitimately be killed if that were the only way to save other lives, would himself in another situation be saved at grave risk to the lives of the very same policemen—i.e. if that man alone is in need of rescue because he has gone off his rocker and is threatening to jump from the ledge of a building twenty stories up.

This is the moral economy which regulates the use of force *within* political communities, where it is both *morally* and *legally* binding. This same moral economy is *morally* if *not* legally binding upon the use of force between nations. It will become *both* legally and morally binding if ever there is world law and order abolishing the nation-state system. War may *in fact* be more than an extension of politics in another form, but the *laws* of war are only an extension, where war is the only available means, of the rules governing any use of political power. We are not apt ever to "abolish war" if we keep on denying that there is a morality *of* war, which is only a concise summary of right and charitable reason in the simultaneous *justification* and the *limitation* of the use of power necessary to the political life of mankind.

To summarize the theory of just or civilized conduct in war as this was developed within Christendom: love for neighbors threatened by violence, by aggression, or tyranny, provided the grounds for admitting the legitimacy of the use of military force. Love for neighbors at the same time required that such force should be limited. The Christian is commanded to do anything a realistic love commands (and so sometimes he must fight). But this also prohibits him from doing anything for which such love can find no justification (and so he can never approve of un-limited attack upon any human life not closely cooperating in or directly engaged in the force that ought to be repelled).

This means that nuclear war against the civil centers of an enemy population, the A-Bomb on Hiroshima, or obliteration bombing per-petrated by both sides in World War II were all alike immoral acts of war; and that Christians can support such actions only by dismissing the entire western tradition of civilized warfare that was originally born in the interior of that supreme compassion which always seeks if pos-sible to wound none whom by His wounds Christ died to save. This theory of just and severely limited conflict has guided action and served as the regulative norm for military conduct for nineteen centuries. If a man cannot irresponsibly forsake those who need to be saved from an oppressor, neither can he directly and indiscriminately attack innocent people in order to restrain that same oppressor. If to protect his own children he should resist an aggressor, that gives him no leave directly to intend and directly to do the death of the aggressor's children as a means of dissuading him from his evil deeds.

If the just-war theory did not already exist, Christians would have to invent it. If in the fullness of God's time and the emptiness of ours, Christ came into our present world (instead of when he did), then would the just-war theory still have to be produced. Then would Christian thought bring together the notions of justice lying around in the Renais-sance and the Enlightenment (if you can imagine these periods without their Christian background) as St. Augustine and other great Christian thinkers brought together the notions of justice lying around in the Graeco-Roman world, galvanized them into action, elevated and firmed them up, illumined and sensitized the justices of men to produce severer restrictions upon the forms of human conflct which the Christian or any truly just man can ever believe justified. Had I the space I could derive the same moral restrictions upon the use of force from the ethical per-spectives of the Old Testament. These would have been productive of a remarkably similar just-war theory, had Judaism been the predominant influence in western civilization.

I can only briefly indicate that this distinction between combatant and non-combatant never supposed that the latter were to be roped off like ladies at a medieval tournament. The fact of twilight, as Dr. John-son said, does not mean you cannot tell day from night. So with non-combatant status, and the difference between discriminant and indis-criminant acts of war. Moreover, it was never supposed that non-com-batants were immune from all damage but only from direct, intended attack. The range of indirect, unintended, collateral damage might be quite large. Moreover, closeness of civilian cooperation, in contrast to some degree of remoteness from the force used, was sufficient to bring the civilian under the category of "combatant." But these qualifications were never the same as "enlarging the target" to include the whole of civil society as a legitimate military objective, directly damaging whole peoples in order to get at their leaders and fighters. Translated into modern terminology, this means that just or limited warfare must be *forces*-counter-*forces* warfare, and that *people*-counter-*people* warfare is wholly unjust.

At stake in preserving this distinction is not only whether warfare can be kept barely civilized, but whether civilization can be kept from barbarism. Can civilization survive in the sense that we can continue in political and military affairs to *act civilized,* or must we accept total war on grounds that clearly indicate that we have already become *totalitarian* —by reducing everyone without discrimination and everyone to the whole extent of his being to a mere means of achieving political and military goals? Even if an enemy government says that is all its people are, a Christian or any truly just man cannot agree to this.

Now pacifism teaches people what massive deterrence is built on. It "teaches people to make no distinction between the shedding of innocent blood and the shedding of any human blood. And in this way pacifism has corrupted enormous numbers of people who will not act according to its tenets. They become convinced that a number of things are wicked which are not; hence, seeing no way of avoiding 'wickedness,' they set no limits to it." [2] That is to say, pacifism teaches people to believe that there is no *significant moral* difference, except in the *ends* sought, between murder and killing in war. It seems incredible to accept that anyone really seriously believes that soldiers are only "licensed murderers" and that murderers are only unlicensed soldiers. Yet, at the operational level where the thoughts of a multitude of human hearts shall today be revealed, this seems to be what it comes down to. The desperate attempt to maintain the current state of non-war by indiscriminately aiming weapons at people, and a fervent attempt to abolish war by declaring it in any shape to be a wickedness to which no moral limits can or should be applied, lie down peaceably together in the declaration by both parties that there is no moral economy that should or can govern the use of armed violence.

It has certainly to be admitted that all the wars of the past have been conducted more or less justly, more or less unjustly; but attacks on civilian life have been *peripheral* even if often carried out. In former ages

[2] Walter Stein, ed.: *Nuclear Weapons and Christian Conscience* (London: Merlin Press, 1961), p. 56.

it simply took too much muscle to fight war unlimitedly. You will understand the point on which present-day politics squirms, and military strategy squirms, if you see that in the nuclear age the nations are trying to make *unjust war* the *central war,* and to *base* strategy on the deliberate aim of attacking cities. They will never succeed in basing politics or purposive military strategy on such an inherently irrational and immoral plan of war.

They will never succeed in making war "carefully" by such planned disregard for the moral economy governing the use of force as an extension of the moral economy governing any purposive use of political power. It seemed reasonable for President Kennedy to say in his speech at Frankfurt, Germany, "The United States will risk its cities to defend yours because we need your freedom to protect ours." [3] This seems reasonable because the risks are still in the state of non-war. The *plus* in front of that policy statement is within a parenthesis preceded by a *minus* sign, as shall be revealed if we ever factor the equation. Then the pluses will all become minuses. For it cannot make sense for the President to say, "The United States is *now,* this moment, accepting the destruction of its cities in order to defend yours, which are also now being destroyed along with the Russian cities, because we need your freedom to protect ours." If one perseveres in thinking the thinkable (because it is the actual, present) state of non-war all the way through to an actual war conducted in the fashion apparently planned, he will have thought an unthinkable and a politically undoable action. He will have factored the massive deterrence—or retaliation—equation, and found that the pluses within the parenthesis all become minuses.

The traditional teaching about the conduct of war taught us that it is never right to intend or do wrong that good may come of it. Nuclear weapons have only added to this perennial truth a morally insignificant footnote: it can never do *any good* to intend or do wrong that good may come of it.[4]

[3] *The New York Times,* June 26, 1963.
[4] In Chap. 11, "The Limits of Nuclear War," pp. 248–58 below, I argue that deterrence sufficient to keep war limited and just need *not* rest on the intention to do murder. This is a significant correction of the treatment of the morality of deterrence in my book *War and the Christian Conscience* (Durham, N.C.: Duke University Press, 1961).

CHAPTER 7

The Case for Making
"Just War" Possible*

A recent editorial in *worldview*[1] expresses evident dissatisfaction with political "realism" and "prudential" ethics as by no means an adequate contribution of religious ethics to politics in our times. It continues by noting that the nature of modern weapons has given religious pacifists powerful new arguments that have not been adequately answered. It is symptomatic of the ills of religious ethics today, and of political and military doctrine, that the editorial writer gets from the limit he places on "realism" and "prudential" politics to the need for reopening a discussion of pacifism by a quite uncritical rejection of the only genuine alternative there is. He states as a conclusion no one today would think of challenging, that "previous norms for the 'just' war have, for all practical purposes, been rendered obsolete"; and demands that religious leaders find out quickly whether they have anything to say about the destructiveness of modern warfare and not "salve" their "conscience by repeating the ancient rules for a 'just' war—rules which have

* This and the following chapter first appeared in John Bennett, ed.: *Nuclear Weapons and the Conflict of Conscience* (New York: Charles Scribner's Sons, 1962), pp. 143–170, copyright © 1962. The present chapter was a paper prepared for a Special Advanced Seminar of the Council on Religion and International Affairs (then the Church Peace Union), meeting at Highland Park, Illinois, 1960.

[1] "The Pacifist Question," *worldview*, Vol. III, No. 7–8 (July-August 1960), 1.

as much relationship to an all-out modern war as such a war would have to the bow and arrow." [2]

Now obviously, you cannot indict the concept of the just war for drawing up a moral indictment of all-out nuclear warfare as intrinsically immoral; nor should anyone simply dismiss the distinction between the just and the unjust conduct of war because men and nations have the power (and are in fact planning) to violate this distinction. Too frequently the just-war theory is said to be assuredly false or irrelevant or outmoded by people who would not confront the actual policies of their nation with these criteria even if proved true. Translate the traditional terminology distinguishing between just and unjust warfare into contemporary language distinguishing between counter-*forces* and counter-*people* warfare. At once it will be seen that the position that counter-forces warfare alone can be justified for arming the political purposes of a nation may reasonably be proposed as a truth to be acknowledged in military doctrine. It is certainly not irrelevant or anachronistic to say this; and the consciences of men may be not "salved" but awakened if this is said clearly by the moralist and, in collaboration with competent weapons-analysis, concretely *to the point* of the dilemma we confront in modern warfare. The present chapter undertakes an initial step in this direction; first explaining *why,* under the shaping influence of Christian ethics, criteria for just conduct were enunciated by the theory of civilized warfare in the West, and then proceeding to clarify the exact *meaning* of these criteria.

I

It is convenient to begin with a quotation from a Roman Catholic, who is perhaps a "just war" pacifist, concerning "thirteenth century principles . . . as a minimal statement of the Christian ethic," not exhaustive or preclusive of a "higher aim." These principles, writes Robert Hovda, "made an exception (that's what it was) to the commandment 'Thou shalt not kill' in the case of a soldier or other military personnel on the opposing (clearly unjust) side in a war. The basis for this exception has been the fact that such a one is cooperating directly in the unjust action of his government and that he is therefore materially if not formally 'guilty.' Generally, moralists extended this exception to include other citizens who were cooperating *directly* in the war effort." [3]

---

[2] Cf. editorial, *worldview*, Vol. II, No. 6 (June 1959), 2: ". . . it is more and more agreed that the concept of a 'just war' is an anachronism."

[3] *worldview*, Vol. III, No. 7–8 (July-August 1960), 8.

However, it is only when the commandment "Thou shalt not kill" is viewed *legalistically,* and only when the actions that are licit or illicit under it are viewed *externally,* that the Christians who formulated the just-war theory can be said to have made, in regard to killing another human being, one, single, clearly defined and limited *exception,* and nothing more.

Those persons "formally" directing or participating in the military forces, or "materially" yet closely cooperating in the force that should be repelled and can only be repelled by violent means, these persons are—this theory states—legitimate objects of *direct* violent repression. The justification of warfare and of Christian participation in it was not actually an exception (certainly not an arbitrary one, or a compromise from the purity of Christian ethics), but instead an *expression* of the Christian understanding of moral and political responsibility. This conclusion was not simply the result of importing into Christian ethics certain conceptions of natural justice from Stoic and other ancient philosophies. Nor did the theory always simply result in a bifurcation of public morality, based on justice, from private morality, based on love—that love which required the early Christians to withdraw altogether from the resistance of evil by political and military means. Instead, intrinsic within the new foundation laid by Christ for the entire conduct of his disciples was the conviction that love and mercy are the fulfilling of the law, of natural justice, and of the meaning expressed in the commandment, "Thou shalt not kill." When in doubt as to the actual action required by this command, one had simply to consult again the requirements of compassion incarnating itself in serving the concrete needs of men. Therefore in the ancient theory of just war, Christian conscience took the form of allowing any killing at all of men for whom Christ died only because military personnel were judged to stand, factually and objectively, at the point where, as combatants, resistance to them was judged to be necessary in responsibility to many other neighbors. The combatant stood at the point of intersection of many primary claims upon the Christian's life with and for his fellow man.

This still included undiminished fellow humanity with the enemy soldier; yet he was not the only one to take into account. The claims of many others had also to be acknowledged and realistically served in the only way possible. In this world and not some other, faithfulness to all our fellow men, and not only to the enemy, must somehow be enacted. Jesus did not teach that his disciples should life up the face of another oppressed man to be struck again on the other cheek. Out of neighbor-regarding love for one's fellow men, preferential decision among one's neighbors may and can and should be made. For love's sake (the very principle of the prohibition of killing), and not only for the sake of an abstract justice sovereign over the political realm in separation from the private, Christian thought and action was driven to posit this single "exception" (an exception only when externally viewed): that forces should be repelled and the bearers and close cooperators in military force should be directly repressed, by violent means if necessary, lest many more of God's little ones should be irresponsibly forsaken and lest they suffer more harm than need be. This, then, was not really an "exception," certainly not an arbitrary one; but a determinate expression of justice and mercy. It was an *expression* of the Christian understanding of political responsibility in terms of neighbor-regarding love. It was, and is, a regrettably necessary but still a necessary and morally justifiable expression of our being with and for men, as Christ was *the* man *for* other men. Christian love was the influence that shaped this conclusion. Therefore, the just-war theory states not what *may* but what *should* be done. This does not preclude a "higher aim" in personal relations if here one's own goods and life alone are at stake. It does not even preclude higher aims in politics, since as Augustine wrote, "it is a higher glory still to slay war itself with the word than men with the sword, and to procure and maintain peace by peace, not by war." But there can be no higher aim in military affairs, weapons-policy, or among the goals of military establishments, except of course the prevention or deterrence of war by means it would be just to fight with.

This was the origin of the judgment that war can on occasion be justifiable in Christian conscience, and military forces or personnel (and close cooperators in mounting the opposing military force) be legitimate objects of direct attack. By the same stroke definite limits were placed upon the conduct of war by surrounding *non-combatants* with moral immunity from *direct* attack. Thus, a love-inspired justice going into concrete action fashioned rules for practical conduct—at once justifying war and limiting it. The Christian is commanded to do anything a realistic love commands, and he is prohibited from doing anything for which such love can find no justification. If combatants may and should be resisted directly by violent means to secure a desired and desirable victory, this also requires that non-combatants be never directly assaulted even to that same end. When out of Christian love or from definitions of justice inspired by love it was concluded that the death of an enemy might be directly intended and directly done for the sake of all God's other children within a just or a just endurable political order by which God governs and preserves human life in a fallen world, this also meant that such love could never find sufficient reason for directly intending and directly doing the death of the enemy's children in order to dissuade him from his evil deeds.

Thus, western political thought did not until recently stand clothed only in an "aggressor-defender" concept of warfare, nor did it justify any sort of reply believed to be technically required to stop an aggressor. Warlike action was not justified, until recently, merely by a calculation of the future consequences and choice of the lesser evil in aiming at hypothetical results. Of course, no right action aims at *greater* evil in the results. But this does not mean that every action that prudently aims at good or less evil consequences is therefore right and is to be done. There is also a morality of means, of conduct, or of actions to be put forth. Since at least everyone seeks peace and desires justice, the *ends* for which wars may legitimately be fought are not nearly so important in the theory of the just war as is the moral and political wisdom contained in its reflection upon the *conduct* or means of warfare. Unless there is a morality applicable to instruments of war and intrinsically limiting its conduct, then we must simply admit that war has no limits— since these can hardly be derived from "peace" as the "final cause" of just wars. Certainly Christian ethics did not first concern itself with estimating the consequences. Instead, out of responsibility *to* God *for* all men before God, Christians sought to discover the meaning of just and loving *present* action toward them. Since it was for the sake of the innocent and helpless ones that the Christian first thought himself obliged to make war against an enemy whose objective deeds were judged to be evil and in need of restraint by any just and feasible means, how could he ever conclude from this that it was permitted him to destroy some "innocents" for the sake of other "innocents" closer to him in natural or social affinity? Thus was twin-born the justification of war and its limitation by the moral immunity of non-combatants (and the immunity of *remote* material cooperators in the force which should and had to be repelled).

This states *why* the theory of justifiable warfare was developed in the Christian West.[4] Whether this theory has any longer any bearing

---

[4] Here one must simply voice sharp disagreement with Hans J. Morgenthau ("The Demands of Prudence," *worldview*, Vol. III, No. 6 [June, 1960], pp. 6–7). It is not the case that "the natural aspirations proper to the political sphere—and there is no difference in kind between domestic and international politics—contravene by definition the demands of the Christian ethics," or that "it is *a priori* impossible for political man to be at the same time a good politician—complying with the rules of political conduct—and to be a good Christian—complying with the demands of Christian ethics." The just-war theory bridged the "unbridgeable gulf" Morgenthau thinks he sees. Its genesis shows that, as Christian ethics goes into actual practice, it fashions and shapes itself into principles for the direction of concrete action. Of course, no proposal for the *direction* or guidance of action can be a simple factual summary of the context in which that action is to be put forth. Only for the most abstract versions of natural law, however, is it true to say: "The gap between the rational postulates of natural law and the contingencies of the concrete situation within which man must act and judge is just as wide as the gulf which separates the demands of Christian ethics from the rules of political action, In truth, . . . both gaps are identical." If that is the meaning of the natural law, then it must be insisted that the theory of just conduct in war had nothing to do with it, but arose rather from a concretely

upon the conduct of nations is, however, a question that cannot be answered without first gaining a more complete and accurate understanding of the meaning of the norms expressed in terms of the ancient theory. Nothing can be more irresponsible, and less conducive to disciplined reflection in an area today sorely in need of being subjected to rational control, than to dismiss the just-war theory on a mistaken understanding of it—as often happens today, from different points of view, by political realists and by resurgent pacifism. To come to terms with these terms will be our next undertaking.

II

In order to comprehend the meaning of "non-combatancy," it is necessary to understand a number of primary notions or distinctions fundamental in the traditional moral rules for the just conduct of war. The following may be cited as most important: (1) The distinction between "formal" and only "material," and between "close" and "remote," cooperation in the force that should be repelled. (2) The distinction between the "guilty" who are legitimate targets of violent repression and the "innocent" who are not. These are very misleading terms, since their meaning is exhaustively stated under the first contrast, and is reducible to degrees of actual participation in hostile force. (3) The distinction between "direct" and "indirect" attack. It was never supposed that non-combatants were morally immune from indirect injury or death on however colossal a scale, if there is proportionate grave reason for doing this. This has sometimes been expressed by saying that death to the

---

oriented Christian love in-principling itself in responsible ways to serve actual man within the fabric of political life and institutions. Not without further examination should we agree with Morgenthau that, in the political sphere, man "is precluded from acting morally" and "the best he can do is to minimize the intrinsic immorality of the political act" (by choosing "the lesser evil"), or that "the best man is capable of is to be guided by the vision of a life lived in compliance with the Christian code and to narrow the gap between his conduct and that code." All this presupposes an asserted gap—between Christian ethics and politics, or between natural law and political decision—which the criteria of just action in war asserts it has at least partly bridged—not leaving the entire leap to technical reason or to that prudence to which Morgenthau appeals. Finally, it should be pointed out that Morgenthau's view that the gap can be cut down, not by any shaping of principles of political conduct, but only by the strategy of choosing the lesser evil, under the "vision" of a life lived otherwise, places him in the position of not being able even to understand correctly John Courtney Murray's remark that nuclear weapons are "from the moral point of view . . . unshootable." That, he says, is "because of the consequences of shooting them." This chapter will demonstrate that this is only the *last* reason (while a sufficient one) for calling multi-megaton weapons morally unshootable.

innocent may be "permitted" to result "accidentally" from an act of war primarily directed against military forces. But if the word "accident" is used, it is in a philosophical or technical sense, and not with its usual meaning. For the "permitted" killing of non-combatants does not just happen to take place. It is foreknown and foreknown to result as a necessary effect of the same action that causes the death of political leaders or military personnel who are its legitimate targets. This brings us to (4) the analysis of acts of war as (like many other human actions) having double or multiple effects, and to the so-called "rule of double effect." The latter requires that a distinction be made between (a) killing that is directly intended (in the subjective order) and directly done (in the objective, physical order) and (b) killing that is only permitted even if it is *indirectly* done (i.e. also *caused*) by the same action that causes the death of men who are its primary targets. Acts of war which directly intend and directly effect the death of non-combatants are to be classed morally with murder, and are never excusable. If the excuse is that victory requires this, then we would be saying that the end justifies an intrinsically wrong means or that men may be murdered in order to do good. A desired and desirable victory may, however, justify conduct in warfare that causes the death, and is foreknown to cause the death, of non-combatants *indirectly*. This would *not* be directly to do evil that good may come of it. There is a significant moral difference between the destruction in obliteration warfare which is deliberately wanton and murderous, and the destruction and death that is among the tragic consequences of counter-*forces* warfare. This distinction is not determined by the amount of the devastation or the number of deaths, but by the direction of the action itself, i.e. by what is deliberately intended and directly done. This permits there to be foreseeable evil consequences acceptable among the multiple effects of military action.

Whether these latter effects are acceptable, or not, must be assessed by prudential reason balancing good and evil, or lesser evil, consequences. But first one should be able to discriminate between acts of murder and acts of war. Indiscriminate bombing or counter-people warfare stands indicted as intrinsically wrong. In this sense, multimegaton weapons are "morally unshootable." To use them indiscriminately or deliberately against *society*-targets would be the direct murder of the innocent as a means of victory. This, however, does not condemn every enlargement of legitimate military targets in the course of weapons-development, much less the *unavoidable* enlargement of the indirect effects of counter-forces warfare. Multi-megaton weapons may also be "unshootable" in this second sense: because we are, in the last place, forced to conclude that there can be no greater evil than the *consequences* of using them. Therefore, after having permitted and prohibited actions by an analysis of the intrinsic nature of each, it has yet to be determined whether military action lawful in itself should actually be done. This requires (5) a prudential estimate of the consequences to see whether there is in the good effect sufficiently grave reason for also indirectly producing the evil effect. Thus, the traditional morality of war locates in the last place a calculus of probability and a morality of the ends in view. In the end, proper place should be given to sitting down to count the costs of a proposed action. While an effect cannot justify any means, one effect can justify another effect because of the greater good or "lesser evil" in one than in the other.

In recent years, bellicists and pacifists have united to declare that every act of war as such is intrinsically immoral. These alike declare the just-war theory no longer applicable—bellicists, to the end of engaging in war without moral limitations; pacifists, to withdraw from it altogether; and many so-called Christian realists, with moderation placed only upon the political objectives for which, they say, wars should ever be fought (and *through* the ends, upon the means). In order for either of these parties to make a beginning toward reaching one of these conclusions, it is first of all necessary for them to misunderstand the criteria for the conduct of war and the rules of civilized warfare. Terms are used imprecisely in order to discredit the quite precise notions of the moral doctrine of war that has prevailed in western history. Therefore, the concept of "non-combatancy" has not been proved wrong by sound moral or political or military analysis. It has been rejected before having been understood. Thus, the traditional analysis of the morality of war has been thoughtlessly rejected, and the necessary totality of modern war largely conceded.

How can the "facts" of warfare between modern industrial and metropolitan societies prove that there are now no non-combatants when this conclusion depends in every respect upon whether we have in our heads such notions as the moral significance of the degrees of proximity or remoteness of cooperation in unjust aggression, and the distinction between direct and indirect killing? Too often in Protestant and in secular writings on the subject of morality and war it is also erroneously supposed that *direct* killing is the only kind of killing that one undertakes to justify in a doctrine of war; and so it has come to be an unquestioned maxim that, for war to be justly conducted, non-combatants have to be clearly and in detail distinguishable from combatants. Moreover, we would have to be sure not only *who* these people are but also that *where* they live is not within or near any legitimate target area, and that none will be slain or injured as an unavoidable indirect consequence of direct military action. As a result of faulty analysis of the morality of war, if today the moral immunity of non-combatants from direct attack is not simply ignorantly ridiculed, the nullity of it is assumed as a premise rather than as a conclusion to be reached by disciplined moral reflection. On this understanding of the matter, any act of war is either an immorality to be done out of military necessity or an immorality never to be done out of Christian love; and there are no significant moral distinctions to be made among warring actions except between those that succeed and those that do not succeed in obtaining victory, or between means that are proportionate and those disproportionate to the end of victory.

Plainly, it is necessary for most people to come to terms again with the terms of the ancient limits of civilized warfare. It is the *concept* of non-combatancy that has first been jettisoned from our minds; and this has happened because the *concept* of degrees of cooperation, the *concept* justifying the repulsion of objectively "guilty" forces as well as those "formally" or personally responsible for their direction, the *concept* of an indirect yet unavoidable and foreknown effect alongside the legitimately intended effects of military action, or the *concept* of double effects flowing from the same neutral or good action as cause, bringing along with the good result also a tragically necessary evil consequence in the limited, not directly intended, yet foreseen destruction of civilian life (still not the same as wholesale murder, nor the same as a single murder)—all these notions have eroded from the minds of men. *This,* then, is the reason we are prey to the illusion that modern industrial society has completely changed the nature of warfare, and not simply that mass defection from sound moral reasoning has rendered wholly inapplicable or indeed senseless any attempt to conduct war in accordance with the carefully constructed concepts of traditional Christian morality.

Of course, non-combatants are not in modern society roped off like spectators at a medieval tournament. In the theory of just war they never had to be. We only have to know *that* there are babies among the civilan population of any enemy nation, we do not even have to know that there are any grown men and women deserving to be classed as non-combatants in order to know *with certainty* that warfare should be force-counter-forces warfare, and calculated attack be limited to legitimate military targets. There are many people, other than infants, going about their little human affairs whom a loving justice should surround with immunity limiting violence; and to know this we do not need to know *who* or *where* they are. This moral limit still holds, even if it had to be admitted that responsible political and military action must now place civilians with their moral immunity from direct attack in far greater danger even in a justly conducted war than ever before in human history, because (it might be asserted) there are many more legitimate targets than ever before and because the firepower of even a just war and the indirect effects of even its right conduct have enormously increased.

III

The difference between justifiable and wholly unjustifiable warfare can perhaps be better grasped from an examination of some current mistakes. In modern warfare, it is said, "all human and material resources are mobilized," and only "small children and the helpless sick and the aged stand outside the war effort. . . . Total war, in this sense of the involvement of the whole nation in it, cannot be avoided if we have a major war at all." [5] Now, who ever defined a "non-combatant" in such a fashion, as one who "stands outside" of any relation to his nation's action? Who ever meant by a non-combatant a person who, to be one, would have to be utterly helpless, and incapable of any activity at all with important results for the common weal? Evident in such an undiscriminating definition of the "involvement" of a whole nation in war is no conception of the significance of degrees of remoteness or closeness of cooperation in a nation's war effort such as was essential in any definition of the moral immunity of non-combatants in the past. The foregoing statement, therefore, constitutes no objection at all to the application of the moral rules of warfare even in the case of two modern industrial societies locked in a war of attrition. Even more can it be said to have no force at all to nullify the distinction between counter-forces and counter-people warfare with present and future weapons which insure that wars will be fought quickly and not out of inventories. That brief period of western history when counter-*factory* warfare was supposed to justify counter-*people* warfare has now come to an abrupt end.

The traditional distinction between combatant and non-combatant, it is asserted, today is "far less clear" than in the past. Evident here is no conception of the fact that, in the moral choice between direct and indirect killing of civilians, or between counter-forces and indiscriminate counter-retaliatory warfare, this distinction *does not need to be clear*. We do not need to know *who* or *where* the non-combatants are in order to know that indiscriminate bombing exceeds the moral limits of warfare that can ever barely be justified. We have only to know *that* there are non-combatants—even "only small children and the helpless sick and aged"—in order to know the basic moral difference between limited and total war.

This same mistake, in my opinion, was made by Professor John Bennett, who ordinarily writes with discernment upon this subject. "It has become increasingly difficult," he writes, "to distinguish in detail

[5] "The Christian Conscience and Weapons of Mass Destruction," The Dun Report of a Special Commission appointed by the Federal Council of the Churches of Christ in America, 1950, pp. 10–11.

between combatants and non-combatants and sometimes the teaching about the just war has been legalistic at this point, if we grant that the use of military force is ever justified at all." [6] That unexamined statement is not worth having; and upon examining it two remarks should be made: (a) *Careful* statements as to the just conduct of war ought not to be dismissed out of hand as "legalistic." (b) To prohibit the *direct* killing (while allowing the *indirect* killing) of non-combatants, it is not at all necessary to distinguish them "in detail." We have only to know that anyone is there—children, the aged, the sick, barbers, cobblers, and Latin school teachers among the people we intend to obliterate by "enlarging the target." We only have to know that there are any civilians, whose lives are made the *intended*, direct object of violence, who are not now closely supporting the military force it would be just and necessary to resist by force limited to this.

A second instance of the misuse of the concept of non-combatancy is to be found in Bennett's correct insistence that the "official scientists" have been morally insensitive in their disregard of the effects of continued nuclear testing upon future generations, and his assertions that, while the Communists may sacrifice people now living to a future goal, we are in danger, by these tests, of sacrificing people yet unborn to present political goals. Whereupon he writes: "I think that the traditional distinction between combatants and non-combatants in war does not fit the present realities, but, on any showing, future generations should be regarded as non-combatants." [7] The assumption of the latter part of this statement seems to be that without revising the rules for the just conduct of war no action could ever be justified which brings about the death of non-combatants, and surely this has helped to produce the disparagement of the concept of non-combatancy in the first part of the statement. However, it was never supposed that non-combatants should be morally immune from being killed, but from being *directly* killed. It cannot be shown that nuclear testing is *intrinsically* wrong simply because there are evils among its effects. Here the question is whether one effect is sufficient to justify another. The question is whether there is proportionately greater good or lesser evil intentionally sought among the effects that can only be secured by testing which also unavoidably permits some grave evil effects to fall upon future generations.

Such is the only justification for most human actions and most of the inventions that have made civilized life possible on this earth. Here there is no question of using persons as a means, or justifying an inherently wrong means because some good may come from it. In general, it

[6] "Theological and Moral Considerations in International Affairs," issued as background paper for the Fifth World Order Study Conference of the National Council of Churches, in Cleveland, 1958.

[7] Letter in *worldview*, Vol. II, No. 11 (Nov. 1959), 7.

is really quite astonishing how American public opinion concentrates upon the moral problem posed by these tests, since a planned policy of nuclear retaliation is much more clearly immoral. The death and devastation contemplated in the case of all-out nuclear war would be both *directly willed* and *directly done* as a means, while the death brought about by nuclear testing *as such* is only *indirectly willed* and *indirectly done* as one among several effects of the tests. The first is murder (to be justified by no calculation of consequences); the second is tragic (probably to be prohibited, if the proportionately greater good or lesser evil expected to result from weapons-tests is not important enough to warrant our accepting the bad effects of testing—and if these cannot be controlled or avoided).

We were told in the Council of Churches' Report we have been analyzing that it is now "practically impossible to distinguish between guilty and innocent. Certainly men who are drafted into uniform may be among the least guilty." [8] Who ever clothed non-combatants with moral immunity from direct attack by first investigating their innocence in the highest subjective and personal sense? Who ever declared combatants (or the "guilty") to be legitimate objects of direct attack or counter-attack simply because, unlike mercenaries in the past or men drafted today into "democratic" armies, they are more personally guilty than the rest of their countrymen? The statement that conscript armies, made up of men who may not wish to kill, are *therefore* made up of men who are not *unjust* aggressors and this gives no one the right to kill them, assumes that the point was to prove the guilt of combatants in a fully personal sense. Against this stands the notion of objective or functional guilt because of status in the forces that should be repelled. Against this stands also the fact that for many centuries after participation in war was said to be justified for Christian conscience, it still was never allowed that, when one's own life or goods alone were at stake, the evil intention of a clearly guilty assailant gave the Christian any right to resist or wound or kill him whom by his wounds and death Christ came to save. No amount or kind of guilt in the fully personal sense as such gave any man the intrinsic right to kill another. Instead, the permission and the duty to do this arose because of the place where the bearer of hostile force stood in relation to God's other children, and to their need to be served by Christians in the existing order of the common life by the maintenance of a tolerable justice for them. Of course, the "formal aggressors" are clearly guilty; the political commanders are among the legitimate targets if one knows who they are and can get at them. But an ordinary soldier's "guilt" is his objective and direct participation in the military offensive that has for love's sake to be repelled; and the "in-

[8] The Dun Report, pp. 10–11.

nocence" of non-combatants means their lack of crucial relation or the remoteness of their cooperation in the prosecution of the war.

This demonstrates, it seems to me, that in rejecting as invalid the quite discriminating concepts of the just-war theory, all too many people have first employed insufficiently articulated terms, or block-buster concepts, all to the end of obliterating the moral wisdom deposited in the traditional view of the morality of war. No wonder, then, that we were morally ready to use blockbusters, and now metropolisbusters, in actual fact! War first became total in the minds of men. Why this happened among religious people, who should have remembered their traditions and who should cultivate conceptual clarity in moral analysis, can perhaps be partly explained by the effort to persuade the pacifists, as World War II approached, that in no way could they avoid "contributing to the war effort." Pacifist Christians may have been wrong in the religious and political judgments they made in refusing direct participation in war; but they were certainly not wrong in discerning a significant distinction between civilian and combatant status. (Pacifists make this distinction *for themselves* and *their own* society, while refusing to make the same necessary distinction between the people and forces of the enemy, which entails acceptance of positive responsibility to resist the latter by military means.) On this distinction hangs the discrimination between war and murder, between limited and unlimited war, between barely civilized and wholly uncivilized, even if technically efficient, military action.

At stake also in this discrimination is not only the defense of civilization against total war, but against totalitarianism as well. In stating so blandly that practically no one "stands outside" the war effort and no one is "innocent" and there is no one who may not be directly killed for some good cause, have we not in principle included practically everyone, to the whole extent of his being, within the direction of the common life toward political goals? When men wage wars, if they do not maintain a relation *of non-relation,* or remote relation, between the civilian life of a nation and its fighters, they have already in principle totally politicized human life. So much is at stake in restoring the laws of civilized warfare, of fighting, if we must, in a just manner for the preservation of just orders of life. Anything else is technically efficient barbarism, no matter what "values" may be our objectives or the names we use, like fig leaves, to cover our unseemly acts.

The Dun Report which we have been following, rejects, of course, "war in which all moral restraints are thrown aside and all the purposes of the community are fully controlled by sheer military expedience." The question is whether the "moral restraints" not to be thrown aside have sufficient substance and careful enough articulation to provide any guidance for the military conduct of nations. A consequentialist ethics limits behavior only by subordinating it to limited and just ends. "Moral restraints" are placed mainly upon wanton killing, on savagery that kills without reckoning. Thus, it is pointed out that some methods of fighting "cause more pain and maiming without commensurate military decisiveness. Some are more indiscriminate . . . We cannot, therefore, be released from the responsibility for doing no more hurt than must be." Now, we have seen that the church's teaching about morality and warfare calls—in the last place—for a prudential calculation of consequences that may be expected to follow from inherently lawful, right, or indifferent action. The proportionately greater good or lesser evil in one effect of such action must justify producing a lesser evil effect, or else the action, in itself licit, ought never to be done. But in the above statement this principle of proportionality, or the prudential balancing of effects, stands almost entirely alone in determining the meaning of "indiscriminate" or wanton action.[9] One should not kill without "reckoning"; and in the main he reckons only the consequences.

Robert L. Calhoun's objection to this was to the point: "The norm of practically effective inhibition turns out to be, after all, military decisiveness; and beyond ruling out wanton destructiveness, Christian conscience in wartime seems to have chiefly the effect (certainly important but scarcely decisive) of making Christians do reluctantly what military necessity requires." [10] After all, manuals enunciating standards for the Housing, Care, and Surgical Handling of Laboratory Animals rule out of bounds the use of methods that cause laboratory rats more pain and maiming without commensurate medical or scientific decisiveness; and they are quite prepared to lay down the moral law that no one engaged in medical research can "be released from the responsibility for doing no more hurt than must be." Clearly, a political morality that focuses on motives or ends only, and gives over entirely to prudence and judgments of utility the determination of the way and means to these goals, has already reduced human beings to the level of creatures to be managed and controlled in any way that may be believed to be commensurate with the attainment of political and military goals. While

---

[9] The Dun Report, p. 12. And see pp. 13 and 14: "The real moral line between what may be done and what may not be done by the Christian lies not in the realm of the distinction between weapons but in the realm of the *motives* for using and the *consequences* of using all kinds of weapons. . . . We have found no moral distinction between these instruments of warfare, apart from the *ends* they serve and the *consequences* of their use" (italics added). But between motives, on the one hand, and ends and consequences, on the other, stands the nature of the *act* itself, which may be moral or immoral; and this too is not *primarily* a discrimination among weapons as such.

[10] Calhoun's dissent in the Dun Report, p. 23.

one should not do people more damage than need be, and with proper motives and objectives, still on such a view they are already merely and wholly *means*.

A different estimate of the Dun Report as a whole might be reached if the principle of proportionality were not so central in determining the "sense" in which it says Christians have to reject total war—if, in other words, another clear statement in this Report could be regarded as still more fundamental in the logic of its moral argument. For there are said to be "real distinctions . . . to illumine and help conscience in its trouble"; "the destruction of life clearly incidental to the destruction of decisive military objectives, for example, is radically different from mass destruction which is aimed primarily at the lives of civilians, their morale, or the sources of their livelihood." If this judgment had been placed first, and fundamental to all other considerations, a different evaluation of this Report would be required. This would be to say that we may be decisively prohibited from calculating the military decisiveness of *some* proposed acts of war in an attempt to justify them from their supposed results. Instead, the judgment just cited is given as an "example"; and it is immediately followed by the conclusion that "in the event of war, Christian conscience guides us to restraint from destruction *not essential to our total objectives*." [11] That obviates entirely the distinction between counter-forces and counter-people warfare; and it provides little "guidance" toward the limitation or alteration of the shape warfare has assumed in the present day.

Professor John Bennett, to whom critical reference has already been made, gave clear utterance to the criteria for the just conduct of war when he wrote that "the use of weapons to slaughter civilian populations, recklessness in regard to future generations, and the destruction of the fabric of national community and of civilized life are opposed to all that the churches have taught in the past." Concerning massive deterrence, he asks: "Should deterrent power be thought of as directed against the opponent's power to strike or against the whole population in the hope of deterring the will to strike? If the latter is the objective, we are again in the realm of unlimited terror and unlimited striking power and an unlimited arms race. If the former is the objective there may be a better chance to avoid the errors that result from panic. Also the former objective raises a less acute moral conflict than the latter. Do we know what the present presuppositions of the U.S. government are on this matter?" [12]

Perhaps the following comment should be made concerning Bennett's summary of the moral limits upon warfare in terms of prohibiting

[11] The Dun Report, p. 13 (italics added).
[12] Bennett, *Nuclear Weapons*, p. 7.

"the destruction of the fabric of national community and of civilized life" in the enemy nation; and upon his judgment that warring action is "intrinsically evil" when it "takes as its target of attack, whether intentionally or not, the recuperative powers of the enemy" or the "fabric of national community" in a nation at war.[13] Such formulations of the criteria for the just conduct of war are of considerable worth. Certainly Christians and just men should have regard for the uniqueness of the various peoples of the world in their traditions, ways of life, and distinct contributions to the enrichment of mankind. The nations also are creations of God; and the world would be poorer without any one of these creatures of His.

Yet, it seems clear that such statements of the principles that should limit warfare are *reducible* to the more fundamental principles surrounding civilian life with moral immunity from direct repression. It is to be feared that, unless this reduction is carried out with conceptual clarity in the analysis of morality and warfare, we have not yet elaborated the firmest possible moral guard against total war. Moreover, it seems to me that Christian love, expressed in principles of justice that suit it, does not first of all fashion itself in terms of regard for the fabric of community life, nor does Christian faith, going into political action, take effect primarily in fidelity to the recuperative powers of an enemy nation. Not nations but first persons are elevated to citizenship in another City and to a destiny kept between themselves and God which prohibits any man from reducing them wholly to the status of means useful in attaining some historical goal in the life of the kingdoms of this world. The neighbors and companions God has given us are primarily persons, within the separate national traditions He has provided for them and for us. Bennett's way of articulating the point at which the conduct of war becomes intrinsically unjust seems clearly derivative. Logically and Christianly, it is predicated upon the claims and obligations pointed out in the traditional doctrine. At most, it is an articulation that helpfully supplements the ancient formulas.

It is true, the rule that only the enemy's military forces should be directly attacked, and not people in general, does not derive simply from

---

[13] Unpublished paper, American Theological Society, 1960. Strike "whether intentionally or not," since an intrinsic *moral* evil cannot be without intention. [David H. Smith, Department of Religion, Indiana University, contends in an unpublished doctoral dissertation on the social ethics of John C. Bennett, that while this prohibition of attacks upon the fabric of an enemy society and its recuperative powers appears to be a formulation of the principle of discrimination, it is actually to be viewed as a formulation of the principle of proportion (defining *excessive* destructiveness). If this is true, this would explain why Professor Bennett in his writings on Vietnam can continue to speak of war's killing and destructiveness as *inherently* immoral, and say that while a Christian should be prepared to *do this* to prevent greater evil our action in Vietnam cannot be justified. See below, Chap. 20, p. 479.]

a consideration of them as persons, as, for example, the bearers of rights before God. Yet when a loving regard for fellow men draws close to them amid the realities of politics and military affairs, it discerns significant distinctions to be made within the activity of war itself. It takes into account persons' specific function, or lack of function, in the war itself in order to save as many as possible from being absorbed into the *thrust* of war. We must recognize this as the proper conduct of war if what is justly due is illuminated by the highest loving regard for men. Christian love does not simply hover over the realities of political life, as a vision of how life might be lived otherwise. It incarnates itself in the actualities and provides itself grounds for action by fashioning discriminating judgments between acts of war proposed to be put forth. The principle forbidding indiscriminate warfare pertains to the nature of warfare itself and its own proper laws—so long as this human action remains, by the skin of its teeth, a rational activity at all, so long as war is even conceivably a purposive extension of national policy, so long as war barely remains an affair in which a human being at all above the level of the beasts of the field can ever justifiably participate, or (to go higher and yet lower for a comparison) so long as engagement in war has not been reduced merely to an exercise of technical reason and efficiency.

The just-war theory cannot be repealed; it can only be violated. It states the limit beyond which war as such becomes in itself a wholly non-human and non-political activity, and the point beyond which military force becomes senseless violence, and our weapons no longer weapons of *war*. This is not because war has an "essence" or "nature" but because man has; and because political society has a nature to which military means must be kept subordinate. The distinction between "combatants" and "non-combatants" asserts that there is both some relation between a civil society and its fighters and yet non-relation or remote relation between them. The maintenance of this distinction, or of this distance and subordination in the relation of combatants to the society they defend, is of the very essence of war that may under any circumstances be chosen by men who have not wholly lost all political morality and their political reasons. Push-buttons may be able to launch retaliatory and counter-retaliatory warfare, but political man with all his faculties in exercise cannot do purposefully any such inhuman deed.

The problem today is "just war," limited war. This is not a description of the facts, opposed to other descriptions. It is rather an imperative statement, a political imperative which points the way in which alone, through intelligent moral action in direction of national policy, warfare can be enclosed again within the political purposes of nations from which it has escaped. This is the case for making just war possible. There is more to be gained from a concerted effort to make just war possible than from attempting to "prevent" war without first (or also) altering the shape it now has in reality and, first of all, in the minds of men.

IV

Exactly how counter-forces warfare can again be made possible cannot be fully explained here. In fact, no moralist alone should undertake to do this, since that is primarily the task of the weapons-analyst and the statesman in shaping policy under the guidance and in the context of the regulative criteria for the purposive conduct of war. Nevertheless some concluding remarks[14] may be addressed to the astonishing fact that the just-war theory still appears outmoded and irrelevant to an age that gives the name of "realism" to proposals that are more "out of *this* world" than the reflections of any medieval theologian upon the morality of war.

Some say "hard" verification standards must be included in any arms control or other agreement, until an open society is here.

Thus Edward Teller opposes the suspension of nuclear tests without the most stringent enforcement of the agreement by inspection. At the same time he writes that "the idea of massive retaliation is impractical and immoral," that responding to evil with much greater evil is "contrary to our sense of justice"; and he calls for *limited* nuclear war to be designed, the limit on size and targets to be determined, apparently, only by what "best serves the military purpose of that conflict." This affords no *decisive* limit upon ever increasing firepower directed against populations. How, may we ask, can a man alive today endure this prospect? The answer is: Teller's faith is built on nothing less than a quite utopian hope, namely, that a world of "open" societies can be achieved in time, "freedom to exchange information" be "guaranteed by enforceable international law," secretiveness become reprehensible, and "a strong and widespread condemnation of all practices of secrecy may in the long run have a strong effect even on those countries which value this form of security most." Can any proposal be more apolitical in today's world? If "a gradual and well-planned abandonment" of secrecy can claim to be a realistic and relevant proposal, even more can be claimed for a plan of graduated, unilateral steps to make counter-forces warfare possible.[15]

[14] For more extensive reflections oriented in the direction of national policy decisions, see my *War and the Christian Conscience: How Shall Modern War Be Justly Conducted?* (Durham, North Carolina: Duke University Press, 1961) pp. 307–324.
[15] Edward Teller, "The Feasibility of Arms Control and the Principle of Openness," *Daedalus*, Fall, 1960, pp. 792, 794, 795, 797; later published in book form by George Braziller, Inc.

Another expert writes: ". . . For arms control to succeed, secrecy among nations must become disreputable." [16]

Others say "soft" verification because an open world of peace loving peoples is already immanent. In contrast to Teller, those who believe that an agreement to cease testing should be negotiated with less rigorous verification, and who rely on this as a step toward further agreements that may control war and armaments without changing their present shape, often provide themselves with other exits into another world than this. This may be the world rule of law, world government, a world without war, a world in which nations can't fight if they want to and can't want to; or, short of these achievements, "people" inspection stations and fewer veto-free on-the-spot inspections because, in negotiating such an agreement, it may be possible for every nation to become "entrapped" in its own propaganda, leading to an "increase in the probability that some individual or individuals will identify with the inspectors instead of with their government and will expose illicit activity." Ideally, we know the kind of propaganda which will make a government most completely a prisoner of its own moral leadership in the cause of international peace through arms control or general disarmament, and which tends to perfect the system of "people" detection, "the propaganda which will make cheating hardest is propaganda in which a nation's top officials repeatedly tell their people that it is their duty to cooperate with an arms control and inspection system." [17] The world in which we live, however, is one in which the Russian negotiator, upon the resumption of the test negotiations in March, 1961, renounced his country's former agreement that an inspection system be under a single director and proposed instead a three-man inspectorate composed of Communist, Western, and Neutralist representatives in which Russia would have a veto; and this is a world in which what the Russians call "control without disarmament" already seems to them to be barely disguised espionage.[18] Moreover, "the Soviets undoubtedly look on their secrecy as a military asset. In allowing it to be pierced by inspection, they consider they are making a separate or additional, sacrifice of their military potential." [19]

These opposites meet in their common expectation that force can be banished from human history. No wonder the more realistic just-war theory is overlooked!

[16] Ithiel de Sola Pool, "Public Opinion and the Control of Armaments," *Daedalus*, Fall, 1960, p. 995.

[17] Ithiel de Sola Pool, "Public Opinion and the Control of Armaments," *Daedalus*, Fall, 1960, pp. 989–990.

[18] Cf. Wm. R. Frye, "Characteristics of Recent Arms Control Proposals and Agreements," *Daedalus*, Fall, 1960), p. 741; and Jerome B. Wiesner, "Comprehensive Arms-Limitation Systems," *ibid.*, pp. 920–921.

[19] Robert R. Bowie, "Basic Requirements of Arms Control," *ibid.*, p. 714.

Less obviously is this still the assumption behind current policies for the deterrence of war by means of apparently hardheaded schemes for stabilizing (while maintaining) counter-people deterrence. We need to examine carefully any proposal that would make weapons of reprisal "invulnerable" by submarine and other means of mobility, and then base arms control and the prevention of war (i.e. the *unjust* war built into such weapons-plans) upon the "stabilization" of this system. Such may undoubtedly be the military posture of the United States in the 1960's; and some of the best intelligences in this country have devoted themselves to the solution of the problem of how current technological developments in the weapons field can simply be moulded into invulnerable, stable systems. A statesman today needs to ponder long upon the essentials of any such proposal, and meditate upon it, perhaps as if in a reverie. We will attempt to anatomize his dream in the following chapter.

CHAPTER 8

The Hatfields
and the Coys*

If President Kennedy sits down with the recent Arms Control issue of *Daedalus,* before he can say "Stockpile" he might with a little imagination tell himself the following tale as a symbol for the present world situation with which statesmanship must deal. The subtitle of this story might be phrased, "My, How Feuding Has Changed!" or "What's Wrong Won't Work." The theme is not that of a positive pragmatism, which holds that military conduct is *right* because it works. It is rather that of a negative pragmatism, which holds that inherently wrong actions cannot be made to work. Morally unshootable weapons or ways of using them cannot be made politically shootable by any kind of technical arrangement. Morally un-do-able *military* conduct can be shown to be politically unsuccessful in the present age.

In its shifting scenes, this tale summarizes the successive weapons policies on which this nation has relied in recent years. First we go to the 1950's.

Down in the mountains of Tennessee where for decades there has been fun and feuding, the Hatfields and the Coys suddenly one day found themselves in a most extraordinary posture toward one another. High up on one ridge, the eldest Hatfield discovered in the sights of his rifle the youngest Coy gurgling in a cradle, while at the very same moment the

* Revised from the final section of my chapter in John Bennett, ed.: *Nuclear Weapons and the Conflict of Conscience* (New York: Charles Scribner's Sons, 1962), pp. 159–170, copyright © 1962.

eldest Coy on the opposite ridge draws deadly aim at the youngest Hatfield lying on a quilt on the porch. Each knows, and knows that the other knows, that this is the case. For some weeks that seem a very long time indeed, each tries to improve his situation by calling on all the other Hatfields and Coys to come and station themselves at various places in the hills, each aiming at the last human life on the other side. The deterrence is truly "massive"; and if this system is ever used it will have failed completely. It looks as if effective feuding has been abolished. Such has long been the desire of the few sentimental ones born from time to time in both families; and now technology has achieved what religion never could. While the lion and the lamb have not exactly lain down together, the Hatfields and the Coys seem capable of forever standing there together, since each sustains the other and prevents his firing. This is in effect a condition, it is supposed, equivalent to mutual total disarmament. Since neither could fight if he wanted to he cannot want to. This seems so clear that strategists on both sides have declared that not so many guns are needed; that one has only to be able to deliver unacceptable damage; that "overkill" is not needed; and that a finite amount of deterrence is enough. War has been stopped. Only a few of these weapons seem to suffice to banish the use of force from human history, while the rest of society can devote itself to chewing sugar cane and making moonshine whiskey (the obvious ends of policy: consumer goods in an affluent society).

Then begins the second scene of the first act of this drama, without any alteration in the weapons systems or in the external military postures. There takes place a radical and subtle change simply because both gunners have second thoughts. Each began by saying in effect: "I'll not strike first unless you do." Then the next moment each realizes that the other must strike first before his enemy does. Both sides begin to quake with fear because each realizes that this system of deterrence, this way of banishing force from human history, is quite unstable. Each begins to suspect that the other may launch a surprise attack, indeed that he should launch a surprise attack, in order to pre-empt against the launching of his own surprise attack (which is equally necessary), and *that* pre-emption in turn would have to be pre-empted, etc., etc.

Mutual "anticipatory retaliation" is always about to take control of this system, consisting of only first-strike weapons, which was supposed to unarm both sides. This is not because both sides are in danger of *mis*calculating, but because they are in danger of calculating *correctly*. On second thought, these first-strike weapons are of no use except for striking first. This is the case because each side knows that he who does not strike first loses everything. He therefore expects the other to strike first, and he expects to be expected himself to strike first. Each does what he expects to be expected to do. He strikes first in order not to be the second who is struck. Each does this. Thus, wonderful to behold, we have on *both* sides a *defensive* war fought with unlimited aggression. Each side can justify its action by bringing it under the category of legitimate defense; yet each must strike first and all-out, in order to have any defense at all. Douglass Cater calls this "the theory of immaculate aggression." [1] If each calculates *correctly*, war will break out. The only reason it doesn't is that politics is never a rational enough human enterprise. The question has now become: When is a surprise or pre-emptive attack *not* justified—on both sides? At *no* moment is a defensively motivated first strike without justification! An almost automatic two-sided defensive war has been built into these massive first-strike weapons, as long as their bases are *vulnerable*. Thus, "*immaculate* aggression" or "anticipatory retaliation" has practically been read into the computers of both sides. Each will act as expected, because of how he expects the other side to act and himself expects to be expected to act. Therefore, both will strike first. Both must become limitlessly aggressive—all for the sake of defense, so long as no limitation has been placed on the weapons it is willing under any circumstances to use even in retaliation. On second thought, massive deterrence tends to produce the war it thought to prevent forever. Surprise attack is the only reasonable *use* to be made of these weapons. They do not deter or abolish war; rather, they tend always to produce it.

Meantime it has become apparent that ordinary feuding has not been deterred. Under the umbrella of deterrence, the grown Hatfield and Coy boys continue fighting whenever there seems an opportunity to increase their power-control of the valley in face of any weakness in conventional forces. Each time this occurs, Hatfield says firmly, "No one should doubt our resolution"; and Coy exclaims, "We will bury you." The side wins which acts as if it is the more capable of wholly irrational action, since each knows that the system exceeds any of the reasonable purposes feuding ever had. So far as the main threat, or "central war," is concerned, they work on each other's minds and not with physical force upon each other's bodies. But war has actually not been abolished; we have only attempted to exceed it. And the side most bemused by this possibility loses in every encounter of real power.

In the second act of this drama, we go to the 1960's. Technological changes take place which seem capable of abolishing surprise attack itself —without, however, removing the immobilization of politics and the confusion and partial immobilization of ordinary feuding and fighting as an extension of purposive policy, especially among the peace-loving Hatfields. The promise of invulnerable bases is that they will prevent surprise attack, and stabilize this system. We find a way to protect the guns and

---

[1] "Foreign Policy: Default of the Democrats," *The Reporter*, March 10, 1955, p. 23.

the gunners, if not the babies. Some of the Hatfields—the peace-loving ones—fall into wells, and begin to take aim through periscopes. These are Minuteman missiles. A way is found to harden and protect the guns. The gunners begin to move around, so that you don't know where they are. The bases are placed on mobile railroad cars, planes, barges, and submarines (*Polaris*). The retaliatory forces are made *invulnerable* to surprise attack.

This act of our drama also has two scenes. While still aimed at baby Hatfield and baby Coy,[2] counter-*people* warfare seems miraculously to have been transformed into counter-*forces* warfare. Only counter-*forces* war seems now to be possible since it would be necessary for either side first to find a way of getting at the other side's guns before using his own in the way originally intended (or in the way it was originally intended that by them the other side would be deterred from using his in the way *he* originally intended). Plans for "cooperating with the enemy" in tacit agreements to maintain the mutual "invulnerability" of deterrence, and arms control schemes to "stabilize" the deterrent gain wide currency, especially among the Hatfields.

After this flight of fancy, our statesman may have some sober thoughts that will cut athwart basing national policy on any such expectation. While still daydreaming and before altogether returning to the real world, he might even reflect for one moment as a moralist. If so, he will conclude that it would be totally immoral to "stabilize" the deterrent and "prevent" war by such means without fundamentally altering war's present shape *even if this succeeded*. Still somewhat in the mood for myth-making, he might suppose that one Labor Day weekend no one was killed or maimed on the highways; and that the reason for the remarkable restraint placed on the recklessness of automobile drivers was that suddenly every one of them discovered he was driving with a baby tied to his front bumper! That would be no way to regulate traffic *even if it succeeds* in regulating it perfectly, since such a system makes innocent human lives the *direct object* of attack and uses them as a mere *means* for restraining the drivers of automobiles. It would even have to be assumed that the drivers will tacitly agree never to remove the baby from the bumper, since that would destabilize the entire system of controls! Against such a proposal it obviously should be said that restraints and penalties

---

[2] In fact the danger they are in has been *increased:* The oceanic system is an "improvement" over land-based missiles not only because invulnerable to surprise attack and not only because it can make for a delayed and measured response; but also because the smaller warhead on submarine-based missiles, "with possibly a lesser degree of accuracy as compared with ground-based missiles, makes them *less of a threat to the enemy's retaliatory forces and more of a genuine deterrent*" (i.e. more useful only in reprisals against populations.) T. C. Schelling, "Reciprocal Measures for Arms Stabilization," *Daedalus*, Fall, 1960, p. 905.

ought to be objectively brought to bear only upon *the drivers* of automobiles, even if this means the abandonment of the hope of saving the lives of every human being (guilty and innocent alike) who venture upon the highways on any holiday weekend. The rational and only just thing to do, if we wish no longer to accept the necessity of the number of deaths that repeatedly take place in the face of vain moral injunctions to drive carefully, would be to introduce basic changes into the machines that are driven, by compulsory safety devices and built-in maximum speeds of forty miles an hour, and enforce with heavier penalties the laws defining the proper conduct of drivers.

But in the real world of political and military encounters, the question is: *can* any scheme hope to succeed which accepts retaliatory strategies directed against populations, and only tries to stabilize these deterrent forces and perfect the mutual invulnerability of counter-people weapons? It would have to be tacitly agreed that baby Hatfield and baby Coy will not be protected directly, and a piece of sheetmetal never be placed between them and the bullets. A successful civil defense program on either side of the valley would not be impossible so much as it would be undesirable, for to succeed in protecting the last possible survivors of such defense plans if they are ever used would be destabilizing to the very system calculated to prevent its having to be used (always without any basic alteration in the design itself of war and defense). Here, the morality of the matter insists on obtruding, for this defines what is politically wrong in all such products of man's artistic, technical reason in designing weapons, arms control, and deterrence systems. No government can *effectively communicate* to its people the fact that it is accepting the complete reversal of a proper relation between a nation and its armament. It cannot tell them, so that they feel it along their pulses, that old ladies and children are now the "fighters" to be maneuvered into position in the struggle for national advantage;[3] that civil defense is a weapon that perhaps should not be used; that a "race" in shelter programs might be exceedingly dangerous and the Russians may even now be mounting this in a clandestine manner;[4] that it is *the arms* alone that can be and are now sought to be protected, and not the nation, except as a hoped-for consequence of protecting the *forces;* and that it is essential to *this* precisely that the people generally be left with no protection.

[3] ". . . In the kilomegaton age evacuation of cities may have replaced general mobilization as the most provocative step short of war that nation can take." (Arthur T. Hadley, *The Nation's Safety and Arms Control* [New York: The Viking Press, 1961], p. 29.)
[4] ". . . The Russians must be watched closely. For should the Soviets start a massive shelter program, America must immediately respond." (Arthur T. Hadley, *The Nation's Safety and Arms Control,* p. 102.) To build shelters would give little protection, but it would "permit a surprise attacker to remove his hostages" (*ibid.,* p. 101).

Moreover, task forces of Hatfields and Coys are already at work out in the woodshed developing anti-gunnery gunnery (anti-submarine warfare[5] and anti-missile missiles[6]). Their barns are said to contain stores of bacteriological, chemical, and radiological weapons. These capabilities for total war cannot of themselves be miraculously transformed into counter-forces weapons. Nothing will automatically insure that germs will have first to be let loose on the forces of an enemy bearing these same weapons before one would dare use them in attacks upon civilians or in civilian reprisal. Not only in active defense but in offensive plans as well there may be an upsetting scientific breakthrough that will make vulnerable every supposed invulnerable system of deterrence and destabilize any system of supposedly stable arms control erected upon the preservation and use of counter-*people* warfare (or its use for deterrence). ". . . We are having a complete technological revolution in the art of war approximately every five years. . . . Technological progress is so rapid that there are almost bound to be doctrinal lags," [7] in any of the proposed schemes for subduing our galloping war-technology *only by means of that technology itself* without any decision to alter the weapons themselves.

Exposed to view is the fact that the Hatfields and the Coys cannot make war or *make defense* in any such fashion that accepts as its premise a fundamental reversal of the subordinate relation of arms to the fabric of a nation's life and its purposive policies. Faced with such manifold difficulties, it would seem that the eldest Hatfield (if he is a realist) would rather make some gesture in the direction of indicating to the chief Coy that he is willing to lower his rifle and direct his aim upon the *forces* opposing him and not upon the babies. Graduated steps to make just war possible would seem to contain as much or more promise than delicate schemes for attempting to stabilize the altogether extraordinary and fluid

[5] President Kennedy, in his first military budget message, did *not* omit antisubmarine warfare from his expanded emphasis on non-nuclear weapons, while at the same time counting heavily on the supposed invulnerability of our own Polaris submarines from Soviet attack (*The New York Times*, March 29, 1961). Also the *Times* reported on May 15, 1963 an agreement between the United States and Great Britain to inaugurate on a 100-mile range in the Bahamas a $95 million *underseas* weapons testing center. Finally, on May 31, 1964 this same newspaper reported the complaint of Secretary of the Navy Paul Nitze that "we are not removing from the enemy submarines the protective mantle of the unpredictable ocean as quickly as we had anticipated." To all this the question most urgently to be asked is: *Where went those tacit agreements about leaving the bases invulnerable for deterrence's sake?*

[6] "It is important to note that a missile deterrent system would be unbalanced by the development of a highly effective anti-missile defense system and *if it appears possible to develop one, the agreement should explicitly prohibit the development and deployment of such systems*" (Jerome B. Wiesner, "Comprehensive Arms-Limitation Systems," *Daedalus*, Fall, 1960, p. 935; italics added).

[7] Herman Kahn, "The Arms Race and Some of its Hazards," *Daedalus*, Fall, 1960, pp. 765–778.

situation in which one now finds himself as head of a powerful feuding family.

Moreover, if Hatfield listens to the more sober among his advisors they will be heard making plans for what to do should deterrence fail and weapons have to be used. Making just war possible may then appear as feasible as making the fighting of a thermonuclear war feasible (and thereby making deterrence credible).[8] Our statesman may have read in the book just cited an apology for resting the whole defense of the nation at its core upon "the rationality of irrationality." This is defined as follows: "The Rationality of Irrationality war corresponds to a situation in which neither side really believes the issue is big enough to go to war but both sides are willing to use some partial or total committal strategy to force the other side to back down; as a result they may end up in a war that they would not have gone into if either side had realized ahead of time that the other side would not back down even under pressure." [9] A "committal strategy" to make *credible* a nation's resolve to go through with a "rationality of irrationality" policy may be compared to what might work to deter one's opponent in the case of two hot-rod drivers playing the game of "Chicken!" by racing their cars at break-neck speed toward one another, each with his left wheels on the *wrong* side of the white dividing-line in the middle of the road, to see which will give in first and pull over to avoid a collision: one or both drivers might *strap the steering wheel* in order to make it mechanically necessary for him to carry out this irrational action.[10] Thus, Kahn asserts that in this uncertain world "it is just possible that the enemy, in spite of our best thought and preparation, may (either because he is clever, or because he or we have made a miscalculation) develop a technique which *he believes* will destroy more than 80 percent of our strategic forces on the first blow. We wish to assure him that *even if he thinks he can be this successful he is still in serious trouble.* To the extent that he could rely on our using our small remaining force 'sensibly,' this might not be true." [11] Thus, *stabilized* counter-people deterrence, or the supposed technological diversion of this into counter-forces warfare, not only may but, to be maintained, *must be planned* to break down into actual, irrational, purposeless counter-people retaliation. This whole effort to impose limits upon thermonuclear war depends upon the rationality of *committal* to irrational behavior, to which it inevitably returns. Kahn knows very well how alone this can be done: not by contemplating the beauties of the contrivance

[8] Cf. Herman Kahn: *On Thermonuclear War* (Princeton, New Jersey: Princeton University Press, 1960).

[9] *Ibid.*, p. 293.

[10] *Ibid.*, p. 291. Or see Kahn's article, "The Arms Race and Some of its Hazards," *Daedalus*, Fall, 1960, pp. 756–757.

[11] *On Thermonuclear War*, p. 185.

while it is working to deter surprise attack, but by thinking through and planning our *committal strategy* for when it may not work. "If there were some politically acceptable accident-proof way to make this kind of retaliation completely automatic," he writes, "it would be sensible to put it into immediate effect"; and he unflinchingly calls attention to the fact that the idea of using our forces finally with insensible sensibility against an enemy's society, rather than against his forces, is *not* credible "*unless we really intend to do it.* If we are only *pretending* that we would do it, the credibility and therefore the deterrent value of our force is almost certain to be lessened by the automatic and inevitable leaks. While we can probably keep the details of our war plans secret, it is most unlikely that we can keep the philosophy behind them secret." [12] In other words, to have "the courage of rashness" we must simply strap the wheel; and the stabilization of invulnerable deterrent forces depends on guaranteeing that this has been done, by some determination *equivalent* to the mechanization of the ultimate political-military decision.

Having learned about the rationality of irrational systems, our statesman can be instructed by another sober weapons analyst in what might realistically be called "the virtue of vice" or "the humanity of inhumanity" as the foundation upon which to base this nation's policy, while providing also for the eventuality that such a policy may not be able to be "virtuously" stabilized and therefore may not work. T. C. Schelling believes that it may be virtuous and wise to keep people hostage and integrate the weapons directed at them into plans for preventing a war directed upon them. ". . . Weapons," he writes, "may be more stabilizing and less aggressive if they are more capable of civilian reprisal than of military engagement. A standoff between two retaliatory forces is in some ways equivalent to an exchange of hostages; and 'inhumane' weapons, capable of inflicting damage but not able to go after the enemy's strategic forces, *acquire virtue* because of their clearly deterrent function and the lack of temptation they give either side to strike first." [13] This type of arms stabilization depends not so much on formal agreement between the two powers as upon tacit agreement on the part of each to direct its policies to this end. It calls for "mutual arms accommodation" to have and to hold hostages; for "reciprocated unilateral actions and abstentions." [14] Making *decisions*, even some *unilateral* decisions, that this should be the shape of war, of defense and deterrence, lies at the root of the matter. Yet in the end Schelling faces the eventuality that the surface wisdom, virtue, humaneness, and rationality of this

[12] *Ibid.*
[13] "Reciprocal Measures for Arms Stabilization," *Daedalus*, Fall, 1960, p. 892 (italics added).
[14] *Ibid.*, p. 904.

system may break down and disclose that upon which it is based: purposeless war, vice, inhumanity, and irrationality.[15] He discusses not only the possibility and actuality of an outbreak of thermonuclear war, but also *how on earth* either side can then manage *to surrender,* even *unconditionally* surrender; [16] and what terms should be exacted of a surrendering enemy. "In the future, at the close of a general war, one might have to allow the conditionally surrendering enemy to retain some retaliatory weapons, these being the only kind that two major powers can use to enforce promises from each other. . . . Certainly more drastic measures than any that have yet been considered [to 'safeguard against surprise attack'] might be the minimum requirement of a conditionally surrendering enemy." [17]

Plainly this will not only have to be *allowed,* and allowed a *conditionally* surrendering enemy. This would also be a minimum *requirement,* and a requirement also in the case of an *un*conditionally surrendering enemy, if we are going to stabilize armaments after the war as was attempted before. After deterrence "fails," the next war after that could then be "prevented" only by basing deterrence again on the preservation of war and the deterrence of war in its present shape. This gruesome conclusion follows unless we take hopefully reciprocated but yet persistent graduated unilateral steps to make counter-forces warfare possible. No wonder Kenneth Boulding writes: "The grotesque irony of national defense in the nuclear age is that, after having had the inestimable privilege of losing half (or is it three quarters, or all?) our population, we are supposed to set up again the whole system that gave rise to this holocaust!" [18]

The fact is that contemporary weapons analysts are not simply using pure reason, in the form of technical reason wholly stripped of moral *scientia,* in producing their designs for invulnerable weapons systems and arms control. They are using pure reason interfused with

---

[15] Since "commitment" is necessary. In "The Retarded Science of Military Strategy" (*Bulletin of the Atomic Scientists,* March, 1960, 16:103–106), Schelling writes: "We have learned that a threat has to be credible, that credibility may depend (inversely) on the pains of fulfillment for the one who makes the threat, and that to make it credible one has to get 'committed' to its fulfillment." (Or see his *The Strategy of Conflict* [Cambridge, Mass.: Harvard University Press, 1960], p. 6.)

[16] If under a test suspension or arms control agreement an enemy may not be trusted, why, "in circumstances infinitely more desperate, when a one-hour pause in the war may be of strategic benefit to somebody, if they send us an urgent message acknowledging their guilt in the war and proposing that we preserve our world by letting them surrender to us, are we likely to be able to do anything?" (T. C. Schelling, "Reciprocal Measures for Arms Stabilization," *Daedalus,* Fall, 1960, p. 913.)

[17] T. C. Schelling, "Reciprocal Measures for Arms Stabilization," *Daedalus,* Fall, 1960, p. 914.

[18] "The Domestic Implications of Arms Control," *Daedalus,* Fall, 1960, p. 858.

moral themes and judgments furnished them by characteristics of the American ethos. They are persuaded by this that it is possible to banish the use of force from human history; and that, when force is actually used (because of the stupid, aggressive, and evil wills of some men) there then supervenes a state of war to which no norms or limits apply. There used to be an oscillation in successive periods of time between all-out peace and all-out (aggressor-defender) war. Contemporary proposals for arms controls based on the total deterrent represent the final product of this ethos. Their distinctiveness is only that they may claim to have banished force and provided in advance for the irrational use of violence in one timeless scheme. There is no hope for purposive political applications of power or for survival unless it is possible to break decisively with this modern doctrine of warfare; [19] and, on both counts, in "peace" or in "war," make just war possible. This should become the regulative context of political decision and of the exercise of technical reason in designing weapons, war, and deterrence systems, in the present age. There is no other course of action, if, as President Eisenhower said, the great powers are not "doomed malevolently to eye each other indefinitely across a trembling world." We need fight-the-war plans that may be less "deterring," but whose consequences are less catastrophic *when* deterrence fails.

I said there were two scenes in the present act in the drama of the Hatfields and the Coys. The entire act is based upon the invulnerability of nuclear missile bases. The first scene attempted to stabilize this system while retaining the direction of the warheads upon populations. The second scene is an unfinished thing. It was inaugurated by Secretary Robert McNamara's announcement in June, 1962, that United States' policy would be to direct the firepower primarily upon *forces*. At least Hatfield signalled to Coy that he was willing to redirect his aim. This opened the possibility of "graduated" rather than "extended" or massive deterrence, and of graduated, limited war should deterrence fail. These will be the themes of a number of the following chapters in this volume.

[19] Cf. Robert M. Tucker: *The Just War: A Study in Contemporary American Doctrine* (Baltimore, Md.: The Johns Hopkins Press, 1960); and Chap. 3 above.

CHAPTER 9

Turn Toward Just War*

The story of the Tower of Babel can teach us a great deal about man's political life. Mankind began at a time before time when "the whole earth was of one language, and of one speech." Then men said to one another "Go to, let us build us a city, and a tower whose top may reach unto heaven; and let us make us a name, lest we be scattered abroad upon the face of the whole earth." It is sad to report what happened to that first United Nations, at a time (if we are to believe the tale) far more auspicious than ours for the union of mankind and for the ability of peoples to understand one another. The Lord (so the report reads) confounded their language, that they might not understand one another's speech—"and they left off to build the city" (Genesis 11:1–9).

The political life of mankind goes on perennially under the sign of the verdict at Babel. Will not a profound student of politics today (church politics or state politics, local or national, domestic or international) be driven to conclude that all this goes on as if that verdict has not been set aside? It is as if political science gives knowledge of the life of mankind on the underside of that divine decision.

Each man calls to another, every group and nation calls to the others, as they build in every age the City of Man. Each tries to communicate to the other workers his plan for the whole edifice. They strive for vision of the whole, and for agreement on this. Excellent plans these are, some better than others. But it turns out that each thinks he is making the plan for the center of the tower, and he imagines his neighbor to be working on some less worthy part of the project. The vision every

* First appeared in *worldview*, July–August, 1962, pp. 8–13.

man and every nation has is "a view of the universal"; it is not "a universal view." And so there arise disagreement and dissension in the best of causes. Doubtless nothing men see of truth will ever be lost. Doubtless their blood and sweat and tears have meant something. But they have all been subjected to the divine overruling.

Nothing this triumphantly secular age can do will undo that verdict—neither Politics 201, nor UNESCO, nor American Field Service student exchanges, nor touring ballet dancers, nor Operations Crossroads, nor the Peace Corps. This does not mean that these things are not very good indeed, and certainly to be done. It means only that the good land we may hope to possess by them (and I will add, by the skillful use of diplomacy and by responsibility in the limited use of force) is a down-to-earth, creaturely good in the meanwhile of man's historical existence, the whole length and breadth of which is lived on the underside of that verdict at Babel. A person who practices his religion with enthusiasm should also engage in every building operation in the earthly city with somewhat less expectation than the final unification of mankind. His enthusiasms in politics will be characterized by a sense of limitation; and by an acceptance of the fact that we who build do not understand one another's speech nor do we look out upon even our common projects with the same eyes.

The New Testament tells us that the verdict that drove men into separation over the face of the whole earth was, once upon a time, reserved by God's own act. On the day of Pentecost, the Spirit of God filled this world to overflowing and enabled the Apostles to speak so that men "out of every nation under heaven" exclaimed in amazement, "Behold . . . how we hear every man in our own tongue, wherein we were born" (Acts 2:1–8). So were the separated reunited, and foreigners made to understand one another like men of the same country. But what they heard and understood were "the wonderful works of God" (verse 11) and not, as before and elsewhere, the wonderful works of men.

That was a decisive moment in the history of the City of God. The Spirit of God came to be with men and granted them foretaste of the heaven every man and nation lives in want of. But on that day, no less than on the day when God uttered an eternal No to man's attempt, living in his own name, to build a tower-top reaching unto heaven, politics was radically de-divinized and secularized. Political activity still goes on much as before, under its own sign. Since Jesus Christ was not the political Messiah many of the Jews expected, since his Kingdom in this world is not of it, the union of men of every race and nation which is found in Jesus Christ does not also mean their political unity or agreement. As long as the Bible contains the book of Revelation, it ought to be impossible for Christians to suppose that the political life of mankind is anything other than a realm of "patient endurance," or for us to fail in the faith that it is God who shall finally wipe away all tears from men's eyes and not earthly happenings. We live in Two Cities, and not in the one world of the City of Man under construction.

This puts politics in its place, and frees men for clear-sighted participation in it. Absolutely related to the Absolute, we should be content to be relatively involved in the relative. Then politics can be best conducted; decision and action can be what they are worth. This only *de-mythologizes* the role of politics, and men are free to think of it as highly as they ought to think, and not make unearthly demands of it.

Most of the symbols in which modern men express their political faith are also in need of being *de-mythologized*. For example, in one of the great halls at the United Nations building in New York, behind the speaker's dais, there is a great mural representing two different myths about human history, one super-imposed upon the other. Both myths are entirely alien to Christian beliefs, and both also quite questionable. There is the figure of the phoenix being reborn every five hundred years out of its own ashes. This hope in cyclical recurrence is not ours.

Behind the image of the phoenix is represented a linear view of man's history: at the bottom, ages past out of which our present civilization has arisen; in the middle, the present with its struggles and perils; and at the top—running off the top, as it were—the uncompleted future. The artist did not know what the future holds, and so he did not picture it fully; but he believed he knew what it would be like, and so the bottom is somber and dark, the present in lighter colors, and the future brighter still. This hope in a progressively better future is not ours; but it is the *mythos* of the modern age. And the *mythos* lives on. "Obviously," wrote Adlai E. Stevenson in a getting-down-to-brass-tacks article in *The New York Times,* "we need not expect to attain this well-nigh Utopian goal ('general and complete disarmament') easily or quickly. That would be like seeking to reach heaven at a single bound."

Who can stand before the bell at the United Nations dedicated to "absolute peace" (a gift of the Japanese people) and not—if his mind has been formed by the Bible—feel the urge to prophesy, in the words of St. Paul (in Athens, the cultural center of the ancient world): Ye men of New York and of the modern age, I perceive that in all things you are too superstitious . . . Whom you ignorantly worship at this altar to the unknown god, him I declare unto you (Acts 17:22, 23).

This but means that "peace" is not something men or nations "race" for. Jesus better said: Blessed are the peace *makers.* To the end of the earthly city of patient endurance, and of wars and rumors of war, blessed are the peace *makers.* Only on the underside of this verdict, as on the underside of the verdict at Babel, can we grasp rightly the nature of politics. Then can we see that the United Nations is what it is, to its great credit and for the justifiable if limited hopes of mankind—a community of porcupines gingerly attempting to draw close to one another for the warmth each needs in winter time; or (to change the figure) workers on the foundations of some City of Man who will get along better if they do not presume to hope fully to understand one another; or (to say it politically) a babbling if erudite assemblage of the representatives of nations, whose common interests and agreements are perilously poised over diverse particular concerns none will or should give up entirely. It is idle to suppose that the threat of nuclear war has changed the nature of porcupines, nations or politics, when we know that none of God's mighty acts, or his past verdicts in judgment and for the saving of mankind, has changed this. Christians no more believe in the determination of history by the "means of destruction" than they believe, with the Marxists, in the determination of history by the "means of production." The very nature of politics requires us to turn toward just war.

The weapons in existence today have made the "unjust" conduct of war (present but peripheral in all wars of the past) into the central war. This requires us to search again into the wisdom contained in this distinction between just and unjust war, to see what light it can throw upon the path along which statesmen today must walk.

The just-war doctrine provides the clue to a sound analysis of why massive deterrence is wrong and won't work. It is the factor that is missing in discussions of weapons procurement. And it will be the regulative doctrine of policy decisions if ever we emerge from a multinational world into a world governed by international organization and courts of justice. These three points can be only briefly explored here.

A great power today needs to probe, more deeply than the American people and their leaders have yet done, the almost irremediable contradictions between *deterrence* and effective *defense,* between deterrence and the use of force in the effectuation of national policy.

We ought not to listen to what our statesmen and military planners *say* when they are only trying to bolster the credibility of deterrence upon the *mind* of an enemy, if we want to find out what are our actual fight-the-war plans. Whether the public is or can be made aware of this or not, our military planners know very well the distinction between discriminate and indiscriminate conduct in war; and all their writings assume that this distinction can still be made today in actual warfare. Still, what it may be reasonable to *say* in order to deter war has not been clearly enough separated from what it may be reasonable to *do* in order ever to fight a war. By keeping a potential enemy confused about what we are actually going to do if he resorts to arms, we confuse mainly ourselves. We jumble together what we suppose to be reasonable deterrence with proper means for the actual conduct of war and we conclude from this that there might be conditions under which massive nuclear retaliation would be justified. A first step toward grasping the need to turn national policy in the direction of "just war" is the realization that such plans already exist but that we are sheltered from them by the supposed requirements of deterrence.

Glen H. Snyder's book *Deterrence and Defense,* for example, clearly shows that cool-headed military analysis is quite aware of the inherent contradictions between deterrence and defense. The more deterrence you "buy," the less defense; and vice versa. This book shows also that, in calculating the alternatives for policy, distinctions can be made between "all-out counter*city* retaliation" and "all-out counter*force* retaliation," and also between (and this is discussed at greater length) *"limited* counter*city* retaliation as a bargaining tactic" and *"limited* counter*force* retaliation" (italics added). There is a distinction expected to be made between destroying *cities* and destroying *forces,* and between unlimited and limited warfare (and this distinction has to be and can be made even when the former of these pairs of alternatives is chosen).

Yet religious leaders of SANE persuasion often select their military experts from among those who hold the most horrendous military opinions. They declare roundly that all war must now be total, or that it will escalate by *necessary* connections into total war. These religious leaders often tell statesmen and the military that the distinction between limited or unlimited counter*city* retaliation and limited or unlimited counter*force* retaliation *cannot* be made. It seems almost as if they mean to say that this separation *ought* not to be attempted. They seem resolved to keep war total in order to hope that in that shape it can be proscribed, and they are provoked most of all by proposals for the limitation of conflict. This seems to them like saving war when it was just about to be abolished. Instead, it should be the answer of the American people, or at least the churches, that these choices between various weapons systems and various war plans are not reducible merely to how much defense and how much deterrence you want to "buy"; but that at stake in these decisions are moral values as well, the justice of war, and the just conduct both of warfare and of politics among the nations.

Not only religious people but statesmen and war planners as well suffer from the same grand illusions. They dream of perfection in deterrence. For them, technology may now do what religion never could, namely, banish the use of force from human history. Preparation is made for the war that cannot be waged and not for war that can be (in the hope that hereby no war will ever have to be) waged. The greatest powers are vastly more interested in unusable force than in usable force.

A recent illustration of confusion in high places was the remarks of Franz Josef Strauss, West German Defense Minister, upon the idea that, if hostilities break out in Europe, a "pause" should be sought before nuclear weapons are ever used in the hope that before the fighting reached an upper "threshold" some settlement could be reached. "I am neither a criminal nor a fool," said Herr Strauss, "I am not against a pause or a nuclear threshold" in actual war plans. But he said he was against any discussion of these things, because such discussion would have "the inevitable outcome that the credibility of the deterrent is weakened." Herr Strauss necessarily made reference to the "natural justice" of warfare by equating "criminal" political and military policy with utterly "foolish" policy. He also asserted that "our whole Bundeswehr [armed forces] concept, training and education is based on the necessity of fighting a conventional war to a certain limit." We may, therefore, ask whether his reluctance (while he was discussing them) to have those limits discussed exhibited only that necessary ambiguity that must be maintained about what a commander intends to do with fight-the-war weapons in order that these may also serve to deter-the-war.

The answer to this question must be negative. There was more at work here than a military commander's need to keep uncertain what he is going to do with his fight-the-war weapons in order that these same weapons may serve to deter. Strauss' statement shows that an entire gulf has opened up between fighting a war and deterring war, and/or between force and policy. He went on to say: "I am a firm believer in the strategy of the deterrent . . . I do not want to contribute to weapons of war once again becoming a means of national policy. And if we do not have a deterrent that is credible, the only alternative is war as an element of policy." If saying loud enough and thinking hard enough that it is so can make it so, then the only useful force in human history is unusable force. This force would be both criminal and foolish ever to use—except in non-use, which can be maintained if we declare often enough that we are, of course, going to use it, you can't tell when.

Yet surely the only exception to be taken to Clausewitz's famous dictum that war is the continuation of politics by other means is to the implication that may be drawn from this (or may have been contained in it) that it is entirely *indifferent* whether a nation's basic policies gain expression or effectuation by peaceful or by warlike means. Many conditions of peace are better than war in the best of causes; and since this is true, it very much matters whether arms or other forms of power and influence are chosen to defend or to effect political policy.

But a complete separation between force and policy has been the most disastrous illusion of men in the modern period. This, and not an ordinary need to keep ambiguous what one is going to do with the arms he has, is the fundamental question today.

So we have the spectacle of great powers absurdly attempting *always* to act politically with only peaceful means as the instrument of their purposes, while these same powers accept total nuclear war as a possible instrument of policy. And each of these claims is accompanied by *ideological* statements that *this* is the sole posture.

Today or tomorrow in the multi-national world in this nuclear age there must come a "turn toward the just conduct of war." If anyone asserts, in view of how horrendous even just war would be today, that this requires instead a radical "turn toward peace," he need only take one more look to see that this "turn" is with some confidence believed to have been already taken. It is impacted, in fact, at the heart of the system of deterrence. Massive deterrence lives by this unearthly confidence that total peace can be insured by means of weapons that have no other purpose; and by virtue of a complete separation between force and policy.

For nations cannot sunder force from policy before war comes without also institutionalizing the same separation after war comes. They cannot act by a belief in the total injustice of war as such, before it occurs, without also, after it happens, conducting war with total injustice and with no discernible connection with any national purpose, not even survival. Renouncing all resort to arms as a matter of policy requires the adoption of war plans which promise, before war comes, to prevent the policies of any nation from ever taking up arms, and, after war occurs, to prevent arms from ever taking on any purposeful policy.

The perfectionistic goal of banishing force from human history as the main justifying ground for having weapons (deterrence) means that *technically* there not only *is* no purpose governing their use but also that there cannot and need not and *should* not be. The political objectives of the nations are supposed to be pursued by legitimate political means only, under the umbrella of a self-fulfilling renunciation of the use of force. This is the high-flying aspiration of deterrence. It claims to outlaw war. But the system can credibly claim this only if it is also the case that, if the system fails and has to be used, we have provided in advance for fighting the war unlimitedly and to none of the ends of national policy. Thus a theory of "immaculate," total aggression has been read into our instruments, because the attempt is being made, by those instruments themselves, to banish any future use of them as instruments of war.

Thus, massive deterrence seems a sensible policy while we contemplate the beauties of the contrivance for completely separating force from policy and banishing the use of force from the world where policies are effected. But to do this, the system *has* to be planned to break down into completely purposeless warfare. Deterrence is a legitimate military posture with a totally illegitimate and offensive *arriere pensée*. It may even work better (because more credible) if it is perfected to possess this totally offensive *arriere* mechanically, without any *pensée*. If total nuclear war ever occurs, this we will not be able to understand unless we understand that it *had* a purpose, a totally non-political, limitless purpose, namely the banishment of force from human history and the outlawing of war. You cannot separate force from policy before the war without justifying the separation of force from policy in the course of the war, i.e. without justifying intrinsically purposeless war.

We do not immorally adopt different standards for a time of peace and for the time of war. We do not say that in war the end justifies any means, while in peacetime ends and means must both be morally acceptable. Instead, the ethics of peace and the ethics of war depend upon the same categorical imperative: that resort to force be forever banished. Not just any end justifies any sort of means to attain it: this we know well enough in peace or in war. But this single supreme end, the exorcism of policies extensible into the use of force, justifies any means that seem technically most likely to attain it.

It is not because of immorality or amorality in politics, or by adopting a double standard, that we have given over to technical military reason the sole determination of the conduct of war. We have done this because of the conviction, as Robert W. Tucker writes in *The Just War*, that "only technical questions remain to be solved." The rejection of force as a matter of policy has already certified any indispensable military means to attain this. Our moral certainty that it is right to separate force from policy in peacetime, and always wrong to connect them, continues to operate in time of war. A "good," "virtuous" and "rational" system is the one that promises to afford us all-out peace in time of peace and all-out war in time of war.

We devised a "war" to prevent all war. God may let us have it, just as he let Adam have the chaos he asked for. In the American ethos, there used to be an oscillation in different periods of time between all-out peace and all-out war. Deterrence systems can only claim to have secured both these things at once, in one timeless scheme. Deterrence is the final product of this ethos in which all-out peace and all-out war go so well together. It is simply the result of our conviction that anyone who ever goes to war for any purpose deserves capital punishment. Weapons technology has only given us the capacity to carry out the sentence. Weapons had little to do with our judgment that this verdict pronounced upon a whole nation is right. Such is the result of placing the supreme goal of banishing force in the center of the military system. In peacetime, there can be no other goals to compare with this; in wartime there can be no controls beside this, because there still are no other goals than a "peace" in which politics and men and nations alike have been put to death.

Since no link between policy and force can be found before war comes, none can be found after it occurs. There is no possibility of forging a connection between force and policy after war has begun without going back and reestablishing this connection during the period before war's start. This is why it will be hazardous business for the nations of the world (who have already turned toward peace with a vengeance) to "turn toward just war."

A nation, and especially a great power, needs a settled and accepted doctrine of the use of armed force (sometimes); it needs a doctrine of the limitation of such force and the proper conduct of war; and it needs armament and weapons systems than *can be used,* if need be, in subordination to the fulfillment of policy. This brings up the question of the weapons we are procuring for ourselves. How far the citizens and political leaders of the United States are from even asking the pertinent question about our weapons can be illustrated from the debate a few years ago about the Air Force's B-70 bomber, or its RS-70 (reconnaisance strike) version. In this prolonged dispute, there was public discussion about inter-service rivalry, about the rivalry between Carl Vinson's Armed Services Committee and the appropriations committees of the House, about whether the Congress has constitutional power to "direct" the President to procure two hundred and fifty of these bombers by 1967 or whether it has only the recourse of impeaching the President if he does not spend the funds appropriated by Congress for this purpose, and about whether this "last of the manned bombers" may be necessary before our missile delivery systems are completed later in this decade or whether to the contrary the B-70 will be obsolete before it can be produced in any numbers. But we hear only incidental reference to the choice between "limited" or "general" war as an instrument of national policy that may be at stake in this decision (one such reference is to be found in Jack Raymond's "News of the Week" article in *The New York Times,* March 11, 1962). We hear no full scale discussion about whether the manned bomber may not be more *accurate* for attack on legitimate military targets than missiles can ever be. We hear no debate about the weapons needed in a possibly justifiable fight-the-war-with-some-purpose policy, in contrast to terror weapons by means of which it is hoped to deter all war.

Yet Col. John Glenn has spoken eloquently of the need for a man at the controls of ships in the exploration of outer space. Do we not need as much human discrimination when we target in on an enemy's forces or his people? Is it enough to say that several missiles on an area are a less expensive way to destroy the target? Moreover, among the reasons given for the resumption of nuclear testing in the atmosphere was the judgment that it may be possible for an enemy to shower a whole area with electronic forces that will render missiles inoperative even when they are hardened underground, and there was in any case the great need to study actual nuclear effects to see how missiles are going to operate in a "post-attack" environment. Meantime, crucial political decisions are being made with no focus on the criteria of just, limited, and legitimate conduct in war, and these decisions about weapons procurement may commit this nation to more rather than less indiscriminate means.

Modern war first became total when the British RAF adopted a policy of obliteration bombing during World War II; and there is reason to believe that they need not, and perhaps would not, have done this if they had had ships. The totality of war was, in part, determined by procurement decisions made years before. In the meantime, also, the churches, whose tradition calls for precisely the limitation of weapons to be debated, engage in a "race for peace"—a kind of sack race in some macabre carnival mood on a picnic ground some distance from the real decisions that are shaping man's political destiny at this very hour. And no churchman can condemn, with good conscience, the present reliance of the U.S. on massive weapons, unless he confesses also that, during the period we began to develop it, a general Christian pacifism (and perhaps the lobbying of the social action agency of his own church) contributed to this reliance by a sweeping opposition to a more equitable and universal military service.

If ever our multi-national world becomes a world ruled by law and by institutions for effectively and equitably resolving international disputes, the guidelines for it will have been provided by the just-war doctrine. This becomes clear when we remember that the peace, order, and justice achieved within the domestic life of nations simply puts into practice the criteria of justice in the ends and means of proper political conduct that define the justice of civilized military conduct. These are *limited* means and ends, and are our unavoidable responsibility for seeking and defending the justice to be dispensed between contending parties.

In the way a police force performs when choice must be made between one life and another, it can be seen that domestic political enforcement discriminates between the bearer of hostile force who must be stopped and the "innocent" bystander (or non-combatant). It is never just to "enlarge the target" and deliberately and directly kill any number in a crowd of people as a means of preventing some criminal from injurious action. The police fire with discrimination. They make a modest and limited defense. We do not allow them the right to get a criminal's children into their power as hostages and to threaten to kill them in order to "deter" him.

Yet the source of the justice of this limited use of force is evidently to be found in "social charity." This is clear from the fact that a man, who legitimately could even be killed if that were the only way to save life, would himself be saved at grave risk to the lives of firemen and police, if he alone is in need of rescue because he has gone off his rocker and is threatening to jump from the ledge of a building twenty stories up.

What is missing from international relations are simply the ways domestic society defines the just cause among men. The justice of, and limitations upon, human conduct or upon the legitimate means to be used, are the same. It is always disheartening to hear Christian people say that the norms governing the domestic use of force do not apply between nations. International relations are a moral jungle, it seems to them; and, *non sequitur par excellence*, only "peace and non-violence" can be applied there. The truth is simply that within nations the *moral* control of the use of armed force has attained *legal* definition, just as *human* rights are also *legal* rights in civil society. Our multi-national world is characterized only by the absence of legal status for the guarantee of human rights, the absence of judicial resolution of conflict, and the absence of legal institutionalization of the moral distinction between legitimate and illegitimate use of force to be found in the proper objectives of restraint and repression in the conduct of war.

Whoever agrees that this is the problem agrees also that there must take place a turn toward "just war" in the political relations of nations. For there can be no hope that our multi-national world can move toward international justice upon the premise that, unless and until the rule of positive world-law defines and produces justice, there is no distinction to be made between the just use of armed force and an unjust resort to purposeless and wholly indiscriminate violence.

CHAPTER 10

When "Just" War
Is Not Justified*

In addition to "just cause" and "just conduct," there is a third criterion which must be applied before resort to war can be said to be finally "justified." This is the test of prudence, of expediency, counting the cost, or weighing in a balance the good and evil effects that any war is bound to cause. This requirement of "proportionate grave reason" has given rise to significant developments both in the Communist theory of "just war" and in contemporary Roman Catholic and Protestant thinking about the justice of war. Before taking up the trends in papal teaching, let us look first at the signal developments in Communist doctrine.

While Communist theory has, so far as I know, no definition of "unjust conduct," it does have (as any justification of war must have) its own understanding of "just cause." In Marxist-Leninist doctrine any class struggle leading to war makes that war just; and specifically, "a just war is a non-predatory, liberatory war." Today, this means not only defensive wars and revolutionary wars but also "wars of national liberation." [1]

But this definition of revolution, defense, and national liberation as the cause that renders war just is insufficient, by itself, to tell Com-

* An address presented at the "Nuclear War Institute," West Baden (Ky.) College, now Bellarmine Theological Seminary (Aurora, Illinois) of Loyola University, November 9, 1963.
[1] Y. A. Korovin, et al, Academy of Sciences of the USSR, *International Law* (Moscow: Foreign Languages Publishing House), p. 402.

munists when or whether to fight a war. What is just according to the Communist or according to the Western sense of justice means only that resort to arms would be, so far, licit or permitted; not that this is forthwith to be done. Therefore, there has developed a test of prudence or proportionality which has eroded war's fatal inevitability in Communist doctrine, without however discarding the orthodox Marxist-Leninist doctrine of "just cause" or adding to it a test of "just conduct." This is the key to Russian revisionism and "coexistence," in contrast to Chinese intransigence.

Thus, Edvard Kardelj, writing in 1960, asserts that the Marxist-Leninist distinction of just from unjust wars was not intended to give "any absolute scientific or political evaluation"; and that this doctrine "cannot possibly mean that the working-class should be for a war or should even fight in a war which may be just." [2]

> The classics of Marxism and Leninism have always emphasized that it is not the mere justifiedness of a war that should determine the attitude of the revolutionary proletariat to it, but the part that war plays in the whole complex of international developments. Even very just wars can have a reactionary effect. For this reason, Lenin considered that it would be wrong to support a war, however just in itself, if that war were to excite reactionary consequences on a world scale.

> The formula about just and unjust war as interpreted by the Chinese turns into a peculiar mystification, the sense of which is that you may not fight for peace if any war which interrupts peace is a just war.[3]

Obviously there are considerations other than "justice" in the sense of just cause that have to be reckoned before determining the final "justification" for engaging in war.

The foregoing shows the emergence of *jus contra bellum* replacing *jus ad bellum*. This development comes from within the Communist doctrine of just war itself, and from its own moral economy in assessing the use of force. Perhaps there are other ways of "fighting for peace," and better ways to achieve the final triumph of Communist "justice." This strikingly resembles the development in papal teachings, where also it is not the mere "justifiedness" of a war that determines one's whole attitude toward it. This development was, indeed, anticipated in the Western just-war doctrine almost from its beginning, in its principle of expediency or proportionality.

Thus, it may not be the "justice" of the Communists that is ap-

[2] Edvard Kardelj, *Socialism and War* (Beograd: Jugoslavija Publishing House, 1960), p. 89.

[3] *Ibid.*, pp. 89, 91. (For the above, I am indebted to Lynn H. Miller: "The Contemporary Significance of the Doctrine of Just War," *World Politics*, January, 1964.)

proaching a meeting with Western conceptions of justice. It may merely be that they are discovering that the use of force has multiple consequences which must be weighed against one another—leading to the conclusion that it is wrong to engage in a war, however just in itself, if this leads to greater evil. This is the doctrine of coexistence; and it can happen that, in the nuclear age, this *jus contra bellum* will provide the basis for new institutions with worldwide powers. If so, this will be not so much because mankind's "justices" became one, but because the common principle of expediency or proportionality in the use of power requires it, in order for violent means to be subdued and connected again with minimal political goals. This test seems apt to make "nuclear pacifists" of us all.

At the same time, however, it has to be noted that those whose method of war is "revolutionary" war, or insurgency or subconventional war, have to date no sufficient reason for believing that *these* "just wars" may finally be unjustified because resorting to violence even in just insurgency causes is likely to lead to greater evil. Insurgency war has not been "deterred" as generally as nuclear war. *Therefore* there is no "coexistence" at this level.

Still, in the main the extraordinary destructiveness of modern warfare is convincing people on all sides of conflicts that even "just war" may not be "justified." This impact of the objective nature and horror of modern war can be seen in recent papal teachings and in the thinking of Roman Catholic moral theologians, and, somewhat less well articulated, among Protestants. Indeed this will be the tendency in the mind of anyone who shares the intimidation which the danger of nuclear war has added to any decision to resort to arms.

In his Christmas message, 1944, Pope Pius XII declared, "The theory of war as an apt and proportionate means of solving international conflicts is now out of date," and at Christmas, 1948, he condemned "aggressive" war as "a sin, an offense, and an outrage," and modern total war, unless it could be in self-defense, as "a crime worthy of the most severe national and international sanctions."

Interpreting Pope Pius' words, John Courtney Murray affirms that, for all Roman Catholic Christians, "the use of force is not now a moral means for the redress of violated legal rights. The justness of the cause is irrelevant; there simply is no longer a right of self-redress; no individual state may presume to take even the cause of justice into its own hands." The right of self-defense was left standing, while the right of self-redress, to *repair* some already accomplished violation of justice, was withdrawn by Pius XII. But in answer to the question, How can this sin in the moral order, defined by the Pontiff, be now transposed into a crime in the international legal order? Murray could only reply: "Pius XII did not enter the formidable technical problem, how this legal transcription of a moral principle is to be effected." And to this he appended the following somber notation: "This problem has hitherto been insoluble." [4]

It is obvious that the spirit and teachings of John XXIII are, if anything, even more set against *jus belli* as an inherent attribute of national sovereignty. When the objectives of nations are in contention, he wrote in *Pacem in terris,* "the resulting disagreements must be settled not by force . . . but rather in the only manner which is worthy of the dignity of man, i.e. by a mutual assessment of the reasons on both sides of the dispute, by a mature and objective investigation of the situation." "Men are becoming more and more convinced that disputes which arise between States should not be resolved by recourse to arms, but rather by negotiation," the encyclical affirms at another point. Because of the ever deepening problem of war in the nuclear age, there is not in *Pacem in terris* any reference to a right of recourse to arms *ad repellendas iniurias,* in self-defense, such as there was in Pius XII's Christmas messages which removed only the right of redress. Because John XXIII was silent about the right of self-defense, war seems in his teachings to be in no case a just resort of policy; and a mature and objective assessment of the situation in order to negotiate a settlement seems all that could morally be done by states.

Because of his natural law optimism, because of the overriding importance today of "the principles of human solidarity," and because of the perfection of justice in the Pope's mind by Christian charity, John XXIII believed litigants, even though they are nation-states, to be capable of such dignified "mutual assessment." He went further than Pius XII did toward spelling out how this sin in the moral order—using armed force—might be transcribed effectively into a crime in the international legal order. Still, a chief question about *Pacem in terris,* now and in the years to come, will be whether to it must not be appended the same somber verdict: "This problem has hitherto been insoluble." This has to be said, even while also saying that John XXIII correctly identified the chief problem facing statesmen today as the "structural defect" in the nation-state system itself which frustrates the wisest and the best-willed efforts to secure world peace.

II

There is a single sentence in *Pacem in terris* over which men will divide in their views of political ethics in a nuclear age. These divergent

[4] "Morality and Modern War," (New York: Council on Religion and International Affairs, 1959), p. 10.

paths are expressed in two different English translations of the sentence in question. The first is the translation *authorized* by the Vatican, which was for many months the *only* and is still a widely circulated version of the text: "It is hardly possible to imagine that in the atomic era wars could be used as an instrument of justice." This is an *erroneous* even if widely influential translation of the *official* Latin version. The second translation reads (with variations): "Thus, in this age which boasts of its atomic power, it no longer makes sense to maintain that war is a fit instrument with which to repair the violation of justice." This is the correct translation.

I propose now to play out two "scenarios." One will be to draw out the entailments of the authorized (and incorrect) translation for political ethics. Then secondly I will do the same for the accurate translation. For us at this point to "unpack" both translations of the Pope's statement will afford the fullest exposition of present-day Catholic teaching in regard to war, and subordinately the authority of an encyclical in the formation of Catholic conscience. Most importantly, this will be to clarify the options for a sound political ethics in the nuclear age.

If John XXIII had written that "it is hardly possible to imagine that in the atomic era war could be used as an instrument of justice," surely there was at work in his mind the requirement that there be a reasonable proportion between the injury caused by any use of force and the good effected or the graver evil prevented. He would seem to be saying that, in the nuclear age, it is now impossible for statesmen to establish any rational relation between the just ends of policy and the means of violence that are available to them. In not expressly holding open self-defense as a possible justification of resort to arms (as did Pius XII), John XXIII would seem to be saying that in the atomic era it is hard to imagine any circumstances in which *any* sort of war (and not only *nuclear* war or some types of nuclear war) could be justified, because there is now no reasonable expectation that the good effects will justify the evil effects or the good accomplished warrant the evil let loose.

Such a sweeping assertion could be questioned, if this had been the Pope's meaning. It is a simplicist assertion to say that, in the whole range of possible resorts to arms, even by the major powers, there is none that could be an instrument of justice in the atomic era. On this interpretation of the Pontiff's statement, it would simply have to be said that he was wrong. This was and is the interpretation given his statement by Roman Catholic pacifists, and by others as well.

On another interpretation even of this translation, however, and especially of the opening words, "It is hardly possible to imagine . . . ," John XXIII only, but definitely, provided the *framework* of cost-benefit in which the use of force has always to be calculated. He did not presume to draw, even on this translation, the *conclusion* of all argument concerning the possible justifiedness of war in the atomic era.

The question whether the Pontiff meant to state a sweeping and doctrinaire anti-war conclusion may be compared with the question whether he meant to replace doctrinaire anti-communism with an equally imprudent and doctrinaire pro-communist or pro-reconciliation position. In both cases, he calls instead for a proper exercise of political prudence. When speaking of the possibility of *détente* between East and West, Pope John wrote that "whether this moment has arrived and also to lay down the ways and degrees . . . are problems which can only be solved with the virtue of prudence"; and moreover, he said, such decisions "rest primarily with those who live and work in the specific sectors of human society in which [the] problems arise." As with the pope's warning against doctrinaire anti-communism, so with his severe warning that "it is hardly possible to imagine that in the atomic era war could be used as an instrument of justice." Both are directives to the laity on how they should proceed; and therefore, neither is entirely preclusive of the conclusions the layman who is expert or any citizen may reach in the practical order.

If this were the Pontiff's word to the "Apostolate of the Laity," what sort of word is it? Perhaps, the last section of *Mater et magistra* will illuminate what follows also from *Pacem in terris*. There, the Catholic layman, who lives and works in the political sector and engages "in the formation of institutions that in their finality are temporal," is told in no uncertain terms, of course, that he should in all secular matters "look, judge, act" within the terms of the general and specific moral teachings elucidated by the encyclical. The structure which these words give to the last part of *Mater at magistra* originated, indeed, with the lay-Apostolate in Belgium, and they entered into the encyclical's statement to and for the entire Church through their adoption by the Belgium hierarchy. Thus did the lay-Apostolate share in the Apostolic office as this shared in the Petrine office.

Mater et magistra affirms that while "Our sons" are to exercise their own professionally qualified judgment in spheres where they are expert and their own personal moral judgment, "it is equally necessary, however, that they act within the framework of the principles and directives of Christian social teaching." Otherwise, among other things, "they can even cast into discredit that very doctrine which in spite of its intrinsic value, seems to be lacking in a truly directive power." For any moral teachings not to remain "merely abstract ideas," they must be "translated into deeds" and "reduced to action." It belongs to the Apostolate of the Laity to do this; and not only to *act,* but also to *look* and to *judge* in these terms.

As applied to *Pacem in terris,* these words, of course, direct the layman first of all to his responsibility to "look, judge, act" toward the formation of international "public authorities" that will correct the structural defect which statesmanship suffers in the present system of nation-states. But if the Pontiff did not put his own prudence in the place of the citizen's and the magistrate's prudence in the matter of "openings to the left" or in regard to opportune "moments" for reconciliation which "can happen" in the present or the future, and if he did not supplant the layman's prudence in the formation of political institutions that can better serve the international common good, is it likely that he meant to render a conclusive prudential judgment replacing what the layman who lives and works in the political or the military sectors of society may find to be the case concerning war as a possible instrument of justice in the atomic age? Surely, the fact that he did *not* mean to do this—and not any fatherly hesitation—would explain the qualifying, opening words (in this translation): "It is hardly possible to imagine . . ." This must certainly be the interpretation, when we remember that the question itself, whether, when, how, and in what manner or degree war may be an instrument of justice in any age, is precisely the question political prudence must finally settle, and which only political prudence can settle, when on other grounds the justifiedness of resort to arms is clear.

It can never be right to resort to war, no matter how just the cause, unless a proportionality can be established between military/political objectives and their price, or unless one has reason to believe that in the end more good will be done than undone or a greater measure of evil prevented. But, of all the tests for judging whether to resort to or participate in war, this one balancing an evil or good effect against another is open to the greatest uncertainty. This, therefore, establishes rather than removes the possibility of conscientious disagreement among prudent men.

Yet this point is today invoked on all sides with the greatest assurance. A man's perception of the fact-situation is invoked as if this were a truth in the moral order, or a premise in a syllogism leading to theoretical certainty. "There can be no greater evil than war" or "no greater evil than nuclear war," it is said; or, less modestly than Pope John, and less correct as a guide for practical wisdom, "In the atomic age, war *cannot* be an instrument of justice," or "no form of nuclear war can be." Not only are the perceptions of the fact-situation summarized in these conclusions absolutized. Not only is it strongly suggested, from the point of view of these universalized perceptions of the facts, that only the stupid or the wicked will make any other calculation. It will also be *insisted* both that these perceptions of fact cannot and *ought* not to be corrected in those who possess them. And it is often said that the objective *facts* perceived (i.e. that any war today will inevitably produce more evil than good in its manifold effects) cannot and *ought* not to be changed even if war could be saved as an instrument of justice.

"However, despite the rhetoric of proportionality," writes Professor Richard A. Falk, "we have no adequate way to quantify, or otherwise render precise, the relation between the cost of and the benefit from the use of force. Therefore, our moral agency leads us to make intuitive distinctions that emphasize the continuing need to justify force by some sense of the cost-benefit relationship." [5] And the fact-situation to which we must apply some sense of the cost-benefit relationship is one in which "we must face the *unequal* and *uncertain risks* of various kinds of warfare and the *imponderable* risks of different forms of totalitarian encroachment." [6] It is simply not the case that the certainty and objectivity of a moral rule is guaranteed by a logical relationship between the scope of the rule and the controversial facts to which it is to apply. Ethics and politics are simply not exact sciences—especially not the principle of prudence itself. When, therefore, John XXIII stated in *Pacem in terris* (if he did) that "it is hardly possible to imagine that in the atomic era war could be used as an instrument of justice," that was the *framework* for analysis and not the conclusion of all thought on the subject. It is the responsibility of defense establishments to find the way to relate means of violence rationally to the ends of policy, and to not fight all the war—or many of the plans of war—they are capable of fighting today.

Perhaps an analogy may be helpful here. In the encyclical *Humani generis* it is stated concerning the theory of "polygenism" that "the faithful in Christ cannot accept this view, which holds that either after Adam there existed men on this earth, who did not receive their origin by natural generation from him, the first parent of all; or that Adam signifies some kind of multitude of first parents; *for it is by no means apparent* how such an opinion can be reconciled with what the sources of revealed truth and the acts of the magisterium of the Church teaches about original sin, which proceeds from a sin truly committed by one Adam, and which is transmitted to all by generation, and exists in each one as his own" (italics added). Here the Pontiff seems to be deciding once and for all between two theories about truth in the natural order—polygenesis from many stocks or monogenesis from one stock—and making it a *conclusion* for all Catholic biologists that polygenesis must be false because of its incompatibility with the dogma of original sin.

Yet, I am told that when *Humani generis* was issued, Jesuits all over the world read the words, "it is by no means apparent how such an

[5] Richard A. Falk, *Law, Morality and War in the Contemporary World*, Princeton Studies in World Politics: No. 5 (New York: Frederick A. Praeger, 1963), pp. 40–1.
[6] *Ibid.*, p. 4.

opinion can be reconciled . . ."; and said, "The Holy Father is asking us to *show* how polygenesis, if it is a truth of the natural order, can be understood to be compatible with revealed truth."

I mean in no way to ridicule this response—certainly not I who have frequently been dismissed by my fellow Protestant ethicists as a Protestant Jesuit, indeed as worse than Pascal's Jesuit. To the contrary, this response seems to me exactly right, and in it is disclosed the strength of the Catholic synthesis of the truth of revelation and the truths of reason, and also the way to understand the theological reflection and the researches of reason which go on before and after papal pronouncements set forth the framework or the guidelines within which Catholic thought is to proceed. The words, "it is by no means apparent how . . ." were, then, both a warning and an invitation—an invitation to Catholic biologists to "look" and "judge" again whether they have correctly apprehended the truth about the genesis of man, to Catholic theologians to think and judge again whether the doctrine of original sin has been formulated with entire adequacy, and to them both to consider how the truth, which must be one, from these two sources is to be understood and to be understood coherently.

Is it far-fetched to suggest that the statement of John XXIII, if it reads, "it is hardly possible to imagine that in the atomic era war could be . . .", was a comparable warning and invitation to moral theologians and to laymen in the political and military sectors of society? This statement girds them not with ready-made conclusions and solutions but with the framework and with admittedly severely limiting guidelines within which the moralist's reflection and the layman's looking, judging, and acting are to proceed if they are to proceed rightly. The moralist should think and judge again whether he has comprehended rightly the justice of war. And the layman, himself in conscience a moralist also, should look and judge again, and take manifold actions in his calling, to find out whether in the atomic era war could possibly be or be made an instrument of justice.

I, at least, shall not believe that by *Pacem in terris* the Roman Catholic Church became a "sect" in relation to the military establishments of all nations—not until I hear this declared in plain English, or you might say, plain Latin and not in English variously influenced by the Italian text. A sectarian Catholic pacifist would doubtless say that the Catholic layman in the Pentagon is still joined with him in the supernatural life. A Protestant sectarian would doubtless say that the laborer in the Pentagon may be "sincere," or that his motivations are not to be questioned, or that he may love the Lord Jesus. But in both instances a sectarian pacifism would say that he cannot possibly have a Christian vocation to do what he is doing in the natural order, in politics, and in military affairs. More than a conflict of prudential judgments and of perceptions of the fact-situation will be asserted to be at issue. The laborer in the Pentagon will be declared to be not only wrong, but also, if he is not simply stupid or invincibly ignorant, culpably wrong, since it is believed to be antecedently evident—from reading the encyclical's statement in this translation as a binding conclusion—that war cannot be an instrument of justice in the atomic era; or because of the Protestant pacifist's belief that the nuclear age has revealed, as it were from on high, directly to all but the obdurate in heart that Christian love cannot possibly be made compatible with trying to make war any longer an instrument of Christian political responsibility. A Christian who is an undersecretary of defense is, of course, by supernatural grace or his sincere discipleship in his private capacity a member of the body of the church. But in his public capacity what he is doing is rather like running a house of prostitution for the restraint and remedy of concupiscence.

I do not believe that a Catholic or any other Christian has thus become a sectarian in regard to the sphere where the *military* problems of the nuclear age have to be solved. Nor do I believe that any Christian church should, by always speaking only of *jus contra bellum* and never of justice *in* war, flee so far away from its responsibility to address, through the laity it instructs and inspires, the most crucial problem facing politics today.

It may be that the pontiffs have withdrawn, morally, the right of war more completely than, even in *Pacem in terris,* a single world public authority is adumbrated. More important to notice, however, is the fact that no amount or kind of *adumbration* of world public authorities that should take the place of the nation-state system can of itself withdraw the right of war. This can only be accomplished by an actual political reordering of the world, to which the papal teachings point, and can only *point*. Therefore, John XXIII seems, but only seems, to have withdrawn morally the right of war more rapidly and completely than our existing or probable or presently possible international institutions enable a responsible statesman to follow his teachings.

There are those, of course, to whom the *conclusion* to be drawn by political prudence is already obvious: in the whole range of possible resorts to arms by major powers, there is none that could be an instrument of justice in the atomic era; nor can any reforms in strategy, however radical, hope to control military weapons so that war could conceivably serve the cause of an ordered justice or a just peace. Whoever believes this ought not then to conclude that international politics can now be based merely on impartial assessment of justice and upon negotiation. It is not the omnicompetence of negotiation or men's will to have peace, but world public authority, that can supplant the right of war. Whoever believes that there can be no connection between justice and modern war ought to conclude that the nation-state is moribund, and must rapidly be replaced by a more inclusive public authority capable of exercising force in a just and effective manner. Only the public authority of a world community can provide the legal transcription of the tendency in modern papal teachings to withdraw, morally, the right of war. These two things are opposite ends of the same see-saw: the moral right to use force cannot go down faster than the public authority and enforcement of a world community is organized.

The question, "Is 'just war' possible today?" means: "Can we learn to subordinate violent means again to political ends, while still maintaining the nation-state system?" If this cannot be done, then a world public authority is the only alternative. If, on the other hand, world public authority cannot now be achieved, and *until* it is established and the nation-state curbed, the responsibilities of statesmen in our structurally defective international order must still include possible resort to arms. Peace and justice are not linked by an unseen hand, as pacifists and the deterrence people both suppose, nor can the political life of mankind endure without the use of force.

The crisis which nuclear technology has brought upon politics is at bottom the critical question of how policy is to gain enforcement. This crisis can be exhibited from within the just-war doctrine itself. These are the clinchers of the argument within which political responsibility must now be determined. From the principle of proportionate grave reason we seem to be required to judge that it is immoral to resort to armed force; and from the justice of many a cause, that it would be immoral *not* to use force when all other *available* means have been exhausted. If this correctly expresses the moral dilemma of the nuclear age and if both horns of this dilemma are correctly stated and neither can be shown by a calmer calculation to be incorrect or altered by a manifold effort of political and strategic thought and action, *then* we must move to give ourselves other means—or rather, we must move to give ourselves another source or subject of political agency than the nation-state, capable of rationally relating means of violence to the ends of policy. The most immoral position of all would be to assume—numbed as we are by the intimidation we share in the face of nuclear weapons—that justice and peace no longer require that powerful means be used. One way (justly limited war) or another (world government), the need to use force and to arm policy with usable power cannot be abolished.

To assert that the right of war can be morally withdrawn no more rapidly than world public authority is achieved—two ends of the same see-saw—simply asserts a *logical* and the *actual* connection between these two things. This is *not* an account of the *origin* and development of more inclusive political communities or a historical *description* of how smaller sovereignties are ever supplanted. It is certainly not a *prediction* that, because of the *terror* of nuclear weapons, world public authority will rapidly be organized, so that in principle the right of war has already vanished from among the duties of states. In the political life of mankind, and despite the powerful longings of the entire human family, there is in fact another dilemma, namely, that we would not need world public authority so desperately if the nations and peoples of the world were anywhere near ready for it, or their "justices" anywhere near agreement. Moreover, a world public authority, organized to solve the crisis that has come upon the use of power, and an authority powerful enough to subdue the problem of nuclear weapons, would necessarily be tyrannical unless there is a genuine world community based on common values and a common understanding of justice.

A realistic analysis of the United Nations affords an illustration of the fact that the right of war remains with states so long as it has not *in actuality* been replaced by superior political initiative and authority.

All of the member states in the United Nations were pledged to refrain not only from the *use* of force but also from the *threat* to use force for the settlement of international disputes [Art. 2 (4)]. So far, the United Nations was an honor society. The charter provided, however, that the Security Council, upon the premise of the solidarity of its permanent members, would be an instrument for enforcing by means of the overwhelming power of its permanent members acting together, policies in behalf of the world community. This was to have been the chief instrument for carrying out the purposes stated in Article 1 (1): "Take effective collective measures for the prevention and removal of threats to the peace, and for the suppression of acts of aggression or other breaches of the peace. . . ." Notice that it was understood that something other than "acts of aggression" might be substantial "breaches of the peace" and vital challenges to the security of the member states and of the world community. Notice also that not only "breaches" of the peace but also "threats" to the peace or situations likely to lead to later breaches were to be promptly prevented and removed.

That was in its inception a powerful organization of the longings of mankind. Even in the Charter itself, however, there was one exception: when Security Council action could not be effectively present the right of war was not attempted to be withdrawn from the member states. "Nothing in the present Charter shall impair the inherent right of individual and collective self-defense if an armed attack occurs against a Member of the United Nations, *until* the Security Council has taken the measures necessary to maintain international peace and security" (Art. 51, italics added). The nation or group of nations acting against a breach of its peace had only to report to the Security Council, and when it had acted presumably yield to its superior authority. The assumption was that with regard to "threats" to the peace a right of national or regional initiative need not be reserved to the members, since there would be time for an alert Security Council to anticipate and remove any such threats.

When it appeared there was no post-war solidarity among the wartime allies, when the great powers proved to be unable to act unanimously, when indeed the veto became an instrument of the cold war between them, and when relations between the great powers began to manifest constant threats to the peace and many actual breaches of it, it was evident that one end of the see-saw, elevated by the Charter, descended sharply. The other end at once went up. Presumably, there is now no "until" qualifying "the inherent right of individual or collective defense." At least, this is not the radical requirement it once was expected to be. Although the Assembly "united for peace" in the Korean war, and although it has been able to act in the face of some threats and uses of armed force, it can only be said to have performed better than the Security Council *did,* but not better than the Security Council was *expected* to perform when the right of war was so far withdrawn by the Charter. This means that, while there exists an obligation of some sort on the part of the members to "take it to the U.N." just as surely as they are also morally obliged to refrain from the threat or use of force, the United Nations still cannot be termed a legal transcription or effective organization of these moral requirements. The inherent right of individual or collective self-defense remains with the member states, certainly to greater degree than the Charter intended. There it will remain "until" the member states are persuaded that the United Nations can, and has the will, to organize and enforce peace with justice. And if the right to act against aggression remains with the member states until the United Nations does this for them, the same can be said of the prevention and removal of "threats" to the peace or vital challenges to the security position of a nation which stop short of actually breaching the peace, or "breach" it in other ways than by acts of open, armed aggression.

One of the regional organizations recognized by the Charter is the Organization of American States. In the relations among the states of this hemisphere it is again evident that non-intervention as a declaratory policy requires a regional organization of power to keep the peace and to remove threats to the peace. The O.A.S. has declared often enough that the presence of a communist regime in the hemisphere allied with the international communist bloc is an intolerable threat to the American system of free and independent nations. It has certainly condemned the subversion the Cuba regime is conducting (in 1967) against Venezuela. At the same time the member-states of the O.A.S. are pledged to non-intervention in the affairs of other states. Yet the O.A.S. itself cannot find the will or the means to intervene collectively in the affairs of a state which, by openly or covertly intervening in the affairs of other states, poses a threat to the peace and the independent development of the nations of the hemisphere. It is evident that the right of war in response to direct aggression, and indeed the right of intervention to repress the sources of covert infiltration, remains with an individual state until the O.A.S. has the will and the power and the organization effectively to replace this responsibility of a member state.

It may be that the United States should not or could not have provided military assistance to the democratic regime of the Dominican Republic when this was requested during the night the military coup succeeded. But this ought not to have been because of some *a priori* principle which declares that intervention is never right or that the use of armed force can no longer be an instrument of justice. The democratic government of Venezuela certainly has the right to "intervene" in Cuba to stop at the source Cuba's intervention in Venezuela. Whether that country has the power and whether the exercise of this right would be wise is another question. Upon a "sphere of influence" theory of the great powers, the United States should long ago have destroyed the Castro regime in Cuba to stop its interventions in Venezuela. All this can be said, while also stressing that hemisphere enforcement needs rapidly to be organized precisely in order to provide a legal transcription of the declarations the O.A.S. has often made against both unilateral intervention and communist penetration in the hemisphere, and to deprive its member states of the right and responsibility of dealing with breaches of and threats to the peace and security of their own and of other societies and with threats to the hemispheric order of independent states itself.

By the "uniting for peace" resolution, it was hoped to transfer the peace-keeping, threat-removing powers of the Security Council to the General Assembly of the United Nations. This has been frustrated mainly by the fact that the United Nations has not the power to interpose its own policies and enforcement between the great powers *or the small powers* unless they agree to it. The growth of peace-keeping threat-removing machinery has been frustrated also by the influx into membership in the United Nations of a great many new nations who seem to believe that it is sufficient simply to declare that resort to armed force can no longer be an instrument of justice or of enforcing a positive settlement. One need not ignore the very great significance of the peace-keeping activities of the United Nations in order to observe that this has been largely in the form of interposition where the parties to a conflict agreed to it, or even wanted this to save face. The General Assembly has too readily accepted the American "doctrine" that politics is an extension of management in another form and that armed force can never be a proper extension of politics.

The recent determination on the part of certain nations to assign certain of their military forces to United Nations' command, and the

clear linkage made not only between disarmament and a carefully preserved security balance between states but also between disarmament and
the development of U.N. armament, are signs of a movement in another
direction. But unless and until the United Nations becomes an effective
organization of authoritative decision-making and an instrument of enforcement, statements like that of Dean Acheson (April 30, 1951) that the
United Nations action in Korea "never contemplated the use of force to
accomplish its political objective in Korea, which is the establishment of
a unified, independent, and democratic country" (although this might
have been accomplished as an "incidental effect"), or statements like that
of President Eisenhower during the Suez crisis that "I do not believe that
another instrument of injustice—war—is the remedy for these wrongs,"
and statements to this same effect made in or by the United Nations—
all will remain ideologies hanging in mid-air with no competence to remove the right of war from among the duties of the nation-states.

If these statements, like the mistranslated statement in *Pacem in
terris,* mean to withdraw morally the right of war in order to point the
nations to the formidable task of organizing a world political authority,
they have a certain validity. If however they mean, or are used, to dis-
guise the fact that U.N. diplomacy is at present diplomacy based on
carefully protected national sovereignties, or to beguile the peoples of the
world to believe in the omnicompetence of negotiation to resolve all disputes and reach the settlement of every conflict by "peaceful" means,
such statements can only prove damaging to the cause of peace with justice.[7] They can only unnerve national resolution, or exhibit this, where
no other source of political resolve has effectively taken its place.

With regard to all such statements on the part of statesmen seeming to renounce the right of war while the nation still stands as the highest effective authority, it simply has to be said (as John Courtney Murray
said of Pius XII's Christmas messages) that they do not "enter the formidable technical problem, how a legal transcription of a moral principle
is to be effected." Then the question is, how, in the years to come, mankind is to avoid the somber verdict, "This problem has hitherto been
insoluble"!

The task ahead is formidable indeed, when one remembers the
variety of "justices" there are in the world, and especially the variety of

[7] Such statements in *Pacem in terris* (to the effect that there can be hope in
negotiations only if these proceed "from inner conviction") have already been interpreted, and not without some justification, to mean that "the way to conduct negotiations is not to permit them to fail" (Stanley Kunitz in *continuum,* Vol. 1. No. 2
[Summer, 1963], 232)! Since it takes *two* to negotiate in any such fashion, the adoption
of such an attitude toward negotiation by any single nation would mean its premature
surrender. This also would raise the question why it ever helped to create the dispute
in the first place by adopting a firm policy on the issue it now is "resolved" shall
not fail to be settled by peaceful means.

understandings of justice that are the basis of concrete cases of dispute even when the nations agree on generalities. In addition to the problem posed by the increasing Balkanization of the world, and by the multitude of concrete claims to justice at issue, there is the powerful dynamism of contemporary world political life. A *status quo* world political authority could not hope to keep the peace and remove threats to the peace. It could not hope to provide mankind a "changing order changing orderly" [8] unless the decisions it became competent to make and to enforce could be radical and thorough-going ones. It would have not only to provide means for the settlement of disputes between powers more or less content with the existing world order. It also will have to provide some equivalent for "the central legislative role in world politics" which armed force served in the past,[9] and some equivalent to war as the "institution" capable of replacing old and decadent political stabilities with new ones and at points of stress basically reordering the existing world political order itself.

III

There is another and more correct translation and interpretation of the crucial statement about war in *Pacem in terris*. "The Pope Speaks" translation, in contrast to all other American translations, reads: "Thus, in this age which boasts of its atomic power, it no longer makes sense to maintain that war is a fit instrument with which to repair the violation of justice." [10] This reading would bring John XXIII's teaching into line with that of Pius XII, if Murray is correct in saying that the latter, in obviously excepting defensive wars, meant to proscribe two of the three traditional reasons for recourse to war—*ad vindicandas offensiones* (to gain vindication against an offence) and *ad repetendas res* (to retake the thing)—but meant to leave standing the third: *ad repellendas injurias* (to repell injury, to resist an armed aggression). On this interpretation (which seems to be sustained by the official Latin text) John XXIII left open the possibility that war might well be an instrument for repelling an injustice that is being perpetrated but is not yet accomplished.

[8] In his Christmas Message, 1963, Pope Paul VI spoke of "the dynamism of the elements from which peace must result," and of the "component parts" of "peace of well-balanced *motion*"—in contrast to Augustine's definition of peace as the "tranquility of *order*."

[9] Richard A. Falk, "Historical Tendencies, Modernizing and Revolutionary Nations, and the International Legal Order," *Howard University Law Journal*, Vol. 8, No. 2. (Spring, 1962), 128.

[10] In the Latin: "Quare aetate haec nostra, quae vi atomica gloriatur, alienum est a ratione, bellum iam aptum esse ad violata iura sarcienda."

The assertion that John XXIII no less than Pius XII left standing the justification of defensive wars in the atomic era, and perhaps even the use of nuclear weapons in defensive war, and said only that war is no longer "a fit instrument with which to repair the violation of justice," is supported by the historical studies concerning the traditional doctrine of just war undertaken by the Center for Peace Research at Creighton University in Omaha, of which E. A. Conway, S.J., is the director. Indeed, the policy-proposal involved here is fully explicated only by some attention to the asserted findings of this study.

The contention of these studies is not only that the medieval theologians Vitoria and Saurez made a complete distinction between defensive war on the one hand and, on the other, wars initiated for the purpose of repressing or correcting "injurious actions" of some kind other than armed attack, generally some infringement of rights, customs, or laws. The contention also is that the limitations surrounding and the moral economy governing the use of force (just cause, just conduct, proportional grave reason) were applied *only* to the latter case, and not to the case of defense against armed aggression. Vitoria and Saurez, it is asserted, did not believe that "defensive war" required moral justification or was subject to legitimate limitation. It was rather "an involuntary act" forced upon an innocent political community, which was not then required to justify or limit its response as it should do in the case of "voluntarily" taking up arms to repair some previous violation of justice.

An historian cannot but welcome this splendid historical reconstruction, if it is correct, all the more because of its boldness. A moralist, however, must raise questions of a different order. This proposal would mean in the moral order, if I understand it, that for Roman Catholics there would no longer be any "just-war theory" to be applied or any of the tests and limits that applied only in the case of "involuntary," i.e. aggressive, war. This conclusion would now follow because Pius XII and John XXIII have withdrawn the right of war in cases to which these tests ever had reference (namely, *initiative* in the use of force), while both Pontiffs have left standing the one case, namely, defensive war, to which they never had reference. This would mean that, in an opposite way from the way Catholic pacifists read the developments in papal teachings, the just-war theory has become in an atomic age a mere abstraction.

What then must a Christian moralist say to this? Surely, that this would only show that the just-war theory itself, as this existed in the past, is greatly in need of revision. We would have to move to apply to the case of defensive war the tests which in the past governed only the "offensive" initiation of armed conflict. This would mean prohibiting, even in defense, violation of non-combatant immunity and the proscription of "defensive" counter-society warfare. Or it might only mean the ready realization that, while this may not have seemed a needful test in the past, the defensive weapons the nations now have in their arsenals clearly open the question whether and how we are going to defend anything by them. That is to say, the test of rationally relating means to ends even to the end of a good defense, and of making sure that the society defended is not sacrificed by its own means of defense and by its own plan for defensive war, implicitly assumed in the past, must now be explicitly applied to assure the conduct of a proper defense. Whether by revising the traditional theory to apply to the case of defensive war the tests of "discrimination" in the conduct of "voluntary" war or by applying to such a war the test justifying the effects by making sure the good are greater than the evil effects makes no great difference, since today these two criteria so nearly converged upon the same conclusion in any assessment of the morality of war.

Thus, on the assumption that it can be shown that the tests for determining the justice of war never applied in the past to the case of defensive war, the first task of the Christian moralist would be to make sure that these tests and limitations do so apply now and in the future. Secondly, and this is perhaps even more fundamental, the constructive moralist would have to contend that if Vitoria and Saurez believed that there are no moral judgments to be made concerning acts of *self*-defense, this could only be because they were *late* medieval schoolmen who stood furtherest removed in time (and unfortunately also far removed in the inner structure of their thought about justice in war) from the Gospel ethic from which the just-war theory first arose. A Christian whose mind and whose justice is formed in any measure by "social charity" cannot premise one-half of his treatment of the problem of war upon the idea that *self-defense* is a "natural" right, and indeed so "involuntary" as to be intrinsically justified without more ado and therefore exempted from any of the limitations which justice and political prudence should impose upon "voluntary" resorts to armed force in which one takes the initiative. Here there is no shadow remaining of the Gospel ethic which requires that the enemy—even the enemy who strikes first—should be held in peculiar regard. Life and not death, his life and not his death, ought to be chosen in intention and so far as possible in actuality. Because of Jesus Christ who "first" loved us and him, no natural ethic can be given the primacy, and certainly not the premises of a spontaneous "involuntarism" which preserves ourselves in existence while claiming exemption from all norms or controls simply because of the injustice of the enemy's aggression. The genesis of the just-war theory in the interior of an ethics of Christian love[11] seems to be erased from memory and no longer of

---

[11] This ground was traversed at greater length, and the point demonstrated in regard to Augustine and Aquinas, in Chapter Three on "The Genesis of Non-Combatant Immunity" in my *War and the Christian Conscience* (Durham, N.C.: Duke University Press, 1961).

any effect in Vitoria and Saurez, if in fact they placed moral limits only around taking the initiative in a "voluntary" resort to arms. Not for nothing did the first formulators of the limits and responsibilities of engagement in just war still deny the "natural" right of defending one's own life if that alone is at stake! Not for nothing did all the theologians of the past discuss the justice of war under the heading of charity and its subheading peace, which is a work of charity!

Beyond this it would have seriously to be questioned whether the right of war to correct wrongs other than armed aggression can *in actuality* be completely withdrawn so long as the right of defense is left standing. Do not these stand or fall together, or to the same degree remain? I do not pretend to know what may have been the full meaning of that justice that may have needed repair, or of those infringements of rights, customs, or laws short of armed attack which were believed to be a possible justification of initiation of war so long as the direction of military power was within a unified Christendom where legitimate political leaders acknowledged themselves to be governed by the same overarching laws, customs, and rights. But surely the equivalent of this today is violated by the "threats" to the peace discussed above, and by fundamental challenges to the freedom and independence of nations that are also a challenge to the security of all, which however need not take the form of armed attack across boundaries. The distinction between defense and offense is notoriously difficult to make; and nations cannot be required to delay responding to serious threats until the point where the peace has been breached. If it will require world public authority to remove from them the right of defensive war, it will certainly require world public authority—and an alert and effective one, at that—to supplant a nation's responsibility to respond, perhaps with arms, to vital challenges to its own security and to the system of independent nations. President Kennedy's firmness and restraint in dealing with the Russian missiles in Cuba was a clear example of the exercise of a nation's right to meet serious challenges and to answer sudden changes introduced into the security balance by a restrained but definite threat to use force unilaterally prior to any actual breach of the peace. If he had waited for O.A.S. action instead of getting O.A.S. concurrence, or taken the problem to the United Nations, and *if* this had significantly delayed or weakened the response made, that would have been a politically wrong action, and defective in responsibility to all other free and independent nations no less than to our own.

The President not only had a just cause in taking this initiative. He also adopted immediate goals and methods (i.e. blockade) that were restrained. Whether his action is called "voluntary" because it seized the initiative to correct wrong, or "involuntary" because it was only a response to an aggressive act that however made no actual *use* of arms, the same moral economy in the use of and threat to use force still applied, and was applied. The President's plight, and ours, and that of all peoples, was that he had or believed he had to invoke the additional threat to use nuclear weapons in an unusable, immoral manner. The radical correction of this situation requires the governance of all wars and warlike threats, "defensive" or "offensive," by just-war tests and limitations—until such time as a world public authority makes this no longer a necessary and awesome responsibility of the statesmen of individual nations. The morality of deterrence, or the just discriminations to be made concerning the deterrence apparently held in reserve during this military encounter and which were necessary to preserve limits upon it, is a formidable moral problem that must be taken up elsewhere in this volume.

Before closing this discussion of justice in war and in actual military encounters, however, it should be pointed out that the two preceding paragraphs have offered an interpretation of a modern equivalent of warlike initiative *ad vindicandas offensiones* (to gain vindication against an offense). I have interpreted the correction of an infringement of "rights, customs, and laws" (which the popes have sought to withdraw morally from the duties of states) in terms of the correction and removal of *threats* to peace and order. Until such time as a world public authority effectively assumes this responsibility, a nation and particularly a nation that has had world leadership thrust upon it cannot renounce its initiative in making the world "safe for diversity," [12] diversity within a world order of free and independently developing nation-states. This, then, is the equivalent of those rights, customs, and laws that more or less governed in the medieval world. The right to use and threaten force will remain with the Nations now struggling to become United until that goal is accomplished.

Perhaps John XXIII did not mean to withdraw, morally, the right of war or the use of threats of war to remove wrongs other than armed aggression in this sense of removing serious threats to the peace. His words, "alienum est a ratione, bellum iam aptum esse ad violata iura sarcienda," if this is translated "as a means for gaining redress for violations of rights," do seem to have a more antiquated flavor.[13] If this is the reading, and if the Pope meant more or less trivial irritations and violations of customs and agreements which it is "alien to reason" to fight about, then he withdrew something that is clearly removable by the decision-makers of the nation-states as presently constituted. Through U.N. diplomacy and many a U.N. agency they have already reached agreements not to fight *ad vindicandas offensiones*, and to resolve less than vital disputes by means other than war.

[12] President Kennedy in his American University address.
[13] This is the translation made by Louis B. Sohn when he sought to correct the authorized English version (*continuum*, Vol. 1, No. 2 [Summer, 1963], 249).

But these words, and the Pontiff's flat, unqualified statement that it is "alien to reason" and "no longer makes sense" to make war for this cause, have considerably more significance if one puts out of mind medieval notions of insults, customs, rights, offenses, and laws; and if instead we understand him to say that "it no longer makes sense to maintain that war is a fit instrument with which *to repair the violation of justice.*" [14] This proscribes war *ad repetendas res* (to retake the thing, or territory). George H. Dunne, S.J., understood this to be the Pope's primary meaning (even from the most widely circulated but erroneous English translation of the crucial passage):

> There are those among us who still think that war can be an instrument of justice, who, whether they explicitly avow it or not, think that Hungary, or Poland, or the Ukraine can be liberated by means of war and who nourish the hope of eventually precipitating a war of liberation.
>
> This is sheer folly. John XXIII knows it as such. He knows that in the atomic age war as an instrument of justice is unimaginable. [15]

On this view, the Pontiff has morally withdrawn the justice of *wars of liberation,* for the repair of previous injustices that have already accomplished their effect on the political map of the world, while he left standing a possible justice in a war undertaken to repell some new injustice now in course of being done. Shall we add to this the repulsion or removal of threats and severe challenges to the *pax-ordo-justitia* of the world that may be put forth long before overt aggression occurs?

But this places us on the horns of another dilemma which no reader of *Pacem in terris* should forget or ignore. It is *this age* (and not the Pontiff)—this age "quae vi atomica gloriatur," "which glories in" or "boasts of its atomic power"—that has made just wars of liberation unimaginable (in some if not in all theatres), and has rendered it nearly or entirely "alien to reason" to maintain that war is a fit instrument with which to repair ancient or more recent violations of justice. Since the rule against just wars of liberation, to the degree to which this is in force, depends upon the deterrent effect of nuclear weapons themselves, we are driven on to an inquiry into the justice in deterrence. In the words that immediately preceded the statement we have been examining, John XXIII acknowledged "that this conviction owes its origin chiefly to the terrifying destructive force of modern weapons. It arises from fear of the ghastly and catastrophic consequences of their use." In short, the proscription, as alien to reason, of resort to armed force as a fit instrument with which to repair the violation of justice was a judgment drawn by

[14] *The Pope Speaks* translation (italics added).
[15] "John XXIII's Latest Miracle," in *Ave Maria*, May 4, 1963.

applying the principle of proportion in weighing the effects of starting a war—even a war which has "justifiedness" in itself—in the nuclear age.

This means that to dismantle the balance of terror would have the effect of making just wars of liberation—justified in themselves, according to various conceptions of justice abroad in the world today—possible again, and on all sides. Without deterrence, the repair of many a violation of justice would cease to be so alien to reason. Without deterrence, i.e. without the atomic power of which this age boasts, just wars of liberation would likely make sense again, or they would do so in more instances. Remove these weapons with their terrifying destructive force, and the nations would again be able to imagine, indeed it might become sensible for them to imagine, that war can be invoked for the purpose of repairing injustice.

It is clear, therefore, that the injustice of war which is so urgently stressed by the encyclical depends *meanwhile* upon the justice of deterrence; and that for the duration of this *meanwhile* before world public authority is established, an analysis of the justice and the injustice in war today is thrust back upon an analysis of the justice and the injustice of deterrence.

CHAPTER **II**

The Limits
of Nuclear War*

The writing of this chapter was begun in the context of a deeply distressing event. For seventeen years of the nuclear age no leader of the Western world indicated any doubt that military policy should be based on President Truman's judgment that an entire city is a legitimate military target. The "massive" deterrence of the Dulles era, when the United States still had a monopoly of atomic weapons, has now been supplanted by "balanced" deterrence from hopefully invulnerable bases. Arms control and measures to lessen the danger of surprise attack and of accidental war have been proposed, and conventional and "unconventional" military capabilities have been strengthened. But during these years there appeared to be no crack in the official acceptance of cities as choiceworthy targets for total destruction.

Then in June, 1962, Secretary of Defense Robert McNamara delivered the commencement address of the University of Michigan. In this speech, which had the approval of President Kennedy, he said: "The United States has come to the conclusion that, to the extent feasible, basic military strategy in a possible nuclear war should be approached in much the same way that more conventional military operations have been regarded in the past. That is to say, principal military objectives, in the event of a nuclear war stemming from an attack on the Alliance,

* First appeared in a pamphlet published by The Council on Religion and International Affairs, 170 East 64th Street, New York, 1965.

211

should be the destruction of the enemy's forces, not of his civilian population."

Instead of a chorus of "Amens!" from the millions of decent citizens of this country, Christian and non-Christian, hardly a single voice was raised to say, "*That* is certainly the upper limit of what we ever want done in our behalf, if for no other reason than that it is clearly the upper limit if indeed it is not more than the limit governing what can ever be done in defense of anything by means of nuclear weapons." Hardly a "civilized" person was reminded by the Secretary's words that the proscription of direct attack upon a whole society is the oldest and most well-established rule of civilized warfare. Hardly a Christian was reminded by the Secretary's words to seek from his own traditional teachings practical wisdom for the direction of public affairs. Hardly any of the leaders of religious and public opinion stepped forward to support the most significant change (or suggestion of change) in military policy in nearly two decades of the nuclear age.

Instead, the opinions expressed were stereotyped and evidenced as much inertia as can exist in the vast and sprawling defense establishment which McNamara is struggling to subdue and direct. Perhaps resistance to McNamara's proposal was to be expected from our allies.[1] When we think of the magnitude and complexities of our interlocking systems of defense, "doctrine" is almost bound to lag behind realities. It is not surprising, therefore, that C. L. Sulzberger reported from London that this novel "nuclear defense theory, based on counterforce rather than countercity strategy . . . produced confused reactions in Europe," or that he concluded two weeks after the policy was announced: "It is now dead." [2] Yet it is surprising and most distressing that individual leaders of opinion manifest not much greater freedom to explore "new" doctrine.

Instead of support for this or any other effort to limit the nuclear holocaust for which the two great powers now stand ready, one heard only sterile protests that our leaders were again trying to make us grow "accustomed" to the idea of fighting a nuclear war. Instead of applauding the announcement as a policy of definitely *limited* feasibility, the public widely regarded it as simply one more assertion of the limited *feasibility* of nuclear war. The *Christian Century* damned with faint

---

[1] *The New York Times* reported (August 9, 1962) that Franz Josef Strauss, West German Defense Minister, " 'is giving up hard' on a strategy based largely on nuclear weapons." Herr Strauss apparently believes not so much in a credible fight-the-war policy as in deterrence that "begins at the battle line" with tactical nuclear weapons and goes to the grave line, by means of massive nuclear weapons targeted mainly on cities.

[2] *The New York Times*, July 9, 1962.

praise—because the editors apparently know in advance that any thoughtful effort to un-target the cities is bound to prove impossible. It will show "the essentially unmanageable nature of these weapons," and direct us again with single-minded attention to "the importance of preventing any war from starting."

"So vast is the destructive capacity of nuclear weapons that their effects could not be confined to military objects," said the *Century*, sweeping aside any distinction between effects that cannot be confined and deliberately enlarging those effects by targeting on cities. "Would the United States," it asked rhetorically, "be prepared to remove military installations from the vicinity of its great cities, where some of them are now located?"—as if war plans must now and for the future be ruled by the stupidity of congressmen who secure the location of missile bases in their districts near large centers of population where there is an unemployment problem; and as if the fact that Tucson, Arizona and Plattsburg, New York and Omaha, Nebraska and Colorado Springs, Colorado are now legitimate military targets means that this must necessarily remain the shape of modern war. "In making his proposal Mr. McNamara has rendered a service," the *Century* concluded, "but probably not the one he intended to render. What he has really done—or so we hope—is to strengthen the argument of the Committee for a Sane Nuclear Policy that the only safe way to manage nuclear weapons is to abolish them as one step in a plan of complete disarmament." [3]

THE ALTERNATIVES OF POLICY

So far public opinion in this country seems to ignore the difference between 25,000,000 dead as the probable result of all-out counter-force warfare and 215,000,000 dead as a result of all-out counter-city warfare between the great powers.[4] We seem to turn away from any effort to make counter-force nuclear war, if it comes, fall far, far short of all-out. So, in addition, do we gloss over the qualitative moral distinction between tragically killing or sacrificing human beings as an indirect result of knocking out military targets (counter-force warfare) and the murderous policy of deliberately killing them in totally devastating counter-city warfare. The only ground for hope is that our leaders who must make the decisions will not be so irresponsible. Richard Fryklund re-

[3] Editorial, July 4, 1962.
[4] C. L. Sulzberger's report, *op. cit.*, of the estimates on which McNamara's policy shift was based. These, of course, are very uncertain figures.

ports, at least, that the shift to counter-forces strategy has been in the making for the duration of this administration, and he always writes of the decision in the past tense.[5]

Still, this is a decision that will have to be not only our actual policy but our *declared* policy. More than once it will have to be declared, and massive manifold actions will have to be taken in accord with it, if there is again to be a well-understood boundary and a mutually accepted limit in the conduct of war. This will require the support of an informed and morally sensitive people. When one asks why the just conduct of war is the last thing people want to talk about or to believe possible, or why they do not demand that governments make only limited nuclear war possible (if there is to be nuclear war) or limited war (if there is to be war at all), the answers are hard to give except in terms of a breakdown of the tradition of civilized politics that is without parallel.

Yet these distinctions among possible strategies have long been made by weapons analysts. Glenn H. Snyder, for example, discusses at some length the choice between "all-out counter*city* retaliation" and "all-out counter*force* retaliation," and also between "*limited* counter*city* retaliation as a bargaining tactic" and "*limited* counter*force* retaliation." [6] And Herman Kahn spells out in some detail the difference that exists and *can* be drawn between "Counterforce plus Countervalue," "Straight Counterforce," "Counterforce and Bonus," and "Counterforce plus Avoidance" in the choice of strategies.[7] Moreover, two other such books have recently appeared: one analyzes "limited strategic warfare"; [8] the other, based in part on interviews with highly-placed Pentagon officials, offers a reporter's analysis of a "no-city" strategy (Kahn's "Straight Counterforce" or "Counterforce plus Avoidance") in contrast to "pure-city," "cities-plus" or "devastation" war plans.[9]

Thus, there stands on one side counter-value warfare; pure-city, cities-plus, and devastation war; controlled or unlimited counter-city retaliation; counterforce-plus-countervalue, or counterforce-and-bonus; and limited strategic city reprisal. These all aim at civilians, except for the sort of "counter-value" warfare which proposes to allow time for cities to be evacuated. On the other side stands counter-force warfare; no-city war; controlled or unlimited counter-force retaliation; straight

[5] *100 Million Lives: Maximum Survival in a Nuclear Age* (New York: The Macmillan Co., 1962). The Pentagon studies and debates go back to early 1960.

[6] *Deterrence and Defense* (Princeton, N.J.: Princeton University Press, 1961), pp. 68–79.

[7] *Thinking about the Unthinkable* (New York: Horizon Press, 1962), pp. 65–68.

[8] Klaus Knorr and Thornton Read, eds., *Limited Strategic War* (New York: Praeger, 1962). In this volume, this concept includes both limited strategic city reprisal and limited strategic attacks on forces.

[9] Richard Fryklund, *100 Million Lives: Maximum Survival in a Nuclear War* (New York: The Macmillan Co., 1962).

counter-force or counterforce-plus-avoidance. Only counterforce-plus-avoidance may be called a just way to conduct war, since traditional and acceptable moral teachings concerning legitimate military targets require the avoidance of civilian damage as much as possible even while accepting this as an unavoidable indirect effect.

This chapter defends the thesis that counter-force nuclear war is the upper limit of rational, politically purposive military action. Two ways are commonly taken to avoid this conclusion, and another uncommonly. Those who magnify the difficulty and undesirability of adopting a policy of making just war possible usually do so because:

(1) they believe that general disarmament is about to be accomplished and therefore no plans should be made for the use of any weapons, nuclear or other; or else because

(2) they believe that balanced deterrence can be stabilized and kept perfect enough to insure that nuclear weapons will never be used except in their non-use for deterrence.

In these two schools, extremes meet. They are brothers under the skin who believe so strongly in peace by disarmament (whether unilaterally or by treaty or by technical contrivance by which the weapons will neutralize themselves) that as a consequence they see no need for thinking about the upper limit of sanity in the actual use of nuclear weapons. The conclusion that "pure-city" is the only way in which nuclear war can ever be fought, or the judgment that "pure-city" is the aim the weapons *should* have, is thus "the favorite [strategy] of influential civilians whose eyes are actually on disarmament rather than defense," [10] or who, at least, find it impossible to be active on two political fronts at once. And not only civilians.[11] Even Prussians are pacifists of this new breed. So Franz Josef Strauss, West German Defense Minister, explained why he did not want even to *discuss* plans that actually exist for controlled fighting in Europe by saying that the inevitable outcome would be that "the credibility of the deterrent is weakened. . . . And if we do not have a deterrent that is credible, the only alternative is war as an element of policy." [12]

Therefore, no steps *should* be taken to plan to fight war justly against forces if you believe that peace by deliberate disarmament can soon be achieved; and no such steps *need* be taken if you believe that weapons technology can keep the nations permanently disarmed and no future rational decision-maker need ever decide to fire these weapons. Most, if not quite all, of the arguments against counter-forces warfare (its instability, for example) have absolute peace as their premise; and the latter is, one way or another, believed to be a genuine—and the sole—

[10] Fryklund, *op. cit.*, p. 42.
[11] Cf. General Pierre Gallois, *The Balance of Terror: Strategy for the Nuclear Age* (Boston, Mass.: Houghton Mifflin Co., 1961).
[12] *The New York Times*, March 1, 1962.

option today.[13] There is an inner logical connection between indigenous American pacifism and the Strategic Air Command with its motto, "Peace is our profession." "Pacifistic deterrence" has been our policy, our hope and our faith. Only if fighting a possible war is understood to be a governing purpose of a military establishment will inherent limits in the design of war seem choiceworthy. It is always easier to plan murder and mutual suicide, and somehow despairingly more pleasant too, than to plan for defense and the survival of the nation.

There is no way to avoid thinking about militarily feasible and politically purposive warfare. Against the first of these positions, it must be said that nuclear weapons and armaments in general are unlikely to be scrapped soon, if ever. Against the second, it must be said that "balanced" deterrence and invulnerable weapons systems do not preclude the need to think about believable fight-the-war plans. Instead, the opposite is the result. The more the great powers think they have achieved for the moment a nearly automatic neutralization of nuclear weapons, from bases it will take years to find a way of attacking, the more the world is prepared for local war, for conventional and unconventional war. The more, too, will it seem possible to make a controlled use of tactical nuclears, and after that to expand the war to controlled attacks upon an enemy's strategic forces and then to engage with him in a cold-blooded exchange of a few cities.

The third, and more uncommon way, of going around or beyond counter-forces warfare is to envision a slow lobbing intercity exchange as, under some circumstances, the decision of statesmanship. It is this proposal of "limited attacks on cities," or "controlled counter-value" war or "counterforce-plus-bonus civilian damage," which should be examined in depth. In doing so, I shall regard the limited exchange of cities as a lower limit of pure-city or of unlimited counter-value war, and not as simply a variant or upper limit of controlled (or even all-out) counter-forces warfare. Those analysts who fail to note here an essential distinction have failed to observe the point at which, in making a courageous effort to "think about the unthinkable," they themselves began to think about the un-do-able.

Herman Kahn's book, *Thinking about the Unthinkable,* bears in its title reference to the contribution for which we are all indebted to him and to other weapons analysts. Some actions and events have been termed "unthinkable" because they are unpleasant to consider, or because they

---

[13] For this argument in expanded form, see my "Dream and Reality in Deterrence and Defense," *Christianity and Crisis,* Vol. xxi, No. 22 (Dec. 25, 1961), 228–232; "U.S. Military Policy and 'Shelter Morality,'" *worldview,* Vol. 5, No. 1 (Jan., 1962), 6–9; "Correspondence," *worldview,* Vol. 5, No. 3 (March, 1962), 6–9; *War and the Christian Conscience* (Durham, N.C.: Duke University Press, 1961), and Chap. 9 above.

disturb our customary ways of thinking, or because we are weak in our determination to overcome the problem and submit it to the most rigorous rational analysis. Other proposed actions, however, are "unthinkable" in the far different and deeper sense that they are morally or politically "un-do-able." Properly to think about the unthinkable requires that we be open to the possibility that such effort will lead beyond the mere delineation of many possibilities for choice and action, which are distinguishable only extrinsically and in terms of consequences. That man is not quite resolute in thinking about the unthinkable who does not know that he may one day think something that is, in and of itself, un-do-able. He has not much confidence in his own powers of rational analysis who does not know that he can perfectly well think the "unthinkable" which will remain unthinkable in the sense that it is, for human agency, un-do-able.

A first illustration of this is to be found in what analysts say about policies based on the "rationality of irrationality." There is a point where a fundamental irrationality of at least some of these policies becomes evident in the fact that, we are told, one must irrevocably "commit" himself to doing them. That is to say, there are some actions that cannot be *done* at the time they are to occur. For them to occur, human agency and rationality must be placed in suspense at the time of occurrence. One must get himself bound by some artistic contrivance or, better still, by acting as if he were a force of nature, before the event happens or before the (wrongly termed) "action" is to take place. "Committal strategies" cannot, in the extreme instances, be located in the ethical and political sphere. Instead, ethics and politics are abolished by the adoption of such strategies, for the simple reason that they put human agency out of commission. They are designed to do precisely this.

In this day when action and the principles of right action have been so far reduced to techniques, Aristotle's distinction between "making" and "doing" reasserts itself at the heart of any consideration of "committal strategies." "Making," he said, always has "something beyond itself" as an objective, whether this be a poem, a physical artifact, a weapons system or a social system. In contrast, in ethics and politics "the very well-doing is in itself an End." [14] Right and wrong doing are to be found in the nature of moral and political agency itself and not first of all in any of its external results. Of course, from any "well-doing" a lot of "making" results. Even so these are not the same.

The fundamental questions of ethics and politics have to do with "the very well-doing" that in and of itself is an end and norm of action. This question is simply avoided by schemes that plainly annul human

[14] *Nichomachean Ethics*, 1140b.

agency at the place and time of an event's occurrence. Extreme "committal strategies" cannot be the result of an exercise of practical reason which Aristotle rightly called "doing." As un-do-able actions, they can only be contrived by "Art," an exercise of practical reason properly called "making"; or, we might say today, as a consequence of social "engineering." Today, those who manage to believe the un-do-able to be actionable accomplish this in large measure by virtue of what Jacques Maritain calls a "merely artistic view of politics" and of military conduct.

I once improved on Herman Kahn's use of the game of "Chicken!" as an analogy to the game of deterrence. The driver who wants to make *certain* he will win this game (to "deter" the other driver and force him to pull over before their vehicles collide) can do so by being the *first* to strap his steering wheel and communicate to his opponent that he has done so and now *cannot* pull over even if he wanted to do so.[15] This is how one must contrive to do the un-do-able. He must effectively rule out human choice and agency at the time a totally irrational action is to be produced. He must get himself totally committed, and he is not totally committed if any "doing" remains to be done. Neither at the time of deterrence *nor before* has he made a human *political* decision, or chosen means apt to political ends. Neither in the event nor before does he put forth a political deed. *Before,* he did an *artistic* thing, beautiful to behold, whose whole meaning was to rule out choice and to make the exercise of political wisdom impossible at that later moment. This is the only way to think, and to think how to do, the un-do-able.

Now I find Kahn saying this same thing more clearly than in his earlier book, *On Thermonuclear War,* in which he stated that "Doomsday" deterrence machines would be unchoiceworthy (un-do-able) even if they might work. Or, rather, I find him stepping back and forth across the line between the unthinkable that has not yet clearly been thought and the unthinkable that, the more you think about it *with political judgment,* is inherently un-do-able. Out of his own writings our present point can best be made, namely, that this line exists between right and wrong political choice, and it is not one to be discovered merely by calculating numbers killed or saved or by engineering the values marched by in various scenarios. The boundary governing moral and political choice is rather to be discovered in the mind and judgment of the observer stimulated by "War and Peace Games" to think about "doing" and about what is worthy to be done, as a just man would make the choice and perform the deed. Scenarios and "War and Peace Games" are altogether to be praised for what they can do to enlarge our knowledge of actual and exceedingly complex cases moving, as they must, through time. They stimulate the imagination, and if in no other way the oppos-

---

[15] Cf. Chap. 8, p. 174 above.

ing "team" insures that no fact or riposte or consequence is neglected.[16] This has always been the service of actual or hypothetical "cases" in moral and political reasoning: they require and enable informed concrete decision to be made. But, in an earlier age, this exercise was for the purpose of illuminating and stimulating *judgment* concerning what is to be done or not done, and not only to enable a man to *imagine* some "unthinkable" situation that might possibly face him in the future. Since Herman Kahn has probably run through more scenarios than anyone else, and since he is also a moral man concerned with the conduct of politics and war, it is helpful to observe him making judgments concerning the to-be-done and the not-to-be-done.

Before examining his position, I will insert here the opinion that the morality of war, and distinctions between just and unjust, rational and irrational, human and inhuman conduct, would be clearer in Kahn's writings if these distinctions were not trammelled from the beginning, and turned into seemingly *technical* judgments only, by the conviction he shares with most modern men that since war as such is immoral, no *moral* judgments can be made concerning the way it is conducted. In short, if there is no distinction to be made between killing and murder in the calculated (*vs.* wanton) acts of war between nations, then only technical questions remain to be solved. For example, the *numbers* the computers tell us will be dead will be the only basis for choice between, say, counter-forces warfare and limited strategic city exchanges for bargaining purposes.

"Rationality of irrationality" policies cannot be said to be useless in politics. It was certainly true that, in the case of many delegates to the U.N., "the apprehensions created by Mr. Khrushchev's boorish actions in the General Assembly outweighed their dislike of such behavior," and that these delegates became "more disposed to go along with Soviet demands." [17] Nevertheless, *extreme* "rationality of irrationality" policies obviously become irrational again. For a nation to go to *total* committal

[16] Litigation in our law courts and our "adversary" procedure are also ways of reenacting the case and making sure that all the relevant facts will be found and brought to bear upon the decision. Here, however, members of the jury, deciding as to the facts of the case, also bring their sense of justice and injustice to bear on it; and rules of law, in which they are instructed by the judge, are not only positive laws "making" right but also depositories of collective judgment as to the justice or injustice of similar cases. Moreover, judge-made law provides a growing edge of decision-making in which the justice or injustice of a specific aggregation of personal and impersonal facts is determined. It is one thing to mount procedures apt in determining facts and for thinking the unthinkable action one is enabled and almost forced by these procedures to think through concretely. It is another thing to judge that the unthinkable is criminal. War and Peace Gamesmen should remember this.

[17] Thomas J. Hamilton in *The New York Times*, Oct. 30, 1960.

policies is obviously to step over the line into action by contrivance, despite the fact that the action is politically un-do-able. Total committal to irrational action turns diplomacy or statesmanship itself into a Doomsday machine whose parts are erstwhile people.

This, it seems to me, Kahn now says more clearly. He spells out more fully what it would take to deter irrational action by irrational action. One must say convincingly, "One of us has to be reasonable and it is not going to be me, so it has to be you." [18] "One of us has to be responsible and it isn't going to be me, so it has to be you." [19] Now, how can this be contrived effectively, and effectively communicated? The enemy has to be convinced you are "stark, staring mad" [20] or

> totally reckless, oblivious to the danger, out of control. These objectives can probably be met best by getting into the car drunk, wearing very dark glasses, and conspicuously throwing the steering wheel out of the window as soon as the car has gotten up speed.[21]

> The side using this tactic tries to act like an unreasoning force of nature or, at least, a rigid human being. It tries to point out, implicitly or explicitly, that, "One does not argue with a hurricane, one seeks shelter in a cellar or suffers the consequence. Why then do you argue with me?" This tactic is particularly effective upon bystanders.[22]

Yet Kahn knows that this cannot be *done*, certainly not by a free society or by a government responsive to the will and responsible for the weal of a free society. He writes that

> thermonuclear threats . . . must look and be both prudent and rational. We cannot go around threatening to blow up a major portion of the world, or attempt to get our way by looking insane and dauntless. These strategies might be available to a totalitarian nation. They are not available to us, a democratic nation in a democratic alliance. Strategies overly dependent on resolve, on committing first, on extreme use of the rationality of irrationality, are not likely to succeed if attempted by the West.[23]

And immediately after one of Kahn's most extreme statements of how "best" to play this game of deterrence by total committal, he writes:

[18] Kahn, *op. cit.*, p. 78.
[19] *Ibid.*, p. 130.
[20] *Ibid.*, p. 79.
[21] *Ibid.*, p. 45. Also see p. 188. "The youthful degenerates' game would be a better analogy if it were played with two cars at an unknown distance apart, travelling towards each other at an unknown speed, and on roads with a fork or two so that one is not even certain that he is on the same road as his opponent" (p. 187).
[22] *Ibid.*, p. 179.
[23] *Ibid.*, p. 124.

If we must play the game, we should play it soberly, with clear vision, and in full control of both our capabilities and our emotions, even if doing this results in serious competitive disadvantages. We must do this in order to have both the appearance and reality of responsible leadership.[24]

In both the foregoing passages, Kahn plainly calls for never *being* or *appearing* to be totally committed to action that is so irrational it can never be politically done by free and present decision. Certainly, the upper limit of the politically do-able would be to appear to have strapped the wheel or thrown it away, but not actually to do so. Given the *deterrent* value of "this *appearance* of irrationally inexorable commitment," one would want to provide for the possibility of revoking the apparently irrevocable, since "if deterrence fails . . . it would then be irrational to carry through the commitment." [25] There may even be "some advantage in not using too extreme a 'rationality of irrationality' strategy," because, if you neither are nor seem to be totally committed, the enemy may actually do only what *he* can do purposefully, then and there at the time of action.[26]

Still there are passages in *Thinking about the Unthinkable* in which Kahn seems to hold open for adoption strategies which he himself has plainly stated ought never to be chosen, and which, his own analysis makes clear, *cannot* be "done" except by "making" ourselves do them (if that is to be called "doing"). He writes, for example, "*It can make sense to commit oneself irrevocably to do something in a particular eventuality, and at the same time it may not make sense to carry out the commitment if the eventuality occurs.*" [27] Yet far more frequently, as I have shown, Kahn says *this cannot make sense*. Certainly not the actuality of it, and likely not the appearance either. This is not surprising, for we should have known all along that rational purposive action cannot contradict itself, or ever be "made" to do so. "Making" cannot take the place of "doing," nor contrivance replace responsible decision in the moment of action, nor can Art supplant Politics, if men remain men.

WAR AS A TEST OF WILLS

Policies of extreme committal to irrational behavior are only one illustration of where one is driven when war is regarded as primarily

[24] *Ibid.,* pp. 188–89.
[25] *Ibid.,* p. 68.
[26] *Ibid.,* p. 69.
[27] *Ibid.,* p. 45 (italics mine).

or exclusively a trial of wills or a test of resolve. There is no end here, no limits. Limited strategic war involving controlled city exchanges or limited counter-city retaliation *as a bargaining tactic* offer another illustration of war in which the sides aim to "prevail" *primarily* by demonstrating resoluteness. This, too, is "unthinkable" in the sense that the more you think about it the more it will seem manifestly "un-do-able." But first, a word should be said about war as a trial of wills in contrast to war as a trial of strength. (War, of course, always involves both these encounters.)

In war as a trial of wills, what one side does is determined primarily by its calculation of what the other side expects of it, or what is required for its resolution to be broken. Analysts in our day have developed an entire science of purely voluntaristic games of strategy simply by abstracting the encounter of the wills and minds of the combatants (always a significant aspect of military engagements) from other factors. For purposes of analysis one sets aside any consideration of war as a resort to a controlled collision of bodily forces, war as a trial of physical strength, or war as the challenge and response of national entities each with concrete policies to be defended or effected. Where will and resolve are at issue, the question is not what would I do if I were the enemy seeking to enforce some definite national policy by possible resort to arms. The question is, rather, what would I do if I were he, wondering what he should do if he were wondering what I would do if I were he . . . ? In the determination of radically voluntaristic policy, the focal point is each side's expectation of what the other expects it to expect to be expected to do. Such is the result of our present-day attempt thoroughly to "spiritualize" the conduct of war. Such is the result of trying to elevate war from being mainly a trial of strength directed toward some controlling objective, and of transmuting it into a test of resolve which has no other purpose than to prove who wins in a battle of wills. There is no limit or end to this. One is guided only by "what he expects the other to do, knowing that the other is similarly guided, so that each is aware that each must try to guess what the second guesses the first will guess the second to guess and so on, in the familiar spiral of reciprocal expectations." [28]

Much of the language of the foregoing paragraph presupposes that a nation's strategy is framed as a *response*, though an empty response that takes shape only, or mainly, in terms of what it expects another (so far) empty expectation to expect of it. You have the same conflict of wills, each empty and formless until it is filled by the other, if it is supposed that one is on the "offensive," trying to "bargain" with the other, to break his resolution, or to deter him from further action. Thus, the determina-

[28] Thomas C. Schelling, *The Strategy of Conflict* (Cambridge, Mass.: Harvard University Press, 1960), pp. 54, 57, 87.

tion of strategy takes place almost wholly within a meeting of the wills and resolves of the combatants, in the sense that what each must be willing to do in order to "win" is determined by what the other is willing to do. This goes on to mutual destruction, or until one gives up and turns away, or until the strange notion comes to the mind of one or both of them that warfare has no limit or purpose unless it is predominantly a trial of strength.

American voluntarism was the source of this nation's confidence in deterrence. "The strategy of deterrence has assumed that this requirement of an ever triumphant will could be satisfied, if only because strength of will must somehow be proportionate to nobility of purpose. If our heart is pure, our hand will be steady, or at least steadier than the aggressor's." "To convince the adversary that we would act in the manner threatened, it is indispensable to convince ourselves that we would so respond. As long as we believe, others will believe. As long as others believe, they will not act. The key to a successful strategy of nuclear deterrence lies wholly within ourselves." [29] So, deterrence is a technical contrivance for doing what religion never could accomplish and the Christian religion never proposed (i.e., banish the *use* of force from human history), backed by an infinitude of correct anticipations of our anticipation of an enemy's anticipations, and so on.

The same American voluntarism is the source of our confidence in extreme "rationality of irrationality" policies, and it also has given birth to the thought that it is feasible and proper to fight a war of controlled counter-city retaliation *as a bargaining tactic*. The question is not primarily whether cities can be deliberately exchanged with coolness and control enough to prevent this from at once becoming a spasm of counter-city devastation. To this there is a prior question: whether exchanging cities for bargaining purposes and to play on the will of the adversary and break his resolve has not already transgressed the limits that are clearly present when war is understood as a trial of the actual military strength of nations. War as a test of the limitlessly variable "strength" of resolve may go as high as strategic city exchanges. War as a test of real strength to defend or effect objectives can and will go no higher than counter-forces warfare. A nation determined to play a game of wills to the end, and resolved to will in accord with the internal "rationality" of a radical voluntarism, never will discover that there are any limits in resolutely willing to win this game of hostile wills in conflict. Not here is to be found any *ratio* in the *ultima ratio* of the arbitrament of arms. A nation comes upon no boundaries in this upward spiral, so long as proper acts of war are believed to arise not primarily out of concrete policy but

[29] Robert W. Tucker, *The Just War: A Study of Contemporary American Doctrine* (Baltimore, Md.: The Johns Hopkins Press, 1960), p. 185.

out of contending wills. Unfortunately, in this a commander can show his resolution in no other way than by proving he is willing to sacrifice one or more of his own cities; and one must reduce an enemy's cities to rubble as a means of getting at his resolution. This is the very definition of the unjust conduct of war.

Fighting a war has its obscure *ratio* only when the conduct of war is subordinated to the civil life and purposes of a nation, to its concrete civilization, values, and policy objectives. The will to fight and the manner of fighting must be governed and controlled by the pre-eminence of society, and the effectuation or defense of its policy, over the use of armaments. This relationship is lost sight of when war becomes a matter of one will "prevailing" over another, and the destruction of an entire city is made a mere means of "demonstrating" resolution, or is used to "symbolize" one side's willingness to go higher unless the other "chickens out."

Although analysts of the strategy of abstract conflict of wills would probably regard themselves as cool-headed rationalists in comparison with the warm-blooded "engagement" and passionate "involvement" recommended by contemporary existentialist philosophy, these schools are nevertheless brothers under the skin. The latter abstract from the structures of the person and the substance of inter-personal relationships and concentrate attention on only an *aspect* of the meeting of person with person, namely, the limitless capacity of self-consciousness to include in its consciousness the other's consciousness which in turn is determined only by its consciousness of the first person, and so on *ad infinitum*. Some existentialists reduce inter-personal relationships to a trial of wills or a test of resolution to "prevail," just as some analysts have pictured conflict between groups or nations. This is the secret meaning of the statement that counter-value warfare can, as a test of wills, have only *quantitative* limitations. This really means that there are no limits, except that quantity of destruction which will cause one side to give up first. If there had been more resolution to continue fighting (as there certainly might have been) the quantity would have been higher. No *ethical standards* are to be discovered for *inter-personal* behavior unless encounters between persons are imbedded in the nature of the persons and their good. No *political* limits are to be discovered for inter-national relations unless encounters between groups are imbedded in the structures of civil societies and their good. The wills and resolves of men must come down from aloft, they must return from their self-transcending "freedom" and limitless transcendence of the other in order to find that there are some things they are *bound not to do,* by the very nature of personhood, the very nature of political society, and the "natural justice" of warfare that is a purposive trial of strength with some controlling objective in view. The controlling goals in warfare may, of course, be "political effects objectives" which range far more widely than "battlefield objectives." [30] But surely, that contest is no longer "war" which has become a mere will to become demonstrably more resolute than someone else, by means that are not basically intended to insure that choiceworthy political effects will follow.

WAR AS A LIMITED STRATEGY

Analysts who have managed to think this "unthinkable" thing—limited counter-people war—give evidence in what they say about it that in this they have begun to think about the "un-do-able." It is instructive that, in his recent book, Herman Kahn leans away from Controlled City Reprisal toward Controlled Counterforce even more than seemed to be the case in his first and major work, *On Thermonuclear War*.[31] He finds greater difficulty thinking about situations in which an exchange of cities might seem justifiable in actual execution, and (most significantly) he states with substance and at length the political reason for not *doing* in this regard what he and other analysts have *thought* with some exactitude while playing war games. The same judgment—that controlled inter-city warfare is actually an un-do-able plan of war—finds support also on almost every page of the latest study specifically devoted to *Limited Strategic War*.[32] To be sure, none of these analysts recommends such a war; they say only that "limited strategic war is a *possible* war; to fight and prepare for such a war is a possible strategy." [33] My contention, however,

[30] Cf. Morton H. Halperin, *Limited War in the Nuclear Age* (Center of International Affairs, Harvard University, 1962).

[31] Princeton, N.J.: Princeton University Press, 1960.

[32] Edited by Klaus Knorr and Thornton Read (New York: Frederick A. Praeger, 1962), with chapters by each of the editors, and by Herman Kahn, Herbert D. Benington, Morton A. Kaplan, Arthur Lee Burns, Clark C. Abt & Ithiel de Sola Pool, and T. C. Schelling. My discussion of this volume of essays of necessity ignores significant differences among these authors.

[33] Knorr in *Limited Strategic War*, pp. 5–6. "Limited strategic war" entails *long range* exchanges; and this may mean (1) limited attacks on strategic *forces* or (2) limited strategic attacks on *cities;* and the latter in turn may mean attacks (a) on *evacuated* or (b) on *populated cities.* In commenting on a volume of essays which analyses all these possible types of war under the heading of "limited strategic war," I cannot avoid using the term "limited strategic war" mainly to mean controlled counter-populated-city exchanges, which I deny is a plan of war at all possible to be done. At the same time it should be clear that I mean to allow that "limited strategic war," in the other senses, may possibly be done and justly done. Certainly, limited attacks on strategic *forces* conforms to the principles of *legitimate* military conduct. While unthinkable in one sense, such a war is not un-do-able. One has to be more cautious, however, in describing the conditions under which "counter-value" warfare that engages in exchanges of cities allowed to be evacuated might be do-able, or could be a possibly legitimate military action.

is that even such a statement by a researcher goes too far, or not far enough toward decision. It is a possible war and a possible strategy in the sense that one can think of it after having not done so before: it is thinkable and possible in this sense. But it is not a strategy that can be chosen and put into effect by rational statesmanship, least of all by the government of a free society.

1. Limited nuclear attack on populated cities is only a limiting case of general nuclear war, and partakes of the same insanity. The fact is that weapons analysts are only able to think of a war of controlled city exchanges as a *possibility for choice* by almost forcibly channelling their not inconsiderable intellectual powers in this direction. They manage to think *limited city* exchanges to be do-able by resolutely concentrating their attention upon all-out general nuclear war as the *only* alternative to the one they are considering at the moment. This means that they first think of unlimited attack or unlimited retaliation, and then and by the aid of that unspeakable horror they manage to think of a limitation just short of that as possibly choiceworthy and do-able. Thus, Kahn writes: "*If the only alternatives are* between the all-out mutually homicidal war and the city exchange, bizarre and unpleasant as the city exchange is, it is not as bizarre and unpleasant as complete mutual homicide—even if a confusing and obsolete doctrine seems to make the latter the more conventional response. *It is precisely the value of this model that it jars me into adjusting intellectually* to the changed character of modern war." [34]

Klaus Knorr writes that limited strategic retaliation is "absolutely speaking, a calamity" so great that "a rational person will consider it only if all available alternatives are appreciably worse." [35] To be sure, he seems to believe that there may be a *number* of alternatives that might be worse; and he even implies that, if strategic forces become more stable and invulnerable, this *might* be a form of war frequently resorted to. I suggest, however, that this can be done, or genuinely considered only if the *sole* alternative is to go higher still, i.e., to go rapidly to all-out counter-city retaliation. This, at least, is what Knorr's conclusion seems to mean: "From every conceivable point of view it looks like a bad war and a bad strategy. But the question remains whether the available alternatives may not be, or may not come to be, more absurd and worse; and the possibility cannot be ruled out that *our* choices, *and* our opponent's

[34] *Thinking About the Unthinkable*, p. 134 (italics added). Or see p. 133: "The comparison should be made with the destructive all-out war, and the reader must fully understand that, *at least in our model*, this destruction really is total. Everybody is killed. Nobody is left. In these circumstances I believe one could expect the decision makers to prefer the controlled city exchange to the all-out war."

[35] *Limited Strategic War*, p. 11.

choices, may become as absolutely bad as that implies." [36] There is only a short distance between the most violent use and *this* "least undesirable" use of nuclear weapons. The fact that *any* city-exchanges seem equally undesirable, or nearly so, produced the first significant attempt to procure for this nation a wider range of choices: McNamara's move toward counter-forces warfare. Significantly, in his concluding comment on these essays, T. C. Schelling writes: "the concept of limited reprisal is something that a rational decision-maker can invent or discover in five minutes, once he is in a situation in which general war is an appalling prospect, a local tactical campaign is ineffectual, and inactivity and withdrawal are intolerable. It takes an act of intellect to *exclude* this kind of strategy from consideration. . . ." [37] It also takes an act of intellectual surrender to base strategy on city exchanges without making every effort to procure for ourselves other alternatives.

2. Whenever another pair of possible wars is in mind—when the analyst contrasts limited counter-value or counter-city warfare with limited counter-forces war—it seems very clear that the latter is choiceworthy for far more than quantitative reasons. Counter-city or counter-people warfare is bizarre, whether it is limited or unlimited. Doubtless there are distinctions to be made according to whether such war (fought between commanders proving their resolve by means of their cities and people) is partially or totally destructive, whether one of the contending wills seeks to bargain and to prevail over the other in measured terms or goes all-out against that other will. There are distinctions of objective importance in comparative damage to the societies and in the number of casualties. But, in addition to these *quantitative* comparisons, there is also a *qualitative* distinction between counter-city and counter-force which soon discloses itself in the midst of cool calculations of one-city-for-one or five-cities-for-one. No person can remain content with saying, "fifty cities is a lot to lose," or contemplate for long actually *doing* the fighting of a war in which "Both A and B will run out of cities before B runs out of missiles." [38] So there are qualitative reasons to recommend that, as an upper limit, nuclear warfare limited to counter-force be designed, if there is to be nuclear war, and for as long as there remain any nuclear weapons.

3. The Knorr and Read volume reveals quite clearly the abyss of infinitude and illimitability into which a strategic city exchange has already plunged. To this there are no real boundaries; and to speak of "quantitative" limitations is misleading and dangerous language. Even the understandings reached during the fighting will be arbitrary ones

---

[36] *Ibid.*, p. 30.
[37] *Ibid.*, p. 257.
[38] Cf. Kahn, *op. cit.*, pp. 138, 142.

maintained only by encounters of resolve. It is true, the bargaining is not only over survival or prevailing. It is also over "the criteria of behavior permissible in the nuclear age;"[39] such war is "a contest to define the rules of the game"[40] while the game is being played. The "teachers" must themselves be "learning" what they are going to will this war to be.[41] As Thornton Read puts it: if "strategic punishment is limited voluntarily," then it not only influences bargaining but is itself "also a subject to bargain about"; "when punishment is limited by the will (rather than the capability) to inflict it, every tactical engagement becomes an individual case of tacit bargaining."[42] An aspect of war that has always been present in it has now become its whole content: war now has to be "conducted according to rules that are themselves subject to tacit bargaining,"[43] for example, whether the cities exchanged are equivalent or accepted by the other side as an indication of equivalent or greater resolve. The expression Read uses, "a pure punitive contest," is itself probably too restrospective. This strategy is, on the contrary, primarily prospective: one side is teaching the other "strategic foresight." In contrast, punishment has an appositeness and therefore may have limits, which are not to be found in war whose purpose is to convince your opponent that you have irreversibly passed (by slow motion, to be sure) to higher levels, because you are irrevocably committed to "appositeness *plus*" following each exchange. The side wins which first effectively communicates the fact that it will take two cities for one.

What then can Kaplan mean by saying that "limited strategic retaliation depends on and appeals to the inherent rationality of the players"? He means: "It induces them to think in cooperative rather than in strictly competitive ways. . . ."[44] But the writers of other essays make abundantly clear that this spiritualizing of conflict into cooperation only means "shared intimidation."[45] Only the optical illusion suffered by voluntarists and idealists could encourage anyone to imagine there must be more limits to this than in limited conventional war.[46] The more the players are lion-hearted and resolved to prevail, the more obvious it becomes that there are no boundaries to be found simply by pooling intimidation. On the contrary, each contestant must strive to demonstrate to the other that he is inexorably going higher. No matter how slow

[39] Kaplan in *Limited Strategic War*, p. 149.
[40] *Ibid.*, p. 154.
[41] There are "probably intolerable 'expenses' of the educational program." Burns in *Limited War*, p. 168.
[42] *Ibid.*, pp. 82, 84, 86.
[43] *Ibid.*, pp. 82, 84, 86.
[44] *Ibid.*, p. 158.
[45] Knorr and Schelling in *ibid.*, pp. 21 and 247.
[46] Kaplan in *ibid.*, p. 159.

the pace up the scale of "value" exchanged, that side wins which appears most like an ascending force of nature. The "heart of the problem" for each contestant, once limited strategic retaliation has begun, is that he must "by individual examples . . . achieve the credibility of *an irreversible trend*." [47]

The way to win such a war is to get in the car, cold sober, with 20–20 vision and with the steering mechanism in perfect working condition, but with an accelerator so contrived that it will press itself very, very slowly to the floor unless and until the car's radar picks up a beam which tells it that the other car has pulled off the road or that its driver has retarded his speed. T. C. Schelling's comment at the end of his volume is worth noting, concerning a "mistake that one can be seduced into," and, he seems to imply, one made by some of the contributors. This is the supposition that "to conduct war in the measured cadence of limited reprisal somehow . . . gives it rational qualities that it would otherwise lack." Instead, writes Schelling:

> The situation is fundamentally indeterminate as far as logic goes. There is no logical reason why two adversaries will not bleed each other to death, drop by drop, each continually feeling that if he can only hold out a little longer, the other is bound to give in. There is no assurance that both sides will not come to feel that everything is at stake in this critical test of endurance, that to yield is to acknowledge unconditional submissiveness.

It is cold comfort that the foregoing statement is preceded by the sentence: "Even if this kind of warfare were irrational, it could still enjoy the benefits of slowness, of deliberateness, and of self-control" [48]—except that here Schelling inadvertently makes backhanded reference to another kind of rationality in the conduct of war than the "rationality of irrationality." A slow lobbing value-for-value war, like deterrence by threat of massive retaliation, can best be conducted by providing in advance for making an increasingly "choiceless choice." [49] This can be done, at the time and in the increasingly un-do-able fashion it has to be done, only by "making" oneself actually or apparently less and less the doer of it.

4. The fact that controlled city exchanges are an "un-do-able" way to conduct war becomes evident in the fact that Kahn can think this "unthinkable" only by thinking of its being done *once*. "It is, in fact, hard to imagine a 'controlled' city exchange or similar limited Countervalue at-

[47] Abt and de Sola Pool in *ibid.*, pp. 220–21 (italics added).
[48] *Ibid.*, p. 255. Also see Knorr, p. 5: "Only in a crudely descriptive and arbitrary sense would it be possible to say where limited strategic war ends and 'unlimited' general war begins."
[49] Cf. Benington in *ibid.*, p. 123.

tack being used more than once in two generations," he writes. "If used once, the shock might be sufficient to cause drastic and irreversible changes in the international order that would make repetitions unlikely." [50] He lists the objections against limited general war in order of increasing importance, and places last the objection that "surely even if it worked once or twice it will eventually escalate into all-out war, and that would be the end." [51] Whereupon Kahn comes down heavily on the side of this objection:

> It is, in fact, inconceivable to me that such a system could continue. The objection is less to the strategy than to the model of two nation states both armed to the teeth, both regularly playing a version of the juvenile game of chicken, and yet both somehow expecting the system to last for a long time. I do not believe that this is possible. The proper, possibly the only, way to view this type of controlled war is as an attempt to use what influence one has, while one has it, to "vote" on the system which replaces our current deterrent system with its negotiation and resolution of disputes and political objectives against a background of threatened mutual homicide. One possible effect of a controlled exchange might be a heightened sense of crisis and danger plus a greater realization of the two nations' mutual interest in developing a better system—this could end in a détente. [52]

Surely this says as plainly as anything can that controlled nuclear reprisals against cities is not a proper form of war at all. Into this none of the definite objectives of a nation are extensible at the time of the action —except, of course, the objective of changing the system. The scenario describes a critical *transition* from city reprisals to purposive action. In itself, it cannot be politically *done*. If it is thinkable as being done only once before another line of action takes its place, and if city exchanges cannot even be done once with the expectation that the system is going to last for a long time, then the task of statesmanship is to think through such a critical transition without engaging in it and to initiate action that can continue, if need be, in behalf of definite policies.

If what Kahn supposes is what happens, let this not be called a plan of war among others that can be drawn up. It is rather a catastrophe that exceeds all the limits of warfare, for the purpose of teaching our-

---

[50] Cf. Kahn, *op. cit.*, p. 63.

[51] *Ibid.*, p. 133. Some contributors to the Knorr and Read volume seem to believe that limited strategic war may frequently be used in an era of balanced and invulnerable missile bases. But those who suggest this are using the term "strategic war" to mean strategic counter-forces warfare. Thus Morton Kaplan writes that he "tends to believe that, *unless limited strategic nuclear war reaches the city-busting stage,* it can probably be used at least several times." (*Limited Strategic War,* p. 161, italics added.)

[52] Kahn, p. 135.

selves, and the world, a lesson that might have been otherwise learned simply by taking a little thought *within* the limits war now has, as a just barely purposive extension of politics. For the scenario which begins "the morning after" city exchanges is as follows:

> . . . the President of the United States might send a copy of this book [Granville Clark and Louis B. Sohn, *World Peace Through World Law*, (Cambridge, Mass.: Harvard University Press, 1959)] to Premier Khrushchev, saying, "There's no point in your reading this book; you will not like it any more than I did. I merely suggest you sign it, right after my signature. This is the only plan that has been even roughly thought through; let us therefore accept it. We surely do not wish to set up a commission to study other methods of organizing the world, because within weeks both of us will be trying to exploit our common danger for unilateral advantages. If we are to have a settlement, we must have it now, before the dead are buried." [53]

Instead of even once doing the unthinkable which is "un-do-able," it might even be possible to think in another (habitually) unthinkable direction: "serious, tough-minded study of world government or other 'alternatives' might even result in a scheme's being devised that could be negotiated without the pressure of war," [54] or rather without contriving a catastrophe illegitimately called "war" to "make" ourselves think politically. In any case, it is significant that most of the viable war plans Kahn runs through in his volume *Thinking About the Unthinkable* (in settings that are more imaginable in real political encounters than the *one* model that can ever give counter-city reprisals an apparent choice-worthiness) are controlled counter-force, or this *plus avoidance* of civilian damage, even when this seems to sacrifice some military advantage!

5. Finally, there are internal considerations, as well as external ones, why even limited city exchanges must be judged politically un-do-able, especially by the government of a free-society, un-do-able even once in the expectation that such a system will continue:

> If every time a hard decision has to be made, a major portion of the country has to be risked; if every time a country's diplomat walks into a hostile conference room, every man, woman and child feels threatened; if every time a nation stands firm against aggressive probes panic seizes the hearts of many of its citizens, then many citizens will simply adopt an attitude of denial or apathetic fatalism. Others will call for "peace" at any price with such intensity that their governments will have to get out of their way. There may even be some who will say, "Better a fearful end than endless fear." Responsible political life is likely to suffer dis-

[53] P. 148.
[54] P. 150.

astrously as a result of a combination of apathy, denial, and hysteria. The trouble with "negotiating" in this atmosphere is that, to put it mildly, it is not likely to produce thoughtful, considered suggestions or programs. It will instead invite blackmail and deception by the government which is in better control of its people, and irresponsible rigidity or destabilizing weakness by the government which cannot manipulate its people.[55]

This says as plainly as anything can that war plans based on the premise that civilian lives and property are to be sacrificed indiscriminately or made the object of attack in planned city exchanges, however controlled, are imaginable only in a world in which legitimate political activity has already been strangled. Men, cities, and politics have already been put to death in thinking this unthinkable thing that is also, in and of its very nature, politically "un-do-able" conduct in war. This is not a surprising conclusion, since the "natural justice" of counter-forces warfare defines the upper limit of the use of force which is politically justifiable.

To this reader, the most interesting chapter in the Knorr and Read volume is that by Clark C. Abt and Ithiel de Sola Pool on "The Constraint of Public Attitudes." This is an inquiry into whether the strategy under consideration can "satisfy the constraints of the politically possible." [56] This, happily, is "not, in any rigorous sense, a researchable subject," [57] except by means of speculative scenarios. The response of people, and particularly of a people who have a measure of influence on their government's decisions, to an actual city exchange is in no sense comparable to their reaction to the destruction of an entire town by a natural disaster, nor even to their probable reaction to damage of the same magnitude that may be the unavoidable side-effect of counter-forces nuclear war. To speculate about what their reaction will be is, I believe, to speculate about the rudiments of the just-war doctrine that still makes its presence felt.

The most these authors seem able to say in behalf of a counter-city war plan is that "the strategy may still be worth planning for if it can be a contingency policy, available for use if public opinion turns out to tolerate it. . . .[58] Even the idea of folding this war away in a contingency plan is not actually supported by their findings of probable fact. It is true that during the time of actual execution one possible public reaction counterbalances another. Perhaps the people in threatened cities "would channel their fears and anxieties into the direct self-protective actions of evac-

[55] Pp. 214–15.
[56] *Limited Strategic War*, p. 199.
[57] Knorr in *ibid.*, p. 23.
[58] P. 204.

uation rather than into civil protest." [59] Perhaps, on the other hand, "substantial portions of the people living in the cities threatened with prompt counter-reprisals, *if given time to make their opinions known on the matter,* would be violently opposed to the United States' initiation of limited reprisal against Novosibirsk." [60]

The question, however, concerns civil protest not only during the execution of this strategy, but also *before, during,* and *afterward,* unless politics has already been put to death before cities and people are. Statesmen cannot long remain, if they ever are, isolated from the civil life it is their function to serve. Therefore, "the major inhibition felt by the President would be his *perception* of what public opinion was likely to be *after* the crisis." To be prepared to fight a counter-forces war requires a "community" fall-out shelter system, correlated with private shelters. To be prepared to fight a counter-city war, however, would make it rather dangerous for the statesman to allow the people thus to congregate, since "large communal shelters in cities might be the scene of considerable political agitation that might have both immediate and long-term effects." [61] People must be isolated from one another if a decision-maker is to be sufficiently isolated from them to make this a do-able policy. Free political life would have to be put to death if this is the way a nation's survival is to be engineered. This analysis is revelatory of the inherently non-political character of this supposed strategy. It means that "many of the problems that may result from the adoption of a policy of limited retaliation could arise if the policy were even considered with sufficient seriousness for people to believe that it might be undertaken." [62]

So there they stand, these "spiritualized" conquerors, each seeking to "prevail" by throwing cities to rubble, as wealthy dandies in San Francisco used to fight their "duels" by throwing gold dollars into the Bay until one of them had the will to do so no longer. It is evident that the people of one of the selected cities will have to be put out of politics before they can knowingly agree to their own government's arbitrary resolve to use them in this game of tit-for-tat. And it would be *their own* government's resolve and not that of the enemy alone, since if this game stays limited everything will depend on the enemy's attacking no more cities or cities only a little larger than those we have "signaled" him to take out by

[59] P. 215.
[60] P. 214.
[61] P. 215.
[62] P. 237. Under this strategy, the relation of the people of our cities to their government domestically is the same as the relation of a smaller ally to an alliance thinking of adopting this policy, if the ally is apt to be offered as target or more of a target. See, in *Limited Strategic War,* Arthur Lee Burns on "The Problem of Alliances."

our own immediately prior choice of targets from among his cities. This is a war that is supposed to be fought slowly up the range of the "value" we and the enemy have agreed to place on cities in order that the sacrifice of them will, in turn, effectively signal to the enemy our determination to go only somewhat higher than he.

So there they stand, these "spiritual" warriors, as they engage in a war of nerves, each saying to the other, "There, you see, one of us has to be rational, and since it's not going to be me, it has to be you, or you first." This war of "value for value"

> can be regarded as a late and perhaps last desperate move in the *economization* of war and world politics. Arms and men are more or less scarce means having alternative uses; resources such as cities, fertile country-sides, and even stable social systems are, in one aspect, economic goods— as implied in the strategic term countervalue.[63]

The people of a country cannot knowingly accept their complete inclusion in this process of the *economization* of politics by which they themselves are reduced to the status of values in exchange. No government responsive to their will or responsible for their weal can conduct war in this fashion. In contrast, the civil damage collateral to actually fighting a counter-forces war will seem rationally directed to some purpose, and it is intended to be, even if the damage proves as extensive or more. As with massive or balanced deterrence, so with value-for-value war that has none but the quantitative limits which the weakness of one side's resolve may allow: these war plans are intrinsically intolerable. Both are tolerated only because people don't think about them or because people who think about them stand several steps back from thinking through the actual doing of them, or because they think grimly that, if only we have these wars in preparation and are strong enough in our will to use them, why, then none of them will ever have to be used.

On the other hand, no one should blink at the fact that the transformation of "political man" into "economic man" may have proceeded so far in the contemporary period that it has become an irreversible trend in this civilization. Then modern man will sooner or later destroy himself. This will be because of his merely quantitative evaluation of human life and of ethical and political conduct, because of the economization of politics, and his lack of capacity for political agency and for making sound political judgments concerning the do-able and the inherently un-do-able. These things increasingly characterize all of the realms of decision. This leads, in international relations, to a nation's unquestioning acceptance of the supposed rationality of counter-value warfare.

[63] Burns in *ibid.*, p. 170.

SUGGESTED POLICY DECISIONS

The "just conduct" of war proscribing deliberate direct attack upon non-combatants, and the primacy in war of weapon-to-weapon trials of strength over a contest of wills, are not, of course, immediately *constitutive* of policy decisions or war plans. But these are *regulative* of such decisions, so long as war remains in any measure a definite purposive political act.

I will venture here to suggest a series of policy decisions which seem to me imperative at this hour for the free world's security. These suggestions are put forward with a great degree of reluctance, since I do not believe that ethico-political analysis extends so far beyond providing regulative moral guidance. Not every decision, not even every important decision, is an *ethical* decision, and many exceedingly important choices are the business of statesmen and of experts other than the moralist. Still, with the aid of other experts the following suggestions can be made for steps that need urgently to be taken. None of these decisions waits on international agreement. Each must be *declared* policy, and each can at least begin to be put into effect by "unilateral initiatives."

1. This nation, and other nations of the West, need increasingly to procure forces for sub-conventional and conventional warfare, and at the same time to repair in public consciousness a doctrine of the possible and just use of such forces. Of course, it may be said about conventional forces that we lost that "arms race" with the Russians long ago, or rather never sought seriously to enter upon it. It is also true that the strength needed for conventional warfare would require a change of heart in that "economic man" who bears the name of the free world taxpayer. He must be told in no uncertain terms that his unexamined reliance on deterrence of total war by threat of total war and mutual homicide policies are themselves of a piece with his unwillingness to prepare for any real trial of strength. He must be told that he is in mortal danger precisely because at every level of warfare he is so completely non-political and unpurposive. Hoping to banish the use of force by threatening unusable force, he only banishes usable force and pulls the nerve of action. It is an ominous weakness in the West that the enemy can heat a crisis to almost any temperature knowing that the West will be no better prepared after the event. Men will be called up, it is true, but we now give a crisis-maker the luxury of knowing in advance that very soon the *status quo ante* will be restored.[64] The free world taxpayer must be awakened

[64] On the same pleasant summer evening in August, 1962, the "Seven O'Clock Report" showed film and the voices of reservists complaining how useless their call-up

from the dream of deterrence; and he must be told that we cannot make unjust, inter-city warfare measurably more of an impossibility without making just or counter-forces warfare again a possibility. This means, first and foremost, strength in conventional arms; and there is no analyst who does not say that NATO could match the mythical Russian "hordes," and the whole free world could do this at every point of probable vital challenge.

If religious opinion has any influence on public opinion, and that in turn on high-level policy decisions, then a false Christian identification of the peace of God with the peace of the earthly city must bear a share of responsibility for this nation's reliance on war that can never under any circumstances be fought, and its simultaneous abandonment of the sort of war that can be used. No churchman can condemn the one without condemning the other. He cannot in good conscience oppose the present reliance of the U.S. on massive weapons unless he also confesses that, during the period we developed this reliance, a general "Christian" pacifism contributed to it and to our present design of war by a sweeping opposition to a more equitable and universal military service. In 1948, for example, it required only a one- or two-man social action lobby of the Presbyterian church and a few telephone calls to prominent Presbyterians in Oklahoma to determine the vote of one representative which was decisive in Republican caucus in bottling up a universal training bill in committee and in insuring that it never reached the floor of Congress for debate.[65]

2. This nation should announce that as a matter of policy we will never be the first to use nuclear weapons—*except* tactical ones that may and will be used, against forces only and not strategically against an enemy's heartland, to stop an invasion across a clearly defined boundary, our own or one we are pledged by treaty to defend. This would make it

---

was ten months ago, and a commentator's analysis of the evidences that Russian military might was being mobilized in support of another Berlin crisis about to be created.

[65] See R. Morton Darrow, "The Church and Techniques of Political Action" in *Religion in American Life*, ed. by J. W. Smith and Leland Jamison (Princeton, N.J.: Princeton University Press, 1960), Vol. II, 186–87. The author considers only the technique of making religious opinion politically effective, not the substance of the matter.

After a nuclear war, the survivors may well ask concerning the complicity of the churches and "peace" groups in the assistance our government gave to the enemy in killing people he did not want to kill—by locating missiles near populated cities and by failing to construct a national system of community fall-out shelters. If this question is asked, the answer can only be that such resulted from the effort good people of the previous age made never to grow accustomed to the idea of nuclear war, from their resolve instead to avoid war altogether, and from the natural kinship between their views and *pacifistic deterrence*.

unambiguously clear that tactical nuclear weapons will be used if need be against any invasion, even by conventional forces. The threat would be believable, because of the clearly declared limits which state that the use of nuclear weapons will be defensive only and that not even in reply to an invasion will we first use nuclear weapons "offensively" against an enemy's territory or his strategic forces. This would make it unnecessary for the President of the United States constantly to warn off a possible invasion of Europe by words that allow the possibility of our initiating the use of nuclear weapons in a strike against Russian cities or against her strategic bases. This proposal may be called the right of first defensive use of nuclear weapons against invading forces, or a commitment to use nuclear weapons first only over one's own territory.

This proposal has been made by Paul Nitze,[66] and more recently by Leo Szilard [67] and Thornton Read.[68] While Szilard's formulation should be looked at to see the significance of the inclusion of this policy decision among the tenets of a Council for Abolishing War, the fuller and sounder analysis by Thornton Read affords us the clearest way to elaborate further the meaning of this second policy proposal. Thornton Read has written most eloquently and forcefully concerning the value of preserving the distinction between conventional and nuclear weapons as such, of preserving the fear the people of the world have of ever again crossing this boundary, and of channelling this fear into a proposal for neutralizing nuclear weapons in a system of international sanctions against their use.[69] Without even invoking the danger of escalating from tactical to massive nuclear weapons, he has satisfactorily demonstrated the essentially escalatory character of tactical nuclear weapons themselves, because of the relation of their weight to their fire power in comparison with conventional explosives, a relation which places a great gulf between conventional weapons and tactical nuclears as possible instruments of controlled warfare.[70]

Thornton Read does not lightly find virtue in a proposal involving a possible first use of tactical nuclears. The fact is that he can do so only because he thinks it may be possible to link legitimate first use of tactical nuclears with another well-understood limit, namely, national boundaries,

[66] *East-West Negotiations* (Washington Center of Foreign Policy Research, 1958), pp. 28–36.

[67] "Are We On The Road to War?" *Bulletin of the Atomic Scientists*, April, 1962.

[68] "The Proposal to Use Nuclear Weapons Over One's Own Territory," Unpublished paper, Center of International Studies, Princeton, 1962.

[69] *A Proposal to Neutralize Nuclear Weapons.* Center of International Studies, Princeton. Policy Memorandum No. 22, Dec. 15, 1960.

[70] "Counterforce Strategies and Arms Control," Center of International Studies, Princeton, March, 1962 (unpublished); and *Limited Strategic War*, pp. 72–77.

which may serve to sustain an even more important agreement concerning the rules of conflict. This is his proposal for defensive first use in or over one's own invaded territory. Such a declaration of policy is, of course, a positive assertion of legitimacy which requires, and makes it possible to declare, that not even to stop a massive conventional invasion will we use nuclear weapons offensively first. *This possibility we now hold ambiguously open* for ourselves in order to "strengthen the deterrent." Yet in view of the destruction an offensive first strike over an enemy's territory would immediately let loose over our own, it has become increasingly unbelievable that we would ever employ this threatened "plan" for any of the definite military or political objectives involved in recent crises. Thus, the proposal is that we publicly renounce that first use of nuclear weapons which we can really mean to renounce, while asserting a defensive first use of tactical nuclears tied to the repulsion of an invasion across a conventionally defended boundary.

> National boundaries have the same sort of clarity and symbolic significance as the distinction between conventional and nuclear weapons. Crossing the nuclear threshold has, in fact, been compared to crossing a national boundary. Both limits are unambiguous and both are the focus for strong feelings.
>
> The proposal to use nuclear weapons defensively combines two sharp and unambiguous discontinuities in the spectrum of violence and says that crossing a clear-cut geographical boundary justifies the opponent in crossing the equally clear-cut discontinuity between conventional and nuclear weapons.[71]

It may also be added that the qualitative discontinuity between counter-force and counter-people warfare is tied in with boundaries, if nuclear weapons are ever justifiably used. The side using nuclear weapons justifiably would have every incentive to limit their destructiveness and to maintain sufficient conventional forces either to hold the border or to slow an invasion so that civilians could be evacuated from between the lines. Moreover, "the region that is fair game for a nuclear attack is not only clearly defined and small in area; *it does not even exist until the aggressor creates it.*" The objective in this use of tactical nuclears will not be "victory" but defense strictly understood as sealing the border. "At the border there would be a discontinuity in the life expectancy of enemy soldiers. In crossing the border residual life expectancy would drop from, say, fifty years to fifty minutes. This would establish a powerful incentive

[71] Thornton Read, "The Proposal to Use Nuclear Weapons Over One's Own Territory" (Unpublished). Subsequent and undesignated quotations are also from this document.

not to cross and would create serious problems of morale for the aggressor."

This is certainly a clear case of "just conduct" in a first resort to nuclear weapons. It is counter-forces warfare surrounded by the additional limitation of the aggressor-defender distinction. And it allows "bargaining" and an encounter of wills in which rules of warfare may be agreed to, created, preserved, or enforced. Here the aim is not "to bind a potential violator through his sense of honor" but "to influence his behavior by creating in his mind expectations as to how we will respond." This is its superiority over a simple proscription of aggression.

At the same time, in contrast to our present policy which admits the possibility of a first initiation of nuclear warfare over an enemy's territory, "the advantage of the more restrictive rule is that it is more credible" and therefore more likely to deter invasion in the first place as well as more likely to bring about tacit agreements to limit nuclear war by restricting it to forces. The point is to "emphasize the distinction between the defensive and the offensive use of nuclear weapons so that it becomes a focus of expectations comparable to the nuclear-conventional distinction." Breaching the latter distinction may serve to enforce the former. This proposal is, therefore, also a struggle over the rules of warfare. "An aggressor having superior conventional forces would try to establish the rule that nuclear weapons should not be used at all. The defender would want to establish the rule that nuclear weapons could be used defensively but not offensively." But this is far removed from a limitless struggle of empty wills, each only reflecting the other, *disconnected* from encounters of real power.

Before going on to my third point, a comment may be inserted here concerning Leo Szilard's formulation of this proposal that *"America could and should adopt the policy that, in case of war, if she were to use atomic bombs against troops in combat, she would do so only on her own side of the prewar boundary."* [72] Against the objection that it is an odd war, indeed, in which weapons with the greater destructive side-effects are reserved for use over one's own territory, Szilard gives the obvious answer: "I do not know to what extent West German cities could be spared by a judicious tactical use of atomic bombs by American forces, but I do know that if America were to use bombs beyond the pre-war boundary, West German cities would be destroyed by Russian bombs." In comparison with "the simple pledge renouncing the use of the bomb" altogether, the proposed commitment "would be easier to keep and therefor it would be a more believable pledge" (though Szilard does suggest that "it would be possible for Western Europe to build up within five

---

[72] Quoted from "Are We on the Road to War?"

years conventional forces to the point where it could renounce the use of atomic bombs against troops in combat in case of war").

To announce unilaterally, as Szilard proposes, this limitation upon any first use of nuclears requires us also to renounce unilaterally *"plans which call for a first strike against Russian rocket and strategic bases in case of war"* and to renounce *"the policy of 'deterring' Russia, with the threat that America would resort to such a first strike in case of war."* The "general *deterrent"* would be given up; and in urging this surely Szilard is correct when he says that America would not "lose much by giving up the threat of strategic bombing because the deterrent effect of such a threat is negligible unless the threat is believable," which increasingly it is not. A *second* strike, however, should be maintained, as a threat and a promise, in case *"American cities or bases are attacked with bombs, or if there is an unprovoked attack with bombs against one of America's allies."* Szilard's use of the word "bomb" for all nuclears is inexact, of course. He probably means to justify an attack first upon the stratetgic *forces* of an enemy who has used tactical nuclears offensively on the territory of our allies. If so, the above statement amounts to a crucial point yet to be considered in Read's rule for restricting legitimate use of nuclears to one's own territory, namely, that any violation of this rule will, for the first time, make offensive strikes legitimate over the enemy's territory. Szilard's present proposal shows that when a powerful intellect (even though his mind is the mind of a scientist) focuses attention on the grave problem of war today, he will be driven to follow the lineaments of the just-war doctrine in his policy proposals.[73]

[73] Szilard's mind wanders from the problem of concrete political and military policy, and his political objectives "which must be pursued in the next couple of years" turn into "steps" which must be taken toward a more lofty goal, and are of value only if they lead to this goal. These policy proposals, which surely are worthwhile in themselves to limit war, are only "in order to make the present danger of war recede to the point where attention could be focused on the task of abolishing war."

No one would deny that attention must be given to this task, but it must be political reason and political action which attend to it. Unfortunately, in Szilard's case it is "scientific" reason instead of the political reason he exercised in the concrete proposals. These are all set in the context of the formation of a "Council for Abolishing War." This Council is to have "fellows (who are all scientists)" and would elect a board of directors, on which "membership would not be restricted to scientists." A panel of political advisors, of course, would be assembled. The scientific Council would by these means formulate two sets of objectives. "To the first set belong those objectives which can not be attained at the present time through political action because it would take further inquiry, and perhaps even real research to know, in concrete terms, what needs to be done. To the second set belong those objectives which can be pursued through political action because it is clear what needs to be done [presumably Szilard's concrete policy proposals]." A *political* movement will be brought into being to enable us to back away "from purposeless warfare. *Scientific* research may then tell us how to abolish it altogether." Thus, "the combination of a few per

Something like this is what anyone will come up with if he focuses attention on how we are to "back away from the war to which we have come dangerously close," and to which we still stand too dangerously close.

3. In the foregoing, we have bracketed for the moment the ques-

---

cent of the votes and the sweet voice of reason might turn out to be an effective combination."

A conversation between Szilard and Polanyi is not, I think, untypical of this sort of reasoning. Polanyi said that, since it might be suicidal for people to be *overly* generous, "perhaps the rule ought to be 'Be one per cent more generous to people than they are to you.' This should be sufficient . . . because if everyone were to follow this rule, the earth would, step by step, turn into a livable place." [An alternative name for Szilard's Council is "Council for a Livable World."] To which in reply Szilard summed up the phenomena in human nature and politics which theologians have always called the boundless "sin" of man, by saying, "each is bound to think that he is 30 per cent more generous than the other"; and he proceeded to slay this with a rule: "Perhaps if we were to stipulate as the rule of conduct 'Be 31% more generous to others than they are to you' such a rule might work." Everywhere in this article Szilard describes the men he wants in his proposed Council and movement as men who have an adequate "historical" point of view, meaning (I think) men who believe the bomb has completely changed the nature of history and of politics and who are as a consequence resolved to reconcile the nations by rules and abolish war by additional research in the time provided by the foregoing concrete political proposals. This is exceedingly *un*historical and *non*-political reasoning.

This may seem needlessly harsh on that great man and generous spirit who is Leo Szilard. I have already paid tribute to his concrete proposals as disclosing the very anatomy of just and rational conduct in war. But one cannot forget the fact that Szilard was also the first to propose that *counter-value* warfare be planned and, if need be, put into execution. ("Disarmament and the Problem of Peace," *Bulletin of the Atomic Scientists*, October, 1955, pp. 297–307.) Once he also speculatively proposed a variant of Kahn's Doomsday deterrent machine: cadres of Russian demolition experts under New York City and an American demolition team under Moscow, to make certain neither side can ever fire their massive weapons because neither *can* want to, and because both are now *bound* to want peace. ("The Mined Cities," *Bulletin of the Atomic Scientists*, Dec. 1961, pp. 407–412.) To such proposals the ascendency of the scientific mind in politics almost invariably comes. (For an excellent study of scientific advisors in government, the undeniable political character of their "scientific" advice, and the additional confusion introduced by the fact that they often fail to acknowledge this, see Robert Gilpin: *American Scientists and Nuclear Weapons Policy* [Princeton, N.J.: Princeton University Press, 1962].) Such proposals are in play because of the ascendency of "making" over principles for the guidance of political agency and inherent in proper "doing." One must question, not the present proposals themselves, but whether they are soundly grounded. Is not Szilard and the "scientific" mind generally just a special case of the modern mentality which out of limitless passion for peace on earth might be willing to design and do unlimited war? Was it because he simply became convinced his former proposals could not be "made" to work or because he began to think politically that Szilard wrote his recent article? Does *he* understand that his concrete proposals were born out of the morality of war's conduct which has validity in a multi-national world long before and apart from the descent of peace?

tion whether the first use of tactical nuclears only between the front line and the border crossed is a rule we want simply for the five years needed to mount adequate conventional forces, or whether this self-imposed rule of war should be regarded as a permanent part of justifiable resistance to conventional invasion in a nuclear age. Should the United States have as its ultimate goal the preparation of conventional defense so that as soon as possible it can accept a prohibition of *any* first use of nuclear weapons?

The more one thinks about a policy of using tactical nuclears defensively, and unilateral initiatives to try to govern war in this fashion, the more it seems a possible choice for the nations of the world for the entire age in which nuclear weapons have been invented. At least we are forced to ask whether it is only for the time being that security for the free world and the peace of the entire world could be based on this proposal. If this first use of nuclear arms can be tied to the resistance of aggression across well-understood and conventionally well-defended boundaries, will not free world security and world peace be less in danger? Will not this be better than an absolute distinction between conventional and nuclear explosives as a basis for the peace-keeping machinery of some future international organization? Or, on the contrary, ought we to begin now to strengthen conventional forces with a view to placing all nuclear weapons in a class by themselves as illegitimate weapons (like bacteriological weapons) which may be possessed to deter their use by an enemy but never used first even in self-defense? [74]

In whichever way this question is decided, it is of great importance that freedom-loving and peace-loving people realize that to renounce the first use of any weapon is a matter more of what they do than of what they say. "To the extent that the Communists are unable to defeat the conventional forces of the free world without resorting to nuclear weapons, the practical effect will be our renunciation of the first use of nuclear weapons." [75] This means that at the moment we may have simply presented the Russians with the ability effectively to renounce the first use of tactical nuclears in the European theater.

4. Nuclear capability must be maintained for use in counter-force strikes over an enemy's territory. These strikes would have a dual purpose: first, to prosecute the trial of strength and destroy or decrease an enemy's forces and the force he can muster on the battlefield; secondly,

---

[74] There is an excellent summary of the arguments for eliminating *any* first use of even tactical nuclear weapons from Western military policy in Halperin, *op. cit.* He, however, does not explicitly consider the possibility of tying first use to a self-imposed and announced policy limiting the use of nuclear weapons to one's own invaded territory.

[75] Henry Kissinger, *The Necessity for Choice* (New York: Harper, 1960), p. 91.

to punish any violation and thus to enforce if possible the rule which we declare by word and by action we have imposed on ourselves, namely, that while defensive first use of tactical nuclear weapons is legitimate, not even in answer to this will we tolerate the use of tactical nuclear weapons offensively over the territory of another nation. Both these purposes indicate that nuclear weapons over an enemy's territory should first be used against *tactical* objectives, munitions dumps, supply lines, bridges, etc. If *nuclear* weapons are used to do this, their use will both prosecute the war and be a signal that the right to do this was granted when the enemy first used nuclear power offensively across another nation's boundary. The reasons for the limitation of these retaliatory strikes to tactical targets, however, will have to be declared again and again and communicated to both the enemy and neutral nations.

If *tactical* targets are clearly the objectives of an answering offensive use of nuclear weapons, the distinction Thornton Read makes between these two uses may be a little too severe:

> The defensive use is primarily to act on the opponent's capability, to deny him territory. The offensive use is rather to act on his will, to punish him and to communicate to him our resolve and our determination not only to defend our territory but to uphold the two rules he has violated, namely the rule against conventional aggression and the rule against the use (or first use) of nuclear weapons against another nation's territory.[76]

Acting upon his will is, of course, important, perhaps now of added importance, but one is still engaged in war to deny him territory and cause him to withdraw. Moreover, in acting upon his will one is doing so by just and limited counter-force means, and with the objective of achieving possible political effects in societies and in the international system that will endure beyond the conflict.

5. We come now to the "no-city" strategy discussed in the first parts of this paper. The statement of U.S. policy that McNamara presented in his University of Michigan address, if carried out, would place as wide a "firebreak" as possible between a war of exchanges involving strategic counter-forces and counter-city strategic warfare. There should also be a "firebreak" between conventional and tactical nuclear warfare—by, for example, not equipping the same troops with both types of weapons—and another between strikes against tactical targets and strikes against strategic forces.

We ought not to say at once that, in the nuclear age, "a main con-

---

[76] "The Proposal to Use Nuclear Weapons . . . ," p. 29.

sequence of limited war, and a main purpose for engaging in it, is *to raise the risk of general war.*" [77] Since "general war" ambiguously embraces both attacks on an enemy's strategic forces and attacks upon his cities, this implies that a main purpose of engaging in any form of limited war is to indicate that we are prepared to go to massive retaliation against cities. This is to regard the main purpose of any of the forms of limited war as a simple trial of wills. We ought rather to say that one of the consequences and one of the purposes of limited conventional or tactical nuclear war is *to raise the risk of counter-force strategic war.* A nation which first makes use of tactical nuclear weapons to resist a conventional aggression, for example, says by that action that it may be finally willing to use strikes against the enemy's homeland tactical targets or missile bases to impose on him its self-imposed rule that nuclear weapons are to be used only defensively and to punish any violation of this limit. The latter is clearly one purpose of nuclear war at the first level. Its main purpose is to seal the border and defend the country. Its main purpose, in any case, is not to raise the risk but to preserve a limit, and to conduct *the war* against *the war* that has been mounted.

Moreover, the risk which the defender raises is still counter-forces warfare and not the mutual destruction of societies. The will to fight "counterforce-plus-avoidance" can be signalled to the enemy, can work to keep war limited and enforce tacit or declared agreements about the rules of war in international law, *only* if one is able to fight such a war marked off as clearly as possible from "general war." One must have the ability to carry limited counter-force warfare to the enemy's own territory in order to bargain effectively about the limits and rules by which war is to be fought.

6. Just as it would be wrong to say of unconventional, conventional, or tactical nuclear war that it is *nothing but* deterrence during the war, so it is also wrong to say that a no-city strategy "is nothing but deterrence during a war." Counter-force strikes over an enemy's territory, and preparations to limit war to this, do replace the assumption of massive general deterrence policy (so far as it is possible to deter a rational enemy *before* the war starts) with the assumption that "it surely is possible to deter that rational enemy from going to city destruction even if the war starts." [78] Such deterrence during strategic strikes against forces is only an aspect of even this war whose principal purpose is to enforce *lower* limits, punish violations of them, and in any case decrease the enemy's military capability and affect the balance of power

[77] T. C. Schelling, "Nuclear Strategy in Europe," *World Politics,* Vol. XIV, No. 3 (April, 1962), 421.
[78] Richard Fryklund, *100 Million Lives,* p. 89.

in the world after the war is over. Still, all forms of limited war, including counter-force strikes over the enemy's territory, do have this additional purpose of reducing his will to fight, or to fight in certain ways, by indicating our possible willingness to go higher still.

The capstone of this system, which includes war at any of the lower limits in a nuclear age, seems finally to be the deterrence of city destruction by the threat of city destruction. Thus, Fryklund sums up the no-city strategy that may now be in the making:

> We adopt publicly a weapon-against-weapon strategy and concede that there are no targets in Soviet cities worth destroying at the cost of our own cities. At the same time, we emphasize that if the Communists start blasting our cities, we will use our hidden invulnerable forces to wipe out their cities. To make the decision easier for the Russians, we see to it that none of our cities or suburbs contain important military targets.[79]

Even if we can say that the Russians and the West have equal reason for policy decisions based on the judgment that "no matter what happens it doesn't make sense to start hitting cities," there stands in the background and in support of this the fact that in the nuclear age city destruction seems to be deterred only by the threat of city destruction in reprisal. Thus, McNamara went on to say in his University of Michigan policy statement:

> The very strength and nature of the Alliance forces make it possible for us to retain, even in face of a massive surprise attack, sufficient reserve striking power to destroy an enemy society if driven to it. In other words, we are giving a possible opponent the strongest imaginable incentive to refrain from striking our own cities.

This question of continual massive deterrence, to which any consideration of limiting policy decisions seems inevitably to be driven, is my concern in the following section.

REPRISALS

In the foregoing, I have argued that the no-cities, or counterforce-plus-avoidance, policy is the only just and sensible way to conduct war; that weapons analysts have sometimes overlooked the distinction between the unthinkable that has simply not yet been thought and the unthinkable that is un-do-able when thought about; that war as a trial of wills

---

[79] *Ibid.*, p. 97.

disconnected from trials of strength becomes an abysmal and unlimited conflict or resolutions; that current discussions of "general" war or "limited strategic war" need to distinguish more clearly between long-range attacks on strategic forces and strategic attacks on cities; and finally I advanced tentatively a gradation of policy decisions designed to set "fire-breaks" between the steps in increasing violence up to the no-cities or strategic counter-force policy. We need now to take up the moral and practical questions involved in "deterrence during the war," which at every stage seems necessary to keep war limited in these ways.

I shall argue that none of the virtues of the limiting policy decisions for which a case can be made, or of war considered only in the context of constant massive deterrence, can invalidate the distinction between the do-able and the politically un-do-able.

It is frequently contended that "both prudence and international law" permit and make it "desirable to carry out reprisals in kind," and that the only question remaining once an enemy strikes one of our cities is how to determine the equivalence to be exchanged moment by moment in counter-value war.[80] Whatever may be the rule of reprisal in international law today, this can hardly be said to settle the question of the justice—the natural justice—of reprisal in kind (or in *some* kinds). If it is unjust for an enemy to destroy our society, the fact that he does or tries to do so first cannot make it any less of an injustice for us to destroy his. William V. O'Brien's judgment concerning this "pernicious institution of reprisals" seems to me to be irrefutable:

> Few rights are more solidly established in the law of nations than the right of reprisal, and few principles have done so much to gloss over immoral behavior with an aura of legality. . . . This exceptional right [of reprisal in kind] applies to all the laws of war. It is supposed to serve two purposes: it provides a sanction for the law and it tends to restore the balance upset when one belligerent uses illegal means.
>
> Obviously, this kind of "legality" is ridiculous. . . . If bombing cities were really contrary to the law of nations, violation of the law could not affect the legal obligation to refrain from such bombings.[81]

Such a law of reprisals can only be described as a product of an age of legal positivism where justice has become something men and nations "make." No wonder they suppose they can make "just" an act that before was "unjust," or unjust when *first* done. With no sense of the difference between the do-able and the intrinsically un-do-able, the nations may

---

[80] Thornton Read, "The Proposal to Use Nuclear Weapons Over One's Own Territory," (unpublished ms.) p. 28.

[81] "Nuclear War and the Law of Nations," in *Morality and Modern Warfare*, ed. by William J. Nagle (Baltimore, Md.: Helicon Press, 1960), p. 140.

well agree that a certain weapon or plan of war should never be used, unless, of course, it is. That excuse must today be called radically into question.

It can be shown that the traditional limits upon the "just" conduct of war were a product not so much of man's sense of justice as of "social charity" determining, in crucial situations in which the use of force cannot be avoided, how force can be directed to the saving of human life.[82] From this point of view—from the point of view of concrete Christian charity—even more than in the context of the natural justice surrounding killing in war, this so-called law of reprisal in kind, if it is proposed as a sovereign and all-embracing rule for conduct, must itself always be condemned. Pure reprisal between persons or between nations will appear especially heinous to a just or Christian man. Neither in interpersonal nor in international relations will a Christian accept the reduction of moral and political agency to this attempt to gain an empty victory of one will over another. Instead, if he is properly instructed and sensitive to the requirements of a love-informed justice, he is apt to call such punishing reprisal of will against will the very epitome of sin and of injustice.

The injustice of the law of reprisal is perhaps hidden from view in impure cases where actually *doing* the reprisal in kind seems clearly connected with accomplishing some definite purpose. In this way an almost self-enforcing system of diplomatic immunity is maintained, and restrictions are imposed upon the travel of Soviet citizens in this country roughly equivalent to those imposed upon American citizens traveling in Russia. Almost all the laws of war in the past have been enforced, to the extent that they have been enforced, by creating the expectation of reprisal in kind. The tendency toward increasing irreconcilability in the actions of nation-states seems to be slowed down by *doing*, on occasion, the expected reprisal in kind, even if in itself the action has no reconciling power.

But then, it ought to be observed that many of these enforcements, which seem to warrant reprisal in kind, involve actions which are not *malum in se*. In a great many kinds of action the nations can "make" right what they want to, and enforce rules they agree to by reprisals in these kinds. What was not inherently wrong when first done but only legally proscribed, can be legitimately done in reprisal. The possibility of massive nuclear retaliation against the society of an enemy who struck first has made clear that the rule of reprisal in kind was never an all-embracing rule for the conduct of men or nations. *This* kind of reprisal can only be justified by a very immoral "moral" system, or by a positivism

[82] See my *War and the Christian Conscience*, Chap. Three on "The Genesis of Non-Combatant Immunity."

that seeks to "make" right in the second place what was ruled to be wrong in the first.

To the argument from justice and the argument from charity may now be added a third argument against ever *doing* the reprisal in kind that is now in question. Today the irrationality and purposelessness of pure punishment is laid bare, and the spiritualization of war into a contest of resolves is exposed as the most *abysmal* of all wars we could contemplate. One can still contemplate it, but it cannot be done except as an act that no longer has political purpose. Such reprisal would be a choiceless choice, an act without a definite end to be attained. For it can no longer be said that reprisal in kind—the kind we are speaking about—will "restore the balance when one belligerent uses illegal means," or defend freedom or civilization, or hold back from destruction any life worth living, or even that it will enforce a lower limit of warfare.

It remains only to be asked whether actually *carrying out* this reprisal in kind is really necessary in order to "provide a sanction" for the lesser laws and rules of warfare which it is urgently necessary for the nations of the world to impose on themselves and one another.

THE JUSTICE OF DETERRENCE

Clearly, staged limitations upon the conduct of war, each stage separated from another by a "firebreak," depend on deterrence during war, and finally upon the hidden and not so hidden *possibility* that one's own cities may come into range. The threat that one's society as a whole and that of the enemy may be subjected to capital punishment seems necessary as an ultimate resort, to support the rule against the capital punishment of any society as a means of war, and to insure that this limitation is observed.

Shall we say this is to be compared to what must be done by any society which wishes domestically to abolish capital punishment for crimes? An exception has to be made in the case of treason in wartime and in the case of anyone who in resisting arrest shoots a policeman in his execution of the law. In this case, a criminal has not only killed a man; he has also challenged the whole structure of the law, and precisely that law which seeks to order human relationships without capital punishment. For that, capital punishment is not likely to be abolished. Shall we say, then, that the nation which resorts to bombing without avoiding civilian damage as much as it can and instead begins deliberately to strike cities has challenged the laws of civilized conduct in war at such a fundamental point that such a society can be justifiably put to death? That nation has, in fact, violently attacked not only another whole people, but also a central part of the whole system by which, it is hoped, counter-society warfare can be abolished now that it has been invented. Is it not just, then, to exact the supreme penalty under these circumstances?

The objection to this line of reasoning, and one that is fatal to it, is that the analogy does not hold. In the case of enforcing the law, even the law which has abolished capital punishment, by *carrying out the deterrent threat* maintained in the minds of potential "cop-killers," the one put to death is the person who threw down the gauntlet to the whole administration of justice. In the case of strategic warfare against a whole nation, however, to do this would be to destroy indiscriminately people who were not "unjust aggressors" as a means of getting at their government (and this, in turn, is now a rather useless endeavor). If this is like anything in the world, it is like shooting the children of the criminal who shot a policeman, or of a soldier who turned traitor in wartime. John Bennett's conclusion here seems to me unavoidable: "We must not deceive ourselves into believing that we could ever justify the use of megaton bombs for massive attacks on the centers of population of another country no matter what the provocation." [83] If a first strike, it would be both wicked and foolish. If a second strike, it would still be wicked and foolish—supremely foolish because when one comes to the actual doing of the act of reprisal in *such* kind it is already abundantly clear that the limitation upon war one hoped to "sanction" can no longer be preserved by the proposed sanction. It would be an act of pure purposeless punishment and retrospective vengeance. One simply cannot argue, as do the proponents of the various forms of limited war, that limited war must be *made possible* today and then say that illimitable inter-city warfare becomes less than an irrational absurdity *because committal to do this* is for the sake of deterrence *during* the course of limited war.

Any politically viable solution of the problem of war today requires that we finally employ a distinction between the *possibility* and the *certainty* of illimitable city destruction, and in deterrence during the war that we carefully discriminate between the *appearance* and the *actuality* of being partially or totally committed to go to city exchanges. The reader should recall at this point the discussion in the first section of this paper of Herman Kahn's contention (or admission) that while the appearance of irrationally inexorable commitment may have its uses, one would need in actuality and in advance to provide for revoking it. A nation ought never to be totally committed to action that is so irrational it can never be done by free, present decision; and even

---

[83] *Nuclear Weapons and the Conflict of Conscience* (New York: Charles Scribner's Sons, 1962), p. 101.

to *appear* to be totally committed may itself be altogether too danger-ous. A nation ought not to communicate to an enemy that it might go to city exchanges without at the same time communicating some doubt about it, if it wants both to remain and to seem to remain a free agent with still some control over its destiny and the course of world politics. The *appearance* of *partial* commitment, or the *appearance* of *possible* commitment, may be enough of a commitment to deter an enemy.

I would be willing to consider adding to the stages of military decision set down in the previous section yet one more. A statesman might consider ordering one of the enemy's cities to be struck after a warning allowing time for civilians to be evacuated. That would be an act of counter-value warfare in which human beings have not been entirely economized; and there may be some argument for it to be found in the changed nature of much property today in comparison with the period when both civilian property and civilian lives were surrounded with moral immunity from direct attack.[84] Whatever be the correct judgment of this possibility, the arguments against ever actually en-gaging in a war of nerves by means of populated cities cannot be with-drawn. Deterrence will have to be accomplished by the deterrent effect of the *possibility* and the *appearance* of the possibility that the sanction of city exchanges will be invoked, or not accomplished at all.

I propose, first, to discuss the moral issues in preserving such a national posture, and to conclude with some remarks upon technical questions concerning the feasibility of limiting war under the deterrence of a possibility we do not intend to carry out. In approaching the moral issues involved in appearing to be willing to do something that is wrong, I shall make use of a volume of essays by British Roman Catholics[85] who follow the anatomy of the just-war doctrine to a conclusion altogether different from mine, namely, nuclear pacifism.

It is never right to do wrong that good may come of it. Nuclear weapons have only added to this perennial truth the footnote: it can never do *any good* to do wrong that good may come of it. Neither is it right to *intend* to do wrong that good may come of it. If deterrence rests upon genuinely intending massive retaliation, it is clearly wrong no mat-ter how much peace results. If weapons systems deter city exchanges only because and so far as they are *intended* to be used against cities, then deterrence involves a "conditional willingness" [86] to do evil, and evil on a massive scale. Granting that deterrence deters before or during the war, and that it supports peace or the control of war, that alone

[84] See Thornton Read, "Counterforce Strategies and Nuclear Weapons," p. 48.
[85] Walter Stein, ed., *Nuclear Weapons and Christian Conscience*. (London: Marlin Press, 1961).
[86] *Ibid.*, p. 23.

cannot justify it. It would be justified "if, and only if, in employing this threat, we were not involved in . . . *immoral hypothetical decisions.*" [87] The distinction between murder and killing in war, or between directly killing combatants and directly murdering non-combatants, posits an ethico-political principle that can only be violated, never abrogated. "Nothing, not even the alleged interests of peace, can save murderousness from evil," [88] and nothing, not even the alleged interest in deterrence during war for the control of war can save the *intention* to commit murder from being evil. Does reliance on nuclear weapons for deterrence hypothetically commit us, here and now, to murder, there and then? [89] If so, such deterrence is wrong, and can never be anything but wickedness. This conclusion would seem to follow from the comparatively simple moral truth that "if an action is morally wrong, it is wrong to intend to do it." [90]

This is surely a correct "finding" as to the moral law. The authors of these chapters, however, intermix with this a certain "finding of fact" which may be questioned. They assert that "deterrence *rests*, in the end, on the intention to use nuclear weapons," not that in some or many of its forms it *may* or *might* rest on either present murderous intention or on a "conditional willingness" to do murder. No wonder the conclusion follows: if this is the case, deterrence "cannot but be morally repugnant for the same ultimate reason as is the use of the weapon held in reserve." [91] The following statement of the case is a better one, and by accenting the first word the fact to be questioned can be stressed: "*If*, then, we find that 'having' nuclear weapons involves intending to explode them over predominantly civilian targets, no more need be said; this intention is criminal, just as the action is criminal." [92] This is the matter of fact that needs to be determined—whether it *is* so, and must or should remain so if it is now the case—before we can know how the moral prohibition of intending to do wrong is to be applied in an assessment of deterrence policy.

The authors of these essays systematically fail to show that there can be no deterrent effect where there is no actual intention to use nuclear weapons directly against cities. They underrate what is pejoratively called "the argument from bluff," while admitting that if this deterred and if

[87] P. 36 (italics mine).
[88] P. 36.
[89] P. 125.
[90] P. 71.
[91] P. 78 (italics mine). [This was the analysis of deterrence which I held in 1961 and set forth in the concluding chapters of my *War and the Christian Conscience.* The moral argument, I believe, remains irrefutable, but findings of fact are not to be deduced from this.]
[92] Pp. 73–74 (italics mine).

this is what deters there would not be an implied "conditional commitment to total war." [93] These essays are remarkably sophisticated, and at many points suggest their own answer. "Having an H-bomb," for example, is no simple matter. It is not only that "having an H-bomb" differs from having a gun "in respect to the nature of the object possessed." One can "have" one or both these instruments with subtly but significantly different ways of "having" them. There is then a considerable difference "in respect to the nature of the 'possession' of the object" that has to be taken into account.[94] The question is whether "possession" of massive nuclear weapons is reducible to the crime of planning to use them over civilian targets. The question is whether "having" or "possession" implies a criminal intention to use them murderously, or a conditional willingness to do so. These questions cannot be answered without first exploring a spectrum of "havings" that may be possible, and indeed desirable. This further exploration of the nature of the "possession" of nuclear weapons which may be possible will determine whether deterrence by means of them before or during any war can ever be judged legitimate.

The technical possibility of deterrence before and during war can now be indicated, as can its compatibility with the moral prohibition of both the use and the intention to use nuclear (or any other) weapons in direct attacks on centers of population.

1. The collateral civilian damage that would result from counter-forces warfare in its maximum form may itself be quite sufficient to deter either side from going so high and to preserve the rules and tacit agreements limiting conflict in a nuclear age. In that case, deterrence during the war and collateral civilian damage are both "indirect effects" of a plan and action of war which would be licit or permitted by the traditional rules of civilized conduct in war. To say that counter-force strikes over an enemy's own territory are licit or permitted is to say that one can morally intend and be "conditionally willing" to engage in such a war. Whether one positively should ever do so depends on the conditions. Collateral civilian damage is certainly an unavoidable indirect effect and, in the technical sense, an "unintended" result of something a nation may and should make itself conditionally willing and ready to do. The deterrent effect, of which we are now speaking, is then, as it were, an indirect effect of the foreseeable indirect effects of legitimate military conduct.[95]

[93] P. 32.

[94] P. 75.

[95] [This was a quite inadequate, indeed, an unfortunate, formulation of this first step in defense of the justice of deterrence. I should not have described "collateral deterrence" as the "indirect effect of forseeable indirect effects" of legitimately targeted nuclear strikes. Instead, this deterrent effect should have been described as a *direct*

One can certainly "intend" to deter in this fashion, and oneself be similarly deterred. Not knowing the tyrannies future history may produce one cannot say whether the one effect of successful resistance to them will justify the direct and the indirect costs. Still we foreknow that these costs may be very great indeed. This is to say that, at least to a very great degree, perhaps a sufficient degree, nuclear warfare is a design for war that is inherently self-limiting upon rational decision-makers without their having to intend to use these weapons directly to murder cities and civilians.

This is not at all a matter of "double-think about double effect." [96] To justify "possession" for the sake of deterrence one does not have to invent possibly legitimate uses for nuclear weapons, such as their use against a ship at sea. Many a military installation in the nuclear age is fifty or more miles in diameter.

2. In respect to the nature of the weapons we possess, there are two possible uses which cannot be removed from them. The dual use the weapons themselves have—the fact that they may be used either against strategic forces or against centers of population—means that *apart from intention* their capacity to deter cannot be removed from them. This means that there may be sufficient deterrence in the subjectively unintended consequence of the mere possession of these weapons. No matter how often we declare, and quite sincerely declare, that our targets are an enemy's forces, he can never be quite *certain* that in the fury or in the fog of war his cities may not be destroyed.

This is so certainly the case that the problem of how to deter an enemy from striking our cities ought not for one moment to impede the shift to a counter-forces policy and to the actual intention to use nuclear weapons only against forces. We should declare again and again, and give evidence by what we do, that our targets are his forces rather than his cities. Since it is morally repugnant to wage war without renouncing morally repugnant means,[97] this should be speedily done, and communicated as effectively as possible to the enemy. Still, without any hesitation or ambiguity on our part, the weapons themselves will continue to have deterrent effect because they have ambiguous uses. They always *may* be used over cities; and no enemy can *know* that this will

---

and a *wanted* effect of the unwanted, indirect, collateral consequences of even a just use of nuclear weapons. For me to revise the language of the text above and remove this mistake would be to attribute to myself a prescience and an aptitude for words that I did not have. This would also prevent the reader from being drawn into the argument over the justice of deterrence as it unfolds in subsequent chapters. Therefore, in what follows this misleading wording will continue to be used until I was forced to supplant it by better wording for the same thought.]

[96] *Nuclear Weapons and Christian Conscience*, p. 57.
[97] Cf. *Ibid.*, p. 82.

not be done. Was McNamara's reserved use of massive nuclear weapons for retaliation in case Russia strikes our cities really necessary, or his declared policy of conditional willingness to do this? Was not this aspect of his speech mainly needed to reassure domestic public opinion which is still so far from supporting any steps toward a counter-force strategy and away from pacifistic maximal deterrence?

Similar conclusions can be reached from an analysis of the "familiar spiral of reciprocal expectations" which is an important aspect of war in the nuclear age. This spiral not only threatens to be illimitable, but it serves as a built-in dampener, which no deliberate policy nor any intention can remove. This is the truth in T. C. Schelling's contention that in the nuclear age all forms of limited war raise the risk of general war, whether intended or not. The point here is not the "threat" of general war because of some technical or human failure or some mistaken calculation. The point is rather that in a nuclear age all war raises a risk of general war by an apparent *possibility* of a *politically irreversible trend*. War creates this risk which we share with the Russians. They can never "be confident that even the lack of resolution sometimes attributed to the United States could guarantee that general war would not result." "It is our sheer inability to predict the consequences of our actions and to keep things under control, and the enemy's similar inability [or our reciprocal doubt whether the other is in control], that can intimidate the enemy," and ourselves.

If war is no longer a matter of making no threat that does not depend on our ultimate willingness to *choose* general war, it is no longer a matter of having to put forth acts or threats that involve a conditional willingness to choose general war.[98] War being sufficiently threatening, a conclusive case can be made for the proposition that massive nuclear weapons should never be intended for use against societies. The nations of the world *should* and *can* devote all their attention and intention to making only just or counter-forces war possible. A single great power *can* and *should* do this, since the other ominous possibility will always remain in the background as a shared and unintended threat.

3. Only now do we come again to the suggestion that the distinction between the *appearance* and the *actuality* of being partially or totally committed to go to city exchanges may have to be employed in deterrence policy. In that case, only the appearance should be cultivated. If the first two points above do not seem to the military analyst sufficiently persuasive, *or able to be made so*, then an *apparent* resolution to wage war irrationally or at least an *ambiguity* about our intentions may have to be our expressed policy. This is a matter, not of the nature

[98] See T. C. Schelling, "Nuclear Strategy in Europe," *World Politics*, Vol. XIV, No. 3 (April, 1962), 421–24.

of the weapons themselves, but of the manner in which we possess them— the "having" of them that might be necessary to sustain deterrence during justifiably conducted war.

The moralist can certainly say to the decision-maker that it can never be right for him to do such a thing as attack an enemy's society, or for him actually to intend to do so, or under any conditions to be willing to match his resolution against that of the enemy by means of populated cities. He can point out to the statesman that it can never be right for him to contrive to "make" the un-do-able intention irrevocable, or to have the intention of doing so. He can even point out where the military analyst will be found saying the same thing about the irrationality of total committal to an irrational act of war, or even of appearing quite unambiguously to be totally and irreversibly committed.

But the moralist must be careful how he rushes in with his ethico-political principles mixed with an assortment of findings of fact and various arguments *ad horrendum*. He must be careful how he spells out his *moral* guidance for deterrence policy. For, on a sound solution of this problem the security of free societies may well depend in a nuclear age which is also an age of "megacorpses," [99] "deracination from humanity," [100] and of "unparalleled moral landslide." [101] The moralist must be careful how he disparages the so-called "argument from bluff" to a morally licit form of deterrence; and he should examine whether the reasons *he* uses to dismiss this argument are telling *moral* ones or rather technical judgments he has gathered to fulfill a prejudice.

The crucial question for the moralist is whether deterrent effects that flow from a *specified kind* of studied ambiguity concerning the intention with which a nation holds nuclear weapons in reserve are *praeter intentionem* (besides or without the actual intention to attack cities) as surely as are the first two types of deterrent effects we have analyzed. To say and to act as if we might go to city exchanges is certainly a form of deception. But, if this can be done without intending to make irrational, immoral use of nuclear weapons, or even with the intention that our weapons be not so used and with the intention of revoking what had never even the appearance of total committal, such deception cannot be said to be based on the criminal intention or conditional willingness to do murder. The first thing to be said then, is that the intention to deceive is certainly a far cry from the intention to murder society, or to commit mutual homicide.

The second thing to be said is in connection with the moral prob-

---

[99] One million dead bodies.
[100] *Nuclear Weapons and Christian Conscience*, p. 31.
[101] *Ibid.*, pp. 125–26.

lem of *deception* in politics and in wartime. A moralist need not slur
over the fact that in all sorts of ways deception may be an evil, just as he
need not slur over the fact that the killing of combatants is evil (though
certainly not wicked). But having said this, it must then be pointed out
that there are deceptions and deceptions. Or rather, the word "deception" ought perhaps to be reserved for any denial of the truth to someone to whom the truth is due, or permitting him to gather from you a
false or inadequate impression concerning the exact truth which, in some
sense, "belongs" to him. If this is a fair statement of the moral rule, then
an experienced finding of fact must be that there are many situations in
both private and public life when withholding the "truth" or even
communicating an inadequate representation of the "truth" is not a lie.
Relative to this, there is a teaching of long standing in the Western
tradition about the virtues of a military commander, to the effect that
there is nothing wrong with his having military secrets provided he does
not pretend that he has none. It would be extremely difficult to support
the judgment that an effective reservation about the use of the weapons
we possess, or about our intention that they not be used over cities, in
any sense belongs to an enemy, or that this information is due to be
given him, if thereby deterrence will fail and war break out and go
whoosh!

Finally, a moralist must raise the question of whether this truth
is not owed to the people of an enemy nation, if not to their military
commanders. In answer to this, it goes to the point to say that this may
be necessary to save *their* lives as well as those of our own civilians. Or
(worse than their death from the point of view of an ethics that does not
place supreme value in mere physical existence) it may be necessary in
order to save them (and ourselves) from a measure of complicity in their
government's conditional or actual willingness to save them by doing
mass murder, or from the *tragedy* (not the *wickedness*) of actually being
saved by murderous intention (if a wrongly willed deterrent worked)
and some of them from the tragedy of living on in a world in which their
lives have been spared in the midst of the greatest possible wrong-*doing*
by a government which in remote degrees of participation was still their
own (if the shared intentional risk does not work). So the question resolves
itself into the question whether it is ever right to withhold the truth in
order to save life, to save from moral wrong-doing, to save from sheer
tragedy. Does the truth that might well be "fatal" in all these senses
"belong" to them? Is it "due" to be given if it can be? Do we "owe" them
a true report that will unambiguously quiet their fears by effectively
communicating to them (if this *can* ever be done) that we have no intention of engaging with their government in inter-society warfare under
any circumstances? I am so far from believing that one ought readily to

justify this deception that it seems to me that the first two types of deterrence must, if at all possible, be made to work. Still, if deterrence were based on a cultivated ambiguity about our real intentions, and if "deception" in an objectionable moral sense would thus in some measure be perpetrated, it would still be an intent to deceive and not an intent possibly to do murder.

Perhaps we should say that we ought to be conditionally willing to strive for this ingredient in deterrence, that is, on the condition that it is necessary to deter and to save life. I do not grant to a physician any right to withhold from a patient knowledge of his true condition; but then I also do not believe that learning the truth about his condition can be demonstrated to be so nearly fatal as, in our present supposition, it would be for an enemy government and population to learn that we do not intend to attack people. A better analogy might be the following one. If you were trying to save a man out on the ledge of a building, threatening to commit suicide and to take you with him, would you withhold from him, and have an obligation to withhold from him, any blandishments, including "daring" him to join you inside for a duel to the death by "Russian roulette" at three paces, with no intention of ever carrying out this dissuasive dare or threat?

The military and political analysts I have consulted do *not* reject as infeasible the sort of "possession" of nuclear weapons for deterrence which we are now discussing.[102] If it is thought to be infeasible now, then the "system" may have to be studied and perfected so that it can be done. For this may be one of those customarily "unthinkable" things which, the more you think about it, will prove to be technically and politically "do-able." If needed, it should be developed in many a scenario. It is on balance, I believe, morally "do-able," as city-busting is not, however much you think about it. Whether this ingredient in deterrence can be adopted and exercised by a democratic society is, of course, a serious question. It requires of a people a mature "ethic of restraint, limits and silence," [103] not moral protest always, much less punitive fury or he-man morality; and it requires a reliance on the morality and rationality of their political leaders not to be expected or (on any policy decision not so crucial) desired in a free society. For this reason, if for no other, all our attention and intention should doubtless be directed toward adopting, declaring, and implementing a policy of counter-forces warfare, with the "collateral" deterrence that policy affords. This is the doctrine which should form the consciences of free men today; and if their consciences

---

[102] Halperin, *op. cit.*, for example, develops at length the distinction between "communication policy" and "action policy."

[103] Cf. Kenneth Thompson in "The Nuclear Dilemma—A Discussion," *Christianity and Crisis*, Nov. 27, 1961.

are thus formed, it may then be possible to add to the "graduated" deterrence of a counter-force policy this last type of non-murderous deterrence.

Then it may be possible to put, not nuclear weapons as such, but the inter-city use of nuclear weapons into a category by itself, so that, while the capability still exists, the intention to attack cities will recede into the background so far as not to have actuality. Things as strange have happened before in the history of warfare. Tribes living close to death in the desert have fought cruel wars. They even used poisoned arrows, and certainly to a limited extent they fought one another by means of direct attack upon women and children. But they knew *not to poison wells!* That would have been a policy of mutual homicide, and a form of society-*contra*-society warfare that would have removed the possibility of any more bloody cruel wars, not to mention peacetime pursuits. In refraining from massive well-poisoning, or in keeping that ambiguous, did these tribes, in any valid or censorable sense of the word, still "intend" to poison wells?

CHAPTER 12

Can a Pacifist
Tell a Just War?

James Douglass himself is one of those Catholic intellectuals whom he describes.[1] He is "moved by reason to justify . . . assent in conscience to the way of peace by means of an ethic of war." He too uses the just-war doctrine as merely a "point of reference" and as a means of "going beyond it." The consequence is that he necessarily misunderstands and misuses the just-war doctrine on the use of force, since that doctrine has not the purpose of surpassing itself.

One can handle the just-war tests in this way, of course, if he chooses to do so. He can attribute to them a cogency and moral persuasiveness sufficient to condemn all war in a nuclear age, just before these tests themselves drop from his hands and the Christian goes beyond them.

With all due respect to the Christian pacifist position, the question most urgently to be raised about the procedure Douglass adopts, and concerning his reasoning, is, Can a pacifist tell a just war? or even, Can a pacifist tell *the just-war tests* and reason with them to the end of clarifying the responsibilities of citizens and statesmen in the international system? Has he not abdicated from the beginning the task of searching out the true meaning of the just-war theory and the requirements this imposes upon us under the conditions of modern war, by giving himself

---

[1] "Anatomy of the Just War," in *The Non-Violent Cross* (New York: The Macmillan Co., 1968).

the premise he wishes to fetch forth from it, namely, that the just-war doctrine can (by condemning all war in a nuclear age, just before it becomes a "relic" in governing political consciences) furnish a negative and transitional ground but not any "essential support" for a life of non-violence and suffering resistance? In my day, this would have been called a prejudiced line of reasoning, suspect from the beginning.

The just-war theory is precisely a theory of statecraft. The charge leveled by Douglass in the end is simply that this doctrine has entailments in statecraft for the political use of armed force. This verdict signals the fact that, all along, Douglass was "going beyond" politics. This necessarily affects everything he has to say about the proper application of the just-war doctrine on the use of force in today's world, and about my writings upon these questions.

We shall have to take his word for it that this is the plight of a great many Catholic liberals today. There is only question whether this is because they are Catholics and Christian, or because they are liberal modern minds. There always was in the Catholic heritage a natural-law or natural-justice optimism which significantly influenced the quest for and definition of justice in war. This becomes quite clear when compared with the politically more realistic, not to say gloomy, comprehension of the just-war doctrine in, for example, Lutheranism. When today this optimism is manifested in a deeper personalistic philosophy, and when Biblical renewal and the claims of the lordship of Christ are brought directly into connection with these humanistic grounds for optimism, the result is the transformation of the cross of Christ directly into a political alternative.

Protestantism has a more complicated understanding of God and man, and of man and man, at "cross-purposes." The one meaning of the word sharpens our apprehension of the other. The political life of mankind goes on under the sign of the cross in both senses. Our political responsibilities must be examined in the light of Christ, but also in the shadows revealed and cast by that light. For this reason, Christian vocation in politics cannot be reduced to "suffering as an alternative opponent of injustice."

In all that I have ever written on the morality of war I have been quite consciously drawing upon a wider theory of statecraft and of political justice to propose an extension within the Christian realism of Reinhold Niebuhr—an added note within his "responsibilistic" ethics. There is more to be said about justice in war than was articulated in Niebuhr's sense of the ambiguities of politics and his greater/lesser evil doctrine on the use of force. That more is the principle of discrimination; and I have tried to trace out the meaning of this as well as the meaning of disproportion in kinds of warfare that Niebuhr never faced. Come to think about it, this may explain why I seem so alone in championing the recovery of the just-war doctrine—since Protestant messianists rushed pell-mell to join forces with the new breed of Catholic messianists in jettisoning the elements of Christian political realism from their thinking. The owl of Minerva (political wisdom), which rested for three decades upon a spokesman for Christian truth, has now taken her flight from among the leading theological voices. It dwells now with secular analysts, such as Robert E. Osgood and Robert W. Tucker. Their book, *Force, Order, and Justice*,[2] with its politicizing of force, would today be regarded as somehow a betrayal of Christ and of Christian conscience. Yet many of its themes were among Niebuhr's generalizations about the political life of mankind. I am rather pleased that James Douglass drew our attention to the fact that the just-war doctrine is not a Catholic doctrine; it is a common Christian teaching about the justice and limits upon the state's use of force, as Lutheran or Calvinistic as it is Roman Catholic.

In any case, the way to unravel Douglass' seemingly demonstrative argument is to read it backward. In the end he states the position which is controlling and trammelling throughout, the norm and outlook from which he assesses the just-war theory, and the stance in relation to which this doctrine is made an expiring functionary.

His point of view is, of course, an honorable and time-honored one for Christians to take. It is "an ethic of reconciliation based on the Gospel of Peace." He calls for a conscience "not only purged of the nuclear sword" (and all other swords as well) but "re-formed in the strength of the non-violent cross," "choosing the world" with Christ by "committing ourselves totally against war and totally to peace on earth." This means not only a call to the individual Christian to accept the cross in suffering resistance, but also a call for the nation somehow to oblige itself to embrace the cross. The latter would certainly be "a cross without takers," but I should think this to be escalated religious language for a man's or a nation's proper refusal to fight a war *unjustly*. Yet Douglass' language is essential to his case, since he wants to elevate political agency to the perfection of Christ. He speaks of the "cross of unilateral disarmament," which wouldn't be a cross if it was a responsible thing to do and not the betrayal that it is. He wants every Christian and everyone to "make justice not war," to choose "a suffering resistance to injustice, rather than a warring resistance."

There are aspects of Protestant experience, history, and tradition that should enable us to understand Douglass' position better perhaps than can Catholic liberalism. There is in Roman Catholic experience and tradition a long history of Christian perfectionism and imitation of Christ. But a vocation for these maximal goals and expectations did not subsume into itself every other minimal, but still moral, political or

---

[2] Baltimore, Maryland: The Johns Hopkins Press, 1967.

personal requirement. What happens when Christians affirm that making justice by suffering and non-violence and never by the sword constitutes the form of all Christian obedience? What happens when perfectionism is made the ground floor of the Christian life? This can best be seen by looking at the sects of the age of the Reformation to which passed the time-honored fervor of Christian perfectionism. Menno Simons founded one of these sects upon the premise that "the sword is ordained outside the perfection of Christ."

It is hard to know how to deal with someone who, like James Douglass, announces the same premise concerning Christian obedience and yet wishes, in the tradition of the great churches, to continue to talk relevantly about politics. This leads him to the conclusion that the sword is ordained nowhere and never at all—at least not in the modern period. Throughout the centuries these two positions have been locked in struggle within Christian conscience: the sword is ordained outside the perfection of Christ (the tradition of the sects); the sword may sometimes be a Christian's secular duty and calling or a requirement of civil right-eousness (the tradition of the great churches: Lutheranism, Calvinism, Roman Catholicism). Douglass abolishes this perennial tension at the heart of a Christian's double wrestle over the meaning of faithfulness to Christ and the meaning of his faithfulness to fellowman and to the claims of political justice. He solves the problem by the simple expedient of proclaiming the perfection of responsible politics. He simply declares that justice-making can now be accomplished by suffering love alone, or that the nuclear age has so radically changed the nature of politics that today this can be the only way to secure the political good.

Since there is really very little actual evidence for such a proposition completely excluding the use of force from political responsibility, Douglass' belief that this is true requires extrinsic explanation. Doubtless there is sufficent *cause* to be found in the horrifying effects of nuclear and many other modern weapons, but there is not sufficient *reason* in this for anyone to conclude that force has been displaced from any connection with justice and peace. Quite the contrary is the experience of our age.

Still it is understandable that many Christians today should be convinced that "nuclear weapons are ordained outside the perfection of Christ"—even if not all war once was—and that all modern war (believed to be programmed inexorably together with nuclear war) must be renounced.

I have never seen how as a Christian ethicist I could ask more of this point of view than *consistency* (plus a little forebearance in trying to understand how there are other Christians who in conscience give another account of their political responsibilities in the world of today). With consistency should go a recognition of the fact that the verdict that

Christ calls us to eschew all but "suffering resistance" and non-violence in the cause of justice will necessarily be productive of a form of sectarianism. A genuinely sectarian Christian who is a universal pacifist prescinds from the history of nations in prescinding from the history of warfare. He radically even if still selectively withdraws from politics; he makes in trust the venture that God has not committed to him (but perhaps to persons outside the perfection of Christ) the use of armed force in justice-making and in peace-keeping.

The nuclear pacifist prescinds from the history of contemporary states in prescinding from this form of warfare or deterrent weapon. And if he adds, from all war in a nuclear age, he even more radically if still selectively withdraws from politics.

He prescinds, for example, from all responsibility for managing the deterrent non-use of nuclear weapons so that their actual use is prevented. At the present moment, he can say nothing but hortatory words about stopping the proliferation of nuclear weapons. A nuclear non-proliferation treaty will require the transmission of *credible* guarantees to non-nuclear (aligned or non-aligned) nations against nuclear attack, nuclear blackmail, or conventional or subversive assault backed by nuclear threat. Douglass has already said he can say nothing but No! to that; he can therefore say nothing politically effectual about one of the necessary conditions for stopping the proliferation of nuclear weapons. The spread of nuclear weapons is not going to be stopped by suffering resistance to them. To stop proliferation will require political acts of refusal on the part of governments, but these will have to be sustained by resolves and arrangements extending nuclear deterrence and by more numerous (not fewer) far-flung tacit or actual commitments on the part of the United States to the security of other nations.

Still it may be true that Christians should specialize in making justice, stopping proliferation, etc., through suffering non-violence and by no type of resorts to armed force. Then we should stop advising citizens and statesmen concerning what they should do in their offices. Let everyone who believes as Douglass does call upon every son of the church to come out of the nation-state (and out of any future world political authority with enforcing power). Let them inform the consciences of statesmen in a position to *do* something *politically* about stopping nuclear proliferation that for Christ's sake they ought not to do that, since this would involve them further in immoral deterrence, and in security arrangements that promise resort to war in a nuclear age. Let them call upon all our fellow Christians to have nothing to do, or as little as possible to do, with any actual use of armed force or with the constant threat of it for the purpose of preventing or deterring war in any form— no matter what may be the calculable consequences of such a policy. Let every son of the Church, in fact, have nothing to do with any means of *resisting* evil (violently or non-violently), not even "suffering resistance" to injustice; let them rather specialize in overcoming evil with good and enemies with reconciliation, while other men to the end of history must needs do otherwise. All honor to James Douglass and Menno Simons! They may be quite correct.

In any case, as I have said, we must take Douglass' word for it that this is the present frontier of Catholic conscience which he represents; and then, of course, that would explain "the just war's moribund state in the Church."

It is quite another thing, however, for him to assert that this is the mind of "the Johannine Church" or was "the mind of the Church as expressed in *Pacem in terris* and *The Church in the Modern World*." That depends on what those documents actually said, and not upon Douglass' simple allegation about what they said in order to assimilate them to his own position. This is not proved by reference to the Italian language behind the official Latin of one crucial assertion in *Pacem in terris*, or by general invocations in the Pastoral Constitution that we must think about war in a new way. An analysis of the text of the Vatican Council document will, I believe, reveal that the council issued a just-war document.

Moreover, Pope John's encyclical *Pacem in terris* issued in a call for new world public authorities correcting the structural defects of the nation-state system under which statesmen labor. That, too, is a fruit of the theory of statecraft entailed by the just-war doctrine on the state's use of force. That is the only way to "go beyond" this doctrine, namely, in the direction of its fulfillment or expression in superior peace-keeping and justice-making powers.[3] The just-war doctrine governing the use of force by nation-states is going to surpass itself, or functionally call attention to its own demise, only in the direction of a structural re-organization of the international system and of new forms of world authority (more apt to achieve the world common good of which Pope John spoke).

It is notable that James Douglass specifically rejects the ultimate goal of an effective peace-keeping and justice-making power beyond the nation-state. He eschews this because—being for once more prudent and calculating than I—such enforcement powers are not, he says, "today a viable way to restore warfare to a legitimate police function." In short, the attempt would not be "useful." He may also believe that this self-sur-passing step beyond just-war statecraft toward new world public authorities cannot be accomplished without tyranny until the justices of men are more in agreement and there is a greater actualization of

[3] See "The Vatican Council on Modern War," Chap. 16 below, and *"Pacem in terris,"* Chap. 4 above.

community among them than is a remote likelihood in the foreseeable future. This was certainly not the Johannine mind. Clearly Douglass moves in an opposite direction in his attempt to go beyond the just-war doctrine by going below it and by availing himself of only suffering non-violence in the service of justice.

II

Douglass divides the present writer into "two phases." One was my age of "technological innocence" when I was "recommending limits which the defense technicians had gone beyond fifteen years before." The other phase came with my greater "technological sophistication." This subtly suggests to the reader that my deliberation and writings on the morality of war have been but a reflection of my technical information. Later the subtlety is abandoned, and replaced by a host of ringing assertions that "the solutions of the nuclear moralist 'work' when . . . they justify those making the weapons work. Reason has become the servant of technique, and the moralist the good conscience of the warfare state"; "so might a manual for the nuclear-age confessional absolve us all of both past and future slaughters"; "if . . . we swallow the conscience pill . . ."; "moralists standing in the wings to complete the creation of a self-justifying vocabulary."

Douglass knows very well that those "two phases" of mine were not in any important respects a reflection of technological innocence and subsequent sophistication, but were altogether dependent upon the moral argument at each stage. I am not at all averse to cutting knowingly across fifteen years in the history of military technology in declaring something to be *wrong,* if the moral argument leads to that conclusion.

It is never right to do wrong that good may come, and anything that would be wrong to do would be wrong to intend to do. My writings have all resulted from trying to find out the meaning of these principles for modern war. In my 1961 *War and the Christian Conscience* I came to one conclusion on the morality of the deterrent possession of nuclear weapons. In the 1963 pamphlet *The Limits of Nuclear War*[4] I took up the matter of deterrence again, examined it more carefully in the light of the just-war-statecraft categories, and came to a different conclusion. This is not self-evidently progress, but neither is it self-evidently wrong; and it was certainly not a matter of following military technology wherever it led, or of justifying anything that works.

That 1963 pamphlet is *not* chiefly concerned to argue "the moral

[4] See Chap. 11 above, pp. 248–58.

THE MORALITY OF WAR

case for 25,000,000 discriminately dead against the prospect of 215,000,000 indiscriminately dead." I took off from those figures, and I remain amazed that anyone can be less sensitive than were McNamara's computers, or that conscience could register no moral difference between these quantities of deaths, taken alone, and (what is more) fail to see a signal and inherent moral difference between a policy of prompt massive retaliation and McNamara's policy of greater discrimination, greater flexibility, greater control, allowing for graduation up or down in our military responses if war comes.

The pamphlet argued, if anything, the moral case for no first use of nuclear weapons except over one's own territory or that of an ally against a massive conventional invasion. That was to invoke another "boundary" to keep nuclear war limited in ways that hopefully might become first policy and then customary international law binding on all antagonists. I was aware (to a degree that I was not in 1961) of the fact that there would have to be forms of not-inherently-unjust, counter-forces nuclear war to sanction and enforce this or any other lower limit upon war today. That brought up the subject of the morality of deterring war and keeping it down to one or another of the lower levels by the possession of weapons that would, if used, likely cause vast death and destruction. I argued that planning to make interdictional and counter-forces nuclear strikes over the territory of an enemy are indeed likely to be disproportionate to every political good except deterrence itself, while still there undeniably would be legitimate nuclear military targets. This being so, my conclusion was that it is not immoral to maintain this sort of deterrence with the aim of preserving lower limits upon wars in a nuclear age.

Against this, Douglass says that I have "escalated the nuclear age meaning of 'discrimination' " or again that I have "escalated tremendously the destructive potential of a 'discriminate' weapon." These are assertions that should be directed at our age, not against me. I only looked to see, having in my mind what I believe to be a proper understanding of the meaning of the principle of discrimination. This principle means that the difference between discriminate and indiscriminate acts of war is *not* to be determined by escalating or de-escalating their "destructive potential" but by the direction or aim of the military action. Mainly, however, I reply that these are only Douglass' allegations. He does not grapple with the *arguments* that go to show that terribly destructive acts of war today are and could still be legitimately targeted, and therefore can legitimately be used in designing deterrence that can lock these very weapons into non-use except for deterrence.

Instead he himself foreshortens the meaning of the principle of discrimination by ordinarily writing "non-combatant immunity." There is no objection to shorthand, of course, except that it is apt to support in the mind of the reader the impression he already has that the immunity of non-combatants meant to surround them with protection from all death and destruction or from excessive quantities of it while still fighting a war. It meant rather their moral immunity from destruction resulting from *direct attacks* aimed upon them. With this in mind, I simply note that modern war, including nuclear war, would cause *disproportionate* civil damage long before it would be indiscriminate (and that therefore effective deterrence need stem from nothing inherently immoral). This— no more—comprises Ramsey's alleged escalation of meanings, my scandalous moral justifications, my deliberately skimming a nuclear holocaust, sealing moral discourse in the absurd. In expressions such as these, I have searched for the moral reasoning, even for arguments to try to refute, and have found none.

It is not only that I fail to find arguments against my own understanding and application of the just-war theory to take hold of and listen to, and then accept or counter them. It is also that I fail to grasp the logic or movement of Douglass' argument. He charges that I justify altogether too much war and find too many moral permissions from analyzing the morality of war in terms of the just-war doctrine. If true, that would seem to demonstrate that modern war is *not* without justification in these terms and according to these tests. But I thought Douglass wanted to show from a study of the just-war theory, and particularly from an analysis of my writings, that its function is morally to condemn all war in the nuclear age. The charge is that I have justified modern war, and even some types of nuclear action in war, from an application of the just-war doctrine on the use of force. The conclusion is supposed to be that actually the just-war doctrine, before expiring, condemns all war in the nuclear age. One can get from one to the other of these positions only by appending a simple unargued notation to the first (derived, I can only suppose, from intuition or revelation or from some source other than moral reasoning) to the effect that Ramsey's "proofs" only show the vacuity or the wickedness of moral reason and the just-war doctrine in a nuclear age.

For example, in regard to the proposals I have made since 1963 concerning the morality of deterrence, Douglass does not press the objection Walter Stein, unsuccessfully I believe, attempted to bring against my moral analysis, namely, that I radically abuse just-war and double-effect categories.[5] That would have been a demonstration that the just-war tests, correctly understood, lead to the negative conclusion Douglass wants from them, namely, a condemnation of any nuclear component in war or deterrence. Instead, Douglass at that point simply proclaims that he would prefer to say that my analysis "testifies eloquently

[5] See Chap. 15 below.

to the irrationality of reason in the Nuclear Age, where truth has been reduced to a component of technique." How he knows this, he does not say, whether from intuition or revelation or some *other* just-war theory. Therefore, there can be no reply to Douglass as there could be to Stein on whether one can and must derive from just-war tests a moral condemnation of all modern war and a condemnation of all types of possibly effective deterrence.

Douglass gives a fair exposition of the three sorts or sources of deterrent effects (in a scale of "graduated" deterrence) whose morality I considered—and whose morality I espoused in the case of deterrence from the expectation of disproportionate collateral damage accompanying legitimate strikes and in the case of shared deterrence stemming from the ambiguous uses modern weapons have in themselves. His response opens with the declaration that Ramsey's case for the justice in deterrence only "illustrates the strains placed on even the most brilliant [elsewhere "torturous"] effort to maintain the justice of war in the nuclear era." But in this instance there is an argument appended that one can, at least, take hold of. The case, Douglass observes, is dependent at every stage upon making a distinction between the felt and shared threat of "massive evil" and "an opposite or moral intention by those judged to be making the threat." Of course! The case has to be that deterrence rests upon evils resulting from war (the collateral damage of any high level modern war), or feared to be possible (the counter-city use of weapons that cannot be withdrawn from them), that should not be directly willed or directly done as acts of war. That follows from the premise that one should not intend or make oneself conditionally willing to do for deterrence's sake something that would be inherently wrong to do in actuality. Would Douglass have that premise withdrawn? Surely not! Yet it is the degree of successful execution of this requirement in my analysis of the morality of deterrence that he brings against it.

Then follows the rhetoric of three sentences: "The first deterrence preserves our good conscience. . . . The second deterrence preserves our good conscience . . . The third deterrence [intending ambiguity] preserves our good conscience . . ." Here read in each case: ". . . puts nuclear weapons in a class by themselves as weapons intended to be not used directly against populations or as not intended to be used against populations even when intending and securing their use for deterrence." That would be a consummation devoutly to be wished; it is in any case the objective of all thinking about the morality of deterrence. "Good conscience" is only an incidental effect, not of central concern and to be secured only if we correctly determine the objective morality of the matter.

Then Douglass sums up my argument by characterizing it as a "theory of non-responsible deterrence" (where I would have thought

"a theory of responsible deterrence" would be the correct characterization
—unless, again, we are to withdraw the moral premise that one should
not intend to do evil in order that deterrence may come of it). It is, he
says, a theory of "non-responsible" deterrence because populations are
threatened yet "from a moral point of view there is no one threatening
them. . . . Responsible agents are nowhere in sight."

That is not rhetoric; it is only a mistake. I have everywhere
contended that to share the threat in the ways I analyzed as components
of a graduated deterrence, to maintain these ingredients of an effective
deterrence, and to intend *this deterrence* consciously and deliberately is
a moral matter. I have contended that the maintenance of the potential
for disproportionate but still limited and discriminating acts of war is
precisely *not* disproportionate to the political good accomplished by
deterrence. Responsible agents are, as it were, everywhere in sight in this
theory of deterrence. Everything depends on the cogency of the moral
argument from the categories of a just-war statecraft. If my moral argument holds, the deterrent possession of nuclear weapons is a responsible
design. If not, the deterrent use of nuclear weapons to secure their non-use
is irresponsible. Deterrence is in no case "*non*-responsible."

It is true that between 1961 and 1963 I became convinced—as
Herman Kahn came later to be convinced [6]—that "the deterrence of a
rational enemy" is "almost a simple philosophical consequence of the
existence of thermonuclear bombs." But Kahn came to this conclusion
from his continuing *strategic* analysis. I came to it from further analysis
of the morality of deterrence, from continuing to ask what *should* be
done to withdraw murderous intention from deterrence and to put nuclear weapons in the special category of weapons intended to be not
used or not indiscriminately used directly against populations as such.
Douglass is heir to Kahn's former contempt of this possibility. That
meant that I was not *primarily* concerned with the *practical* problem of
making deterrence work at the cost of planning to do something inherently immoral. On the point we are presently discussing, it meant
that my proposal of several ingredients in a not-inherently-immoral,
graduated deterrent certainly requires responsible agents consciously to
maintain the system stripped of the immorality of "extended" deterrence
(i.e. deterrence extended downward through all the lower levels of warfare in a nuclear age from an actual threat to destroy populations as
such). This was, indeed, the point of my attempt to demonstrate that

---

[6] His statement reads in full: "Some years ago, I said, with a certain degree of
contempt, that 'some . . . seem to view the deterrence of a rational enemy as almost
a simple philosophic consequence of the existence of thermonuclear bombs.' I recognize
today that these people may have been much closer to the truth than I then thought
reasonable." Herman Kahn, *On Escalation* (New York: Frederick A. Praeger, 1965),
p. 246

the shared threat of something, itself disproportionate if done, is not necessarily disproportionate to possess in force and to use for the high purpose of deterrence and the great good of peace in the world.[7] If Douglass refuses to allow this to be a morally sound proposition, that would be to reject not only nuclear deterrence or deterrence of any war in a nuclear age but deterrence under any previous condition of warfare. Since in all ages war before or during its outbreak has been deterred by the shared danger and mutual threat of disproportionate damage, a rejection of that proposition in morals only exhibits that before the beginning of the argument seemingly on just-war grounds one has already basically prescinded from the history of force in the politics of mankind and from the history of nations.

Douglass charges that my "theory of non-responsible deterrence give the moralist's blessing to all the decision-making, or lack of it, necessary to destroy the world." Not only is my theory one of responsible and, in the ways explained, intended deterrence. I should also say that it gives a moralist's blessing to the decision-making that may save the world from nuclear destruction. In any case, I did not invent nuclear weapons or introduce them into the political life of mankind or place mankind under the unavoidable threats I have analyzed in distinguishing between the morality and the immorality of the actual intentions that we have the option of placing behind these threats or withdrawing from them.

These weapons, moreover, will remain in one way or another in the political life of mankind—in the possession of nation-states in the present international system, or they will be transferred to some future world public authority. Douglass prefers to stand against war or deterrence in any form rather than to stand for the latter, either because he does not think an international authority is now viable or because he well knows that, after the transferral of nuclear policy from the nation-state as its subject to an international authority as its subject, Ramsey would have to make the argument for the morality of deterrence, or for a possibly moral form of deterrence, with agents in and out of sight, all over again and Douglass would be obliged to term that theory non-responsible and finally atrocious.

Douglass' mind wanders from what I am talking about (deterrence) to what he is thinking about (the event if and when deterrence fails because of accident or miscalculation, beside anyone's responsible intention). It is one thing to talk about "spiritualized deterrence" (and, although I would not choose that expression, we had better begin to

---

[7] *Peace, the Churches, and the Bomb* (New York: Council on Religion and International Affairs, 1965), pp. 56–59; Chap. 14 below, pp. 302–307.

talk and act in this direction if we are going to put modern weapons in a category intended to be not used against populations); it is quite another thing to talk about "spiritualized slaughters," of which Douglass falsely accuses me. My finding or judgment of fact is simply different from his on the matter of the inexorable or probable necessity of any such eventuality. He knows that, if I judged that to resort to any war in the nuclear age, or to resort to war "X", or to resort to any use of nuclear weapons would be to put ourselves out of control and to step on an escalator that automatically will take us to counter-society warfare, I would characterize *that first step* as inherently immoral and irrational. Moreover I would also then say that to deter war by actually intending or making oneself conditionally willing to do any such thing would also be inherently immoral. We simply disagree over these findings or judgments of fact.

"It is the besetting sin," writes Robert E. Tucker, of much ethico-political argument today that "it insists upon evaluating the significance of military power largely in terms of its potentially uncontrolled use. The conclusion—that force is no longer a useful or rational instrument of national policy—therefore appears foreordained. . . . If force could once serve the ends of justice (these men say) at present its use can lead only to the greatest injustice. But alter the assumption on which this argument proceeds—consider the function served by military power so long as it is not overly employed or employed only with restraint—and very different conclusions may be drawn." [8] This may be mistaken, but it is not the baptism of atrocities while doing or intending them.

It is instructive to compare the way Douglass comes out of his criticism of the just-war doctrine with the way Robert W. Tucker comes out of *essentially the same criticism* of these writings of mine. Tucker thinks that the position I espouse still cuts quite a hole in the design that deterrence must necessarily have. More important is the fact, that, according to Tucker, a decisive critique of the just-war doctrine on the use of force will serve the function of showing that statesmen and citizens must necessarily adopt another perennial view of statecraft based on "necessity of state." The demise of just-war-statecraft and the failure of its exponents to establish that there are just-war limits upon the actions of states functions to demonstrate that reason of state "affords a justification for any measures deemed essential to the preservation and continuity of the state"; and "as against the injunction that evil must not be done that good may come," a true statecraft "responds that not only may evil be done but that no determinate limits may be drawn to the evil that

[8] Robert E. Osgood and Robert W. Tucker: *Force, Order, and Justice* (Baltimore, Maryland: The Johns Hopkins Press, 1967), p. 226, n. 9.

may be threatened, and done, if necessary for the preservation and continuity of the state." [9] There are no limits, upon the failure of the just-war doctrine (Tucker). On the other hand, no war in a nuclear age could ever be justified upon that same failure, or last dying success (Douglass). Thus have the lion and the lamb lain down together.

It may be that Christians should go with Douglass. But if we do it should be in clear recognition that by abandoning the control of force we will effectually be saying that outside the perfection of Christ someone is ordained—or, by our omission or failure to find a better vocation in the politics of a nuclear age, someone is being left with the necessity—to threaten, to intend and maybe to do directly the deaths of 215,000,000 persons in order to plan to keep the casualties to 25,000,000. I do not believe that that is the sole Christian calling in today's world.

Moreover, if we stand against all war in the nuclear age (and are not citizens of some lesser and non-nuclear power), this should be done in clear recognition of the fact that (if ours is more than a witnessing action and has any effect) our words and action will tend to make it more likely that the United States will use nuclear weapons *first* in some future encounter of power, since we would be undertaking to weaken our nation's resolve to provide itself with sufficient conventional strength and graduated and flexible response below the nuclear level. The way to be a *nuclear pacifist* and at the same time politically responsible would be precisely to stand *for* the possible justice of non-nuclear war today, and to foster and strengthen the means for conducting such a war successfully without resort to nuclear weapons (planning to surrender rather than go to nuclears).

The present writer could easily be persuaded that this should be

[9] *Op. cit.*, p. 323. I responded to an earlier but substantively identical statement of Tucker's critique of the just war. See "Robert W. Tucker's *Bellum Contra Bellum Justum*," Chap. 17 below. Tucker apparently would agree entirely with Douglass' statement that "a morally limited war has already been excluded from possibility in the nuclear age on the level of intention by the global context of nuclear counter-threats which constitute the only (murderous) guarantee of limitation today." In other words, Tucker thinks it to be a necessity of state today to employ a morally unlimited intention to destroy, while eschewing the besetting sin of evaluating the usefulness of military power largely in terms of its potentially uncontrolled actual use. Osgood and Tucker end with a qualified optimism that nevertheless nuclear weapons can be conquered, by prudent statesmanship under the fear of illimitably destructive mutual intentions to destroy. Douglass accepts the reality of illimitability in both senses, both on the level of intention to destroy at the heart of deterrence and the uncontrollable use of nuclear weapons that will come into use. Douglass' mind, at least, is simply a reflection of supposed nuclear sophistication, and so morally he turns away from all war. I think—contrary to Tucker's *realpolitic* and Douglass' abandonment of statecraft—that it is possible and a Christian vocation to do something intentionally about these weapons.

the conclusion from the just-war categories, that this is the place we should attempt to cut across modern military technology and our present war plans. Such a policy supported by religious people would not be for them to move in a sectarian direction or to prescind from the modern history of nations. Still we would have to think about the morality of some form or level of nuclear deterrence to preserve these limits.

I must simply protest Douglass' casting upon me guilt by misassociation in everything he says about Dresden and Hiroshima and the performance of Jagerstatter's confessor. Anyone having the slightest acquaintance with my writings knows that I would never accept those "justifying" briefings before the bombing of Dresden or believe that the crew who inadvertently were told the truth about what they were commanded to do should have said anything other than No! to that. No more than in my 1961 book did I accept President Truman's description of the atom bombing of Hiroshima when he wrote that this was done "in the manner prescribed by the laws of war. That meant that I wanted it dropped on a military target. I had told Stimson that the bomb should be dropped as nearly as possible upon a war production center of prime military importance"—"to avoid, as far as possible, the killing of civilians." [10] In *War and the Christian Conscience*, I clearly concluded from the just-war tests that the obliteration- or area-bombing in the European theater in World War II, the fire-bombing of Tokyo, and the atomic destruction of the two Japanese cities were inherently immoral acts of war.[11] It is not I but Douglass who believes that the just-war doctrine is morally pliable. It is not I but Douglass who thinks it comes down to quantitative increments of destruction. It is Douglass who can find no limits if there is war.

On the matter of selective or just-war conscientious objection, Douglass fails to cite an earlier passage in which I stated (long before this became a celebrated cause) that "it does not seem possible *responsibly* to call for a general discipline to limit the use of force unless the church at the same time makes a decision to support its members who refuse to fight because they believe a particular war to be unjust with the same vigor with which it has in recent years supported the pacifist witness within its ranks and within the nation. This would mean that the church will consciously attempt to obtain in military draft laws some

[10] Harry S. Truman: *Years of Decisions* (Garden City, N.Y.: Doubleday, 1955), p. 420.

[11] One of the books which Douglass cites, by Robert Batchelder (*The Irreversible Decision, 1939–50* [Boston, Massachusetts: Houghton Mifflin, 1962]), for its judgments about Hiroshima was, in fact, influenced in some degree by my *War and the Christian Conscience*.

status for those who refuse to fight unjustly as well as for those who have conscientious objection to all war." [12] Instead he cites a later passage where I was *pondering* the alternative to this, namely, that we might conclude that these tests of political responsibility are addressed principally to the top-most magistrate. Even there I said that on such an interpretation it might still be the case that "just-war refusal to fight in unjust war or in one that makes unlimited use of immoral means" may be the way to address these same political leaders or a way "to bring about the needed limitation on warfare, or what the Christian must do in any case." [13] Douglass' degree of misunderstanding arises, I suppose, from the fact that I tried to ponder all sides of the question of selective conscientious objection before passing to advocacy. In any case, I came down on the side of the democratization of the just-war doctrine not only here but also in my treatment of "justifiable revolution."

This is also the case in the subsequent article on "Discretionary Armed Service." [14] Anyone who wants Christian ethics done in clarion calls, however, must remember two things. The first is that there is a difference between the right in conscience to refuse to fight in a war deemed to be unjust and the legal right or status that might be granted to this in military draft laws. It takes one line of moral reasoning to determine when war is right or wrong and what is right or wrong in war. I have, along this line, consistently reached the conclusion that there is a right and duty in conscience to object to particular wars and to refuse to fight in them, or to engage in particular acts of war deemed unjust. It takes another line of reasoning, however, to decide that there can or should be a law according this moral right legal status and granting the objector alternative forms of national service. Just as not every vice is a fit subject of criminal legislation, so also not every virtue or conscientious action may under given circumstances be a fit subject of legal protection. While I have been more cautious in reaching the conclusion that an enactment of the status of selective conscientious objection is possible or desirable, I have nevertheless not failed to reach this. Any hesitancy on this that rightly or wrongly I may have expressed, however, should not be transferred to the moral right and duty of just-war conscientious objection itself, or unjust-war resistance.

The second thing that needs to be remembered is that the democratization of the just-war doctrine democratizes and places upon the individual every aspect of it. Specifically, the individual is not only in his degree a "lesser magistrate" participating in the public processes

[12] *War and the Christian Conscience,* pp. 128–39.
[13] *Ibid.,* pp. 131–32.
[14] *worldview,* February, 1967. For a more sustained consideration of the question of selective conscientious objection, see Chap. 5 above.

by which a resort to war may be initiated. He is also subject to these processes and determinations in a manner that is to be determined by moral and political deliberation.

In his capacity as a lesser magistrate he shares in the determination of how to apply the tests of justice in war and the justice of this war. Is the cause just? Is there a reasonable chance of success? Of doing more good, or lesser evil, than harm will be done? Is the political good to come proportionate to the costs paid and exacted? What is the meaning of not aiming acts of war indiscriminately upon populations, and what does this require under the conditions of modern war? Is or can the conduct of the war be just, or must or will it violate the moral immunity of non-combatants from direct attack? When participating in these decisions in the public forum, our democratic "magistrate," in giving answer to these questions, knows that they are all subject to still another test that has also been democratized. In his capacity as a deciding magistrate participating in the public processes, he must make *a presumption against war.* He must ask whether the war is undertaken as the last reasonable resort, other methods of conciliation or defense of justice having been given every reasonable trial.

Once the decision is taken, however, and the foreign policy of a nation has undertaken a particular political use of armed force the presumption shifts in favor of the justice of the war that these processes have authorized. It shifts because there is a shift to a *presumption favoring the established or legitimate political processes* by which the decision was made. Before, the individual was a "lesser magistrate" required to know from an examined and critical conscience that the war is just. Now, the individual is a "subject" required to know from an examined and critical conscience that the war is *un*just before he claims to exercise the moral right of objection to a particular war, refuses participation, or resists the war.[15] The democratization of the magisterial capacity in

---

[15] Philip Wogaman is plainly mistaken when he writes that I have overlooked a "stipulation" of the just-war doctrine, namely, that "the burden of proof must be borne by those who conduct the war, not by those who oppose it" ("The Vietnam War and Paul Ramsey's Conscience," in *Dialog*, Autumn 1967, p. 293, replying to my earlier article "Is Vietnam a Just War?" in *Dialog*, Winter 1967). That stipulation has not been "overlooked"; rather I have correctly located it, namely, at the point of the *determination* of foreign policy and the *initiation* of any resort to armed force. The democratization of *this* responsibility to the degree that everyone is and should strive to be a deciding "magistrate" bearing the "burden of proof" if war seems to be the remaining desirable resort, in no way removes the fact that once war is "initiated" and while a nation's course is set every man is subject to these same deciding public processes and must himself now assume the burden of proof that that course and *this* particular resort to arms is unjust. This is not to say *how* he shall bear both political responsibilities, simultaneously and with a constantly examined conscience. It is only to say that this is the question of questions in a democratic political society.

initiating use of force has not removed the fact that every man is also a subject; that too has been democratized. It ought even to be more democratized, by equalizing the incidence with which the burdens of war fall upon citizens, their obligations of obedience to the political processes of which they are also the magistrates, and their duty to serve —unless and until a man knows from an examined and critical conscience that the war is unjust or is being unjustly conducted. This presumption in favor of decisions taken by established and legitimate political authority in a democratic society ought not to be forgotten in forming consciences, preparing the social conditions for the acceptance of and entering claims to selective conscientious objection—or in defending war resisters. This is in no way to withdraw from conscience the moral right of refusal to participate in unjust wars. Quite the contrary; it is an examination of the meaning of doing this, in the context of every man's political responsibilities.[16]

Nothing in the foregoing amounts to giving theoretical support to the moral right of selective conscientious objection while practically rejecting its exercise. The conditions for there being this moral right *are* the conditions upon which in practice it should be exercised. Douglass seems to believe that granting *legal status* to selective conscientious objection should be not only easier to defend but also, it would seem, morally more important than to establish the grounds for the moral right and its exercise. In no case does "ambiguity" about the former spill any doubt upon the latter. Certainly not if Christians should go the way of "suffering resistance"; and if every man should obey his conscience, even an erring one.

Above, I expressed my puzzlement over the logic of Douglass' enterprise in taking up my writings at all. He evidently wants to show

[16] The best recent article on the democratization of the just-war doctrine on the use of force is, in my judgment, Quentin L. Quade's "Civil Disobedience and the State," in *worldview*, November, 1967, pp. 4–9. Professor Quade rightly says, "The principles of Just War become operative only *after* the classic political question is answered: who should do the judging? . . . the question behind the question ['to war or not; how to war if to war'] is who will decide for the nation, or how will the nation decide?" He answers this question unhesitating: "To universalize the scene of Just War deliberation is a worthy objective. It seems simply another way of seeking an enlightened and responsible citizenry, and it would undoubtedly heighten the possibility of Just War principles operating in the political sphere."

Quade is equally right in adding immediately: "But it does not make each Just War practitioner his own government." That is to say, the democratization of the just-war doctrine on the use of force in no sense removes the fact that each practitioner of it is also subject to that same government, subject to the political processes by which the nation decides. It is within this understanding that the case for selective conscientious objection has to be argued. Both Quade and I do so argue, and each of us conclude to selective conscientious objection as both a possible legal enactment and (in differing ways) sometimes a moral right and duty.

that the just-war doctrine affords at least negative support to the way of non-violence by demonstrating that no modern war could possibly be just. He finds that the present writer justifies a lot of modern war or provides out of the just-war criteria a lot of possible justification for modern war. He even exceeds me, and does not note or believe the limits I have drawn *contra bellum*. That is the charge levelled against these writings.

What I find puzzling is that this is supposed to prove that the just-war doctrine serves the function, which a pacifist finds useful, of condemning all modern war, although this does not provide him with the essential and positive foundations of his ethics. The "inherent logic and integrity of the just-war doctrine today demand a stand in conscience against all war." ". . . By its own moral logic . . . taken by itself" we should be compelled "to relinquish all recourse to modern war." But the charge against the writings chosen for analysis is that the just-war criteria have in my hands justified modern war altogether too much.

This would require Douglass to leave off dealing with my writings, and himself exhibit in a better manner the inherent logic and integrity and proper moral logic of that doctrine. I am supposed "with great ingenuity" to have avoided "the doctrine's natural logic against modern war." That places on Douglass the responsibility of using his ingenuity to exhibit that logic in a better fashion.

Therefore, the author turns around full circle, assuming now that Ramsey's interpretation may not afford any such conclusion, and asks whether the doctrine itself, more correctly interpreted, may not have "the theological strength to support the cross of non-violence or conscientious objection." This possibility is only briefly considered in the end. There is the unexceptionable statement that "the basic concern of the just-war theory is not that we should make war but that we should make justice." But then the entire issue on which Douglass' whole case depends is begged in an hypothetical: "*If* . . . war and justice should be seen to have reached an absolute conflict, war as the physical factor in the theory must give way to justice as the ruling moral principle." Any just-war theorist would grant that at once; I at least would abandon the view that some modern war can be justified if I believed there was the slightest evidence that that hypothetical proposition represents the actual state of affairs in regard to force and justice.

Even if it were so, the just-war theory would not be about to undergo transformation into Douglass' "theory of just resistance," from "the value of violence as a form of justice" to "the value of a just refusal of violence." It may not be necessary for international war to be a component of justice, but it is necessary for force and enforcement to be. Nor do I believe that "a warless world would be a lawless world," or that "peace is no responsible alternative." But if we achieve a warless world that is lawful, and make peace the exclusive political responsibility of all men and states, it will be because the just-war doctrine has undergone self-transformation into world political authority with radical peace-keeping and justice-making powers (which Douglass eschews). It will not be because "warring resistance" has been changed solely into "suffering resistance to injustice." There is a "moral alternative to war" in the international system, and this is the transformation of that system.

Still I do not claim to be able, I do not even undertake, to demonstrate that "war's central function," the state's central function, and the world authority's central function, "of *inflicting* suffering and death" is not "directly opposed to the example of Christ in *enduring* these same realities." That may have been the better path to take in His discipleship away back yonder when Christian non-political pacifism and Christian political responsibilism came to this enduring fork in the road.

PART THREE

The Morality of Deterrence

CHAPTER 13

A Brief Preface to the Morality of Deterrence

Before the third session of the second Vatican Council ended in November 1964, there was introduced for brief discussion a statement on nuclear arms. This was a part of "Schema XIII'" which—after much revision—was to become *Gaudium et spes,* or the "Pastoral Constitution on the Church and the Modern World" (finally issued by the Council and promulgated December 8, 1965). On October 12 and November 10, 1964, *The New York Times* published extensive quotations from the crucial Article 25 of the *Schema* then in process of evolution and revision. This occasioned a good deal of discussion in the press and in journals of opinion—not least important of which was the colloquy which began in *worldview,* December, 1964. That discussion focused on Paragraph 2 of Article 25. It was continued by my response to those analyses and comments upon Paragraph 2, and by the same authors' rejoinders to me, published by the Council on Religion and International Affairs early in 1965 in a pamphlet edited by James Finn, entitled *Peace, the Churches and the Bomb.* This dialogue concluded with a counter-argument by the present writer published as an Occasional Paper by the Council on Religion and International Affairs in October 1965 under the title "Again, the Justice of Deterrence." While doubtless the colloquy continued in the minds of the participants, this was the end of it in the public forum. The entirety of this discussion of the morality of deterrence is recommended to the reader of the present section. Only by knowing what *everyone* said can he be drawn into the heart of the argument, and make up his own mind. The pamphlet *Peace, the Churches and the Bomb* with the articles against which I direct my arguments can be obtained from CRIA, 170 East 64th Street, New York, New York.

For our present purposes, a complete version of Article 25 is reprinted. It was from this that the whole discussion had proceeded; it especially revolved around Paragraph 2 which seemed unequivocally to condemn nuclear war. The fact that this paragraph in its present form did not appear in the final version of *Gaudium et spes* is of no consequence if any reader wants to be drawn into a discussion of Christian political ethics. For an analysis of what finally the Vatican Council had to say on nuclear war, see Chapter 16 below. It may be that discussions such as this of the quite inadequate paragraphs of the *Schema* influenced for the better the final accomplishment of the Vatican Council in *Guadium et spes*.

It may assist the reader in following my arguments as they developed in relationship to the statements of the other members of the colloquium to know who were the *dramatis personae*:

Theodore R. Weber is professor of social ethics at Chandler School of Theology, Emory University in Atlanta, Georgia. His recent scholarly research has been on the matter of German theological response to the atomic crisis. Professor Weber is the author of *Modern War and the Pursuit of Peace* (New York: Council on Religion and Inter-national Affairs, 1968).

Walter Stein, an Englishman and a Roman Catholic, is lecturer in philosophy and English literature at the University of Leeds, England. Professor Stein is editor and a contributor to *Nuclear Weapons and Christian Conscience* (London: Merlin Press, 1961), and of *Peace on Earth: The Way Ahead* (London: Sheed and Ward, 1966).

Dr. William V. O'Brien is Director of the Institute of World Polity, Georgetown University. Among other volumes, he contributed to *Christian Ethics and Nuclear Warfare* (Washington, D.C.: Institute of World Polity, Georgetown University, July, 1961), which he co-edited with Ulrich S. Allers, and he is author of *Nuclear War, Deterrence, and Morality* (Westminster, Md.: The Newman Press, 1966).

Dr. Justus George Lawler, a member of the faculty of St. Xavier College, Chicago, and editor of the distinguished quarterly *continuum*, is also the author of *Nuclear War: The Ethic, the Rhetoric, the Reality* (Westminster, Md.: The Newman Press, 1965).

ON MAKING LASTING PEACE
ARTICLE 25 FROM SCHEMA XIII
(*UNOFFICIAL TRANSLATION*)

Among the principal signs of the times there stands out clearly before all men an immense desire for true and lasting peace, although the human race after so many bloody wars is still disturbed by almost continuous conflicts, and is terrified by new weapons capable of destroying the entire human family. In view of this extreme danger the barbarity of war stands out in an entirely new light. For this reason, the Church, the handmaiden of the peace of Christ, has to work with the greatest diligence, together with the entire family of nations which is the family of God. And she wills that peace, which transcends every desire and work of this world, may bear fruit among all people. This Sacred Council, replying to the suppliant voices reaching her from all sides, before God adjures all men, all nations, and particularly the rulers of nations, to be mindful of their very grave responsibility, and in view of the complexity of the situation to work with united forces for the establishment of peace:

1. Peace is made stable and lasting by mutual friendship and mutual help, effectively recognizing the united will to help, or "solidarity," which ought to govern the family of nations. There is no true peace, if wars are only postponed by a parity of weapons for spreading terror, rather than a sincere spirit of cooperation and concord. Therefore, everything that unfortunately divides rather than unites must be adjudged as opposed to peace, and above all any words, doctrines or actions that spread hatred, contempt, vengeance, or unfounded suspicion against any nation or even stir up an excessive patriotism and that burning desire to acquire excessive power. Everyone, therefore, and especially those who exert any influence on public opinion, must speak the things that are of peace, promoting mutual esteem among the nations, gladly extolling the virtues of other nations, speaking only patiently and calmly of their defects, and promoting mutual respect among different persuasions.

2. The controversies that may perchance arise between nations must not be settled by force and arms, but by treaties and agreements. *Although, after all the aids of peaceful discussion have been exhausted, it may not be illicit, when one's rights have been unjustly hampered, to defend those rights against such unjust aggression by violence and force, nevertheless the use of arms, especially nuclear weapons, whose effects are greater than can be imagined and therefore cannot be reasonably regulated by men, exceeds all just proportion and therefore must be judged before God and man as most wicked.*[1] Every honest effort therefore must be made, so that not only nuclear warfare may be solemnly proscribed by

---

[1] Italics added. This is the statement that was debated in the symposium in *worldview,* and in Chapters 14 and 15 below.

all nations and alliances as an enormous crime, but also that nuclear arms or others of like destructive force may be utterly destroyed and banned.

3. Since the terrifying destructive force, which is daily increasing in war arms, is able to cause calamities and horrible destruction throughout the world, and since technological progress, communications, and organizations for peacefully settling disputes are daily proving more effective, it is becoming ever more absurd that war is an instrument suited for the redressing of violated rights.

Therefore the Sacred Council denounces as a ruinous injury inflicted upon the whole human family, and in severest terms censures, the uncontrollable armaments race, inasmuch as it is injurious to and prevents real peace, harmony, and trust among nations, places a great part of mankind in danger of their life, and dissipates the wealth needed for much better things.

The rulers of state should be thoroughly aware of the fact that it is their duty to deliver their people from this danger by agreements which will effectively work out a just peace and at the same time they must endeavor to put out of man's minds all hostility, hatred, and mistrust. Better aids must be chosen to prevent wars and peacefully remove conflicts; among these aids are the following: consistent progress in building up a universal community among the nations, all of which will remain free; an international authority having at its disposal the means necessary to avoid war and to promote peace, so as to bring about conditions in which war of any kind can no longer be regarded as a legitimate instrument, even for the defense of one's own rights.

4. Yet the faithful who believe in Christ the Lord, the Prince of Peace, feel His impelling love and in all gladness follow Him, who by the blood of His cross reconciled all men to God and restored the unity of all in the one family of God, and in His own flesh killed hatred. Let the faithful therefore shun no sacrifice, so that, practising the truth in love (cf. Eph. iv:15), they may in every way contribute toward establishing a lasting peace, which is a sign of the world redeemed. Let them, by their charity, justice, and unity, be harbingers of the peace of Christ.

CHAPTER 14

More Unsolicited Advice
to Vatican Council II*

The articles [by Theodore Weber, Walter Stein, William V. O'Brien, and Justus George Lawler that appeared in *Peace, the Churches, and the Bomb,* pamphlet published by the Council of Religion in International Affairs] on the proposed statement by the Vatican Council on nuclear war are incisive and penetrating. Together they advance the discussion of Christian morality and nuclear war or nuclear deterrence. I, at least, am stimulated to make the following comments.

I yield to Theodore R. Weber ("Questions for Vatican II"), who was there as an "observer," the correctness of his report that most of the conciliar Fathers are in agreement that Article 25 ("On Making Lasting Peace") "proposes to condemn all nuclear weapons" and "means to deny any justification to all nuclear weapons." Yet I cannot agree that "the text seems to read that way." The text reads rather like an ambiguity that was introduced into the deliberations of a solemn assembly by some scribe's poor draftsmanship, by a mistake in punctuation, or insufficient attention to the difference in grammar between a restrictive and a non-restrictive clause.

Suppose the relevant passage read:

Although, after the aids of peaceful discussion have been exhausted, it may not be illicit, when one's rights have been unjustly hampered, to

* First appeared in *Peace, the Churches, and the Bomb,* Pamphlet issued by The Council of Religion in International Affairs, 1965.

defend those rights against such unjust aggression by violence and force, nevertheless the use of arms whose effects are greater than can be imagined and therefore cannot be reasonably regulated by men exceeds all just proportion and therefore must be judged before God and man as most wicked.

Or suppose, as a statement about nuclear weapons, the passage read:

> . . . nevertheless the use of nuclear arms whose effects are greater than can be imagined and therefore cannot be reasonably regulated by men would exceed all just proportion, and therefore must be judged before God and man as most wicked.

If one reads in a single breath the words, "the use of arms whose effects are . . ." or "the use of nuclear arms whose effects are . . ." with no comma before "whose . . . ," the clause is restrictive. Then the whole of the proposed statement makes good sense. It restrictively specifies the sort of weapons, or use of weapons, that would be proscribed by the principle of proportion. It warns persons working in the political and military sectors of all nations that it would be gravely immoral—indeed, "most wicked"—for them to intend to put themselves and their nation's use of arms out of control. It stresses the ultimate irrationality of the "rationality of irrationality" policies, should these ever be put or intended to be put into actual use. It urges upon the consciences of men that the immediate effects of some weapons, or of some uses of weapons, may be more destructive than the ultimate consequences of the injustice they are seeking to repel. It calls attention to the calculus of cost-benefit that must be made even in a justified cause, lest the evil done exceed what one hoped to prevent.

This statement, however, would not presume to substitute the conscience of a church council for the conscientious judgment of men who are expert in military and political affairs. Instead, it would direct them (as said *Mater et magistra*) to "look, judge, act," as they endeavor to "reduce to action" these guidelines from the church's ancient teachings and its present pronouncement. On this construction, the statement on warfare would acknowledge that "what is at issue is the application of the criterion of proportionality to a weapons system," as Mr. Weber says must be the case; and that "this calls for a judgment of probable effect, and the criteria of effect in this instance are technological, political and military," which church Fathers as such know little or nothing about. On this construction, and on this construction alone, the statement is within the competence of the Council, and is in fact sorely needed guidance for the consciences of experts in military strategy the world over. On this construction, the entire statement makes sense.

The objection to be raised would be to grounding a possibly justified resort to arms—in the first part of the statement—exclusively upon the natural right of self-defense. The objection would be that charity, obliging men not to abandon to dereliction any of the suffering victims of tyranny, or not to abandon ordinary men to complete political disorder, is the true source of a Christian's justification for using armed force. This clarification, itself, would *anatomize* why the understanding of the justice of war originally entailed a *positive* undertaking in the service of needy men, even *initiative* in the use of force to correct injustice.

This, then, would locate the present draft-statement in the line of modern papal teachings which have condemned aggressive resort to arms and have ever more limited the use of force (which might be justified in itself) *because of the danger of disproportionate evil.* Neither Pope nor Council, being men of graceful reason, should undertake to withdraw from Christian charity the impulse to serve mankind in every concrete way possible that is not intrinsically wrong. (Here comes in the legitimacy of some determination that rights were violated or are about to be violated by "unjust aggression"; but not necessarily one's own rights alone.) But either Pope or Council may rightly withdraw in principle resort to force when this is seen to do more harm than good or produce greater evil than that opposed, or when the effects "cannot be reasonably regulated" to the attainment of choiceworthy political goals. This is the only sensible construction to be placed upon recent developments in Roman Catholic teachings on war, including the draft-statement now under consideration.

But then, according to my hypothesis, it occurred to someone to cite a class of weapons that might illustrate a possible "use of arms whose effects are greater . . . ," or the sort of thing that "would exceed all just proportion." The words "especially nuclear weapons" were inserted. They were inserted before the restrictive clause in "the use of arms whose effects . . ." A comma was required *before* this reference to nuclear weapons, and of course one had to be placed *after* it. The effect of this insertion, enclosed by commas before and aft, and especially the effect of the final comma, was to transform a restrictive statement about the use of arms that would be most wicked into a non-restrictive statement about nuclear weapons. Or so it seems. The non-restrictive statement "especially nuclear weapons, whose effects are greater than can be imagined . . ." became, thus, a flat statement that all nuclear weapons *in fact* have such effects in *all* their uses, and "cannot be reasonably regulated by men," and are therefore most wicked.

Such a statement of fact is beyond the competence of a church council. It would preempt and replace the conscientious judgment of experts in the political and military sectors of the nations, whose consciences should, of course, be severely warned and informed by principles that are within the Church's competence. Thus it may have come about that, with such a poorly drafted statement before them, many of the conciliar Fathers found themselves in personal agreement, in their capacities as citizens of the various nations, that the verdict of disproportion should be brought against all uses of nuclear weapons. So they were tempted to violate the boundary between priest and magistrate in making judgments based upon the certainty of nuclear escalation, or in ignorance of how fractional some nuclears are. This may be the reason it was then discovered that, as Weber reports, there was "more support for a total condemnation of nuclear weapons than one might have expected."

The presumptive judgment of fact was invited to an even greater extent by the first published report of this statement in the English language. This set the characterization of the effects of nuclear weapons off from the rest of the sentence by the use of the dashes, thus making the statement more definitely non-restrictive—if that be possible—and more sweeping in its prohibition. Instead of a severe qualification of the arms it is ever licit or illicit to use, we have a sweeping and unqualified statement, in the empirical and not in the moral order, about the nature of nuclear weapons as such. *The New York Times* (Oct. 12, 1964) read: "the use of arms, especially nuclear weapons—whose effects are greater than can be imagined and therefore cannot be reasonably regulated by men— exceeds all just proportion . . ." Thus were the conciliar Fathers placed—so far as grammar could do this—under strong pressure from world public opinion, and from what John XXIII called the profound longings of the entire human family, to forget *who they are* and what *the church* is. This will have to be recalled by the committee redrafting the *Schema on the Church and the Modern World*, and by the next and final session of the Council.

It is true, of course, that the context of the statement we are considering lent support to an extreme interpretation of its bad grammar. The next sentence states: "Every honest effort, therefore, must be made, so that not only nuclear warfare may be solemnly proscribed by all nations and alliances as an enormous crime, but also so that nuclear arms or others of like destructive force may be utterly destroyed and banned." [1] Still, the solemn prescription here envisioned has to come from the nations and alliances of nations, and not from church councils. Moreover, we are not told the difference between an "honest effort" to this end, and an ignoble one. All this is in line with the stress Pope John placed upon the need for public authorities beyond the nation-states to remedy the structural defects in the present world order.

[1] *The New York Times,* Nov. 10, 1964. On this date, the preceding paragraph used commas and not dashes.

I cannot agree with Weber's view that the statement, as drafted, sets "absolute limits—immediately—to a particular form of human action," or that it makes immediate unilateral nuclear disarmament "morally mandatory" while allowing that general nuclear disarmament would be better, or that it tends to "confuse the setting of a goal with its achievement" and would immediately remove "the leverage for collective resolutions" in the direction of a less defective ●world order. I cannot agree that there is here an "immediate principled judgment against all nuclear arms." If there is, why did Bernard Cardinal Alfrink of Utrecht, Maximos IV Saigh, Melchite Patriarch of Antioch and the Orient, Bishop Ancel and Bishop Guilhem all stand up to argue that the statement should be revised to make clear the Council's proscription of all use of nuclear weapons? [2]

There is also another reason for saying that there is not in this statement an "immediate principled judgment" in Weber's sense. The statement about nuclear weapons was *not* couched in terms of the moral immunity of non-combatants from direct, intended attack; but it falls instead wholly under the principle of proportion. That principle most clearly of all the criteria for the just conduct of war *refers* the matter at issue to the conscientious determination of the political leaders of the nations. This is also the reason the conciliar Fathers have only to remember who they are, and what the Church is, to be able properly to redraft what they wanted to say to the world on this issue.

Since there is here no intrinsic "immediate principled judgment," since instead direction is given that should help in the evaluation of facts that fall outside the competence of church councils, I cannot agree that the settlement contains two ethics that are at loggerheads. Mr. Weber supposes that it exhibits both a "goal-oriented," and a "principle-oriented ethic" whose requirements are in this instance contradictory; and he argues that "the political work of constructing a responsible and viable peace requires means [at least as "leverage"] that are denied to it by the principled prohibition." Surely, the rational relation of means to ends in politics, which is one aspect of the moral economy governing any use of armed force, also governs the work of political construction and will continue to govern the exercise of new world political authorities when these are achieved. It is entirely consistent for the Council to provide direction for the long "meanwhile," or for what it mistakenly supposes will be a short meanwhile, and also direction for the overcoming of that meanwhile. The one is not a principled ethics of means nor is the other merely an ethics of goal-setting. Under the heading of proportion no such distinction of intrinsically wrong means and ends is to be made.

[2] *The New York Times,* Nov. 10 and 11, 1964.

The warning against disproportionate means requires political prudence virtuously ordering means to ends in the meanwhile; and such prudence in the conduct of politics must go into the construction of any world public authority that may emerge, and can never be dropped from it. This has to be our understanding of it, unless one is to argue that— while it would be "most wicked" to use arms that "cannot be reasonably regulated" and "exceed all just proportion" to any political goals in the nation-state system—it would be good to use nuclear weapons in city-strikes or to use an intrinsically immoral deterrent (if such it is) in order to destroy the nation-state system and to shock the world into engaging rapidly in the necessary work of political construction. (Some such reasoning was at the time Arthur Compton's justification for dropping the bomb on Hiroshima.)

Mr. Weber's interpretation that the present draft allows no time and would promptly remove the leverage for the work of political construction rests on the premise that one cannot distinguish between justice or proportion in the actual use of weapons and the possible morality of their possession for deterrence. "If the use of no nuclear weapon can be justified morally on any ground," he writes, "there is no reason for keeping the weapons beyond the moment in which the truth of the condemnation is accepted." I have questioned whether the statement so unambiguously prohibits any use of nuclears, or should do so. However, even if it should and did, one could not immediately conclude that it is immoral to possess them for the sake of deterrence. And if my hypothesis is correct—that the proscription applies to disproportionate and therefore wicked use of all arms, and especially of nuclears—one could not immediately conclude that "there is no reason for keeping the weapons beyond the moment in which the truth of the condemnation is accepted." This only raises decisively the question about the morality of deterrent use during the meanwhile. That question is not settled, it is not even addressed, by the statement that "*every honest effort, there-fore, must be made, so that not only nuclear warfare may be solemnly proscribed by all nations and alliances as an enormous crime, but also so that nuclear arms or other like destructive force may be utterly destroyed and banned.*"

That statement may be criticized for omitting to take up the problem of controls, as *Pacem in terris* may be criticized for not having detailed the steps to be taken in order to reach the goal of radically correcting the structural defects of the nation-state system. But in both instances, and in the case of applications of the principle of proportion in the meanwhile, it may be that Pope and Council are commendably refusing to substitute their priestly judgments for the judgments and the manifold actions that must necessarily be taken by political leaders, and by political leaders alone.

To this question of mounting a moral deterrent or morally re-shaping the one we have, we must now turn.

II

Walter Stein ("Would You Press the Button?") and Justus George Lawler ("The Council Must Speak") go deep into the question of the morality of deterrence. Any reader who thinks about it must, I think, agree with the *moral argument* these two authors have in common, but *not* with Stein's conclusions or with *all* of Lawler's.

Stein has stated very forcefully the conditions which, if the fact-situation he describes is necessarily and *unchangeably* true, would mean that the Deterrence State is necessarily and unchangeably an atrocity, and must be wholly abandoned. If he is correct, it is quite impossible to mount a moral deterrent, or to alter radically enough the one we have to make it acceptable to a properly instructed conscience.

The question turns entirely upon what commitments are inherent in the Deterrence State. If this is now and must remain a *commitment* to execute city-hostages, as Stein supposes, then as long as we allow any nuclear deterrence to stand we are all involved in and, in various degrees, responsible for constantly doing something that is most wicked. Is "the backbone of nuclear strategy" a seriously intended "threatened incineration of enemy cities"? Stein does not distinguish sufficiently between a declared and a real intention, nor does he question whether there is enough shared deterrence in the collateral damage inflicted by use of nuclear weapons over legitimate targets only. Nevertheless, he is quite correct in saying that an actual, present intention to execute city-hostages is

> no less immediately, and categorically, genocidal for relating to a future hypothetical condition. No doubt there is a difference between murder accomplished and murder in one's heart, but it is not a difference between murderousness and non-murderousness.

Therefore, the question is whether the deterrence that is needed to enforce restraints upon war necessarily and unchangeably depends on an actual, present intention to do murder, or upon a present murderous intention. If something is wrong when done, it is wrong when intended. Stein is therefore quite correct in shifting the argument from the calculation of the *risk* of future enormities to the question of whether any possible system of deterrence in the nuclear age necessarily and unchangeably "involves gravely immoral intentions *here and now*." Do we have, and if so must we have, in our hearts a "constant, absolute readiness to let fly in moral cash what [we] already owe in professional I.O.U.'s" (declaratory deterrence or the apparent intention)? Does deterrence necessarily and unchangeably rest upon an "unconditional, trained and habitual, present consent" to execute city-hostages? Are we engaged, and if so *must* we for deterrence's sake engage, here and now in this "desperate moral self-violation"? If the answer to these questions is yes, then, I agree with Stein, "it is extraordinary that anyone should seriously have thought of doubting the Catholic supreme *magisterium's* competence to pronounce upon these things." It is notable that all three of the contributors to this discussion in *worldview* who are Roman Catholics (Stein, O'Brien, and Lawler) criticize the Council's draft-statement from their differing points of view for not addressing itself to this crucial issue of the morality of deterrence. Stein, however, must simply be told that, while it is obviously within the competence of church councils to pronounce *in moral terms* upon *the moral issue* just stated, it is equally obvious that it is beyond the competence of any church council to make the determinations of *fact,* and of *necessary* fact, that are interwoven with Stein's moral argument. As an individual citizen of a Deterrence State, it is quite proper for Stein to hold these opinions even if they are mistaken. The forceful expression of his conclusions should no doubt contribute a great deal to the discussion of the problem. This yields, however, to another man the possibility that from the same moral premises another conclusion can be reached about the morality of deterrence based on a different judgment about whether deterrence does in fact rest upon murderous intention, and, if so, whether it must necessarily be so grounded or whether it can be radically reshaped by manifold political thought and action. The man who so believes ought not to be virtually unchurched by church councils that go beyond guiding and informing his conscience, even by the severest warnings, to prejudge the present or the future facts.

I need not repeat here the argument that can be made for the possible morality of deterrence, or the possibility of a moral deterrent.[3] This would sound to Stein like the efforts of "a few—mostly just-war thinkers, anxious to square their principles with support of the deterrent —[who] are at pains to explain . . . away [the statements of leaders of government]: either as simple bluff, or as sophisticated equivocations (either way avoiding any real commitment to genocide)." Now that is a remarkable statement, for until now one would suppose that, especially in Stein's view, there is no more important moral challenge facing man-

---

[3] See *The Limits of Nuclear War: Thinking about the Do-able and the Un-do-able,* Chap. 11 above, *contra* the moral and fact analyses of deterrence in my *War and the Christian Conscience* (Durham, N.C.: Duke, 1961).

kind than "avoiding any real commitment to genocide." His easy dismissal of a position he opposes, and his failure to join issue with it, can be explained only by supposing that he does not believe there is a tremendous moral and political significance in finding a way to mount a morally acceptable deterrent in the nuclear age, or in finding a way to reshape the one we have. Unfortunately, a great many Christians and a goodly number of Catholics are today in positions of responsibility where they cannot pass quite so easily over that problem. These are the men the Church will address when speaking to "the world" and to faithful sons of the Church on the question of nuclear weapons.

I have no cause to defend the tesselation of statements Stein cites from government officials to prove that our present deterrence policy is an atrocity. Still, one will not make progress toward the heart of our nuclear dilemma or help in gaining mastery over it if he does not attend to distinctions that are perhaps prior to an understanding of these statements themselves; and, from such a beginning and upon this basis, to help provide shaping redirection to our future declaratory or actual deterrence policy. McNamara's statement that the United States retains "sufficient reserve power to destroy an enemy society if driven to it" does not itself decide the question of whether deterrence of war (and enforcing limits upon war when war comes) depends on the *power* to do this or on the *intention* to do this; nor is *that* question settled by what McNamara may happen to think about it or by what he meant. The same can be said of Eisenhower's statement that the retaliatory power of the Strategic Air Command presents "to any attacker the *prospect* of virtual annihilation of his own country" (italics added). That prospect may simply be *there,* in the weapons, shared and enough to enforce limits in the nuclear age. When Eisenhower chose, as do the statesmen of all the nuclear powers, to "present" this prospect in threatening words ("our bombers would immediately be on their way . . ."), one has still to ask whether the intent *need* be real behind the words for there to be more than enough deterrence. Again, *this* question is not to be settled by reference to what Eisenhower meant. In general, the possibility of distinguishing between a deter-the-war policy and a fight-the-war policy, and also within deterrence policies between declarations and intent, must be held open if one wants to examine seriously the morality or immorality of deterrence.

Finally, it is obvious that a NATO strategy based on "resort to massive nuclear bombardment of the sources of power in Russia" (British White Paper), may entail the bombardment of legitimate military targets. It may, that is, unless one has already yielded to a notion more heinous (if possible) than "the execution of city-hostages," namely, the notion that all persons in a society are its "sources of power," its fighters, its legitimate military targets. I do not defend at the moment either the morality or the feasibility of any of these distinctions. But no one can ignore them and claim to have *thought through* the morality of deterrence.

The last point, however, should be taken up. Long before an actual war reached the upper levels of massive nuclear bombardment of the sources of military power, the destructiveness of such warfare directed even upon legitimate targets is likely to be disproportionate to the good sought or the evil prevented by resort to arms. Long before an actual nuclear war directed against legitimate tactical and strategic targets reached the upper levels of violence, the range of acceptable collateral damage would likely have been passed. If this be the case, then there is deterrence *at work* within the theoretically legitimate target area, because it will exert pressure upon any rational decision-maker to acknowledge that the principle of proportion is simply a summary of political wisdom. At the moment and for years to come, the most important "hostage" deterring the Chinese Communist from massive intervention in Southeast Asia is a quite legitimate target: the nuclear experiment stations and installations located, it can also be said, away from centers of population, on which Red China hopes to build her future power and prestige in the world.

Moreover, deterrence is also *at work* as a "side-effect," so to speak, of the prospect of extensive damage collateral even in "justly targeted" nuclear war. In short, there is a deterrence from disproportionate "combatant" damage and there is a "collateral deterrence," or deterrence from the indirect, unavoidable destructiveness of even tactical nuclear war. This is mutual and enough, without ever thinking of executing city-hostages.

Christian moralists have simply not made the most of the radical difference between "extended deterrence," which hoped to deter conventional wars by suspending everything from massive retaliation, and "graduated deterrence." The latter is geared to flexible and graduated responses. Both in fighting a war and in deterring war, the question is how far up the levels of violence it is necessary to go and how far up one should go in order to have effective means proportionate to the political purposes of war and effective means proportionate to the goals of deterrence. It is *not* a settled question that, in order to have a shared and workable deterrence of the upper levels of warfare today, one must always go *in mente* and intentionally on up to counter-city deterrence.

Legitimate deterrence is the indirect effect[4] of the unavoidable indirect effects (the collateral civil damage) of properly targeted and therefore justly intended and justly conducted war in the nuclear age. It would

---

[4] [Again, I must put the reader on notice that my language was inexact, even mistaken; and that this error was to be improved in the course of the colloquy. See above, p. 252, n. 95.]

seem that Christian moralists should have maximum concern to suggest that the adequacy of a morally tolerable deterrence be fully explored by the statesmen and citizens of the world; and that we should have no interest at all in proving that deterrence policy must go to the top and be altogether suspended from counter-society threats meant to be invoked. I seriously suggest that if one's mind is emancipated from "antebellum" notions that fight-the-war policies and deter-the-war policies require that everything in a nation's arsenal be used for these purposes, he will be impressed by the fact that the "shared intimidation" arising from counter-forces warfare has in it sufficient effect to deter war from going that high on the scale of violence. If actual war today soon becomes disproportionate, then the war threatened soon becomes deterrent enough upon any rational decision maker. One need not wax so horrendous about it. The strategist should ponder well the deterrence there is in the collateral effects before letting an antiquated war doctrine require that more be mounted with the intention of using it. The puzzle is that the nations of the world seem closer to putting massive nuclear weapons in a class by themselves, as weapons intended to be not used, than some churchmen are, who rather insist that their use against cities must be intended for deterrence's sake (which is therefore immoral).

We need to clean up our deterrence system, of course; but mainly we need to clean up our *notions* of deterrence and of what we erroneously suppose this depends upon. It is so certainly the case that deterrence does *not* necessarily involve a present hypothetical immoral decision that one can (almost) agree with Stein's statement (except for the clause set off by dashes):

> . . . Nothing short of a public government resolve to treat non-combatant populations as inviolable, *whatever* the circumstances—the dismantling, that is, of the whole ultimate foundation of deterrence—would now dismantle these built-in commitments to genocide on the part of its servants.

That there should be this government resolve is beyond question. Whether and in what manner this should be by public announcement may be debated. That commitments to genocide, built-in or intended-in, should be dismantled is also beyond question. But there is good reason to believe that these steps would in no sense dismantle "the whole ultimate foundation of deterrence." In fact, it can be well argued that the nuclear powers have already moved a long way toward placing the counter-city use of nuclear weapons in a class by itself, as a "war plan" (if such it can still be called) intended to be *not* used; and, further, that well below counter-city use, deterrence of disproportion and "collateral deterrence" are quite effective. Statesmen may think this way not for

THE MORALITY OF DETERRENCE

consciously moral reasons but because they follow the grain in the nature of present-day politico-military realities. But, then, the teachings about the principle of proportion in warfare and in deterrence simply identify the grain in the nature of purposeful politics. It ill behooves "moralists" to go about imbedding in the minds of people foolish and immoral notions of the necessary nature of deterrence or of modern war.

This Stein does, I am afraid, in his response to Bishop Hannan's speech which pointed out that "there now exist nuclear weapons which have a very precise limit of destruction." Stein reacted to the "appalling irrelevance of the argument, even in its own terms." How prove its appalling irrelevance? By merely citing the *existence* of over-kill stockpiles, and by asking how much of the forces in being are actually directed "towards these primly 'legitimate' targets." To the last question, I venture that the correct answer is: most of the forces have counter-force targets or such alternate use. But if this were mistaken in fact, it is surely irresponsible on the part of a moralist to deride by using the word "prim" any of mankind's present and future efforts to avoid, and to avoid intending, the genocide he himself uses as a criterion in condemning deterrence.

As for the first part of Stein's reply to Bishop Hannan, he should rather have seen and *tried to extend* the relevance of the Bishop's remark, and *made relevant* his own criterion, by investigating ways in which weapons arsenals and systems might be corrected and reshaped into instruments of *proper* policy. This, we shall see, Lawler undertakes to do in relation to "over-kill" capacities. Instead, Stein simply reiterates his own (consequently) appallingly irrelevant fact-judgment: "the fact that it [deterrence] involves massively murderous commitment *in its total structure—here and now.*"

The *moral* truth contained in Stein's article is surely irrelevant unless this becomes the basis for a practical course of action exerting shaping influence upon deterrence systems. His commitment—here and now—to the proposition that deterrence is unreformable, and to the proposition that people must necessarily choose between morality and such peace as deterrence affords, is likely to have appalling consequences. In any case, this confirms—here and now—horrendous notions about the necessary and unchangeable nature of deterrence that are already too widespread. If the Vatican Council chooses to address the central problem of deterrence it should speak exclusively *in moral terms* of the *moral issue.* This might have significant practical consequences, by informing the consciences of men in the military and political sectors. Nothing but confusion, or only irrelevance, could follow upon a presumptive judgment about what must in fact be intended or not intended in order for there to be any or an adequate deterrent effect.

Concerning the effect of pacifism upon actual fight-the-war policies, it was pointed out by G. E. M. Anscombe in the book Mr. Stein edited that pacifism "teaches people to make no distinction between the shedding of innocent blood and the shedding of any human blood. And in this way pacifism has corrupted enormous numbers of people who will not act according to its tenets. They become convinced that a number of things are wicked which are not; hence seeing no way of avoiding 'wickedness,' they set no limits to it." [5] This statement can be slightly revised and applied to the effect of nuclear pacifism upon actual deter-the-war policies. Nuclear pacifism teaches people to make no distinction between the murderous and non-murderous intentions of men in support of deterrence. In this way nuclear pacifism has corrupted enormous numbers of people who will not act according to its tenets. They become convinced that in the matter of deterrence a number of things are wicked which are not; hence, seeing no way of avoiding "wickedness," they set no limits to it.

A final point. This has to do with a requirement that Stein places upon *anyone who has made himself conditionally willing to press the button that will directly kill a million people who are not bearers of the force* it is just to repel. One "gloss" that might eliminate the moral repugnance of such a resolve, Stein writes, would be if such a person "knew, and could know, with 100% certainty that the circumstances in question could never arise." Stein says, correctly, that "even the smallest margin of uncertainty would leave the intention to genocide intact." That is correct because in this case the man has made himself conditionally willing to do something that is most wicked, which only the unconditional, foreknown impossibility of any such thing could remove. Stein simply assumes that he knows, and knows that he knows, with 100% certainty that deterrence rests and must always rest upon a massive murderous commitment in its total structure here and now.

This is worth bringing up, because by this point in the article the reader may have forgotten that the case was *supposed*, and supposed to be "definitive of nuclear immorality." The reader may therefore grant that statesmen who have the burden and responsibility for deterrence must likewise "know, *beyond all doubt,* that the daemons of genocide will never be unleashed." If and only if they had genocidal intent, however, would the smallest amount of uncertainty leave intact a wicked intention. If deterrence does not depend on diabolic intent, no such divine powers to know, *beyond all doubt,* that the execution of city-hostages will never occur in the future would be required of rulers who

[5] Walter Stein, ed., *Nuclear Weapons and Christian Conscience* (London: Merlin Press, 1961), p. 56.

are mortal men. If statesmen intend to mount a moral deterrent and if they intend that deterrence be not immorally used, they need not have a certainty about future contingent events which they cannot have.

III

Justus George Lawler ("The Council Must Speak") has the more balanced view. In what degree this article expresses his own personal opinion it is difficult to tell, since he disavows that it does; and, instead, says that in this "prudential area" he is not going to express what ideally the Council might do but what he thinks practically it can do.[6] He suggests that a more discriminating statement about nuclear weapons should be agreed to by the conciliar Fathers.

> The emphasis throughout the document should be primarily on any weapons that either by the intention of their possessors or by their very nature are instruments of total war. To the degree that it can be shown that even some nuclear weapons do not fall into either of these categories, to that degree, a statement condemning *all* nuclear weapons may be regarded as untimely.

I wish only that Lawler had written that a statement going beyond addressing *the moral issue* of nuclear weapons *in these moral terms* would be wrong in principle, and not merely "untimely." This, indeed, seems to be entailed in Lawler's subsequent remark that "the Council's condemnation of total war should make explicit the immorality of counter-city warfare, and consequently *the unchanging character of the principle of non-combatant immunity*" (italics added). This means, of course, that an American deterrent based on a real resolve to exercise an option to destroy an enemy's entire society, and based in this sense on the possible exercise of the option, must come under condemnation.

---

[6] In his review of my CRIA pamphlet in *continuum*, Vol. I, No. 2 (Summer 1963), pp. 198–210, Lawler held Stein's view of the Deterrence State, only he expressly stated that this total immorality is the only military policy at the present time in the nuclear age. Except for the present reservation about his own "highly personal opinion," and his reduction of some highly moral principles to prudential statements about a practically possible statement which could issue from the Council, I would be inclined to say that in the meantime Lawler may have learned something from the reply I wrote to his first article (which however was submitted too late to be published). In any case, I should indicate that I have been instructed by Lawler's present article concerning some of the conclusions, and the practical steps to be taken, that are entailed in my own analysis of the justice of deterrence.

But then Lawler wanders into details that should perhaps be left to the statesman who has the burden and the responsibility of managing crises and enforcing limits upon war. From the correct premise that a possible willingness to destroy an enemy's entire society would be immoral, Lawler passes at once to the statement (which he believes the Council should also express) that *"the mere appearance* of a possible willingness to destroy it is equally immoral"* (italics added). This is certainly debatable. A condemnation of "the mere appearance" is in no way established by the reference, in his next paragraph, to the fact that for deterrence to be effective it must be "believable" to the enemy. That fact shows only that a moral condemnation of any appearance of willingness or likelihood or the mere possibility of striking cities would, indeed, proscribe and render morally unacceptable any deterrent effects obtained from the fact that the enemy cannot be sure from the appearances or because of ambiguity about our possible willingness. This only says that one fact may lead to another. From the psychological fact that deterrence must be believable, one is lead to suppose the probable necessity of communicating ambiguity about one's real intentions, or allowing the mere appearance of a possible willingness to stand unaltered and unrenounced. One need not defend or reject these judgments of fact in order to know that by citing them or making them Lawler has not begun to analyze the morality of appearances that may help to render deterrence believable to an enemy, and which someone may believe to be a necessary part of deterrence if it is to be adequate.

The assertion that *"the mere appearance"* would be *"equally immoral"* is simply an assertion, and an unexamined one. Even if the appearance is immoral it is not likely the same immorality or an immorality equal to an actual conditional willingness to destroy an enemy's entire society (which is murderousness). Nor is it correct to say that "the ordinary citizen in the threatening nation . . . would be required to acquiesce in what must appear to him as an immoral act." Instead, we should say that (supposing the facts to be as Lawler presumes) the ordinary citizen in the Deterrence State would be required to acquiesce in the *appearance* of what would *be* to him an immoral act. Whether this can be justified is not now at issue, since Lawler no more than brings this question into view. He has only stated the debatable opinion that deterrence requires it.

If the Council takes up the moral question of ambiguity about one's real intentions, in the context of a forthright statement in moral terms about the morality of the use of nuclear weapons in war or for deterrence such as Lawler suggests, the question before it would be, Are mere appearances (of, it is true, a moral enormity) so obviously a moral self-violation and a violation of others that a church council has the competence to withdraw this possibility from among "the laws of deterrence" that may be used if needed in the judgment of the magistrates of a nation, even as the Council can and should withdraw murder from among the laws of war, and murderousness from among the laws of deterrence, because of the unchanging character of the principle of non-combatant immunity?

To answer this question the Council would have to distinguish one sort of appearance from another, and one sort of ambiguity from another. It would have to acknowledge the "threatening" nature of the weapons themselves *quite apart from any intention or conditional willingness to use them all-out,* and also *quite apart from any ambiguity* left standing concerning whether these weapons are intended to be used over cities. The *weapons* are "threatening" even if they have been placed in a class by themselves as weapons intended to be not used. Not all of the appearance of danger can be removed from them; and not all of the possibility of their use, or uncertainty or ambiguity about this in the mind of a potential opponent, can be removed. The possessors of these weapons need have no such intention; in fact they can strip murderousness from their souls altogether; and there remains a deterrent effect that goes beyond "collateral deterrence." Short of intending murderousness into the system, ambiguity need not be intended. With no posturing at all, these remain threatening *weapons*. Again, deterrence is given and received, it is mutual and enough, quite apart from intention. This remains true even after solemn declarations and treaties to the effect that nuclears are not going to be used, or used massively against cities. Only after traversing all this ground would the Council reach the question concerning the morality of securing deterrent effect by leaving standing the "possibility" that they will be used against cities, or cultivating some "appearance" of an ambiguity about this.

Thus, there are important distinctions that have *first* to be drawn in order to isolate the question that is before the house. When I assert that, following these distinctions, the question whether, how, and in what manner the resolve that alone can sustain a moral deterrent should be announced is debatable, and when I say that the morality of a policy of ambiguity (which, I believe, is in fact not needed in graduated deterrence) is also debatable, I mean only to call attention to these questions. It is not possible to enter upon this debate here. The question, however, would be: Have moralists the right to require that a statesman should disclose to an enemy the real nature of and the difference between his actual fight-the-war policy (if this is just) and his deter-the-war and deterrence-during-the-war policy (if this also contains no unjust or murderous intention)? To do so may be wise, for all that the moralist may not be able to say.

Still, Lawler is approximately correct when he writes:

> Even in the case of a deterring force of less potent weapons, for which theoretically there are conceivable targets, it should be emphasized that the mere possession of such weapons in great numbers [I should say, excessively great numbers. P.R.] is also immoral. . . .

I am one of those who have argued that "because an enemy can never be absolutely sure that these weapons [that have dual use] will not be turned against civilian centers, the mere possibility that that could happen constitutes a licit way of augmenting the deterrent effect of justly targeted nuclear weapons." I should say this constitutes an existing, licit deterrent that has in no way to be augmented, in addition to the deterrent effect of the prospect of excessive combatant or target destructiveness and of the shared prospect of excessive collateral damage. This makes it evident that there is no need even to think of intending counter-society warfare for the sake of strengthening deterrence. It is already mutual and enough without murderous thinking.

I almost agree with Lawler that this reasoning is valid "only if the number of weapons in a nation's arsenal were sufficient to destroy nothing but an enemy's military strength." My reservation waits only on the clarification of "nothing but an enemy's military strength." That may or may not be a too rigid requirement to impose on the consciences of political magistrates. If Lawler is saying only that, within the *moral* economy governing the use of force according to the unchangeable principle of the moral immunity of non-combatants from direct attack, there is also an economy of proportion in the use of force over targets and an economy of proportion governing the properly targeted forces to be mounted for the sake of deterrence, he is entirely correct. I suppose that by limiting the quantity of dual-use weapons to the number that might be required to destroy "nothing but" an enemy's military strength Lawler does not mean to deny that a political-military leader has to make a prudent calculation within an ample margin of error or failure. I presume that in deterrence policies he is only ruling out "counter-force plus *bonus* deterrent value," just as one should in fight-the-war policies rule that "counter-force plus bonus civilian damage" (Kahn) expresses the first step in unjustly enlarging the actual target. If we have "gone far beyond the demands of adequacy," then he is correct: "the mere possession—entirely apart from intention—of these superfluous weapons constitutes a direct threat to the enemy cities, and as such acts as an immoral deterrent."

In the course of thus designating the shape of a possibly moral nuclear deterrent, Lawler has incidentally admitted the licitness of some unspecifiable amount of deterrence flowing from the ineradicable ambiguity in the possible use of dual-purpose weapons. This is one sort of "mere appearance of a possible willingness" to destroy cities which he cannot but "acquiesce in." This would seem to be an appearance that cannot be made unbelievable to an enemy. This is worth pointing out, even in the context of his requirement that the possibility of a deliberate immoral use be "erased by an explicitly, formally, and publicly stated intention never to use them over cities." Even this, which is debatable, would not remove all the ambiguity.

Agreeing with Lawler that the Council might speak out in these moral terms against over-kill capacity, I must say finally that neither Lawler nor church councils have the responsibility for determining the necessary margin that may be legitimate to build into any weapons system for use or for deterrence. One way he stated his own opinion concerning the factual calculation to be made in the economy of force was, however, *theoretically* incorrect in a significant respect. This was his remark about the Rand Corporation estimates of the lethal fallout from massive attacks upon military installations. Lawler wrote, "Obviously we have gone beyond any calculation of double effect." Strictly speaking, that was an inaccurate notation. Strictly speaking, these figures disclose that at many or most of the upper levels of justly targeted nuclear warfare we have gone beyond a *proportionate* use of force and beyond the rational ordering of force to political purpose. He rightly says, "Nothing within the scope of man's imagination would render just such devastation . . . "—i.e., render such devastation just to be done, since there cannot be proportionate grave reason for it.

He ought not, however, to have called even this devastation "murder." Acts of war and ways of deterring war can be "unjustified" in two senses: because they violate the unchanging principle of non-combatant immunity from *direct* attack and because they violate the prudential principle of proportion. Lethal fallout from massive megaton attacks on vast military installations comes under the latter category. This prospect and the extent of collateral damage I have invoked in the category of "collateral deterrence," which is mutual and enough without conditionally intending to murder cities. If we are to see clearly and to maintain that there is a moral deterrent that works, we must not deny that two effects are still discernible in many of the levels of nuclear warfare that ought never to be fought, but are permissible to maintain in prudent degree for the sake of imposing shared limits upon resort to violence.

IV

Here may be a point at which William V. O'Brien ("After Nineteen Years, Let Us Begin") is correct in calling for significant revision of the traditional just-war theory when applying this to the crucial question of deterrence. He describes "modern deterrence" as a military posture in which "*disproportionate* (in terms of traditional military utility) threats are seemingly the indispensable means of avoiding general war." However, it seems to me that one has only to grasp the fundamental meaning of the principle of proportion, not revise it fundamentally, in order to cover and "resolve" this case.

A threat of something disproportionate is not necessarily a disproportionate threat. This depends on the gravity of the evil (general war) and the greatness of the good (the peace of the world) toward which the threat is proportioned. Or, during war, whether a deterrent threat is proportionate depends on the gravity of the evil (escalation) and the greatness of the good (keeping war limited) to which the threat is oriented.

One ought not to say that, just as a real threat or intention to do murder is a murderous threat, so also to threaten something disporionate is a disproportionate threat. The cases are not the same. In the matter of the moral immunity of babies from direct intended attack, the *formal intention* and the *material* act are, while distinguishable, of the same quality; and the morality of either does not vary with the number of deaths inflicted. One is not permitted to calculate a prudent number of babies to be directly killed or to be made the intentional objective which sustains deterrence.

The disproportion of which O'Brien speaks is a matter of balancing the good and the unavoidably evil effects of action. Here the *formal intention* and the *material act* are hardly distinguishable, at least in the sense that one never knows the judgment it would be prudent to make except in particular cases where the cost/benefit may and must be counted. One can, of course, formally intend or make himself conditionally willing to do a disproportionate or imprudent deed. That would be an immoral intention, but it would be rather empty of meaning until the agent begins to weigh the good and evil, or the greater and the lesser evils, in the consequences of some specific material action. In the matter of intending to violate non-combatant immunity, the agent need not wait, nor need he orient himself fully upon the specific elements of the action about to be put forth, in order to discern what that means. Taking prudence to be the most immediate guide in all decision and action, in the one case prudence applies to the material world the moral distinction between direct and indirect killing; in the other case, prudence gathers from the conditions surrounding action and from all the consequences flowing from it an estimate of proportion or disproportion.

The disproportion "in terms of traditional military utility" of which O'Brien speaks is a disproportionate act *when done* and only when done or when very concretely contemplated. He is thinking specifically of an act of war which, if executed, would be to exact and reap a greater evil than any good that might come from a justly targeted arbitrament of arms at that level of violence. That would be disproportionate.

But a threat of something disproportionate need not be a disproportionate threat. In the case of a householder whose home is broken into by a "felon," the degree of whose felonious intention or capability is not yet known, the civil law permits him to be killed. Yet we would say that *morally* the householder should use an economy of force. He should proportion the force he uses to the prevention of the evil. He ought to avoid killing even a felon if he can resist the evil by lesser means. Yet we would *not* say that, if the householder is prepared and threatens to do something that may turn out to be disproportionate (because the housebreaker only meant to rob or was rather easily deterred), this would be a disproportionate threat. The householder does not yet know this. Moreover, his threat is oriented toward the prevention of the graver evil, and to the dampening down of the felon's intention and his actions. It is not (as in a householder's justifiable fight-the-felon policy) oriented toward the positing of the *material act* that will be sufficient, and no more than sufficient, to stop him by an actual use of preponderant physical power.

It is obvious that threats that are proportioned to the prevention of *all* of the evil effects of war or to the prevention of the escalation of war's destruction may justifiably go quite high (since there are such great goods and grave evils at stake), and that the question is largely whether prudence has rightly ordered these deterrent threats to these results (or whether, in fact, the threats are counter-productive). It is obvious, indeed, that the material act of war has to face a closer accounting (because actual resort to armed conflict itself pays and produces destruction with which the greater evil to be prevented must be compared) than does a contemplated act or system of deterrence which, presumably, is ordered to its good goals without producing death and destruction.

Of course, the simple moral truth is still applicable, that it is immoral to intend anything it would be immoral to do. This applies as well to any disproportion of means to actual ends. If a deterrent threat here and now genuinely terminates in the doing of a disproportionate act of war, that would be a disproportionate threat. And if the "threat" always and unalterably depends on real intention, that would be a disproportionately immoral (not, however, a "murderous") intention. But the analysis of deterrence has to be fundamentally altered when we take into account the fact that deterrent intention terminates rather in the prevention of the grave evil of general war and in the enforcement of limits upon any actual outbreak of hostilities. These are the great goods toward which deterrent threats are oriented.

When a disproportionate action is transposed *in mente* into a deterrent threat, we ought not thoughtlessly to continue to speak of the *threat* as disproportionate. This may or may not be the case. We need to remember the evil which the threat is ordered to prevent and with which it must be compared. A threat of something that would be disproportionate, and which would exceed any of the reasonable purposes of fighting if carried out, may be *proportionate* when weighed against the graver evil that is prevented by the threat. It can fall within the purposes to which deterrence should reasonably be ordered, namely, the prevention of the much graver evil of general war and the enforcing of limits upon disproportionate military actions by either side. Threats that would if carried out have disproportionate military utility may well have proportionate military utility so long as they are unemployed, and are intended to be unemployed, or so long as they are employed for deterrent effect, to enforce shared limits upon actual fighting, and to keep war itself proportionate to political purposes. There is disproportion here only when done, not when merely threatened; and the threat is well ordered to the prevention of disproportionate evil in actuality. This case is quite different from intending, here and now, to do something that is intrinsically wrong, namely, directly to murder an entire city or society. The latter is murderous now; the former is not yet disproportionate.

Some would, incorrectly, draw an *absolute* distinction between deterrence before the nuclear age and deterrence in the nuclear age. They argue that formerly the leaders of nations sought to deter war by means it would have been proportionate to fight with, while in the nuclear age they must deter war by some means which it would never be proportionately just to use in fighting. The last part of this statement is correct; the first part is misleading. Proportion in the political use of forces for actual military utility and for the sake of deterrence was always a matter of particular political judgments, wisdom, and controls; and *some* deterrent effect was always obtained from the *possibility* that a commander might use his forces imprudently. So far as "disproportionate threats" are concerned, the nuclear age has only increased the degree of deterrence that goes beyond proportionate fight-the-war policies, and increased the danger should this shared deterrent possibility ever be used. It was always possible for nations to get locked into the senseless bloodletting of combatants. The prolonged trench-warfare of World War I, for example, was ordered to no political purpose. Wilson offered unlimited and non-political ends to justify the disproportionate use of the means at hand, or rather, the use tragically in process. Still, this shared possibility was a part of the deterrence of war in that age.

There was always, in this sense, a "threat" of disproportionate uses of force sustaining the balance of power *policies* of the European nations. The threat was not only that an attack would be met by equal force, but by more than enough, enough to exact unacceptable damage. The tragedy was and is that in the nation-state system one can deter war

THE MORALITY OF DETERRENCE

only by postures which, when war comes, tend to drive war on to military actions that are in fact disproportionate. But this exhibits the politico-military problem in any age Not Yet the Plowshares. This is, in fact, the structural defect of the present world order to which John XXIII drew attention. *Meanwhile* there is no substitute for justly proportioned war policies which are the product, of course, of political wisdom and self-control but which are enforced also by mutual deterrence proportioned, as it were, to the evil of war itself and to the goal of dampening down the war. In war there should be a reasonable expectation of a resonable or choiceworthy victory. Deterrence and deterrence-during-the-war keep it that way, by making preemptive negotiation mutually necessary and wise. In any case, disproportion in the use of force may be one thing, while disproportion in the deterrent threat may be another. It is the latter that maintains the former proportion.

In any age Not Yet the Plowshares, which is to say in any age before world public authority with radical decision-making, threat-removing and peace-keeping capabilities, there is no substitute for the controlled use of force and the controlled use of deterrence; and prudence in the one may not be the same as prudence in the other. Each should be ordered to its own ends. The wisdom of political magistrates must do this by their particular decrees.

Nevertheless, it is possible to define, for the instruction of the consciences of political leaders, what would be intrinsically immoral because it is already intrinsically disproportionate in this matter of deterrence. It is possible to describe the sort of deter-the-war or deterrence-during-the-war policies that would be certainly wrong under the criterion of disproportion in the threat, just as it is possible to determine the nature of murderous intention under the heading of the moral immunity of non-combatants from direct attack, and to proscribe either from being used for deterrence's sake.

Just as it is wrong in politics to be resolved to do murder, so it is wrong to be resolved at any point to put oneself out of control, no matter how much peace-by-deterrence results from it. To *commit* oneself to "rationality of irrationality" policies would be the epitome of irrationality and political immorality. To imitate a force of nature that is *bound* to go ever higher in escalation in order to preserve the peace would be a dehumanization of politics which no objectives could justify. Is deterrence-before-the-war analogous to a game of "chicken" in which the winner will be he who first *straps the wheel* and communicates this to his opponent, saying, "Look, one of us has to be reasonable, and since it cannot be me it must be you!"? Is deterrence-during-the-war analogous to a game of chicken in which the winner is he who effectively deters the other by being the first to *mechanize* his acceleration, saying, "Look, I can't stop; my direction and increasing speed are out of my control; you are the one who has to make the sensible choice and turn aside."?

If so, then deterrence would be intrinsically and irremediably disproportionate, and most wicked. Effectively to renounce in advance the control over one's future decision whether to use force prudently for political objectives or to not use additional force in the service of those same objectives—this would be here and now a wholly immoral because wholly disproportionate threat. It would also be too high a price to pay for deterrent effects.

V

We need now, in conclusion, to set the draft-statement on nuclear warfare, the work of the committee that revises it, and the final session of the Vatican Council in the context of developments in modern papal teachings on the morality of war. In sum, these developments have all so far fallen within the principle of proportionate grave reason, and the pontiffs have expressed increasingly stringent applications of that principle. The authors of the present comments are agreed that the Council can say more only by (1) invoking the principle of non-combatant immunity from direct attack and by (2) addressing itself expressly to the moral issues in deterrence. (I would add the moral issues of counter-insurgency, since today deterrence—which *works*, moral or immoral—has made the world safe for insurgency warfare.)

In general, it may be said that the present draft-statement attempts to say more than recent papal teachings have said, but that it attempts to do this still under the heading of proportion, without expressly reasserting the principle which determines legitimate military targets and without consciously paying attention to deterrence as a crucial moral and practical problem. By attempting to say more under the heading of proportion, the draft statement mixes judgments of fact with moral judgments. If it pursues this line, the Council is apt to say disastrously too much or irrelevantly too little; and in its interweaving of factual and moral judgments it is apt to speak not nearly as well as *Pacem in terris*. For this reason, an examination of developments in papal teachings prior to the Council, including *Pacem in terris*, may help to illuminate the contradictions in which the debate has become inevitably involved. This arises largely from the fact that popes or Councils can go only so far in calling attention to the requirement that means must be proportioned to ends, and because such decisions have largely to be referred to magistrates. If the Council wants, within its competence, to say more, it will have to turn in the direction of non-combatant immunity and the morality of deterrence. Thus, it could avoid prejudging in detail the weapons that may be licit for use or for deterrence in terms of proportion alone.

In his Christmas message, 1944, Pope Pius XII declared, "The theory of war as an apt and proportionate means of solving international conflicts is now out of date," and at Christmas, 1948, he condemned "aggressive" war as "a sin, an offense, and an outrage," and modern total war, unless it could be in self-defense, as "a crime worthy of the most severe national and international sanctions."

Interpreting Pope Pius' words, John Courtney Murray affirms that, for all Roman Catholic Christians, "the use of force is not now a moral means for the redress of violated legal rights. The justness of the cause is irrelevant; there simply is no longer a right of self-redress; no individual state may presume to take even the cause of justice into its own hands." The right of self-defense was left standing, while the right of self-redress to *repair* some already accomplished violation of justice was withdrawn by Pius XII. But in answer to the question, How can this sin in the moral order, defined by the Pontiff, be now transposed into a crime in the international legal order? Murray could only reply: "Pius XII did not enter the formidable technical problem, how this legal transcription of a moral principle is to be effected." And to this he appended the following somber notation: "This problem has hitherto been insoluble." [7]

These teachings are all expressions of the test of proportionate grave reason. It can never be right to resort to war, no matter how just the cause, unless a proportionality can be established between military/political objectives and their price, or unless one has reason to believe that in the end more good will be done than undone or a greater measure of evil prevented. This is the reason Pius XII and John XXIII have morally withdrawn the right of war to *repair* long standing injustices or to redress violated rights. But, of all the tests for judging whether to resort to or participate in war, this one balancing an evil or good effect against another is open to the greatest uncertainty. This, therefore, establishes rather than removes the possibility of conscientious disagreement among prudent men.

Yet this point is today invoked on all sides with the greatest assurance. There seems to be great pressure upon and within the Vatican Council to apply and extend the principle of proportion in this fashion. Today, many a good man's perception of the fact-situation is invoked as if this were a truth in the moral order, or a premise in a syllogism leading to theoretical certainty. "There can be no greater evil than war" or "no greater evil than nuclear war," it is said; or, less modestly than

---

[7] *Morality and Modern War* (New York: Council on Religion and International Affairs, 1959), p. 10. See Chap. 10 above for a fuller elaboration of this and the following paragraphs.

Pope John, and less correct as a guide for practical wisdom, "In the atomic age, war cannot be an instrument of justice," or "no form of nuclear war can be." Not only are the perceptions of the fact-situation summarized in these conclusions absolutized. Not only is it strongly suggested, from the point of view of these universalized perceptions of the facts, that only the stupid or the wicked will make any other calculation. It will also be *insisted* both that these perceptions of fact cannot and *ought* not to be corrected in those who possess them and that the objective *facts* perceived (i.e., that any war today, or any use of nuclears, will inevitably produce more evil than good in its manifold effects) cannot and *ought* not to be changed. This explains the ease with which it is assumed on all sides that the restrictive draft-statement of Schema XIII, Art. 25, is an obvious truth, or that it is morally certain that all nuclear weapons have unimaginable effects and cannot be subjected to reasonable control.

"However, despite the rhetoric of proportionality," writes Professor Richard A. Falk, "we have no adequate way to quantify, or otherwise render precise, the relation between the cost of and the benefit from the use of force. Therefore, our moral agency leads us to make intuitive distinctions that emphasize the continuing need to justify force by some sense of the cost-benefit relationship." [8] And the fact-situation to which we must apply some sense of the cost-benefit relationship is one in which "we must face the *unequal* and *uncertain risks* of various kinds of warfare and the *imponderable* risks of different forms of totalitarianism encroachment." [9] It is simply not the case that the certainty and objectivity of a moral rule such as proportionate grave reason is guaranteed by a logical relationship between the scope of the rule and the controversial facts to which it is said to apply. Ethics and politics are simply not exact sciences—especially not the principle of prudence itself. The principle of proportion provides the *framework* for analysis and not the conclusion of all thought on the subject. It is the responsibility of defense establishments to find the way to relate means of violence rationally to the ends of policy, and to not fight all the wars, and many of the plans of war, they are capable of fighting today.

It may be that the pontiffs have withdrawn, morally, the right of war more fully than, even in *Pacem in terris*, a single world public authority is adumbrated. More important to notice, however, is the fact that no amount or kind of adumbration of world public authorities that should take the place of the nation-state system can of itself withdraw the right of war. This can only be accomplished by an actual political

[8] Richard A. Falk, *Law, Morality and War in the Contemporary World* (Princeton Studies in World Politics: No. 5. New York: Frederick A. Praeger, 1963), pp. 40–41.

[9] *Ibid.*, p. 4.

reordering of the world, to which the papal teachings point, and can only *point*. Therefore, Pius XII and John XXIII only seem to have withdrawn morally the right of war more rapidly and completely than our existing or probable or presently possible international institutions enable a responsible statesman to follow them in their teachings. The pontiffs have invoked the principle of proportion to guide the consciences of statesmen, to warn them of the grave consequences of modern war, and to call attention to the very grave structural defect in the nation-state system.

Thus, *Pacem in terris* stresses the need for world public authorities, and it bases its plea on an eloquent doctrine of the rights of man and by reference to the longings of all mankind for peace. There is little analysis of the problem of political power and conflict in this encyclical, or how we are to attain a world of law. The condemnation of war, significantly, is expressed entirely in terms of the principle of proportion. "Thus, in this age which boasts of its atomic power, it no longer makes sense to maintain that war is a fit instrument with which to repair the violation of justice." [10] These words show that John XXIII's teaching is entirely in line with that of Pius XII. Thus, John XXIII no less than Pius XII left open the possibility that war might well be an instrument for repelling an injustice that is in course of being perpetrated but is not yet accomplished. The authorized English translation is obviously mistaken; yet pacifists of all sorts continue to quote it as if John XXIII wrote that "it is hardly possible to imagine that in the atomic era war could be an instrument of justice." Readers of the encyclical should know, and generally they do not know, that the words referring to a repair or correction of some violation of justice (in contrast to preventing some injustice about to be done) are almost a technical concept in Roman Catholic political thought.[11]

Interpreting the teachings of Pius XII, John Courtney Murray says that, in expressly excepting defensive wars, he meant to proscribe two of the three traditional reasons for recourse to war—*ad vindicandas offensiones* (to gain vindication against an offence) and *ad repetendas res* (to retake the thing)—but to leave standing the third: *ad repellendas injurias* (to repel injury, to resist an armed aggression). Before accepting Murray's analysis as an entirely correct account of the present shape of

[10] *The Pope Speaks* translation. In the Latin: *"Quare aetate haec nostra, quae vi atomica gloriatur, alienum est a ratione, bellum iam aptum esse ad violata iura sarcienda."*

[11] The translation of the *Pacem in terris* distributed by the National Catholic Welfare Conference (which is said to be "basically" that issued by the Vatican Polyglot Press but with "many textual changes—some of them important") now reads: "Therefore, in an age such as ours which prides itself on its atomic energy it is contrary to reason to hold that war is now a suitable way to restore rights which have been violated." This was the English edition distributed to the participants in the *Pacem in Terris* Conference in New York City, Feb. 18–20, 1965.

Roman Catholic teachings on war, we need to remember how difficult it is to separate a defensive use of force to repel injury from initiative in the use of force to remove some basic *threat* to the peace that may not yet have breached it. We need also to ask, what would be a modern equivalent of warlike initiative *ad vindicandas offensiones* (to gain vindication against an offence)? It is not entirely clear that the pontiffs have withdrawn or could withdraw the right of war *ad vindicandas offensiones* (in all interpretations of this) along with proscribing war *ad repetendas res* while allowing the possible justice of a war *ad repellendas injurias*. This is doubtful, if the correction of an infringement of "rights, customs and laws" may be taken to include the correction and removal of *threats* to peace and justice which lie behind *breaches* of the peace. Resort to war rests with the nation-state unless this is supplanted by effective peace-keeping and *threat*-removing action by regional or world organizations. Until such time as a world public authority does this, a nation cannot renounce its initiative in keeping the world "safe for diversity," [12] diversity within a world order of free and independently developing nation-states. This, I suggest, is the equivalent of those rights, customs and laws that more or less governed in the medieval world in which this test was first formulated.

Perhaps these words of John XXIII *"alienum est a ratione, bellum iam aptum esse ad violata iura sarcienda,"* should be translated "as a means for gaining redress for violations of rights." That has a more antiquated flavor.[13] If this is the reading, and if the Pope meant more or less trivial irritations and violations of customs and agreements which it is "alien to reason" to fight about, then he withdrew something that is now clearly removable by the decision-makers of the nation-states as presently constituted. Through U.N. diplomacy they have sometimes reached agreements not to fight *ad vindicandas offensiones* when even more important matters were in question, and certainly negotiation has proved capable of resolving less than vital disputes by means other than war.

But these words, and the Pontiff's flat, unqualified statement that it is "alien to reason" and "no longer makes sense" to make war for this cause, have considerably more significance if one puts out of mind medieval notions of insults, customs, rights, offenses and laws; and if instead we understand him to say that "it no longer makes sense to maintain that war is a fit instrument with which *to repair the violation of justice*" (italics added). This proscribes war *ad repetendas res* (to re-take the thing, or territory) and precisely this was the meaning of Pius

---

[12] President Kennedy in his American University address.

[13] This is the translation made by Louis B. Sohn when he sought to correct the authorized English version (*continuum*, Vol. 1, No. 2 [Summer, 1963], 249). Or as the National Catholic Welfare Conference edition reads: ". . . to restore rights which have been violated."

XII's Christmas messages. Even from the more widely circulated but erroneous "authorized" English translation of the crucial passage, George H. Dunne, S.J., understood this to be John XXIII's view.

> There are those among us who still think that war can be an instrument of justice, who, whether they explicitly avow it or not, think that Hungary, or Poland, or the Ukraine can be liberated by means of war and who nourish the hope of eventually precipitating a war of liberation.
>
> This is sheer folly. John XXIII knows it as such. He knows that in the atomic age war as an instrument of justice is unimaginable.[14]

On this view, the Pontiff has morally withdrawn the justice of wars of liberation, for the repair of previous injustices that have already accomplished their effect on the political map of the world, while he left standing a possible justice in a war undertaken to repel some new injustice now in course of being done (*ad repellendas injurias*). This would also include the repulsion or removal of threats and severe challenges to the *pax-ordo-justitia* of the world that may be put forth long before overt aggression occurs. It would leave standing the use of arms *ad vindicandas offensiones* as interpreted above.

But this places us on the horns of another dilemma which no reader of *Pacem in terris* should forget or ignore. It is *this age* (and not the Pontiff)—this age *"quae vi atomica gloriatur,"* "which glories in" or "boasts of its atomic power"—that has made just wars of liberation unimaginable (in some if not in all theaters), this age which has rendered it nearly or entirely "alien to reason" to maintain that war is a fit instrument with which to repair ancient, or more recent but secure, violations of justice.

Since the condemnation of otherwise just wars of liberation, to the degree this has force, depends upon the principle of proportion and thus upon the deterrent effect of nuclear weapons themselves, we are driven back to our inquiry into the justice of deterrence. In the words that immediately preceded the statement we have been examining, John XXIII acknowledged "that this conviction owes its origin chiefly to the terrifying destructive force of modern weapons. It arises from fear of the ghastly and catastrophic consequences of their use." In short, the proscription, as alien to reason, of resort to armed force as a fit instrument with which to repair the violation of justice was a judgment drawn by applying the principle of proportion in weighing the effects of starting a war—even a war which has "justifiedness" in itself—in the nuclear age.

This means that to dismantle the balance of terror without solving the problem of how to mount a moral deterrent or the problem of world order would have the effect of making just wars of liberation—

---

[14] "John XXIII's Latest Miracle," in *Ave Maria*, May 4, 1963.

justified in themselves, according to various conceptions of justice abroad in the world today—possible again, on all sides. Without deterrence, the repair of many a violation of justice would cease to be so alien to reason. Without deterrence, i.e., without the atomic power of which this age boasts, just wars of liberation would likely make sense again, or they would do so in more instances. Remove altogether the destructive force of nuclear weapons, and the nations would again be able to imagine, indeed it might become sensible for them to image, that war can again be invoked for the purpose of repairing injustice on a scale higher than both this age and modern papal utterances have taught us to believe wise.

It is clear, therefore, that the injustice of war which is so urgently stressed in *Pacem in terris* depends *meanwhile* upon the justice of deterence; and that for the duration of this *meanwhile,* before world public authority is established, an analysis of the justice and the injustice in war today is thrust back upon an analysis of the justice and the injustice of deterrence.

Against this background it is evident that more has been at work in the present draft-statement on nuclear weapons than misplaced punctuation or a failure to distinguish grammatically between a restrictive and a non-restrictive clause. The impulse behind the statement and at work in it has been a conscientious effort to go beyond the recent teachings of the Church which we have just reviewed, to break through to a more healing, more limiting, more helpful word. But it is quite impossible to advance a hairsbreadth beyond Pius XII and John XXIII while still staying within the principle of proportionate grave reason and while applying this principle alone to the analysis of modern war, without trespassing upon the responsibilities of political magistrates and substituting questionable ecclesiastical judgments of fact for possibly more instructed ones. For this reason, the Vatican Council should temper its statement on nuclear weapons in recognition of who the conciliar Fathers are and what a church council is, and in recognition of the true nature and limits of its competence. Then, if the Council desires to advance the Church's teachings beyond the formulations of recent pontiffs, it will be necessary for the Church through Council to speak *again* in moral terms about legitimate targets and the unchangeable principle of non-combatant immunity from direct attack, and to speak for the *first* time decisively about the morality of deterrence, the need to mount only a moral deterrent, and the need to follow moral guidelines in order to reshape and render acceptable the nuclear deterrence we have.[15]

[15] [At this point some readers may wish to pass immediately to Chap. 16 for an analysis of what the Vatican Council actually said on nuclear war. The alternative is to proceed with the text—and to be drawn into deep, dark crevices of the morality of deterrence.]

CHAPTER 15

Again, the Justice
of Deterrence*

There is no more important and unresolved issue, or a less discussed issue, before us today than the question of the morality of nuclear deterrence. Twice the present writer has undertaken to find his way into and through this complex moral dilemma.[1] The second instance—the previous chapter—has enlisted statements of different points of view and brought them into direct encounter.

One criticism in particular—that of Walter Stein [which appeared in his article "The Limits of Nuclear War: Is a Just Deterrence Strategy Possible?" in the CRIA pamphlet *Peace, The Churches, and the Bomb*] may be singled out. Mr. Stein does not reduce ethical and philosophical issues to rhetoric. He keeps in view the considerations that should weigh most in Christian conscience, and he sustains a cogent argument. His premises and categories of analysis are close to my own. Yet our conclusions differ widely. It cannot be a matter of indifference which one of us is correct, since the ethical analysis we both use is not a private one. If men should reason about conduct, and about deterrent-action, then one needs to look to his reasons; and we need to grapple with one an-

* Issued October 1965 as an Occasional Paper by the Council on Religion and International Affairs, 170 East 64th Street, New York, New York.
[1] "The Limits of Nuclear War," 1963, Chap. 11 above, pp. 248–58; and the foregoing "More Unsolicited Advice to Vatican Council II," Chap. 14 above. Page citations inserted in parentheses in the text refer to pages in the pamphlet *Peace, the Churches, and the Bomb*, Council on Religion and International Affairs, 1965.

other about the moral dimension in the political judgments we make.

The following reflections may, therefore, have a usefulness beyond the correspondence of interlocutors (which was my first intent).

My central contention [in the article "More Unsolicited Advice on Vatican Council II," here reproduced in the preceding chapter] was that it is moral to mount a deterrent whose effects flow from shared fear of the "collateral" damage unavoidably connected with targeting modern weapons of war, especially nuclear weapons, upon legitimate military objectives. If the latter defines justice in the actual conduct of war, the former is a just form of deterrence. The one is just war; the other is the just use of the non-use of weapons.

Stein calls this "a radical abuse of double-effect categories." In terms of formal argument, here is the crucial issue between us. A great deal depends upon the outcome of this debate, no matter how many don't care.

First, however, a word to the reader who has already been left behind, or who would say that Stein and Ramsey are already remote from any of the real substance of moral decision—especially remote from the elements of *Christian* moral decision-making.

The so-called "rule of double-effect" (with its distinction between "direct" and "indirect" effects) is only but definitely a summary of moral and political wisdom. It tells no one what to think according to some extrinsic norm. It only *anatomizes* how he will think if he engages in moral decision-making and is alert to all the factors involved. It is true that double-effect is a simplification of any actual situation in life, since almost all actions have *manifold* effects; but the rule itself directs attention to all the consequences.

The decision-makers of no human community can avoid judgment in these terms. The United States Supreme Court, for example, availed itself of the *flexibility* afforded by this "rule" when it declared state-action affecting religious practices to be constitutional provided the legislation had a secular legislative *purpose* and *primary effect*.[2] Anyone

---

[2] McGowan v. Maryland, 336 U.S. 420, 422 (1961) and School Dist. of Abington Township v. Schempp, 374 U.S. 203 at 222. "The distinction between a law that is directly, primarily, or purposefully religious and one that is not, has its difficulties," writes Robert G. McCloskey. "But the problem of determining whether or not a law's primary thrust is religious, though not subject to precise solution, would *at least direct judicial attention toward realities and away from presuppositions.*" 1964 *Religion and the Public Order* 3 at 31 (italics added).

At the present moment, in cases that complain against religious pageants and the observance of religious holidays in the public schools or the singing of songs that contain religious references or the author's religious beliefs, the courts are holding that such practices are entirely constitutional provided *the purpose and dominant tone* of the activities is to promote historical, cultural, or intergroup understanding ("The Year in Review," 1964 *Religion and the Public Order*, 205 at 250).

shows himself to be an "absolutist" in applying a neutrality-principle in church-state relations who refuses to think in accord with this "rule," whether he be Philip Kurland [3] or the Presbyterians.[4]

"Double effect" was not patented by Roman Catholic theologians of the sixteenth and seventeenth centuries. It is not a teaching peculiar to Catholic morality. Instead, this explicit summary of moral wisdom belongs to the common Christian tradition. The use by military planners of the concept of "collateral damage" also shows that the difference between directly intended and unavoidable indirect effects must be drawn in any serious thought upon this subject. To dismiss this sort of analysis is to take the path of loose thinking.

Moreover, I have demonstrated [5] (I think) that the heart and soul of it was charity seeking to save human life when not all killing could responsibly be avoided. In other words, the distinction between direct and indirect effects protected as many as possible by surrounding them with moral immunity from direct attack in situations in which that same charity impelled men to resist evil by force of arms directed upon the bearers of the evil that had to be repressed—tragically and unavoidably by direct killing. Thus, the rule of double effect was the immediate result of charity forming the consciences of men, while equally from this same ethical "on-look" sprang Christian pacifism or visiting the sick or the derelicts in prison, etc.

The number of those of my contemporaries who have "rejected" this rule and thus kept themselves free to make impressionistic "situational" judgments—which is a badly constructed form of *intuitionism*

As a final illustration of the importance of determining the primary thrust of any action having manifold effects, consider the *General Findings* of the NCC National Study Conference on Church and State, Columbus, Ohio, Feb. 4–5, 1964. That Conference (Protestant and Orthodox), in attempting to give a thorough account of the norms limiting justifiable state financing of church-affiliated agencies that, like hospitals, perform a public service, stated that "the important considerations here are (a) that the government program must not be aimed *primarily* at the support of religious institutions or objectives, (b) that any support of church-affiliated agencies must be an *incidental* part of a larger program *directed to* appropriate public interests . . ." (6 *Journal of Church and State* 151 [1964]), (italics added).

Yet whenever anyone seeks to determine the primary thrust of military action or the primary thrust of surgical action in birthroom cases that also involve conflict of life with life, and to distinguish this from the incidental effects these actions also have, Protestants especially are apt to cry "casuistry."

[3] *Religion and the Law of Church and State and the Supreme Court* (Chicago, Illinois: Aldine Publishing Co., 1962).

[4] Special Committee on Church and State: Report of the Special Committee on Relations between Church and State in the U.S.A., in The United Presbyterian Church in the United States of America: General Assembly Journal, 1963, 180.

[5] *War and the Christian Conscience* (Durham, N.C.: Duke University Press, 1961), Chap. 3: "The Genesis of Non-Combatant Immunity."

in ethics—about the morality of war, while continuing to refuse in an epithet the "rigidities" of "natural law," corresponds rather exactly to the number of those who have not undertaken to refute this demonstration.

Yet it must be admitted that to analyze the morality of war's conduct in terms of the direct and indirect, the primary and secondary, the intended and the unintended effects of military action is bound to seem "remote" from the primary impulse and norm of the Christian life. Even more "remote" it will seem, to proceed next to speak of the *deterrent effects of the indirect effects* (i.e., of the collateral damage) that would accompany properly targeted military action. Still it is necessary to do this if one is to continue to do Christian ethics, and to show that complex problems are corrigible to its terms and illuminated by them.

It was because of my awareness that the problem of deterrence is one more step removed from discriminating between the justice and the injustice of war's conduct (which already seems abstract and "casuistical" enough to persons content with indiscriminate judgment in these matters), and it was to ease myself and such readers into the use of yet another term ("collateral deterrence") that I wrote: "The deterrent effect of which we are now speaking is then, *as it were,* an indirect effect of the foreseeable indirect effects of legitimate military conduct" [6] and "deterrence is also *at work* as a 'side-effect' *so to speak* (italics added) of the prospect of extensive damage collateral even in 'justly targeted' nuclear war" (p. 46). [See Chap. 14, p. 294 above.]

This seeming verbal hesitation, or rather this warning that here comes a concept to get used to, was unnecessary in Stein's case, since he is quite at home in this sort of analysis. He is wrong, however, in supposing that here my language "shows signs of stumbling" (p. 81) because the thought behind the words lacks inherent conceptual clarity or validity. The thought can be expressed without the verbal easement.

In fact, the more I think about it, the fault lies elsewhere, and goes to an inexactitude at quite another point in the expressions I used. I should have said that it is entirely moral to intend to derive deterrence as, in the objective order, a *direct* effect flowing from the mutual prospect of the indirect consequences of acts of war planned and intended to be properly placed in a nuclear age. Beginning with the concept of collateral damage in fight-the-war-policies, my proposal concerning the morality of deterrence simply takes the next step of analyzing the justice of deterrence in terms of the *immediate and direct* effects upon decisions to go to war, or to escalate a war, that come from the shared prospect of extensive collateral damage (the indirect effects) of even justly fought war today.

[6] Cf. "The Limits of Nuclear War," Chap. 11 above, p. 252.

This, Stein says, constitutes "a radical abuse of double-effect categories" (p. 80). His reason seems to be that these deterrent effects would still be, in the order of subjective intention, directly willed and this would be to will evil in order that good may come of it. I now agree that it would be to will the effects in question *directly*, but not that this is to want or intend evil ends or means.

Stein says quite correctly that "the essential foundation of double-effect analysis is . . . *the principle of moral dissociation.* . . . The basic question . . . is whether we do, or do not, want the effect in question to ensue" (p. 80).

"Collateral deterrence" meets this test in every way. The collateral damage—which is first in order of the effects to be analyzed—is unfortunately in prospect. The link between this and justifiable acts of war cannot be undone with the best will in the world. Thus, the collateral damage itself need not be wanted. Secondly, I shall contend, it is entirely proper to want to deter and to be deterred by this fact.

Civilian death and damage involved in a military strike, or accepted in a nation's plans, need not and should not be "essential" to the purposes of the strategy for the actual conduct of war. The destruction of which we are now speaking must *not* be either "directly indispensable" or "radically wanted" in a nation's *war*-plans.

We are speaking of the unavoidable and radically unwanted damage that still will take place in a policy of "counter-force plus *avoidance*" of as much civil destruction as it is possible to avoid. It is the prospect of *this* that deters. We are not speaking of any measure of additional, purposefully essential, radically wanted or indispensable civil destruction such as would be entailed in "counter-force plus *bonus* civil damage."

The latter would be, in the objective order, murderous military action; and in the order of subjective intention it would also be murderous, because one cannot purify his heart of the action by making an inward effort to not want something deliberately done, or by wanting and yet not wanting these extra consequences at one and the same time. Any deterrent effects that sprang from deliberately extending the number of civilian deaths that are in prospect would be as wrong as that original decision itself: such deterrence should never be wanted.

But such are *not* the consequences we have in mind under the heading of genuinely "collateral" damage; and such is not the meaning of "collateral deterrence." I shall try to show that there is no reason why we should not want the immediate and direct *deterrent* effects of the prospect of extensive collateral damage, which itself remains unavoidable yet is and remains radically unwanted in *fighting* a modern war.

The first order of consequences to pay attention to (and never to be forgotten later in the argument) are consequences that are indirect, non-essential, morally quite unwanted, yet physically unavoidably connected with taking out some important military target. This is the first step in my argument, and the basic point in the "model" I propose for understanding the morality of deterrence. Here, at the (logical) beginning, the connection is decisively broken between willing or doing evil and any subsequent or second order deterrent consequences that follow from the unavoidable magnitude of collateral damage. There is, first, a graduated scale of prudently acceptable → prudently unacceptable collateral damage which the conduct of war, justified in itself, would bring. There is, secondly, a scale of increasing mutual deterrence that comes from contemplating this prospect.

Both are "permitted": the first because "indirect"; the second, because as a means it arises directly from the prospect of the first (already justifiable) thing and because it is entirely commendable to want deterrence as an end. If it is tragic, though certainly not wicked, that justifiable acts of war by means of modern weapons entail extensive collateral damage, it is at most tragic, it is certainly not wicked, that we should be deterred by knowing this.

Although first in order in my model, collateral damage is an *indirect* effect. It is *primary* for my argument that civil damage be *"secondary."* Then there are, in the model and in the argument, second order consequences that follow in the matter of deterrence.

Shall we call these second order deterrent effects "secondary"? I now see that I was misled by the ambiguity in the term "secondary"— which in ordinary usage may mean "second in order," in logical order or in the steps of an analysis, but which in moral discourse means "indirect." I meant to affirm that for deterrence's sake it is clearly possible to justify intending to use, and be used by, the immediate (deterrent) effects of the likely indirect (collateral) effects of even "justly conducted" warfare in the nuclear age. Thus was I misled, and misled Stein. I rightly had in mind that collateral damage is, in technical language, a "secondary" effect that would be wrought in accomplishing the "primary" result wanted. But then, upon directing my attention and the reader's attention to another consequence, a "second" one at work in the posture of deterrence, that follows immediately from the prospect of the extensive collateral damage that would occur even in such a proper defense policy (if this had ever to be put into execution), I mistakenly thought of this as "secondary" (as it is in general usage) to the (technically) "secondary" effects of justly conducted war.

The excuse for this error can only be that I ventured to enter dense and unexplored territory where every man needs, if possible, to keep his head clear by the aid of another. I ought to have written: "The deterrent effect is the primary or a direct effect of the foreseeable indirect effects of legitimate military conduct" and "Deterrence is at work as an immediate effect of the prospect of extensive damage collateral (the prospective "side-effects") even in 'justly targeted' nuclear war."

From act (A) arises directly the destruction of military objective (T) and also, by indirection, (C) civil damage. If from (C), when future, hypothetical and merely in prospect, comes directly and immediately into the minds of reasonable men (D) deterrent effects, it would seem entirely licit for them to want (D). Of course, it might still be argued that (D) is "indirect" since it is an extension of the indirection of (C). Even so, I erred in saying that (D) would be an indirect effect *of the* indirect effect, or a side-effect *to the* side effects, which are the civil damage. The case is that through (C), when future, hypothetical and in prospect, comes the (D) of which we are now speaking; (D) is in some sense attached to (C); not, like (T), or (C) itself, to (A). It is better, I now think, to say that (D) is a direct consequence than to say it is an indirect consequence of the prospect of (C).

The reason for choosing to say that (D) follows here and now directly from future (C), rather than claiming that (D)-effects themselves are indirect, because they are an extension of the indirection of (C), is as follows: It is necessary that we be able to affirm that (D) can be "radically wanted," that it is not only licit but commendable to put one's will into postures of deterrence, and not be psychologically dissociated from them. Stein has put his finger on the crucial point that it is not customary in moral analysis to speak of wanting *in*direct effects.

In any case, I believe that he simply brings against my moral analysis the substance of what I regard as most valid: that this deterrence can and should be wanted. He is betrayed into this position not only because of infelicities or inaccuracies in my use of language for my meaning, but also because he pays greater attention to the incidentals of double-effect categories (which he thinks I abuse) than to the moral realities these categories were designed to protect.

This leads Stein to violate one of his own first principles, i.e. that the issue turns upon commitment *here and now* and not upon some future, hypothetical situation. My view is that we should here and now want the deterrent effects *here and now* to ensue. We need *not* want the collateral damage itself to ensue there and then in some hypothetical future. We need not here and now want those actual damages there and then. We simply know that they may, and justly may, ensue. So are we actually deterred. Or, in Stein's language, the shared *"menace"* to populations is essential, indispensable, morally wanted for the purposes of our strategy (p. 83, italics added); yet the *destruction* of populations is never directly wanted, neither here and now nor there and then. Not even the collateral destruction of populations is ever directly wanted, either now or later.

Stein allows his mind to run off toward the hypothetical future. That future becomes real; extensive civil damage is actualized—collaterally, Stein admits, and perhaps justly. Then with this damage conceived to have been already done, Stein imagines that deterrence arises *retrospectively*, from effects which, while indirect in that future war itself, would have presently to be made to bear the additional weight of directly intending the doing of those effects in order for us to derive deterrent benefits *backward* into the here and now.

This is not at all the situation. Deterrence is always *prospective*. The posture of deterrence need involve here and now no immoral hypothetical commitment to do or to will there and then something that is inherently immoral. It only involves a present willingness to do in the there and then something that would then be justifiable. If collateral damages would be licit when done, it is surely not wrong to envision them, while yet un-done, as morally and factually possible to be done, and to deter and be deterred by the prospect. If just-war policy legitimately involves (A)-acts productive of (T)-destruction and (C)-collateral civil damage, then a just deterrence policy may include deriving from estimates of (A)-capabilities a realistic anticipation of the "menace" of (T) plus (C). Such a prospect will be immediately deterring.

To say otherwise leads to one or the other of the following conclusions (or discloses them among our premises), which seem to me manifestly absurd: (1) Justice in war limits its conduct to (T)-target destruction and justice in deterrence limits it to the effects of anticipating just (T)-destruction; (2) While justice in war may involve (T)-target destruction plus necessary "secondary" civil damage, justice in deterrence can take into account only the future, hypothetical destruction of (T)-military objectives. Either of these views would justify only what I call deterrence from "disproportionate 'combatant' damage"—a first and a "lower" form of deterrence than "collateral deterrence." (3) There is justice neither in any sort of war nor in any sort of deterrence.

From the manner in which Stein struggles to avoid going to collateral deterrence, I suspect that his real point of view is the latter. While he does not expressly reject the justice of war as such in the nuclear age, his argument against deterrence in a nuclear age goes to the point of deterrence (and war) in any age, shape or fashion. In no period of military history have the targets been roped off from the non-combatants like the knights from the ladies at a medieval tournament. In no period has fighting been deterred or dampened down from anticipation of excessive combatant damage alone. Deterrence as such, and not only nuclear deterrence, must include deterrence from anticipation of disproportionate noncombatant damage. If such nuclear deterrence cannot be justified, neither was the deterrence of any fighting in the past. This adds up to saying that neither war nor the security of peace can be justified in any age Not Yet the Plowshares. Afterward, of course, neither will be problems commanding the attention of moralists.

In order to secure some perhaps clarifying analogies, I shall now introduce three hypothetical situations in which the foreknown immediate and direct effects of what are "first order" collateral effects may be "radically wanted" here and now, essential to the present purpose, and indispensable to the total action undertaken. The first and third cases are, in my opinion, entirely justifiable, involving no moral disordering of will or of action; the second is unjustifiable. The question is, To which is deterrence from the prospect of disproportionate collateral civil damage most analogous?

In his book *The Time Has Come*,[7] Dr. John Rock describes briefly a series of exceedingly significant scientific experiments, extending over the years 1938 to 1954, which he carried out in cooperation with a colleague at the Free Hospital for Women in Brookline, Massachusetts. "Our procedure," writes Dr. Rock, "was to schedule operations on women who required hysterectomies at times when we estimated they would be ovulating. . . . We utilized the (quite necessary hospital) waiting period, and the cooperation of many highly fertile women, to acquire accurate records of their cycles as well as dates of coitus. This data helped us to estimate when fertilization could occur if an egg were present—and thus to time the operations—with some assurance. . . . When we concluded our series in July 1954, we had operated on 211 patients and secured thirty-four ova, ranging from a two-day, two-cell egg to a seventeen-day ovum already implanted in the uterus."

Now, it is difficult to say from this sparse and somewhat equivocal account what was actually done in these experiments, which were of enormous importance for scientific knowledge and fruitful of undeniably good consequences, in assisting both human fertility and birth regulation, in all ages to come. The questions to be raised have to do with the means, even as these are the crucial questions concerning the morality of war and the morality of deterrence. I will be making suppositions, if-statements, for the purpose of securing possibly fictional, illustrative cases. I do not mean to say what was actually done in the experiments from which my analogies arise. And, of course, any objection to either the actual or my fictional cases would fall to the ground if one initially rejects the assumption, which I ask to be made here for purposes of the argument, concerning the *human* nature of unborn life from the moment of impregnation.

The operations were *required* and urgent because of some damage to the uterus that was, as the moralists say, "entitatively distinct" from whether it was pregnant or not. Hospital delay in scheduling the

---

[7] (New York: Alfred A. Knopf, 1963), pp. 184–85.

operations was necessary, and indeed ordinary. In the normal course of events, over a period of fourteen years and 211 hysterectomies (which number could have been indefinitely increased by extending the research), it was going to be the case that any number of unfertilized ova would be destroyed in surgery and also any number of fertilized ova killed. The latter were clearly justifiable as indirect or secondary results of justifiable primary medical practice, as indeed are indirect abortions at any later stage of fetal growth. No moralist would say otherwise than that in the hysterectomies as such the principle of psychological dissociation pertained. The death of the fetus, where present, could have been non-essential to the purpose, dispensable and radically unwanted. Moreover, there is no universal affirmative obligation that women requiring hysterectomies should cease from the performance of the marriage act lest they become pregnant.

These were the basic factual and moral elements. Additional factors, however, were introduced when a research program was begun. In order to advance the goals of studying micro-generative stages and processes—of fertilized ova no larger than the period at the end of this sentence—plans had to be made and records kept of ovulation, of coitus and of the various periods of time between coitus and the time the operation was performed. (This is to be compared with having deterrence in view and not only the primary and secondary effects of the surgery of war itself.) The pure knowledge and the practical goods to be gained from this series of experiments may be described as arising *immediately and directly* from very grave indirect or collateral consequences of properly targeted surgical action. The question is whether one can be psychologically associated with *these* beneficial results, can want them or make oneself the subject of purposes to which they are essential, without perpetrating a moral violation upon oneself and upon other human beings (in this case, on our supposition, the nascent lives).

Everything depends on how this was done or the way these benefits were brought into prospect. At this point, two quite different factual analyses are possible, and upon the two cases two opposing moral verdicts should be delivered. Collateral deterrence is, in my judgment, like the first; and Stein, it seems to me, thinks it is like the second case. Whichever one of us is factually correct about the meaning of having collateral deaths in prospect is right in his moral judgment upon deterrence. If I am in error about this, then I have abused double-effect categories in applying them to the complexities of the deterrence-situation. If Stein is in error, then he abuses the situation in order to make a routine and a negative application of double-effect categories. The hypothetical cases are as follows, and in each case the analogy with deterrence should be clear:

1. It *might* have been the case (I do not say that it was the case)

that Dr. Rock and his associate *here and now* simply provided themselves, by keeping careful records, with an accurate account of what happened. They made exact findings of all that went on (and of course they did this, where possible, as it was going on). They accumulated many a "scenario" of ovulation, coitus, time of operation, and ovum: the stage of development reached by the time of operation, and its condition as to location and development. By patient research, and even by extending the experiments to other hospitals, they could certainly have secured a complete picture of the micro-genesis of a human being, with no crucial evidence missing (i.e. lacking no ovum as it was on one of the days of its life from time zero to the seventeenth day). They need not even have operated at a certain time in order to kill at that time for the purpose of securing these findings. They could simply have noted here and now (and in advance they could have taken into account the values immediately to be derived from noting) what was or was to be unavoidably and collaterally death-dealing, in the *there and then* of the operation. The women collaborators need not have been encouraged to have coitus at a certain time before the scheduled operation in order to become pregnant in order then to stop the pregnancy and thus secure a fertilized ovum x-days old. In fact, to avoid any suggestion of this, the women need not have known the purpose of the records they kept.

Thus, the indirection of any incidental killing of new life that would take place and did take place could have been brought scientifically into prospect without either the doctors or the women radically wanting to destroy innocent human life. They need not have put direct intention, even secondarily, into the killing that took place indirectly. Yet the doctors could, without blameworthiness, want all the goods in pure knowledge and for medical practice that were the immediate fruits of controlled attention to the indirect killing often involved in hysterectomies. The situation would not be altered if, for some weird reason, required hysterectomies *always* involved indirect killing (as does every major military action). The doctors could still take note and plan to take note of such collateral deaths, and deliberately seek any goods that they conceive may be the immediate and direct results of such systematic medical research—where, it is evident, none of these goods would be attainable *were there not the incidental deaths* in the nature of the case to be anticipated.

So it is with deterrence from the prospect of extensive collateral civil death and damage in modern warfare.

2. It *might* have been the case (I do not say it was the case) that Dr. Rock and his associate "perfected" the series of experiments by deliberately encouraging patients requiring hysterectomies to get themselves pregnant shortly before the operation was scheduled. Or, knowing the operation was planned the women may have grown careless in their

"birth regulation," or, knowing that the purpose of the records they were keeping included the study not only of ovulation but the study of fertilized ova as well, they may have wanted to cooperate by securing in themselves an impregnated ovum by the time of the operation.

This would have been purposeful complicity here and now, in one degree or another, in the bringing of human life under the knife—even though the kind of killing that was in prospect was in the there and then of the operation, collateral. In the subjective order, the deaths as such, and not only the knowledge to be gained from studying them, would have been radically wanted, purposefully essential here and now, and indispensable to these human decisions and to the total action that was undertaken. This is not to be excused simply by virtue of the fact that thereafter, in the objective order, the deaths were unavoidable and collateral to a required and entirely justifiable surgical operation.[8]

Stein must believe that *in this way* in collateral deterrence the deaths as such, and not only the prevention or limitation of war, are radically wanted, purposefully essential here and now, and indispensable to the present choice to deter and be deterred.

Such is not the meaning of deterrence from the shared prospect of extensive collateral damage. Not one more human life has to be brought under the destructive force or into the peril that falls indirectly and unintendedly upon the population unavoidably implicated in the destruction of military objectives. And to use realistically anticipated collateral deaths and destruction (which will take place anyhow unless war is deterred) consciously as a part of an intended scheme of mutual deterrence does not mean that in any wicked way that killing is wanted: the killing is *not* wanted, yet the foreknowing of it deters. This is why I say that the present immediate and direct (deterrent) effects of the indirect effects of future justly conducted warfare may be radically wanted as a factor indispensable to the security of peace. This is the meaning of deterrence from the prospect of extensive collateral damage.

3. A final analogy can be constructed from the case of a woman who requires a hysterectomy after repeated cesarean sections.[9] To secure

---

[8] Besides the above alternative interpretations of the nature of Rock's actual series of experiments, it is not possible for us to suppose that the doctors simply varied the *time* of the operations *after* discovering the women who were pregnant. This was excluded by the fact that only the first seventeen days in the life of an ovum were studied. The ova were known to be fertilized, implanted in the uterus, etc., only after the operations. The deliberate scheduling of required hysterectomies upon women known, in the ordinary course of events, to be pregnant in order to secure specimens of fetal life at two months', three months' development, etc., would have been an entirely different situation from any we have to suppose here; and so far as I can see this would be morally an entirely legitimate procedure.

[9] See John C. Ford, S.J., and Gerald Kelley, S.J., *Contemporary Moral Theology, Vol. II: Marriage Questions* (Westminster, Maryland: Newman Press, 1964), pp. 328–37.

our comparison it may be necessary to make one or two suppositions that are not ordinarily the case in such indirectly sterilizing operations. A woman's damaged uterus cannot likely withstand another pregnancy. Suppose that this medical determination is not made at the time of her last birth by cesarean section, but afterward. The required operation is scheduled. Then suppose that the woman discovers she is pregnant again.

If the operation is performed the death of the fetus would be as indirect as the sterilization. The pregnancy and the weakness of the uterus are, as the moralists say, "entitatively distinct" even though there is no danger to the woman's life from the one without the other. "It is true that the danger would not arise without pregnancy; but it is also true that pregnancy is not the only factor contributing to the danger. The other factor is the pathological condition of the uterus itself. Neither of these factors is sufficient of itself to create a danger of uterine rupture; both are required. That is why the elimination of either factor would remove the danger. . . . [W]ith at least equal causal immediacy the operation removes the other factor, the pathological organ [and the surgery need not be primarily directed at the fetus]." [10] The principle of psychological dissociation applies. The death of the fetus need not be radically wanted; it is not essential to the purpose or to the total operation which is intended and done primarily to remove a damaged uterus.

Suppose that, nevertheless, the woman is "deterred" by the "menace" to her child, and resolves to try to bring it to term before having this operation. Is there anyone who would say that to be deterred she has to want the future, hypothetical death of her child as indispensable to her resolution, or even that she must radically want the "menace" to its life? She only has to know this. To be deterred from even a justifiable operation she has only to know its unavoidable connection with the collateral killing. (T)-target destruction plus (C)-collateral effects produce one degree or another of perfectly natural and morally commendable deterrent pressure in her mind and upon her will, whether she decides to go through with the operation now or to postpone it. This is clearly the present immediate direct effect of the prospect of the indirect effects in this case. She can want to be deterred without wanting the killing. Precisely the latter is what she wants to avoid. She need not even want the menace in order to be glad it is there, exerting its pressure upon her, for the sake of saving life that through no wickedness on anyone's part is yet tragically in grave danger.

This is the closest analogy I can think of to deterrence from the prospect of the extensive collateral death and destruction even in justly fought warfare today. Since the ingredients in the moral situation are not

[10] *Ibid.*, p. 332.

altered by the language we use (but our language should rather be perfected in order adequately to sort out the true nature of the ingredients), I can see no reason why we should not say that the "menace" is "wanted" —provided we discriminate more than one meaning of "wanted." Perhaps Stein impacts into his expression "radically wanted" only the meaning of wanting *the deaths* in question *directly*. If so, then, it has to be said that there is more than one way how a word means (as contemporary philosophers put it). The woman does not want and she need not want her child *to be menaced*. But since the child is irremediably subjected indirectly to menace in what for her would be an entirely justifiable operation, she can without any malice at all *want the menace* to help her sustain the courage she will need in the months ahead. She certainly should not want *to be relieved* of the pressures of this menace upon her resolve. She can, in this sense, want the menace for the purpose of her strategy. Just so, "the menace to populations can be essential, indispensable, morally wanted for the purpose of our [deterrent] strategy" (p. 83), provided we distinguish in the terminology we use between this and "radically wanting" the unavoidable, collateral deaths *done* and do not mean to enlarge the extent of the menace unalterably involved in justly limited war.[11]

It is all the more important to analyze deterrence in this fashion because this is not merely a matter of shared *fear*. It is also a matter of sharing *security* in the expectation of reasonable political conduct. Deterrence means mutually and effectively *communicating* a reasonable assurance to an enemy that we will not act irrationally, that we too are deterred. We may know from the weapons we have that he should be deterred from pressing very far up the scale of modern war, because of the terrible collateral costs he would pay long before cities are brought directly into range and even if they are never directly attacked (which we do not intend). We may have the confidence that we are not going to initiate strikes at such a level of violence. But when we stand at a distance from the question who can be trusted to act rationally in this regard, and do not simply pose the single question whether a potential *enemy* is effectively deterred, we realize immediately that deterrence must be mutual, that we must also effectively communicate assurances to such an enemy concerning *our own* future action. We have as much

[11] [I am grateful for the appreciative and perceptive review of many of my writings on war and political ethics by Richard A. McCormick, S.J., of the Bellarmine School of Theology in the "Notes on Moral Theology," *Theological Studies*, Vol. 27, No. 4 (December 1966), 607–654. Yet for the record I should point out that it was not I but Stein who chose the word "menace" (p. 320, above), by which term the foregoing discussion proceeded. Also I will note that I do believe that one has not fully grasped the subtleties of deterrence unless he understands that we are in fact trying to deter ourselves (be deterred) as well trying to deter a potential enemy. See *ibid.*, p. 643.]

interest in this as he. We have as much interest in ourselves knowing that the enemy has been given credible assurances against escalation from our side as we have in knowing this about him. Thus *we* need to be deterred and to know that he knows it as much as we need to know that he is effectively deterred. We are all liable, subjectively, to the sin of wanting an enemy people *to be menaced,* instead of wanting the menace for deterrence's sake. For collateral deterrence to work, however, the latter is necessary and not the former; and this must be mutual. With regard to our own people as well, deterrence involves making this distinction: *wanting the menace that is there* for its assured pressure upon our own and our government's resolution, without wanting people to be menaced, much less wanting the collateral deaths *done.* Rather like the woman's strategy of deterrence upon herself.

Therefore, one should meet Stein's challenge head-on, when he says that "the basic question . . . is whether we do, or do not, want the effects in question to ensue" (p. 80). That depends on the *effects* in question: the deterrent effects, yes, the collateral destruction itself, no. And it depends on the "wanting" that is in question: to want the prospect, given that it is there, for the sake of the deterrence, yes; to want the prospect to be there in the first place, no; but to recognize that it is there in building deterrence-policy, yes.

II

In addition to deterrence from disproportionate combatant damage with its associated deterrence from the prospect of extensive collateral damage, I analyzed two additional respects in which nuclear weapons deter, and may morally be used to deter.

The first of these additional deterrences is the effect that unavoidably and irremovably follows from the fact that a great many modern weapons, including a great many nuclear weapons, have dual uses. They can be properly used against military objectives or they can be improperly used against populations (or against such objectives but so as to secure also *bonus* civilian terror and destruction). This dual possibility inheres in the nature of the weapons we possess, not (and not yet in the argument) in the manner in which we possess these weapons or the way in which we signal that we might possibly plan to use them. They have the military potential, they *can* be used as effective counterforce weapons or as effective counter-society weapons. Neither of these capacities can be removed from them so long as these weapons endure and are known to men. One can lean against the counter-society use of these weapons, people can denounce and governments can renounce this use as much as they please, and yet the possibility of such use will remain inherent in the weapons themselves. There is deterrence that is mutual and may be quite enough inhering in the weapons themselves that are possessed even without any government intending-in any additional ambiguity concerning its possible use of them. There is a deterring ambiguity, or potential for use, inhering in the weapons possessed and not in how or for what purpose we possess them.

This deterrence is at work at the present historical moment in the pressures upon political reason toward a non-proliferation, non-acceptance agreement.[12] Deterrence from the uncertainty inherent in the nature of weapons that, while capable of being used in prosecuting war against military objectives, have also the ineradicable capability of being used directly against populations, is effectively present wherever there is any pressure upon political reason toward the prevention of war today, or its limitation, toward the settlement of disputes by non-violent means, toward a non-proliferation agreement, toward a nuclear disarmament agreement, or toward some new world public authority. Surely no one would say that deterrence in the nuclear age arises *only* because there is such a thing as a 100-megaton bomb whose sole use would be against people indiscriminately, or *only* because there is over-kill, or *only* because the nations fully intend to use dual purpose weapons against entire societies, or merely because they haven't declared yet what they are going to do. If these are not the sole ingredients in deterrence, then there is also partially or entirely effective deterrence from disproportionate combatant death and damage, and partially or entirely effective deterrence from the prospect of extensive collateral damage, and effective mutual deterrence from the danger to peoples that is simply inherent in the capabilities of nuclear weapons, without anyone waxing genocidal about his proposed use of them or deliberately cultivating ambiguity about the use that he might adopt. We had better analyze these deterrences step by step, lest it be said by some future generation of mankind which may come into the security of peace under a world public authority that the entire present generation was made sin for them and that out of our murderousness here and now came their final peace.

Unfortunately, Stein opens his comment (p. 82) on the sort of deterrence now under discussion—that which inheres in the weapons themselves, and not in our ambiguous manner of possessing them or in any intention we may have—by describing this as a "further form of *counter-people deterrence*," and moreover one proposed as "a licit way of augmenting the deterrent effect of justly targeted nuclear weapons."

[12] If only the most massive counter-city deterrence works and if only this sustains the rest, a good argument could be made, as some French theorists have reasoned, to the effect that the deterrence which is there in nuclear weapons can be more perfectly arranged by *encouraging* proliferation.

"We must first note," he writes, "the word 'augmenting.' " But that was Lawler's word (p. 34), not mine! Stein fails to note that, after quoting Lawler, I immediately stated (p. 53 [see also p. 301 above]) that I would say rather that "this constitutes an existing, licit deterrent that has in no way to be augmented. . . . [T]here is no need even to think of intending counter-society warfare for the sake of strengthening deterrence. It is already mutual and enough without murderous thinking." I shall have to rely upon the reader to gather from the CRIA symposium, pp. 300–302 above, and from pp. 253–4 above of "The Limits of Nuclear War" a better account of this ingredient in deterrence.

Stein's slip is all the more remarkable since in all my thinking upon the present point I have built upon a distinction (to which I was first introduced by the excellent volume of essays edited by Stein[13]) between two ways how the expression "having a bomb" means: the "possession" of nuclear weapons may be understood, first, "in respect to the nature of the object possessed" and, secondly, "in respect to the nature of the 'possession' of the object." It is only when we come to the latter that the question of the morality of "augmenting" deterrence arises.

It has to be acknowledged, of course, that this deterrence which inheres in the weapons possessed, inheres in them because of a possible use of them that inheres first in any actual process of prosecuting legitimate warfare with them or with any modern weapons as means. At issue here is whether it is correct to treat some of the possibilities that are simply present in the course of actually fighting a war with fractional nuclears, or any war today, as possibilities in the nature of things comparable to the capabilities that are merely there in the nature of the weapons themselves here and now and not in the hearts of any of the actors. It is always possible that these weapons may be used against societies, and this possibility cannot certainly be known by a potential enemy to have been effectively excluded (no matter how often it is declared). He is deterred, and so are we, by this fact in the nature of warfare today; and no one need intend that this be the case, or even intend to be ambiguous about it. He cannot remove this powerful deterrent, even with the best intention in the world. There are fearful prospects inhering in the process of fighting a modern war. This *possibility*, these prospects *are* counter-society, but they need not be *intended* in order to be *there*, in the nature of nuclear weapons and in the fighting of any war today. This is an actual, but not directly intended, ingredient in deterrence that is surely frightening enough—again without waxing genocidal in our deterrence systems.

[13] R. A. Markus, "Conscience and Deterrence," in *Nuclear Weapons and Christian Conscience*, ed. by Walter Stein (London: Marlin Press, 1961), p. 75.

By several steps in escalating the argument, however, Stein misunderstands deterrence from the *possibility* that counter-city strikes will take place in the course of fighting a modern war. First, he equates the fact that a potential enemy cannot know with certainty that dual purpose weapons will not sometime be used against his cities (*this* is what deters him!) with an actual uncertainty on the part of the deterring nation or lack of control for which it has made itself responsible. Secondly, he equates *necessary* acceptance of some *risk* of uncontrolled action with responsibility for putting oneself entirely out of control. The possibility becomes the probability becomes uncontrollability. What one knows *could be* becomes the same as doing so maximally, with no discrimination made in degrees of "could" and with no recognition of the fact that, after any responsible government has deprived deterrence of all the risk that can be removed from it, the deterrence now in question arises from the "could be" that remains, or rather from the possibility that remains in and cannot be excluded from the mind of a potential enemy. So Stein can write that "it is immoral to participate in preliminary activities . . . that could, uncontrollably, release the uncontrollable . . ." (p. 83).

Thus, thirdly, he takes the deterrence in question out of the context of limited, graduated response as a military policy and out of the context of graduated deterrence, in which this ingredient in deterrence inheres as a limited additional and unavoidable risk. I certainly was not speaking of deterrence from the prospect of uncontrollably going to the absolutely uncontrollable. Then no wonder, fourthly, my "threat by default" or from "inability" to predict or from any degree of irremediable uncertainty in control becomes for Stein almost or quite the equivalent of *automated* massive deterrence in which the first Russian bomb that falls on us sets the whole thing off (p. 83). Then no wonder my suggested deterrence from taking account of the risks in the realm of *political* and *military* expectations and responses is equated with the *mechanical* risk in various ways to play Russian Roulette (p. 83). To engage in the latter calculus of statistical probabilities is certainly homicidal from the beginning because it entails the *certainty* that eventually someone will be killed: you *know* that the gun *will* go off. In deterrence from the ineradicable possibility of city-strikes, you don't know that your opponent's won't.

In any of the realms of human existence, discriminating and not sweeping judgments are called for. So the "could be" that deters must be discriminated and graded and should not be proscribed *en masse*. In a similar way the courts of the United States found that in order to render responsible judgment in difficult cases the test of "clear and present danger" [14] in free-speech cases had to be refined. This was first inter-

[14] Schenck v. United States 249 U.S. 47 (1919).

preted as a test of *"sufficient* danger of *substantial* evil," [15] and then as a test requiring the court to measure the *"gravity* of the evil discounted by its improbability." [16] Because of the dependence of peace, justice, and security upon deterrence, and because the morality of deterrence must be subjected to analysis in its own right, I do not believe that even a proscription of *any* use of *any* nuclears as immoral would carry with it the conclusion that it is only by prompt unilateral nuclear disarmament that one can avoid immoral implication in the fact that until that is accomplished an immoral act *could* be done. Of almost no realm of human activity requiring control is it correct to say that "the inherently immoral act must be put out of reach" (p. 70, Weber). In all or almost all human affairs, the gravity of the evil must be discounted by its improbability; yet the remaining probability or possibility is there to deter.

Stein supports his extreme interpretation of the deterrence now in question by citing (p. 82) comments I made that were based on T. C. Schelling's analysis of how "in a nuclear age all war raises a risk of general war by an apparent *possibility* of a *politically irreversible trend."* I may have let my remarks at this point[17] run in too close parallel with Schelling's. If so, this was because I expected my earlier criticism and modification of Schelling[18] to carry over to this point, and not to be forgotten by the reader. There it was expressly argued that "we ought not to say at once that, in the nuclear age 'a main consequence of limited war, and a main purpose for engaging in it, is *to raise the risk of general war'. . . .* We ought rather to say that one of the consequences and one of the purposes of limited conventional or tactical nuclear war is to *raise the risk of counterforce strategic war";* and by doing *this,* preserve an earlier and a lower limit. That was to set this further ingredient in deterrence in the context of graduated military responses and in the context of "graduated deterrence" where it belongs.

Even so, a *possibility,* and an *apparent* possibility at that,[19] of a politically irreversible trend is a far cry from an actually irreversible trend or from uncontrollably releasing the uncontollable. The latter, or by any preliminary deeds of omission or commission to bring oneself within an irreversible trend toward genocide, would be as immoral as Stein thinks it is. The former is not *what* he thinks it is (and also it is

[15] E.g.: Gitlow v. New York 268 U.S. 652 (1925).
[16] Dennis v. United States 341 U.S. 494 (1951).
[17] "The Limits of Nuclear War," Chap 11 above, p. 254.
[18] Pp. 243–4 above.
[19] Even Lawler—whose premises and conclusions are very like Stein's—distinguishes between the appearance of a *possibility* and an apparently possible *willingness* ("Moral Issues and Nuclear Pacifism" in *Peace, the Churches, and the Bomb).* Lawler and I, therefore agree that while ambiguity relating to an overkill deterrent is immoral, ambiguity relating to an arsenal *adequate* to legitimate military ends is moral (pp. 86–87).

a far too extreme because indiscriminating and ungraduated statement of what I was talking about).

III

Only now do we come to an ingredient in deterrence that involves the sort of "possibility" or "*apparent* possibility" that would entail "augmenting" anything. All that has gone before involves simply the acknowledgment of or the prospect of what is irremediably there in the nature of justly planned warfare in a nuclear age. It may be argued that the deterrences so far discussed are not sufficient all together to compose an *effective* deterrent. Nuclear pacifists and massive militarists alike argue that only mass murderousness can finally deter and limit war; and both agree that the prospect of the destructive violence inherent in any justly conducted war with modern weapons would not be enough. However that may be, I do not think it is possible to demonstrate that the foregoing elements in deterrence are in any way morally wrong.

There was one more question that had to be posed concerning an additional ingredient or level of deterrence that still is not *ab initio* ruled out by the judgment that no nation should commit itself or make itself conditionally willing or committed or ever actually intend to go to city-exchanges or general counter-people warfare. This is the possibility that an opponent might be deterred by a deliberately intended *ambiguity* about what the deterring nation plans to do, or by omitting to declare what one will not do. (Declarations, communications to the enemy, treaties, and tacit agreements, cannot remove the *inherent* ambiguity but perhaps they can remove any intended ambiguity.) What about intending into or not withdrawing from the system of international relations the possibility or the apparent possibility that an enemy's cities will under some circumstances deliberately be destroyed?

Here again I shall have to let that solitary individual (the still interested reader) gather from pp. 254–8 above and from pp. 299–302 above the argument that can be made for the probable morality of this form of deterrence. I am obliged, however, to take up what Stein calls (p. 79) my "very significant shift" or my "strategic retreat" between the article "The Limits of Nuclear War" (Chap. 11 above) and the preceding chapter (1965). The question here is two-fold: whether I still judge the so-called "deceptions" necessary to maintain a deterrence policy based to an extent on ambiguity to be "obviously" *not* "a moral self-violation and a violation of others"; and whether I still believe this deterrence to be an indispensable background for all the lower deterrent capabilities. The answer to the first question (which is the only question I ever meant to address) is that I see no reason for making any alteration in my moral reasoning to the justification of this form of deterrence. The "deception" involved in a deterrent policy of ambiguity is not a "lie," because it is *not* the withholding of the truth from anyone to whom the truth is due.[20] In the preceding chapter I did not judge it necessary to traverse that ground again, but only to formulate the question correctly, which is: "Have moralists the right to require that a statesman should disclose to an enemy the real nature of and the difference between his actual fight-the-war policy (if this is just) and his deter-the-war policy (if this also contains no unjust or murderous intention)?" The answer to that question still seems to me to be in the negative. I immediately went on to say that there may be practical reasons even if there is no decisive moral reason why a statesman should nevertheless make his policies quite clear: "To do so may be wise, for all that the moralist may not be able to say" (p. 52 [see also p. 300 above]), i.e. may not be able to say anything in the area of the wisdom peculiar to the expert in a position of political or military responsibility, or not be able as a moralist to reach an affirmative answer to the questions posed above.

If Stein is right in observing some shift of emphasis on the practical matter of whether the deterrence of bluff or ambiguity is indispensable (so that all the lower forms of deterrence we have reviewed are but "extensions" suspended downward from this one) then I suppose that I am in trouble—since according to the principles and procedures governing my "moral office," I should not be in the business of constructing any argument that *depends on* the answer to this question. (Neither is Stein entitled to decide such like questions of fact on the way to any ethical conclusion.) In my original essay, I plainly stated only that deterrence effected by studied ambiguity *might* be necessary and I bracketed the whole discussion by an hypothesis: "*If* the [lower degrees of deterrence] do not seem to the military analysts sufficiently persuasive, *or able to be made so,* then . . ."[21] They are the ones to say whether ambiguity

[20] Lawler had reason to know ("The Limits of Nuclear War," Chap. 11 above, pp. 254–8) that I not only, first, distinguished a policy of "deception" from murderousness as, even if immoral, not the same or an equal immorality; and, secondly, argued that it is not an instance of the forbidden falsehood. He ridicules the former contention and fails to address the latter, crucial one (p. 89).

[21] Chap. 11, above p. 254 (first italics added). Incidentally, Stein's footnote #14 on p. 82 of the present symposium is misplaced. That quotation went to the point of deterrence from those possibilities or apparent possibilities that would have to be augmented by ambiguity, not to the point of deterrence from possibilities or apparent possibilities in modern just war that have in no wise to be augmented (to which Stein attached it). The result of this slip is to make me seem "uncomfortable" about the morality of the latter deterrent effect. This is *certainly* moral, it seems to me, while deterrence from calculated ambiguity or from ambiguity about one's willingness that is not attempted to be removed is *probably* moral (to use the traditional notations).

In addition to hypothetical expressions of statements of fact, I think it en-is indispensable; I (to speak presumptuously) am the one to say whether, even so, it is moral; or (to speak more correctly) to submit such considerations and reasons as seem pertinent to me to the community of ethical discourse. And whoever justifies something morally also proscribes something morally; and that was going on all the time in these attempts of mine to render deterrence corrigible to reflective moral judgment.

If there was this shift concerning the military necessity of calculated ambiguity to sustain deterrence, I can only offer an explanation. This is that for the past two years I have frequently given lectures before college audiences in this country on the subject of the morality of deterrence. On these occasions the most vociferous protests to the effect that this final form of deterrence *is not necessary* and would be very unwise and hard to manage have come from scientists in the audience, many of whom had been just lately on one or two year leaves of absence to work in the U.S. military establishment or to engage in some contracted piece of research relevant to national defense and world security.[22] Perhaps I grew weary trying to make a moral argument about something I was repeatedly told was unnecessary, or I too quickly quit trying to explain to more practical men than I the virtue of unpacking a hypothetical case and the clarification of moral conduct that may be derived from such an exercise. After all, not only such men but moralists also often mistakenly suppose that to do this is to *recommend* the hypothesis as a course of action.

In any case, I must simply place this report by the side of Stein's

---

tirely appropriate to use the words "may" or "might" frequently in *ethical deliberations* and at important points in reaching a moral judgment upon some situation. For this reason, in his critical review of my 1963 pamphlet, Justice George Lawler accused me of adopting an "oblique," hesitant, and "subjunctive" manner of speaking about questions on which one should be clear and incisive, with, indeed, "subjunctive ambiguity" and "verbal pleonasm" (*continuum*, Vol. 1, No. 2 [Summer, 1963] 198–210). It now appears that I am guilty of "triumphant truism," victorious quotation, and "pontificating" from under a "supreme adjudicating mantle" (pp. 85, 86, 88). Doubtless the logic of rhetoric can render all these charges consistent with one another, and show me how to triumph with a "may" and a "perhaps." Since, however, I am not endeavoring to compose a literature for the ages, but only trying to get at the truth if at all possible by means of ethical argument, it is more important to note my agreement with St. Augustine against the grammarians of his day, that no one ought to be "more fearful of perpetrating a barbarism than, having done so, of envying those who had not"; and that, for all our hereditary rules of speech and writing, it is more important to know what is and what is not the meaning of murdering a human being, and to trace out the logic of moral action, than it is to fail to aspirate the first letter of "a *uman* being" (*Confessions*, Bk. I, Chap. xviii).

[22] Likewise is O'Brien's response on the related matter of definite threats: ". . . There is much to be said for bone dry honesty to oneself and to one's enemies (not to mention one's friends) when it comes to making threats. . . . [I]t seems better to threaten and, to the extent that this is practical, to seem to threaten only what one is actually prepared to do if the deterrent fails" (p. 99).

comparable statement that he thinks "it is very doubtful whether military analysts, as a body, would be prepared to endorse a minus-[deliberate ambiguity] deterrent" (p. 80). That is neither here nor there in settling the question whether a plus-deliberate-ambiguity deterrent is moral. Since, for example, Stein and I are agreed that a plus-executing-city-hostages deterrent would be an atrocity whether or not the military believed this to be indispensable and even if they would not endorse a deterrent minus this intention, it is hard to see why Stein introduced the above finding of his about what military analysts may be prepared to endorse concerning a minus-deliberate-ambiguity deterrent.

The explanation is doubtless something we share. In moral analysis generally some conditions of fact must be assumed. The assumed facts will be in one way or another "interwoven" with the moral analysis. But the trick is to take care not to make moral capital out of assumptions of fact or assumptions concerning the judgment of experts that may from time to time have to be brought in. Professionally, I should have no interest in proving a moral deterrent to be an effective one; and Stein should have no interest in proving the only effective deterrent to be necessarily immoral. Nor should we have any inordinate concern to prove the existing deterrent systems to be morally acceptable or unacceptable. Even if one of us happened to have the competence, and even though as citizens we must make up our minds concerning the factual aspects of policy questions, such judgments do not fall within the jurisdiction of our moral office as writers on ethical questions. But, of course, our ethical reflection begins with the facts we know or think we know, and it returns some judgment upon them. The validity of these judgments depends, however, primarily on our moral reasoning and only contingently upon the correctness of the judgment of fact we happen to believe. The only way to tell whether a supposed factual situation is morally tolerable or intolerable is to be concerned primarily with the determination of what would be morally tolerable or intolerable in a specific area of action supposing certain conditions of fact. Perhaps Stein and I ought both to sit looser to our "facts."

IV

Until we do, I am in a quandary over how the remaining issues between us are to be joined. Perhaps the ground on which we stand to grapple could be cleared if I posed several questions.

1. Does or does not Stein agree with me that church councils may pronounce in *moral* terms on *the moral issue* in questions of public policy, but that it is beyond their jurisdictional competence to make

determinations of *fact* or of what facts must necessarily be? At first, he seems to agree: that distinction, he writes, is "definitive . . . of the obvious," although he regards it as more than a little "peremptory." Yet the very next sentence affirms that "it is not obvious why *the actual facts I cited and analyzed* are . . . so obviously beyond the competence of a responsible body of judges" (p. 75). Certainly no facts are to be set beyond the competence of a responsible body of *judges,* but some matters of fact are beyond the competence of a body of *ecclesiastical* judges. Here the word "competence" refers to their jurisdiction or responsibility, not to their wisdom or the actual knowledge of the facts some of the representatives at a church council may happen to have.

Stein, however, moves rapidly away from his initial admission that my description of the task of moralists and of church councils is "definitive . . . of the obvious." By the next page the whole case rests upon our ability and "competence" to settle matters of fact, or upon the self-evidence of these facts. It is "strange," he writes, "to be 'told' " that " 'it is beyond the competence of any church council to make the determination *of the actual facts and reasons* interwoven (as Ramsey, here, for the moment, concedes) with my moral argument' " (p. 76). By that I conceded nothing, neither Stein's so-called "actual facts" nor—and this is the chief point, let the facts be whatever they are—his *reliance* in a course of moral reasoning upon a given set of facts, nor his final definitive moral judgment upon the supposed facts. The latter would be the *application* of moral judgment to an actual case, which is the business of men whose responsibilities are in the military and political realms.

It is because I separate procedurally between the task of moralists and church councils and the task of the statesman, and I am afraid Stein does not do so in the areas of his certainties, that I seem to him to make "warily restrictive comments upon the Council's competence in these matters." Also for this reason, he gets the impression that mine is a "correspondingly trustful belief on behalf of . . . governmental self-assessments" (p. 75). This is a crucial issue between us, and it does not revolve around who trusts whose assessments. It is rather a matter of who should make the final assessment of *actual* situations or cases. Statesmen may not always be wise. They may indeed be very foolish. In a given instance some moralist or church council may know better. But the statesman is still the magistrate and the church is the church, whose business it is to comment *in moral terms* on *the moral issue* in public questions and thus to guide and form the conscience of the statesman, whose business it is to know and judge the actual facts.

Of course, any moral argument must have facts interwoven with the moral reasoning. Still, everything depends on how this is done, if the moralist is not to exceed the limits of his jurisdiction (perhaps all the more tempted to exceed the limits of his professional competence *because* he happens to have an actual competence in the matter at hand). The facts interwoven, whether these are believed to be real or are only a construct for the sake of the argument, must remain hypothetical and not become a reliance. If moralists or church councils arrive at conclusions that depend on the facts being thus and so, and not otherwise, then the role of the statesman in knowing the facts and finally determining a moral course of political action would be invaded.

Professionally, I myself do not know what would be "a competent determination of *present* moral *facts*" (p. 77). At least that would not be my language, if I wanted to say that I thought we who belong to the community of discourse about ethics could make a competent determination of the guiding moral principles or the shape of the valid moral analysis that is relevant to the fact-situation and to proposals in the matter of deterrence (whatever these may be). Nor do I know what is a "categorical *perception*" (italics added); and can only say that if Stein discerns in my writings certain "apparent withdrawals of categorical perception" (p. 75), this is because I am resolved to avoid reliance on any perceptions of fact that may be included and that must be interwoven with my moral analysis. This is why as a moralist I had to shift the *emphasis* from judgment upon the facts to clarification of the moral judgments themselves, and so wrote: "We need to clean up our deterrence system, of course [presumably, this was my "categorical perception"]; but mainly we need to clean up our *notions* of deterrence and of what we erroneously suppose this depends upon" (p. 47 [see also p. 295 above]).

In my capacity as a citizen, of course, and in discussions in the public forum (unlike writings addressed to my fellow Christians *as such,* to professional ethicists, and to church councils), I do not deny, I in fact affirm, that I with every man must arrive at judgments of fact and of value, at some determination of present moral *facts,* and some categorical perception of the situation as it is and as it should be. This simply means that every citizen must make up his part of the public-policy decision. He is a lesser magistrate. He has his particular measure of jurisdictional competence to think through to the end an application of the moral principles governing political action. Let us hope he has the actual competence to do this.

The issue here is rather like the one which would be raised if someone demanded from a moralist a "competent determination of present moral *facts*" and a "categorical *perception*" in the matter of distinguishing between fornication and adultery. Some morally uninstructed practical men are apt to reply to this question by saying that they have tried them both, and that to them there wasn't any difference! To which the best answer is that they need to clarify their categories, and that this would then improve their categorical perception of the difference between one case which is adultery and another which is simple fornication. These concepts refer to "rules of practice," and not directly to actual or fictional cases falling under them. No cases fall under these concepts and no one ever perceived a case of either adultery or faithfulness in marriage unless there was the marriage covenant as a moral rule of practice.

So it is with the difference between murder and killing in war, and the difference between murderousness and legitimate deterrence. These concepts are crucial to the rules of practice which define the civilized conduct of war and the justice of deterrence. We moralists need to clarify these categories, orienting our discussion upon but not in dependence on present and possible future fact-situations, since this would help everyone's categorical perception and assist in the determination of present moral facts (or, better said, it would improve anyone's moral judgment upon the facts) which he must make in the office of magistrate or citizen.

Does Stein really agree with me that Christians, moralists, and church councils *as such* are to debate moral issues in moral terms and not yield to any *reliance* upon any reported factual situation for their findings? Despite his opening concession that this is definitive of the obvious, I suspect that he does not. This concession is withdrawn not least of all by his reference to some moralist's "categorical *perception*" or his judgment of "present moral *facts*".

In the only meaning I can assign to these notions, they would mean that the mind of the moralist is furnished with the power to make what Kant called "synthetic *a priori*" judgments. Instead, the "perceptions" and the "moral *facts*" seem to me to be the determinations of prudence on the part of men in the political and military sectors applying the relevantly formulated categories of morality to the specific cases and dilemmas they face.

2. So far I have been speaking of the stance to be taken toward any actual present facts or judgments of fact that we may think we have access to. The next question is this: Does or does not Stein agree that in order to discover and properly articulate the "moral guidelines" needed "to reshape and render acceptable the nuclear deterrence we have" (p. 66 [see also p. 313 above]), or to make *any other judgment* upon it, we moralists ought not to assume in the course of the argument that the actual, present facts are unalterable? It is not we who are writers on ethical subjects who should draw the final conclusion (even if this were correct) that, because of certain *necessary* facts, deterrence is necessarily immoral.

In his reply Stein made a valiant attempt to avoid making judgments of *necessary* future fact. This he did, however, by emphasizing all the more his certainty about the present, actual facts. My first question

339

was addressed to that. I deny that we as moralists are "competent" to be right on that subject; and I deny that any view of the present, actual facts should enter *decisively* into a discussion of the morality of deterrence. Otherwise, we will never arrive at determinations of morality in terms that can clearly assess morally the facts we know or think we know, or be of any assistance to the practical man in assessing the facts he judges to be facts.

Now to take up the question of judgments of *necessary* future facts and therefore, the question of conclusion to the *necessary* immorality of deterrence. I think I was not wrong in understanding that, for Stein, among the present, actual facts of the matter stands the *irreformability* of an effective deterrence. In short, his argument went to the heart of deterrence *as such;* and it is difficult to see why he should now withdraw this attempted universal or "synthetic *a priori*" judgment, and say in reply to my proposals for a *possible* moral deterrent that he only meant to speak of our present, actual one. I think I was not wrong to suppose that he meant to argue and did argue that "nothing short of . . . —the dismantling . . . of the whole ultimate *foundation of deterrence*— would now dismantle these built-in commitments to genocide on the part of its servants" (p. 22). I grant that grammatically and in the context of the Air Commodore's testimony, this may be taken to read: "nothing short of dismantling the whole ultimate foundation of *our present, actual* deterrence would now dismantle these built-in commitments to genocide on the part of its servants." That reading, however, would bring us again to Stein's categorical perceptions of present facts, among which stands the irreformability of the present deterrence and the ineffectiveness of a moral one. Stein himself sums up the universal and necessary truth he takes from this man's testimony by repeating in his reply to me that this shows "the Deterrence State's *actual present* dependence (*as well as* 'necessary' dependence) upon a nuclear personnel willing to press the button murderously . . ." (p. 76). Surely then, I was not altogether wrong to give the clause set off by dashes itself this additional weight of meaning. Although grammatically another reading was permitted, I took the clause to have the meaning Stein still says, in effect, that it has. This is the reason I removed it before agreeing with the passage as a whole— except for wanting to keep open for later discussion and for official decision the question of public declaration of everything a nation would thus remove from the foundations of deterrence itself (pp. 47, 77).

Again, in his reply Stein states that "a justly limited deterrence strategy is a contradiction in terms" (p. 82). That was supposed to be a conclusion out of my own mouth, made necessary by the fact that I used such words as "enforce" and "punish." These, of course, are words that are perfectly proper to use in ethical discourse, and meanings or effects it is perfectly proper to want in politics. Both domestically and internationally, enforcement and protective retribution are ingredients in the nature of political rulership. It is only "pure" (?) retribution, vengeance, punishment for punishment's sake, or punishment that is *not* connected with enforcing limits that are wrong. No reader could doubt that I spoke always of enforcing limits and punishing transgressions of those limits. There is nothing wrong with that, unless one wants to withdraw from the political life of mankind.

Yet Stein takes these categories as *self-evidence* of the immorality of deterrence. This alone is sufficient to show that his argument, or the premises with which he starts, go to the heart of deterrence itself *as such* (and I should say would annul government itself) and not alone to the immorality of our present, actual deterrent. To enforce and to punish become "punitive" (Stein's word, already with a different nuance of meaning); and to want anything "punitive" is necessarily "counter-people" in the structure of the act and in the heart of the agent. How is it possible to enforce limits and punish transgressions without meaning to enforce and punish? The need to mean to do so is an indispensable basis even of counter-force strategies and collateral deterrence. Then comes the already built-in conclusion: Ramsey's *"logically inevitable failure* to empty this punitive element of moral intention . . . demonstrate[s] that a justly limited deterrence strategy is a *contradiction in terms"* (pp. 81–82, italics added).

That is like saying that deterrence deters. That enforcement enforces. Punishment punishes. So deterrence is wrong simply because as a matter of fact it deters, and is intended to do this. To affirm that enforcement does not enforce and is not meant to would be a "contradiction in terms," and to undertake to demonstrate that deterrence does not deter and is not meant to would end in "logically inevitable failure." No one can empty out the enforcing, punishing, deterring element he means to invoke in showing how this could be morally done. Therefore, I think I am not wrong in saying that it is not either some possible future deterrent or our present, actual deterrent that seems to Stein to be morally intolerable. It is deterrence itself *as such*.

Stein's view is based *either* on an attempted "synthetic *a priori*" judgment that deterrence is necessarily immoral, *or* on what amounts to an *analytic* definition of deterrence as necessarily immoral because of the very meanings that the idea of deterrence itself logically contains. (Under question #3, the latter interpretation will receive additional support.)

Taking his departure from these premises, Stein regards the Deterrence State in about the same way capitalistic society was viewed by Friedrich Engels. Everything that is real within the realm of deterrence is bound to become unreasonable after a while; hence, it is already by definition unreasonable, it is afflicted with unreasonableness from the very beginning. Everything that deters deserves to perish. And everything that is reasonable within the heads of men is destined to become real, however much it may contradict the existing seeming reality of the Deterrence State. That day will be hastened if only churchmen will forget who *and where* they are as members of the church militant, and bear witness to what human political community will be like in the End-time when all the nations of the world will become the kingdom of God and of his Christ. From this point of view, anyone who thinks it important to make and apply moral distinctions within the present stage of history is bound to seem "constantly to run together the deterrence strategies we do have with the deterrence strategies we might have" (p. 76), and to weasel not a little in the moral condemnations he is willing to underwrite.

3. The foregoing should make clear that I think I already know Stein's obvious answer to my third and final question. Does Stein believe that as a matter of fact only "extended deterrence" can *effectively* deter war before it breaks out or deter it during a war in the nuclear age? Or is he willing to discuss the morality of deterrence on the factual assumptions made possible by graduated deterrence and to inquire without bias into the possible sufficient effectiveness of this? Is he committed factually and in principle to the proposition that *only* a plus-city-hostages deterrent deters and that this atrocity is what alone is at work in any of the seemingly effective lower levels of deterrence? Or will he look with me into the possibility that a minus-city-hostages deterrent would be quite enough shared danger to place adequate limits upon political and military decisions in this age? To raise this question is to come to a final assessment of where we are in connection with the respective judgments of fact to which neither of us is quite entitled but which nevertheless are unavoidably interwoven with our moral argument.

When at one of those famous Washington cocktail parties I was told by a man in the next to the top echelons of the Pentagon, in the early days of the Kennedy administration and at the beginning of our policy of limited, flexible, graduated response, that the President had been briefed that *no matter what happened* it didn't make sense to start striking cities, I was inclined to believe this; and to believe that our policy was the ambiguous no-cities one it should, at most, be. To the contrary, Stein believes it to be a fact that military strategy is "autonomous," concerned only with the use of violent power which is subject only to its own "vigorous automatic logic." There is for him, a closed system of universal law controlling the facts and the "logic" of deterrence (which Stein sums up in a decree which, like that of a deistic creator, thenceforth abandons the world of power to its own devices and to operation in accordance with its own laws): "You cannot deter unlimited force by force and at the same time limit your force according to extra-deterrent limits" (p. 78).[23] This is Stein's *analytical* definition of the meaning necessarily contained in the *idea* of deterrence. It is not based on experience of the matter.

Of course, in one sense—and a purely *formal* one—it has to be admitted that there can be no "extra-deterrent limits" contained in a scheme of deterrence, or in any deterrence scenario. *Any* consideration brought into view counts as an *intra*-deterrent factor. But in the present context, in which Stein assumes that only more force limits force, it seems clear that an extra-deterrent limit means an extra-force limit. This is what gives him the proposition that you cannot deter unlimited force by force and plan at any point not to keep on going higher or at that point to introduce some "extra-deterrent limit." That premise (or analytical *notion*) happens to be false: the limitation of force by force has always involved also extra-force limits, deterrence has always involved extra-deterrence limits in this sense, because the original forces limiting one another have extra-force or *political* purposes. But Stein's "law"—as long as he holds it—precludes him from even inquiring whether deterrence can have extra-force, extra-deterrent limits and still deter. Thus from a deductive notion of deterrence he is committed as a factual matter to "extended deterrence" as the only preventive of or dampener upon war in the nuclear age.

Therefore there is more at work in our divergent factual judgments about the nature of the present deterrent than the fact that Stein is a Britisher somewhat positioned to favor nuclear neutralism in politics while I am an American who is positioned to have somewhat more concern for the conscience of the people who are under the hard necessity of mounting and operating the defense system that has the most deterring effects, and do not want hastily to make them "mortal sinners" if they are not to be so judged from a more careful examination. The facts may not be subject as Stein supposes them to be to an "iron law of atrocity," or atrocity by the definition of deterrence.

At one point even Stein relaxes his military "You cannot . . ." and says only that "*in most cases* the strategic 'ground rules' designed to limit a possible nuclear war, remain *heavily* dependent upon a transgression of moral limits" (p. 78, italics added). What is this but an admission that in some measure strategic analysis is not set up to refuse every possible extra-force, extra-deterrent *material* limit and that military planning might not be absolutely impervious to the introduction of moral

---

[23] Stein's complementary *moral* premise is simply a circular statement of the plain truth: "You cannot be subject to unconditional moral limits and at the same time escalate these limits to accord with conditions of limitless license" (p. 78). That is correct but uninformative, since it only indicates the presence of moral limits limiting the license.

and political considerations? If it is true to say (p. 78) that the vast majority of strategic analysts do not attempt to propose a deterrent at once militarily *and* morally adequate, this may be due in part to the fact that we moralists haven't given them much help. In fact, Stein's iron law of atrocity reads: "*They* (the military analysts) *cannot* deter unlimited force by force and at the same time limit their force according to extra-force, extra-deterrent limits."

Strategic analysis is probably more highly advanced in the United States than in any country in the world. Yet, during the years this has developed, there has always been a number of military planners who believed that the barrier between the use of conventional and the use of nuclear weapons, even though it is a non-rational barrier, should be preserved and strengthened in the minds of men and in the councils of nations. At the present moment there is said to be a growing body of opinion, reaching high in U.S. government circles, which believes that American security and world peace and security would be greatly improved if nuclear weapons were "banned" not only by Vatican II and all sorts of other congresses but by international agreement as well, without worrying as much as we have in the past about getting perfect inspection. What would this be except by political purpose and action to introduce an "extra-deterrent" limit among the deterrent limitations that are not so autonomous or automatically logical after all, and whose "laws" are not impervious to considerations other than greater force preponderating over lesser force on up to an intended unlimited force that alone deters throughout the scale?

Yet on the yonder side of the line drawn by international agreement banning nuclears (or on the yonder side of any other extra-force limit introduced into the international system), there would remain an effective deterrence from the nature of existing weapons and from the irremovable possibility of non-compliance and from the fearful consequences of any breach of such a treaty or tacit agreement. In other words, the forms of deterrence whose morality I have analyzed would go to work enforcing the extra-deterrent limit in the agreement, each meshing with the other. The forcible pressure of deterrence guaranteeing the agreement would not replace the extra-deterrent importance and authority of the agreement introduced into the international system.

Much the same can be said of CBR (chemical-biological-radiological) mass weapons. These weapons are generally held in a class by themselves as weapons intended to be not used. CBR deterrence consists, formally speaking, of *both* the extra-deterrent limits imposed upon military and political encounters between nations by tacit and expressed agreements *and* (at least) the ingredients of deterrence I have been discussing in connection with nuclear weapons. If this is the case with regard to non-rational extra-force boundaries based on the physical nature of weapons alone, there would seem to be no reason to dictate in advance that deterrence of the use of force by force cannot mesh with deterrence of the use of force also by appeal to qualitative moral and political boundaries.

In the present symposium, O'Brien stated his opinion that "we have already drifted into a situation where the first use of any nuclear weapons is, if not immoral, contrary to an unwritten rule of the customary international law of the nuclear age" (p. 100). If that is or is becoming the customary international law, that would be an extra-force, extra-deterrent factor in the international system, while in turn the sanctions enforcing such a customary law must be the various ingredients in deterrence that I have analyzed. Evidently O'Brien does not believe that the *only* sanction enforcing such a lower limit in customary law is or would have to be the threat of massive counter-society warfare, or that the removal of this threat would dismantle the whole ultimate foundation of deterrence. For, in his campaign for "bone dry honesty," O'Brien wrote: "I am not at all sure we can much longer permit the *impression* to exist that we would in some circumstances initiate nuclear counter-city warfare, no matter how salutary an effect this impression seems to have for our deterrent posture in the short run" (p. 100).

In the preceding paragraphs I have mentioned a number of extra-force, materially extra-deterrent factors that may very well be or be made a part of the total scheme of things deterring or regulating war in the nuclear age. The proper answer to Stein's military analytic: "You cannot . . ." is an experiential, political: "Who's trying to deter unlimited force by force alone?" Then let us get on with the discussion of rational politics and the justice in war and in deterrence in the nuclear age.

Stein's contention that "you cannot deter unlimited force by force and at the same time limit your force according to extra-deterrent limits" only discloses his analytic definition of deterrence. It also reveals that he has set force and morality or politics apart in two quite different worlds. No one that I know proposes to limit force only by more force, or by availing himself of no extra-force factors. If such were the fact-situation, then of course (and by definition or by the splitting off of force from politics), any sort of war and any measure of deterrence is already in some nonsense world of limitless violence. If deterrence is bound to become this in the end, it is already so from the beginning. But this is not the real world of politics even—or especially—in this excessively violent age. Just as I ventured the opinion that most nuclear weapons are in fact targeted on military objectives, so I will venture to say that few if any deterrence-scenarios that have been played out have failed to introduce extra-force, materially extra-deterrence limitations also.

The question is why Stein is under the compulsion to reduce all force to the maximum violence that is possible today, to "extend" the working of any and all deterrent effects downward throughout the scale from unlimited, licentious murderousness, and to cling to the quite pre-nuclear proposition that only the actual destruction of all that can be destroyed, and commitment to do this, would be dreadful enough to deter anyone from his political purposes.

In part, this is because Stein's is only an analytic or deductive definition of "deterrence" from which he draws forth the conclusion that deterrence means trying to deter limitless force only by force, because that is what deterrence *means*. Thus is deterrence *by definition* "extended."

In part, also, this must be because Stein is more a pacifist than he is a nuclear pacifist. He wants finally to separate force from politics and politics from physical force. The nuclear age seems to offer the opportunity of doing what religion never could, whenever before religion sponsored non-historical undertakings. Therefore all the force there is and any deterrence there could be must end up in or "extend" from an immoral, non-political use of force. The principles and limits and tests of the just war which were erected on the understanding that force and politics and morality *are connected* (and which can certainly be used in the justification and limitation of systems of graduated deterrence) must be annulled in the very use of them in a moral argument by showing that the fact-situation obliterates all distinctions and automatically sucks everything into the uppermost violence or into most wicked threats. This is the moral capital derived from the facts supposed. All deterrence must perish because nothing but an immoral deterrent by definition deters.

In any case, Stein cannot have his deterrence cake and eat it too. He cannot deny the probable or possible effectiveness of a minus-city-hostage deterrent, and then say that " 'side-effects' are subject to the principle of proportion" (p. 83). This principle simply says that in the world of cost-benefits you never get away from the responsibility of being prudent, and that for the statesman not everything that is imprudent can be reduced to paying total cost for no benefits (i.e. extended deterrence based on total war). The principle of proportion simply anatomizes how statesmen will think in counting the costs of achieving their political purposes. How can they be obliged to count the cost unless they rightly fear some costs? Long before there are no-benefits-and-total-costs there will be abundant reason for political purposiveness *not* to resort to higher costs. This is all I mean by saying that the prospect of mutually unacceptable side-effects in modern war collaterally deters enough, without going deliberately to a plus-city-execution deterrent. As I said before, "if actual war today soon becomes disproportionate, then the war threatened soon becomes deterrent enough upon any rational decision maker. One need not wax so horrendous about it" (p. 47 [see also p. 295 above]).

Nor do I think it consistent for Stein to deny efficacy to minus-city-hostage deterrence and at the same time allow his common humanity to respond to my expression "counter-force in its *maximum* form" [24] by noting that this is a "disturbingly pregnant qualification" (p. 81 [see also p. 252 above]). My article on paragraph 25 of Schema XIII contained a better statement of the deterring prospects I had in mind: "Long before an actual war reached the upper levels of massive nuclear bombardment of the sources of military power, the destructiveness of such warfare directed even upon legitimate targets is likely to be disproportionate to the good sought or the evil prevented by resort to arms" (p. 46 [see also p. 294 above]); and again: "at many or most of the upper levels of justly targeted nuclear warfare we have gone beyond a proportionate use of force and beyond the rational ordering of force to political purpose" (p. 54 [see also p. 302 above]). If Stein does not as a *matter of fact* believe this, then he ought not to find my statement so *disturbing*. If he does, then he must agree that a moral deterrent might be effective. This would reduce the issues between us to the debate I have with O'Brien: whether the threat of something disproportionate is always a disproportionate threat (pp. 54–58 [see also pp. 302–6 above]).

V

There is one point in Lawler's response that is worth considering at this place. He believes that "the principle of proportion is implicit in the principle of double effect" (p. 88). This he affirms in order to justify calling by the name of "murder" any gross violation of the principle of proportion.

Without knowing exactly what "implicit in" means, it is clear that Lawler here telescopes together two of the criteria governing just conduct which moral reflection in the past has held *distinct* but inseparable in rendering judgment upon actions. An act may be gravely wrong, for one thing, because its primary thrust is to kill the innocent: that is murder. The same act, or another act, may be gravely wrong, for another thing, because of serious disproportion between its good and evil effects. The problem is to establish and keep clear the relationship between those two distinguishable tests. Lawler's view entails a serious confusion of the categories of moral analysis which it is better to keep clear and both applicable in all cases.

Actions, such as acts of war, having manifold effects may be disordered from justice because the primary thrust of the act was directed

---

[24] See above, p. 252.

toward the evil effect or toward some enlargement of it, or such actions may be disordered from justice because the primary good consequence was not worth paying and exacting the price of the evil effects. Either or both ways, there was a moral self-violation and a violation of others. These criteria are always valid, always distinct, yet always inseparably related in judgment concerning actions having manifold effects, some of which are evil.

The relation between the tests seem to be as follows: While the second criterion (the principle of proportion or prudence) is regulative of the "side-effects" *to be done,* it does not make or un-make them as "side-effects." That depends on the verdict under the first criterion. Of course, as O'Brien points out, "in concrete instances counter-force strikes might be threatened or made in such a way as to cause so much 'collateral' destruction to non-combatants that the claim that they were 'only counter-force' would be ludicrous on its face" (p. 99). But that is a verdict under the *first* criterion. In order to say this, or to say that "withholding one's intention" makes no difference in determining the direct objective of the action, one does not yet need to raise the question of disproportion. (The action may also have been gravely wrong because seriously imprudent, in that the strike wasn't worth the candle anyway.) One does not calculate a prudent number of babies to be murdered (directly killed) for the sake of any good consequences; but one tragically may and must calculate the prudent number that will unavoidably be killed as a side-effect of military operations whose goal and other consequence is expected to be the saving of many more from slaughter direct or indirect. Murder is never ordinate; but unfortunately a good deal of killing may be. So prudence rules, but it does not initiate or obliterate the discrimination of side-effects.

As for Lawler's case of tremendous lethal side-effects in nuclear war, it is better, it alone is correct, to say that the action this case supposes to take place would be *gravely wrong* under another *species* (a gross and deliberate violation of prudence or of proportion) than to say that "murder" was committed (unless on evidence that the action proceeded from a deliberate enlargement of the target or extension of the area of civil destruction, or was counter-city in the first place). Which judgment to make is difficult to say so long as the fact-description only tells us that the action was a megatonnage attack on "the Soviet Union" causing tremendous lethal fall-out. But loose language does not render the situation incorrigible to moral analysis; and when analysis of it is made it will not be found that proportion or prudence in its ruling or finally deciding role "negates" the other and morally more basic principle that murder be not done.

One does not have to emphasize that he considers simple fornication very, very wrong by calling it adultery. No more should a violation of the principle of proportion in fighting a war be called murder in order to say that such would be a grave moral violation. Which *species* of a violation of the rules of practice governing the political use of force the case entailed is not settled by the numbers *as such* in the RAND estimate of casualties, no more than whether an act was fornication or adultery or a marriage act is settled by a physical description of the action that took place.

It is better to say with Stein that " 'side-effects' are *subject* to the principle of proportion" (p. 83, italics added), than to say with Lawler that "if there is a radical disproportion between the good intended and the unintended but inevitable evil consequences, the principle of double effect is *negated*" (p. 88, italics added). Lawler merges the two criteria into an indiscriminate one expressing horror (a commendable emotion, of course, but not to be used as a category in ethical deliberations), while Stein rightly relates the two *distinguishable* criteria. Instead of saying that "there is no principle of proportion" (p. 88, italics added), one should rather say that in the case supposed the principle of double effect was first violated and then the principle of proportion was also violated; or that even had the conduct in question passed the test that justifies only the indirect killing of non-combatants it still would have been proscribed because grossly disproportionate to any political purposes sought to be obtained or protected thereby.

Of course, simply to say I didn't *intend* to kill so many or so many non-combatants helps not at all. Whoever said that it did? But neither is what I actually did to be resolved by the numbers or the extent of the damage either. The disproportion does not make me a murderer. All these are questions falling under the first criterion, and they are certainly subject to determination under that heading without invoking the second in order to get oneself classified as a monstrosity, a "disproportionate murderer."

Keeping the categories clear and distinct, however, does not alter the fact it would be equally sinful though morally a different kind of offense if a military commander knowingly does the death of an inordinate number of people in a just war while striking some legitimate target that was not important enough to be worth it. I myself have sometimes spoken of the *moral* economy governing the use of force (non-combatant immunity) and of an *economy* governing the use of force (the principle of proportion). This language may have been misleading, if anyone supposed that a conscious violation of the latter was any the less a moral self-violation and a violation of others. My language stressed that non-combatant immunity is intrinsic to the action itself with no prudential reference as yet to the totality of the consequences of the act, while the principle of proportion takes all the effects from the first time into account. Anyone who believes, however, as I do, that prudence is a virtue believes also that imprudence is *vicious* (though of a different *species* from murder), and that it is gravely *wrong* to act in violation of the requirement that force must be proportioned to greater good effects (or greater evil prevented). Whether the conduct is murderous must be taken up first, because one doesn't justify a proportionate number of murders; and this, of course, is not settled by the agent's withholding his intention while doing direct killing. Then whether the killing in question is to be permitted to take place collaterally entails an application of the principle of proportion which, as Stein says, "subjects" side-effects to final testing—justifying them in one situation, proscribing them in another.

Of course, it is the case—whoever said otherwise?—that "if I know that I will kill a thousand innocent civilians in the act of killing one combatant (he being an insignificant soldier), I cannot believe short of insanity, that I intend only the latter." But this is a question that arises and has to be settled in any assessment of an action under the first criterion. This does not wait to be resolved by finding the action to be in violation of the principle of proportion "implicit in" the principle of double effect. In the case supposed, no matter how disproportionate the effects, my "direct" and "indirect" killings do not become one and the same. Instead, *no one was killed indirectly* (unless it was the combatant whose death was incidental to all the rest). I enlarged my target and killed a thousand or a thousand and one directly. That was a violation of the moral immunity of non-combatants from direct attack. Double-effect was by no means negated by proportion, although the latter criterion supplements in this instance the condemnation of what was done. The act was inordinate primarily because ordered to the injustice of murder; it was also inordinate because disproportionate in that in this instance no sound calculation of good and evil effects could warrant what was done (which, however, I am not permitted even to begin counting because of the first verdict).

It is not difficult, however, to imagine a case in which I may foreknow that I will unavoidably kill a thousand innocent persons in an act whose primary thrust is directed to the elimination of one combatant (he being a commander who plans to blow up a city of a hundred thousand tonight at 9:30 p.m. and who alone knows how he will accomplish this, I having no alternative way of preventing him in time). That would be neither a violation of non-combatant immunity from *direct* attack (it would not be murder) nor a violation of the principle of proportion (it would not be an imprudent decision).

Let us next take three or four actual cases that may suggest the merit in following the tradition in holding these criteria clear and distinct if always related to one another. At this point I might rest my case simply by pointing out that it is *all forms* of consequentialist ethics in the modern period that are agreed on reducing the criteria into one by allowing the *final* adjudication of prudence to become the only test. The extreme alternatives meet—Better Dead or Better Red, nuclear pacifism or the proponents of a drastic "victory" over communism—in that the sole test applied is proportioning cost-effects to good-effects; only a different calculation is made in estimating the good or evil consequences of one or another course of action.

One casts up no such extreme alternatives, instead one's mind is focused upon more of the elements in complex military and political decisions, and one can see that there is no meat-axe solution of them, if he holds both criteria distinctly in mind and uses both in analyzing the ingredients of the action or decision that is under consideration. The tests, related as explained, are helps to the pondering heart that does not want to escape from any of the reality in the midst of which a man's or a nation's responsibility must be determined.

During World War II, some of the prominent leaders of world Judaism tried to persuade the Allies to bomb all of Hitler's concentration camps and extermination ovens, even though this would certainly kill all of the inmates at the time of the action. They reasoned that more innocent victims would be saved in the time that would elapse before the camps could be reconstructed and their genocidal work be going again, than lives would be lost "incidental" to destroying the target-camps and personnel that should justly have been repressed. Perhaps the war could even be brought to an end before the furnaces could be rebuilt. Now, I do not know the full details of the secret parleying that went on, nor the reason the Allies chose more conventional and perhaps more costly methods of "liberating" the camps. But if the details set down here are accurate, there were no reasons of morality except those that political prudence dictated for decision in the negative. Neither objectively nor subjectively would the inmates of the camps have been the objective attacked, though they were known to be certainly killed in great numbers.

Surely the decision rested with prudence, because even side-effects are "subject" to the principle of proportion. Would more lives be lost than likely would be saved by this drastic action? Perhaps the Allies were "deterred" by the possible imprudence of such a decision. The collateral deaths seemed too great a price to pay for the somewhat uncertain good effects in prospect. If this was the reasoning, the statesmen were thinking through the problem as best they could.

It is to be hoped that they were not trammelled by any notion that the action under consideration, even if it were disproportionate, would be "murder." Or by the objection that statesmen cannot discern or control the future. What is a magistrate if he is not a man who must rule the political world and shape the future for good as far as he can see into it by what he decides and decrees? The risk cannot be taken out of decisions based on estimates of cost/benefits according to the principle of proportion. What was not done in this instance and was believed to be prudent may in fact have been imprudent (costing more lives). If the camps had been bombed, on the other hand, that too might later have been judged to be a needless sacrifice of life for which there were not (as it turned out) more than commensurate benefits in lives saved. These are the ingredients of most if not all political and military decisions. It is to be hoped that in this case the decision was not trammelled by an anticipated sentimentalism in the publics these statesmen served, which knew not how to think with proper distinctions in mind or were lacking in sense of the awful responsibilities of magistrates.

My second illustration of the use of these two tests of the justice in actions is the situation created by the urgent question of the moral conduct of counter-insurgency warfare and by the recent invention of incapacitating, nauseating gases and their programming for use in riot control and as a possible means of successfully opposing insurgency more humanely. Too many have too quickly slapped the notation "immoral" upon any such weapons. No such notation belongs on any weapon, but only on a weapon's use or the action for which the weapon is intended.

It cannot, I think, be denied that incapacitating gases would be a more humane means of war in some, possibly frequent, insurgency situations. In short, if such weapons are feasible, they *prima facie* qualify as better weapons of war because more humane. Merely noxious gases would make possible less combatant destructiveness, and less of the associated collateral civil damage, because they would make it more possible to sort out combatants from non-combatants and to select among the people the sides are fighting over.[25]

Then why not immediately revise the rules (the extra-force, extra-deterrence limits) governing CBR deterrence at present, and which the ingredients of deterrence in these weapons themselves and from prospect of their possible use helps to make more or less secure? The answer can only be found (and this may or may not be a correct conclusion) in the disproportionate and uncontrollable consequences that would likely follow upon acceptance of the use of these new weapons of war. This is not obvious in the first instance. Doubt concerning the justifiable use of incapacitating gases arises only when one tries to anticipate any enemy's probable response to our first use of incapacitating gases, and then our response to that, etc. Would an adequate riposte on his part have to be the use of deadly gases, or epidemic diseases against populations; and would our only response to his response be to go to general war? Would our self-imposed limitation of gas warfare to the more humane means be

[25] See Julian Pleasants, "Gas Warfare: Reflections on a Moral Outcry," in *Commonweal*, Vol. LXXXII, No. 7 (May, 1965), 209–212.

a rule that could be enforced (and transgressions of this punished) by means that themselves are still limited and capable of being kept graduated? Have our military planners played out enough scenarios to know that there are obvious boundaries at which to agree to stop, once the non-rational boundary that at present prohibits CBR warfare has been replaced by even a more rational rule humanizing warfare in the immediate areas over which incapacitating gases might first be used effectively?

If not, then the step better be not taken. Still, it is important that in reaching this negative conclusion we be clear from which test we reached it. No one should permit himself the luxury of feeling no qualms about this decision, or turn his face away from the awful evil effects he would be saying we should continue to accept the doing of lest still worse effects follow. In effect, this decision means that because of the best, rough judgment a prudent calculation can make of all the possible consequences, we had better prosecute war against insurgency by running M113's zigzag across lakes and streams on whose bottoms lie for hours hidden insurgency fighters breathing through straws, crushing their bodies and watching bloody hands and arms and legs rise to the surface, rather than spreading a gas over the area which will cause these men to vomit and be captured.[26]

My third illustration of the principle of discrimination will be a brief consideration of the most serious violation of it in our times (which was *also* a violation of the principle of proportion).

David Irving in his account of *The Destruction of Dresden*[27] asserts that, in the bombing of cities on both sides in World War II, before Dresden "the fire-storm had been merely an unforeseen result of the attack; in the double-blow on Dresden [during the night of Feb. 13-14, 1945] the fire-storm was to be an integral part of the strategy." [28] Even if it is truer to say that previous to Dresden the fire-storms were a *foreseen* result of attacks upon cities where there were major military objectives, the fact that Dresden was of no military importance at all commensurate with the destruction let loose upon it, that it was an undefended city[29] swollen with refugees, and that achieving the maximum destruction of human lives without discrimination through fire-storm and by concentrating on residential sectors and not on industries was "an integral part of the strategy"—all this defines the wickedness done at Dresden.

---

[26] See Malcolm W. Browne, *The New Face of War* (New York: The Bobbs-Merrill Co., 1965), pp. 15–16.

[27] (New York: Ballantine Books, 1965), pp. 122.

[28] The fire-storm was to light the way for the second wave of bombers in their unprecedentedly deep penetration into Germany, if the weather lifted and the first wave was lucky enough to start the storm.

[29] "In the whole of Germany, only twenty-seven night fighters had taken off to ward off the mightiest air raid in history" (*The Destruction of Dresden*, p. 137).

This was an immoral act of war of the same order as dropping the atom bomb on Hiroshima; and of the two cities Dresden was the greater evil in that almost twice as many innocent people were deliberately and directly killed (135,000 as compared to 72,000).

Dresden burned for seven days and eight nights.[30] That was evil. Sixteen hundred acres of the city were devastated in one night, compared with less than six hundred destroyed in London during the whole war.[31] "For the first time in the history of the war, an air raid wrecked a target [city] so disastrously that there were not enough able-bodied survivors left to bury the dead." [32] That, even, might have been only a tragic evil. "Giant trees were uprooted and snapped in half. Crowds of people fleeing for safety had suddenly been seized by the tornado and hurled along whole streets into the seat of the fires; roof gables and furniture that had been stacked on the streets after the first raid were plucked up by the violent winds and tossed into the centre of the burning Inner City." [33] That is terrifying; but, after all, it was Ash Wednesday in a world in which, as the Psalmist sayeth, the innocent perish all the day long. Viewing Dresden as an important communications center, it should be noted that the railway complex was operating again within less than three days.[34] That might have been one of the accidents of war, in that the raid simply failed to destroy its objective.

One comes to the decisive moral element, however, when he notes with amazement "the extraordinary precision with which the residential sections of the city were destroyed, but not the important[?] installations";[35] and when one reads that on the maps used in briefing the bomber crews "there was not one railway line crossing the sector marked out for carpet bombing." [36] Thus were the fire-storm and general civilian destruction integral to the plan of attack. Far from failing to accomplish its objective, the bombing of Dresden was a complete success. The strategy

---

[30] *The Destruction of Dresden*, p. 171.

[31] P. 168.

[32] P. 172.

[33] P. 177.

[34] P. 192. Industrial recovery was also swift and electric power was available again within twenty-four hours (p. 220).

[35] P. 194.

[36] P. 131. The tribute paid to man's moral sensibilities in order to accomplish this wickedness ought to be noticed. Despite the fact that little or nothing in the plan of attack sustained it or was commensurate with such an objective, "the Master Bomber and his navigator had been instructed that the purpose of the attack was to hinder the railway and other communications passing through Dresden" (p. 131). Intelligence concerning Dresden was almost entirely lacking, because of what amounted to a tacit agreement that Dresden and Oxford would not be bombed; yet "somehow the information became distorted by the time it was passed on to the aircrews themselves" (p. 149). This whole volume is an impressive demonstration of how men are mutually deceiving and self-deceived when they do grave wrong.

for the destruction of Dresden contained both elements that lawyers tell us are necessary and sufficient for the capital crime of murder: there was the *mens rea* (the intent or purpose) and there were objective characteristics in the deed actually done corresponding to a paramount intention to kill the innocent directly as a means to ulterior goals believed to justify such means. This made Dresden a violation of the first rule of civilized warfare (the principle of discrimination). It was a planned violation of the moral immunity of non-combatants from *direct* attack.

If I know that I will kill a thousand innocent civilians in the act of killing one combatant (he being an insignificant soldier), I cannot believe short of insanity that I intend only the latter or that I did not do murder. But this is a question that arises and has to be settled in any assessment of an action under the principle of discrimination. This does not wait to be resolved by finding the action to be in violation of the principle of proportion. In the case supposed, no matter how disproportionate the effects, the principle of discrimination still applies and the distinction between direct and collateral killing is not abolished. Instead, the first verdict must be that *no one* was *killed indirectly* (unless it was the combatant whose death was incidental to all the rest). I deliberately enlarged my target and killed a thousand or a thousand and one directly. That was a violation of the moral immunity of non-combatants from direct attack. A judgment of disproportion supplements in this instance the condemnation of what was done. The act was inordinate primarily because it was directed to the injustice of murder; it was also inordinate because of the extreme disproportion between the good and the evil consequences (or, if you prefer, between the lesser evil prevented by killing the soldier and the greater evil of so much additional killing).

Suppose, however, a case in which I foreknow that I must unavoidably kill a thousand innocent persons in an act whose primary thrust is directed to the elimination of Hitler and his General Staff—or one combatant only, he being a commander who plans to blow up a city of a hundred thousand tonight at 9:30 p.m. and who alone knows how he will accomplish this, I having no alternative way of preventing him in time. That would be neither a violation of non-combatant immunity from *direct* attack (it would not be murder) nor a violation of the principle of proportion.

My final illustration of the correct way to use the tests of non-combatant immunity and of proportionality (distinctly but together) in assessing the morality of action is to return to my proposal that deterrence from disproportionate combatant and collateral civil damage and from the other ingredients of deterrence that may morally be in prospect provides a way of meshing together the moral requirements and the force requirements. My analysis depends on the admission that *as a matter of fact* a good deal less than limitless violence is apt to deter anyone from his political purposes. It also depends on keeping the categories clear and distinct in judging deterrent-action, i.e. it depends *as moral analysis* on keeping the scale of collateral deterrence or deterrence from disproportionate damage entirely distinct from deterrence from planned murder.

Let everyone know that I at least have never argued that you can deter the limitless use of nonsensical force which modern nations *can* exert, if they are resolved upon it or blunder into it, by a limitless exertion of contrary force, by threats, by morality, or by anything else. It makes very little sense to talk about anything other than the force and the deterrence that can be of service to politics. It is better not even to worry about all that other violence than it is to join the ranks of those apolitical and irresponsible men who every time a nation resorts to a responsible use of force in a just and necessary cause announce: "This could lead to the destruction of all mankind." That is the fallacy of misplaced deterrence. And the nations are all too well deterred without it.

The precarious peace and security of the world depends on the effectiveness of a moral deterrent: this is the chief concern of this chapter. But since peace is not the only political value, this should be no man's sole concern. Deterrence is not the sole or always an unqualified good in politics. It is not always the case that the more we are deterred the better. This is because justice and the precarious realizations of justice in the world depend on nations and citizens who are not always too much deterred from responsible action, including responsible military action and initiatives. This is the other side of the coin in any proper analysis of justice in war and in deterrence; and it should be noted here, although the emphasis in this discussion has been upon the value of deterrence and how this may morally be mounted.

My view of both war and deterrence in the nuclear age entails a revision of the requirement that, in resorting to a use of armed force, there must be a reasonable expectation of success. Or rather, it entails an understanding that this requirement was drawn up before this age in which the most obvious use of the available violence, if not the actual weapons themselves, exceeds the legitimate purposes of war. Today no resort to force would be justifiable if it had to be demonstrated in advance that this will save us from massive destruction. But since we ought not either to attribute such massive wickedness to an enemy or do it ourselves, there may be a reasonable expectation of success in a use of armed force in defense of justice so long as it is war as an extension of politics that an enemy fights. Beyond this, of course, nothing can defend anything.

The justification of a possible resort to armed force today in war or for deterrence's sake ought not, under the rubric of reasonable expectation of victory, to be made to bear a burden of proof it never had to bear in former ages. Today, a military policy based on "victory," and a means test requiring a reasonable hope thereof, is bound to be an immoral and a politically irrational policy. So also in designing a deterrent. That ancient prudential proviso must now be understood to mean a reasonable hope of *reasonable* victory, not of an irrational one. This was, in fact, all that was ever meant by this requirement. Since "victory" is meaningless on both sides if war is immorally total, reasonable expectation of victory must now mean the preservation of an ordered justice provided less than all the means are used and by a use of less than all the means of violence available. This is why justifiable resort to arms by either side in the nuclear age must proceed under an overarching policy that may be called "preemptive surrender," [37] or (if one prefers less boldness in speech) "preemptive negotiation" or a "constant readiness to adopt a policy of preemptive negotiation for a settlement at that point where the use of force is about to become inordinate or dis-ordered from justice." That is to say, either side should be prepared to stop if it seems likely that war will escalate into a purposeless use of violence. The fact that an enemy may use his weapons indiscriminately, and today has the weapons to do this, does not make it politically purposeful for us to do so. Nor does the fact that he may and can do so remove from us the responsibility to preserve, if and so long as we can, an ordered justice in the world by just and limited means. The requirement of reasonable expectation of victory cannot be interpreted to mean that, since today a totally immoral and irrational enemy could destroy us, we have no right and duty to preserve freedom with justice by forceful means—or that we have a right to presuppose in advance that he is totally immoral and irrational, and to use his hypostatized satanism as an excuse for weakness in our own political resolution or for dismantling deterrence altogether.

A theory of war or of deterrence must not depend exclusively on reciprocity or tacit agreements, however important these may still be, because when the time to resort to war has come the time for many of the unilateral initiatives that await reciprocity has passed. A no-cities fight-the-war policy and a minus-executing-city-hostages deterrence policy, of course, depends on introducing an initiative that does not wait or depend on reciprocity. There has been in the literature a great deal of discussion of unilateral initiatives which only invite reciprocation and

[37] John Courtney Murray, S.J.: *Morality and Modern War* (New York: Council on Religion and International Affairs, 1959), made the best comment (at p. 16 and footnote 7) on "losing" as "a function of winning" (Clausewitz), and upon the connection of this with the moral requirement that there be a solid probability of success in any legitimate use of arms. His remarks were called forth by "the hysteria that swept Washington . . . when the Senate voted, eighty-two to two, to deny government funds to any person or institution who ever proposes or actually conducts any study regarding" surrender.

depend on this for continuation; but that is not what is meant by the justice of war or of deterrence. I submit that a reader of any of my writings on the nuclear dilemma should know that where I find inherently immoral conduct in war or murderousness in deterrence, there I find a place for unilateral action that in no sense awaits reciprocity.

I simply contend also that this is the only sensible politics or deterrent in the nuclear age. One has only to recall the footnote to morality which the nuclear age has written: It can never *do any good* to do wrong or to intend to do wrong that good may come of it! It is an interesting and significant fact that so many good people today remain quite unconvinced that equally good consequences will follow from doing right (unless, of course, the Russians reciprocate), more unconvinced than were the Pentagon computers. These computers were fed any number of possible nuclear war situations, including of course situations in which Russia would have to reciprocate or might do so, but including also situations in which Russia does *not* reciprocate. No possible inter-city nuclear war was found in which the United States would not suffer as much, or more, damage from engaging in that sort of defense! The same holds for an *actual commitment*, for deterrence's sake, to make war by means of cities. One could have known this without computers, which simply demonstrated quantitatively that to *use* massive nuclear weapons against the whole of an enemy's society will in fact not defend anything. For the United States to stick to a no-cities policy after Russia went to the indiscriminate bombing of cities would, of course, not save our cities; but neither would our going to a cities policy (if by "cities" one means the fabric of our society with its freedoms and institutions and values, whose preservation should be the political purpose in ever fighting any war, and which may not survive even if many numbers do). This is simply a report of the fact that it may not be possible to avoid the destruction of our society by these weapons. But to avoid the execution on our part of an immoral plan of war would not leave our cities open to any more destruction. To intend not to do this is the only sensible politics in the nuclear age. Therefore, moralists and practical men alike need to explore all the ingredients of deterrence that fall under this rule of practice, and we need to carry out any and all of the manifold actions that may be required to secure a moral deterrent.

VI

I am personally most troubled by Walter Stein's contention that a government cannot maintain nuclear deterrence from which *its own* murderous intention to use nuclear weapons against a whole society has been removed without still "authoritatively leading its own subjects into a gravely sinful consent" (p. 80). If an enemy is deterred by bluff and ambiguity about the actual use to be made of these weapons, will not the immoral consent of our own people be aroused and implicated to the same degree that an enemy's people have cause to fear or its government to be deterred? The statement just quoted was made, it is true, when discussing the sort of deterrent effect that might be secured by *intending* ambiguity into the system; and, strictly speaking, the objection does not apply in the case of the other types of non-deceptive and assuredly legitimate deterrence that are likely, in my opinion, to be more than effective enough graduated deterrence in the nuclear age.

Yet throughout Stein is concerned about this problem; and rightly so, even if this consideration does not, upon examination, prove to be a "clinching argument" against the Deterrence State. "The clinching argument [is] that, 'even if a government could, somehow, ingeniously remove that built-in demand for murderousness from its nuclear personnel,' it could not, with the best equivocations in the world, ensure that *the rest of us*, including millions of the Bishops' pastoral charges, be effectively shielded from genocidal consent" (p. 76).

That statement, if true, is sufficient not only to fault any and all efforts to put nuclear weapons in a class by themselves as never intended to be used *against societies* while retaining such weapons for the sake of their deterrent effect in limiting the possible and actual use of nuclears to other targets. It would also fault any governmental resolve to place nuclears as such in a class by themselves as—all of them—weapons intended to be not used, while retaining them (in the possession of the nations or of some future world authority) for the sake of shared deterrence-during-the-war to avoid any full-scale use of *conventional* weapons by either side, for the sake of deterring war itself, or, for that matter, mutually to deflect international disputes into peaceful resolution through diplomatic channels. Finally, unless I am mistaken, it would fault as inherently and ineradicably immoral here and now those conditions which led Pope John XXIII to declare that "it is contrary to reason to hold that war is now a suitable way to restore rights which have been violated." "This conviction," he wrote, "owes its origin chiefly to the terrifying force of modern weapons. It arises from fear of the ghastly and catastrophic consequences of their use." [38] If effective nuclear deterrence cannot in any way be said to be moral, then none need fear unless some or a great many other people are implicated in genocidal consent; and if none need fear the destructive force of properly targeted nuclear weapons, then, to start wars to correct established injustices would no longer be in violation of political reason.

[38] *Pacem in terris*, Par. 127.

Again, Stein's argument if valid, reaches to the heart of deterrence itself, and not only to the deterrence-system we now have.

Still he is quite correct, there is a crucial moral issue in not leading people generally into gravely sinful consent and there is a need to shield them from genocidal intentions or commitments. In passing, Stein has provisionally allowed that in a proper deterrence system it may be possible to remove the requirement of murderousness from nuclear personnel. He conceded this in order to focus attention on the moral problem that would still remain in view of the inculcation of murderousness in the public mind if this is necessary to the system. This seems necessary *only* in the case of deterrence from intended-in ambiguity about how the weapons are intended to be used.

The beginning of an answer to this moral objection is to take seriously Theodore Weber's suggestion that the criteria governing the just use of weapons have primarily to do with "ordering the responsibilities of the office" (p. 71) held by the topmost decision-makers and (I would add) by all military personnel below the top level who yet are required to intend or not intend anything in order for the deterrence to be effective.

The just-war theory and the understanding of political community on which this was based assumed a hierarchical distribution of degrees of responsibility for official actions and for one's action as a citizen or as a soldier. Thus even in democratic societies, and in an age when the right of "conscientious objection" has come to the fore, the proper expression of this right is to say that a person may or should in conscience refuse military service when he clearly knows and judges he is in a position to know that the action he is commanded to do is unjust. A favored position is given to what Socrates called "the conscience of the laws" even when individual conscientious objection is granted its rights and claims to a higher obedience are admitted into a Christian theory of politics. Why is this so? Because otherwise political community would break apart into a congeries of individual conscientious opinions no one of which has any reason to concede any priority to any other. This is the meaning in saying that the criteria serve first of all as a means primarily of ordering the responsibilities of the *office* (that of the topmost magistrate and those of all the lesser magistrates as well).

This means that Weber's second possibility is not a simple alternative to the first interpretation, but one that has also always to be invoked while understanding it in the light and in the context of the first. "The criteria serve as a means . . . of deciding *whether* they should occupy their respective offices" (p. 71). But this is not a possible *primary* service of the criteria (as Weber says, at the dots above, it may be). Instead, the criteria governing justice in politics, in war, and in deterrence serve primarily as a means of ordering the responsibilities of the offices held by men everywhere in political community where they are emplaced or for ordering the roles in society they may seek to occupy. Then, secondarily and consequently, these criteria help men to decide whether they should occupy their respective offices, seek to change while occupying these offices, or if possible abandon them. In thus applying the criteria, men should conscientiously object (only, but definitely) when they know that "the conscience of the offices" is doing and ordering them to do something that is obviously unjust.

How should this understanding of a Christian's participation in the earthly City be applied to the moral issues raised by a citizen's complicity in deterrence? It seems to me clear that the private individual can in good conscience will what his government wills in the matter of deterrence from disproportionate combatant damage with its associated deterrence from disproportionate collateral death and destruction. Whoever disagrees with this disagrees that war could ever be a just instrument of justifiable national policy. He conscientiously opposes involvement in war itself, and so he conscientiously opposes being implicated in deterrence of war by justifiable war-means. The Christian pacifist may be right, and the just-war Christian may be wrong; but this is where the difference lies. By the criteria the pacifist uses he draws the line at another point and says that he cannot willingly occupy the office that his government, by basing itself on justice-in-politics criteria, has used in defining the responsibilities of a citizen. So he is a pacifistic conscientious objector, who says that he knows that his government did something obviously unjust in thus ordering the offices by criteria other than those he is impelled to obey.

Whoever uses just-war criteria, however, or the morality governing the political use of force, in determining whether to occupy his citizen's office would have reason to object to his government's ordering of the offices in terms of deterrence from disproportionate combatant and its unavoidable non-combatant damage *only* if he is soberly convinced that he knows that the use of weapons planned to meet any eventuality is actually disproportionate or that the threat is disproportionate *as a threat,* or is convinced that he knows better than the higher magistrates that the cause is unjust for which his nation stands, etc. These would be forms of "just-war conscientious objection."

The question of a citizen's complicity in what for him might be a real willingness and for his government only an apparent willingness to execute city-hostages only arises in the case of deterrence from ambiguity or cultivated uncertainty in regard to whether a nation's war-plans include direct attacks on cities as a contingency under some circumstances. If this element of deterrence is practiced, can a government avoid leading its people into gravely immoral motives? How in fact can it shield them from murderous thinking and from genocidal commitments out of hatred and mortal despair? This is a crucial question Stein brought up, and to which he insists an answer be given.

At this point, I would gladly complete the shift from minus-city-hostage-but-plus-deliberate-ambiguity deterrence to collateral-deterrence-plus-inherent-uncertainty-only, if I could forget the men in positions of political responsibility for all the order there is in the world and if I could reformulate the only question that is mine to answer: Have I, as a moralist, the right (if I could) to *require* this shift, this denial, of *them?* I have already said that the collateral damage and the irremovable uncertainties are a certainly moral deterrent, while the deterrence of which we are now speaking has only probable morality. The most basic reason for only hesitatingly or subjunctively reaching a conclusion justifying a deterrence based on studied ambiguity is that (as Lawler wrote) to be believable to an enemy *this* deterrent "must also be believable to the ordinary citizen of the threatening nation" (p. 89). The objection is that this will lead him to will it, or at least it may not be able to be managed so as to shield him from willingness here and now to be defended by some future, directly mass murderous deed. He may even demand that his government make itself willing to do this thing in which he sees his only protection. He may even out-race his government and demand to be assured that even if all he values is lost, the other side must have purely punitive (i.e. non-protective) retaliation inflicted upon it.

It is possible, however, to begin to unpack an average citizen's relation to his government's deterrence from ambiguous willingness so as not to leave him so indiscriminately black in his intentions as the objection supposes. I have only a few questions to raise in this connection, without asserting that the points I will make, which I believe are valid, add up to the entire removal of the objection.

The deterrent has to be "believable," as Lawler says, not only to an enemy government and its people but to the people of the deterring nation as well. But what exactly has to be believed? We should not assign more or anything other to the necessary intentionality of the people of the deterring nation than has to be believable to a potential enemy for this ingredient of deterrence to work. An enemy has only to believe that we *might* be willing to destroy cities; he has only not to know that we will not. He is deterred from the uncorrected ambiguity about our *possible* willingness.

Mixed with considerable doubt, this still remains a deterring possibility. The ordinary citizen of the deterring state need believe no more; and, anyway, believing this possibility is not the same as, on his part, willing it. The people of the deterring state, it would seem, are under no necessity of intending wickedness, nor need they be led by the government into it. They need only believe that their government might, as it sometimes says, be willing to go to city exchanges. They need only not know that the government will not. This is enough to sustain politically a government's refusal to make every effort to clarify its intentions. The people need only to allow there to be some ambiguity and a possible lack of congruence between their government's declaratory deterrence policy and a rational and politically purposive fight-the-war policy. This is far from genocidal consent.

Anyone can tell that the people of any major Deterrence State have a large amount of incredulity about what their government would actually do. A grave problem of politics in the nuclear age is precisely the alienation of the people from government, but this is *not* the moral problem Stein identifies as a peoples' being led into willful, intentional genocidal wickedness in support of a government's deterrence policy. The people notice, of course, that government leaders often say they have enough reserved strength to destroy an enemy's entire society, but they also hear these same leaders say that nuclear war would be monumental foolishness and to no political purpose any nation has in the world. Precisely the problem in managing deterrence this way is that it renders a people as ambiguous as the government is attempting to be, not that it inculcates murderousness in all their hearts.

When the deterrence from the uncertainty inherent in the weapons and inherent in the course of using modern weapons in an actual war was in question, that had to be written: deterrence from the apparent *possibility*. When now deterrence from intended-in ambiguity, or not-declared-out ambiguity, is in question, this has to be written: deterrence from a *possible* willingness. To say deterrence from a possible *willingness* would put too much stress on a government's necessary measure of *willingness*. It is not easy to see why deterrence from a merely *possible* willingness *need* inculcate an actual willingness or genocidal consent on the part of the people in order for this to be sustained in the mind of a potential enemy.

Why is it not possible, at least, for a member of the politically conscious part of the public to say to government leaders who are mainly responsible in military affairs for "ordering the offices": "Whatever are my policy-level disagreements with your policies, I only but definitely will conscientiously object to what you are doing on our behalf when I know that you are planning and actually intending an attack on an entire people and ordering my office so that I would be required also to intend or cooperate in a genocidal war or deterrence policy. Until then, I will and intend, not, it is true, what sometimes I hear you say, but that alone which should ever be willed by anyone or politically done in these matters." [39]

[39] I can fairly hear Lawler exclaiming: "irrelevant and impertinent casuistry," "monstrous cerebralization," and "utterly deracinated perverse academic abstraction" (*Continuum, op. cit.*) or "impressively convoluted latinity" and "tortuous olympian ex-

As for not shielding people from genocidal consent or leading them to consent to genocidal *commitments,* when I ask myself who is most responsible for this in our age I cannot answer "government leaders" and exculpate publicists and leaders of opinion of all sorts, editors, teachers, churchmen, moralists, etc., who often seek to save the world by inciting extremes of fear and extremes in moral condemnation that responsible leaders know better than to share or inculcate. It cannot be successfully denied, as I wrote, that "nuclear pacifism has corrupted enormous numbers of people who will not act according to its tenets. They become convinced that in the matter of deterrence a number of things are wicked which are not; hence, seeing no way of avoiding 'wickedness,' they set no limits to it" (p. 49 [see also p. 297 above]). This can be restated in terms of leading people to or not shielding them from genocidal consent. To teach people to make no distinction between the murderous and non-murderous intentions of governments in support of deterrence will in the end inculcate intentional genocidal consent in the hearts of many a person who can see no way of insuring peace, justice, and security without this indiscriminate emotion, even if the purpose of the moralist was to secure the opposite response of inculcating in them an entire breach with the Deterrence State and with all that murderousness on which alone, in his opinion, such a state can be based.

I must speak carefully here. A just-war theorist on the one hand and proponents of nuclear pacifism and of dismantling deterrence on the other hand are *both* concerned to discover and to determine the *objective responsibilities* of statesmanship in our age. They are not concerned, either of them, primarily about the *subjective guilt* that may be inculcated in someone who hears or reads them, who is convinced of the moral truth in the position set forth and yet finds himself unwilling to do it or unable to will what he sees to be the only right thing to do in the matter. Such a man is then implicated in consents he knows to be immoral.

This should not stop us, however, nor should these considerations be the moralist's chief concern. The church of Jesus Christ to which by grace I, at least, adhere is a company in which a moral theologian is only an ordinary Christian endeavoring to push out as far as he can the frontier-

---

egesis" (85, 88). Yet I think that the above expresses the warm and diversified truth about the average citizen's participation in deterrence. And lest any utopian who hails by a circuitous route from John Calvin affirms that I exhibit only a Lutheran "dualistic" view of church and state, I will cite Edmond Cahn's *The Predicament of Democratic Man* (New York: The Macmillan Co., 1961). This book contains a great deal of profound wisdom about cutting down to its right size a man's sense of guilty complicity in the actions of his government, while at the same time maintaining the appropriate responsibilities of democratic man.

meaning of the practice of a charitable and rational justice and to draw forth all the actions and abstentions that this requires (and so sometimes he must say "may" and "perhaps" at morally crucial points, without fear lest some "layman" resolve this opinion into practical *certainty*, and thus be led to do something that may in reality be objectively wrong). The ordinary Christian layman should also be a moral theologian to the measure that he can, and he should reduce his own remaining subjective incertitudes to the practical certainty required for his own responsible practice. We Christians all together will be altogether better witnesses to one another if each of us does his best to keep clear the range of his reasons and the various degrees of conviction with which he holds them; and if each himself remembers that no one can remove the venture and the risk from his Christian living.

I suppose that Stein fears that I may lead, without good reason, people into complicity in *objectively irresponsible* action, even as I fear that he may lead them without sufficient cause into subjective genocidal guilt—if anybody paid any attention to these writings and proposed to form his conscience or his action by them. This, it must be said, is, on a parity, the risk in writing anything on a significant moral subject. Yet, there is perhaps this slight difference: that, in debate which aims at discovering the truth of the matter, Stein brought up genocidal consent on the part of the people generally as a "clinching argument" against the possibility of a responsible conduct of deterrence by any government.

Stein and I both may have reason to long sometimes to retire from our semi-public forum where so much depends on the consents and actions of people that we (barely) might provoke. There might be some protection from the risks of our profession to be found in the privacy of the confessional. There, priests are accustomed, and not without reason, to allow a certain amount of ambiguity to remain in the advice they give. They sometimes withhold the full moral truth they know. Where the pastoral concern for souls is the chief concern, it may be necessary to shield the penitent from the full measure of subjective guilt and deadly consents that might be his, and in which the priest would have some complicity, if the full measure of the moral truth is communicated to him at once. Instead, a little ambiguity is permitted in order to bring him along a course of education to know, to will, and to do only that which is truly right in Christ's service to all mankind.

Such a course is not open to Stein or to me. The convictions we have won by grace or reason or graceful reason have to be uttered, no matter what the risks in indirect, unintended consequences. I would be the first to contend that priests and ministers are the true moral educators of men in a culture that has not lost its religious bearings. A culture that has lost its religious bearings, however, is one that has also lost the substance of its morality. A moralist may have a bit more to do, until the Lord sends out again his Word over the waters. He might yet have some influence upon the moral ethos out of which the statesman comes to his task of "ordering the offices."

PART FOUR

The Second Vatican Council
and
A Just-War Theory of Statecraft

CHAPTER 16

The Vatican Council
on Modern War*

The Pastoral Constitution on "The Church in the Modern World" adopted by Vatican Council II and proclaimed by Pope Paul VI in Council on December 8, 1965, deserves the admiration of non-Catholics the world over. This is the longest, it may be the greatest, achievement of the Council. Certainly the several parts of this Constitution are uneven. On the matter of religious liberty, there was a background of decades of serious debate among Roman Catholics from which the Council drew its wisdom. In contrast, the discussion of Christian marriage as this relates to the question of contraception can scarcely be said to have begun among Catholics. This part of the schema is correspondingly weak—except that it ought to be said that the traditional formulations, including those of Pius XI, represent a precipitate of the reflection and the insights of Christians over centuries on marriage and sex ethics which is often not matched by the *ad hoc* pronouncements of non-Catholics having in view the solution of world problems.

In contrast to both religious liberty and marriage and the family, the Council's statement on the morality of modern warfare had to be drafted without the benefit of any considerable consideration of this problem by the Church's moral theologians in the modern period. The Council's attempt to draw lines not previously articulated or refined in long

* First appeared in *Theological Studies*, Vol. 27, No. 2 (June 1966); and in *Theology Today*, Vol. XXIII, No. 2 (July 1966).

debate seemed not apt to produce a helpful or a theologically sound result. In addition, news reports emanating from Rome during the weeks before the statement on war was brought up for final consideration seemed to indicate that the test was going to be how much the fathers of the Council would condemn in the specific advice they ventured to give the world's statesmen.

Now that the Constitution has been issued, there is some value in just reading it, listening to what it straightforwardly says, and thinking about the meaning of it without benefit of the Latin or a historical account of each paragraph, draft, or amendment to throw light upon the text.[1]

My thesis can be stated in advance. It is that the many virtues of the Council's statement on modern war and the self-imposed limits upon what was said spring from the effort that was made to speak not only to the whole church but *for* the whole church, not only for the whole church but *to* the entire church wherever its sons are, and not only to men of good will everywhere but to them *in the name of the whole church*. Nothing could be better calculated to induce responsibility in the utterances of a church council than this self-understanding of what it is doing, nor more apt to eliminate utterances and resolutions to which Christianity as such cannot be committed. Catholics believe, of course, that this is a fine constitution because the bishops of the whole world were speaking. *That* would be impossible for other church councils and assemblies to emulate. But it is not impossible for all Christians, when they seek to speak some healing word to the world and to the whole church, to undertake to say only what can be said for the whole church and on the basis of Christian truth. Even so, church councils may err; but they will certainly err—in a triumphalist direction—if they do not try to do this.

So did the Second Vatican Council, "having probed more profoundly into the mystery of the church" and other intramural matters, turn to address itself "without hesitation, not only to the sons of the church and to all who invoke the name of Christ, but to the whole of humanity." The "holy synod" could speak without hesitation because it did not undertake to say everything that humanity or even all the sons of the church need to hear in this or in any hour, but only what can and may and must be said on the basis of moral values and spiritual truth the church as such is competent to know something about. For this reason, the entire Constitution is informed by an articulate and articulated Christian social theory, a doctrine of man, human rights, etc.; this is not limited to an opening paragraph or so, which is then followed by the

---

[1] We shall use the translation contained in *The Documents of Vatican II*, edited by Walter M. Abbott, S.J., and Joseph Gallagher (New York: Guild, America, and Association Presses, 1966), pp. 199–308.

maximum specific advice about the solution of urgent problems. Not even the urgency of the problem of modern war tempted the Council to succumb to its own conjectures about specific policies. The limit upon its recommendations and condemnations came not from compromising this view with that (though this, of course, went on), but from remembering all the sons of the church and men everywhere in the political and military sectors, in the armed forces of the nations, in huts of poverty because there are arms, in prison for conscientious objection, secretly troubled or not enough troubled in conscience. Above all, the impulse and the limit came from endeavoring to say as fully and adequately as possible what can and may and must be said in Christ's name and only what can possibly be thus said by the whole church to all who bear and do not bear His name.

It is not without significance that Part 2 of the Constitution, addressed to "Some Problems of Special Urgency," comprises only forty-eight numbered paragraphs. This is preceded by forty-five paragraphs setting forth the church's understanding of the dignity of the human person, the common good, the norms applicable to political community, etc., as these are to be seen in the light of Christ. Even the second part, dealing with urgent contemporary problems, is interlaced with paragraphs bearing titles like "Some Principles for the Proper Development of Culture." Some *principles!* Under this heading falls also everything the Council permitted itself or was impelled to say on modern war. Call the premises of Christian utterance upon social and political questions "principles" or by some other term, there must be ground on which *the church* makes these utterances and not some other "lesser corporation" within or throughout the modern nations. "It is highly important," the Council reminded itself, "that [there be] . . . a clear distinction between what a Christian conscience leads them to do in their own name as citizens, whether as individuals or in association, and what they do in the name of the Church in union with her shepherds." It is also not without significance that, immediately preceding the paragraphs on war, the church's claim to freedom "to teach her social doctrine" is expressed in terms of her right "to pass moral judgments even on matters touching the political order, whenever basic personal rights or the salvation of souls make such judgments necessary." If these warrants seem too individualistic, they should be corrected by everything John XXIII and the Vatican Council say about "social justice and social charity." All these are the Christian warrants, constantly in mind as the council fathers addressed themselves to urgent world problems. If these grounds upon which conciliar judgments are made is kept clear, if churchmen in that capacity try always to speak for the whole church, this will ordinarily be a quite sufficient self-denying ordinance, and a better one than compromise for dealing with partisan proposals. In any case, they are the only warrants we have, even if not infallible, and ones too rarely used in Catholic and Protestant assemblies that have a less awesome sense of history than prevailed at Vatican II.

II

The statement on the morality of war attains to three successive climactic utterances around which the whole and all its lesser statements can be organized. In the first of these the fathers of the Council use words that gather to themselves the maximum *moral* authority. This comes after a number of paragraphs that summarize the fact-situation and contain only a few ethical counsels. Then it is written:

> With these truths in mind, this most holy Synod makes its own the condemnations of total war already pronounced by recent Popes, and issues the following declaration:

> Any act of war aimed indiscriminately at the destruction of entire cities or of extensive areas along with their population is a crime against God and man himself. It merits unequivocal and unhesitating condemnation.

This declaration had been cited in garbled accounts from Rome as the Council's condemnation of any and all forms of nuclear war or of any use of nuclears in war.[2] It is, of course, no such thing. It is far less than that as a policy statement, far more than that as a statement of principle.

In earlier paragraphs the Council adverted to the pontiffs' provisional justification of wars of defense, but in such a way as to anticipate its own reassertion of the moral immunity of non-combatants from direct attack in any war. "War has not been rooted out of human affairs," it said; and thereupon it asserted the only sound thing that can be said about the right to war: "As long as . . . there is no competent and suf-

---

[2] A news dispatch from Rome, Dec. 7, published in *The New York Times*, Dec. 8, 1965, p. 23, without actually misquoting the text of the schema at this point, nevertheless gerrymandered its sense and mixed together this proscription of indiscriminate conduct in war with some of the preceding sentences describing factually what *can* be done with modern weapons. The result was that unthinking readers had some reason to suppose the Council was about to "condemn nuclear weapons," their use or possession. The dispatch said that the schema under consideration "calls the use of nuclear weapons of mass destruction 'a crime against God and man himself.' " A fair reading of the full text cannot support the conclusion that the Council condemns outright any and all use or any and all possession of "scientific" weapons. An unbiased reading will also, I judge, see that the words "aimed indiscriminately" are simply ordinary language for what is expressed in the technical language of moral theology or ethics as "non-combatant immunity from deliberate, direct attack."

ficiently powerful authority at the international level, governments cannot be denied the right to legitimate defense once every means of peaceful settlement has been exhausted." Then, calling attention to the difference between "the just defense of the people" and "the subjugation of other nations," the Council moves to higher ground than the aggressor-defender distinction. It does this in two parallel statements that follow immediately upon its reference to "just defense" and "the subjugation of other nations." These statements are: "Nor does the possession of war potential make every military or political use of it lawful.[3] Neither does the mere fact that war has unhappily begun mean that all is fair between the warring parties." What is never fair it later declares in terms of the principle of discrimination in all justifiable acts of war. Here we have a plain movement from emphasis upon the judgment that the use of scientific weapons may be censured because while resorted to in defense they actually in the objective order amount to the subjugation of other nations (aggression), over to emphasis upon the judgment that a use of scientific weapons may be censured because it violates the moral immunity of civil life from direct attack. The latter test becomes uppermost.

The reference to "recent popes" immediately preceding the Council's declaration prohibiting indiscriminate acts of war is more than a little misleading. Recent popes have been more largely concerned to draw the distinction between defense and aggression and to deny that aggressive war can possibly be just, than they have been concerned to clarify the main ground on which total war in all its forms is to be condemned. It is the special virtue of the Council's statement that it reasserts the principle distinguishing between discriminating and indiscriminate actions in the conduct of war.

For some recent papal statements, in contrast, the use of modern weapons in war was apt to prove disproportionate and thus in effect to shift a war begun in defense on to the "attack" (because of its inordinate destructiveness). In his Christmas message of 1944, Pope Pius XII declared: "The theory of war as an apt and proportionate means of solving international conflicts is now out of date"; and at Christmas, 1948, he condemned "aggressive" war as "a sin, an offense, and an outrage." Falling under this aggressor-defender distinction, his condemnation of modern

[3] "Nec potentia bellica omnem eiusdem militarem vel politicum usum legitimum facit." The first of these two sentences was omitted from the translation "endorsed" by the bishops and published in *The New York Times*, Dec. 8, 1965. Moreover, the words "by the same token" which were then inserted into the second sentence by the translator, and have no warrant in the Latin, left the unfortunate impression that what's "fair between the warring parties" rests upon the same ground as the distinction between "just defense" and "the subjugation of other nations." This translation, which is the one still circulated in pamphlet form by the National Catholic Welfare Conference, has been improved in the Guild, America, Association Presses edition which we are using.

total war as "a crime worthy of the most severe national and international sanctions" contained, therefore, the important reservation: unless this could clearly be in self-defense. Pope John XXIII's condemnation of modern war is also in terms of the test of proportionately greater evil; and, within this, he too proscribes aggressive war: "Thus, in an age such as ours which prides itself on its atomic energy, it is contrary to reason to hold that war is now a suitable way to restore rights which have been violated" (*Pacem in terris*). Thus John XXIII no less than Pius XII left open the possibility that war might well be an instrument for repelling an injustice that is in course of being perpetrated but is not yet accomplished. This would be defensive war; and concerning this the recent pontiffs seem mainly to have had in mind the warning that because of the destructiveness of modern weapons a defensive war is apt, objectively, to amount to the same as the aggressive total subjugation of an enemy people. The Council repeats all that had been said against war fought aggressively to restore rights, and the judgments upon modern war in general that arise from an application of the test of proportion. Then it resoundingly reasserts an altogether different criterion: the test of discrimination.

The force of modern papal statements before John XXIII was, in rejecting the justice of aggressive wars to redress established wrongs, to affirm that the use of modern scientific weapons could not be just unless this was possibly defensive. The good Pope John could not bring himself to say anything expressly about this possibly permissible use, even while he repeated his predecessors' condemnation of aggressive war in the course of directing attention to the need for world public authorities. Now the force of the Council's elevation of the principle of discrimination (or the moral immunity of non-combatants from direct attack) into a prominence not heretofore accorded it by recent pronouncements of the magisterium is to say quite clearly that not even defensive use of the newer scientific weapons can be approved unless this could possibly be discriminating in the sense explained. In short, the justice even of defensive war is now submitted also to the test of discrimination. Before, a probable prohibition of the use of massive weapons was based on the spectre of disproportionately too great evil which would violate the limits of defensiveness. Thus the chief warning was against the danger that, once begun in defense, a war may pass to the subjugation of another nation because of its excessive destructiveness. Now the chief concern is lest, once a war is begun in defense, we may suppose there is no further test of justice in the conduct of military actions between the warring parties.[4] This further test is the principle of discrimination.

[4] One effort of Philip M. Hannan, Archbishop of New Orleans, at the Council was almost bound to fail, namely, his apparent effort to eliminate the proscription of aggressive war altogether from the mind of the Council and have it declare wars to

III

The Council's resounding declaration of the principle prohibiting direct attack upon civilian life as such is preceded also by sober references to what *can* now be done in war. "The horror and perversity of war is immensely magnified by the addition of scientific weapons." We may pause to reflect upon the use of this strange expression "scientific weapons" in a statement that, according to the press reports, was supposed to be on *nuclear* war. Did the Council fathers deliberately choose to speak of "scientific" and not of "nuclear" weapons because of what everyone knows the great powers are capable of doing with other *new* scientific weapons in their arsenals besides nuclears? Or to stress that conventional explosives can also be used indiscriminately, as in World War II *before* Hiroshima? In any case, the effect is to enlarge our judgment concerning the morality of war's conduct by not limiting the governing principle in its declaration to a particular weapons-system.

". . . Acts of war involving these [scientific] weapons *can*," the Council points out as a matter of fact, "inflict massive and indiscriminate destruction, far exceeding the bounds of legitimate defense" [and, we may add, violating all that is "fair" between warring parties even if defense is legitimately still in view]. "Indeed," the statement goes on, "*if* the kind of instruments which can now be found in the armories of the great nations *were to be employed to their fullest,* an almost total and altogether reciprocal slaughter of each side by the other would follow . . . ." That too is a finding of present facts that cannot be denied.

These factual considerations "compel us to undertake an evaluation of war with an entirely new attitude." This turns out to be a very old principle, indeed, governing the political use of force; but the new attitude is that "men of our time must realize that they will have to give a somber reckoning for their deeds of war" in terms of the moral principle the Council has the spiritual authority to declare. Then it is that

---

redress wrongs again to be licit. This went too much against the statements of recent pontiffs. There is, of course, no reason in principle why non-combatant immunity and proportion may not be said to be the norms governing the political use of violence, while backing further away from absolutizing the aggressor-defender distinction (which is the misshapen relic of the just-war doctrine that modern man is capable of grasping). In fact, there is need for moralists and church councils to make it clear that, unless and until there is a world public authority with interventionary threat-removing authority (such as the United Nations' Charter said the Security Council should exercise through the unanimity of the great powers), it will sometimes be just for a nation to initiate a use of force against threats to its peace and to world order. The only way to avoid this doctrinal conclusion and shift would be to pack political and military initiative into an extensible notion of "defense."

the statement moves from these references to actual and hypothetical factual conditions, to deliver its declaration *in moral terms* upon the *moral* discrimination to be made in any political or military decision in face of these existing capabilities and ominous possibilities.

The cardinal point in the declaration is not a condemnation of any use of nuclears in war. It is rather a call to the citizens and magistrates of all the nations to clarify their consciences in terms of the basic principle governing the use of these or any other "scientific" weapon.

The present writer confesses that he may be inordinately gratified to find that the Vatican Council's statement is so decisively controlled by the principle of discrimination. This test has now been given far greater prominence than it had in any of the statements of recent pontiffs. For some time now, if one had believed the Catholic "liberals" on this question (who are not so much "just-war pacifists" as they often are pacifists without benefit of the just-war principles), it seemed more likely that the Roman Catholic Church would renounce adherence to this principle of discrimination in its eagerness to condemn nuclear war as such (because it is necessarily disproportionate, or because objectively defense by nuclears would be a case of "immaculate aggression," or for any other reason). That would have left the present writer exposed on his other flank! Yet I do not think my professional and personal concern for this outcome alters the fact that, on a plain reading of its statement, the Council has signally reaffirmed the moral immunity of non-combatants from direct attack, and left it for citizens and statesmen to determine the prudent application of this principle in the specific decisions that this requires.

The paragraph that follows, as well as those that approach, this climactic utterance enforce this interpretation of the Council's meaning. Measured by this principle, "the unique hazard of modern warfare" consists in the fact that "it provides those who possess modern scientific weapons with *a kind of occasion*[5] for perpetrating just such abominations," i.e., acts of war aimed indiscriminately at the destruction of entire cities, which the Council fathers had just condemned unequivocally and unhesitatingly. Now, the expression "a kind of occasion" is worth pausing over.[6] The "hazard" in the nature of modern weapons is an "occasion," not a compulsion; "a kind of occasion" that may lead to immoral acts of war, not the necessity of this eventuality. The Council fathers recognize and urgently warn, it is true, that through an "inexorable chain of events [which we call "escalation"], it [i.e., modern warfare] can urge men on to the most atrocious decisions." Still, this is the unique *hazard* of modern war, not a necessity that this be so. Having stated the moral

[5] *"Quasi occasionen"* (". . . furnishes, as it were, an occasion . . .").

[6] It can be compared in its cruciality to the expression, a "peace of a sort," which alone the Council concedes to be the virtue of the deterrent possession of these scientific weapons.

terms in which the atrocity of an "atrocious decision" is to be measured, the Council does not entrap itself in false findings of fact that presume that modern war has put human freedom out of control. In fact, the opposite is the premise of this very warning about "inexorable" chains of events: *"That such in fact may never happen* in the future, the bishops of the whole world, in unity assembled, beg all men, especially government officials and military leaders, to give unremitting thought to the awesome responsibility which is theirs before God and the entire human race."

IV

The second crucial utterance is the treatment the Council gives to the fact and to the morality of deterrence. "To be sure," these weapons are not amassed solely for use, but for deterrence. Then follows a statement of plain fact, namely, that "this accumulation of arms . . . also serves, in a way heretofore unknown, as a deterrent to possible enemy attack," and they may be considered a part of "the defensive strength of any nation." In the next statement of fact, however, the Council's judgment upon deterrence begins to emerge in the (properly?) disparaging words chosen to express the sort of peace deterrence insures: "Many regard this state of affairs as the most effective way by which *peace of a sort (pax quaedam)* can be maintained between nations at the present time."

The Council is not concerned to assay these facts as such. It allows them to stand for what they are, or for what responsible people in the political and military sector may judge them to be. Across words that concede the possible necessity and value (such as it is) of deterrence (*"Whatever be* the case with this method of deterrence . . .") and across words that anyway put deterrence in its place ("peace of a sort"), the Council is concerned rather to direct sons of the church and mankind in general to the work of political construction needed to alter fundamentally these conditions. This is the third great pillar of this statement on warfare, to which we will come in a moment.

Here it needs to be pointed out that the Council says nothing that removes the morality from deterrence, or removes responsibility for this from among possible Christian vocations. It is true that the peace that deterrence assures is not "the peace that passes understanding." It is not even a very good worldly peace; it is only a peace of sorts. The Council does not shirk its responsibility for calling attention to the fact that, in terms of worldly peace, deterrence is "not a safe way to preserve a steady peace. Nor is the so-called balance resulting from this race a sure and authentic peace."

Still nothing in all this says that responsible decision and action in regard to deterrence falls below the floor of the *morally permissible*. In this regard, Protestants need to take care how we read Roman Catholic pronouncements, for we are accustomed to think that there is one Christian thing to be done; and that once the positive task of political construction has been identified, all Christians should be wholly engaged in this only. Such, however, is not the Catholic outlook, which rather preserves the importance of determining both what is permitted and what is or would be better to be done.

Read with this background in mind, there is no reason for separating what is said here about the justification of deterrence in terms of a "peace of a sort" from an earlier, more seemingly positive statement: "Those who are pledged to the service of their country as members of its armed forces should regard themselves as agents of security and freedom on behalf of their people. As long as they fulfil this role properly, they are making a genuine contribution to the establishment of peace."

The expression "peace of a sort," which deterrence insures, was well chosen, in the argument of this statement and in the dynamics of its composition at this point, to bend even this lower good toward the better that has yet to be done. Not even the counterproductivity of deterrence, therefore, which the Council goes on to stress, is capable of removing the actual justifiedness from deterrence that has already been stated in this low key. For surely it has to be granted that "disagreements between nations are not really and radically healed" by deterrence, however effective; these disagreements may actually be exacerbated whilst peace of a sort is maintained. Moreover, "the causes of war threaten to grow gradually stronger" in that "extravagant sums are being spent" on deterring war by scientific weapons, and not on relieving worldwide poverty and starvation. "Therefore, it must be said again: the arms race is an utterly treacherous trap for humanity, and one which injures the poor to an intolerable degree. It is much to be feared that if this race persists, it will eventually spawn all the lethal ruin whose path it is now making ready."

I do not see how the most "just-war" Christian imaginable, or a firm believer in the justice of deterrence, can possibly disagree with these statements. He must concede and indeed insist upon their truth, especially in the light of the *sole* realistic alternative to continuing to preserve an unsteady peace by partially contradictory means to which the realistic contours of this analysis of deterrence is designed in the end to compel our attention.

V

When the Council fathers come at last to a discussion of this, the third and last principal point they have to make, it is across ominous words of thanksgiving: "Warned by the calamities which the human race has made possible, let us make use of the interlude granted us from above and in which we rejoice." It takes nothing from the theological ultimacy of that statement to remember that any good Catholic believes that God in His providence works through "secondary causes," and to apply those words about "the interlude granted us from above" also to the over-arching edifice of deterrence by which an unsteady peace is maintained in our time. However merely permissible the just works of deterrence may be, sons of the church and other men of good will working in the military and political sectors are surely making a genuine contribution of sorts to the establishment of peace and the security and freedoms of peoples. They are, in fact, also doing the will of God, who in His ruling and overruling providence grants us this interlude from above. This is true even if—especially if—the church as mother and teacher of men has truly caught a glimpse of the dilemma they are in because the instruments of this "peace of a sort" may also be "a kind of occasion" for abominations. A Protestant, at least, should find nothing unfamiliar in this statement of the paradoxical nature of Christian service on the frontiers of military and political responsibility. Reinhold Niebuhr is supposed to have taught this generation (who are liberally on the way to forgetting it) that "to serve peace, we must threaten war without blinking the fact that the threat may be a factor in precipitating war." [7] Nothing can remove the potential and actual counterproductivity of preserving peace by deterrent threats to use instruments of war. Therefore, it seems to me that the Council's analysis of deterrence and its minimal morality is quite accurate. It might have made clear that the preservation of an unsteady peace should be by the deterrent threat of not indiscriminate acts of war; but even so, its somber view of the nature of deterrence would have needed no change.

It was, of course, on the matter of deterrence that most of the behind-the-scenes political maneuvering went on at the Council. An account of this will doubtless read like an exercise in the arts of parliamentary compromise, of amendments and counteramendments, of paragraphs won or lost. If the Holy Spirit did not speak infallibly through these seem-

---

[7] "From Progress to Perplexity," in *The Search for America*, ed. Huston Smith (Englewood Cliffs, N.J., 1959), p. 144. The threat of war, of course, also serves the pedagogical purpose of moderating the policies of governments.

ingly alien human actions and counteractions, I believe that the whole of the church here represented found its voice, and that we are fortunate that no one segment or position in the church was able to speak through council to the whole church and to mankind its necessarily limited opinion.

Some wanted an unqualified endorsement, in today's dangerous world, of the possession of nuclear weapons. These would, while deploring the origins of the present world situation, have said that in concrete fact the possession of weapons for deterrence may be viewed as "the last road to peace now remaining in the world." A paragraph to this effect in the original draft was eliminated, because it would have prevented the Council from pointing to a better road to peace that ought never to be regarded as closed. The victors in this seemed to be those who felt that if the Council could not condemn the possession of nuclear weapons, it ought not at any rate to approve them expressly; it should refrain from sanctioning them. But neither did this voice of part of the church become the voice of the whole church to all of its sons. The result was the "peace of a sort" statement we have analyzed. Mere compromise? I think not. Instead, a reasonable whole of the Catholic Church speaking the approximate truth for the whole church to itself and to the world.

One effort that failed would, if successful, have rendered the statement substantively a less valid and realistic account of deterrence. This was the effort of eleven prelates (of whom only five were from the United States), inspired by Philip M. Hannan, Archbishop of New Orleans, to remove the ambiguity from the justification offered for deterrence. If Robert C. Doty correctly reported the viewpoint of this group of bishops, they understood the schema to say that the mounting stocks of nuclear weapons aggravate *rather than* lessen the danger of war.[8] They wanted the Council to say forthrightly that deterrence lessens the danger of war. Doubtless, others wanted the Council to say that the possession of nuclear weapons only aggravates. The fact is that the statement adopted by the Council does not say that possession of these scientific weapons aggravates *rather than* lessens the dangers of war. It says rather that deterrence lessens *and* aggravates, aggravates *and* lessens, the dangers of war. Compromise? I think not. Instead, an approximately true statement of the situation arrived at by the Council fathers when they sought to speak for the whole church. The Council might have said that when deterrence lessens the danger of war at one level, it aggravates war's causes at another; that the deterrence of nuclear war puts something into the making of revolutionary wars or wars of insurgency (or, at least, takes something from curing the causes of these wars). But the

[8] *The New York Times,* Nov. 17 and Dec. 5, 1965.

Council ought not to have said that deterrence prevents war, no ambiguity about it, no counterproductive tendencies within it.

To the weightier matters of the laws of present-day political responsibility we must now turn.

VI

The interlude granted us from above is rightly to be ransomed by finding means of "resolving our disputes in a manner more worthy of man." "It is our clear duty," the Council states, "to strain every muscle as we work for the time when all war can be completely outlawed by international consent."

But the Council fathers apparently believe that the new order of a "sure and authentic peace" replacing the present one will not rest on consent alone, or the will to peace by itself, or a mere determination of the will of statesmen to resolve disputes in a manner more worthy of men.

There must be a real political order which, while it can be brought into existence without conquest or tyranny only by the manifold works of international consent and political construction, still cannot then be broken by mere disconsent. It will be a world order of enforceable law and justice. "This goal undoubtedly requires," the statement reads, "the establishment of some universal public authority acknowledged as such by all, and endowed with effective power to safeguard, on the behalf of all, security, regard for justice, and respect for rights." Thus, the Vatican Council makes it clearer even than *Pacem in terris* that a *single* world political authority is needed ever to change this peace of a sort into a steady peace in the world. In expressions drawn from the language and the intent of the original Charter of the United Nations (whose realism has been rendered more nugatory by subsequent developments in U.N. practice), we may attribute to the Council fathers the belief that only a universal public authority with radical and justly used decision-making capabilities, interpositional peace-keeping and interventionary threat-removing powers can safeguard security, justice, and rights on the behalf of all; and that only the achievement of just world government will remove from among the burdens and responsibilities of the leaders of the nations the right and the duty to maintain a very unsteady peace. Until then, it will remain *among* the duties of statesmanship (though, of course, not its only responsibility) sometimes to resort to war on behalf of a juster order and a relatively more secure peace. This can be done, of course, only by the costly instrumentalities available which of themselves partially defeat these ends, by scientific weapons designed and used (or used in their deterrent non-use) by mortal men who are not culpable for doing the lesser permitted good they can do, and by means that (unless extreme care is taken in the exercise of man's freedom to control his political action or unless we can move the world political system out of this "meanwhile") hazard or may occasion the actual happening of abominations.

The Council's hopeful vision is not left in prospect only. ". . , *Before* this hoped-for authority can be set up," the Council declares, "the highest existing international centers must devote themselves vigorously to the pursuit of better means for obtaining common security." This word—some Protestants might call it a "middle axiom" between the ultimate ideal and the present actuality—is addressed to sons of the church and to all men who are at work at the highest existing centers of political power in "Europe," the Organization of American States, the Organization of African Unity, etc., and at the United Nations itself. The call to them is *not* simply that they ought always to negotiate so that negotiations may never fail. It is rather that they should put their minds to perfecting world and regional political institutions at every level so that the structural defects shall be removed, that presently render it impossible with the best will in the world for the leaders of the nations to insure a steady peace and a just security. The road to any better peace than the peace of sorts that deterrence partially insures requires a manifold work of political intelligence to make it possible to will and to do the works of peace in the future without self-contradictory resorts to international conflict or to costly and dangerous, yet not necessarily immoral, deterrence-systems. Radical world political reconstruction is a rational requirement in the nuclear age. This is not optional, but mandated.

When now we consider the entire thrust of the Vatican Council's statement on war, it is relevant to ask of all who desire to form their consciences by this declaration, Who most falls under its judgment? This is no longer Luther's question, Can a soldier also be saved? Or can a crisis-manager who wields deterrence also be saved? The central question behind which the Council seems to have placed the full weight of the spiritual authority accorded it by any who do would be the question, Can anyone, citizen or political leader, who believes not and labors not for the radical political reconstruction of the nation-state system, can he also be saved?

To take an illustration, what are we to say of all the sons of the church, or what ought they to say, who in any measure shape the public opinion and policies of those Central and South American countries (notably Mexico) who adamantly opposed strengthening the collective decision-making and interventionary military capabilities of the Organization of American States at the recent meeting in Rio de Janeiro? The principle of non-intervention is precisely not a principle of world or regional order. It is only a reflection of the asserted impermeability of every member of the nation-state system (which is only a state of war, defining war as a perpetual inclination thereto). This supports no sort of peace at all, but only the structural defects which are bound to make peace impossible. When, therefore, Secretary of State Rusk told the eighteen Latin-American delegations that "we ought to be prepared to move fast and effectively and, if possible, together when a dangerous situation arises in the hemisphere," [9] he by the not so subtle suggestion behind the words "if possible" pointed to the need, in the absence of better means, for there to be from somewhere some threat-removing capabilities in and among the governments of men in this area. He was only but definitely suggesting the need to maintain a peace of a sort in the absence of the instrumentalities of a steadier peace (among which is *not* the principle of non-intervention). If this regional organization or if the world in general is not ready for or capable of organizing new public authorities, without conquest or tyranny but by consent, that can and will "safeguard, on the behalf of all, security, regard for justice, and respect for rights," then the crisis-manager wielding deterrence and soldiers regarding themselves "as the agents of the security and freedom of peoples" are left alone to discharge their responsibilities, in the last resort, for a sort of peace. And what are we to say of all the liberal sons of the church and men of good will in the United States who regard "taking it to the United Nations," as this organization is now constituted, as always the sufficient and only thing to do, and always to be praised because this is a way to achieve reconciliation among the nations, a way to achieve peace without government or without the enforcement of a collective will upon the recalcitrant wills of any member, and a way by which they can be "involved" in all the world's problems without being tragically, i.e., militarily, involved in them? In all this it is quite clear, if the Council is correct, who of all these parties are brought before the seat of judgment in today's world and most condemned.

VII

The Council's statement on war is significant also for its inclusion of a reference to conscientious objection to military service. This is notably not set forth as a "right" as such, but instead is located in the midst of a discussion of "agreements aimed at making military activity

[9] *The New York Times*, Nov. 23, 1965.

and its consequences less inhumane." "Moreover," the Council asserts, "it seems right that laws make humane provisions for the case of those who for reasons of conscience refuse to bear arms, provided however that they accept some other form of service to the human community." The view here seems to be that the defense needs of a nation (and the corresponding duty to bear arms) can and should be administered in such a way that this does not require too burdensome enforcement upon those who have conscientious scruple against such service. As men and governments are bound to do everything possible to effect improvements in the frightfulness of war, so they should seek to hold in check the punishment of conscientious objectors or the enforcement of military service upon them; and out of feelings of common humanity such persons should be granted alternate service.

This will not be acknowledged to be an adequate analysis of the "right" of conscientious objection by a number of other Christian churches. By the same token, the latter often have not articulated an adequate understanding of public authority and its conscience in relation to that of the individual citizen. Perhaps these have something to learn from the Roman Catholic comprehension of the meaning of and need for authority in any community. "If the political community is not to be torn to pieces as each man follows his own viewpoint," the Council remarked earlier in this chapter on the life of the political community, "authority is needed. This authority must dispose the energies of the whole citizenry toward the common good . . . , [acting above all] as a moral force which depends on freedom and the conscientious discharge of the burdens of any office which has been undertaken." Only where there is political authority and among citizens an acknowledgment of political authority can there be primary political community among men. And the Council seems to be saying that where this is the case, it ought to be possible for the government directing the energies of all toward the common good partially to humanize the effects of war by granting alternate national service to conscientious objectors.

In any case, the fathers of the Council regard the juridical order to be a moral order, and they state that when authority is so exercised, "citizens are conscience-bound to obey." Yet it is in the midst of expressing the primacy and moral substance of the political order and its legitimate authority that the Council comes closest to formulating a "right" of conscientious objection. This is notably in a context that first states the sense in which even an illegitimate public authority should still be obeyed: ". . . Where public authority oversteps its competence and oppresses the people, these people should nevertheless obey to the extent that the objective common good demands." Then the Council declares: "Still it is lawful for them to defend their own rights and those of their fellow citizens against any abuse of this authority, provided that in so doing they observe the limits imposed by natural law and the gospel."

Since it is evident that the Council fathers regard military service still to be a moral act, falling among those things that may be objectively required for the common good, it is also evident that the statement about conscientious objectors remains a statement about the humanization of war's effects to be arranged and granted by governments. In this light, the citizen's rights against a political authority are a corollary of his general duty to disobey any civil authority that oversteps the limits drawn by natural law and commands him to do something contrary to the gospel. It is exceedingly doubtful that the Council meant to suggest that military service in general falls outside these limits, or that objection to such service in general could be a duty, or that, where granted, conscientious-objector status or alternate service is anything more than one more element in humanizing war itself and removing another of its many untoward effects upon men.

Still, this tradition in the Christian understanding of political community and of a citizen's political responsibility needs to give more thought to the question of "just-war conscientious objection," if ever this talk about just civil disobedience and the limits drawn by natural law and the gospel is to be reduced to action or to become an acknowledged form of citizen responsibility. By the same token, those Protestant communions in which today there is a good deal of sound discussion of the need for the government to exempt from military service young men who have conscientious objection to a particular war only (which would be "just-war objection") could not then shirk their responsibility for the positive instruction and formation of consciences in terms of a proper understanding of political obligation contained in the just-war principles. This doctrine is scarcely understood in the legalist-pacifist version of justice in war that is today all too widely received even among Roman Catholics. No nation can grant draft exemption to conscientious objectors to particular wars if it is widely believed among the people that the tests of justice in war are mainly ways of securing peace by discrediting one by one all wars. They are rather directives addressed to statesmen and citizens concerning how within morally tolerable limits they can and should protect and secure the relatively juster cause by resort, if need be, to a political use of armed force.

There is not space here to give further consideration to this important subject.

VIII

The Council fathers know, of course, that not even world government is going to insure peace—not at least the peace the Council has in mind. It is not only structural defects in the world political system that have to be corrected. The *causes* of war have also to be uprooted. Among these causes are poverty, economic inequalities, population pressure, etc. But the Council's statement probes to even more fundamental causes. "If peace is to be established," it affirms, "the primary requisite is to eradicate the causes of dissension between men. Wars thrive on these, *especially on injustice.*" Without a dynamic justice there can be no world political authority that is not tyrannical or imposed by conquest. Without justice there can be no *pacem in terris.*

The present writer sought to tell the participants at the Pacem in Terris Conference at the New York Hilton Hotel, Feb. 18–20, 1965, that while one might accept the principal political teachings of that encyclical without believing Pope John XXIII's *theology,* it was quite impossible to do so without accepting also the pontiff's *philosophy,* i.e., the understanding of natural justice and human rights that undergirds everything he said upon the subject of peace.[10] So also of the Council's statement on war. In this sense one can say after Vatican II, as one can after John XXIII, that "the fact that there are different ideas of what constitutes *pacem in terris"* and different notions of what constitutes and builds up peace on earth may be "the final source of human division" and of war.[11]

It looks remarkably as if one can also add that the Council's political teachings cannot really be believed without also believing its *theology.* In addition to injustices (or disagreements as to the very meaning of justice) that cause discord and foment wars, there are other causes. These other causes, the Council notes,

> . . . spring from a quest for power and from contempt for personal rights. If we are looking for deeper explanations, we find them in human jealousy, distrust, pride, and other egotistic passions.
>
> Man cannot tolerate so many breakdowns in right order. What results is that the world is ceaselessly infected with arguments between men and acts of violence, even when war is not raging.

[10] *Pacem in terris,* ed. Edward Reed (New York: Pocket Books, Inc., 1965), pp. 188, 191–92.

[11] John Cogley, "The Encyclical as a Guide to World Order," a background paper for the planning session of the Pacem in Terris Conference in New York City, Feb. 18–20, 1965, inserted by the Hon. Claiborne Pell in the *Congressional Record,* Thursday, May 21, 1964.

While the truth of these statements would seem to drive men to look for a savior, the Council continues instead to speak of the need for "unwearying efforts . . . to create agencies for the promotion of peace." Still, I think it true to say that the words I have just quoted probe the causes of strife so deeply that it is questionable whether one can believe the hope the Council holds out for peace on earth without believing its theology of ultimate reconciliation among men. Then the question is one concerning this theology itself: whether this affords grounds for hope in an earthly peace or hope in an ultimate peace that is not of this world. If both injustice and animosities must be removed from among men, if the peace of which we are speaking will evidence a regard for justice and mutual respect for the rights of all, and if world security will finally rest in these achievements and upon the consent of all and not in new political institutions that are established by conquest or maintained by any measure of tyranny, if distrust and pride and other egotistical emotions that rupture the harmony of things must be uprooted, that would seem a reasonable facsimile of the kingdom of God.

Our brothers in Christ who wrote those words, and the Council that adopted the statement, which finally penetrated to the fact that human conflicts are rooted in human sinfulness that is not going to be expunged without redemption, were apparently not unaware of the borderline between this age and another to which simple realism had driven them. In the midst of those somber words they fittingly paused simply to confess our fallen social existence and to describe how the entirety of this human life of ours will appear in the final judgment upon it by the coming age in which their hope was fixed: "Man cannot tolerate so many breakdowns in right order." [12] This is the political reality that is laid bare when man's existence is penetrated and fully revealed in the light of Christ, or in the light of an authentic peace on earth that can only be described as the restoration of the historical socio-political order to harmony.

[12] "Many cannot bear so many ruptures in the harmony of things" was the translation first issued (*The New York Times*, Dec. 9, 1965). Actually the Latin words do not by themselves form a complete sentence. *Cum tot ordinis defectus homo ferre non possit, ex iis consequitur ut, etiam bello non saeviente, mundus indesinenter contentionibus inter homines et violentiis inficiatur.* A more accurate translation would be: "Since man cannot bear with so many weaknesses [i.e., the defects just mentioned: 'jealousy, distrust, pride, and other egotistic passions'], it follows from these things that, even when war is not being actively waged, the world is unceasingly beset by contentions between men and by violence." This sentence, with the rest of the paragraph, clearly expresses the view that the state by its enforcement and its organization of the use of force is a restraint and remedy for sin. Not only because a secure peace is a great good but also for the negative reason that the causes of discord are so profound and universal, there must be unwearying efforts to create and perfect governmental agencies that promote peace or at least keep violence from becoming unbridled.

That statement should be set by the side of a luminous sentence in the opening paragraphs of the encyclical *Pacem in terris*. The pontiff was introducing his theme of the sense of natural justice in the hearts of all men when he seemed suddenly struck by the fact that the actual affairs of men contrast rather sharply with the supposition of the single propensity to justice and order in their hearts, and with also the harmonies of non-human nature. "How strangely does the turmoil of individual men and peoples contrast with the perfect order of the universe!" wrote Pope John XXIII. "It is as if the relationships which bind them together could be controlled only by force." Now has the Council also probed the causes of human historical conflicts so far as to come upon the sinfulness of man in which most of them root, and it has spoken so realistically of everything that would be needed to "build up peace" that salvation from sin could not be omitted.

What then should be said concerning a document that acknowledges quite clearly that the present "peace of sorts" depends on wielding deterrence, which cannot imagine a better peace except by perfecting powerful instruments of security and new instrumentalities for the solution of outstanding problems, and which finally cannot imagine a truly steady peace or an authentic peace with justice and freedom without presupposing the removal of envy, distrust, pride, and all other egotistical passions from the human heart and from relations among men, groups, and nations?

It has simply to be said that this understanding flows naturally enough from bringing all the perspectives of Christian theological ethics to bear upon the problems of politics; and that unless extreme care is taken in excising the Council's political teachings from its theology, the men of good will who do this are exceedingly apt merely to have their world-historical utopianism confirmed. That, in turn, will only add idealistic fury to the ruptures in the harmony of things that many cannot bear; and this will finally render mankind ungovernable.

It is clear that everything that the Council says *proximately* or *remotely* needs to be done to build up peace falls under the heading of a man's response to God the Strength of all covenants, to the coming action of this our God who saves men into a world of enduring covenants, to the redemption toward which the human race is in destination.

It is clear that everything the Council says concerning the morality of deterrence and the need for new security arrangements and a powerful new world public authority falls under the heading of man's response to God who mercifully preserves and governs a fallen world through the restraint and remedy of evil by coercive means.

It is clear that the Council's signal reassertion of the principle surrounding non-combatants with moral immunity from direct attack and its confidence in the justices of men fall under men's response to the goodness of God's creation as this is Christianly understood. For that goodness entails that politics be governed by the respect that should be accorded even in war to the image of God in man, to that sacredness in the temporal order who is man. The principle of discrimination is a requirement in the nature of things and in the laws of war when that nature and these laws are illuminated by what Christ teaches us concerning the protection of the weak and the little ones on earth, even in our struggles to maintain for them an order of justice and liberty. The resulting severe commandment is that, even in war, we ought never directly to take the life of anyone who is not the bearer of the force we are under the hard necessity and the ethico-political obligation to oppose.

These are the theological foundations of the three successive climactic utterances around which the Council's entire statement on war and most of its lesser propositions can be organized. This statement is a consequence of the response of the Council fathers to the action of God in all the actions that politically and militarily have come upon us in the modern period. The Council's formulations are the fruit of Christian political reason connecting every political consideration with the *whole* idea of God.

The Christian man and every man lives between the time of the fallen creation and the redemption of the whole creation. His problem in trying to tell what he should do falls within the dialectic between the here-and-now of fallen existence and the there-and-then of a restored human reality. At his peril he ignores either of these dimensions, by failing to take responsibility for the preservation of real political order in the world or by failing to take responsibility for introducing radical changes into the existing world political system. Stripped of its *prima facie* optimism, this seems to be the position which results from taking seriously the statement on war issued by the Vatican Council, i.e., from interpreting it as a treatise in Christian theological ethics.

At all times we must decide between the respective claims of preservation and government and of the higher and fuller forms of community toward which God preserves the world by these means. It is better to say that at all times our decisions will be *in between* these respective claims. They will be choices and actions composed by reference to *both* these claims.

We are obliged always to be inaugurating some new line of action. Since God does not preserve the world in order only to preserve it but to perfect our human social existence, man's own action is set in motion from simply upholding things as they are to aligning them more to accord with the perfection of human covenants. While any new line of action must be practically possible, this is not a very narrow limit, since "the possible" has not a determinate meaning in human affairs. Instead, we are obliged to open new paths and reform existing institutions, having always in mind that the first step and then the second, etc., may be needed in order to *make possible* what was previously impossible. Thus an ethics of redemption has bearing upon every possible reconstruction of the world political order that does not unfit it for serving as a real order serving liberty and justice among men. This the Council says we should be doing in the time of God's patience and in the places where we are.

Yet all action that has in view the actual transformation of the world political system must be located in this world and not some other. A man must take care that his zeal and idealism is not a matter of high-minded rebellion against the governor and preserver of the existing world. This means that a political order is worth something only if it is real, and not merely ideal. Any order is better than none at all. Since God in His governance of the fallen creation desires in His mercy to keep at bay chaos and disorganization and the destruction of every human political dwelling place which would be the final consequences of sin, men must preserve politically embodied justice and even a peace of sorts. Reordering the political world must begin here and not elsewhere; and any new ordering of the life of mankind will be worth something only if it is real and not merely ideal. This means that any transformation of our political life will have to be actual, just, and enforceable. When setting out on the radical new pilgrimage to which men are called in the politics of the nuclear age, we are obliged to take responsibility also for this.

CHAPTER 17

Robert W. Tucker's *Bellum*
*Contra Bellum Justum**

A statement of Jacques Maritain has recently become quite a consolation to me. "Moralists," he wrote in *Man and the State*, "are unhappy people. When they insist on the immutability of moral principles, they are reproached for imposing unlivable requirements on us. When they explain the way in which those immutable principles are to be put into force, they are reproached for making morality relative. In both cases, however, they are only upholding the claims of reason to direct life." [1]

For which aspect of the professional work of a moralist Professor Tucker has the greater distaste, it is difficult to tell. Any attempt to show

* First appeared in *Just War and Vatican Council II*, by Robert W. Tucker, with commentary by George G. Higgins, Ralph Potter, Richard H. Cox, and Paul Ramsey, published by The Council on Religion and International Affairs, 170 East 64th Street, New York, N.Y. 10021, 1966. This chapter is located here because of its connection with what the Vatican Council actually said on nuclear war. In contrast with any other chapter in this volume, in this essay the present author was required in answer to Professor Tucker's original article to expound and defend the just-war view of politics against an allegedly more *realistic* view of politics. Instead of the more familiar posture of "justifying" ("saving") war, I was forced to do intellectual battle for the moral limits upon war. I regret that it is not possible to publish Professor Tucker's essay along with my own. I can only hope that the present chapter will lead additional readers to that defense of realistic statecraft; to the other comments besides my own contained in the pamphlet cited above; and to the volume which Robert W. Tucker and Robert E. Osgood have recently published, *Force, Order and Justice* (Baltimore, Md., Johns Hopkins Press, 1967). Also see Chap. 12, pp. 271 f. above.
[1] (Chicago: University of Chicago Press, 1951), p. 74.

how moral principles work in political practice and in the conduct of war is like trying "to square the circle." The constituent elements of statecraft, Tucker believes, must revolve in a closed circle. The quest to define *legitimate* military necessity or *legitimate* reasons of state is bound, therefore, to eventuate either in the renunciation of statecraft or in the renunciation of morality.

Either of these contentions, taken alone, would be sufficient. It is interesting to note that Tucker thinks it worthwhile to undertake to prove both. Unless I misread him entirely, he is concerned to uphold not the necessities of statecraft alone, but the moral evil of these necessities. He writes about the state not like a seasoned and somewhat cynical practitioner of politics, but like a Socrates who himself would seek a private station and not a public one because of what he sees must be done for and by the state. Whenever some formulation of *bellum justum* threatens to become relevant to the ultimate safety of the state and of service to the political good, this must be demonstrated to have "emasculated the doctrine." The doctrine, it is insisted, must be square, lest the circle be successfully invaded or the statesman's task be illuminated by ethico-political insights that are not reduceable to the prudent wielding of quantitative increments of force in defense of the state.

Both Tucker and the pacifist insist that in statecraft—especially in the nuclear, deterrent state—evil must be done in order that good come of it. Tucker insists on this in behalf of the necessity of doing that evil when need be; the pacifist, in order to abandon statecraft. When the proponents of *bellum justum* attempt to cut down that evil by a proper political morality their undertaking is resisted by both as a betrayal of moral principles. The pacifist knows a lot about morality and what's evil; Tucker likewise knows very clearly what moral principles would be if there were any or any relevant to politics. Both also agree that to moralize the politics of the nation-state would mean to abandon its statecraft. This means that Tucker and the pacifist are in agreement as to the nature of "power politics." This is not surprising in an age when morality is a-political and politics is a-moral. Only Tucker is keener than most, in prosecuting this two-pronged objection to all attempts to "just-ify" force.

I

We will take up first the statement on modern war in the *Pastoral Constitution on the Church in the Modern World* issued by Vatican Council II, and Professor Tucker's comments on this.

The central declaration of the Vatican Council is its proscription as "a crime against God and man himself" of "any act of war aimed indiscriminately at the destruction of entire cities or extensive areas along with their population" (¶ 80). The fact that this is the most important statement of the Council is signalized by its use of the word "condemnation" this once in any of the sixteen promulgated Constitutions, Decrees, and Declarations, running to 103,000 words, issued by Vatican II. The Council did not even formally condemn atheism; yet, in language freely used at all previous councils but rarely by Vatican II, it condemns acts of war aimed indiscriminately at the destruction of entire cities with their populations.

Professor Tucker says that this prohibition is open to three possible interpretations, namely, that acts of war should not be aimed at the destruction of entire cities because this would (1) violate the moral immunity of non-combatants from direct attack, or (2) cause greater evil than any good resulting from such strikes, thus violating the principle of proportion, or (3) be tantamount to the "subjugation of peoples," and therefore in violation of the proscription of "aggressive" wars by recent Pontiffs even though the war had its origins in legitimate defense.

It seems obvious to me that the first is the only plausible reading. Either of the other explanations are strained. If the intention had been to condemn a certain kind of acts of modern war only because these actions would violate either the principle of proportion or the prohibition of aggression, the Council would have said simply *the destruction* of entire cities, etc. Instead it proscribes any act of war that is *aimed indiscriminately* at such destruction. This is another matter. The only reasonable explanation of the Council's choice of words is that this is *ordinary* language which expresses simply and forcefully what is meant by the more *technical* language of *bellum justum* enjoining the moral immunity of non-combatants from deliberate, direct attack.

Tucker himself remarks upon the "interesting, if not significant" omission of any express repetition of the recent denials that "aggressive" wars can possibly be just. Reference to this is not, as a matter of fact, lacking. The Council made "its own the condemnations of total war already pronounced by recent Popes," and that reference was enough, as it went on to introduce its own most solemn declaration. There are more references than this one.

Moreover, the second and third reasons are always *connected* in recent teachings: "aggressive" wars to restore violated rights, etc., cannot possibly be just *not* because wrongs should not be righted but because of the disproportionate evil that would be done in attempting to uproot an already established injustice, e.g., by wars of liberation.

Perhaps, as Tucker says, the Council considered this to be so evident as not to require lengthy reiteration either of the injustice of all aggressive wars, or of the ground for this judgment in disproportion (which, as a test, is everywhere expressed). In any case, if either or both of these explanations of the Council's central condemnation are correct, why did not the Council affirm this even more simply and directly instead of couching its meaning in the words ". . . aimed indiscriminately . . ."? Language forbidding aggressive wars and forbidding vast destruction that amounts to the same, while permitting just defense or permitting proportionate evil or permitting proportionate defense, has in recent years become quite customary in the Church's address to the problem of war and peace.

To explain why the Council invoked such familiar themes in the extraordinary language of its central condemnation would be far more difficult than to explain why, intending to invoke the rather complex doctrine of non-combatant immunity, it chose the simpler words ". . . aimed indiscriminately . . ." for a new emphasis it wanted to introduce into the Church's guidance of men in the face of modern war.

If this is correct, Tucker asks, "Why did the Council not affirm the rights of the innocent even more simply and directly by stating in traditional terms the principle of non-combatant immunity from direct attack?" The answer to that question is that such language is *not* familiar. It is rather the technical language of moral theology, and this is a pastoral constitution addressed to all mankind in which it was proper to use other language for the same idea. If even Tucker has not yet rightly grasped the meaning of the moral immunity of non-combatants from direct attack as this is comprehended in moral science, the Council is rather to be commended for simply declaring that it is most wicked to aim indiscriminately at the destruction of entire cities or extensive areas along with their population.

The point here is quite clear. For there to be any capital "crime," not only in the legal order, but the "crime against God and man" of which the Council speaks, there must be *mens rea* as well as the objectively evil deed. It is not a sin or crime without both: not only the destruction, the disproportion, not only the subjugation or annihilation of great numbers among the adversary, but also *the aiming of* acts of war *indiscriminately* upon entire cities.

Moreover, not only had the Council in many other paragraphs directed attention to the grave danger that any modern war will do greater evil than the evil it prevents or the good it secures (the principle of proportion). It has also *not* neglected to repeat in the clearest possible terms the recent papal teachings limiting just war to legitimate defense and calling attention to the danger that war begun in defense may, because of the nature of modern scientific weapons, easily become in the objective order tantamount to the prohibited aggression. "It is one thing to undertake military action for the just defense of the people, and something else again to seek the subjugation of other nations" (¶ 79), the

Council pronounced in *principle*. Then it remarked as a matter of *fact* that "acts of war involving these weapons can inflict massive and indiscriminate destruction far exceeding the bounds of legitimate defense" (¶ 80).

It is not reasonable to suppose that in the Council's central condemnation it chose more obscure language to express something said more clearly in other paragraphs; or that it introduced the reference to aiming indiscriminately at the destruction of entire cities and areas along with their population in order to say no more than that this destruction as such would be excessive or beyond the limits of just defense or both. Instead, we have to conclude that the Council chose less obscure, more familiar, and less technical language to express the principle of discrimination than the language in which moral theologians usually analyze the meaning of this principle and justify and explain it in terms of the moral immunity of non-combatants from direct attack.

The language was well chosen also because it enabled the Council at one and the same time to direct attention to the "central war" now planned and designed by the nuclear powers as a consequence of applying in statecraft only the constituent element of responding to the threat and use of force by quantitative increments of the same threats and force. To have approached the overriding issue facing today's world by first of all expressing the principle of discrimination in terms of the general moral argument for the immunity of non-combatants from direct attack would have focused attention upon any and all comparatively minor acts of wrongdoing in war, and not upon where the abomination is most clearly to be found. This Tucker seems to demand of the Council when he lays down the requirement that we be told "the *acts* that are absolutely forbidden"—or else he proposes to run away with the conclusion that the Council came instead to a "near emasculation of this immunity" in what it said about "entire cities" and "extensive areas" (p. 45).[2]

I agree with Professor Tucker that in its analysis of deterrence and the morality of deterrence the Council leaves standing the assumption that we may intend to do evil that good may come (fn. 34). But in the matter of the actual conduct of war the Council has clearly declared, in its "unequivocal and unhesitating condemnation" of "acts of war that aim indiscriminately at the destruction of entire cities," that the nations ought never, in the actual prosecution of war itself, to do evil that good may come. Perhaps the Council should have said that deterrent postures that rest upon aiming indiscriminately at entire cities, if this requires that we make ourselves conditionally willing to go to such acts of war, are equally to be condemned. Then it would have made a beginning

[2] Page numbers in parentheses refer to Robert W. Tucker, *Just War and Vatican II: A Critique.*

toward a fuller analysis of the morality of deterrence. But then I fail to see why Professor Tucker thinks it important to direct against the analysis of the morality of deterrence which I have proposed not so much the objection that this would mean the renunciation of statecraft as the objection that I too have emasculated the doctrine as such and (quoting, significantly, a Catholic pacifist) "abused" double-effect categories in using them (p. 37; n. 26). Apparently, a moralist must remain as "square" as the Council is silent on the morality of deterrence lest the nature and valid requirements of statecraft be addressed relevantly.[3]

The most revealing encounter between Tucker's position and the Council document takes place in a fairly obscure footnote (p. 45; n. 32). Here we find his premises disclosing themselves as premises and not arguments. The Council's central declaration, he writes, "leaves open the possibility that any act of war 'aimed discriminately at the destruction of entire cities' may not be forbidden, unless, of course, the destruction of cities is, by definition, an indiscriminate act." Then, Tucker continues, the statement would be "simply redundant rather than ambiguous. Instead it should read: 'any act of war aimed at the destruction of entire cities . . . is indiscriminate and is a crime against God and man himself.' "

Of course, the prohibition of any act of war aimed indiscriminately at the destruction of entire cities leaves open possibilities which the Council does not address, such as the possibility that the destruction of an entire city may be the consequence of a discriminating act of war. It is Professor Tucker, and not the Council, who in the main would deduce the intention of an act of war, its aim, and its moral quality, backward, as it were, from the destruction wrought. One might frame for the Council a statement that verbally begins with a sweeping condemnation of the physical destruction of entire cities, like the one of Pope Pius XII condemning modern war unless, of course, this could be in self-defense. The reformulation would read: "An act of war that destroys entire cities or extensive areas along with their populations is a crime against God and man himself, unless of course such acts are or could be aimed discriminately at the destruction of proper military targets."

In no case, however, is the Council's most solemn declaration either redundant or ambiguous. It cannot be reduced to a sort of *synthetic apriori* or synthetic redundancy which merely holds that the physical destruction of cities is by definition an indiscriminate act. Neither is it to be reduced to a logically analytic redundancy which merely announces that an indiscriminate act is by definition forbidden because it is indiscriminate. After all, quantitative economy in the use

[3] See "The Vatican Council and Modern Warfare," Chap. 16 above; also Chapter 15 above.

of force is able to prohibit wanton, indiscriminate destruction of cities in war (unless, of course, the destruction could be prudent or proportionate to the ends in view). Instead, the words "aimed indiscriminately" plainly rest the validity of the condemnation upon the prior category of murder and upon distinguishing this from indirect, unintended killing in war which is not aimed at. At the same time, the words "the destruction of entire cities and of extensive areas along with their population" lay hold on and encompass what may be the central plan and design of modern war. It thus proposes to be an ethico-political statement about proper and improper conduct of statecraft, and one that shows the immediate relevance of a rock-bottom moral principle to the determination of the constituent elements of legitimate or illegitimate appeals to military necessity. As such, the Council's most solemn declaration has to be faced and endorsed or disapproved by political consciences.

II

In any discussion of the claims of reason to direct statecraft, against or in modification of the claims of necessity, it is of first importance to distinguish the unchanging principles which govern the use of force from the practice which these principles (if there are any) require from age to age because of the changing shape of warfare.

The objective of combat is the incapacitation of a combatant from doing what he is doing because he is this particular combatant in this particular war; it is *not* the killing of a man because he is a man or because he is this particular man. The latter and only the latter would be "murder." This is the indestructible difference between murder and killing in war; and the difference is to be found in the intention and direction of the action that kills. From the requirement that just acts of war be directed upon the combatant and not upon the man flows the prohibition of the killing of soldiers who by surrender have taken themselves out of the war and incapacitated themselves from continuing it. The men are not to be killed when effective combatancy is no longer in them, since all along it was the combatant and not the man who had to be stopped.

From this also flows the cardinal principle governing just conduct in war, namely the moral immunity of non-combatants from deliberate, direct attack. This is the principle of *discrimination*, and in it there are two ingredients. One is the prohibition of "deliberate, direct attack." This is the immutable, unchanging ingredient in the definition of justice in war. In order to get to know the meaning of "aiming discriminately" *vs.* "aiming *in*discriminately," one has only to pay attention to the nature of an action and analyze action in a proper fashion. The second ingredient is the meaning of "combatancy–non-combatancy." This is relativistic and varying in meaning and application. As Tucker says, "combatancy–non-combatancy" is a function of how the nations and their forces are organized for war, and it is in some measure a function of military technology. In this he is as correct as, we shall see, he is mistaken when in the same fashion he seeks to fix the meaning of "deliberate, direct attack."

There are at least three constituent elements in the moral life and in any ethical analysis of morality. There are first the *motives* of the agent and any other ingredients that may, so to speak, be in his head or in his subjective consciousness. There is secondly the *intention* of his action. And there is thirdly the ultimate ends or consequences of the action. Each of these has to be reckoned in a complete appraisal of morality. While the terms moralists use vary, ordinarily *goodness* or its opposite are said to characterize the motives of agents; *right* or *wrong*, the intended shape of the action; and *good* or *evil*, the ultimate effects.

Since the moral immunity of non-combatants from direct attack is a doctrine that rests upon an analysis of the intentionality of actions of a military sort, the *pons asinorum* for understanding the meaning of this requires that the intention of the action be always distinguished from the motives of men (and from anything else that may be in their heads besides intentional aims) and from the final, expected consequences of the course of events set going by those actions. Any collapse of these elements into one another will be a mistake. This is what accounts for most of the gross misunderstandings of what is even proposed by proponents of the principle of discrimination in the political use of violence. This also accounts for Tucker's evident misreading of the meaning of right conduct in *bellum justum*.

Tucker seems to agree that the subjective motives of men should be largely set aside in trying to penetrate the meaning of *just conduct* in war. He says that subjective consciousness is too "indeterminate," by which I judge he means that motives and the subjective states of agents are too various and variable to be of much help in determining the meaning of just conduct or of prudent conduct in politics and in military strategy. This is correct, however important the motives of men are in character analysis and even if moral motives and character are not without significance in the conduct of affairs.

Presumably the death of combatants ideally should not be *wanted*. *Wanting* the death that is done to combatants and *not wanting* the death done to non-combatants cannot, then, be the meaning of the principle of discrimination surrounding the latter with moral immunity from direct attack in war. Still Tucker fails to maintain this distinction between whatever else may be in the heads of human agents and the intention of their actions, or between the intention of an action and its ultimate consequences.

He collapses *foreknowledge* of unavoidable death and damage to civilians collateral to the destruction of legitimate military targets into the meaning of *intending* or meaning to kill them. Anything I *knew* would happen must be an undifferentiated part of the meaning of what I meant or intended to do. This is simply a flaw in ethical analysis that cannot withstand examination. If motives such as hatred or subjectively wanting or not wanting the killing are not decisive in determining the intention of the action, neither is knowledge of the attendant results along with the intended results sufficient to obliterate a significant moral and political distinction between these two sorts of immediate effects of all acts of war. Indeed, in one important respect Professor Tucker's language is not apt or technical enough to lead him to a right understanding of this teaching in the theory of *bellum justum*. He correctly speaks of *direct* and *indirect action*. But then he speaks in parallel fashion of *directly* or *indirectly intending* something, where the doctrine speaks instead of intending or *not* intending something. The deaths of non-combatants are to be only *indirectly done* and they should be *unintended* in the just conduct of war whose actions may and should be, and are intended to be, directed upon combatants and legitimate military objectives. This aiming of intention and of action is entirely compatible with *certain* knowledge that a great number of civilian lives will unintendedly be indirectly destroyed. (Both are quite different from *wanting* either from malicious motives.)

Thus, Professor Tucker deduces the intention of an act of war from the consequences that are foreseen. In fact, he is inclined to deduce intention from the nature and objective amount of the destruction done. When this latter step has been taken, the excellent start that was made by distinguishing between wanting and intending something remains in the words only, and is of little usefulness in the analysis of military plans and actions. Because Professor Tucker finally believes that intention is as indeterminate and variable as motive, he rightly locates motives in the hearts of men where they have no immediate significance in analyzing statecraft or acts of war, and he wrongly deduces or determines the intentions of political agents and of military actions by reference to events in the objective order alone. Between the motives of men and the total consequences of their actions, the meaning of intention is squeezed out.

This simply makes it impossible for Tucker to grasp the meaning of "aiming indiscriminately," or the meaning of the intention. Thus the actual aiming and the actual or the foreseen destruction are telescoped together, or at least the meaning of the intention is given by the destruction foreseen. But since he wishes to retain the word "intention," and wishes to use it in political analysis at least to refute *bellum justum*, he gives it a meaning it never had in that theory.

In only extreme cases will it appear to be proper to move from events in the objective order to the attribution of intentions to agents or to their actions. If I use a sledge hammer to kill a fly on my neighbor's bald head it may be not unreasonably supposed that I had a grudge against my neighbor in my motives and also that by my action I *meant* (intended, "aimed") to do him harm. This might be called getting bonus-neighbor-damage while prosecuting man's war against the insects, if indeed killing the fly was not itself incidental to the aiming of my destructive act upon his head. Similarly, from the extensive destruction of Dresden, from the cruciality of the vast fire-storm to the plan of attack (to light the way for successive waves of bombers), it is not unreasonable to conclude that the destruction of the railway complex was incidental, even if we had no other evidence for the fact the railway complex was not even aimed at.

In general, it simply has to be said that these days we are better able to analyze play-acting than moral action. We speak of the "intention" of a drama as something in the play, in the action itself, not to be identified with everything the author thought he was writing. Similarly, the intention of a human action cannot be identified with everything the author thought or knew, or thought he knew, about the total consequences. Beginning in the *aiming* of the action, the intention of an act then includes the main *thrust* of it upon its immediate objective. There is, thus, a distinction between what is directly done by the thrust of action and what is incidentally, indirectly done attendant upon this thrust. Only the immediate objective is subjectively intended; the other foreseeable effects are *un*intended.

This brings us to the need to distinguish the intention of the act and its immediate effects from the ultimate consequences. The intention or thrust of the action is by no means directed immediately toward ultimate consequences, but toward the production of an immediate event that is reasonably believed itself to be productive of those future good consequences. Professor Tucker magnifies the doing of evil that good may come, first, by falsely implying that everything foreseeably done in the event was in some sense intended and then, secondly, by lumping everything done in the event (including collateral civilian deaths) without differentiation into the "means" by which politically good consequences are obtained. This too is a mistake in the analysis of action.

Perhaps an illustration will demonstrate more clearly what is at stake in distinguishing between the immediate effects of action (some intended and direct, others unintended and indirect) from the ultimate good consequences an action seeks to serve. The intention or present thrust of action concerns immediate effects, not the ulterior purposes or objectives. The latter may be *good* and yet the intention (the direct immediate *thrust* of the action) may be *wrong*. Indeed in some respects it would be more correct to say that the motives of men rather than their intentions are oriented upon ultimate objectives. While granting that this may only be a verbal convention, it has at least to be said that the "intention" of which *bellum justum* speaks is not fixed on ultimate ends. Perhaps we need to change the convention and speak of intention in two different senses. There would be intention (1) to indicate the usage of this word in *bellum justum*. Then there is intention (2) to indicate the meaning Tucker gives to this word.[4] But this is certain: Tucker's meaning cannot be used to interpret the meaning this word has in *bellum justum*, or to refute that theory by proving it ambiguous. It can only be used to displace it, and thus to instate another understanding of morality or of statecraft, or both. Before coming fully to grips with Tucker's displacing definition, I will stick with the convention, and ask:

What is at stake in not collapsing the intention of human actions into orientation upon the ends produced?

Take the case of mortal conflict between the life of a mother and her unborn child. It is well known that Roman Catholic teaching prohibits, in this conflict between equals, *direct* abortion as a means of saving the mother's life. Suppose someone wants to contend against this verdict and to justify *direct* abortion in such cases. Unless he denies the premise that the unborn child is a human being, it will not be sufficient for him simply to *assert* arbitrarily that direct abortion is the right action because this will save the life of the mother. The goodness of this ultimate result was never in question. No one doubts that the proposed medical action will respect the sanctity of the mother's life. The question that was raised is whether direct abortion is not in every way incompatible with any remaining regard for the sanctity of the nascent life.

In order for anyone to wrestle with his Catholic brother over the verdict forbidding direct abortion, he will have to propose another penetration of the intention and main thrust of this action and its immediate effects. He will have to say something significantly different from the Catholic view about direct abortion *as an action brought upon the child*. If instead he prattles endlessly about saving the mother's life he shows only that he does not know where the argument is, since that ultimate good was never in question. It helps not at all to say that we

---

[4] This distinction between two sorts of intention is related to the distinction Ralph Potter made—in his comment upon Tucker's essay—between two sorts of "evils." My "intention (1)" may be linked with Potter's "evil$_1$" (the evil *consequences* of action) that may not be "morally reprehensive" ("evil$_2$"). See p. 58 of *Just War and Vatican Council II*, cited at the beginning of this present chapter.

should do what a charitable reason requires in the final consequence, since the question is whether every shred of respect for the sanctity of nascent life must not be abandoned ever to do such a thing (direct killing of the innocent) for the sake of those consequences. No one ever doubted that the proposed action has effects that are ultimately charitable to the mother. It is therefore no argument to say that it is. The issue to be faced is whether the present action demonstrates (in its intention and in the shape of its primary thrust in the world and in its immediate effects) any remaining recognition of the fact that the littlest and least important human life has a sanctity that is not wholly to be denied in anything we now do.

This is precisely the issue raised by proponents of the moral immunity of non-combatants from direct attack (or, more briefly, the principle of discrimination) as a principle that should govern the political use of violence. It is no answer to affirm that there are ultimate ends which statecraft must have in view, even the preservation of a just or humane political order as a safe dwelling place for the human beings remaining alive and for future generations of men all of whom have a dignity and sanctity which should be respected. It is not enough simply to reiterate that this is a good and proper end of politics, with the implication, without argument, that to this all else is properly menial. The question that was raised was how the ends of the state can be served by plans and acts of war that evidence some remaining respect for the sanctity of persons now alive and with whom we are presently engaged. The proposal was that, if one focuses attention upon the intention and thrust of present action, it will be evident that acts of war *aimed indiscriminately* at the destruction of entire cities and extensive areas along with their populations cannot possibly be compatible with any remaining regard for the sanctity of human life as such. The contention is that if one is going to justify killing in war this must be intentionally limited (in the sense explained) to combatants and to the destruction of legitimate military objectives, and that one's just regard for the dignity of manhood and one's resolve not to reduce this to a mere instrument of statecraft will manifest itself in non-combatant immunity as a regulative principle. It is no answer to this argument to proceed to collapse the intention of present action into the ultimate ends of statecraft, the goodness of which no proponent of *bellum justum* ever meant to question. What would be required, in order to refute the traditional understanding of just conduct in war, would be another penetration of the present intention and thrusts of acts of war and their immediate effects that seeks to show that non-combatant immunity or the principle of discrimination does not adequately express the justice governing present action and intention. What is required would be a reforming and not a displacing definition of intention. I venture to believe that such a properly targeted rebuttal cannot succeed.

III

Professor Tucker is quite correct in saying that it is only when we come to the means permitted in warfare that we find "a significant conflict between the necessities of the state [as he conceives these] and the demands of *bellum justum*" (p. 21). He is led somewhat astray by his use of the word "means." "Means" are not right or wrong. Only "conduct" is: the conduct or "the manner of warfare."

There are two principles governing the conduct of war: proportion and discrimination. The principle of discrimination forbidding deliberate, direct attack upon whole cities and areas with their population apparently opens up the greater gulf between necessity of state and the requirements of political morality. Still this begins to be the case with regard to the principle of proportion. Let us look first at what Tucker says about this, and ask whether he has in this connection properly located the beginning of a difference between *bellum justum* and his own view of statecraft.

Professor Tucker writes (p. 18) that a "proportionality of effectiveness" is permitted in international law. This means economy in the use of force, or the proportioning of means of violence to the effective protection of endangered interests or values. This he contrasts with a "proportionality of value" which he says characterizes *bellum justum*. This, I take it, means not only proportioning means to ends along the single track of protecting the *endangered* interests or values. It means taking account of other values as well. Since the use of force not only protects values but must pay costs in other values, the values preserved need to be proportioned to the values sacrificed through the use of force. Whatever be the meaning of the permissions and requirements of international law, it seems clear that the requirements of a realistic statecraft and the requirements of *bellum justum* must be in agreement in this respect. Surely, both the conduct of statecraft and the just conduct of war enjoin not only the use of the force and no more than the force needed effectively to protect endangered values, but also the reckoning of those values against the values that will be destroyed in the course of that same use of force. The principle of proportion, in short, is no more than a counsel of political prudence. One should not only use effective force and no more than that. One ought also to count the costs of doing this (even effectively doing this), and weigh all the cost/benefits.

Admittedly, this justification of and limitation upon the use of force does not tell the statesman what to do. It leaves this for him to decide by virtue of political prudence. It is precisely a worth of the principle of proportion that this enables no man to bring against statecraft an extrinsic norm. But this is not to agree with the charge that "a prescription the converse of which is manifestly absurd can tell us very little that is meaningful about how men ought to behave." Tucker seems to regard this as a weakness in the "proportionality of value." This means no more than sound statecraft counting all the costs/benefits as well as effectiveness in protecting the values that were threatened. Such counsels of prudence are by no means useless because their converse (Be imprudent! Pay more costs than the benefits are worth!) is manifestly absurd. Moreover, a "proportionality of effectiveness" is likewise a prescription the converse of which is manifestly absurd. The worth of these propositions, or of the use of them in analyzing sound statecraft and justice in the political use of violence, stems from the fact that men and statesmen very often do things that are manifestly absurd, led on by rhetoric, bravado, and inflexible postures. Moreover, a "proportionality of effectiveness" is no more informative. When Churchill made the decision to stand against Nazi Germany he could not then have known that a few months later Hitler would make the stupid mistake (fighting on two fronts by his attack upon Russia) which proved Churchill's decision to have been a politically prudent one. He could not have known this whether the standard he consulted was that of a realistic statecraft (national self-interest, defending the "self" and independence of the state, or a proportionality of effectiveness alone) or whether the standard was a broader conception of the common good (counting all the cost/benefits according to a proportionality of value). Tucker's campaign against the *bellum justum,* and in this instance against its proportionality of value because it is "devoid of substantive content" (p. 18; n. 13), is carried so far that it must turn against his own conception of one of the constituent elements of statecraft.

However, it may be that by "proportionality of value" Tucker means, in a somewhat inept choice of words, to refer to taking into account more than one's own national good in the calculation of cost/benefits that would justify or forbid resort to arms. If so, then a proportionality of value would be different from the proportionality of effectiveness governing the conduct of a narrow statecraft and enshrined in international law. It is true that *bellum justum* requires of political prudence not only a calculus of all the values paid but also of the values exacted, even of an adversary. It envisions an international system which, while properly described as a state of war, ought not to be termed a non-moral state of nature.

Therefore, justice in the conduct of war, even the prudent conduct of war, meant some reference to harmonizing the national common good to the common good of all men and nations. I suspect that the traditional principle of proportion always assumed that there might be some costs too great, even when exacted of an adversary, to be worth the value protected on one's own part or for the good and safety of one's own state. The present writer does not believe, any more than Tucker does, that there are any "wandering nations" which, like our father Abraham, are called or answer the call to go out from the integrity of their selfhood into a far country which they know not. But short of this, there is an inclusion of the values of other peoples as well as the values of one's own which *bellum justum* seeks to acknowledge in international relations even when there is war. The nation is not *the absolute* even if none is Abraham. Perhaps Tucker has not made enough of the difference between his own view of statecraft and that contained in *bellum justum* which begins to emerge here even in the meaning and application of the principle of proportion in justifying or forbidding political resort to violence.

In turning from proportion to discrimination in assessing intrinsic justice in the conduct of war, we need to note that these are different tests but that both are always needed in determining the justice of warfare. One test without the other, or one instead of the other, can never lead to the verdict: this is justifiable to do. We also need to note that, of the two, the principle of proportion or political prudence provides, in face of the destructiveness of modern warfare, the greatest pressure toward redefining *jus ad bellum* as *jus contra bellum*. This has been a parallel development in international law and in *bellum justum* (vide: modern papal teachings). But the stress on limiting "the manner of warfare" by forbidding acts of war aimed indiscriminately at noncombatants and combatants alike has been to the point of defining *jus in bello*, not to enforcing *jus ad bellum* or *jus contra bellum*. This is so much the case that one of Professor Tucker's main objections to the principle of discrimination proscribing direct attack upon non-combatants in the conduct of war, strangely, seems to be that this test, taken alone, allows for a far higher level of violence in legitimate ripostes than are prudent today or proportionate. Only he does not seem to know that this principle of discrimination is not to be taken alone. Nor should he imply that anyone must be either stupid or morally insensitive who says that a certain plan of war, e.g., tactical nuclear war or counter-insurgency war, as the nations are presently organized for war, might be a quite discriminating plan of war, while the destructiveness of it may or may not be a disproportionate cost to pay or exact for the political goods at stake. There are two *connected* principles.

Tucker is altogether correct, however, in resisting the reduction of the principle of discrimination to "in effect, another form of calculation." There are *two* principles.

> it is not enough to argue that one may never do evil that good may come because the good will not come (only the evil),[5] or that the evil act will corrupt the actor and thereby defeat his ends . . . , or that the means cannot be separated from the ends but are themselves the ends in the very process of coming into existence. . . . If certain means are to be absolutely forbidden they must be forbidden quite apart from these considerations. If certain means are to be absolutely forbidden they must be forbidden because of their intrinsic evil. If one may never do evil that good may come, it is not—or not primarily—because the good will not come but simply because one may never do evil (p. 22).

Professor Tucker is also quite correct in ascribing to the theory of *bellum justum,* at the point of gravest potential conflict with "reasons of state" which he identifies, the implied verdict that "the state cannot be considered a supreme value for men" and also (if the state is instrumental to other values) the verdict that those values which "the state, and perhaps only the state, may serve to protect also cannot be considered supreme" (p. 23). It is, indeed, because and only because human lives possess a dignity and value which transcends the state and all the values the state serves to protect that, in the service of the state and in the exercise of statecraft, there are limits to those individuals who may be deliberately made the objects of attack in war.

Finally one can grant that "it is only where the prohibition against the deliberate killing of non-combatants is considered absolute that a clear conflict *may arise* between the necessities of the state and the requirements of an ethic which presumably sets limits to those necessities" (p. 24; italics added). This possible conflict, however, has to be *proved*. A political ethic that "sets limits" to the exercise of statecraft does not therefore go *contrary* to the vital interests of the state. It may only indicate among its necessities its choiceworthy necessities (and even Tucker's necessities of state are "necessities" for choice).

---

[5] We should note, however, at this point that the moral judgment "it is never right to do wrong that good may come" is neither withdrawn nor weakened by referring anyone who argues that this would call for the abandonment of statecraft to the footnote the nuclear age has written to this perennial truth: "it can never do any good to do wrong that good may come of it." The latter simply affirms the compatibility of morality with statecraft. "Acts of war aimed indiscriminately at the destruction of entire cities . . . are a crime against God and man himself" is not a true ethico-political statement *because* it is also the case that such a war would be self-defeating statecraft. Morality may be prudent without being moral *because* it is prudent.

IV

It is time now to grapple more closely with Tucker's displacing definition of the intention that governs the meaning of non-combatant immunity from direct attack. At the outset it should be clearly stated that he is quite at liberty himself to hold his particular understanding of intention. Such a view of the intentionality of acts of war would then be entirely consistent with the necessities of statecraft as Tucker conceives these to be, since it is in fact drawn forth from this understanding. His interpretation could then be used to *assert* the *irrelevance* of *bellum justum.* The latter and "reasons of state" would simply be squared off in opposition to one another as doctrines of state: abandon justice all ye who enter statecraft; abandon statecraft all who seek to act justly in politics and in military affairs.

But Tucker's displacing definition cannot be used to show the emasculation of the theory of *bellum justum* by its proponents, since plainly it is he who holds this understanding of it, and not they. I confess that this interpretation of the issue posed by Tucker may be fairer to its author than a reader may suppose to be substantiated by a first reading of his essay. Most of the time Tucker *does* seem to be offering *an interpretation* of the meaning of non-combatant immunity and of the intention entailed in direct attack proposed by *bellum justum.* He *does* seem to be proposing an explanatory or even reforming definition (one that better states the meaning of the theory itself) and not a displacing one. If this is the correct reading, then, Tucker's account of the doctrine is simply a mistake he has made while doing political philosophy.

He begins auspiciously and comes close to rightly apprehending the meaning; yet in the end he drives to a point most remote from it. He begins auspiciously, by noting that in "the moral immunity of non-combatants from deliberate, direct attack" there are two concepts in need of separate definition. This opened the way toward an affirmation that "non-combatancy" when correctly understood indicates how the principle of discrimination can be relatively and variably applied in the practice of war, while "deliberate, direct attack" when correctly understood indicates the unchanging element in the principle. At once, however, both these features of the definition of the immunity, and not only the meaning of non-combatancy, are defined by Professor Tucker by reference to objective events in the world or the objective destruction brought about by acts of war. Thus he barred himself from an understanding of "aiming indiscriminately."

Still he does begin auspiciously by clearly defending the fitness of the notion of non-combatancy in the direction of war's conduct. We should follow him in this, and not the ordinary critics of *bellum justum*.

Who are the "innocent" who are not to be deliberately attacked?

Tucker answers this question with a categorical statement that "unless the very concept of non-combatant status is itself suppressed," the difficulties over the precise characteristics requisite for this status "are not likely to prove intractable" (p. 25). If, as he remarks in a footnote at this point, the distinction "is far more relative and pragmatic in application than is commonly admitted," proponents of *bellum justum* should be among the first to admit this. There can be no reason for anyone to resist the notion that the meaning of combatancy-non-combatancy has been and will continue to be "dependent both on the manner in which states organize for war and on the technology with which they conduct war." Only a legalist-pacifist employment of the *bellum justum* doctrine would think of supposing otherwise, in the hope of bringing peace by discrediting one by one all wars, or all modern war. Since *bellum justum* proposes to indicate to statesmen how within tolerable moral limits they may make use of violence in the preservation of the state's politically embodied justice and in defense of its "self" and independence, how could it be otherwise than that this distinction governing just conduct in war should be relative to the shape of war in any period Not Yet the Plowshares? This being so, I fail to see why Tucker later on waxes so eloquent in condemning the seeming moral insensibility of my defense of the possible justice (so far as non-combatant immunity alone is concerned) of counter-force nuclear strikes in an age when there are military establishments fifty or more miles in diameter and legitimate targets deeply buried.[6] Moreover, to argue that non-combatancy is, unlike sub-

---

[6] Again, it is not discrimination defining *jus in bello*, but prudence or proportion transforming *jus ad bellum* into *jus contra bellum* in the face of the destructiveness of modern war that imposes the more severe limits upon the state's use of violent means. This calls for radical revision of Tucker's judgment that there is an irrepressible conflict between *jus in bello* and necessities of state. The more severe limitation upon statecraft will already have arisen from a principle that is undeniably inherent in its proper exercise, namely, prudence or proportion. Moreover, the principle of proportion is controlling over the principle of discrimination in determining whether it is finally *just to do* even those actions in war that can be shown to be discriminate. Thus, Tucker is entirely mistaken in saying that any proponent of *bellum justum* would contend that the evil effects of counter-force nuclear strikes, "whatever might be said of their proportionality or disproportionality, would still not be the doing of evil" (p. 32). Knowingly to do a disproportionate act is wicked (since prudence is a virtue), even on the excuse that only legitimate targets are attacked. Note 26 to p. 37 contains a more accurate statement of the case: "Even if we were to accept the view that the 'indirect effect' of killing half a population would not be the doing of evil [read: "would not be indiscriminate," since there are two tests of the evil] there would still remain the question of the proportionality of the action."

jective innocence, susceptible to "objective determination" is not to argue that it is susceptible to *certain* determination. True enough, the determination of non-combatancy depends upon the "subjective appreciation" of what constitutes this status in one or another organization for war, on the part of our political leaders and citizens alike in public deliberation. But one is not concerned with the subjective appreciation of something that is itself subjective, namely, guilt or innocence. It was surely a gratuitous remark (and one that may indicate that Tucker scarcely appreciates the fact that *bellum justum* is a doctrine of state-craft, for statesmen, to be determined in its application by statesmen) for him to write: "In the subjective interpretation of this behavior [constituting non-combatancy] there is no apparent reason for according greater weight to the insights of Christian moralists than to the insights of others" (p. 25; n. 19). Of course not!

What is the meaning of deliberate attack upon non-combatants? This, Professor Tucker rightly says, is the question that "pose[s] very considerable difficulties"—far more difficulties than the question of who are, or whether there are any, non-combatants—and he then proceeds to demonstrate that he himself has not yet surmounted the main difficulty he points out in understanding the meaning of this immunity. He asserts summarily, and without an attempt at demonstration by a careful analysis of the meaning of "direct" and "indirect" attack, that the qualification of the prohibition of direct attack by the permission of collateral non-combatant destruction (or some instances of this qualification) is "to be explained in terms of military necessity. . . . The scope afforded to the principle of non-combatant immunity has always been dependent upon the scope afforded to military necessity" (p. 26). Thus the prohibition of deliberate attack upon non-combatants really means that belligerents may take those measures required for the success of their military operations unless these are forbidden by one or another positive law of war.

What seemed to be introduced was an endeavor to render tractable the very considerable difficulties in the way of understanding the meaning of "deliberate attack." This trial ends, in the very same paragraph, with an essay on the vagaries of men or the history of injustice in war (only we cannot tell this unless first the meaning of direct attack has been fully understood). Let it be said that this notion is better expressed on p. 28.[7] But here at the outset Professor Tucker has introduced

[7] "What *bellum justum* does require is that in attacking military objectives the death and injury done to noncombatants be beside the intention—at any rate, beside the direct or positive intention—of the attacker, that this death and injury done to non-combatants not constitute a means for achieving an otherwise legitimate military end and that, finally, the evil effect of the action not prove disproportionate to the good—

his theme: non-combatant immunity from direct attack (not only "non-combatancy" but "direct attack" as well) must derive its meaning in one way or another from what is done in the objective order. Damage done that was foreseeable, for example, must have been "intended."

"Non-combatancy" is a category whose meaning varies from age to age according to military technology and the way nations are organized for war. But "direct" or "deliberate attack" in the statement of the immunity is not relative. This means, of course, that the meaning of the immunity varies *in its application* from age to age; but not that the meaning of deliberate, direct attack is a relative matter. The reason for this is that the concept of "direct attack" gives the shape to *an action* (its intention and thrust) while "non-combatancy" is a function of the bare facts of military organization.

Tucker argues from the admitted relativity of non-combatancy as a category to the relativity of "deliberate, direct attack" as a category. This is a mistake.

His misstep is plainly evident from the topic he takes up immediately after having introduced, as a separate question, the meaning of "direct attack," and the unsupported assertions about this that we have cited above. On p. 26 we find ourselves dealing with "the concept of military objective." Surely this is a return to the first question (pp. 24–25) concerning non-combatancy. At least, a discussion of the meaning of "military objective" is far closer to a further probing of the meaning of combatancy than it is to being an extension or further grappling with the problem of the meaning of deliberate attack, concerning which there were "very considerable difficulties" to subdue. Tucker first analyzed the meaning of the immunity into the two questions, concerning non-combatancy and concerning deliberate, direct attack. This is the only fruitful approach. But then he collapsed these categories again without having probed deeply enough the meaning of "deliberate attack" which steadfastly governs the meaning of the immunity and of just *conduct* in war.

In any case there is no reason to disagree that the nature of a

---

or, at any rate, the morally sanctioned—effect." This more adequate comprehension of the meaning of the intention and direction of action is, however, promptly confused again by the unsupported assertions that *bellum justum* "for the most part . . . deduces intent from these consequences," "by inquiry into the character of the means he has chosen." In the next sentence, the correct approach again emerges: "The character of the means . . . is in turn determined by inquiry into *the action itself*"—only to be buried again by the words: "above all by inquiry into the *consequences* that might have been reasonably expected to follow from the action" (pp. 28–29; italics added). In Section II above, I attempted to set down an account of "intention" that is apt to unpack the confusion in these expressions, and correct them—on the assumption that Professor Tucker meant to offer us a reforming or interpretative definition and not merely his own displacement of the traditional meaning.

military objective is a function of the manner in which societies organize for war. This is the "same dependence" the category of non-combatancy was allowed to have. But the same dependency is nowhere proved to pertain to the meaning of deliberate, direct attack.

Of course it is the case—taking the immunity as a whole, in both its crucial aspects—"that the scope of the immunity accorded the civilian population is largely dependent upon the meaning given the concept of military objective and that the concept of military objective varies with the character of war" (p. 26). This only means that *bellum justum* is a doctrine of statecraft. It proposes to tell the statesman how, even in war, reason can direct life (as Maritain put it). But in no way does Tucker demonstrate his assertion that the meaning properly to be given to a *legitimate* military objective depends on the meaning given by military necessity, or that the meaning of the intentional aim can be inferred from the scope of the destruction.

Apart from the semblances of plausibility (p. 27) that have their explanation in the vagaries and pretensions of men in the fog and fury of war, there are only three ways to accomplish this reduction of the meaning of non-combatant immunity to the scope of military necessity. One way would be to show that non-combatancy (and military objective) as a category is quite indeterminate. A second way would be to demonstrate that in some past or present organization for war everyone in a society is a fighter without any distinctions of degrees of remoteness or proximity to its military power. Professor Tucker does not undertake to show either of these two things to be the case. Indeed, he affirms that a definition of non-combatancy is tractable. The remaining way would be to show, by a careful examination of the meaning of "deliberate, direct attack" as a rule of practice specifying the meaning of just and unjust conduct, that this in principle does actually depend upon the variable meanings given to the concept of military necessity. Perhaps the reason Professor Tucker does not undertake to probe the meaning of direct attack so deeply is that he knows that this will prove the opposite. For here we come upon the "immutable principle" for which the admittedly variable meanings of "non-combatancy" and "military objective" show the application—producing the concept of *legitimate* military necessity.

Tucker's cardinal assertions have no weight, if he meant to give us an interpretation of *bellum justum*, and not his own view of statecraft in another guise. "Whether the death and injury done to the innocent is directly intended or is beside the intention of the actor is *determined by the scope of this death and injury.*" That is a palpably false account of the doctrine of just conduct. Given this false account, *of course* how much death and injury will be regarded as violating non-combatant immunity will vary, "whether consciously or unconsciously, by the claims of necessity." Then *of course* Hiroshima will be regarded as a legitimate military target!

Professor Tucker's comment upon a statement of mine about whether "in the objective order" an immediate effect of action is "incidental" or essential to the action's thrust and intention is: "This is clearly a matter of *quantity* then—of objective consequences" (p. 29; n. 21). Again a palpable error—and moreover one made without first investigating thoroughly the meaning of "incidentality" proposed by the doctrine in question.

There is further confusion for want of doctrinal clarity. "Ordinarily," Tucker begins without noticing that the terms of *bellum justum* are *not* the terms of ordinary language, "we regard a *certain* effect as a means to an end if that end cannot be secured without this effect, if the realization of the one is dependent, and is known to be dependent, upon the occurrence of the other" (p. 30). This statement (which might pass muster if we stress the words *dependent*) is then used to support the conclusion that the death of the innocent "in the course of attacking a military objective is as much a means as is the destruction of the military objective." The latter effect "could not be secured without destroying a great number of lives; but this fact, if unavoidable, does not make their deaths "as much a means." "Where," writes Tucker, "the one effect, destruction of the military objective, is a means to the end of victory in war, the other effect, the death and injury of non-combatants, is indirectly a means. . . ." The notation upon this sentence should be "So far, so good," provided you know the meaning of "indirectly a means," which is anyway not a good expression for the thought. But then Professor Tucker discloses that he did not know the meaning of "indirectly a means" of victory, by going on to say that the other effect, the death and injury of non-combatants, is "*directly* a means to the end of destroying the military objective." It was not; rather were the civilian deaths incidental, however foreseeable, to the destruction of the military target which was the direct means of victory. Unless, of course, the commander was going about unjustly getting bonus-civil-damage construed as a means of victory. But we could not even know this without knowing the meaning of direct, deliberate attack in distinction from unavoidable, foreseen, collateral damage!

Both effects must be considered as means, we are told. There is in this paragraph, it is true, reference to the notion of "intent" as voiding (Tucker says avoiding) this conclusion. In this reference Professor Tucker shows an awareness that intention is not synonymous with wish or desire in ordinary language or in the terminology of *bellum justum*. "We may not wish or desire something to happen, yet may intend it to happen." The direct killing of combatants may be an example of this. But then Professor Tucker substitutes for the confusion of intent with *desire* another confusion—of intent with *foreknowledge*. We may not wish a consequence, he writes; but "even so, we intend this consequence if we know that it will result from a certain action and nevertheless take this action." This is simply a grave error in both psychological and moral analysis—and poor reporting of the *bellum justum* doctrine if that is still under scrutiny. "To intend," we are told, "means to have in mind as something to be done or brought about." Something *to be done*, yes. But whether to have in mind something *to be brought about* is synonymous with intending it depends altogether upon how this is envisioned to be brought about. It depends upon knowing the meaning of intentional aims, and of what is called in the language of moral theology the "indirectly voluntary."

The footnote to this paragraph (p. 30; n. 22) contains an acknowledgment that there is a significant distinction to be drawn between "positively intending" the one effect and "indirectly intending" the other effect. This might be enough to permit Tucker his own use of language if he concluded only that *in this sense only* both effects are "intended." Instead he claims too much: "Objectively, we still intend the one effect *just as much* as we intend the other effect" (italics added). Likewise one can almost but not finally permit him his language about "means": "[The indirect means] too is a means, though it is a means that may be distinguished from the means that is directly intended or positively permitted." This statement shows both an understanding of the traditional doctrine and seems to acknowledge the importance of some of its cardinal distinctions in the analysis of just action in war. To press on in the right direction calls for eliminating the use of the expression "indirectly intended" and "indirectly a means." Where Professor Tucker says "indirectly intended," the doctrine under scrutiny says "*un*intended but indirectly *done*."

Tucker prosecutes his war against the moralist's verdict that one should never do or intend wrong that good may come into the citadel of attacks *upon combatants*. This must, it seems, not only be done but also judged to be evil, for there to be statecraft. Are we to "positively intend" the death of combatants; is this a "good effect"? The upshot of these questions for Tucker's argument is again to make both of the effects of a military action equally *means* (the one "positively permitted," the other "reluctantly permitted") to the repulsion of injustice which alone can or should be "positively intended" as an ultimate end. This preys off a further confusion between the ultimate or ulterior end or goal and the immediate effects, which alone are in question in the analysis of the nature of present intent and action. Still, Tucker will have to make up his mind whether he means to say that the positive or reluctant permission or intention or doing (whatever the language he finally adopts) of these effects as means is *right* because of the ultimate end, or *wrong* because of the killing and destruction. His view of statecraft would seem to entail the former, but his *bellum contra bellum justum* requires him to say the latter, in order to undercut the ethical verdict that it is never right to do wrong that good may come. In any case, Tucker should know that Christian moralists do not agree with him that only the ulterior effect should be positively intended. Nor do they accept his verdict that to intend and do directly the death of combatants is to do evil that good may come. I myself prefer to say that the intention of combat is the incapacitation of a combatant from doing what he is doing; it is not the killing of a man because he is a man. Others have said instead that the "unjust aggressor" may be killed directly and that to do this is not morally evil. (It undoubtedly is a tragedy and a physical evil; but this is not in question.)

Perhaps it would be helpful to introduce here a few illustrations in which the "scope of the death and injury" remains the same whatever be the intention. From these cases it may be seen that the meaning of the intention can be reasonably and "objectively" discriminated from the "incidentality" of other effects falling unavoidably *within* the scope of the destruction. From these cases we can also see the *importance* of making this distinction even in cases in which the objective damage remains the same. This will prove that, so far as the theory under discussion is concerned, it is incorrect to define what is intended or what is the means leading to the manifold effects of action simply in terms of the objective consequences.

An obstetrician has two women as patients. Both have cancer of the uterus requiring prompt surgical action to remove it. One is pregnant, the other is not.

In both cases it is possible to know the intention of the surgical action. Whether the death of the fetus is directly intended or is beside the intention is clearly *not* determined by the scope of the injury. It is not a matter of quantity. The death of the fetus is *not* a means to saving the mother's life simply because this end cannot be secured without that effect. Nor should it be said that the fetal death is *as much a means* as the destruction of the cancerous uterus, which is the legitimate surgical objective. The doctor does not intend that consequence simply because he *knows* that it will result from his surgery and nevertheless performs the operation. To have in mind the death of the fetus that will be brought about is *not* his intention. He does *not* intend the one effect as much as he intends the other effect. Unless of course he was going about getting bonus-fetal-damage. However, we could not determine whether he was or was not meaning to kill the fetus without first knowing the meaning of the direct intention and thrust of proper surgery in this instance. The other case, of the non-pregnant cancerous uterus, shows that this discrimination can be made rationally even in the case of the pregnant woman. In both cases the means of "victory" was the destruction of the diseased uterus, and not also, in the one case, the foreseeable collateral, "incidental" death of the fetus.

The intention of combat and the result of action is the incapacitation of a combatant, not the killing of a man. *Objection:* He is killed in any case. The "scope" of the injury is the same. The consequence is the same. *Reply:* Yes, but the importance of distinguishing the main thrust of an act of combat from the unavoidable, foreseeable attendant killing of a man even when these produce the same objective event becomes manifestly clear when one asks about the treatment to be justly accorded soldiers who incapacitate themselves as combatants and take themselves out of the war by surrendering. The rule of practice that captured soldiers are not to be killed, and which protects them from gross mistreatment, is a dictate of the justice *inherent* in the conduct of war as a barely human enterprise. This is a regulative principle, a rule of civilized warfare itself. Its bearing upon the conduct of war may not be that captured soldiers ought never to be killed (in fluid, jungle situations in which the "non-combatant" is liable to return quickly to the status of combatant, there being no stockades in which to insure that he will remain a non-warrior.) The bearing of this rule of practice in war may be instead the requirement that every effort be made to implement this limit upon the killing in the entire shape, manner, and "institutions" mounted in the conduct of war. This illustration should also serve to indicate something that is too often forgotten when one hears ethicists discussing the moral dimensions of the political use of violence. The upshot is never mainly the definition of culpable individual acts or agents—defining "sin" and making "sinners"—but rather the criticism of institutions and practices. Thus is *bellum justum* a theory of statecraft.

The "incidentality" of killing the man to stopping the combatant is not determined by objective consequences or by the scope of the death. The incapacitation of a combatant is the means, not the other effect without which this cannot be secured. One need *not* intend this other consequence he knows will result beside the intention and beside the prime objective of combat, if, knowing killing to be unavoidable, he nevertheless engages in combat. The case of the surrendered soldier shows this clearly to be the case, whatever may be the vagaries and furies of men. Justice in the treatment of the man after surrender helps us to see the discrimination to be made in analyzing the difference between "killing in war" and "murder." This shows that the distinction between objectives is *there,* and can be drawn.

During World War II, some of the prominent leaders of world Judaism tried to persuade the Allies to bomb all of Hitler's concentration camps and extermination ovens, even though this would certainly kill all of the inmates at the time of the action. They reasoned that more innocent victims would be saved in the time that would elapse before the camps could be reconstructed and their genocidal work be going again, than lives would be lost "incidental" to destroying the target-camps and personnel that should justly have been repressed. Would this have been to do evil that good may come? Prescinding from whether the proposed action would, or would likely enough, have achieved the proportion of effectiveness and value expected (which would be sufficient reason for declaring that this should not be done), we need to ask, would such strikes against the concentration camps have been deliberate, direct attacks upon the innocent no less than upon the furnaces?

The answer to this is clearly, No. This shows that one does not deduce intention from the consequences. In this case, also, whether the deaths are directly intended or beside the intention cannot be determined by the scope of the death and destruction. Incidentality is not a matter of quantity, even where the quantity remains the same and cannot be altered by any difference in the intention. The death of the inmates was not a part of the means to the end in view simply because that end could not be secured without this effect. Their deaths were clearly *not* as much a means as the destruction of the target-furnaces, An immediate consequence known to result would not have been the intention of this action. To have in mind something that will unavoidably be brought about is not the same as aiming at it. No one would actually intend the secondary effect just as much as he intends and directs the action in question upon the target of the other effect. Unless of course there were latent anti-Semites in the Allied high command who might have intended to get bonus-inmate-damage. But (apart from character-analysis) we could not reasonably and objectively tell whether this was so or not unless it is possible to know first the meaning of deliberate, direct attack upon legitimate military targets. The fact that the action would have been carried out exactly as proposed had there been intelligence of a certain lucky day on which the camps would be empty of inmates provides in this instance a clarifying test-case like the woman who was not pregnant and the combatant who has surrendered in the foregoing illustrations.

These are hard cases, deliberately chosen because they are hard cases, or rather because they demonstrate the determinate meaning of the intention of an action without varying the scope of the destruction.

The importance of this analysis in the theory of *bellum justum* is, of course, that without the principle of discrimination in one's doctrine of statecraft and in the conduct of war there is no reason to limit the scope of the destruction and increments in the use of violence by any reference to whether the "targets" are populations or not. It would be a proportion of effectiveness alone that gave preference to the one or the other. This world already knows what that means, even if there seems to be some considerable difficulty in coming to know the meaning of "aiming discriminately" among the laws of war.

No less a realist than Herman Kahn can tell the difference, without preferring one to the other, between war-plans and military strikes that aim to get bonus-civil-damage as part of the means of victory and one that aims at counter-force-plus-avoidance of as much civil damage as possible. This does not seem to be a distinction that can even be made in the minds of men if Professor Tucker's replacing definition of intention is correct. It should in any case be clear who has emasculated the doctrine of *bellum justum* in the course of interpreting it.

V

There remains the question whether *bellum justum*, correctly understood, provides a *viable* theory of statecraft at the point of the state's use of violence in modern war.

Tucker makes an initially profoundly true contention that no matter what are the higher values the state serves, and despite the hierarchy of values in human political communities, a "realistic" statecraft nevertheless holds true if only the state is a *necessary* condition to these higher human goods. The state's "self," territorial integrity and independence may not be the supreme good. The state may be only a *conditional* instrumental value, inferior to all the rest. However, the state is a *necessary* condition to the higher values it serves. Therefore, when the chips are down, it is *as if* the state were the supreme value. Provided the state is a necessary condition, the state is *functionally* the supreme value. A *necessary* condition of all the other political goods must be protected at all costs. This the state will do, and *should* do, for the sake of those superior, unconditional values to which it is a necessary condition. The fact that in politics there are values superior to the safety of the state does not, therefore, open the way to any moral limitation upon the practice of statecraft. Precisely for the sake of those other values which the state serves and to which it is an indispensable condition, the safety of the state must be insured. Thus, the basic value is more important than all the rest, precisely because it is a necessary condition to all the rest. As an argument, this seems a clincher!

However, the requirement that statecraft insure the safety of the state needs to be correctly understood even at this initial and most fundamental level. Tucker seems to believe that what seems true when the chips are down proves that the practice of statecraft is a closed circle. He seems to believe that acceptance of the principle that each individual should be considered a moral finality in himself would not require a modification but *the end* of statecraft. Instead, the premise that when the chips are down there are no "wandering nations" stems precisely from the fact that only man has a moral finality in himself, and the state does not. Since the state is *only* a conditional value having no moral finality in itself, the safety of the state should be insured precisely for the sake of generations of men who do have moral finality and for the sake of the unconditional ends constituent of the common good.

Professor Tucker judges that a realistic statecraft requires that the moral finality resident in individual men be dismissed from politics. He should have concluded instead that the first requirement which this principle itself places upon the conduct of statecraft is that a nation's "self" be defended for the sake of finalities it has not.

This is enough to open the question whether acceptance of the principle that each individual has moral finality in himself would in other respects put an end to statecraft. Perhaps Tucker has simply misstated what is entailed by the moral finality resident in men, and found *this* to be incompatible with statecraft.

The next step is to bring into attention those many situations in which the state is a *condition,* even a *necessary* condition, to the attainment of higher political goals, but is not a *sufficient* condition to their attainment. From this the correct inference is that the state must do *more* than preserve its own safety, or that more must be done in the political community if there is to be sufficient condition for the unconditional ends to be realized in the common life. There may even be other *necessary* conditions besides the safety and independence of the state. The proper conduct of statecraft, then, will require the provision of not only all the necessary conditions but also the sufficient conditions, and all the *necessary and sufficient* conditions in directing the community to the common good.

I presume that Tucker would not disagree with this, provided only that the safety of the state is not removed from among the necessary conditions. He need not even disagree that, in view of the requirement that the conditions be sufficient, nation-state statecraft entails abundant and urgent concern for the health of the international system and the common good of mankind.

The final step, however, brings us to the crux of the matter. The fact is that not only is the state an insufficient condition in the privative sense, requiring that far *more* be done to make the conditions sufficient than preserving the state's "self" and independence by wielding quantitative increments of force. The fact is that the modern state is positively insufficient, not merely negatively so. Something *other* may need to be done. Because of the nature of the weapons into the use of which the politics of the nation-state today may extend, "necessities of state" may quite readily contradict, frustrate, and destroy those very values which the state exists to serve. The state as necessary condition may become destructive of the goals to which it is ordinarily a condition.

"Reasons of state" are valid only so long as the state itself has reason. Not that the nation-state has automatically ceased to be necessary. The dilemma is rather that the state while continuing to be in some sense still necessary may in the pursuit of its own safety today readily contradict those very goals for which it is necessary and which alone justify its "reasons of state." We must now say that the state's *raison d'état* depends for justification upon the state's *raison d'être*, which brings us again to the goods the state is supposed to serve. Rather, this was always the truth of the matter; today it is only evident beyond question. The argument that, since the state is a necessary condition, the safety of the state *functions* as the supreme value *even if it is not*, can no longer serve when that will likely *contradict* all the values it conditions. Only inflexible political reasoning can today continue along this course.

We must say not only that *more* needs to be done for there to be sufficient conditions for the attainment of the goals of politics. That should have been said all along. Instead we evidently must now say that *something other* must be done than simply to preserve the safety of the state when to do so precisely de-conditions, contradicts, and would destroy the values and finalities which alone give warrant to the state's conditional value. It can no longer be argued that because the state is a necessary condition its safety *functions* as the supreme value. In an age when the state in seeking its safety can prove positively *dis*functional as a condition (and not only insufficient), resort must be made again directly to those unconditional values and finalities which before or ordinarily warrant the exercise of statecraft *as if* the state were the supreme value. We must proceed again to adduce from these higher values and finalities better insight into the proper conduct of statecraft, along the same route by which we initially derived the basic moral reason for the state's "reasons of state," the functionally supreme necessity of its necessities, the choiceworthiness of choosing its safety before all else. The supreme ends of political community have actually become conditional, and necessarily so, and conditional to the safety of the state, in an age when the routine pursuit of these goals through the safety of the state may destroy both these values themselves and every condition for the successful pursuit of them. This is the *bouleversement* the nuclear age has accomplished!

There are two ways to make renewed appeal to the goals of political community and the finalities resident in men in reconstructing the politics of the nuclear age and our understanding of statecraft.

One way is to appeal to the goals or ends or values served by statecraft and ask again what this requires in and of the conditions. This will mean severely but prudently limiting the means it would ever be just to employ to save the state, in accordance with the principle of proportion, a proportion of effectiveness and of value. This has been the pressure to perfect institutions of an international order, correcting the structural defects of the nation-state system. This is the impulse behind endeavors to proscribe in customary international law, or by agreement, all but defensive wars, first use of nuclears, etc. This was the main emphasis of modern Roman Catholic (papal) teachings until the Vatican Council added to these limitations of prudence and proportion upon the exercise of statecraft its own additional and most solemn condemnation of aiming indiscriminately at the destruction of entire cities with their populations. (The latter is a definition of right conduct in war that follows from renewed appeal to the finalities resident in man himself.)

This is also the argument of many political scientists, notably Hans Morgenthau; and, resting as this does on a principle plainly inherent in the exercise of statecraft, I do not suppose Tucker would at all disagree. (In fact one of his charges against proponents of *bellum justum* is that they seem to him to be morally insensitive in justifying more destructiveness under the principle of discrimination than prudence or proportion would allow.) "I would say without qualification," writes Morgenthau, "that a thermonuclear war, however begun, cannot be justified on moral grounds." The reason he gives for this verdict is as follows: "The moral evil inherent in any act of violence is mitigated by the end the act serves. . . . Nuclear war destroys the saving impact that good ends exert upon evil means. For nuclear war is not only irrational, in that it destroys the very end for which it is waged, but, by dint of that irrationality, it is also immoral in that the destruction of the end for which it is waged renders its moral justification impossible." [8] In short, thermonuclear war removes the reason from reasons of state, and destroys everything that ever gave warrant to necessities of state.

The other way—an additional, not an alternative way—to renew appeal to qualities of political justice that today have become functionally fundamental to the proper exercise of statecraft is to attend to the finality in man himself which politics should serve and not contradict even in acts of war. This is the principle of discrimination forbidding acts of war aimed indiscriminately at populations as a means of "victory" or to save the state. The question is, Does this afford needed insight into the meaning of statecraft that is both proper and relevant in the world of today, or would it require, as Tucker believes, the abandonment of statecraft?

[8] *Christianity and Crisis*, Dec. 11, 1961, p. 223.

The prohibition of organized direct attack upon populations has become an evident, constituent element of statecraft today. This has become evident in the concept of the "central" war for which the nuclear nations are organized. All along, direct killing of innocent non-combatants was wrong. Moreover, while wrong it was usually *beside* the main thrust or plan of war, since (however much injustice was done in war's conduct in the past) this was peripheral and it required too much muscle to fight wars most or all of the time by civilian genocidal acts. Today such acts have become easily within reach of modern military technology (nuclear and non-nuclear). Therefore, another principle besides proportion has been laid bare in the anatomy of statecraft and in the use of force as an instrument of policy. This must be both discriminate and proportionate. Today the validity of *bellum justum* as a theory of statecraft has been thrust upon us. This is ever more evident to everyone except the defenders of old-line reasons of state and the pragmatic policy-makers and crisis-manipulators.

The small but important virtue of the limitation which the principle of discrimination imposes upon statecraft, or rather reveals to be in the nature of a proper statecraft, is the absolute prohibition of total war in all its forms. This can never be an apt exercise of statecraft. The principle of discrimination discloses the final irrationality and immorality of pure "rationality of irrationality" policies, tit-for-tat city-exchanges played out to discover who is more resolutely determined to do any and everything for the safety of the state.

Tucker invokes political prudence which begins to operate much lower in the scale of violence to place limits upon the use of force. He then benefits by bringing this against proponents of *bellum justum* who have sought to show how the prohibition of deliberate, direct attacks upon civil life, taken alone, would work out in practice in the direction of political life in the nuclear age (and in this age of subversive warfare—which is total war at the subconventional level). He forgets that *bellum justum* includes also the requirement of political prudence or the proportionate use of force no less than does his own theory of statecraft, and that discrimination is never to be taken alone.

As a consequence his readers are apt to forget that, when taken alone, prudence and proportion, which begin to impose earlier limits, have in the spectrum of violence thereafter nowhere to stop, or no reason for stopping anywhere. They are apt to forget that Tucker's theory of statecraft would not rule out the possibility of going to city-exchanges for reasons of state, to preserve the state's "self," integrity and independence in however self-contradictory a fashion.

This may only be to say that central violations of the principle of discrimination have been proved in the nature of modern warfare to be the highest form of imprudence and a political use of violence that cannot be proportionate to any good to come of it. To say this is not to say that war aimed indiscriminately upon populations is wrong *only* because disproportionate in means to ends. It is to say rather that this would be wrong for *both* reasons. It is to say that this would be wrong because it is a direct violation of the finality resident in men *and* that no good but only extensive political evil can ever come of it.

It is difficult to understand why Tucker is such a purist in moral reasoning (and therefore a purist in his theory of statecraft) that he demands to be shown that one should never wage war indiscriminately even though a very great deal of good will come from such a strategy. This is simply not the way the nations are presently organized for war. The fact is that they are organized for war in ways that cannot fail to destroy both the state's conditional value and all other conditional and unconditioned values in the political life of mankind. There has taken place a *convergence* of the two principles in placing limits upon meaningful statecraft. This is altogether different from saying that acts of war aimed indiscriminately are wrong *because* only the mutual destruction of states can come from it and not their safety. Because of this fact, no doubt, practical men are being driven to the roots again, to renew direct appeals to fundamental norms governing the use of force, in order to discern in the distinction between legitimate and illegitimate military targets the meaning of legitimate statecraft today. Mankind's slow and tortuous discovery of any political values or the achievement of insight into how to act rightly in our historical existence has always been by discovering these things to be *incarnate*.

We are not apt without such appeals to the ultimate finalities to begin to put nuclear weapons in a class by themselves as weapons intended to be not used, or not used over primarily population objectives, or to put them in a class by themselves as weapons intended to be used only in intentional non-use for deterrence's sake. Below this in the theory of *bellum justum* are all the limits of disproportion on which alone Tucker and Morgenthau seem to want to rely, as in the main did Papal teachings before the Vatican Council. The peoples and nations in the modern world, however, are not apt to proceed further in transforming *jus ad bellum* into *jus contra bellum* without more than this, without also the force of *jus in bello* (non-combatant immunity) upon political consciences.

There is a final point that is so obvious that it should not be necessary to call attention to it. Of course more is needed than aptitude in perceiving the "natural justice" which governs the political use of violence. More is needed than political prudence determining *jus ad bellum* or *jus contra bellum* and determining, in the last resort, *jus in bello* in so far as this means economy in the use of force or threats. More also is needed than *jus in bello* forbidding the fighting of the central indiscriminate war that is possible today. More is needed than *jus in bello* requiring instead that such use of these weapons be intended never to be done; and that their deterrent use be subdued until either this intended use is taken out of national deterrent-systems or, if that is not possible, a radical political reconstruction of the present international system is accomplished that can exercise statecraft in a new way stripped of the necessity of ever intending to use violence massively against populations.

In addition to the tests and impulses to justice that are inherent to the nature and meaning of a proper statecraft, there is also need for all sorts of "positive laws" and agreements and institutions among men and nations that go beyond all this in specificity, and place further limits upon the exercise of statecraft in this age of violence. There is really no reason to be found in the justice of war itself for forbidding aggressive war and allowing only the right of self-defense, or for forbidding the use of a certain weapons system as such. Still there may be needed additional rules of practice in the building of a more orderly international system, and some of these rules of practice may be additional specifications of the requirement of prudence. Today there may be growing consensus or a "customary international law" forbidding *first* use of nuclear weapons, or any use of any nuclears. Perhaps explicit international agreements should be made formalizing such customary international law on these and many other matters.

It has always been an assumption of political theory in the Western world that, while there are moral principles in the "state of nature" among the nations that are regulative of resort to war, men can nevertheless improve on the state of nature. Theirs is a task of law-*making* and institution-building. We are not apt to do this, I would argue, if we are persuaded that there is no law to be *found* in the state of nature, in the nature and meaning of statecraft and regulative of its proper exercise. But the final point to be made is the need, even so, for the further specification of law and institutions in the international order.

It is odd that anyone should suppose that a proponent of *bellum justum* in attempting to revive some memory of the minimal requirements upon the conduct of politics even in a state of nature among the nations should, because of the justifications and limitations he *finds* among the laws of war, be supposed to be lacking in cognizance of the need for further specifications of *jus ad (contra) bellum* and *jus in bello*, or that he should be accused of denying the need for a manifold work of political reason and action in the making of international law and in constructing new formations of the political life of mankind that will help to moderate and proportion political means more rationally to political ends. It is not *bellum justum* that has no room for positivism in statecraft. It is rather an entirely positivistic viewpoint has no room for justice among the constituent elements of statecraft.

PART FIVE

Vietnam and Insurgency Warfare

CHAPTER 18

How Shall Counter-Insurgency War Be Conducted Justly?*

"Modern war" is not nuclear war. Instead, the possibility of nuclear war has made the world safe for wars of insurgency. The balance of terror, which some foolishly thought would compel peace, produces instead a multiplication of wars. The military strength of the nation-state, which we thought made it impossible ever again to have a successful revolution, has led instead to an era of revolutionary wars. The possibility that any war may escalate into all-out nuclear war makes insurgency wars, in many areas of the world, an increasingly feasible choice. The fact that it would be nonsense for nations ever to fight the "central" war, or all the war they are today technically capable of fighting, produces "peripheral" wars. When the security and order of the world depends on arsenals of *militarily* useless weapons (nuclears whose use is their deterrent non-use), you can be sure that insurgency, subversion, and disorder can win victories with meager weapons that have at least this virtue, namely, that they can be used in support of somebody's purpose or policies. Thus, at the heart of the great strength of the modern state there is weakness (as Mao Tse-tung, Ho Chi Minh, General Nguyen

* A paper presented at the annual meeting of the American Society of Christian Ethics in Evanston, Illinois, January 21–22, 1966.

Giap, and Che Guevara discerned). And in the weakness of the present guerrilla there is strength: better to strike and run away, and live to fight another day; and if there are enough of him who endure long enough they may bring down a whole nation without ever winning a conventional battle. This will remain the military situation for decades to come.

Therefore the type of warfare that deserves to be called truly "modern" is "insurgency" warfare, "subversive" war, "sub-limited" or "sub-conventional" war, "revolutionary" war or "wars of national liberation," "guerrilla" war or the "war of the flea" [1]—or whatever you want to call it. There can be no doubt that the most urgent, practical, military and political question during our lifetime is, How is it possible, if indeed it is possible, to mount an *effective* counter-insurgency war, and to deliver such retribution upon it that future insurgency will be deterred, and thus the precarious, politically-embodied justice in the world be given some protection?

That, however, is not my question. Mine it is rather to ask, How is it possible, if indeed it is possible, to mount a *morally acceptable* counter-insurgency operation? Among the many considerations that are relevant to a decision that it is politically wise and necessary to resort to arms, and among the several considerations that determine the justice of a war, I shall restrict my remarks to the justice of war's *conduct*. This is to prescind from questioning the justice of the cause, the end for which the war is fought, and from making any judgment about the comparative rectitude of the social systems, the regimes, and nations that may resort to war. I shall ask (in words that were the sub-title of a book[2] I published in 1961), How shall modern war be conducted justly? The contemporary meaning of that question can only be grasped if we formulate it to read, How shall counter-insurgency war be conducted justly?

II

In determining the justice of war's conduct there are two criteria or tests that are applicable. These are the principle of discrimination and the principle of proportion.

First, a word about the meaning of and the relation between these tests—before we get down to insurgency cases. The principle of dis-

[1] The title of a book by Robert Taber (New York: Lyle Stuart, 1965). "The guerrilla fights the war of the flea, and his military enemy suffers the dog's disadvantage: too much to defend, too small, ubiquitous, and too agile an enemy to come to grips with."

[2] *War and the Christian Conscience* (Durham, N.C.: Duke University Press, 1961).

crimination is shorthand for "the moral immunity of non-combatants from direct attack." This does not require that civilians never be knowingly killed. It means rather that military action should, in its primary (objective) thrust as well as in its subjective purpose, discriminate between directly attacking combatants or military objectives and directly attacking non-combatants or destroying the structures of civil society as a means of victory. When this distinction is made, it becomes clear that the latter is the meaning of murder, which is never just even in war; while the former is the meaning of the killing in war which can be justified, including the collateral and foreseeable but unavoidable destruction of non-combatants in the course of attacking military objectives.

An exact analogue to discrimination in the conduct of war (and one which shows that this principle means to refer *both* to subjective intention and to the objective direction of the act) is to be found in the ruling of the United States Supreme Court that state-action unavoidably affecting religious practices in some of its consequences may nevertheless be constitutional provided the legislation had a "secular legislative *purpose* and *primary* effect." [3]

The second test of justice in the conduct of war is the principle of proportionality. All that Reinhold Niebuhr ever said about politics and war falls under this heading, since the principle of proportion says simply that nations, statesmen, and citizens are acting responsibly when they choose and vigorously support policies and decisions which are likely to secure the lesser evil (or the greater good) among their mixed consequences.

In summary of the two criteria governing the justice of war's conduct, an act of war may be gravely wrong, for one thing, because its primary thrust and purpose is to kill the innocent: that is murder, which no good end can justify. The same act, or another act, may be gravely wrong, for another thing, because of a serious disproportion between its good and evil effects in comparison with the mixed consequences of another deed that might have been actualized instead.

The meaning of these two "rules of practice" in warfare can perhaps be made somewhat clearer by considering the different meanings the expression "doing evil" has in connection with the one and the other criterion. Under the first test, "doing evil" means doing evil directly, having in view some good end or consequence to come from it; and that

[3] McGowan v. Maryland, 336 U.S. 420 at 422 (1961) (italics added). For other illustrations of the meaning of the distinction between "primary" and "secondary" effects *and* intentions, see above Chap. 15, p. 315, n. 2. I have elsewhere shown that at its heart this distinction originated historically, and logically always must arise, from charity seeking to deal with difficult cases in which the good alone cannot be done. This "justification" does not fall within the purposes of this paper. We must rather proceed to the "doing" of political ethics.

is inherently wrong. It is inherently wrong because of the nature and structure of the action itself, without yet counting all the costs. That is, the agent's primary purpose (if not his ultimate prediction or expectation) was the doing of an evil (for the sake of a subsequent good, of course) and the primary, direct, immediate effect was this evil. Under the second test, however, "doing evil" means doing the *lesser* evil among manifold consequences of a *not indiscriminate* act. In this sense and when one comes to count the costs "doing evil" is not always wrong. It is not immoral to do the lesser evil from among consequences that are more evil. In fact, not to do so and to allow a greater evil to prevail would be gravely wrong. Anyone who identifies every sort of "doing evil" with wickedness simply has not faced the fact that most actions—whether they are in the personal or the political or the military realms—have many consequences and not one effect only. Some of the effects of not indiscriminate actions are good, some are evil; some, a greater or a lesser evil; some, a greater or a lesser good. To choose the least evil that can be done is to choose the good that alone is possible. So there should be a proportion among the good and evil effects of an action; the good accomplished or the evil prevented must be sufficient to justify (in a comparison of effects) the evil that is unavoidably also done. This is the principle of proportion, or the requirement of prudence, in any course of conduct that can finally be justified and termed right. There must be a calculation of the costs and the benefits that flow from any action that itself is not wrong, before one knows whether to do it or not.

In summary, actions, such as acts of war, having manifold effects may be disordered from justice because the primary thrust of the act was deliberately directed toward the evil effect or toward some enlargement of it, or such actions may be disordered from justice because the primary good consequence was not worth paying and exacting the price of the evil effects. These criteria are always valid, always distinct, yet always inseparably related in judging actions having a number of effects some of which are evil. Like any two persons of the Trinity or the two natures of Christ, the principle of discrimination and the principle of proportion ought never to be either confused or separated.

The relation between the tests seems to be as follows: the ends justify the means, since nothing else can; but they do not justify *any* means. The means which no ends can justify have to be determined by the principle of discrimination. The statement that only the ends justify the means is a statement falling under the principle of proportion; so understood, it is unquestionably correct. The statement that the ends do not justify the means (or are not capable of justifying any and all means) is a statement falling under the principle of discrimination; so understood, it too is unquestionably correct. The principle of proportion is regulative of all actions that are finally *to be done;* prudence governs in determining the effects or consequences that ought ever to be let loose in the world. Especially in politics, only the ends justify the means.

Yet proportion or prudence or judgments concerning the lesser evil among the ends of action have nothing to do with whether something is the direct object of the action's impact and something else the collateral or side-effect unavoidably also produced by the action. That depends on the verdict under the first test, the principle of discrimination. This test can and should be independently applied, and an assessment of any proposed action should first be made in terms of discrimination, in order to determine the actions that are ever permissible. Then one has to choose, from among actions that are morally tolerable because they are not indiscriminate, those actions that should actually be done because of an apt proportion between their good and evil consequences.

Thus, one does not calculate a prudent number of babies to be murdered (directly killed) for the sake of any good consequences (such as getting at the government); but one tragically may and must calculate the prudent number that will and may be killed as an unavoidable side or collateral effect of military operations targeted upon the force to be repelled and whose goal and other consequence is expected to be the saving of many more from slaughter or from an oppressive tyranny, or in order to preserve in the international system accepted patterns in the actions of states on which grave consequences depend. Murder is never ordinate; but unfortunately a good deal of killing may be. Direct attacks upon a civil population can never be justified; but unfortunately—in this world to date—a good many incidental deaths and extensive collateral damage to civil society may still be knowingly done lest worse befall. So prudence rules, but it does not initiate or obliterate the discriminations that should first be made as to who is and who is not a legitimate military target.

So there are two ingredients in the moral economy governing the use of force: discrimination and proportion. Non-combatant immunity assesses the action itself with no prudential reference yet to the totality of the consequences, while the principle of proportion takes all the effects for the first time into account. An action having multiple consequences, some of which are evil, must pass both tests before it should ever be actually done. Since prudence is a virtue, to do deliberately an imprudent or a disproportionate evil is vicious. It is seriously wrong, and not only "inexpedient," to act contrary to the requirement that the use of force, which also invariably produces evil, can be justified only if it is likely to achieve greater good effects (or greater evil prevented). Still, whether the conduct is murderous must be taken up first, because one doesn't justify a proportionate number of murders. This of course is a question that is not settled by reference to subjective intention alone; we must also take into account the objective nature of what was done, the structure and outward nature and direction of the action as such. One must ask not only whether one *wanted* but also whether one *did* kill the innocent *directly*.

III

We must now apply the principle of discrimination and the principle of proportion in order to reach an assessment of the morality of insurgency warfare and the morality of counter-insurgency.

When today insurgency resorts to arms, it avoids striking the government's military forces with military means. Instead, it deliberately strikes the civil population, or a selected number of the civil population, in order to subvert a whole country's traditions and institutions and to bring down the government. The moral quality of such action, though perhaps not the extent of the damage, is like making fire-storms or city-busting an integral part of military strategy at the conventional or the nuclear level.

Of course, modern revolutionary wars are the most political kind of warfare that can be imagined. Of course, the insurgents win the allegiance of people by many other appeals; and when they gain control they often "out-administer" the government. It is not impossible for their cause to be the more just one. So did the Allies have greater justice on their side against the Hitler regime. Still what we did to Dresden was wrong, and not only because of the body-count or the extent of the damage. No matter how much a person who passionately believes and perhaps correctly believes in a revolutionary "just cause" may squirm on the point of the argument, he can avoid being impaled on it only by asserting that "just conduct" need not be taken into account in any resorts to violence.

In order to analyze the morality of the conduct of insurgency warfare, it is not necessary to examine the program of "national liberation." Instead, we must focus attention upon what happens when insurgency resorts to arms. The fact that insurgency wins by many other appeals; and resorts to terror, when it does, only in the form of *selective* terror, may be sufficient to qualify it under the requirement that cost-effects be wisely proportioned to what are believed to be good-effects. But consequences are not the only test. There is also the principle of discrimination, and this cannot justify selecting only a comparatively few among the non-combatant population to be made the direct object of attack. There are not a prudent number of babies to be murdered in order to dissuade their fathers from their evil deeds. Neither are there a prudent number of villagers, or petty officials and their families, to be disembowelled in the village square in order to dissuade others from allegiance to the existing social processes and institutions. If it is not incorrect to say that the strategy of contemporary insurgency in its (even in its minimal) use of violence is to strike selectively the civil population in order to subvert the country and to gain control of what's left of the government, then it is *correct* to say that this is an inherently immoral plan of war, no matter how many benefits are supposed to accrue from it.

The chief question, then, concerning any *counter*-insurgency operation is whether it can be effective without adopting a military strategy that is, like that of insurgency, morally intolerable. Can insurgency be countered only by strikes deliberately directed upon the civil population, or select portions of it, as a means of getting at the insurgency forces? Is it possible successfully to oppose these revolutionary wars without joining them in direct attacks upon the very people we are undertaking to protect? Are insurgency and counter-insurgency *both* bound to be warfare over people as a means of getting at the other forces?

There is evidence for believing that during the Japanese occupation of the Philippines, the Huk guerrillas pinned down in the islands a large number of Japanese forces only by terrorizing their own people more than the Japanese did. This may have contributed significantly to final victory in a war prosecuted at another level primarily against forces, even while plans were in the making for direct and indiscriminate attacks against civilians in the fire bombs over Tokyo and the A-bomb over Hiroshima that brought the war to an end. Still it is true to say that selective and not so selective terror were peripheral to the main war that was going on. What has happened in "modern" war—both at the highest nuclear level and at the sub-conventional level—is that the injustice that was peripheral even if widespread in wars of the past has now become the central war. In particular, the problem posed by insurgency warfare is whether modern warfare, by becoming more and more political in nature and correspondingly more and more selective and coldly calculating in its attacks upon the lives of non-combatants, has at the same time become irremediably indiscriminate (in the moral if not in the merely quantitative meaning of that term) by an entire rejection of the moral immunity of non-combatants from direct attack. Can counter-insurgency abide by the distinction between legitimate and illegitimate military objectives while insurgency deliberately does not?

Perhaps the term "counter-*insurgency*" contains the suggestion that the insurgency forces are the direct object of counterattack. If so, this term entails a plan of war that is significantly different from that of contemporary insurgency itself. (According to another possible and widely accepted interpretation of the expression, however, "*counter*-insurgency" entails the belief that only "defense" against "aggression" is ever justified, with the implication that if this is the reason for resorting to arms there is nothing more to be said about it. Such a view not only makes too much of the test of who first crossed under the legal boundaries or who struck first. It also contains the suggestion that the manner in which a defensive war or a *counter*-insurgency operation is conducted can find its warrant in proving that someone else did something dastardly *first*.) If an act of war is *malum in se,* if selective terror is intrinsically wrong conduct, then the doing of such an evil by one side can never justify the doing of the same evil by the other side in return. "Retaliation in kind" is justified as "protective retribution" only when the kind of retaliation is not intrinsically wrong. If only proportion governed the justice of retaliation, then only wanton or excessive punishment could be ruled out, i.e. retaliation disproportionate to the protection in view or to deterring such acts in the future; and all or any kind of actions needed to do this would be justifiable. If, however, the principle of discrimination is among the laws of war, if this also governs the practice, then not all retaliation in kind can be justified. This depends on the kind. There are some forms of retaliation that ought never to be done, not even for the sake of deterring barbaric acts of war in the future and enforcing the rules of civilized warfare itself. Just so, domestically, we say that there are "cruel (and unusual) punishments" that are not to be justified simply because they "punish," deter future violation, and thus sustain the legal order.

I believe that there can be and should be a counter-*insurgency* that meets the tests of just conduct in war, while insurgency does not. (Insurgency does not, if I have not incorrectly described the facts concerning how contemporary revolutionary warriors who are politically weak, idealistic, and impatient proceed to leave the field of community-building where their energies might be constructive and attempt to gain power more quickly and to bend a whole society to their will by the use of armed force upon selected civilians.) The meaning of a morally acceptable "counter-*insurgency*" operation is suggested by where I place the italics in that expression. This entails, of course, that counter-insurgency should primarily be directed to defeating insurgency by political and economic means, since that is the challenge thrown down by insurgency and the only way finally to come to grips with it. But we are prescinding from that in order to concentrate attention on the use of armed force that is needed in extension and in defense of even the best political purposes. Counter-insurgency as a military operation can and should make the insurgent forces the primary object of attack. That it *should* do so is clear, if there is the principle of discrimination and not only the principle of proportion morally regulating every political use of violence. That it *can* do so becomes clear if only we have in mind a correct understanding of the meaning of the principle of discrimination as we seek to apply it to the admittedly difficult situation and turmoil (the "quagmires") created by insurgency.

In order to understand the principle of discrimination and correctly to appeal to this in ethical analysis, one must understand that (1) this requires not the avoidance of all death and damage to civilians (which, of course, is impossible), but the withholding of *direct attacks* upon them and thereafter understand that the amount of collateral destruction that is morally acceptable is governed entirely by the principle of proportion); and (2) a "combatant" means anyone who is an actual bearer of the force one seeks to repress by resorting to arms. While in conventional warfare this seems easily determined by whether or not a man is in military uniform, it is still the case that (a) persons in command positions are "combatants" even though they wear tweed suits; (b) closeness of material cooperation may define a civilian as a "combatant"; (c) a man still in uniform after he surrenders is not one of the "combatants" it is just to repress; yet (d) it can be questioned whether a soldier who has surrendered may not remain a "combatant" in some fluid, jungle warfare situations in which it is impossible to insure that he will stay "surrendered." Guilt or innocence in the sense of malice or good will (even if it were possible in war to weigh hearts) would scarcely assist us to apply the principle of discrimination in the conduct of war.

In contemporary insurgency, the fact is that a peasant is often a civilian by day and a combatant by night. Others are close cooperators all or some of the time, and therefore technically combatants also. In short, the decision of the insurgents to conduct war by selective terror results in a situation in which a whole area is inhabited mainly by "combatants" in the ethically and politically relevant sense that a great number of the people *are* from consent or from constraint the bearers of the force to be repressed. "There is no profound difference between the farmer and the soldier," wrote Mao Tse-tung;[4] and so saying made it so. *The insurgents themselves* have enlarged the target it is legitimate for counter-insurgents to attack, so far as the principle of discrimination is concerned; and it is therefore mainly the principle of proportion that limits what should be done to oppose them. Since in the nature of insurgency the line between combatant and non-combatant runs right through a great number of the able-bodied people in a given area, male or female, above, say, ten years of age, and since anyone may cross over this line in either direction by the hour, it is not the business of any moralist to tell the soldiers and military commanders who are attempting to mount an effective counter-insurgency operation that this cannot be done in a morally acceptable way because under these circumstances they have no legitimate military target. In devising a military riposte, it will not be those who are directing the counter-insurgency who illicitly enlarged the target and chose to fight the war indiscriminately. Instead

---

[4] *Mao Tse-tung On Guerrilla Warfare*, translated by Brigadier General Samuel B. Griffith USMC (Ret.) (New York: Frederick A. Praeger, Publishers, 1961/65), p. 73.

the tragedy is that they *have* an enlarged legitimate target because of the decision of the insurgency to fight the war by means of peasants. Whether because he is idealistically persuaded or terrorized, many a South Vietnamese lad qualifies as a combatant without malice. It is a terrible human tragedy when American soldiers discover among the casualties after a Vietcong attack the body of a twelve-year-old boy, his maps on him, who an hour before had shined their shoes near the compound; but I do not see how it is possible to accuse them and not the Vietcong of the wickedness.

Also it is the insurgency and not counter-insurgency that has enlarged the area of civilian death and damage that is legitimately collateral. When war is planned and carried out by an opponent on the principle that the guerrilla lives among the people like a fish in water, we may be justified in accepting the destruction of an entire school of fish (and the unavoidable and foreknown destruction of a great many people intermingled with them) incidental to the elimination of the guerrillas, provided only that the elimination of the school of fish is important enough to the whole course of the war the winning of which is judged to be the lesser evil (or greater good). In other words, again it is proportion and not discrimination which counter-insurgency is in peril of violating. The principle of discrimination has already been violated by the practice of Mao Tse-tung's maxim,[5] with the result that not only is the category of combatancy enlarged but also the extent of permissible collateral damage. Of course modern revolutionary wars should be opposed, if at all, primarily by political means. We should attempt to withdraw the water and see what then happens to the fish. Still when contemporary insurgents resort to arms in support of their policies, this is the way it is done. It is therefore the shape of insurgency warfare that defines the contours of the legitimate combatant destruction with its associated civil damage that it may be just to exact in order to oppose it, subject to the limits of proportionately lesser evil. The only way to avoid this conclusion is to suppose that the just-war theory is a device for abolishing war by a (false) definition of discrimination and insuring perpetual peace by a shiboleth. Instead, the just-war theory establishes the limits and tests that should surround justified resorts to arms in a world where there is yet no peace and many new wars, in order to insure that the precarious justice politically embodied in this world can be preserved and not left defenseless in the face of selective or non-selective terror.

[5] "The [people] may be likened to water and the [army] to the fish who inhabit it." "With the common people of the whole country mobilized, we shall create a vast sea of humanity and drown the enemy in it . . ." (Q. by E. L. Katzenbach, Jr.: "Time, Space, and Will: The Politico-Military Views of Mao Tse-tung," in *The Guerrilla—and How to Fight Him,* ed. by Lt. Col. T. N. Greene (New York: Frederick A. Praeger, 1962), p. 14).

It is true that Mao Tse-tung stressed *political* warfare as the primary meaning of his fish-water maxim. "It is only undisciplined troops," he wrote, "who make the people their enemies and who, like the fish out of its native element, cannot live." [6] And in his "Three Rules and Eight Remarks," the rules are: "All actions are subject to command, Do not steal from the people, Be neither selfish nor unjust"; and the eight remarks read: "Replace the door when you leave the house, Roll up the bedding on which you have slept, Be courteous, Be honest in your transactions, Return what you borrow, Replace what you break, Do not bathe in the presence of women, Do not without authority search the pocketbooks of those you arrest." [7] Still I think it cannot be denied that the guerrilla immerses himself in the medium in which he swims when he *fights* no less than when he is making friends and influencing people. Selective terror is definitely also one of the actions that are "subject to command." The injunctions that the guerrilla avoid offending people may not unfairly be compared, in the crucial point, to the standards of personal conduct sought to be imposed upon the élite Nazi troops. Although the former is a social ethic and the more apt means of political, revolutionary war, while the latter was a rather arbitrary personal ethic, *neither* supplants nor basically changes the nature of the selective and the not so selective terror used in the conduct of insurgency by violent means. Both as a political movement and in its resort to arms, contemporary revolutionary warfare proposes to "mobilize the common people of the whole country" and to "create a vast sea of humanity and drown the enemy in it." Such is the new shape of an otherwise shapeless sort of warfare. This defines who and where are the targets that are legitimate in the conduct of counter-insurgency, and it also tragically defines how extensive is the collateral civil damage morally acceptable under the principle of discrimination.

To draw any other conclusion would be like, at the nuclear level, granting an enemy immunity from attack because he had the shrewdness to locate his missile bases in the heart of his cities. Instead of saying that we have no legitimate targets because of the extensive civil damage unavoidably associated with knocking out such missile bases, the case is rather that the enemy deliberately enlarged the extent of foreknown but collateral civil destruction in his attempt to gain a privileged sanctuary by adopting a military posture which aims at success by making hostages of more of his own population. If in U.S. policy it were possible to mount an effective deterrence by Morgenstern's "oceanic system" of Polaris submarines *alone,* and if it is possible to secure graduated and flexible military responses below and at the nuclear-missile level by locating *none*

---

[6] *Mao Tse-tung On Guerrilla Warfare,* p. 93.
[7] *Ibid.,* p. 92; and Greene, *op. cit.,* p. 6.

of these military bases on territory where people live, then we would have to say that it was grossly immoral for us to have made Omaha, Nebraska, and Colorado Springs, Colorado, legitimate objects of enemy attack. The onus of the wickedness cannot then be shifted to acts of war which in the future may destroy these cities in the course of destroying the bases and command posts. No more can the onus for having placed multitudes of peasants within range be shifted from insurgency to counter-insurgency.

Still it is the case that the principle of discrimination with its distinction between combatant and non-combatant can be shown to be intrinsic to proper counter-insurgency operations. This is still the regulative norm, as can be seen from a brief examination of the "strategic hamlet" program. This counters insurgency by attempting to withdraw the water to see what then happens to the fish. This program of "civilizing" was a success against the insurgents in Malaya, because the terrain was not so lush as in South Vietnam, because the source of guerrilla recruitment, supplies, and intelligence was an identifiable part of the population (the Chinese), and because the program was not financially corrupt or used to impose a dictatorial control over the country (as in the Diem regime). Yet as a strategy it is clear that the strategic village is an attempt to impose controls on a situation created by the Vietcong, in which all or almost all of the people are "fighters" and many, many more have been placed in peril collaterally, by enabling the combatant and the non-combatant in every man to come out and to settle down into a way of distinguishing one man from another and telling who and where he is. Thus, the principle of discrimination governing just conduct in war is the regulative norm of a central part of the counter-insurgency effort in South Vietnam. Just so, the moral immunity of a surrendering soldier from execution is still valid, even in jungle situations in which it may not be possible to guarantee that he will not promptly become a fighter again if he is not killed: the requirement is still relevant in that every effort must be made, compounds should be constructed if at all possible, etc., to enable the non-combatant to be securely distinguishable from the combatant.

Suppose, however, that the "strategic hamlet" program does not succeed in enticing the non-combatant to become separated from the combatant. Suppose it has not succeeded in a given area of the country. Suppose there are entire areas controlled and "militarized" by the Vietcong. At this point political and military decisions are to be limited and determined by the principle of proportionately lesser evil; and we must now follow out some of the options this entails. In no case can a moralist ignore the fact that a very large number of the "adult" population of an area may in fact be "combatants" and thus not immune from direct attack. Nor can the moralist deny that the remainder of the people in a given area may have been brought within range of legitimate collateral destruction. No more can the moralist or the church or churchmen *as such* determine that the collateral civilian destruction necessary in order to defeat the insurgents cannot be a lesser evil than an insurgent victory. Since the amount of combatant destruction and the amount and quality of the collateral civil damage is governed by political prudence, this is the crux of the decision statesmen must make. Private individuals and groups of citizens, of course, should contribute to the democratic debate that in its measure forms public policy. Christians who engage in this debate do so out of the inspiration of their faith, no doubt; but they do not bring to it any particular instruction that foretells how the proportionately right national decision should be made, or that enables them in advance to attach the label "immoral" to one and not possibly to another of the alternatives.

In a situation such as we have described, one alternative falling under a judgment of proportionality is a decision that an additionally destructive counter-insurgency operation should *not* be set in motion, even though it can pass muster before the principle of discrimination when this is correctly understood and applied. While in the situation supposed a given area may not be morally immune from direct attack because of the dispersal of the insurgency forces in it and while the civilian inhabitants generally may have been brought within range by insurgency's maxim and practice of war, the wisest policy (the lesser evil consequent to the tactical alternatives) may be to throw a sanitary cordon of some sort around this area while the attempt is made slowly but effectively to apprehend the guerrillas and to extend the strategic hamlet program of "civil-ization." This is the "ink-spot" or the "oil-spot" strategy; and, clearly just in itself, this may (under some circumstances) entail proportionately less evil in the effects that flow from mounting an effective counter-action.

This is one alternative, but it is clearly not the only alternative. Other options may also be in accord with the rules of practice governing the political use of armed force. The foregoing, however, encompasses the main features of the war in South Vietnam until early in the summer 1965 when the decision was made no longer to fight the guerrillas mainly as guerrillas but *preemptively* to escalate the war into a limited conventional engagement. The U.S. and its allies could have chosen then to lose the war. We must therefore explore this and other alternatives in the face of which political and military leaders, and an informed citizenry, must chart the course to be taken. In assessing the present actualities and proposals for the future, both political and military, our reasoning can and may and must be in terms of the same two rules governing political decisions, and particularly governing a decision to use *or* not to use increments in military force or to exercise in a new way a nation's power to dissuade.

IV

The situation we have been supposing, where the insurgency controls large areas of the country under attack and the guerrillas fight from behind and between the people, was the actual state of affairs early in the year 1965. Then the U.S. and South Vietnamese governments pre-emptively escalated the war in order to frustrate an expected attempt of the insurgents to launch into their final stage of conventional or positional warfare and possibly cut the country in half during the monsoon season. I propose to examine in this section a number of alternatives to the decision that was taken, and a number of the political and military alternatives that still are before us. In each case the concern will be to examine how one goes about making such decisions responsibly. This will be to expose to view the moral anatomy of political decision-making. While we will have in mind the particular and urgent problem of South Vietnam, it should be clear that not altogether dissimilar situations will arise in the future. An examination of the alternatives before us now— which range from a negotiated surrender to further escalation of the war —and an examination of the circumstances under which one or the other actual or proposed policy might recommend itself to the not indiscriminate and the not deliberately imprudent mind of a statesman may help us in thinking about the general meaning of the political responsibilities of the citizens, including the Christian citizens, of one of the great powers.

1. There was, of course, the alternative of "losing as a function of winning" (Clausewitz). This is still an option to be considered with a mind open to all that is at stake in any political decision. It is often forgotten that discriminating between direct attacks on combatants and direct attacks on non-combatants does not mean to immunize the latter while justifying the limitless killing of combatants.[8] Surely, guerrilla war-

---

[8] Even John Bennett, in a book for popular distribution, has contributed to spreading the rumor that I, by my writings on non-combatant immunity from direct attack, imply that it is a rather good thing, or a not very evil thing, to kill combatants. See his *When Christians Make Political Decisions* (New York: Association Press, 1964), p. 86; and again in *Foreign Policy in Christian Perspective* (New York: Charles Scribner's Sons, 1966), p. 120. Bennett, of course, does not fail to elaborate the principle of proportion; and he knows very well that this governs combatant and all other destructiveness in war. The "relative innocence," subjectively, of men in or out of the forces has nothing to do with either principle.

fare in some circumstances, even if an extensive and inclusive meaning of "combatant" is quite correct to use in determining who and where are the bearers of the force, would have to be compared to the senseless blood-letting of the nations' strength through the killing of combatants in the trenches of World War I. Just as this was disproportionate to any of the political purposes at stake at the outset of that war, so also to continue to prosecute counter-insurgency may be inordinate or disordered from any political purposes that can be gained by continuing to pummel a country by fighting the insurgents where they are. A negotiated surrender cannot be ruled out from a proper calculation of costs/benefits. While in "the war of the flea" it may be discriminating enough to strike at the fleas everywhere on the dog, the dog may prefer to die of exhaustion from scratching instead of being bruised to his death from internal injuries. There may be for him no proportionate reason for choosing between these alternatives.

In this connection this has surely to be said: inordinate and morally intolerable damage may be the unchoiceworthy result of unduly restricting counter-insurgency to the country under subversive attack. To force one-self to fight the insurgent by fighting with him over all or by fighting with most of the people in a particular region where one cannot tell the differ-ence between combatant and non-combatant, where in fact one has reason to believe most are combatants or close cooperators and almost everyone is unavoidably within range of justified collateral damage, rather than to strike the legitimate targets where are his source of command and supply north of the border, simply because this age assigns more sanctity to legal borders even when subversion violates them than it assigns sanctity to the life of a peasant—or to do this out of unreasoning fear of escalation or of the Chinese communists—this would be certainly immoral. Should that sort of legally concentrated but unlimited counter-insurgency war-fare become the only alternative, further resort to arms would no longer have the justification that the retribution inflicted was "protective" (i.e. ordered to the greater good or lesser evil effect) and we should negotiate some sort of settlement earlier than we may. At least, this might be the verdict if the welfare of South Vietnam were the only commonweal at stake in the outcome.

2. There is also a range of alternatives that may prudently be chosen, given the contours of insurgency warfare, which involves escalat-ing the war. The air strikes in North Vietnam have to date certainly abided by the principle of discrimination, in that the objectives have been the ground-to-air missile bases and interdiction targets such as bridges and roads used to supply men and materiel to the insurgency in the south. The evidence for this is not only that the city of Hanoi has been spared, but mainly that the elaborate and highly vulnerable irrigation system, on which the economy of the country and the livelihood of countless

peasants depends, has been carefully avoided. There remain additional legitimate military targets in North Vietnam that can still be attacked, such as rail lines from Red China, or Haiphong harbor, used to supply the war in the South by land and by sea, which can be put out of commission by discriminating bombing or by underwater demolition teams with a minimum of loss in lives of both combatants and civilians.

In any case, the decision to bomb or not to bomb North Vietnam, the question whether to include additional or fewer targets, and the question whether to increase the bombing or instead to announce a pause of three weeks—these are all questions falling under a judgment of proportion. The issue is, Which policy increases the likelihood of a just and a stable settlement? Which has greater costs or fewer benefits in its results? Anyone who debates these questions with an "absolute" standard in mind, namely, that *any* increment in the use of force is always wrong and *any* decrease in firepower is always right, simply does not understand the nature of political and military encounters. Since we have indicated our willingness to begin "unconditional discussions" [9] and since there

---

[9] The signers of *The Call for the March on Washington for Peace in Vietnam* (*The New York Times*, Nov. 23, 1965, p. 29) slander their own government and misinform domestic and world public opinion when they state that "The Johnson Administration has now been caught rejecting the peace talks it says it wants to end the Vietnam War." That statement is supported first of all by reference to Eric Sevareid's article in *Look* Magazine (Nov. 30, 1965) on "The Final Troubled Hours of Adlai Stevenson." The quotations from Sevareid's article, however, are grossly gerrymandered! In the first place, dots . . . are the only indication of why, according to Stevenson, McNamara (or someone in the U.S. government) may not have wanted to agree to begin talks with the North Vietnamese in Rangoon, Burma, *in the early autumn of 1964*. The omitted words read: ". . . the South Vietnamese government would have to be informed and . . . this would have a demoralizing effect on them." That may or may not have been a good reason; but it states the reason. These words state that not just any sort of peace talks were ever wanted (and a responsible power can say no less). In the second place, and this is a more important omission, Sevareid's account of this incident as reported to him by Stevenson, goes on to say (at the very point *The Call* leaves off quoting him!) that "*at the time of this incident, it was official American policy* that the fighting would go on until North Vietnam 'left its neighbors alone'. . . . *In other words, the Communists would have to quit first. It was not until April, in his Baltimore speech, that President Johnson changed all this* and announced that the United States was willing to negotiate for peace without preconditions." In other words, the Johnson administration was "caught" publicly changing its policy in April, 1965! It may be that our present announced policy should have been adopted earlier (as Stevenson believed); or it may be argued that our present policy departs too much from that which prevailed in the early autumn of 1964. Perhaps, in hope of saving on the "costs" to be paid and exacted, we are now liable to sacrifice too many of the political "benefits" that can be realistically expected to be forthcoming from negotiations to which no terms are set in advance. In either case, "the Johnson administration" seems to have "been caught" from time to time doing its perhaps meagerly best to make decisions that are in accord with the requirements of proportion or political prudence.

If it is true that "the war will ultimately end at the conference table," it is

are channels open by which North Vietnam and the Vietcong could easily indicate their willingness to reciprocate by not using the spared bridges and roads for further build-up in the south or their agreement to explore the possibility of a settlement with the South Vietnamese government and ourselves as the assisting power, it may be that a pause in bombing would only let worse befall and that this would be taken to indicate a lack of resolve on our parts. At the moment of this writing, it is evident that the Vietcong are willing to accept a thousand casualties if they can inflict a hundred on the U.S. forces, because at that rate they expect to win the war on the streets of the United States and in our minds.[10]

also true that the "peaces" arranged at conference tables have heretofore ultimately ended in wars. *Any* basis of negotiation is, of course, better than *none ever;* but this does not argue that the negotiation that is possible at any given time is better than judging that there is not yet a basis for a settlement that has some hope of success. A present basis of negotiation may not be as good as *none yet.*

It is arguable, of course, that the Johnson administration has been less than candid with the American public. But no political principle requires that our political leaders assay the worth of peace-feelers by a public debate about each one of them; or requires that the total circumstances surrounding a decision to make peace—or a decision not to do so yet—need not be carefully weighed in terms of the costs/benefits that are realistically to be expected. If a government is not to be censored for having political and military secrets in attempting the difficult task of negotiating war and negotiating peace, perhaps the "crime" of the Johnson administration was that it pretended to have none.

[10] Ho Chi Minh wrote Linus Pauling that "the Vietnamese people highly value" the demonstrations going on in the U.S. against the war in South Vietnam. And on Nov. 28, 1965 Seymour Topping reported as follows in *The New York Times*:

"The communist leaders evidently believe that American public opinion may exercise a decisive influence in persuading the Johnson Administration to retreat on the Vietnam issue. The shaping of American public opinion, therefore, is of prime importance.

"This may explain the costly frontal assault tactics recently adopted by the Vietcong and infiltrating North Vietnamese troops. The principal motive may be to inflict maximum casualties on American troops so as to excite anxiety in the United States and lend momentum to the anti-Vietnam war movement.

"These analysts also think that it is unlikely that the Vietnamese Communists will adopt a flexible attitude toward negotiations while they are encouraged to believe that the Johnson Administration eventually may yield under pressure of mounting hostile opinion at home."

This is not to say that the demonstrations should not be held! But it is to say that peace pledges such as the students at Oxford signed as Hitler came to power, the present anti-war demonstrations during wartime, and alike the maintenance and exercise of the precious right of dissent all are political actions that have costs their doers should recognize along with their expected beneficial consequences. Verbal protests sent also to Hanoi do not alter this fact. However the present war is ended, it may be the case that a number of additional casualties will have been paid and

On the other hand, it may be that the destruction is already disproportionate to any good consequences that *can* be gained. Decision in these terms is among the terrible responsibilities of statesmanship; and churchmen and moralists can only direct the statesman's attention to the calculus of costs/benefits in terms of which such decisions have to be made. We can also uphold and moderate responsible politico-military decision on the part of our leaders by ruling out from our own minds and from the minds of our fellow churchmen and fellow citizens those naive, extreme alternatives, namely, that when victory for the right is in prospect there is no need to count the costs, or that the justice embodied in political institutions can be preserved without paying and exacting military costs.

3. The U.S. bombing of the central highlands and other areas of South Vietnam that are in the control of the Vietcong seems on the face of it more indiscriminate than the bombing of selected military targets in the North. The use of our advanced technology as a way of avoiding a decade of counter-guerrilla warfare on the ground is bound to occasion the greatest qualms of conscience in anyone who knows that the conduct of war should be both discriminating and proportionate if it is to be a barely human and a politically purposive enterprise. What should be said concerning bombing raids, launched from Guam, upon target areas (Vietcong "strongholds") in South Vietnam? These raids, like any other actions in war, may be (a) indiscriminating (in which case one need not ask whether more good or less evil consequences are expected from them), (b) indiscriminating and also disproportionate (if one incriminates them *also* in terms of their mixed effects), (c) discriminating yet excessive acts of war in that they result in greater evil than the good to be gained, or (d) neither indiscriminate nor disproportionate.

While one's first impulse is to say that (a) or (b) must be the correct verdict, I believe that a correct assessment of the bombing in South Vietnam in terms of a *correct understanding* of what discrimination does and does not require will reveal that the debate should be between (c) and (d). In the foregoing, it was argued not only that the conduct of contemporary insurgency warfare is wrong in itself (in that it selectively attacks non-combatants directly); but also that it vastly enlarges the number of people in the territories controlled by the in-

---

exacted because of the peace movement which to be justified finally does not escape from itself falling under the rule of proportionately lesser evil. On the other hand, the Vietnam protest movement might be *politically* justified because risking or sacrificing the lives of some is the only way to save (on this view of the stakes) excessive loss of lives. It is not only that dissent is worth it, taken alone; dissent during wartime must be worth *the lives* taken. Especially in such a *political* warfare as insurgency starts, a decision to dissent is rather like a decision to use increased force; either may be *tragically wrong;* neither is inherently wicked!

surgents who should be regarded as combatants; and that, by the guerrilla practice of moving and fighting in the midst of the people like fish swimming in water, insurgency is responsible for extending the scope of possibly legitimate collateral death and damage in an entire area. This is the original wickedness that can only be compared to protecting one's forces by locating missile bases in the middle of a metropolis. In reply it may, of course, be contended that, even if this is the manner by which contemporary revolutionaries propose to seize power, the situation is no longer the same in territories over which they have established control. There, it might be said, one has a "government," not a revolutionary war. This is doubtful, in view of the fact that this year so far the Vietcong have disembowelled, decapitated, or shot four hundred village officials and grenaded scores of buses and taxis.[11] Granting that there is considerable difference between contemporary revolutionary war and the revolutionary shadow "government" of a "stabilized" area, the *moral* issue that should be pondered is whether the situation is then so radically different that we can no longer say that the guerrilla attempts to make a virtue of fighting behind and between the people among whom he lives, and thus presents the counter-guerrilla with an enlargement of the target, with its associated areas of secondary damage, which then it is quite legitimate for him to strike. Moreover, in the notably civilian area controlled by the Vietcong, namely, the Mekong Delta, the war has proceeded more gingerly, ambush by ambush; our very effective "air cavalry" is a discriminating weapon; and it can be contended that the strongholds in the highlands that have been bombed are as a matter of fact base areas.[12] Then the question is whether there are not military objectives in South Vietnam that measure many miles in diameter. When the Sixth World Order Study Conference meeting in St. Louis recommended that the U.S. "alleviate the desperate plight of non-combatants in South Vietnam by immediately restricting aerial bombardments within the country to military targets," its resolution was based on an entirely too restrictive notion of a military target or else on an erroneous assumption as to the facts. There is good reason to believe it recommended that our present policy be carried out.

The weighing of all these considerations in reaching a conclusion justifying or not justifying bombing guerrilla-held territories is quite difficult. One can "admire" in a certain sense those who do not have any doubt about their judgments; but, to say the least, no one should emulate or be swayed by public pronouncements that confuse and mislead public opinion by using an entirely false notion of the principle of

[11] See William Tuohy's "A Big 'Dirty Little War'" in *The New York Times Magazine,* Sunday, Nov. 28, 1965.
[12] See the report by Charles Mohr on "Rising War Worries Vietnamese in South but They Stay Loyal," *The New York Times,* Nov. 28, 1965.

discrimination. Thus, *The Call to the March on Washington for Peace in Vietnam* affirmed (under the heading of "atrocities") that "all of the brutality practiced by Vietnamese on Vietnamese of both sides is of *small scale* besides the enormity of the suffering, crippling, and destruction visited on combatants and non-combatants alike by the U.S. forces in the indiscriminate use of weapons far too powerful to be confined to the supposed foe."[13] This may be an "enormity": that it is has to be proved in terms of cost/benefits, taking into account all that is at stake and weighing this against the cost/benefits of genuine alternatives. But the assertion that weapons are being indiscriminately used because they are "far too powerful to be confined to the supposed foe" is *ab initio* mistaken. The principle of discrimination never required that the use of weapons be "confined" to the foe. To "prove" that the stepped-up action in South Vietnam is an atrocity because it necessarily causes a large number of civilian casualties, and *therefore* is *indiscriminate,* must simply be set down as an effort to stop a war by using an erroneous notion of what would be a discriminating one. The fact that The Call was signed by a number of leading intellectuals and ministers shows a breakdown of the tradition of justice in warfare that is almost without cultural parallel. When the leaders of public opinion show themselves not even to be within hailing distance of a discriminating understanding of the principle of discrimination, by using a notion of just conduct in war to which no war was ever supposed to conform in order to try to stop this one, then it is not surprising that in the present age some military leaders and analysts would use no notion of discrimination at all in the regulation of military action.

Still the least that can be said, and I think the most, is that the question whether the bombing of "stabilized" Vietcong "strongholds" is discriminating enough raises initially grave doubts about the morality of this action. The resolution of this question depends on one's answer to this more basic question, Has the insurgency itself presented us with an enlargement of the target with an associated area of vastly increased secondary damage? And the least that can be said concerning the question whether, even so, the destruction entailed is incommensurate with a realistic estimate of the political benefits that there is hope of gaining is that no one should surrender to certitude concerning his own prudential judgments or impune the motives or the wisdom of men who disagree. Nevertheless we know that there are enormities in the action in South Vietnam that can only be warranted by greater enormity in the alternatives that would befall without this action; and we certainly know that (because of the inchoate character of insurgency) counter-

[13] *The New York Times*, Nov. 23, 1965, p. 29.

insurgency is most apt to violate the principle of proportionately lesser evil.

Not only so; but there is something problematic about reaching the conclusion that acts of counter-insurgency may be discriminating enough but yet are in grave peril of becoming disproportionately destructive. In modern war at the nuclear level, the fact that nuclear strikes can conceivably be discriminating and yet be excessive leaves us with a problem instead of the solution to one; this presses thoughtful men to search for other more flexible, more graduated and moderate responses. Just so, in modern war at the sub-conventional level where war again threatens to become "total," it is not enough to devise solutions that show that effective counter-insurgency operations are in accord with the principle of discrimination but still are likely to be excessively destructive. This paradox of a justly-discriminating-yet-unjustly-excessive means or plan of war drives thoughtful men to search, for example, among incapacitating gases, for other more discriminating and minimal responses with which to arm counter-insurgency. The ethical issues raised by this quest for less destructive or more humane means to be used in counter-insurgency warfare will be considered in the following chapter. Paradoxically, many of the same people who regard the use of napalm and the bombings in South Vietnam as an unjustifiable enormity because these weapons are self-evidently indiscriminate would also judge that the use of more discriminating weapons, if they are gaseous, would be even more *self-evidently* atrocious. SANE has become an exceedingly degraded word in our language!

4. There are also a number of broader military questions falling under a judgment of proportion; and there are all sorts of political decisions that have to be made as we come to negotiate a settlement at the conference table. Each raises the question whether there is an actualizable alternative that is apt to produce a lesser evil in all its consequences than the destruction caused by that measure of resort to arms needed to secure a more favorable political solution, or whether an increment in the force employed may not make a stable political solution more difficult.

All the available studies of insurgency as an exceedingly political form of warfare, and of the political and military means necessary to defeat it, warn that the military factor cannot predominate over the political, or an outside assisting power become more prominent than the local government to which the allegiance of the people must be won. The only effective way to assist in fighting guerrillas as guerrillas seems to be the system of "counterparts" in which the local government is both militarily and politically in command. This precisely failed in South Vietnam. But then the war should no longer be regarded as a classical guerrilla war. It is now a "limited" war approaching the scale of the Korean action. What can be the justification for this?

It is likely that to warrant the present scale of destruction one has to see the connection between South Vietnam and the independent development of all the people of Southeast Asia, and the balance of power in the world at large. Unfortunately the dog which the fleas have now singled out for most massive assault is not the only one whose comfort and life is at stake. The "domino" theory is inaccurate for Southeast Asia only because it suggests too rigid an image to represent a situation in which the task of government is more like running a footrace in a carload of peas.

Perhaps it could still be argued that a merely face-saving solution in South Vietnam would not weaken the security of Thailand so much that the latter would be too much of a price to pay for a temporary solution in South Vietnam which would bring to an end the present scale of destruction. That might buy time in which to assist in strengthening Thailand, whose forthcoming attack by insurgency was publicly announced long ago by the peripatetic Chou En-lai, which threat was repeated as late as early this year (1965) by Foreign Minister Marshal Chen Yi of Red China, where the formation of the Thai Patriotic Front has been announced by Peking Radio. Thailand would seem in some respects to be a better "battle ground" because of its traditions as a country that was never under French colonial rule. In other respects, it is a more difficult country to aid against contemporary insurgency because of a large minority of Chinese in its population and because of the presence in the country of a great many Vietnamese "refugees." The latest events in the terrorism that has already begun in northeastern Thailand was the murder of twenty-four local political officials and school teachers disclosed on Nov. 26, 1965.[14] If not Thailand, then India —unless one wants uncharitably and self-interestedly to "spiritualize" politics all the way back to fortress America by giving economic aid but never political and military aid to countries other than our own. Perhaps (with a stress that is heavy with irony) we should aim only to show in South Vietnam that we cannot be defeated *by military means* (but are willing to accept defeat by the kind of peace we agree to).

Again as always in questions requiring that greater and lesser evils or goods in all the consequences be weighed in the balance, he who discusses such questions on the assumption that to use more force always leads to worse results simply is not exercising his capacity for political prudence.

5. For anyone not antecedently convinced of the single overriding absolute principle that the triumph of Titoist types of communism is in

[14] *The New York Times*, Nov. 27, 1965.

general the greater good, the fact that the success of the "war of national liberation" in South Vietnam would liberate the whole of that traditionally anti-Chinese nation into a nationalistic form of communism would only change the factors to be weighed in any judgment of proportion. It would only lead to the conclusion that, since such a national communism is not so gravely evil as the Chinese, or so dangerous to the world at large, less should be paid and exacted by war's destruction to save from coming under "nationalistic" communist domination a people who might still be saved from it; and to disagreement over whether this can still be done or not. It remains the case that no Christian and no man who loves an ordered liberty should conspire with communism in coming to power. (This is a different question from whether it is possible to serve God in a communist land.) Then there arises an obligation to assist others in resistance to communism, even in its more "liberal" forms, if there are actual alternatives. This political obligation disappears, of course, if it cannot be done; or if to do so would produce greater evil than the evil prevented. These, then, are the questions: whether what ought to be ought to be politically done, whether what ought to be politically done ought to be politically done by us, whether there is power commensurate with these responsibilities of a leading democratic society, and finally whether what ought to be politically done by us can be prudently done.

Depending on the outcome of such political reasoning as this, different answers will be given to the question whether we should agree to negotiations with the Vietcong—"a primary combatant" (thus reads *The Call for a March on Washington for Peace in Vietnam*). So was Franco "a primary combatant" against the Spanish Republic. That too was a civil war as well as one supplied from abroad. A decision now to designate the Vietcong as "a primary combatant" in a sense warranting it a primary shaping, much less a controlling influence on the political settlement will have about the same effect as the U.S. decision to embargo shipments of arms to the Spanish Republic. Those who judge these effects to be the lesser evil will judge this to be the thing that should be done. But nothing in such a possibly prudent present decision will prevent both civil wars from being dress rehearsals for wars to come—which prospect ought not in prudence to be altogether disregarded and ignored in reckoning the consequences.

6. Suppose, next, that the present or some future level of the war in South Vietnam impels Hanoi to come to the conference table (coupled with the world-political situation as a whole, including pressure from Russia—which country by our present resistance has not been left free to compete with impunity with Red China for the direction and acceleration of these insurgency wars). The political questions then arising are all of them questions of political prudence that are not

to be settled by any absolute judgment that the earlier the cease-fire the better or that any basis of negotiation is better than none yet. On these widely-accepted premises, the result could be comparable to what happened as we brought the Korean conflict to a close. Bernard Brodie has described this as follows:

> When the Communists showed an interest in discussing an armistice, which they communicated through the Russian delegate to the U.N. headquarters in New York, Mr. Truman immediately stopped an offensive which our forces had recently initiated and which was going extremely well. This was done for the sake of making a gesture—a sort of good will gesture. We tend to feel it is morally good to make such gestures. We learned soon afterward that at the time we stopped our offensive, the Chinese Red Armies had been in a state of incipient collapse. Our relaxation of pressure gave them a chance to save themselves, to restore their army from a condition of absolute demoralization. It of course also relieved the pressure on the Communist negotiators. The result was that the negotiations for the termination of that war dragged on for something over two years. I submit that had we continued that offensive until an armistice was actually signed—as nations at war have always done in the past—the negotiations would have lasted a few days to a week rather than over two years, and the terms would have been much more favorable to us. Further, the Chinese would not now be calling the United States a "paper tiger." One perhaps dismisses this kind of label, saying it does us no real harm. I think it does. I think it does us harm in a way that may ultimately cost lives.[15]

Since the Chinese transferred their weapons across their continent to be used in Southeast Asia, this "gesture" may be said, by remote but definite steps, to be now costing American lives. General Giap and Ho Chi Minh know well enough that you cannot win at the conference table anything that *it seems evident* you could not win on the battlefield, or are not resolved to win.

7. Should the 1954 Geneva Accords be made the basis for negotiation? Perhaps, but not without searching thought about this proposal, and by a politically prudent decision that is altogether free from the objective malice contained in the thought that peace is worth any price. The "essentials" of the Geneva agreements which today are most often recalled seem to be an excellent position to which to repair. These are: the "regroupment" of all forces and the erection of temporary administrations north and south of the provisional military demarcation line which has now become the boundary between North and South Vietnam; the eventual withdrawal of all foreign military forces; promises that the interested foreign powers will not arm forces within

---

[15] "Morals and Strategy," in *worldview*, Sept. 1964, p. 6.

Vietnam; a prohibition against military alliances, i.e. the neutralization of Vietnam; the peaceful reunification of Vietnam; and the self-determination of the Vietnamese people. Little exception can be taken to any of these principles—except that the first is hardly consistent with the proposal that the Vietcong be recognized as a "primary combatant" and negotiations opened with the National Liberation Front.

It ought not to be forgotten, however, that there were other "essentials" in the 1954 Geneva Accords. Those agreements were also so essentially lacking in effective inspection and enforcement procedures that the signators should have known, and probably did know, that they were in no sense creating an instrument for the pacification of politics and the government of men in that area of the world. Nor would similar pious accords be a responsible political act in any other place on earth or at any other time in human history. It ought not to be forgotten that (whatever the reason South Vietnam refused to sign the Geneva agreement), the U.S. refused to sign because it had failed to prevent the concessions Mendes-France was willing to make to Ho Chi Minh in order to conclude quickly a war France had already lost on the battlefield and in France itself. The "control commission" had no freedom of movement to inspect for violations of the agreement. Within the so-called control commission there was instituted the first achievement by Russia of the "troika" principle. And, finally, the commission could only "report" violations to Great Britain and Russia, the co-presidents of the conference. This immobility and the "troika" (Poland's veto over any judgment of violation India and Canada might agree on) made the agreements impossible to enforce, even if enforcement had been prearranged. *For these reasons* the United States emphasized, in its separate announcement that as a non-signator it would abide by the agreements, that this was contingent upon no other nation violating them.

These facts are pointed out not to compel prudence to reach the conclusion that the 1954 Accords could never be the basis for fresh negotiations, but to point out that these are the considerations political prudence must take into account. Perhaps a negotiated patch-work is the best solution permitting us time to enforce politically and militarily other ramparts; but then we should be conscious of the fact that we are using the conference table only to make it clear that we cannot be defeated *by military means,* and that it is by political means combined with the insurgency which is certain to continue that the South Vietnamese will be allowed to succumb to a "national communism."

8. A more ominous projection of the future course of events than compelling the negotiation of a stable and enforceable solution comes to mind when we remember that, no matter how successful we may be in frustrating the insurgents' effort to launch themselves into positional

war and win the final victory, there is no need for them to come to the conference table because of this. They can simply return to the lower levels of guerrilla warfare. This prospect is contained in the comments of a good many American observers and analysts, to the effect that all we have gained is time—time to correct the mistakes of more than six years during which counter-insurgency did not succeed in stopping the insurgency. We have only "stopped losing the war." We may yet face the harsh prudential decision whether we are going to defeat the guerrillas as guerrillas. The political reforms necessary to do this, necessary to withdraw the water to see what then happens to the fish, are inherently good and well worth doing. But the cost entailed by the necessary military means can perhaps best be indicated by the fact that during the eleven years in which the British successfully fought the subversion of Malaya it required 6,500 man-hours of patrolling or lying in ambush even to *sight* a single guerrilla; and of ten sighted, nine escaped; and by the estimates of some experts that it takes fifteen counter-guerrillas to defeat a single guerrilla if we are not going to join him in making morally "total" war on the people by means of selective terror. It may be that the war will be ended by early negotiation. It may be, as General Maxwell Taylor suggested,[16] that the end will come by the quiet cessation of Vietcong activity and the "eventual dissolution" of the guerrilla apparatus. There is, however, this third, and it is a harsher, alternative. We may discover in the very marrow of our bones and in the horror hollows of our hearts that de-escalation has greater costs per benefit than escalation.

V

To the foregoing "political fragments" may be added the following "concluding unscientific postscript" on the role of principles in political decisions, on the role of the church in fostering apt political principles in the societies in which it lives, and finally a supplementary explanation of how I am making up my mind (and how I judge any Christian ought to make up his mind) about revolutionary wars.

Theoreticians quite rightly speak of the national common good (or "interests") and the world common good, of order and justice, of *lex, ordo,* and *justitia,* etc., as—all of them—terminal political values. They speak of determining political responsibility in an area of congruence among these ends; and of the need to secure them by the use

[16] *The New York Times,* Oct. 28, 1965.

of force in the government of mankind.[17] We quite rightly speak of the principle of discrimination and the principle of proportion governing a proper use of armed force.

When all is said and in all that is done, however, we must ask how these principles function or should function in the actual decision-making process. None of these concepts are drawn from another world and extrinsically imposed upon the political realm. If they were, they would, alternatively, too greatly constrict the statesman's decision in reaching a solution to his problem or provide him too ready an escape from his quandary over finding the right thing to do. These principles do not tell him what to think. They rather tell him how he will think and does think when he is thinking in a politically responsible fashion. They are, in sum, intrinsic principles which *anatomize* the nature of politically responsible action. A decision's act of being proper politics (its *bene esse*) will have at least these components. Political *agency* is itself (as Aristotle knew) a moral act; and "government" (in our forefathers' understanding of the word, unfortunately not in ours) is in itself a matter of morality. The task is to analyze what this morality is. If there was current among us a proper understanding of ethics or politics it would be impossible to make such statements as: "Any *military* decision to use [x] would most certainly be made in the light of other important factors such as political, economic, health, and *perhaps even moral considerations*." [18]

It is not to deny the regulative power, and moreover the universally regulative power, of these general principles if now we go on to say that how they function in a statesman's conscious deliberations or the value of calling these theories to his attention are rather different questions. As one of the theoreticians, I, of course, believe that it is worthwhile to clarify the meaning of discrimination, proportion, etc. Any of these concepts may serve to enlarge the statesman's or a citizen's awareness of forgotten political realities or goods. The principle of proportion serves to jog us loose from notions that if the cause is right there is no need to count the costs or from the notion a political good can be secured without costs. The principle of discrimination serves to remind us of the fullness of the respect due to the human beings who are not to be wholly politicized or militarized for the sake of some supposed future state of affairs through any present action óf ours that upturns the proper

[17] See, for example, my own articles, "The Uses of Power," *Perkins Journal of Theology*, Vol. 18, No. 1 (Fall 1964), 13–24, and "The Ethics of Intervention," *The Review of Politics*, Vol. 27, No. 3 (July 1965), 287–310; Chaps. I and II of the present volume.

[18] *Chemical-Biological-Radiological Warfare and Its Disarmament Aspects*. A study prepared by the Subcommittee on Disarmament of the Committee on Foreign Relations, United States Senate, August 29, 1960, p. 23 (italics added).

relation between arms and men, between forces and political communities, even in a justifiable resort to the use of force. This should jog us loose from the notion that revolutionary causes are so just and so good that these ends can justify *selective* terror.

Still, it is impressive how little our political leaders may need or be able to think about these norms in their day to day, crisis to crisis, lives. This is true not only of my categories, but of any concepts, such as, for example, the *"real* national interest." That, too, is an abstraction, in that it is always regulative in political decisions in such fashion that, combined one way or another with other norms in the statesman's mind and in a nation's ethos, it is always *being concretely applied.* No politico-ethical norm is *first* thought out and *then* applied. In the flux of pressing circumstance the focus of attention is properly almost always on the particular case, never on the perspective-giving and the regulative concept. This is true, without taking anything from the validity of political principles—even if, to understand this, we have to say that particular political decisions are always about to have been right or wrong.

Two instances reveal the awesome responsibilities of magistrates in ruling by particular decrees. Arthur M. Schlesinger, Jr., reports that President Kennedy believed that "there was a *point* at which," if U.S. assistance in South Vietnam became too massive, it might "turn Vietnamese nationalism against us and transform an Asian civil conflict into a white man's war"; still he increased our military and other forms of assistance because "the fact that the Vietnamese seemed ready to fight had made him feel that *there was a reasonable chance of making a go of it. . . .*" [19]

The second instance concerns modern "conventional" war. If Churchill had consulted Britain's "national interests" in 1940, even if he had consulted Britain's *"real* national interests," he might have made as fast and favorable an armistice with Germany as possible. Instead, he, too, believed there was a reasonable chance of making a go of it; and he could only risk this, since he could not know that Hitler, months later, would make a miscalculation that was to enable Britain to survive. Churchill's decision and leadership, when taken, were about to have been right; he could easily have been about to have been wrong. This is ordinarily the case in international affairs in regard to decisions that turn upon a proper application of the requirements of proportion. Well do I remember the much-publicized charge against Churchill made by a Roman Catholic Archbishop (the fact that he was Irish and by nurture somewhat anti-British was surely not irrelevant) to the effect that some of the utterances with which Churchill rallied the British nation were "immoral"

[19] *A Thousand Days: John F. Kennedy in the White House* (Boston: Houghton Mifflin, 1965), as reported in *The New York Times,* Nov. 25, 1965 (italics added).

on a strict or on any construction of the principle of proportion! While the requirement that greater and lesser evils be weighed is never suspended, great decisions are often made in answer to the question whether it is just possible that this risk may be more justifiable than that; and some of the most noble political decisions have been made in terms of a resolve ventured in the face of impenetrable uncertainty. Since *nothing is the wave of the future,* such noble ventures conform, after all, or do so as it turned out, to the principle of proportion, provided only that the course taken was not foreknown to be predetermined to fail or to cost more than the end was worth. Thus it is probable that the decision of the Johnson administration to step up the war in South Vietnam was made in the belief that there was still "a reasonable chance of making a go of it," in not only stopping the subversive aggression but also deterring it in the future so that other countries in that part of the world can be preserved from similar assault. This is not to contend that these decisions were not tragically mistaken; but it is to contend that the outrageous excesses of our public debate over Vietnam, and particularly the charge that these decisions were "immoral," demonstrates an astonishing failure to understand the nature of political decisions—and on the part of adults and intellectuals who should know better, a reprehensible failure.

This argues, I believe, that church pronouncements (in domestic politics also, but certainly in foreign affairs) should, to say the least, be "minimalist" and not "maximalist." After all, it is the deliberately imprudent mind, it is any policy that for the sake of the idea of "victory" consciously does not count the cost, and it is the deliberately uncharitable mind that draws back from paying the costs necessary to achieve beneficial results in the political order, that are to be censored. And no perspective upon politics more definitely *refers* the matter to be decided to the statesmen and to the *public* forum than the principle of proportion. It is true that men need to be reminded of this important guideline in the formation of foreign policy. It is true that the principle of discrimination is a more substantive moral limit upon acts of war, and this basic test of the justice of war's conduct needs to be urged in season and out of season. But even in connection with the principle of discrimination, members of ecclesiastical councils should listen to experts in the political and military sectors and learn from them the new shape war may have assumed in any age, and thus learn to know the meaning of a present application of the principle of discrimination. Churchmen cannot, because *the principle* cannot, determine the cases to be subsumed under it. Moreover, when an understanding of the meaning of discrimination has been reached (from a dialogue between moralist and magistrate), it will certainly not be among moralists or in any church forum that the decision will be made that one account and not another of permissible collateral death and damage is ordinate to the issues at stake. It is the deliberately indiscriminate mind and the deliberately imprudent one that should be censored. A determination of the exact meaning of discrimination and finding the proportionately lesser evil in the conduct of politics and war are both, in different ways, finally the task of the magistrate and persons in their citizen capacities.

Today, Christian comment upon foreign policy evidences but little concern to press relentlessly the requirements of discrimination as these may be shown, by the manifold work of intelligence on the part of the moralist and the technical expert alike, to bear upon modern warfare. The word is most often used with a mistaken meaning that could not be more irrelevant to actual decisions of state in this or any other age; and when the true meaning of this requirement is exhibited, one couldn't be less interested. This seems to yield too little for "prophetic" voices to use in criticizing the government! Better stick to the principle of proportion in which we all are expert, and which defines right action altogether in terms of consequences. Any assemblage can, of course, construct a historical prediction that has verisimilitude; and there are always a number of these guesses, supported by all sorts of facts, to which to succumb; and, if they are non-governmental, to bring in "prophetic" criticism of present policy and in support of some other policy. This does, indeed, yield maximalist church pronouncements jurisdictionally beyond the competence of churchmen *as such.*

Something like this is always the nature of democratic discussion of public policy. Probably the churches are able to predict the good and evil consequences and to propose policies falling under the principle of proportion about as well as any other group within our society. Suppose these policy recommendations are the best yet proposed; they would still, I suggest, be questionable church actions. For then the church blurs the distinction between itself and all other groups in the society who in any measure participate in the formation of the public mind; and it inordinately seeks to assume in the name of the church decisions that belong to the realm of the state. Unless it can be made clear in what way Christian instruction can as such substantively lead to these conclusions, then this is simply to put the engine of religious fervor behind a particular partisan political point of view which has as much and no more to recommend it than if it had not emanated from a church council. This confuses the realms of church and state, of moralist and magistrate (or citizen); and it undoubtedly secures maximalist resolutions.

The shrewdest device yet for accomplishing this purpose is the reservation that the resolutions and pronouncements on all sorts of subjects advising the statesman what he should do which issue from church councils do not represent "the church" but only the views of the churchmen who here happen to be assembled. Thus, a group of concerned Christians free themselves from having to weigh their words lest they falsely commit the church and speak an inadequately Christian word to this age, and of course they are not in the position of the statesman who has to bear responsibility for any cost/benefits he may have left out of account. One can scarcely imagine a situation that to a greater extent invites irresponsible utterance. "The Pastoral Constitution on the Church in the Modern World" issued by Vatican Council II may be an imperfect document, but at least that council has not only addressed the modern world and has not only spoken *to* the whole church. In doing *this*, it has also placed upon itself the requirement of speaking *for* the whole church; it has tried to be *the whole church speaking*.

The opening words of the report in *Christianity and Crisis* (Nov. 15, 1965) on the proceedings and findings of the Sixth World Order Study Conference, meeting recently in St. Louis, seem at first reading to be heavily laden with irony: "That 463 people from all sections of the nation could in a three-day meeting draw up and reach agreement on policy statements on all the major—and many of the minor—foreign policy issues affecting our country seems incredible. That, in addition, they listened attentively to eight addresses more or less pertinent to the subjects under discussion would tend to make this a minor miracle." Those words were surely meant to call in question the worth of any such findings. Or so it seems until the correspondent's concluding remark that "the very fact that the delegates felt impelled to speak so forthrightly on a number of controversial issues is reassuring in a day when the pressure to conform to Administration policy on foreign affairs is so strong." Is that damning with faint praise? Is the meaning only that the expression of almost any opinion so long as it is opposed to something is a sign of health in our society? That would be to say that in this instance a church assemblage did something that is indirectly good for the state because it was contrary-minded, no matter what was the substance of its resolutions. But the matter is not to be left on that ground. The final verdict upon the St. Louis conference, we are told, depends on how "zealously" these "goals" are pursued by the National Council of Churches' International Affairs Commission and its participating communions. In short, although procedurally the conference did not speak for the church and did not *require itself* to say no more than it judged could be said *for* and *by* the church as such, its "goals" (agreed to in three days on a great many of the major and minor questions of this nation's foreign policy) are now very definitely to be spoken *to* the church as precedental determinations of responsible Christian decisions and action in the political life of this nation. Freedom and dissent within the church, of course, will not be coerced. Still these resolutions become a part of the fabric of "positions" taken (through a confusion of roles) by churchmen in the past to which appeal can and will be made in the future practically to unchurch anyone who (within the limits of the principles that should instead have been addressed to him) properly exercises his competence as a citizen to reach opposite conclusions about foreign policies and the not indiscriminate acts of war that serve the greater good or lesser evil.

As long as this situation prevails it will not be our Christian patrimony that is being appropriated or Christian insights and principles that are probed, revivified, and exhibited in their relevance (so far as this can be shown) to the crucial decisions of men in this age. Instead it will be some amalgam drawn from that late product of western culture and now spread like a veneer over all the world, namely modern liberalism (God save that word for better usage, since I cannot!). Of this it simply has to be said that by these views modern man will continue in the best of causes to place himself on the rack, and that on this understanding of political community mankind will finally become ungovernable at home and abroad. Unless and until a way is found by which the church can reappropriate its own heritage of political insights, then it will continue to be the case that Christians will only exacerbate domestic political debate in its extreme conservative-liberal question-begging polarization. And we shall continue to allow it to be supposed that from somewhere in the Christian understanding of human life we have been given to believe such foolish notions to be true as that disarmament (nay, even general and complete disarmament) can be achieved without first resolving outstanding political conflicts, or that the weaker the U.N. becomes as an apt decision-making, threat-removing, and peace-keeping body the more the nation-state has the right only to load it with more enormous problems to solve, or that the multi-national system will work and requires no fundamental revision if only neighbors will leave neighbors alone (non-intervention). The situation at the moment is, I should say, that even Reinhold Niebuhr signs petitions or editorials as if Reinhold Niebuhr never existed! [20]

VI

Finally, in objection to the foregoing analysis of justice in the conduct of insurgency warfare it may be asked whether I mean with Luther to side always against those who make revolution and with those who oppose it. Neither in theory nor in practice is this the conclusion to be drawn.

[20] [For a full-length elaboration of the foregoing vindication of the church's address to the world and a critique of its recent address, see my *Who Speaks for the Church? A Critique of the 1966 Geneva Conference on Church and Society* (New York, N.Y. and Nashville, Tennessee: Abingdon Press, 1967).]

In practice, even if a revolution happens to be wholly unjustifiable because it uses means no end can warrant and seeks ends for which no political means are apt and is on balance evil in its worldwide consequences, it does not immediately follow that the United States should oppose it militarily. Not all that should be should be politically done; nor all that politically should be done should be done by us; nor all that should be done by us can be done. This is a world in which many have perished, more will; and there shall be revolutions and rumors of revolutions, but the end is not yet. We can agree with those who say that the U.S. is not a self-appointed world-policeman, if this is meant to make an unbending principle of our responsibility to use our power to affect events beyond our borders. The reexamination, revision, and possible contraction of our far-flung alliances and commitments is a legitimate question falling under the principle of proportion.

Still the pressure of a charitable concern for mankind will be toward the assistance of as many as possible of those who need help where there are means apt to do this, and where we (or we alone) possess these means. Senator Frank Church's call for a reexamination of our foreign involvements is good, except for *the ease* with which he concluded for reasons of state, Santo Domingo, yes; Vietnam, no! [21] A nation's responsibilities are indeed to be located within an area of congruence between the national common good and the common good of other peoples; but these are not fixed areas of overlap. They are permeable boundaries, and boundaries that can be construed narrowly or with a deeper sensitivity to the meaning of each. The Christian influence in our nation, it would seem, should be in the direction of including within the scope of national policy as much of the world common good as is realistically possible, and toward this nation providing itself with usable power, and the use of power, commensurate with these responsibilities so far as this can be done.

One thing this administration's declaratory policy and that of those who oppose it have in common: a belief that in the political world of the nation-state system neighbors are to be expected to leave neighbors alone. To see that they do would, indeed, be an illimitable task for the U.S. to assume. It is *conceivable* that there might be a world organization with radical decision-making, threat-removing, and peace-keeping capabilities which would insure that nations left one another alone. It is *conceivable* that the U.S. and Russia might agree *to enforce something* (what, doesn't much matter, e.g. non-proliferation of nuclear weapons, or a Kashmir solution, or something else) and this would be

[21] "How Many Vietnams and Santo Domingos Can We Afford?" *The New York Times Magazine*, Sunday, Nov. 28, 1965.

the beginning of the hegemony of the two great powers insuring that neighbors leave neighbors alone. Neither of these conceivable solutions is possible now or possible without tyranny. But it is quite *inconceivable* that one hundred and seventeen or more sovereign nations, great and small, will leave one another alone. In short, non-intervention is not a principle of world order, without some ordering power. This is only a lure always on the edge of political realization which is sometimes helpful, sometimes harmful to bring to bear on concrete decisions. It is the crisis in the government of mankind today. And this describes the world situation in which the citizens of a great power must somehow chart their nation's course. While a charitable concern for the world's plight should not lead to imprudent burden-bearing, it would seem that Christians should also not welcome every redrawing of the circle of the national good which because more restrictive in its inclusion is ever more expansive in its exclusion of neighboring-peoples in this one world. Are there not a number of signs in our current debates over foreign policy that evidence a return to that state of affairs during Hitler's early years which Robert Lowry Calhoun, himself a pacifist, reported with deep personal shock to us who were then students at Yale Divinity School that there was a good deal of traffic between the office of the midwestern branch of the Fellowship of Reconciliation and the America First Committee located on the same floor of an office building in Chicago?

As for theoretical approval or disapproval of revolutionary movements, I *do* mean always to side with the doctrine of justifiable revolution as this was developed out of the just-war theory (hedging revolution with the same limits) by Calvinists of the second generation and beyond. I do mean *not* to side always with those who make revolutionary wars and against those who oppose them. I do mean not to side indiscriminately with revolutionary movements because their cause may be just. For Christian conscience the killing of an enemy or the destruction of an oppressor were alike always such an evident *prima facie* violation of *agapé,* that these actions required justification in terms of countervailing requirements of *agapé;* and this squeeze upon the definition of right conduct produced those severe limits upon the conduct of war or of revolution. It also produced the politics of an ordered liberty that has prevailed to date in the Puritan political heritage. Revolutionary violence was no more to be approved than international conflict, unless either could be shown to be possible within the stated rules of practice and the justice that a charitable reason could discern to be properly regulative of these last resorts in politics. Therefore, political action before that point was pacified and disciplined to live within compromise and to pursue limited ends by moderate means only. This was productive of that understanding of liberty in an ordered community life which alone deserves the name of liberalism.[22]

This makes me—I grant, I know, I even affirm and celebrate— "parochial." Nor should a Christian with this particular patrimony have it otherwise, in a vain effort to become the universal man of the future by now becoming extremely rootless and other-directed. It may be that these same sound political principles are possible on the ground of other religious cultures; but they are not yet in evidence in many parts of the world. In any case, whatever the coming world civilization may be like, it will not be what it should be and might have been unless one of the strong vectoral influences going into it is the religious and political tradition of which we are the heirs. It is of peerless importance that the justification and these limits, and these limits as well as the justification, morally regulative of revolutionary movements no less than of wars, gain voice. It may be possible for there to be an original invention of a politics of ordered liberty on other religious and cultural grounds, or from the pressures toward this from the nature of political life itself. Still ecumenical politics and that coming world civilization are not likely to be the same if there takes place here and now a "treason of the clerks" among the heirs of western, Christian civilization.

What, however, has happened among us?

Domestically, there are a good many Christians who take pride in deliberate identification with what is called "the freedom movement" in distinction from "the civil rights movement"; and who defend and practice the violation of social disciplines and violations of "social due process" or the production of "creative social turmoil" because the urgent end in view is believed to justify any effective means to secure it so long as these means are "non-violent." That justification must simply be set down as a foreign importation into American life, an extra-Christian norm imported into what's left of Christendom, and by no means a sufficient discrimination as to the methods to be used while effectively struggling for political goals. While we may have proceeded along the way toward proving to the theorists of insurgency warfare that guerrillas can operate effectively in urban situations, provided they avoid awakening counter-resistance by using violent or too violent means, Christians who have been beguiled to this view of our domestic political life because of the genuine Christian impulses everywhere at work in this movement must simply be told that every revival of religion in the last hundred years has revived less of it—including the current revival of religion in the streets. These phenomena may have

[22] See the chapter on "Justifiable Revolution," in my *War and the Christian Conscience*, pp. 114-133.

the form of godliness and be evocative of much religious enthusiasm and idealism. But, the substance afforded by many of the great Christian concepts with their perspectives upon man's collective and historical and political existence are exceedingly lacking. It is not at all surprising that there are disciplines and restraints upon a responsible exercise of liberty within a democratic and constitutional political order that are also often lacking—except those born out of the extensible notion of non-violence.

Looking out upon this age of worldwide political turmoil and violence, there are those among us whose single, overriding political norm seems to be the justification of radical social revolutions wherever they may be occurring, threatening to occur, or in need of occurring. This position is given Christian coloration under the rubric of "what God is doing in the world" in our time. This comports well with the fact that for decades Protestant Christian ethics, expressed in maximalist pronouncements, has been articulated in terms of consequences or the principle of proportion alone. It is, indeed, a conclusion aptly drawn from systems of thought lacking in any other general political premises and lacking the principle of discrimination governing also in resorts to force, or any real understanding of this. This is the position that seems to be in the ascendency in much "ecumenical" Christian ethics today and in many seminaries where young men must be given a quick word and an obviously relevant word to speak in this generation.

The trouble is that the word is entirely too relevant to be profound, or to contain any proper guidance for Christian decision and action. This is in fact a new parochialism, and an exceeding narrow and dangerous one at that. What God is doing in the world is not identified with Jesus Christ—political reflection proceeding then upon this basis, in this light, and in the darkness cast by the shadow of this light upon human existence. Instead, what God is doing in the world is said to be making revolutions. Doubtless, any theism would say these do not occur without God's doing; but a Christian theological ethics should have more to say than that upon this subject, and it should not yield the primacy to other categories of analysis in telling what Christians should do in revolutionary times.

What is this decisive identification of God's present action with revolution but another version of the "God wills it" of the Crusades, the Moslem and Christian holy wars of the past, the unlimited religious wars that racked the sixteenth century until politics was moderated by becoming secular, another version of Hitler's wave of the future or the still unqualified reliance of Communists upon determining what's right by whether or not it is in line with the direction they discern in historical events? One may reply, of course, "Not those, but these revolutionary upsurges, are what God is doing in the world; these are in some sense *just* where those were not." But not all of the justice of war is concentrated in the justice of the cause or the end in view; and unless one knows something about the discriminations to be made and the limits to be acknowledged along the way toward achieving victories for a greater justice he has already *in mente* unleashed unrestrained violence in the means and methods of revolutionary war—*particularly* if the cause *is* just.

At a more theoretical level, what has happened in the "what God is doing" school of Christian ethics is—in the absence of the full range of Christian perspectives upon politics—an identification of human freedom (and man's moral decisions) with man's *consciousness of* his determinations. This is to try to give Christian coloration to the Hegelian-Marxist understanding of man.[23]

Thus, God as Christians know Him is reduced to what is going on in the world and man's responsibility is reduced to consciousness of his determination by the revolution that is going on—if only he can find out the exact meaning of that! Since it is very difficult to find this out, man's responsibility is reduced to surrendering to his own conjectures about the indeterminate future. This is the final consequence of consequentialist ethics in the modern period—a paradoxical conclusion from a viewpoint that was supposed to celebrate Man the Maker in comparison with the role assigned to him in those dreary views of the past that are supposed to have beset men behind and before by too greatly exalting the determining call of the living God. Yet such is the upshot of some contextual decisions about what Christians and our nation should be doing in foreign affairs. At least those who espouse this point of view should not accuse anyone else of parochialism. It passes belief that some who find in the concept of contemporary revolution a way to get leverage for escape from a fuller articulation of Christian insights in politics (which are said to be "western") thereupon propose "free elections" and "self-determination" in South Vietnam! I say, this passes belief; but not really so, if we recall that one must have *something* to say when he ventures to discuss politics.

It is better to begin with the assumption that God is more than man's revolutions, and man is more than consciousness of his supposed historical determinations; and that this "more" is precisely what is at stake in Christian knowledge into God and into man. Then on this

---

[23] In only a page or two Harvey Cox in *The Secular City* acknowledges the problem of distinguishing between what God is doing and what he is not doing in all that goes on. The main thrust of his book is such as I have described: man's proper response is to be found, in the main, in consciousness of his secular determinations. This influential book also displays one of the least attractive virtues of the systematic mind, in that any objection is included in a paragraph already prepared for it earlier in "the system." The objection will turn out to be a defense of "town virtues."

basis, Christian ethics poses the question, What does *this* God who reveals Himself, this God above what god is doing in the world, require of us men in the midst of these revolutionary times? Our answers may differ in detail, but common to them all will be the unswerving pursuit of a more just order for men to dwell in without seeking here the Kingdom of God, a prudent service of every concrete human need by all not indiscriminate means no matter how messy, a moderation of revolutionary expectations (ends), and specific moderation of the means ever to be put forth by men for any historical cause.

CHAPTER 19

Incapacitating Gases*

The question of the use of incapacitating gases in conducting a counter-insurgency operation is deserving of full and separate treatment. The pressure to do this, upon the minds of thoughtful and conscientious men today, I have said, arises from the fact that the tactics and strategies that can effectively counter contemporary insurgency without violating the principle of discrimination (when this is correctly understood) are still apt to prove excessively destructive and in violation of the principle of proportion. In the tension between proportion and not-indiscriminate acts of war, we are forced to ask, Must the justice embodied in existing political institutions be left at the mercy of insurgency and revolutionary war, because to oppose it successfully seems bound to do more evil than the evil prevented or the good secured? This is an urgent question today not because insurgency is apt to seize upon those purely lethargic and wholly traditional societies whose rulers ought perhaps to be violently overturned, but precisely because it is far more apt to seize upon those societies that have begun to move, where reforms are being instituted, where there are already rising expectations on the part of at least a significant minority of the people pressing steadily upon the government. These are the situations in which the task of political reconstruction and the extension of ordered liberty for a human dwelling place is so enormous that patience and social disciplines are going to be required of all persons capable of leading the people in nation-building, upon everyone capable of contributing to social change and nation-building; and there

* A portion of a previously unpublished paper on counter-insurgency warfare printed in this and the foregoing chapter, presented at the annual meeting of the American Society of Christian Ethics in Evanston, Illinois, January 21–22, 1966.

is going to be needed a government that can govern as well as progress.

Are there more humane weapons of war today, and should these be used in opposing insurgency? In addition to tear gas customarily used in riot control, there are the newer nauseating gases. In the arsenals are also tranquilizers and nerve gases capable of "turning all the enemy population into pacifists," but capable also of being used in a more discriminating way. There are ultimately harmless ways of making a soldier perfectly happy so long as he is in a horizontal position, but dizzy and unable to function if he is erect. Instead of using violent means to seal a border against infiltration and which if effective reduce an attacker's residual life expectancy from, say, fifty years to fifty minutes, it is possible to lay down a cloud within a three mile limit this side of the border which will stick there and not be blown away and which will increase his chances of going to sleep or becoming dizzy from, say, 2% to 98%. Thus, among the means of chemical warfare one does not have to think only of lethal gases. And even among the means of biological warfare one does not have to think only of indiscriminate mass weapons which are lethal. In addition to *contagious* epidemic diseases which even if not deadly are certainly immoral because they are indiscriminate, there are *non-contagious* non-lethal infections which on the face of it would seem more humane to use *on target* than napalm or bullets.

The programming of these weapons for use in riot control and as a possible means of opposing insurgency more humanely and more discriminatingly has raised new moral issues—or rather they raise the same age-old moral issues in a startlingly new way. Too many have too quickly slapped the notation "immoral" upon any such weapons. No such notation belongs on any weapon, but only on a weapon's use or the action for which the weapon is intended (or the action for which alone it can be used, as in the case of epidemic diseases). And, of course, it is quite impossible to discuss these issues rationally with anyone who is so ill informed of the meaning of the principle of discrimination that he formulates his emotional distress or sense of strangeness upon hearing about the existence of these "weapons" by calling attention to the fact that someone in the battle area is liable to die of a heart attack from a like astonishment.

It cannot, I think, be denied that incapacitating gases might be a more humane means of war in some, possibly frequent, insurgency situations. If such weapons are *feasible* (which is the judgment military experts must make) they *prima facie* qualify as better weapons of war because more humane. It may be important, however, for us to unpack the meaning of "humane" in this connection; and to say that these weapons seem to make it possible for the conduct of counter-insurgency warfare to be both more discriminating and also less destructive (more proportionate) *in the target area.* Merely noxious gases would make it possible to sort out combatants from non-combatants, and to select from the people the sides are fighting over, in situations where the insurgents are making war from behind and between the people and where therefore (except for these weapons) it might still be discriminating enough and possibly the lesser evil to strike with more violent means the already enlarged target with which we are presented. Also, incapacitating gases would make possible less combatant destructiveness and less destructiveness in the surrounding area of collateral civil damage. By markedly lessening the consequent evil, this would *raise the threshold of effective resistance* that can be *morally* justified because of the politically prudent proportion between the expected evil and good effects of the military action. These both (discrimination and proportion) are ingredients in any definition of humaneness in the conduct of war; and on both counts the use of tear and nauseating and other noxious gases would seem to qualify as choiceworthy weapons of war in the target area.

On September 8, 1965, *The New York Times* reported an investigation, possibly leading to court martial, of a use of tear gas by Lieut. Col. L. N. Utter in South Vietnam. Confronted by a situation in which fifty Vietcong guerrillas were hiding in caves and tunnels shielded by between 350 to 400 women and children, Colonel Utter decided against using fragmentation grenades, flame throwers, or automatic weapons. He felt that tear gas was the most humane way to dislodge the Vietcong, and he used it in what was described as a "completely successful" operation. But since General William C. Westmoreland alone has the authority to authorize the use of tear gas or any of the incapacitating gases, it had to be determined whether Colonel Utter was aware of the ban on his own local action. In this way, he was not punished for his humaneness; he was "constructively" presumed to be ignorant.

In centralizing authority in this matter in the supreme U.S. military commander in South Vietnam, the United States is at the same time holding open the question of its rightful use of these weapons. At some point in a possible projection of the war in South Vietnam, for example, the question will arise as to what should be done about the Ca Mau peninsula, which has been largely bypassed so far, has been "administered" by the Communist for many years, and is a low-lying area largely devoted to the production of rice. Shall this area be brought under the control of the legitimate government by "search and destroy" tactics that are bound to be quite destructive of civilian life? One reason for maintaining the symbol and as much as possible of the substance of legitimacy in the government is that the use of discriminating, merely incapacitating, weapons can be held within a category not too far distant from riot control, the suppression of rebellion, and the reimposition of law and order in that region; just as, perhaps, some persons may be assisted to contemplate calmly the possibility of using these newer weapons by thinking of them as a means of some future U.N. peace-keeping operation. But then anyone should know that the "laws of war" are the same as the laws governing the use of force domestically—only within nations they have legal enactment and controls.

In the flurry of excitement and scandalized world opinion over an earlier use of non-lethal gas in South Vietnam, Julian Pleasants, research associate of the Labund Laboratories at the University of Notre Dame, wrote an article entitled "Gas Warfare: Reflections on a Moral Outcry." [1] He protested against the moral outcry. The author himself is a symbol of the issues at stake for Christian conscience, and an illustration of the fact that the same divine charity that leads some to pacifism leads others to the essentials of the just-war theory. He was once a member of the Catholic Workers—the group of Roman Catholic pacifists and radical social activists to which the young man belonged who recently performed in front of the U.N. the act of self-immolation which he believed to be his religious obedience. In the latter instance agony over the horrors of modern war led one man to do something that has heretofore in the western moral tradition been regarded as an inherently wrong act. He treated humanity in himself—as Kant said it—as a means only. In the case of Pleasants, the same sensitive conscience led instead to sober reflection concerning the requirements of humanity in war itself.

To the objection against conscientious self-immolation, it may be replied that this is exactly what a soldier does in the case of both himself and the enemy combatant. Perhaps then it ought only to be said that both killings—that of oneself in protest and killing in war—are *prima facie* violations of basic elements in Christian morality, that they both would require justification; and that heretofore in the western tradition the killing of self or of another in war declared in one's private capacity

[1] *Commonweal*, May 7, 1965, pp. 209–212. Pleasants argues for the morality of using chemical agents. He points out that most of the wars of the past have been won by "involuntary germ warfare," and he allows that "there is much to be said for germ warfare if only it could be delivered where it was needed." Still, the fact is that unlike chemicals "a microbe has a life of its own"; by rapid passage through a series of animal or human bodies it can build up virulence. "A disease germ spread abroad over a wide area might find new modes of transmission, and might be so altered by rapid serial passage from one person to another as to become a very different disease. Germ warfare is indeed a Pandora's Box, yet weighed against an alternative of atomic war, some form of it might be far the lesser of two evils." In other words, this author rejects germ warfare because it is likely to be disproportionate in its consequences beyond the immediate target area. Questions of this order, as we shall see, also introduce, in a different way a number of countervailing considerations in the matter of finally justifying warfare by incapacitating chemical agents. The case for them is not nearly so evident as Pleasants supposes when he is considering only their immediate greater humaneness. He does not ask what follows next, or prevents there from following the first step certain more destructive and indiscriminate consequences.

and on one's private authority have been considered to be acts no end could justify.

Pausing to ponder this possible penetration of the truth in the two cases would lead to reflection upon the significance of a view of political community that retains a proper ordering between individual conscience and "the conscience of the laws" embodied in some political authority. In theory that never meant, from the thirteenth century through the truly liberal periods of modern societies, a denial of the right and duty of individual conscience to stand against the public authority, refusing to fight in a war. It meant only but definitely that the individual, before claiming conscientious resistance, assumed responsibility for knowing better than the public authority and for knowing that in this instance its commands were contrary to fundamental moral right. Does the current asserted conscientious dissent signal an end to the age of relativism about man's ability to know fundamental moral right? Or does it signal the final triumph of egalitarianism over liberalism and over the moral substance political community requires, with its orderly if only provisional priority of consciences? The present writer has witnessed by the miracle of TV, on-the-spot interviews with *some* banner-waving anti-Vietnam protesters who said they would, of course, fight in their country's war if they could know it was just; but, they said, in this instance they just didn't know for sure. That reverses the burden of proof— or, if that is too strong, the burden of moral persuasion—necessary to an acceptable notion of conscientious objection and to political community as such. We shall return to this distinction between *incapacitation* as the objective of warfare and immolation of self or of another.

Julian Pleasants acknowledges the psychological resistance to the use of these new weapons, and the obstacle of our present conventions concerning them. But that is neither here nor there when the question is their reasonable moral justification or condemnation. "If we are to be prevented from doing what is more humane because the action has the connotation of being less humane, then humanity has been defeated by words," he writes. "It is a gruesome thought that we must gun down and burn people because it is [considered] cruel to nauseate them." The incapacitating chemicals are in fact both a more humane and a more effective means of warfare. In comparison, the atom bomb is "a weapon so inefficient that it must destroy practically everything in order to achieve anything." In war research, the chemical may be the only corps that is making moral progress. From the point of view of morality, the principle to apply is that of *minimum force*. The objective in warfare always was the incapacitation of forces. Heretofore that could be accomplished only by a great amount of killing. Now the objective can be obtained directly by incapacitating chemicals. Now happily the (sleeping) lion and the lamb may lie down together! Whether to use these new weapons would seem to be not an optional but "a *necessary response* to the moral requirement of minimum force." Therefore, the author concludes, "unless we are complete pacifists or completely amoral" we must approve of these weapons on the ground that they achieve "the minimum force necessary with the least destruction of human life and culture."

As with other terms in ordinary language—"doing evil," "the end justifying the means" or not, and "humaneness"—so also now this principle of "minimum force" needs to be unpacked and its full meaning in any treatment of the morality of warfare made clear in terms of the principle of discrimination and the principle of proportion which are neither to be separated nor confused together. If "minimum force" narrowly construed *means* the same as the proportionately lesser evil in combatant destructiveness plus collateral damage, then Pleasants has made only one part of the case that needs to be made for using incapacitating agents. Moreover, if "minimum force" means only prudently counting all the costs/benefits, this may finally require that Pleasants' conclusion be reversed when we take also into account all the consequences beyond the immediate target area of stepping across the convention against using gaseous weapons.

The fighting in the Pacific that was necessary to dislodge the Japanese from their island strongholds provided an isolation of combatant destructiveness from questions of discrimination. This in retrospect can be taken as a good illustration of Pleasants' case (except that he is concerned also to lessen non-combatant destructiveness). The choice that a military commander had to make at that time in the war in the Pacific was between ways of inflicting *death* upon combatants (and so incapacitating them). There is much evidence to show that lethal gas is no more inhumane, when so used, than the lethal weapons that were actually used. Yet the decision was made in terms of supposed greater humaneness. While there may be no rational grounds for distinguishing between lethal gas and lethal flames or lethal bullets (provided each is lethal, and difference in damage to survivors comes not into the reckoning), there is good reason for preferring directly incapacitating agents to either, as the following account, I think, makes evident:

> . . . At the time Iwo Jima had to be taken in 1945, war gases were available to the American commander. They were not used, not for fear of retaliation, but on humanitarian grounds. Instead, explosives and flame were used to dislodge the Japanese. In the end, almost all 21,000 defending troops were killed, and this country suffered 7,000 dead marines and 18,000 other casualties. With gas [the deadly gases then available] the same result would have been obtained on the island, but the airfield would have been intact, and 25,000 American casualties would have been avoided. If the new incapacitating agents had been available, it is con-

ceivable that neither side would have lost any appreciable number of men.[2]

The objective of combat is the incapacitation of a combatant, *not* his death. Heretofore, this assertion has been regarded as at best a strange subtlety. The existence of incapacitants, however, are an aid to the intellect in taking up again the question whether it is altogether nonsensical to say that while killing one does not *intend* to kill. (Of course, one intends victory, justice, etc., as ends; but the question is what one means to do with *this* man: kill him or incapacitate him from doing what he is doing?) Inadvertently, the chemical corps may have made a contribution to the devious history of moral theology! For the "incaps" do return our reflection to a possible greater validity in Thomas Aquinas' first formulation of the "rule of double-effect" than I, at least, once thought it contained.[3] As long as an enemy combatant had to be and was done to death it seemed nonsense to say that this was not what was wanted. Subsequent centuries, therefore, improved away Aquinas' formulation, since it seemed dishonest to say one was withholding the intention to kill directly, while still killing a man. Now that what is done in war might be the combatant's incapacitation and not his death, it again makes some palpable sense to say that what was wanted (as *means*) even in killing him is his incapacitation and not his death.

This may also enable us to probe more deeply into two sorts of cases: conscientious suicide and conscientious killing in war. When one thinks about it, a soldier who kills an enemy combatant need not want his death as means, he need not *in a certain morally relevant sense* directly do his death. He rightly wants (and this is one way to express the meaning of directing violence upon forces) and he directly does the enemy's *incapacitation* as a combatant; and so far, at least, in the tragic evil of war, killing is the only way to incapacitate him. Similarly, a captured soldier who swallows a "suicide" pill does not want or directly will or do his own death; he *incapacitates* himself from living under conditions for the next few days and months during which he fears or knows he will disclose to the enemy military secrets on which his cause and comrades depend. Or a man may perhaps justifiably take his own life because that is the only way, in the face of medical science's determination forcibly to prolong his dying, for him to *incapacitate* himself from becoming a carefully tended cadaver that will accumulate medical bills and bring financial disaster upon his loved ones.

[2] *Research in CBR: A Report of the Committee on Science and Astronautics.* The U.S. House of Representatives, Eighty-Sixth Congress, first session, House Report No. 815. Department of the Army Pamphlet, No. 3-2, March 1960, p. 12.

[3] *Summa Theologica*, II-II, Q. 64, art. 7; *War and the Christian Conscience*, pp. 39–49.

I do not say that these reflections remove altogether the charge that all such killings "treat humanity whether in oneself or in another as a means only"—when that is the only means of incapacitating oneself or another. Still it is more correct to say that in all these cases the person does not take human life in his own hands; he rather takes incapacitation (his own or another's) in his hands.

Then the question is whether the same can be said concerning the recent cases of self-immolation. I think not. In these instances, the persons took their *lives* in their own hands. They treated humanity in themselves wholly and directly as a means only to an altogether extrinsic historical end. They entirely reduced their existence to this end. What they meant to do to the man standing there was his *death* for the sake of a consequence believed to justify it. They did not mean to do only incapacitation to the man standing there; and in them were still unspent capacities, and around them in the needs of men many reasons for not thinking their incapacitation to be justifiable in itself. They did not mean to incapacitate themselves from doing what they were doing ordinarily in the world (and that would not have been justifiable). Standing there, they did not mean to incapacitate themselves from doing what they were doing *then;* and what they meant to do and did *then* was *death* (and such an action no end in this world can justify). A soldier's killing in battle can be more readily warranted. The judgment that these desperate acts of self-immolation were possibly justifiable, perhaps even admirable, stems from a gradual South-Vietnamization of western morality (which, I cannot but judge, found entrance in part through the western liberal's acceptance of the morality of indiscriminate acts—or only quantitatively limited acts—of non-violent direct action so long as the cause of the protest is just).

Let us now return to the matter of a proposed use of incapacitants in a situation where the foe is *not* isolated from civilians, i.e. in counter-insurgency warfare. The assertion that such use has merit because these weapons will greatly lessen combatant and non-combatant *destructiveness* cannot be separated from (though this can and should be distinguished from) an assertion that such use would first of all be a discriminating one or even that these weapons would permit greater discrimination. The moral *economy* governing a use of force is comprised of both proportion and discrimination; and both features of this economy ought to be remembered in any discussion of the meaning of *minimum* force (even if the latter expression seems semantically appropriate enough to be used for the one feature only).

It must be possible also to say both things *in favor* of a decision to use "incaps" in modern warfare because it has certainly to be said that these new weapons are *subject* to the principle of discrimination no matter how non-destructive they are. Just so, "non-violent direct action" is subject to the principle of discrimination correctly understood as having to do with who is "non-violenced" and how. Such conduct is by no means to be justified simply because it is not destructive of life or because the *motive* of the agent is charitable or because it is "discriminating" in another meaning of that word when this is understood to require only a restrained, apt, and rational relation between the means and a limited and achievable goal in the struggle for a just cause. The latter is consequentialist ethics on any showing; and it provides a by no means adequate limitation upon the social and political conduct it seeks to justify. Neither does the non-destructiveness of incapacitants alone justify their use. I still judge, therefore, that my reasoning was correct in 1961: "The horror we feel in face of such possibilities[4] is not lessened by the fact that the destruction of lives is not aimed at. The distinction between actual killing or not killing, or the relative 'humaneness' of such applications of power, is not the issue; but rather the obliteration of the distinction between counter-*forces* and counter-*people* warfare." "One should therefore know whether the destruction or immobilization of civilian life as a whole is the sole aim and the sole use of these modern means of warfare before judging them to be intrinsically immoral." [5] A project or a plan of war designed to get a whole people in one's power even with only psychological or other non-lethal effects, and without permanent damage to anyone, simply exceeds the proper purposes of war, which are to alter or dissuade that people's will as this has come to be expressed in its government's present political policies when these are extended and empowered in the world by

[4] Herman Kahn's illustration of what might be done by way of producing only psychological effects on "the enemy": "It is not at all inconceivable that if the North Koreans invaded South Korea again in 1965 [sicl] we would be able to keep all of North Korea continuously saturated with chemicals or organisms that reduced the efficiency of the exposed inhabitants markedly, but did not injure them permanently" (*On Thermonuclear War* [Princeton, N.J.: Princeton University Press, 1960], Lecture III, Chap. X, p. 485).

[5] *War and the Christian Conscience*, p. 228 n. 7 and p. 227. Then as now, I would be forced to reject Richard J. Krickus' judgment that the "CB taboo" has one of its roots in the principle of discrimination. And reject as well his statement: "Paul Ramsey may be taken as representative of the just-war school on this issue, and he has declared that the use of incapacitants against non-combatants is as immoral as are lethal weapons" ("On the Morality of Chemical/Biological War," *Journal of Conflict Resolution*, Vol. 9, No. 2 [June 1965], 208). That characterization is all the more remarkable since Krickus earlier in his article quoted from the context of the passages I have just cited in the text above, and he understood me rather better at that point (*ibid.*, p. 202). Yet Krickus is not unrepresentative of contemporary thought: he simply does not understand that the principle of discrimination governing just conduct never required that lethal *or non-lethal* weapons be "confined to the foe" but that and only that the non-combatants unavoidably involved be not directly attacked with deliberate intent.

its armed forces. One doesn't attack a whole people non-lethally in order to get at the government, and then call that the entire meaning of "humane" politico-military action.

To say that the use of "incaps" is subject to the principle of discrimination does not, however, entail that they must be "confined to the foe" in the sense that for them to pass muster before this rule in the practice of war one would have to insure that no one except the guerrillas felt his eyes irritated by tear gas or was nauseated and no one except infiltrating soldiers was made dizzy. The concept of discrimination does not exclude, it specifically includes, the justifiability of collateral damage in the use of "incaps" or any other weapon; how extensive this should be falls under a judgment of proportion. This means that everything that was said in the previous chapter about the enlargement of the number and sorts of persons legitimately classifiable as combatants and the enlargement of the area of collateral civilian damage by insurgency's maxim and practice of fighting between and behind people has now to be brought to bear upon the question we are now considering. In brief, if Colonel L. N. Utter would have been justified in using flamethrowers and explosives in those tunnels and caves *so far as the principle of discrimination is concerned,* a use of "incaps" in that situation would also have been clearly justified under this principle. Were or were not those women and children within collateral range of any weapon? If this question could be answered in the affirmative, then the destructiveness of explosives might still make the action proportionately wrong to do because of greater evil than good effects; and the non-destructiveness of incapacitants might then reverse *this* judgment. While the merely noxious effects of not indiscriminate acts of war are a clear gain, non-destructiveness cannot render any particular conduct in war discriminating in the first place. There are those who would argue that, although Colonel Utter rightly felt he had a better weapon he was forbidden to use, use of the *violent* means available to him would not have been indiscriminate (because the women and children were within range through no agency of his, not in this isolated instance alone but by the deliberate design of insurgency warfare) *and* that this not indiscriminate action would, tragically enough, have been proportionate. The last part of this judgment could find support in the importance of not letting those fifty Vietcong escape, the importance of this particular action to the whole course of the engagement, and all that is at stake in not letting insurgency succeed in using its "weakness" in this fashion to cause social commotion and bring down a whole people's fragile social and political institutions. In this way one would proceed to try to answer the question whether the unavoidable death of those 350–400 women and children, and similar casualties that unavoidably occur collaterally by use of any of the means yet devised to mount a counter-insurgency operation, are the lesser or a greater evil. Perhaps such collateral deaths from a lethal weapon would have been grossly disproportionate. Even more certainly, then, the use of tear gas would be proper in similar not indiscriminate acts of counter-insurgency. In fact, the use of incapacitants would be morally required because they are less destructive in their consequences *in the battle area*. If now or in the future there are incapacitants that are also *more* discriminating in the sense that they make it possible to target on the forces to be repressed *more exactly* or *separate* them in the strike itself to a greater extent from the environing civil life or *reduce* the area in which non-combatants will be collaterally damaged non-lethally, that would be an additional virtue in such a weapon of war. At the moment the most telling point to be made is simply that a not indiscriminating use of incapacitants would raise the threshold of the effective resistance that can be *morally* exerted while reducing the violence that otherwise threatens to bring counter-insurgency under condemnation as a violation of the principle of proportion. Incapacitants, however, are not to be used as mass weapons or for the sake of mass "casualties" and mankind will rue the day the first nation begins to "enlarge the target" to include people as direct objects of attack on the excuse that the means used are not lethal.

The foregoing analysis simply repeats in the case of the use of incapacitants in war *everything* that should be said concerning the use of incapacitants in quelling social commotions within a nation. This is as it should be. The laws of war are the same as the rules governing any use of force. Incapacitants in the hands of the police force, of armies, or of the forces of some future regional or world organization capable of radical decision-making, interpositional peace-keeping, and intervention-ary threat-removing action are subject to the same *moral* limits; only in the first are these moral limits legally instituted and violations of them subject to adjudication and enforcement. The police should doubtless under some circumstances allow a criminal or a man gone berserk to escape when he has shielded himself behind seven women and children (to choose the ratio Colonel Utter faced) rather than risk hitting them. If his escape alone is what is at stake they would choose this rather than destroy innocent lives. But if he is continuing to fire upon other people from behind this shield, their deaths being collateral to the thrust of an action that will prevent his action from continuing, then under these circumstances their deaths also along with his might be the lesser evil. If, however, incapacitants are available to the police force they would be obliged to use the less destructive means. This would, at the same time, raise the threshold of the effective repression the police would be justified in employing while lessening or removing its destructiveness. In any case, the target area and the range of civil life collateral to this (to which lethal or non-lethal means may be applied—directly to the one, unavoidably to the other—according to the principle of discrimination) are defined by the social commotion and the magnitude of the social commotion, and not by the police.

Why not then immediately revise the rules and the widely accepted conventions now prohibiting chemical warfare?

The answer can only be found (and this may or may not be a correct conclusion) in the disproportionate and uncontrollable consequences that seem likely to follow upon acceptance of the use of these new weapons of war. This is not obvious in the first instance. Doubt concerning the justifiable use of incapacitating gases arises only when one tries to anticipate an enemy's probable response to our first use of incapacitating gases, and then our response to that, etc. Would an adequate riposte on his part have to be the use of deadly gases, or epidemic diseases against populations; and would our only response to his response be to go to general war? In other words, if a nation steps across this non-rational but existing barrier in order to de-escalate the violence in the target area, there immediately arise questions both in and far beyond the area where this greater humaneness was first practiced. There then is danger of escalation through a number of unconventional weapons systems which have in common only the fact that they are gaseous or micro-biological.

In one way this is a familiar problem falling under the principle of proportion. In conventional explosives the escalation is quantitative, and then across the nuclear barrier the escalation would again be quantitative along the same spectrum of violence. To begin the use of incapacitating gas in warfare would create a peril of escalation that (apart from its unfamiliarity) would be perhaps easier to think through and to devise controls in advance. The fact that there are, under the heading of gas, a large number of weapons each different in nature from the others and with clear boundaries between them would seem to make it easier to prepare "firebreaks" and stopping places beyond the steps taken in the first place to make war more humane. Yet there is danger that war would move rapidly through the class names, chemical and biological, the lethal as well as the non-lethal; and that these weapons might be directed at mass casualties sooner than weapons we are used to.

Here we have an extraordinary situation in which the principles of discrimination and proportion in the battle area may be in conflict with the final judgment of proportion when all the possible consequences of thus humanizing war are taken into account. It may be that war *should* remain as destructive as it now is in order to remain at all controllable.

In removing the boundary between explosives and gases we would be imposing on ourselves, and seeking to secure tacit agreement from an enemy or to impose on him a number of rules instead. It may be that the move should be only to the legitimacy of the use of *tear gas* in counter-insurgency, taking full advantage of the conventions in the use of this to which we have been accustomed. Then there would be the boundary between incapacitants and lethal gas that would have to be made clear as the new self-imposed rule we mean to enforce on warfare, if the step is taken to go to nauseating gases alone or to other incapacitants. In all this there would be another self-imposed rule that we would be trying to get accepted as the new extra-force limit that both sides agree to. This would be the understanding that incapacitants are legitimately to be used only in and over one's own territory or that of an ally to stop insurgent assaults. If insurgency did not in practice agree to this, if it began to use incapacitants upon the territory of the country under attack or if it used lethal gases in reply, the protective retribution and enforcement to be used would need to be prepared.

All these questions may be summarized in a single question, Is the first act of using incapacitants already an act that is out of control? If it is, it is inordinate and ought never to be done no matter how humane it may be in the first instant. Would our self-imposed limitation of gas warfare to the more humane means be a rule that could be enforced (and transgressions of this punished) by means that themselves are still limited and capable of being kept graduated? Have our military planners played out enough scenarios to know that there are obvious boundaries at which to agree to stop, once the non-rational boundary that at present prohibits chemical-biological-radiological warfare has been replaced by even a more rational rule humanizing warfare in the immediate areas over which incapacitating gases might first be used effectively?

If not, then the step better be not taken. Still, it is important that in reaching this negative conclusion we be clear from which test we reached it. No one should permit himself the luxury of feeling no qualms about this decision, or turn his face away from the awful evil effects he would be saying we should continue to accept the doing of, lest still worse effects follow. In effect, this decision means that because of the best, rough judgment a prudent calculation can make of all the possible consequences, we had better prosecute war against insurgency by running M113's zigzag across lakes and streams on whose bottoms lie for hours hidden insurgency fighters breathing through straws, crushing their bodies and watching bloody hands and arms and legs rise to the surface, rather than spreading a gas over the area which will cause these men to vomit and be captured.[6]

My own view is that, if I am not in error in forecasting decades of

[6] See Malcolm W. Browne, *The New Face of War* (New York: The Bobbs-Merrill Co., 1965), pp. 15–16.

revolutionary upheaval, men and the existing conventions about the weapons to be used in military conflict cannot long withstand the pressure exerted upon them by a "social charity" that is now informed of the fact that it is not impossible to make at least many military engagements and the government of mankind a far, far less destructive business. A charitable reason may be able to find a way to think through the problem of imposing further limits and enforcing other rules upon warfare when the prohibition of incapacitants is breached in the direction of humanization.

CHAPTER 20

Farewell to
Christian Realism*

One remaining element of "Christian realism" in Dr. John Bennett's statement[1] seems to me entirely mistaken; or else he has not exactly stated what he means. "What we do," he writes, "and permit [no distinction drawn between these two kinds of action] in Vietnam" is "intolerably evil in itself." "We are involved in acts of inhumanity that are morally intolerable," he affirms without qualification. Yet he asserts: "I might have to say of them in some circumstances that as by-products of an action to overcome a still greater evil, they would not be sufficient to cause me to reject the action."

On one reading, that would be like giving up sin during Lent and returning to it afterward—for the sake of choiceworthy consequences, or less evil ones. For nearly a decade, the present writer has tried to refute such a merely consequentialist understanding of political "responsibility" among Protestants of the realist persuasion. Apparently without success. It still seems to me obvious that one should not first define some political or military action as "intolerably evil in itself" or as "*morally* intolerable" and then make ready to perform it under some circumstances.

On another reading, the evil, the death and destruction in question may truly be the "by-products" of actions that can reasonably be ex-

* First appeared in *America*, The National Catholic Weekly Review © 1968 America Press, April 30, 1966, pp. 618–622.
[1] "Christian Realism in Vietnam," in the same issue of *America*, pp. 616–617.

pected to overcome still greater evil. But even to come to this choice between evil and greater evil consequences requires that they be the results
of political and military actions that are *not* intolerably evil in themselves.
One should not first define an action in which we are involved as *morally*
intolerable and then propose to justify it situationally. Either it was not
in the first place, and is not, in itself, a morally intolerable course of action, or no less evil in the results can justify it.

John Bennett, however, holds together two judgments: his *ethical*
verdict concerning the "inherent evil in what we are doing" and his
political "conviction that what we are doing is leading us into a tragic
blind alley." Politics and ethics do belong together; but in this instance
Bennett's conclusion about what our nation's specific policy decisions
should be (which may be correct) overwhelms and foreshortens his ethical
analysis, and his insufficiently examined and sweeping moral judgments
lend force and certitude to his policy recommendations. This, I should
say, is typical of the "consensus" among secular and religious liberals today, whether Protestant or Catholic.

First, to fill in the missing ethical analysis. Bennett should have
paused to grasp the nature of insurgency's use of violence (whether this
is aggression from outside or revolution inside a country, or both). He
should have dissected the basic design of its warfare no less than that of
counter-insurgency. Only then can we tell how to distribute judgments
about the inherent evil of their respective resorts to military force.

One does not justify adultery by saying that it is *selective*. Not even
with the additional finding that with one's various mistresses one mainly
enjoys the finer things of life and has achieved an orderly domestic economy. Neither does one justify deliberate terror in the conduct of war or
revolution by saying that it is selective. Not even with the additional
finding that the insurgents win the allegiance of people by many other
appeals or also by a program of national liberation. The fact that insurgency resorts to terror, when it does, only minimally or only upon
selected people does not qualify it as a discriminating resort to force. That
is simply not the meaning of the principle of discrimination in the use
of means of violence. It is in fact, morally, the meaning of total war. Decision as to the inherent evil of an act of war or revolution cannot be settled by the body count. There is not a prudent number of villagers, school
teachers, or petty local officials and their families that it would be right
to disembowel in the village square to dissuade others from allegiance to
the existing social processes and institutions, all to the good end of destroying the social fabric of a traditional society and taking over and reforming the country.

Guerrilla war by its main design strikes the civil population (albeit
selectively and as rarely as need be) in order to subvert, while striking as
few legitimate military targets as possible. This is an inherently immoral

plan of war or of revolution, and one that cannot be rendered morally tolerable by reference to the social reforms by which insurgency mainly proposes to succeed.

Without invoking the domino theory, it is a fact of life that the nuclear stalemate has made the world safe for insurgency warfare. *This is modern* war! Nor is the threat to just order dependent upon there being an intact worldwide Communist conspiracy behind all such resorts to arms. Guatemala recently elected a *left-wing* government that offers some hope of social progress; the next day, a 24-year-old guerrilla leader took to the hills to gain rule or to ruin; and the military made the first "classical" mistake of scorning him as a "bandit."

The question facing the world for decades to come is whether it is possible to oppose these revolutionary wars successfully without joining them in direct attacks upon the very people a government may be trying to protect while social progress is secured with liberty. Is counter-insurgency, like insurgency, bound to be warfare over people as a means of getting at the other's forces?

Of course, if the guerrilla lives among the people like a fish in water, he must be opposed mainly by withdrawing the water to see what then happens to the fish. This is to say, insurgency can be finally defeated only by social, economic, and political reformation. But what of the military force that must still be used? If the guerrilla chooses to fight between, behind, and over peasants, women, and children, is it *he* or the counter-guerrilla who has enlarged the legitimate target and enlarged it so as to bring unavoidable death and destruction upon a large number of innocent people?

It is the shape of insurgency warfare that defines the contours of the legitimate combatant destruction and the unavoidably associated civil damage it then may (so far as the principle of discrimination is concerned) be just to inflict in order to oppose it, subject only to the limitation that this be the proportionately lesser evil. To draw any other conclusion would be like, at the nuclear level, granting an enemy immunity from attack because he had the shrewdness to locate his missile bases in the heart of his cities. It is rather *he* who has deliberately enlarged the extent of foreknowable but collateral civil destruction in the attempt to gain a privileged sanctuary through a military posture that brought more of his own population into range. The design of insurgency does this to the people of a society it assaults. The onus of the wickedness of placing multitudes of peasants within range cannot be shifted from insurgency to counter-insurgency, any more than it could be called an indiscriminate act of war on the part of some enemy if in the future Omaha, Neb., or Colorado Springs, Col., are tragically destroyed in the course of destroying the bases and command posts *we* located there.

The principle of discrimination governing the proper conduct of war has no other meaning than this. Some call this a "medieval" notion. One should then be able to recognize a medieval fortress when he sees or hears of one buried underground in South Vietnam—command headquarters, munitions factories, stores of rice and intricate tunnels connecting many villages, with openings into countless peasant huts, or under the water in lakes, streams, and rice paddies, by which the guerrillas may fight and run away and live to fight another day through these same egresses. Plainly, there are here extensive areas subject to the laws of the siege; i.e., "catapults" from as far away as Guam may then not be indiscriminate acts of war.

These are unpleasant facts. I did not make them so; originally, Mao Tse-tung did. No Christian or moralist has a right to demand that statesmen or commanders fail to take account of these facts in their policies and plans. This is to suggest, all too briefly, that the main design of the counter-insurgency mounted in Vietnam need not be and likely is *not* an inherently evil or morally intolerable use of armed force—not in any meaning that the distinction between discriminate and indiscriminate conduct in war ever had or should have.

This is not to deny that peripheral to the "central war" against the insurgents there may be taking place many intrinsically wrong actions in this confused and bloody war. (I only say that this is not proved by reference to the bombing of villages, etc., that may in fact lie within a vast Vietcong stronghold.) There are those who say that if *any* of the acts of war violate the canons of justice in war, or injustice is violated by *frequent* actions that, however, do not or need not fall within the main thrust or design of the war, it is still on the whole unjust and no Christian should support or participate in it. This position is far more to be honored than the indiscriminate use of the principle of discrimination that is current today. Still, to uphold it seems to me to uphold a legalist-pacifist version of the just-war doctrine, as if the purpose of this teaching was to bring peace by discrediting, one by one, all wars. Instead, the just-war doctrine is intended to indicate to political decision-makers how, within tolerable moral limits, they are to defend and preserve politically embodied justice in this world.

If by now *America's* avant-garde readers are alarmed, I can only plead: "Moralists are unhappy people. When they insist on the immutability of moral principles, they are reproached for imposing unlivable requirements on us. When they explain the way in which those immutable principles are to be put into force, they are reproached for making morality relative. In both cases, however, they are only upholding the claims of reason [and, I would add, of a rational explication of Christian ethics] to direct life." [2]

---

[2] Jacques Maritain, *Man and the State* (University of Chicago Press, 1951), p. 74.

This brings me to the weighing of lesser and greater evils in the results expected from specific policy decisions. Most of what Dr. Bennett says about Vietnam falls under this head (traditionally called the principle of proportion, which is a matter of prudence).[3] With some of his particular points I wholly agree; with others I disagree; and with most, he and I would find shades of agreement or disagreement between us. We need not enter upon these questions in order to know that neither of us should place the engines of religion and morality behind our particular opinions. A church leader and Christian moralist can avoid this error only by expressly making it clear that he knows that other specific policy recommendations may equally (or as little) claim to be entailments of the Christian faith or proper prudential applications of Christian ethics to today's urgent problems of world justice and order.

Pope John XXIII was more circumspect when he made his "opening to the left." Wishing to strike down a programmatic anticommunism that was rendering political decisions inflexible, he did not presume, upon the moral authority of his religious leadership, to put in its place a naive *unilinear* theory of the development of "diversity and freedom" in the world communist movement. He claimed no prescience about the actual possibilities of political reconciliation at any given time. He did not speak of the Khrushchev era as if it were already post-Khrushchev; nor certainly of the Brezhnev era as if it were already post-Brezhnev (there are already signs that in the future many elements of Stalinism may be restored).

On the contrary, from everything that Pope John had said in general about human rights, the exigencies of human nature and historical movements, he simply drew the conclusion that "it can at times happen" that "meetings" are actually useful. This entails that it can at times happen that they are not, and that issues fail to be resolved by negotiation. "To decide whether this moment has arrived . . . these are the problems that can only be solved with the virtue of prudence." Whether a moment for fruitful negotiation (which should always be held open as a possible occurrence and as an opportunity we seek) has actually arrived is a decision that "rests primarily with those who live and work in the specific sectors of human society in which these problems arise" (*Pacem in terris*, §160).

I agree with Dr. Bennett that our policy makers do not have a monopoly on the relevant information, that their decisions are more influenced by their "general pictures of the world" than by facts they alone possess, and that other pictures of the world and other policy recommendations, such as Bennett's, are needed in the debate over national policy. But such pictures are still the artifacts of political prudence weighing the costs/benefits to flow from particular policies. Suppose we agreed com-

[3] See Chap. 7 above, p. 163, n. 13.

pletely with Bennett's reading and his estimates of the proportionately greater and lesser evils. It would still be the case that there is no such thing as a *Christian* perception of facts or a *Christian* conjecture concerning consequences to come.

The United States certainly has "no past commitment to do *everything* to prevent" a national communism from taking over the whole of Vietnam. There is certainly no valid commitment to do anything inherently wrong to prevent this. Nor is there a commitment to do anything knowingly that is imprudent or that will cause greater evil than the evil we are seeking to prevent. I would say that no Christian should assist communism of any variety in coming to power; we should prevent or assist in the prevention of this if we can. The obligation disappears, however, if we cannot, or if we cannot without causing greater evil in the process. But Bennett's perception of the facts in estimating this is not therefore Christian or prophetic because he disagrees with the government's estimates or with the pictures of the political world that influence our leaders. He may only be more correct than they in his prudent calculations. Then too, the possibility cannot be excluded that in some ways our present policy takes a wider view of the consequences.

This could better be settled, or debated, if we withdraw all prejudicial notions that from Reconciliation can be derived or supported some particular proposal for political reconciliation, or that from Christian insights we can see that mainland China should be admitted to the UN, or that it follows from the Christian's goal of peace with justice that the Vietcong should be one party—or the principal party—to negotiations in Vietnam. The main conclusion to be drawn from the uniqueness of the war against Hitler's terribly evil regime is that only rarely do churchmen *as such* like Karl Barth or Reinhold Niebuhr have the "competence" to call, in the name of Christian responsibility, for specific military resistance at its price—or for a particular peace at a particular political price. What we do in exercising political prudence as citizens and the lesser magistrates in a democracy is another matter.

Of course, a departure from Christian realism is not demonstrated by the fact that some who urged the use of armed force to destroy Hitler now oppose the force that is being used to prevent military victory by the Vietcong. That would be a cogent argument only on the silly assumption that realism requires that all possible wars be fought. The presence or absence of Christian realism is shown in the premises, not in the conclusions. There were once two old women slanging and cursing one another across the street that separated their domiciles. Sydney Smith, the Scottish wit, remarked that they would never agree because they were arguing from different premises. The erosion of "Christian realism" from Bennett's premises is shown far more by what he omits to say than by what his particular exercise of political prudence leads him to say.

484

Christian realism is to be found in the sound articulations of the early Niebuhr in *The Nature and Destiny of Man* or in those of the late Niebuhr in *The Structure of Nations and Empires*. It is missing from the genial, quasi-pacifist pragmatism of many of his disciples today. The political philosophy *operating* (at least) in present-day social and political movements among the leaders of both secular and religious opinion, Protestant and Catholic (less so?), is a rather unqualified optimism that is oblivious both to the chaos and furious consequences that finally, and to the Christian truths that *ab initio,* count against it.

Anyone who berates our government for unclarity about the meaning of "unconditional discussions" should first ask himself what he has done in the midst of a politically immature people to make it unnecessary for statesmen to engage in posturing. Anyone who charges that the United States is demanding "unconditional surrender" of the Vietcong should call equal attention to the fact that the Vietcong very likely believe they can win a pre-negotiation victory for the forces of national liberation,[4] and to the fact that quite a crunch may yet be required to bring them to accept even the status of being only one party to a final settlement. Bernard B. Fall, who is no defender of the U.S. policy in Vietnam, has written: "Let us do away with the nonsense that there is such an animal as 'unconditional discussions,' let alone 'unconditional negotiations.' Both sides have a pretty good idea about the shape of future contacts." [5]

If anyone says that national communism in Vietnam may be the lesser evil of our actual options, he should also give equal weight to what Gen. Gavin called the "fierce fighting" that in such an eventuality will be needed to save Thailand. (If there is a Christian perception of the facts in regard to the Vietnamese Liberation Front, there should be one in regard to the Thai Liberation Front—in Peking!—and in regard to the guerrilla war now well under way in Thailand itself.) He ought also to ponder publicly the possible meaning of Cambodia's slip from neutralism when the war in Vietnam was going very badly, and the return of Indonesia to neutralism now that the U.S. military commitment in Vietnam has been markedly increased. He ought not to take advantage, in any proposals he makes, of the fragmentation of world communism without acknowledging that, beyond geography and historic border disputes and divergent domestic developments, the single most important *policy* "input" that led to the rift between the U.S.S.R. and mainland China was the firm U.S. pledge to defend the offshore islands—a pledge opposed by most of the people now calling for the recognition of Red China. Nor

---

[4] Or a victory by negotiations with Western liberals who are resolved to negotiate so that negotiation can never fail.

[5] "The Year of the Hawks," *New York Times Magazine,* Dec. 12, 1965, p. 113.

should he call for the de-isolation of that government without pointing out that it is likely to take at least one more generation of Chinese leadership before that country learns the value of compromise and negotiation, during which time the pedagogical value of checking her expansionism must not be relinquished.

He ought never to imply that the de-escalation of a conflict is always or in this instance the lesser evil (and certainly not that it is the "Christian" step to take) without a tribute to the costs per benefit paid by the British in order to leave behind in Malaya a socio-political fabric that barely might endure. Eleven years fighting insurgency—in which 6,500 man-hours of patrolling were required even to sight a single one of the guerrillas, of whom one in ten got away—is not obviously a lesser evil. He should never become so transfixed by the "radical right" that he wants the voice of the Church to become only a specific "corrective" of *that* danger. He will rather bring the whole Christian understanding to bear upon articulating principles governing the government of men. He will also be mindful of the equal need of correcting, by an effort of charitable imagination, first in our own minds and then in the minds of our fellow citizens, the fact that none of us has ever seen *televised* a Vietcong take-over of a village or of an area, while we see daily on our screens the "inhumanity" of the war our nation is fighting.

He will remember that the work of charity is to *extend* the area of coincidence of our national interest with the interests of other people (even if this should not lead to imprudent burden-bearing). He will ceaselessly call attention also to the fact that the longing for peace, and cries that we cannot police the world, can lead to an ever more narrow coincidence of Christian impulses with Fortress America. He will lend no credence, not even by silence, to the notion that we can be involved in the world's problems economically, and not politically and militarily (i.e., tragically). He ought not to speak of the danger that U.S. power may be used irresponsibly without saying also that the *primary* problem is that we have inherited world responsibilities that are quite incommensurate with our power. He should remind the modern, liberal U.N. mentality that the capacity of the Security Council to remove *threats* to the peace, envisioned by the Charter, was never achieved; that even the *peace-keeping* capabilities of the U.N. have been further curtailed by its financial crisis and the influx of membership in recent years, until now we should probably speak of "peace *observers*," i.e., observers and regulators of "a peace of sorts" already agreed to by the great or small powers who were parties to a conflict. While "strengthening" the U.N. by using it, he should be ever mindful that one should not jump up and down on a sprained ankle. When (or if) supporting the admission of Red China because the U.N. should be a *universal* forum, he should say also that this will make it even more a *forum* only, and for decades a more exacerbated, frustrated, and frustrating forum. As a consequence of all this, one should unfailingly call attention to the independent initiatives and responsibilities of the United States as a great power within the nation-state system (upon which the U.N. was carefully erected) if a just world order is to be sustained or a juster one be ever achieved.

So could churchmen contribute to the upbuilding of an ethos that might possibly produce the statesmanship needed in the decades to come. As things now stand . . .

Reinhold Niebuhr himself can be quoted in support of the liberal consensus! Writing in the 25th Anniversary issue of *Christianity and Crisis* (Feb. 21, 1966), he gave the following explanation of the difference between the religious and political situation he faced during the years he led the churches to face realistically the perennial meaning of political responsibility, and the task now facing us: "The problem of indiscriminate pacifism in a community in which order and justice are attained not by pure love or pure reason but by an equilibrium of various forms of economic and political power has given way to the problem of curbing pure power in the international realm." What warrant in either theology or politics has Niebuhr ever given us for accepting such a simplicist analysis? Who is trying to shape the world by means of power alone? Where is there power in exercise apart from somebody's notion of responsibility and justice? Where justice not connected with order? Where order or a just order without striking an equilibrium . . . ?

In some such way as this, Christian realism, I judged, ceased to gain voice (upon Protestant premises) at about the *20th* anniversary of *Christianity and Crisis*. The only article in the realist tradition in the Anniversary issue of this journal was the one by Kenneth Thompson— whose name was notably missing from the editors who signed the statement on Vietnam in the next issue. (To have said: "The Following Members of the Editorial Board" instead of "The Editorial Board" would have indicated a proper concern for the range and plurality of particular Christian opinions, more than for impressing the fact of consensus upon the public mind and upon the mind of the Church.) Thus has the spectrum narrowed, and religious journals speaking to the whole Church ceased to speak for the whole Church and for the whole of Christian truth. Thus was the liberal consensus put together again. The manufactured product can be seen from a simple inspection of the sponsorship, speakers, and pronouncements at the recent interfaith Conference on Religion and Peace held in Washington.

From the theological profundities of *The Nature and Destiny of Man* or from the political profundities of *The Structure of Nations and Empires*, it should be clear that neither this nation nor the world can afford the luxury of a Reinhold Niebuhr again, namely, a man who

nudged Christians toward the need to assist in preserving the equilibrium of political power while "that man in Washington" did the same
for the nation as a whole. Ahead of them was a Churchill. As Niebuhr
when sober knows very well, this nation has inherited both power and
responsibility in imperial proportions. This means simply that we are
one of the nations that has the power significantly to influence events
beyond our borders. Whether we do or don't, we *do*. There is need for
more, not less, Christian realism in our premises. It is the premises the
Church is "competent" to affect. The decisions of political prudence upon
those premises are another matter.

CHAPTER 21

Vietnam: Dissent
from Dissent*

The political situation in South Vietnam is simply this: the United States and its allies are engaged there in an arbitration of arms that cannot now be negotiated to a settlement. In the end one side or the other will agree to something it *could* now agree to but will not. Either the Vietcong will accept less than a settlement in accord with the program of its political arm, the National Liberation Front—something other than the pre-negotiation victory it now demands—or the U.S. will agree to surrender South Vietnam to that program as the best thing we *can* do for the Vietnamese and for the world balance of power, at the same time extricating ourselves from the quagmire. This is the meaning of an arbitration by armed force.

The U.S. is not now going to begin negotiations on such a basis, nor will the Vietcong and its National Liberation Front accept being merely one party to an as yet undetermined resolution of the conflict. Unless we have beclouded our political perceptions by wishing it could be otherwise, we cannot avoid this description of the facts in terms of an unavoidable, tragic arbitration of arms.

Because of domestic pressure for peace that does not count the price, the administration was forced into an astonishing effort to distinguish semantically between "unconditional discussions" (which we

* First appeared in the July 20, 1966, issue of *The Christian Century*, copyright 1966, The Christian Century Foundation.

are willing to begin at any time, anywhere) and "unconditional negotiations" (which we are not prepared to accept). In short, we are willing to have *discussed* at a conference even that proposal in North Vietnam's four-point program calling for settlement in accord with the program of the National Liberation Front. But we are not willing to open negotiations with this point already conceded.

Bernard B. Fall, no defender of U.S. policy in Vietnam, wrote in *The New York Times Magazine* as long ago as December 12, 1965: "Let us do away with the nonsense that there is such an animal as 'unconditional discussions,' let alone 'unconditional negotiations.' Both sides have a pretty good idea about the shape of future contacts." This too is the very meaning of an arbitrament of arms. The shape of future contacts and the shape of any settlement that is possible now is well known to both parties. The alternatives are not conditioned political negotiations or that "unconditional discussion" dreams are made of; they are rather surrender by one side or continuation of the present arbitrament of arms until genuine negotiations become possible. These are apparently the unshakable options between which our government must choose if any significant change is to be *now* introduced into this war. Through periods of bombing, and pauses in the bombing, turmoil or quiet in Hue, or stability or instability in the Saigon government, this remains the choice.

It was within the power of the United States to bring peace to Vietnam last January. It is possible today. It will be possible at any time we choose in the coming months. Here is a rough sketch of how it could be accomplished:

Initially the United States would announce its acceptance of Hanoi's four-point program, not excepting settlement in accord with the program of the National Liberation Front. Then a coalition government would be formed in South Vietnam with *decisive* power one way or another in the hands of the N.L.F.

The 1954 Geneva conference could then be reconvened, its participants the communist-led coalition government of South Vietnam and the governments of North Vietnam, the U.S., Communist China, the Soviet Union, France, Britain, Laos, and Cambodia. Under the four-point stand which bars "foreign interference" in a settlement of the internal affairs of Vietnam, the functions of the conference would be limited. The conference would be charged with ensuring that the U.S. withdraw all its troops and weapons from Vietnam and dismantle all its bases. It would also guarantee that there be no foreign military presence in North or South Vietnam "pending peaceful reunification" of the country.

A next step would be opening of negotiations between the "coalition" government of South Vietnam and the government of North Vietnam looking toward reunification of the country through a general election. There would be no guarantee that North Vietnamese troops would be withdrawn from South Vietnam during the election, since Hanoi maintains that the presence of its troops there is a myth. There might be a semblance of international supervision of the elections. But if the elections are agreed to between Hanoi and a southern coalition government already decisively under N.L.F. control, the supervision of elections could in no way cast aspersions on the integrity and legitimacy of that government, which would have come into power by arrangements and concessions made prior to negotiating such subsequent details as elections, the protection of minority groups, etc.

To accept such terms would be in effect to return to seldom-mentioned "essentials" of the 1954 Geneva agreements, essentials which led the U.S. to refuse to sign the agreements. A control commission might indeed be set up, but it would be unable to control and ensure anything because of its near-troika internal nature, its inability to move about and check on violations, its obligation merely to "report" to the presidents of the conference (representing Great Britain and the Soviet Union, who would then do nothing about it). As in 1954, any such instrument is today not likely to create just government in Vietnam or anywhere else. To accept such terms would mean acceding to the surrender of the South Vietnamese to a national communism as the only force capable of organizing the country. Hanoi is quite correct in asserting that its four-point program means no more than the "essentials" of the 1954 agreements.

Now it may well be a realistic, just, and charitable exercise of political wisdom for the U.S. to move toward a peace settlement on such terms, rather than continue by arbitrament of arms to seek to secure the independent political development of the South Vietnamese or achieve a resolution that would involve *effective* international or regional guarantees. Clearly, to move in this manner offers the only exit from further arbitrament of arms in an effort to impel the Vietcong to give up their requirement of what is in effect a pre-negotiation victory. However, so to move might require greater *political* intervention in South Vietnam to force the parties there to agree to form a government in which the N.L.F. holds decisive power and influence. And this could have far graver repercussions throughout southeast Asia—on the delicate balance in Laos, the independence of Thailand, the movements toward genuine non-alignment in Indonesia and (such as they are) in Cambodia —than would have been the case if this solution had been accepted in 1954. Still, a well-tailored surrender of South Vietnam (one that sets aside considerations of *mere* honor and prestige as not of central importance) can be rationally discussed as an option.

Because it is well nigh impossible to compare with assurance the over-all justice of regimes, sincere people disagree as to whether victory for the N.L.F. on the one hand or its defeat or compulsion to some form of genuine political compromise on the other would be more productive of just order in Vietnam and throughout southeast Asia. Some of us used to regard it as a telling piece of evidence of the "justice of the cause" that numbers of Germans were willing to make themselves refugees from their own homeland and displaced persons on the earth, while few were moving in the opposite direction. By this test the million refugees from North Vietnam "voting with their feet," the streams of people pouring out of Vietcong held areas when the control the N.L.F. intends to exert shows its true colors—these are a goodly number of judgments on wherein lies the relatively better political embodiment of justice, in actuality or in prospect. The refugees knew they were walking into a society not regimenting itself to launch into the 20th century, into a society in greater turmoil, one perhaps governed by rascals or inept men. Still they came. The fact that there was not a good European among them, like Paul Tillich or Thomas Mann, should make no difference in the weight given to these living appeals.

From this evidence I would conclude that there is good reason to contend that no Christian should willingly concur in the coming to power of a communist regime, "nationalist" or otherwise, and particularly not in a developing country. If, however, such coming to power cannot be prevented, or if greater evil would otherwise ensue, then of course the obligation disappears; no one is obliged to seek a greater good for himself and his country or for an ally needing assistance if such good is not possible, or is possible at too great cost. Only if this should be the case could we justify abandoning the South Vietnamese to control by the N.L.F. or subjecting other southeast Asia peoples to the repercussions that would then befall their fragile societies.

Public debate in this country can be "cooled" only if those who protest against the U.S. Administration's present policy face this as the issue at stake in the present arbitrament of arms. The President is certainly right in asking (as he did at Princeton) that the discussion be "cooled" in this sense. This was a plea for responsible and honest dissent, not for the suppression of dissent. Instead of speeches about the arrogance of power, his critics need to propose the responsible alternative, i.e. one that can *now* be obtained by a specified use of U.S. power and influence, if there is one in between accepting this Hanoi-Vietcong solution and continuing for now to press the arbitrament of arms. A well-tailored surrender is surely an option. But it ought to be proposed as such. Talks about admitting the Vietcong to the conference table as one of the participants is surely an irrelevant and a deceptive self-deception.

Myriad are the ways in which we twist and squirm to avoid the hard fact that this is an arbitrament by the ordeal of arms. "Give the National Liberation Front a share of power and responsibility," says Senator Robert Kennedy. He knows or should know that "a share" is precisely what the N.L.F. does not now mean to accept. This has been clear at least since the last bombing pause. As Ambassador Goldberg said before the U.N. Security Council on February 2, 1966, there is now "a new precondition—I emphasize a new precondition—more objectionable, not more responsive than before the suspension," that the U.S. must recognize the N.L.F. "as the sole—and I emphasize sole—genuine representative of the people of South Vietnam." This was a "new" precondition only in the sense that 1966 made explicit this unnegotiable demand. This would have been the result of any peace conference in 1965 before President Johnson preemptively escalated the war on the ground in South Vietnam and forestalled a certain Vietcong military victory. The precondition did not then have to be made explicit. It would have been entailed anyway in any favorable U.S. response to so-called peace-feelers earlier in 1965.

The Administration has indicated it is willing to "discuss" even that precondition in order to move the conflict to a regional conference in which, we doubtless hope, a fairer, guaranteed solution will be arranged by Vietnam's immediate neighbors and by all the powers concerned.

But, it is said, President Johnson has not indicated *clearly enough* that the N.L.F. can have a share in the settlement, that all the combatants can somehow be in on the talks, etc. How then do we know they won't accept a share? Anyone who has political perception in exercise, it seems to me, should know that to say or do more than has been said and done already to indicate this would completely undermine any and all political leadership in South Vietnam except that of the Vietcong. It would require massive political intervention by the U.S. in South Vietnam to impel negotiations, and as a consequence the negotiations thus compelled would turn out to be the disguised surrender of the country we are still seeking to avoid. The truth is, rather, that (as Bernard Fall said) the parties have a quite sufficient notion of the shape of the negotiations that would at present be possible. This is exactly why Hanoi and the Vietcong are not yet interested in negotiations. Nor are the U.S. and the non-communist South Vietnamese yet willing to accept the peace we can now get. If we really mean for our government to make peace on the terms on which this can now be secured, we ought to call it by its proper name, and discuss the option rationally.

Perhaps it is understandable that a consensus of vocal liberal religious opinion finds itself unable to look an arbitrament of arms squarely in the face; and acknowledging this, make the recommendations it presumes to make. Ought anyone to be surprised if many vocal voices in the academic community give expression to a similar non-political view of the world?

So also do some newspapers squirm to avoid facing the fact that this is as yet an arbitrament of arms. *The New York Times* in a front page story on April 26, 1966, reported that Vice-President Humphrey "talked for an hour and two minutes to the newspaper executives without once mentioning the prospect of peace negotiations." A few days later that sentence found its way to the editorial page,[1] where it belonged in the first place. Moreover in the adjacent column of that issue of the *Times,* there was a story that fully accounted for the fact that the Vice-President did not mention the prospects for peace negotiations: he did not want on that occasion to discuss our unconditional surrender of South Vietnam! This was the report of a speech by Premier Pham Van Dong of North Vietnam charging that President Johnson turns a deaf ear to that country's four-point demands. The third point calls for settlement according to the program of the N.L.F.; and said the Premier: "To object to this third point is to object to the whole four-point stand" on how to make peace prevail. Precisely! Moreover, they are going to win this, the Premier added, because the U.S. Administration cannot "even soothe ever more acute opposition in the U.S. Congress itself."

It seems evident that this is as yet an arbitration by means of war, that both sides know very well the shape of future contacts and the present conditions for making peace. Only the Vietcong may know better than do the American people that in politico-military conflict you cannot win at the conference table anything that *it is evident* you cannot win or are *not resolved to win* on the battlefield.

One has to go elsewhere than to a Christian view of politics even to understand the animus, the exacerbation, the petulance infecting our public debate and our protests over this war. The explanation is to be found in the utopian notion that the government must be doing something wrong if it has to make political use of violence; in the conviction that it is always possible to negotiate so that negotiation will never fail and yet attain a just peace, or one that will barely hold together; in the belief that if our political leaders don't know all this it must be because they haven't listened to the right people; in the optimistic denial that there can be such a thing as an arbitrament of arms, that conflicts can arise among men and nations that are so unbridgeable that they defy *ratio* and drive nations to the *ultima ratio* of war.

Governed by the illusions under which he hopes to operate in

---

[1] Max Frankel's dispatches and news analysis can profitably be compared with the *Times'* editorial page in estimating whether the latter has a sufficient sense of the complexity of events.

politics, 20th century man is devoted to abstract notions of justice and harmony. With the lead given by liberal religious spokesmen since the collapse of Christian realism and the resurgence of humanistic optimism (no less in the new theology than in the new politics), it is no wonder that the new "revolutionary" left has arisen, that on our college campuses the members of Students for a Democratic Society seem to believe that if only force were not used men would spontaneously attain freedom, democracy, justice, peace, and world order. This is not radicalism but subservience to today's unqualified liberal assumptions. If a man does not want to have a part in modern liberal man's continuing to place himself on the rack, he must resist the utopian expectation that beyond turmoil or tyranny freedom, justice, and order will take care of themselves.

Still there are those who know that no such "philosophical anarchism" is the truth about man's social existence, who know that force still has its just uses and that in the present international system an arbitrament of arms may be among the responsibilities of power, but who voice peace cries where there is no peace on the ground that such a course is needed as a corrective to the bellicosity of the right-wing and as a restraint on our government's policy. Thus in his address at the National Inter-Religious Conference on Peace held in Washington in March, 1966, John C. Bennett said: "If it is true that the President feels stronger pressure from those who would expand the war than he does from those who would restrict or end it now, whatever else we may think about our policy in Vietnam, we should be able to agree on our responsibility to counteract that pressure."

One may question whether responsibility in political utterance can be defined otherwise than by a man's speaking the whole truth as he sees it. Dr. Bennett clearly believes, of course, that to restrict or end the war now is the policy to follow and not only the corrective pressure to exert, and that this can be accomplished now or soon—whether by well-tailored surrender or not is less clear. The question is whether anyone who does *not* believe this to be the responsible course of action to be chosen from among the present political options ought then to pronounce for it anyway, "whatever else he may think," beguiled by the notion that by so doing he can help keep this a *limited* arbitrament of arms.

So it might work out. But to put the engine of religion entirely and always behind de-escalation is a dangerous tactic to adopt. Instead of providing a counterweight to the war hawks on the "right" there is reason to suppose that to call always for restricting or ending the war would instead diminish the board middle base of political support for the government's present policy of firmness and restraint, thus eroding the moral authority for its present position and polarizing public opinion between irresponsible hawks and irresponsible doves. Which way the decision to bomb Hanoi or mainland China's nuclear installations would then go is anybody's guess.

All this means not that dissent should be silenced but that it should be responsible and realistic. What we need to have is real options, not thought-experiments. He who puts forward a proposal for ending the present arbitrament of arms should ask himself how, if he were President, he would upon its adoption manage or reshape our other involvements in southeast Asia and at the same time keep public opinion abreast of the limits of our restrained use of power in the future. If his proposal is in substance for a well-tailored surrender, one ought to discuss it in those terms, and not imply that his is simply a more realistic or more idealistic way to achieve the goals of present policy or more choiceworthy from among those goals than surrender entails. Above all, he ought not imply that admitting the N.L.F. to a "share" in the negotiations is what the Vietcong want and continue to fight for. Nor, conceding this, should he imply that the ensuing "negotiations" would be what western liberals mean by that word. Even if he foolishly argues that the way to defeat insurgency and bring justice and stability in the newer nations and to maintain world order is not by resort to force but through political aid and massive economic assistance, he needs to ask himself whether as President he could count on sufficient domestic support for offering such a costly and radical form of assistance once defeat in the present venture has been accepted. Then he might discover how narrow is the range of choice, how few the actual options, open to the President. Then he might not voice cheap prophecy against the "king" but turn instead to prophesy against the "people of Israel."

CHAPTER 22

Is Vietnam a Just War?*

There is nothing much wrong with Secretary of State Dean Rusk except that he keeps saying that this should be a world in which neighbors leave neighbors alone. Jesus of Nazareth said something like that too. Only we who are Christians ought to know that those words from our Lord do more than point to a *norm* for right human relations. Only platitudes lie in that direction. Those words also bring under judgment the whole of human kind and they reveal in one lightning flash that ours is a fallen existence, that men in this aeon do not and are not going to leave their neighbors alone.

How are we to think Christianly about politics and about the political use of violence in war? A Christian, I believe, must always have two things in mind, one positive, the other negative. He will think politically in the light of Christ, and he will think politically in the light of the revealing shadow thrown by Christ over this our fallen human existence.

This darkness does not envelop that light. Neither does the light diminish, it rather throws, the shadows. So it will be to the end of time when Christ comes to ask not whether there is any peace or even any just peace, but whether there is any faith in the earth. The quickest way to indicate with all the force that can be given it that Christians mean this without qualification, and to tell what we mean, is by a paraphrase of one of Pascal's *Pensées* (¶ 555):

> The Christian religion . . . teaches men these two truths: the grandeur and the justice and the eternal destiny of man and his misery and cor-

* First appeared in *Dialog*, Vol. 6 (Winter 1967), 19–29.

ruption. It is equally important for men to know both these points; and it is equally dangerous for man to know his own nobility without knowing his wretchedness, and to know his own wretchedness without knowing his grandeur. . . . The knowledge of only one of these points gives rise to either the pride of humanists who have known man's goodness but not his sinfulness, or to the despair of atheists who know man's misery but not his dignity. We can have an excellent knowledge of one of these things without the other. But we cannot know Jesus Christ without knowing at the same time both man's worth and his wretchedness.

A Christian in politics takes both into account.

I

First, to accent the negative. Taking into account the shadows cast by the light of Christ simply means "Christian realism" in politics. It means that there is no man, and certainly no collectivity, in which Cain exists no longer (just as surely as there is no man, and no collectivity, in which Abel exists no longer—Abel who was in the providence of God the ancestor of Jesus Christ—or none of the light that leads, as we shall see in the second point, to the need for "just-war" limits upon the political use of violence).

This realism need not be expressed in terms of these Christian dogmatic certainties. Much the same political outlook can be stated in other terms. This Max Kohnstam of Holland did in his address to the 1966 Geneva Conference on Church and Society. Christians need to learn, he said, in dealing with international relations, the lesson we have already learned about domestic society, namely, that "love passes not directly from man to man, but through structures." There are no solutions in international relations but to look inside the existing structures for cracks where a change must take place (Roger Mehl). And meantime, it may be inferred, no one can discharge the political leaders of a nation in the structurally-defective nation-state system from their responsibility for initiatives or actions that sometimes may oblige them to resort to armed force.

The important point Kohnstam made was that structures serve to protect against the unpredictabilities of other collectives, not especially or not only against their evilness (against Cain). The nation-state is surrounded by arbitrariness on all sides: the other is always a stranger and a potential enemy where there are no dependable structures through which identification may pass. The present international system has in it such defects that only the preparation, threat, or the actual use of force can safeguard against the other collective's unpredictability.

This seems to me an important point to stress for Christians in the United States, for the sake of the maturity and understanding we need to have in all that we think and say about the responsibilities of public office. It cannot *simply* be said that the "cold war" is over and that there are now opportunities for reconciliation. To say *only* that would be to identify Christian political ethics with the American *ethos* which in war makes all-out war and after every war, hot or cold, makes all-out peace. The question rather is whether there are cracks where a change in international structures can be initiated and take root, over which reconciliation may pass. It is not that State and Defense prepare always for the worse, when they should have a better picture of the world. It is rather that public officials must prepare for the unpredictabilities, and this means they have to attend to the *capabilities* of other dynamic collectives, not their hypothetical intentions.

Within these limits, we can debate endlessly about the internal changes going on in some communist countries, about the difference between Stalinism and a pluralism of national communisms, or between Russia and China today; about our converging economic interests, and how far communist aggressiveness has abated and to what degree continued frustration of another nation's purposes may be needed in the pedagogy by which those purposes can be moderated and become reconcilable with the interests of others, etc. Still, it is the case that it is the duty of topmost political office to preserve the national common good in the face of the unpredictabilities. No President can or should risk national security, even though he may and should seek to make national interests coincide with the wider interests of others, and he, too, needs to look inside the structures to see where new structures may be possible along which identification can pass.

The nation-state system is in a *state* of war. That had better not be denied in the course of saying that even a state of war is not without moral limits governing it, or in the course of charting the direction in which that system may be changed. It is often said these days that the "just-war" theory is passé, no longer applicable. If this is the case, then truly mankind is left in dereliction. For *jus ad bellum* in the form of *jus contra bellum* provides the moral force behind every effort to make love pass, not from man to man, but through more adequate structures identifying the national common good with the world common good. And *jus in bello* states the tests of a responsible statecraft in the meanwhile—likely a long meanwhile.

It is Christian realism or any other realistic theory of statecraft that has been most lacking in our discussions of Vietnam. One has to go elsewhere than to a Christian view of politics even to understand the animus, the exacerbation, the petulance infecting our public debate and protests over this war. The explanation is to be found in the utopian notion that it is bound to be the case that the government must be doing something wrong if there has to be, or if there has to continue to be, a political use of violence. The explanation is to be found in the conviction that it is always possible to negotiate so that negotiation will never fail, and yet attain a just peace, or one that will barely hold together. Then, of course, if our political leaders don't know this it must be because they haven't listened to the right people. The underlying premise of modern man's political expectations (however disguised this may be by expertise in "area studies") is that there can be "at the same time the free expression of the individual [nation] . . . and absolute social cohesion"—which was J. L. Tolman's definition of all utopianism in politics.[1] The explanation of the petulance of the protests lies in the optimistic denial that there can be such a thing as an arbitrament of arms, a denial that conflicts can arise among men and nations that are so unbridgeable that they defy *ratio* and drive nations to the *ultima ratio* of war.

If there is anything more eighteenth century than the nineteenth it is the mid-twentieth century man in the illusions with which he hopes to operate in politics. We are seized by abstract notions of justice and harmony. With the lead given by liberal religious spokesmen since the collapse of Christian realism and the resurgence of humanistic optimism (no less in the new theology[2] than in the new politics), it is no wonder that the new "revolutionary" left has arisen, and on our college campuses, the Students for a Democratic Society, who seem to believe that if only force were not used men would spontaneously attain freedom, democracy, justice, peace, "government," and world order. This is not "radicalism," but the most palpable subservience to the unqualified liberal assumptions of the present age. No one should let himself "believe in *the* revolution" in this sense, or yield to the utopian expectation that beyond turmoil or tyranny, freedom, justice and order will take care of themselves. One has to break decisively with the premises of this civilization, now unleashed again, and be not of this world, if he does not want complicity in modern liberal man's continuing to place himself on the rack. Extremism today is precisely in the demands placed upon government before ever it would be worth supporting.

II

Secondly, to accent the positive. The justifiedness of possible Christian participation in war can be shown because this might well be a re-

[1] Utopianism and Politics, p. 13.
[2] God is dead, He must be, because secular man is alive and sure to triumph.

quirement of charity—of the light of Christ penetrating man's political existence. It was a work of charity, we would all agree, for the Good Samaritan to give help at some personal cost to the man who fell among thieves on the road to Jericho and who beat him and left him for dead. By one step more, it may have been a work of charity for the innkeeper to hold himself ready to receive wounded and beaten men, and for him to have conducted his business so that he was solvent enough to extend credit to that do-gooder, the Good Samaritan. By another step, it would have been a work of charity, and not of justice only, to maintain and serve in a police force along the Jericho road to prevent such things from happening to travelers. Surely an ambulance theory of Christian charity is not enough, but police action and other preventive actions are needed as well. So some may go only so far as to say that it might be a Christian vocation to serve in the military forces of the U.N. on a peace-keeping mission.

But may it not also be a work of charity, by yet another step, and in the absence of effective U.N. peace-keeping, to resist by force of arms any aggression upon the ordering power or nation that maintains a police patrol along the road to Jericho? Ought a Christian to serve in the military forces of a nation in an international system where there is no effective presence of superior authority but mainly a "state of nature" between the nations? We might reformulate that question to read: What should be done where there is no effective presence of a superior political authority but only "a state of nature" *between individuals?* What do you imagine Jesus would have had the Samaritan do if in the story he had come upon the scene when the robbers had just begun their attack and while they were still at their fell work? Would it not then be a work of charity to resort to the only available and effective means of preventing or punishing the attack and resisting the injustice? Is not anyone *obliged* to do this if he can?

Thus do we come to the first fork in the road for Christian conscience. Some at this point will take the path of pacifism, focusing their attention in Christian love upon the enemy. Others at this point will justify participation in war, focusing their attention in Christian love upon the victims of the hostile force that is abroad in the world. In an address to the 1966 Geneva Conference on Church and Society on "Peace in a Nuclear Age," and before espousing "nuclear pacifism" for all Christians today, Professor Helmut Gollwitzer gave a superb statement of this fork in the road for Christian conscience. "The answer given by Christian pacifism," he said, "leaves to non-Christians that very secular task which requires the greatest love and unselfishness, namely, the use of force; and the answer given by the great churches involves Christians so deeply in the conflicts of the world and in the settlement of these conflicts by the use of lethal force, that it is almost impossible for Christians to bear witness to the joyful message of Christ to their adversaries."

One thing seems to me for sure: Jesus would not have told a parable about a band of Good Samaritans who, confronted by this choice between the robbers and their intended victim, "went limp" on the Jericho road *in the belief that* "non-violent resistance" is qualitatively always more righteous than the use of armed force. The infinite qualitative difference is between *resistance* and *non-resisting*, sacrificial love. If then out of this self-same Christian love and responsibility one makes the decision that resistance is the necessary and most loving thing to do for all concerned, if one judges that not to resist is to have complicity in the evil he will fail to prevent, then the choice between violent and non-violent means is a question of *economy* in the *effective* force to use. The judgment must be one of over-all effectiveness, untrammelled by any prior or absolute decision that non-violent direct action may be moral while violent direct action cannot be.

A Christian who has taken the non-pacifist road must thereafter be concerned with the *morality of war,* and not mix this up with the morality *contra bellum* on which his pacifist brother relies.

He will, first, know something about the intention, direction, and thrust of an act of war if this is ever justifiable. The objective of combat is the incapacitation of a combatant from doing what he is doing because he is this particular combatant in this particular war; it is not the killing of a man because he is this particular man. The latter and only the latter would be murder. From the proper direction of just action in war upon the combatant and not upon the man flows the prohibition of the killing of soldiers who have been captured or who by surrender have taken themselves out of the war and incapacitated themselves from continuing it. The robbers are not to be killed when effective robbery is no longer in them, since it was the robber and not the man who had to be stopped.

From this also flows the cardinal principle governing just conduct in war, namely, the moral immunity of non-combatants from deliberate, direct attack. In this *principle of discrimination* there are two ingredients. One is the prohibition of "deliberate, direct attack." This is the immutable, unchanging ingredient in the definition of justice in war. You have only to get to know the meaning of this in contrast to "aiming indiscriminately." The second ingredient is the meaning of "non-combatancy." This is relativistic and varying in application. "Non-combatancy" is a function of how the nations or the forces are organized for war, and of military technology.

I myself have no hesitation in saying that the counter-insurgency in South Vietnam in its chief or central design falls within the principle of discrimination. It is directed upon combatants as these have organized themselves for war, i.e., among the people like fish in water. No Christian and no moralist should assert that it violates the moral immunity of non-combatants from direct, deliberate attack to direct the violence of war upon vast Vietcong strongholds whose destruction unavoidably involves the collateral deaths of a great many civilians.

Yet this is asserted today by intellectuals and churchmen who have forgotten if they ever knew the meaning of a *legitimate* military target. With such leadership it is no wonder that people march in the streets with banners proclaiming that they prefer education or a domestic Peace Corps to "murder." They simply do not know the qualitative difference between "murder" and "killing in war." While this is to be expected of a complete pacifist, it is neither expected nor excusable in anyone who does not, like the universal pacifist, propose to withdraw from the political life of his nation insofar as politics in the nation-state system must also be organized for the political use of armed force.

What would be quite inexcusable is for anyone who does not take responsibility for the agonizing decision to withdraw rather largely from the political life of his nation in the present, very imperfect international system, then to continue to berate his government with an indiscriminate requirement that acts of war be discriminating in an abstract sense which the definition of "legitimate" targets, "collateral damage," and justice in the "just conduct" of war never meant, and never could mean. The doctrine of justice in war is not a legalistic device for disqualifying, one by one, all wars in this age of insurgency. Instead, the meaning of non-combatancy is always a function of the current organization of nations and forces for war. The doctrine of justice in war is rather an explanation to statesmen of how within tolerable moral limits they should undertake, if need be, to defend and preserve such politically embodied justice as there is in the world.

III

For the rest, decisions in regard to the political use of violence are governed by political prudence. This is to say, whether a particular war should be fought, or whether it should be fought at a higher level of violence for hopefully a shorter time or be de-escalated and fought for a longer time, and many another question one must ask in justifying a particular political option rather than another, depend on one's count of the costs and the benefits, upon weighing greater and lesser evils in the consequences. In technical language, this is called the *principle of proportion,* which requires that the good achievable or the evil prevented be greater than the values destroyed or the destruction involved in any resort to arms.

A deliberately imprudent act that from inflexibility or bravado or for the sake of "why not victory?" undertakes to do more than we can do without greater harm would certainly be wrong. But so also would an uncharitable exercise of political prudence that in order to get on with our own Great Society would be content to do less than we might do for the just ordering of the world and for the good of other people in coincidence with our own, if these goods can at all be secured by anything we do or do not do. The principle of proportion, or prudence, can be violated by acts of omission as well as commission, while the principle of discrimination in war can be violated only by acts of commission. These are the main limits which the Christian who engages in politics knows to govern the political use of violent means. Then no one should fling around the word "immoral" with any other meaning when he is debating these questions, or when he criticizes the Administration's course of action.

On the matter of weighing the greater and the lesser evil, one can only mean to say that the present policy is prudentially wrong—which may be disastrous enough!—not that it is inherently "immoral." If current policy or his own proposal, either one, were the correct course for a charitable political prudence to take, it would hardly be inherently wrong to do it. On the matter of *discrimination* in acts of war, if one is going to use this assertedly "medieval" notion, he should use it correctly, and he should be able to recognize a medieval fortress when he sees one buried underground in Vietnam—beneath villages.

I can briefly show in a figure the anatomy of a charitable prudence in politics and in the use of force, if the reader will think of the three interlocking circles that are the sign for Ballantine Beer in this culture of ours. In the middle there is a small area where the circles all overlap. Around the edges, there are places where two of the circles overlap. But they are not congruent with one another to the whole extent of each circle; there is an area of each that falls outside of all the others.

Let the three circles in turn represent justice, order, and the legalities; or national security, the common good or values of the nation, and the world common good. In the ideal case, the political use of violence would fall in that area of incidence in the middle of the circles; and of course a just and prudent politics will seek to enlarge this area. Ideally, of course, one should use force only in behalf of justice, order, and the international legal system; or in behalf of national security, the national common good, and the common good of all mankind. Less ideal it would be to use force directly in behalf of only two of these terminal values of politics; to locate one's action in the area of overlap of international law and justice, for example, or of international law with security, or in the coincidence of the national with the world common good, or (and this is the ultimate "reason of state") in the coincidence of national security and the values in the common life of a nation. (For a fuller exposition of these ingredients of a proper political ethics, see Chapter 1 above.)

In any case, there are no "wandering nations"—nations who, like our father Abraham, abandon their own established interests and go out into a far country. This is not God's call to the nations. In politics we are called rather to wisdom in the embodiment of these terminal political values and their preservation by means of the monopoly of physical power that can be exerted by an organized community.

In doing this it will sometimes be prudent to do one thing, sometimes another. Thus, Pope John XXIII claimed no prescience about the possibilities of political agreements and peace-making at any given time when he struck down a programmatic anticommunism that would make coexistence forever impossible. From all that he said in *Pacem in terris* about human rights, about the need for justice and "social charity" if ever there is to be peace, about the exigencies of human nature even in ideologues, and about historical movements, he simply drew the conclusion that "it can sometimes happen" that "meetings" are actually useful. This entails that it can at times happen that they are not, and that issues fail to be resolved by negotiation. "To decide whether this moment has arrived . . . these are the problems that can only be solved by the virtue of prudence." Whether a moment for fruitful negotiation (which should always be held open as a possible occurrence and as an opportunity we seek) has actually arrived is a decision that "rests primarily with those who live and work in the specific sectors of human society in which these problems arise" (¶ 160).

Moreover, when Pope Paul VI made the suggestion that the Vietnam conflict be taken to the U.N., this was spoken almost as a prayer. "Who knows," he asked, "if finally an arbitration of the United Nations, confided to neutral nations, might tomorrow—we would like to hope even today—resolve this terrible question? Let us pray to God for this." He also carefully noted that "judgment of political questions" was outside his competence as a religious leader—or that of a Christian *as such;* and he distinguished his long record of appeals for peace from "pacifism, which ignores relative rights and duties in the conflict in question."

In other words, it is for political prudence, and for men (both citizens and magistrates) in the political sector to decide (without imagining any conclusion on this can be derived from their religious faith) whether an opportune moment has arrived when it will be useful to hold meetings for negotiation, to take it to the U.N., or such-like questions.

It required only twenty-four hours to find out that an opportune moment for taking the Vietnam conflict to the U.N. had not arrived.

Senator Morse, who emphasizes the legalities, was told by U Thant in no uncertain terms that responsible political action in regard to Vietnam will have to be located elsewhere. One doesn't jump up and down on a sprained ankle on the excuse that there are ways to use it that perhaps will increase its strength.

In any case, this is enough to show that one has to go elsewhere than to a Christian view of politics ever to understand the animus, the exacerbation, the petulance infecting our public debate over the war in Vietnam and infecting protests against the Administration's policy.

At this point let me say that Christians should endorse completely something that Rabbi Arthur Hertsberg of Kansas City wrote in *The National Catholic Reporter* (Dec. 17, 1965). "It is easy enough," he said, "to defend priests and rabbis and sometimes even columnists and editors, in their right to hold opinions, rooted in their spiritual convictions about the problems of the day. There is in such a defense a rekindling of our high dedication to freedom. Nonetheless, it is particularly important for political and theological liberals to remember that there is at least one other dimension to the situation. The relevance of religion in the modern world cannot mean that there is a direct and clear mandate from God either to get into South Vietnam further or to get out entirely or to recognize Red China tomorrow morning."

This means that the engine of religion or morality cannot be placed behind any person's prudential political diagnosis, or behind the opposite opinions about Vietnam. It is only with this reservation made entirely clear that a Christian, speaking as such, should allow himself to enter upon a discussion of concrete, specific options. A governmental or a non-governmental analysis may be mistaken; neither can be direct implications of Christian faith and ethics.

IV

However, Christians and the churches can very definitely say something about the meaning of discrimination in acts of war. This the Vatican Council did in its central declaration: "Any act of war aimed indiscriminately at the destruction of entire cities or of extensive areas along with their population is a crime against God and man himself. It merits unequivocal and unhesitating condemnation" (Pastoral Constitution on the Church in the Modern World," ¶ 80).

But then, a Christian today will have to be vigilant in telling what this means intrinsically, and in actual practice. He will have to do some sound thinking in this age when quite a number of people not heretofore noted for their contributions to an understanding of moral principles have begun to use the terms "moral" and "immoral" rather recklessly.

We need to examine carefully the case of insurgency and counter-insurgency warfare in order to show what was always the meaning of "aiming discriminatingly" upon legitimate military targets, and the meaning of this in the case of the newer forms of war the world will face for decades to come.

One must pause to grasp the nature of insurgency's use of violence (whether this is aggression from outside or revolution inside a country, or both). We need to dissect the basic design of insurgency warfare no less than that of counter-insurgency. Only then can we tell how to distribute judgments about the inherent evil of their respective resorts to military force.

One does not justify adultery by saying that it is *selective*. Not even with the additional finding that with one's various mistresses one mainly enjoys the finer things of life and has achieved an orderly domestic economy. Neither does one justify deliberate terror in the conduct of war or revolution by saying that it is selective. Not even with the additional finding that the insurgents win the allegiance of people by many other appeals or also by a program of national liberation. The fact that insurgency resorts to terror, when it does, only minimally or only upon selected people does not qualify it as a discriminating resort to force. That is simply not the meaning of the principle of discrimination in the use of means of violence. It is in fact, morally, the meaning of total war. Decision as to the inherent evil of an act of war or revolution cannot be settled by the body count. There is not a prudent number of villagers, school teachers, or petty local officials and their families that it would be right to disembowel in the village square to dissuade others from allegiance to the existing social processes and institutions, all to the good end of destroying the social fabric of a traditional society and taking over and reforming the country.

Guerrilla war by its main design strikes the civil population (albeit selectively and as rarely as need be) in order to subvert, while striking as few legitimate military targets as possible. This terrible terror, while "selective," is not therefore limited or a rarity. In 1960–61 alone, the Vietcong murdered 6,130 and abducted 6,213 persons, or a total of over 12,000. Proportionately, this is as if the U.S. were under subversive assault in which 72,000 prominent persons, crucial in the life of the nation and its community services, were murdered or abducted annually! This is an inherently immoral plan of war or of revolution, and one that cannot be rendered morally tolerable by reference to the social reforms by which insurgency mainly proposes to succeed.

Without invoking the domino theory, it is a fact of life that the nuclear stalemate has made the world safe for insurgency warfare. *This* is *modern* war! Nor is the threat to just order dependent upon there being an intact worldwide communist conspiracy behind all such resorts to arms. Guatemala recently elected a *left-wing* government that offers some hope of social progress; the next day, a 24-year-old guerrilla leader took to the hills to gain rule or to ruin; and the military made the first "classical" mistake of scorning him as a "bandit."

The question facing the world for decades to come is whether it is possible to oppose these revolutionary wars successfully without joining them in *direct* attacks upon the very people a government may be trying to protect while social progress is secured with liberty. Is counter-insurgency, like insurgency, bound to be warfare over people as a means of getting at the other's forces?

Of course, if the guerrilla lives among the people like a fish in water, he must be opposed mainly by withdrawing the water to see what then happens to the fish. This is to say, insurgency can be finally defeated only by social, economic, and political reformation. But what of the military force that must still be used? If the guerrilla chooses to fight between, behind, and over peasants, women, and children, is it *he* or the counterguerrilla who has enlarged the legitimate target and enlarged it so as to bring unavoidable death and destruction upon a large number of innocent people?

It is the shape of insurgency warfare that defines the contours of the legitimate combatant destruction and the unavoidably associated civil damage it then may (so far as the principle of discrimination is concerned) be just to inflict in order to oppose evil, subject only to the limitation that this be the proportionately lesser evil. To draw any other conclusion would be like, at the nuclear level, granting an enemy immunity from attack because he had the shrewdness to locate his missile bases in the heart of his cities. It is rather *he* who has deliberately enlarged the extent of foreknowable but collateral civil destruction in the attempt to gain a privileged sanctuary through a military posture that brought more of his own population into range.

The design of insurgency does this to the people of a society it assaults. The onus of the wickedness[3] of placing multitudes of peasants

---

[3] [Philip Wogaman seems especially offended by this expression ("The Vietnam War and Paul Ramsey's Conscience," *Dialog*, Vol. 6 [Autumn 1967], 294). The distinction is between physical evil and moral evil, between the unavoidable tragedy of war and avoidable wickedness in war. I might have said, "The onus of the *injustice* of placing multitudes of peasants within range cannot be shifted from insurgency to counter-insurgency." If this is "a strange invitation to self-righteousness coming from a Protestant Christian theologian," then we shall all have to stop doing ethics, and there should be no more talk about right and wrong, just or unjustified wars.

While seeming to espouse the just-war tests and only disagreeing with my conscience (my particular judgments on Vietnam), Professor Wogaman in fact abandons the effort to define what is right in war. This is evident from his dismissal of my

within range cannot be shifted from insurgency to counter-insurgency, any more than it could be called an indiscriminate act of war on the part of some enemy if in the future Omaha, Neb., or Colorado Springs, Colo., are tragically destroyed in the course of destroying the bases and command posts *we* located there.

The principle of discrimination governing the proper conduct of war has no other meaning than this. Some call this a "medieval" notion. One should then be able to recognize a medieval fortress when he sees or hears of one buried underground in South Vietnam—command head-quarters, munitions factories, stores of rice and intricate tunnels connecting many villages, with openings into countless peasant huts, or under the water in lakes, streams, and rice paddies, by which the guerrillas may fight and run away and live to fight another day through these same egresses. Plainly, there are here extensive areas subject to the laws of the siege; i.e., "catapults" from as far away as Guam may then not be indiscriminate acts of war. These are unpleasant facts. I did not make them so; originally, Mao Tse-tung did. No Christian or moralist has a right to demand that statesmen or commanders fail to take account of these facts in their policies and plans. This is to suggest, all too briefly, that the main design of the counter-insurgency mounted in Vietnam need not be and likely is *not* an inherently evil or morally intolerable use of armed force—not in any meaning that the distinction between discriminate and indiscriminate conduct in war ever had or should have.

This is not to deny that peripheral to the "central war" against the insurgents there may be taking place many intrinsically wrong actions in this confused and bloody war. (I only say that this is not proved by reference to "the bombing of villages," [4] etc., that may in fact lie within a vast Vietcong stronghold.) There are those who say that if any of the acts of war violate the canons of justice in war, or if justice is violated by frequent actions that, however, do not or need not fall within the main thrust or design of the war, it is still on the whole unjust and no Christian should support or participate in it. This position is far more to be honored than the indiscriminate use of the principle of discrimination that is current today. Still, to uphold it seems to me to uphold a legalist-pacifist version of the just-war doctrine, as if the purpose of this teaching was to bring peace by discrediting, one by one, all wars. Instead,

"strange discussion" distinguishing the sin of murder from killing a combatant in order to incapacitate or stop his combatancy. Here again I am supposed to be "insensitive to the tragedy of all war" and to its ambiguities. Without this distinction (I can only reiterate) there would be no moral ground for prohibiting the killing of prisoners—the possible legitimacy of which Wogaman (strangely) proceeds to draw forth as an entailment of my analysis!]

[4] This was the indiscriminate language used by the 1966 Geneva Conference on Church and Society in condemning recent U.S. actions in Vietnam. Report of Section III, par. 131.

the just-war doctrine is intended to indicate to political decision makers how, within tolerable moral limits, they are to defend and preserve politically embodied justice in this world.

If by now the reader is alarmed, I can only plead: "Moralists are unhappy people. When they insist on the immutability of moral principles, they are reproached for imposing unlivable requirements on us. When they explain the way in which those immutable principles are to be put into force, they are reproached for making morality relative. In both cases, however, they are only upholding the claims of reason [and, I would add, of a rational explication of Christian ethics] to direct life." [5]

V

Determining the greater and lesser evil in accord with the *principle of proportion* and the application of the *principle of discrimination* in the face of some new organization of military forces calls for an exercise of political prudence on the part of magistrates and citizens alike. In the particulars of this no Christian can fault the conscience of another. This is especially the case in judgments whether acts of war directed upon *where the guerrillas are* still may not be doing *disproportionate* damage. In this there may certainly be legitimate disagreement. It may be the case that the conflict in South Vietnam has long since been destructive of more values than there is hope of gaining. If this seems to be the case so far as the Vietnamese alone are concerned, one must not forget that there are more values and securities and freedoms to be reckoned in any judgment concerning the proportionately lesser evil. Tragically, or in God's inscrutable providence, neither villagers nor nations are impervious to one another in our fated and fateful togetherness. Again in the particular decision concerning the greater or lesser evil in the whole of Southeast Asia, no Christian can fault the conscience of another. Then in this no Christian can fault the possible correctness of the conscientious estimations made by his government when he states with all urgency his disagreement with it. And no assembly of churchmen should pronounce—as did the 1966 Geneva Conference on Church and Society—that recent U.S. actions in Vietnam "cannot be justified." [6]

At the time of this writing, President Charles de Gaulle has just made his major foreign policy address in Pnompenh, Cambodia, and signed a joint communiqué with Prince Sihanouk concerning peace in

[5] Jacques Maritain, *Man and the State* (Chicago, Illinois: The University of Chicago Press, 1951), p. 74.
[6] "Structures of International Cooperation: Living Together in Peace in a Pluralistic World Society," Report of Section III, par. 131.

Southeast Asia. One need not—indeed we should not—quibble over the fact that De Gaulle called for a U.S. time-limit for withdrawal of its forces without calling also for withdrawal of North Vietnamese forces from the South. We may yet need the mediation of France if peace is to be established in Southeast Asia; and in this sense De Gaulle's effort to jostle himself into position for this can only be welcomed. He made the opening of "broad and difficult negotiations" dependent upon "the decision and the commitment America would have wanted to take beforehand to repatriate its forces within a suitable and determined fixed period of time."

The objection, if any, should rather be to the fact that De Gaulle did not tie the timetable (two years has been suggested as what was in his mind) for U.S. withdrawal with progress toward the goal of these negotiations which, the General knows, can alone insure peace, namely, that this would be withdrawal in favor of an "international arrangement" "establishing and guaranteeing the neutrality of the peoples of Indochina and their right to dispose of themselves. . . ." Indeed, we Americans have a great deal to learn from the somber realism with which President de Gaulle greeted his own proposal: the time "is not at all ripe today, assuming that it may ever be," and "in any event, lacking this outcome, no mediation will offer a prospect of success, and that is why France, for her part, has never thought and does not think of proposing one."

If only De Gaulle had clearly acknowledged that the time is not yet ripe either for American withdrawal or for getting an "international arrangement" effectively guaranteeing the neutrality of the peoples of Southeast Asia and their ability to dispose of themselves in independent development as nations! But this is a small matter compared with De Gaulle's effort to nudge the forces involved in this tragic arbitrament of arms in the direction of such an arrangement and such withdrawal.

The point to be made here is simply that such an arrangement has *not* been possible since the decision was made at a meeting of the communist party leaders in North Vietnam to aid and abet the insurgency in the South, and that a tolerably peaceful and just arrangement still eludes attainment. This is what the fighting is all about. If and when the day comes on which negotiations are opened that stand a chance of attaining the internationally *guaranteed* neutralization and protection of the peoples of Southeast Asia, no Christian in the United States should suppose that now at last his government has made peace —a just peace—by peaceful means alone, while before we were doing wrong by fighting. Instead, the present use of armed force, no less than somebody's mediation of the conflict, will *both* have served to make such an arrangement possible.

We Christians should, of course, be the first to acknowledge that such a fragile historical outcome is not in one sense worth a single Vietnamese or American life, nor is a life to be exchanged for the values of an entire, more durable worldly civilization that also passes away in the course of time. We have it on the highest authority that the whole world is not worth a single human soul. But to bring this judgment directly into politics would be to compare incommensurables. It would be to weigh temporal accomplishments against a human life which is a sacredness in the temporal and in the political order. This would be to face what Paul Tillich called the ambiguity of all finite sacrifice. This, however, is not the only assessment to be made of the lives sacrificed and taken in political encounters in this world in which political purposes and the use of force are joined by a tie not lightly broken, nor likely to be broken.

The Miami "Appeal to the Churches Concerning Vietnam"*

There are two main ways by which to demonstrate the abstractness of the church's concrete political advice. For all their seeming relevance and particularity, our pronouncements often turn out, upon analysis, to be simply general exhortations.

This happens, first, when these statements responsibly take the form of a balanced set of specifics, condemning or deploring both sides in some unresolved conflict, calling upon both to de-escalate, for example. The second is often the methodology of particular pronouncements when the first fails to produce results. This is for churches or councils of churchmen to continue to deliver incriminating particular political verdicts upon one side only, or upon only one part of the total action, while pleading that since a present particular policy is so certainly censurable, or since the situation is so certainly evil, there *must* be a better alternative that is presently practicable. Men in their capacities as statesmen and citizens, and churchmen everywhere, are urged to use

---

* Adopted and issued by the General Assembly of the National Council of Churches, meeting in Miami Beach, Florida, December 9, 1966. This chapter extends to a post-Geneva conference some of the analyses and themes in my book *Who Speaks for the Church? A Critique of the 1966 Geneva Conference on Church and Society* (Nashville, Tennessee: Abingdon Press, 1967).

their imaginations in searching among several possibilities for a way out that (we churchmen certainly know) must be "less grim" than the present course of action.

Apart from the implicit step-by-step utopianism of these tactics (perhaps because of this), there is nothing much wrong with either of them except that they are not very "relevant." The chief objection to be directed against this seeming relevance, this necessary generality of the church's specific advice, is that it leads us away from the true competence of the church in forming and informing the moral and political conscience of the nations.

It is possible, however, that this form of church address may prove counter-productive in its effects in the public order. The move may not be away from the incessantly censored present policy toward one of the imaginably less grim or ideal ways of eliding, for example, a military conflict into some sort of negotiated solution. The move may rather be toward a *more grim* "way out" that was actually there, or was *believed* to be there or known to be there by the responsible political leaders, but which they might not have chosen if the domestic political base of the present policy had not been eroded by the criticisms of too many good men.

Confronted by that possible "outcome" of churchmen trying to exert a "corrective" by particular pronouncements, perhaps we should go back and ask whether there is not something fundamentally wrong with our first determining that the present course is so certainly censurable that the alternatives are bound to be better. Did we not simply arrive at that conclusion by "agreement" that this is the case "whatever else we may think," and without making quite sure that we know that the present course of action permits of no other characterization than immoral, wrong, unChristian? Did we not simply adduce from this alleged present *wrongness* that there must be a better alternative that is presently practicable?

This, I judge, may well be the way to read the possible effects of one feature—and it is a main particular premise—of the "Appeal to the Churches Concerning Vietnam" adopted by the General Assembly of the National Council of Churches in session in Miami Beach, Florida, December 9, 1966. The present fashion in the ecumenical social ethics and action in and among our liberal churches may bear bitter if quite unintended fruit.

The statement to which attention should be directed is: "We do not acquiesce in the idea that the war must needs be protracted; in our judgment, *this war must be brought to an end soon.*" This affirmation was then made controlling in the concluding list of "statements," or recommendations, which the General Assembly issued. These were issued "in the light of our conviction that *the war must end soon.*" What, we may ask, gave the General Assembly grounds for knowing *that* particular thing about a war in this age in which international affairs are still a matter of encountering powers, in this nuclear age of necessarily limited war, in this age of the protraction of war, in this age of insurgency and counter-insurgency warfare? Was this particular political premise adduced from the idealistic one that there *must* be less grim alternatives?

The point to be made here, however, is that this premise may prove to be a very dangerous one indeed for churchmen to introduce into the ambiguities of present-day politics, for us to address to the church, to our fellow churchmen, and to our fellow citizens in the world of today. The effect may well be the opposite of the intention of that address. There is, after all, another way, in the *opposite* direction from the *moderation* of conflict, for an impatient public or a hard pressed statesman to go in response to religious or moral authority placed behind the particular political judgment that "the war must end soon"! That way seems to be the one now, in the spring of 1967, being taken by this government—and it involves stepping across moral boundaries in the conduct of war which churchmen have done too little to keep clear in the conscience of this nation, while pursuing our passion for policy-making exercises "counting the costs" (Luke 14:25–33) of particular wars and particular peaces.[1] Someone forgot that there was another way in which to go from taking seriously that "corrective"!

Perhaps it was politically and militarily a mistake to try to reduce the "classic" ratio of fourteen counter-guerrilla fighters to one guerrilla by new designs for meeting insurgency with, for example, mobile heli-copter troops in Vietnam; but that was a way to try to shorten the war, to end it sooner rather than later! Perhaps also the level of violence required to prosecute in the North the war *against the infiltration* was a political and military mistake; but that also was a way of trying to implement the premise that the war must be ended *soon*. At the present moment it can certainly be said that President Johnson agrees with the General Assembly of the National Council of Churches in not acqui-escing in the idea that the war must needs be protracted. He too believes the war must be brought to an end soon, if it is possible to do this.

One of these *later* stages of warfare at a higher level violence may, of course, violate political prudence while an earlier level in the conduct of the war did not. But there can be no special *Christian* per-ception of this fact, unless it was also the case that a gathering of Christians would, because they are such, have been able to perceive that counter-insurgency should have accepted the ratio of one to fourteen for

---

[1] The reader may want to refer to a brief article of mine entitled "Over the Slope to Total War?" in *The Catholic World*, June 1967, which forms the concluding pages of the next and final chapter of the present volume (pp. 533–6 below).

a much longer time as the way for the United States to act responsibly in Vietnam, and for us to do the lesser evil or the greatest available good over the longer haul. *If* it is accepted that the business of ecumenical ethics is to deal in the particularities of political wisdom, a very good case can be made for the proposal that all along—or at some point in this scale—we Christians should have begun a mighty endeavor to cut athwart the native American particular premise that the war must be brought to an end *soon!* Instead, out of an ideological conviction that *particular* peacemaking is our province, we have—if anything—strengthened that very perilous doctrine. Without our passion for particular *moral facts* and with a few more of the perspectives of Christian ethics brought to bear upon our political action-oriented *analysis,* we could have known that doctrine to be *ab initio* mistaken.

We Christians ought not to contribute even a widow's mite to the opinion that this war must be over by the next election—if we do not want to have unintended complicity in outrageous crimes. We ought not add any weight to the burden statesmen and commanders bear, who feel that, for the sake of an outcome they must judge is in the interest of this country and much else besides, we as a people will endure a certain number of casualties and degree of political risks associated with warfare for a while, but not the same number of casualties and the same or fewer risks *for a longer time.*

Called up short by this apprehension of the possible consequences of what we have been saying lately, we might be stimulated to think more deeply about our premises. We might be driven to know that the proposition "war (this or any other) must be ended soon" is a sort of baptismal formula uttered over that side of the American ethos which (without us Christians) says anyway "all-out peace" (with all its gradations: de-escalate, negotiate, etc.), the opposite side of which cries "all-out war" and "get it over with." We might be driven to ask by what warrants —Christian, moral, rational, or all three—did the churchmen assembled in Miami presume to ease the conscience of anyone who *agrees* that "the war must be ended soon" from the duty of constantly appraising whether that may not politically and militarily be terribly wrong, and to presume to fault the conscience of any fellow churchman or fellow citizen who presently believes that it is quite wrong.

Even if political "prudence" in the application of Christian moral and political principles (of which I am persuaded) had dictated to *me* that "the war should be ended soon," I should have endeavored to take along with me to Miami two "counterparts" to help prevent me from voting for any such thing to be sent out as a message speaking *unavoidably* for the church to the church, to these men and others as churchmen, and to the world. One would have been Richard N. Goodwin, a "Kennedy man," as adamant as any on "No Wider War" and who favors radical de-escalation of the military aspects of the conflict in Vietnam, but who (I understand) does not believe that these steps would or should lead to static enclaves or could likely be elided into choiceworthy negotiations, but (it may be) to less violent, *longer* war. The other would have been Sir Robert Thompson, who was in charge of the British counter-guerrilla operations in Malaya, which required eleven years to defeat the assaults upon the fragile political fabric the British thought themselves responsible for in that country before getting out. Contrary to the impression given by quotations from his writings by Arthur Schlesinger, Jr., Thompson believes that the United States *should* be in Vietnam (not that getting there was a mistake), and in venturing to criticize the level of violence with which we have conducted the war he has always had in mind that the alternative is a longer war.

I have searched my mind for an answer to the question by what Christian, moral, and political warrants the General Assembly of the National Council of Churches *knew* these men were wrong, and I have not been able to come up with any answer. Let it not be said that the members of the General Assembly of the N.C.C. spoke only *for themselves,* or for the General Assembly as such—no more than that. This would amount to saying that they were only engaging in "adult education" and "democratic discussion"; and, getting to Miami by their evident achievements in the leadership of the churches, that they were only saying what *they* thought. This will not do. Whether representative of the church or not, they spoke *for* the church; and yet, I affirm, that when they said that the war must be ended soon they spoke something that not even *they* believe that no Christian can believe contrary to.

But let us look at other and better aspects of this "Appeal to the Churches Concerning Vietnam." The opening section of the "Appeal" probes deeply enough to have estopped the certitude with which these churchmen asserted that the war must end soon. (To say this as a hope or a prayer—as Pope Paul did in suggesting appeal to the United Nations —is another matter.) Deeper than the current terminology of "hawk" and "dove," this document affirms it to be a fact that "on every basic issue of the war, serious, well-informed and highly motivated people disagree strongly concerning fundamental facts and policies related to them." There are different accounts of the past, and of our moral and legal rights to be in Vietnam. "Present solutions are offered by those who wish to escalate, those who wish to de-escalate, and those who wish a middle ground of military power looking to a negotiated settlement." Deeper even than accounts of the past or detailed predictions for the future, the disagreement among conscientious men—this "Appeal" affirms—"consists of totally different ways of viewing the history, the present, and the future of the U.S.A. involvement in Vietnam."

This is practically to say that conscientious men disagree, and churchmen disagree on Vietnam according as their pictures of the political world in Southeast Asia disagree, and indeed their pictures of the world of politics—illumined as this may be by whatever categories of interpretation they may have in exercise. Since whether the war in Vietnam *must* be longer at a lower level of violence or shorter at a higher level is a function of these pictures of the nature of politics or of Southeast Asia, it is impossible for me to discern why the drafters of the immediately foregoing propositions should also have declared that "the war must be ended soon" with such categorical assurance (unless this was only a hope and a prayer—and then it would have been a confused and confusing *specific* intervention). I will not attribute to them the resolve that, since we are *here* in Miami like Mt. Everest is *there* wherever it is, we will vote *our* opinions which are like anybody else's interventions into our national debate.

This leaves me, I suppose, with *my* problem: how anyone could, as a churchman in council, write and vote for a "conclusion" or a particular political advice as a part of the church's address to the church and to the world with which he knows (and in this instance has just said) "serious, well-informed and highly motivated people disagree strongly" (including integral *Christian* consciences).

Setting aside the possibly calamitous consequences of religious enforcement of the proposition that the war must be ended *soon* and the question by what warrants Christians in council would be justified in thus supplanting the work of political wisdom, the "Appeal" says quite a number of good things. It also says a few things which *all* the Christian perspectives upon political agency could have illumined and corrected (if *that* had been the undertaking, and not specific problem solving).

There can be no objection to the recommendation that the United States be ready to support the United Nations in negotiations "for a cease-fire agreement (including cessation of terrorist activities)." Nor any objection to the proposal that "the judgment, responsibility and action of the United Nations be sought by placing the issue of the Vietnam conflict on its agenda in a manner which will further the initiative of the Secretary General"—especially if that includes initiations to see whether *such* a cease-fire can be secured. Certainly the recommendations concerning United States clarification of its policy in regard to reconstruction assistance and long-range economic development funds for Vietnam and for the whole of Southeast Asia should receive the support of any just and Christian man.

We Christians, however, need to probe very deeply into the topics "The Possibilities and Limits of Multilateral Action," and "The Possibilities and Limits of Unilateral Action," in the international system. There is in this "Appeal" too simple an assumption that "international judgment and responsibility concerning so far-reaching a matter as Vietnam" and other outstanding world problems "is *more likely* to be an earnest of the unity God wills than is a merely unilateral judgment and action" (italics added). In passing the General Assembly admits that "there are occasions upon which a man or a nation must act in spite of disapproval." Yet the former judgment is the controlling one.

This led to a degree of unbalance in bringing God's judgment to bear upon one sort of action only: "Christians cannot permit self-determined, national causes, policies and actions to be identified with the righteousness of God." Certainly not. But the same can be said concerning "a too rigid identification of [a multilateral entity's] self-judging course of action with righteousness." Let both these things be said, and then we might begin to discuss as Christian *citizens* the topics mentioned in the preceding paragraph. Then our discourse could proceed without faulting the conscience of anyone who believes more in the limits than in the possibilities of multilateral action in today's world or in dealing with a specific urgent problem, by self-righteous assertions that may be voiced by those who believe more in the possibilities than the limits of multilateral decision and action, or *vice versa.* Our discourse could proceed without introducing heresy ("divisions") into the life we confess. Did not the General Assembly meeting in Miami extrapolate its picture of a political world in which multilateral decision and action are "more likely to be an earnest of the unity God wills" from that transcendent unity of mankind, even as also it extrapolated its *political* judgment, "the war must end *soon*" too immediately from another peace that is promised us?

Questionable also was the call, "We ask for more candor as regards the following: the efforts of the government to negotiate and replies to them." That reflects too much the present reprehensible judgment that the present administration must be doing something wrong, else there would be peace. It is not only *security* interests of the nation that, as the "Appeal" concedes, require secrecy, but the requirements of diplomacy and peacemaking. One wonders what those who wrote that statement demanding "candor" would now be saying if it had been Lyndon Baines Johnson and not Ho Chi Minh who arbitrarily published weeks later their interchanges concerning conditions for peace that took place at the beginning of the bombing pause in January 1967!

One might even agree with the recommendation that the United States government "give serious consideration to a halt in the bombing of North Vietnam even though there may be no advanced assurance of reciprocal action by the North Vietnamese government." One could agree with that provided only but provided definitely that this had not been coupled with the ideological assumption that either a reciprocal action by the North Vietnamese government *will* follow or fitting conditions for the choiceworthy conclusion of negotiations *must* then ensue. This may or may not be the case. Therefore, anyone proposing that his government make the trial must, if he is politically responsible, have thought the matter through to the point where he says that if these prospects do not materialize he would then support either the resumption of the bombing or a longer counter-insurgency war in the South or both.

None of these strengths in the "Appeal," of course, amounts to an execution of the astounding claim made that "it is the function of the church, when it can find ways of doing so, to propose specific plans for the settlement of the Vietnam (or other) conflict." Nor would any statesman recognize any of this as providing the grounds for a settlement. These are *directions* for the search for a way out, and *not* the only ones that may be needed. Yet the hope that something like "proposing specific plans for a settlement" of the world's problems is the church's business lingers on in the unquestioning assurance with which this "Appeal" affirms that the churchmen assembled as the General Assembly of the N.C.C. certainly knew that the war must be ended *soon;* and who by this statement presumed to usurp the office of citizens and magistrates in making judgment as to the greater or lesser evil in the consequence of that—or of the opposite eventuality.

Not even in "Christendom" would such an astounding claim ordinarily have been made. Richard Hooker defended the proposition that "church" and "state" can be united in the same people, the same "subject"—just as there is nothing to prevent one man being both schoolmaster and physician, although the same man is usually not both at the same time. Nevertheless, these names *can* designate not only the two attributes or "competencies," teaching and healing, but also a single person or persons in whom both attributes inhere. Therefore, in the sixteenth century Richard Hooker defended the proposition that by "commonwealth" we mean a society in relation to all its public affairs (except religion) and by "church" we mean that same society in its religious life. Still, the "judicious Mr. Hooker" knew the difference between the temporal and the spiritual power even when these inhered in the same "subject"—just as one ought to be able to tell the difference between a school teacher and a physician or a gardener even when the same man does the teaching and the healing and the digging.

In the twentieth century the church finds itself living in *diaspora,* in dispersion in a secular world in which those conditions no longer prevail. Church and state, churchman and citizen, no longer designate different capacities inhering in identically the same people. Yet we know far less well how to characterize "the shape of the office" of churchman and citizen in the present age in which citizenship is an attribute we share with many persons who do not share with us membership in the church. Even if all school teachers were physicians, we should be able to tell the difference between teaching and healing. Similarly, the offices and competencies of church and state need not have been confused and ordinarily they were kept rather clear even in an age in which most people possessed both attributes. In the present age when there are a great many physicians who are not teachers, and gardeners are ordinarily not either, the distinction between teaching and healing and cultivating should be at least as clear. In fact it is not: in the churches we are less clear about the nature of the office to be attributed to us and there seems very little reluctance to deal in specific political judgments when speaking for the church or as churchmen.

We live off the lingering hope that our task or capacity may be to "propose specific plans for the settlement of the Vietnam (or other) conflict." This is like expecting the teacher to give the physician specific advice on healing, or the teacher to tell the gardener about digging. *That* is not even what should happen when these attributes all inhere in the same person.

In fact, such a situation contains special dangers that have to be identified and resisted by all who are both Christian and citizen. On specific matters the Christian in us does not supplant the office of political prudence, though those are two names for the same subject. No more should particular church pronouncements seek to supplant, ease, or fault the prudent conscientious judgments of greater or lesser magistrates in the life of the nation. That would be (in another of Hooker's figures) to try to make the two sides of the same triangle (which can and may and must be held distinct) rest upon one another. Because the Gospel of God's peace has been given us, the danger is that as citizens we may suppose that in some way our faith or faith-informed pictures of the world tell us that a given war must end *soon*. Put forward as the overriding consideration in "specific plans for a settlement," that word addressed *to ourselves* is exceedingly apt to incline us unduly to hasty and unwise acts either of war or of peacemaking.

It is equally possible that a longer less violent war and a better mix of political and economic with military action may be the dictate of a charitable political prudence. The Christian in us, however, sent another message to the statesman in us, and to the churches, which had the desired effect of blotting this from view. Our contribution in the public forum was then in the same direction, biasing political wisdom to one particular conclusion: end it soon by the best means possible! At least, we did nothing to cut across that native American premise which is the twin of unlimited war in our culture.

On the assumption that Christians with their fellow citizens influence public policy, and always on the assumption that religiously-based premises addressed to the world influence statecraft, the result may well be that we incline our nation to accept less than the best available peace or to choose greater destructiveness than the peace soon obtainable would justify. I am *not* saying that that piece of worldly wisdom in the "Appeal" was in fact wrong; but that we have no *Christian* warrants for knowing whether it was correct or not; and that if incorrect, the consequence *could* be disastrous. Speaking for the church does not mean proposing particular peaces, or specific plans for the settlement of conflict.

If we learn this lesson, we will be thrown back upon our proper task of clarifying action- and decision-relevant principles of politics that can be characterized as Christian in today's world. If that happened, we would likely remember that to appeal in the public forum for peace and not at the same time equally for justice and order, and to fail to accord these values influence in determining how *soon* peace *must* come, would be to fail to bring to bear the entirety of Christian perspectives upon our understanding of politics. Indeed, to call for peace and not for justice and order as equally ultimate political values would itself come close to being a political immorality. For this reason the N.C.C.'s current special "action for peace" will need to pull the laboring oar against its title, at least, if this is not to lead to the religious sanctification of optimistic secular tendencies toward actual irresponsibility and to the further befuddlement of the American people in this hour of their necessary greatness.

CHAPTER 24

Counting the Costs*

For which of you desiring to build a tower, does not first sit down and count the cost, whether he has enough to complete it? Otherwise, when he has laid a foundation, and is not able to finish, all who see it begin to mock him saying, "This man began to build, and was not able to finish." Or what king, going to encounter another king in war, will not sit down first and take counsel whether he is able with ten thousand to meet him who comes against him with twenty thousand? And if not, while the other is yet a great way off, he sends an embassy and asks terms of peace. So therefore, whoever of you does not renounce all that he has cannot be my disciple.

Luke 14: 28–33.

In these words our Lord mentions kings and builders of towers, but he *speaks* only of the cost of discipleship. These activities have one thing in common, the wisdom of counting the cost. The rest is uncommon. The Kingdom of God is not a pearl of great price; it is a pearl of *inestimable* price for which one sells *all* that he has.

Tower-builders and kings are in a different situation in regard to "cost-effectiveness." They must order limited means to measurable ends, and determine whether the costs are worth it in a world in which nothing is worth everything. The task of statesman and builder is, in a sense, a more calculating one; it requires, in any case, more exactitude amid less certitude and greater ambiguity in measuring costs to goods

---

* A sermon-address delivered at the National (Episcopal) Cathedral, Washington, D.C., Sunday, April 9, 1967 and first published in *The Vietnam War: Christian Perspectives*, ed. by Michael Hamilton. © Copyright 1967 by William Eerdmans Publishing Company. Used by permission.

that are irremediably relative. Even as on another occasion calling his disciples to be as "harmless as *doves*" Jesus cautioned that we also be "wise as serpents," so here he mentions lessons to be learned from the cost-accounting of builders and the responsibilities of statecraft. He remarks upon this world in which the costs and expected goods *can* be *compared*; yet he by these references does not *speak* of these things but instead of man's ultimate good and its inestimable worth.

Nevertheless in drawing one parabolic point from the tower-builder and the king on his way to a larger question, Jesus in some sense and even if in passing commended their practical wisdom and took note of its nature. This perhaps gives us warrant for focusing attention, in our thoughts today, upon the king—upon the direction of statecraft as among the tasks of men, of magistrates and citizens alike.

Jesus said a significant word about the *nature* of this political wisdom: it is largely a matter of correctly counting the costs in relation to the goods to be obtained. This is, in fact, a principal word that through all the centuries Christians have addressed to the world, and to themselves in their offices as magistrate or citizen. (This word is called the *principle of proportion*.) In projecting any policy or putting forth any action that has multiple consequences—some good, some tragically and unavoidably evil or destructive—one should look to see that the good likely to be achieved or the evil prevented is worth the cost, that it is greater than any evil that also will follow. This entails that going to war can only be as a last resort, because other means of securing the good or preventing an evil which in themselves are less destructive should always be tried first. It entails also that, even if a cause is the relatively juster one, a resort to armed force in its behalf must in addition have a reasonable chance of success—else one is liable to do the evil that goes with any war without securing the good that alone could outweigh it.

Two things alone would be excluded from among the possibly legitimate conclusions that men and their political leaders may reach when counting the costs. On the one side, deliberately imprudent decisions—resulting from fear or passion or lethargy or inflexibility or prejudice or blind enmity or from the power of slogans like "why not victory?"—these clearly would be morally wrong. This rules out a decision to use excessive force, disproportionate destruction, or the wanton payment or exaction of costs to no proportionate purpose. On the other side, there could be an *uncharitable* exercise of political wisdom which in counting the good to be done did not cast its net widely enough, and so left out some of the common good of other peoples or some of the common good of all mankind which might have been made effectively congruent with the interests and common good of one's own nation. There is the neo-imperialist danger that we may improvidently try to do too much and there is the neo-isolationist danger that we may uncharitably do too little in the exercise of United States' power. Neither is morally worse than the other. Within these limits, however, no Christian can fault the conscience of another man in disagreeing with him about the costs and/or about what is at stake in such urgent public questions as our responsibilities in Vietnam.

II

If, however, we listen attentively to the world, or if we in our places struggle for the wisdom needed there, we will learn another thing about the meaning of proportioning costs to political stakes. We may call this the insight that comes from the king's wrestle with the tower-builder. The international system may be a Babel, but it is not a tower. This is the reason Jesus described the builder of a tower as *first* sitting down and "counting the cost," and moreover as estimating whether he has enough money to "complete" the tower. That is a comparatively simple calculation, and one that can be tallied up ahead of time. But in politics there are no completed towers. There are no "solutions," no completed edifices. There are only "outcomes."

This is the reason Jesus described the king as already in movement—"going to encounter another king in war." In the midst of this, in the midst of the interaction and forces already at play in the world, he too is described as sitting down *first*. A very peculiar "first" that would be, while he is already going to "encounter" another king!—but, even so, he does not sit down in order to "count." Instead, to "take counsel." If then prudent counsel leads him to conclude that to go further with the encounter that is in process would not be worth the likely costs, or would not likely succeed, he "sends" an embassy "while" the other is a great way off to sue for a better outcome from among the available alternatives. "Peace" it is called, in a world whose *steady state* is that of encountering powers.

Upon his retirement as U.S. Secretary of State, Dean Acheson, among other things, took up furniture-making as a hobby. He is said to have remarked upon the difference between these two activities. A chair, he said, is made to be sat in, and when you've finished you can tell whether or not you made it right. This is not the case with international *policy*. Politics is a kind of *doing*. It is not a kind of *making*— like building a tower. In tower-building your calculations can all be made in advance; and if you fail to be able to complete it you can clearly be mocked, as Jesus said, by all who see the useless foundation you laid. But *not even this* is true of policy-making. You may fail to shape the outcome in the most desirable way, or perchance the outcome will be applauded by the decent opinions of all mankind. But who can say that this eventuality resulted from your "taking counsel"? It is the awesome responsibility of political leadership, and it is the awesome outcome of the in-put of political opinion on all our parts as "lesser magistrates," that we shape the world by what we decree, by what is actually decided and done. Policy-formation gives new shape to the world.

But not even the leader of a great world power has much control over the "outcomes." There are other actors in the international system, whose agency also shapes the future for good or ill—and in any case decisively. This adds up to a destiny—to garble Shakespeare—which shapes our ends *rough*, hue them how we will—or perhaps it shapes them to justify the costs we estimated to be warranted by our political purposes and by what we judged the stakes were. A statesman must always, unlike builders of towers, posit his decision and action in a world in which there is always the action, interaction, and counteraction of others and other forces and influences coming upon him. These all, not he alone, determine the outcome; and then the "outcome" of political problems is again problematic. It is hard to see how any moderately sophisticated statesman in the international system could have an arrogance of power; he is no builder of a project that he can control or complete; he cannot very clearly count the costs because he cannot—he simply cannot—predestinate the benefits he seeks. In this, statecraft is quite unlike building.

This tells us something about the human activity in which political wisdom must stand the test of having been wise; about the meaning to be assigned to the requirement that one must take counsel to determine whether the costs may not be greater than the benefits; and about the meaning of saying that the use of armed force must be only the last resort or that there must be a reasonable chance of success in the outcome. It is simply not at all clear that one may not be able with ten thousand to meet him who comes against him with twenty thousand. This is only what one should take counsel about. The answer is almost never contained in the question.

Whether Winston Churchill used a narrow or a broad conception of British "interests," whether he acted from a grand sense of Great Britain's responsibilities, or from the equivalent of a deeply charitable exercise of political prudence casting its net wide to include the good of mankind when he chose to oppose the Nazi regime, he could not have known that Hitler's stupid decision six months later to attack Russia and fight on two fronts would render his (Churchill's) decision a reasonable one. In World War II, the Greek resistance had little chance of saving Greece from conquest, but it was of enormous consequence to the total outcome. Twenty years ago, President Truman could *not* have known that our assistance to Greece against the communist insurgency would cost as little as it did; he could not have known that Tito would close the Yugoslav border and leave the insurgents without base areas and supplies. Nor, in the continuous stream of events coming upon them, could Presidents Eisenhower, Kennedy, or Johnson determine once and for all that the stakes calling for our support of the South Vietnamese government against insurgents foreign and domestic would be worth a given number of technical and military "advisors" or a given number of combat troops—*but no more.*

Our Presidents simply are not tower-builders. This is simply not the nature of the encounters coming upon the statesman into which he is always going, or the nature of an arbitrament of arms. These things are not to be compared with counting the cost of completing a tower. Instead, there must be a ceaseless and perhaps changing appraisal of the stakes at issue and a ceaseless and perhaps changing appraisal of the costs proportionate to what is at stake, going on at the same time action is being put forth in the context of the actions coming upon us, itself shaping and shaped by those actions.

We can require of the statesman that there be a reasonable expectation of success, but only a *reasonable* expectation—not assurance. We can require of the statesman that resort to force be the last reasonable resort—not the last desperate resort after such prolonged, politically unreasonable trial of other *per se* less destructive means that war will be worse and more destructive when it comes. We cannot trammel public policy with the platitude that any peace is better than any war, or that de-escalation always leads to lesser evil than a higher level of violence, or that negotiation should be carried on upon the premise that negotiation need never fail. Decision as to whether a very great evil must be chosen in order to prevent still greater evil, or as to whether a higher level of violence for possibly a shorter time may not be better than a lower level of counter-insurgency warfare for a longer time, or decision as to whether *this* is an opportune moment for negotiations, or not—these are precisely the decisions that must come from "taking political counsel" amid the claims and actions that have come upon us in this age.

Here again only the extremes on one side and on the other can be ruled out from the conduct of statecraft; and in between no man can fault the conscience of another, or the government's course of action, with which he may disagree; and no man has ground for exacerbating public debate by calling the views he opposes "immoral."

It seems clear, on the one hand, that a *first* resort to arms for political purposes, or a precipitously early resort to arms, must be ruled out as likely disproportionate to the cause however just, or ruled out because one had not the patience to seek out and try the effectiveness of less destructive means, or had not the flexibility about his own vision of justice to accommodate to working with others in the service of it. This is surely the flaw in the revolutionary warriors of the present age, whether these be civil wars or wars that also place a country under subversive assault from beyond its boundaries. It is not only that insurgents' use of violence means selective terror upon civilians by which they hope to destroy the established order and launch a country into the twentieth century according to a predetermined program. It is also that theirs is a *first* resort to armed force, and they often have not the patience or the spirit of compromise and willingness to submit their views of justice to adjudication through public processes or by free and open jar with the views of others with whom they could engage in "nation-building." I speak here not only of an insurgency that may be or may be believed to be fostered or aided by some foreign conspiracy or of insurgency that has laid siege to a wholly lethargic, traditionalistic society. I am thinking mainly of the guerrillas who have taken to the hills to rule or to ruin precisely upon the accession to power of a radical left-wing government in at least two South American countries where there is the will and the opportunity of effecting fundamental social and economic changes in those nations. Surely to resort *first* or too early to force for however just a cause is to remove a limit upon the use of violence with which by the tragedies and efforts of generations past it has been surrounded. Surely, also, only by virtue of placing resort to force in the last place can the political life of mankind in its tortured history ever be tempered or our partisan claims to justice be accommodated into a common good.

At the other extreme, it can certainly be declared to be a grave political wrong to base policy on the principle that it is *always* right to *continue to fight* for the right, or that no matter what the costs paid and exacted heroic action is to be preferred to suing for peace—because one was defending the higher values of civilization, or acting or defending the safety of the state above all, or out of respect for one's *plighted word*, or from duty to the juster cause though the heavens fall!

Between the *first* impatient resort and the *last* desperate resort, however, no certain meaning can be assigned to the maxim that there should be a *reasonable* hope of a *reasonable* victory, or to the principle of proportion requiring the statesman to be constantly assessing, amid the encounters he is always going to meet, the relation of costs to *obtainable* benefits, or requiring him to review whether the great evil he chose in the beginning is not, in fact, turning out to be greater than the "greater evil" he first undertook to prevent. The proviso that a statesman must be reasonably sure of victory for the greatest available good cannot possibly mean that he ever knows in advance enough about his projects to know that, in effect, the other side has no right to resort to force at all since it has no hope of winning for its view of justice. This would be to mistake the nature of an arbitrament of arms. It would be, in the irremediably tragic world of politics, to mistake the meaning of statecraft; it would be to misunderstand how political action shapes the world by what it decrees and is shaped by all the interacting decisions of collective man that are going on in the world. Political agency is definitely not like counting the costs of building even rival towers. This the king knows from his wrestle with the tower-builder over the meaning of counting the costs.

III

There now begins a wrestle between the "king" and Christ—not over the meaning of discipleship absolutely—but over the meaning of discipleship *in a political office*. From the dialogue between Christ and the king, there is still more to be said concerning the political thought and actions of every one of us as "kings" in greater or lesser degree in modern democratic society. In the places where we are decision-makers too, there is wisdom and insight yet to come from an earnest wrestle, doubly, for the meaning of Christian discipleship and for the meaning of political responsibility.

A Christian will think politically in the light of Christ, and he will think politically in the light of the revealing shadow thrown by the cross of Christ over our fallen human existence. This darkness does not envelop that light. Neither does the light diminish, it rather throws, the shadows. So it will be to the end of time. There is no reason why Christians should withhold this consoling word from political leaders in all their dealings with "outcomes."

The commandments of God are, first of all, a revealing *indication* of who and where we all are in this political world. A Christian sees himself, the human condition, and man's historical political life always in the mirror of God's Word. The commands of God show us to ourselves. Thou shalt do no murder, since you *are* a murderer. Thou shalt not bear false witness, because you *are* a liar. The summary of the whole law of God in the commandments, Thou shalt love the Lord thy God with an entire heart and your neighbor as yourself, proves nothing so much as that no man does this. That completes the divine indictment!

Jesus of Nazareth said that this should be a world in which neighbors leave neighbors alone long before Dean Rusk thought of saying any such thing. But these words uttered by the Lord of Heaven and Earth, reflecting in passing upon the "kings" and the kingdoms of this world, do more than *point the way* politics should go. Those words also bring under judgment the whole of humankind and they reveal in one lightning flash that ours is a fallen existence, that men in this aeon do not and are not going to leave their neighbors alone. There is no man and certainly no collectivity, no political community, no nation-state, in which Cain exists no longer.

Our first solidarity is the unity we have with all mankind in suffering, sin, and guilt. For Christians there is nothing surprising in this assertion. This is rather a most ordinary description of the normalcy of the world in which the Gospel of God's redemption is proclaimed. As the distinguished Cambridge historian, Herbert Butterfield, has said: If you take the animosity that is present in the average church choir, prolong it in time by giving this animosity a history and extend it spatially to the larger communities of mankind, you have an adequate explanation of all the wars that have ever been fought in human history!

But what does this mean—the king there in the shadows and modern democratic man will ask—for the conduct of our political vocation?

It means that in the time of God's patience, our political offices must serve to preserve the world against the destructiveness to which otherwise we all would be driven. The state is ordained of God as a "garment of skin" (Genesis 3:21) in which human nakedness may be clothed, and in which men may together find a tolerably secure dwelling place.

This, in turn, means that among the collectives and in all collective action, identification and community and love pass not directly from man to man, but *through structures*. There are no "outcomes" and no right pursuit of better "outcomes," in the large questions of domestic justice, and certainly not in diplomacy and international relations, that do not require us to look inside the existing political structures for cracks or places where a structural change may be initiated and take root—over which a greater political identification of man with man may pass.

No one has expressed this requirement upon good government more pointedly than did Pope John XXIII in a section of *Pacem in terris* on the structural "insufficiency of modern states to ensure the universal common good." "The public authorities of the individual political communities," the Pontiff wrote, ". . . no matter how much they multiply their meetings and sharpen their wits . . . are no longer capable of facing the task of finding an adequate solution to present world problems." This is no accidental failure; rather it is "because of a structural defect [in the nation-state system] which hinders them." There is no way to surmount "problems of world-wide dimensions," there is no way for reconciliation to be inserted into the scheme of things, except by "new juridical arrangements" over which identification may pass.

This is the nature of the world—the Christians, at least, among us should know—in which political leaders must "take counsel" when going to meet the forces coming upon them—to see whether now is the time and in what manner in some area or in some time of conflict viable, new arrangements for the government of men can be brought forth. This being so, no one can discharge the political leaders of a nation in the structurally-defective nation-state system from responsibility for initiatives or actions in that direction which sometimes oblige them to resort to armed force—or from the duty to continue to exert armed force until it becomes discernibly possible to arrange the *instruments* of a just and peaceful order.

This being so, it is appropriate to ask the following questions especially pertinent to those among us who believe that in all things we are supposed to submit ourselves and our whole common life to the judgment of Almighty God. Has not our nation-rending debate over Vietnam proceeded on the assumption that we could start toward peace in Vietnam from some other point or place or planet—from some other "human condition"? Have not many, many persons charged others among us, and the government's course of action, with bad faith in not resorting unhesitatingly to the Geneva agreements—forgetting certain "essentials" of those agreements that made them of necessity (and by no one's "choice") only a stage in an on-going war and no fit instrument for the government of men in that part of the world or for that matter anywhere else at any time in the history of mankind (near-troika in the International Control Commission, this Commission limited in moving about to find violations, and able only to "report" to the Presidents of the Conference—Russia and Great Britain—who, of course, on questions in genuine conflict were bound to veto one another and enforce nothing)? Do we know that the Vietcong and Hanoi are, at this stage in the tribunal of war, willing to accept really viable juridical and enforcement arrangements instead of these agreements? Have not many, many persons charged their fellow citizens, and the government's course of action, with bad faith in not "taking it to the U.N."—without "taking counsel" whether one can go up against the predictable vetoes of both Russia and France in the Security Council and the depleted initiative of the Assembly with any hope of success, and without even *hearing* U Thant's statements that the United Nations cannot resolve this conflict and, even in regard to his own interventions, that it is not practicable for the United Nations to police a "standstill truce"? Have we looked inside the international system and asked whether this is yet the time and Vietnam the problem that may enable some structural change to take root over which identification may pass? Have we not assaulted one another with outraged assertions that the costs are disproportionately destructive and obviously "immoral" when what we mean is that we disagree over what is at stake in this conflict? Have we cried, "This war is unjust" when what we mean is that we find all war abhorrent, and yet have not—like proper conscientious objectors—withdrawn from counseling "kings"? In the shadow of the cross of Christ, can anyone believe that there can be any such thing as "unconditional negotiations"? (Bernard Fall thought not.) Have we put the engine of religion behind de-escalation without backing a possibly longer war; and without undertaking to show how otherwise apt instruments for the government of men can be established? Have we called for a policy of extrication without saying the cost that should be paid militarily to save Thailand or Singapore if that be necessary? If there is an arrogance of power abroad, is there not also an arrogance of conscience on the part of those concerned chiefly with problems at home? Have we disguised a willingness to do more than we should (though worse befall) under the banner of "honoring our commitments"? Alternatively, have we justified a policy of doing less than we might by isolationist concern only for civil rights and the poverty of our own people? When measuring the weakness of interventionary power in Vietnam, have we equally taken the measure of the plight of coalition governments, as in Laos?

Do we not cry, Peace, Peace, where there is no peace? Over such a people Jesus wept; and among us was he crucified. *But Jesus did not tell the king the conclusion he should reach from taking counsel.*

IV

In the wrestle of the king with Christ for the Christian meaning of his political vocation, there is one more thing that we who are, each in his degree, "kings" and decision-makers in modern democratic society know concerning what we should do when going to meet another king in war. This insight comes not from the clarifying shadow of the judgment of Christ over our political existence, but from the *light* He throws upon our duties. There will be those who in integrity of Christian conscience cannot wound any man whom by His wounds Christ died to save; these will become Christian pacifists, withdrawing from all killing in war, and selectively from the politics that may in the last resort lead to the use of force. There will be others who in this same light, and out of the same divine charity, cannot in integrity of conscience see the wounding of man by man continue if by wounding some this can be prevented, and the instruments of a "just endurable" peace be established, preserving rules of practice in the international system guaranteeing that neighbors will leave neighbors alone. These latter will not be able to leave to non-Christians "that very secular task which requires the greatest love and unselfishness, namely, the use of force" (Helmut Gollwitzer).

Those of us who are not universal pacifists will then find our use of force severely circumscribed by the sole purpose that ever warrants any killing in war. The purpose of combat is to stop or incapacitate a combatant from doing what he is doing because he is the bearer of this particular combatancy in this particular war; it is not the killing of a man because he is a particular man (a member of an "enemy" people). Perhaps the same charity that motivated the Good Samaritan in his salvage operation would have warranted using any force necessary to stop the robbers had you arrived on the scene a half hour sooner than he; but it could never justify you in killing the robbers once effective robbery had gone out of them, or been put out of commission. From the proper direction of acts of war upon the *combatancy*—the wounding—that is being resisted, and not upon *the man*, flows the prohibition of the killing of soldiers who, by surrender or capture, have had the combatancy taken out of them. From this flows also the distinction between killing in war and murder; and between *legitimate* and *illegitimate* military targets. (None of these considerations are to be tallied up by body-count or by the quantity of war's destructiveness: *that* was reckoned by "counting the costs.")

[1] This has been the main design of U.S. military actions against North Vietnam. The purpose and the shape of these actions was exactly expressed as raising the cost *of the infiltration* by Hanoi—not stopping it, but raising the cost in men and matériel of continuing it. That was to prosecute the war *against the infiltration*, against the combatancy, against the manner in which North Vietnam has organized and disposed its energies and forces in this war.

But on March 10, 1967, there was an air raid over North Vietnam that can no longer be described in these terms. This was the bombing of the Thainguygen iron and steel complex thirty-eight miles north of Hanoi. The first reports of this action from Saigon described the raid as the first in which United States aircraft had bombed a target that was not directly involved in infiltration of men and supplies into South Vietnam. This was an attack upon North Vietnam itself, upon that society directly, upon the people's stake in their country's future, upon an industrial complex begun in 1959 which when completed would have been the most modern iron and steel factory in Southeast Asia—in the hope of thus getting at the *will* of the regime and driving them to the conference table.

This was to raise the costs *to North Vietnam*, not to raise the cost *of the infiltration*. This was not to prosecute the war against the infiltration. It was not an attack upon Hanoi's prosecution of its infiltration. It was not upon that regime's stake in *continuing the infiltration*. The attack was rather upon the regime's personal and psychological

---

[1] The concluding paragraphs were published as a brief article entitled "Over the Slope to Total War?" in *The Catholic World*, June 1967.

stake in the country as a whole by an attack upon that society itself—which can only be compared to the possible destruction of agrarian aspects of the economy by a direct and deliberate attack upon the dykes.

There can be no justification of this action by appeal to the fact that the Thainguygen plant manufactures some steel that is used ultimately for barges and bridge-sections to replace the damage done by us to interdiction targets. It cannot be denied, of course, that in any war there *are* legitimate industrial targets (factories which can properly be eliminated in pressing the war against the forces that have been organized and as these are organized for war, because these factories serve mainly that purpose). But it is clear that this was an incidental and a purely collateral benefit to our actual aim in striking the steel complex. War products constituted only a small percentage of the plant's output. We aimed to destroy not only that. This was a blow against North Vietnamese society and against the will of that country's rulers by striking its people's stake in their future economic development. It had little to do with stopping the infiltration by raising the cost of *that*. No wonder Robert J. McCloskey knew not what to answer when reporters asked him whether there is "anything which fabricates any construction material in the North Vietnamese economy which could be excluded from the category of legitimate targets." Such other things might be the dykes that help to grow rice!

By this action—and perhaps by earlier sporadic attacks upon thermal power plants—we have stepped upon the slope leading to total war, leading to the area-obliteration bombing of World War II, the fire bombs over Tokyo, to Hiroshima, Nagasaki, and to Dresden *if* the equivalent of these things should prove to be required to break Hanoi's will to fight. Have we not already made ourselves *conditionally willing* to do these things—i.e. *if* raising the costs upon Hanoi requires it—by forgetting the qualitative difference between raising the costs exacted from *North Vietnam* and raising the costs of their continuing *the infiltration?*

Yet by this time we were a people spent—well spent, poorly spent—in outrageous protests over this war. The vocal opinion coming from church and academic circles had already exhausted itself in an indiscriminate use of moral language, crying "murder" and "immoral" and "intrinsically wrong" against military actions that up to now have plainly been directed in their main design against *the infiltration*, or against Vietcong strongholds in the South.

All along, the critics of our bombing in the North have themselves used the quintessential concept of "total war" to characterize the military action which, they say, cannot be justified. The bombing, they say, is only strengthening *the people's morale* and stiffening *the will* of the regime against which it is directed. This has simply *not* been the main purpose or thrust of these actions! The signal failure in our moral reasoning was the implication that with other consequences attacks upon a people *might* be justified—if only such attacks really hurt!

We have spoken of disproportionate destruction as if that means the ratio of civilian to combatant deaths, and not the proportion of the entire evil of war's destructiveness *to what is at stake* in an arbitrament of arms. Or else religious critics of escalation have exhausted themselves in policy-making exercises that stress only the *very good tactical and strategic reasons* why it would not be prudent for the United States to attack the airfields or Haiphong harbor (legitimate targets, surely). Thus we have lost the thread of the moral argument, and have ourselves helped to erode the limitation most needed in governing the political use of violence.

The fact that acts of war against the infiltration also hurt the economy and cause a great amount of destruction does not make North Vietnamese society and its future the target of these actions.

Similarly, the fact that insurgency attacks civilians selectively does not make *that* a *just* use of violence. And the fact that *counter*-insurgency is mounted against the insurgents where they are, i.e. among the people like fish in water, and a great number of innocent people are unavoidably killed, does not make *that* an indiscriminate design of war. Up to now, the "central war" of the United States and its allies has been upon the contours of the war the insurgents, foreign and domestic, have chosen. It is simply *not* an indiscriminate act of war to direct "catapults" upon a medieval fortress buried underground in South Vietnam—command headquarters, munitions factories, stores of rice, and intricate tunnels connecting many villages, with openings into countless peasant huts, or under water in lakes, streams, and rice paddies, by which the guerrillas may fight and run away and live to fight another day through these same egresses. The fact that a great many simple peasants are unavoidably killed is a great tragedy; but it is not a wickedness. It does not mean that we have been "aiming indiscriminately," or even that we have been aiming selectively at civil life, as do the guerrillas.

In any correct use of moral language, this has been a limited war whose conduct has been held within the test of discrimination determining the justice of acts of war. But liberal religious and academic opinion has screamed bloody "murder" or "indiscriminate" war, as if that could ever be proved by the *amount* of the destruction or by the fact that it is not possible to *separate* civilians from combatants, so often that we now have nothing to say when our government may have let loose a real *counter-society* strike in destroying the steel complex on March 10. We have wasted our substance in riotous moralizing. We have confused "counsel" by using words without understanding. We have used the words "immoral" and "indiscriminate" with meanings they never had in assessing the morality of war's conduct. We ourselves have indiscriminately wasted our moral resources for imposing the proper limits upon war—so that now we have not the right words to say in urging upon our fellow citizens and upon our political leaders the absolute necessity of continuing to conduct this war *against the combatancy* and not—for the sake of a quick solution—against another *society*, an entire people and their stake in the future, no matter what the costs in continuing to go to meet the forces that are coming upon us in this age of insurgency warfare.

Rather than continuing to darken counsel many of us—in face of the horror of modern war—ought instead to have gone back to the place where we should have become, in integrity of conscience, pacifists, and ceased to take counsel with statecraft in its resorts to armed force. Then the meaning of aiming acts of war discriminately upon the combatancy might have been kept clear. This is a rule governing the practice of war that may be sorely needed in the days and months ahead.

> Lord, have mercy upon us.
> Christ, have mercy upon us.
> Lord, have mercy upon us.
> In the name of the Father, and of the Son
>   and of the Holy Spirit.
>   Amen.

Index